Chains of Justice

Pennsylvania Studies in Human Rights
Bert B. Lockwood, Jr., Series Editor
A complete list of books in the series is available from the publisher.

Chains of Justice

The Global Rise of State Institutions for Human Rights

Sonia Cardenas

PENN

University of Pennsylvania Press
Philadelphia

Published by
University of Pennsylvania Press
Philadelphia, Pennsylvania 19104-4112
www.upenn.edu/pennpress

Printed in the United States of America on acid-free paper
10 9 8 7 6 5 4 3 2 1

Library of Congress Cataloging-in-Publication Data
Cardenas, Sonia.
   Chains of justice : the global rise of state institutions for human rights / Sonia Cardenas. — 1st ed.
      p. cm. — (Pennsylvania studies in human rights)
   Includes bibliographical references and index.
   ISBN 978-0-8122-4539-4 (hardcover : alk. paper)
   1. National human rights institutions—History.   2. Ombudsman—History.   3. Human rights advocacy—Government policy—History.
I. Title.
JC571.C278 2014
323—dc23
                                                         2013023878

To my parents,
Pura Lerdo de Tejada and Antonio Cárdenas

It is the rising sun, good fortune attends there;
Oppression that was is here lost,
And bound by the chains of justice;
I will imagine each link has eyes,
For those who come to demand justice.

—Indian poet, quoted in *The Ganges and the Seine*,
by Sidney Laman Blanchard, 1862

Contents

1

The Self-Restraining State?

High up the embankment of Agra Fort, next to a sweeping view of the Taj Mahal, is a nondescript archway with a marble plaque. The tablet marks the spot of a legendary chain from the seventeenth century. The unusual chain was according to some accounts made of gold, was eighty feet long, and had sixty bells attached to it, linking Agra Fort to a post by the nearby riverbank. It was known simply as the "chain of justice," and forging it was one of Nuruddin Jahangir's first acts as leader of the Mughal Empire. The plan was for ordinary people to go to the palace and rattle the chain to get the emperor's attention. As Jahangir described it in his memoir, "[I]f those engaged in the administration of justice should delay or practice hypocrisy . . . the oppressed might come to this chain and shake it so that its noise might attract attention."[1] While little is known about whether the chain was used or why Jahangir had it built, most intriguing is the chain's symbolism.[2] It represented a potent idea: individuals suffering injustice at the hands of the empire had a right to seek redress directly from the emperor. Regardless of Jahangir's commitment to justice, the chain may also have helped him extend his rule. From the emperor's vantage point, the chain could rein in dissenting administrators, persuading them to act justly or suffer the consequences. Perhaps most important, the chain might rechannel popular discontent against the empire, making it more likely that the aggrieved would seek justice over rebellion.

Jahangir's chain of justice stands as a powerful if unexpected metaphor for contemporary human rights practice. Though four centuries have passed, modern states and their leaders still act remarkably similarly to the logic that propelled Jahangir. States today routinely undermine human rights at the same time that they create mechanisms to advance those rights. In a global context of widespread and ongoing abuse, recognizing the potentially complex motives underlying the creation of government institutions devoted to human rights becomes crucial. When today's states support human rights mechanisms, they rarely do so without some measure of self-interest, even if the mechanisms themselves prove influential. Like Jahangir's chain of justice, the human rights institutions that states create can have multiple and seemingly contradictory meanings: they can be deliberate attempts to retain and extend state control—not abdicate it—even as they shift the social, political, and legal landscape in unexpectedly significant ways.

Among human rights mechanisms, few are as potentially important but have generated as little attention as national human rights institutions (NHRIs). NHRIs are *administrative bodies responsible for promoting and protecting human rights domestically.*[3] They have proliferated dramatically since the 1990s; and today over one hundred countries have NHRIs, with dozens of others actively seeking to join the global trend.[4] These institutions come under various names (including human rights commissions, ombudsman offices, and public defenders), and they are found in states of all sizes, from the Maldives and Barbados to South Africa, Mexico, and India. They exist in Western countries like France, Germany, and Canada, just as they are emerging in the conflict zones of Iraq and Afghanistan. Across borders, NHRIs also have become exceedingly active, leading to the formation of international and regional networks of NHRIs; a full-blown system of formal accreditation; legal standing in some international organizations; and an accompanying cottage industry of meetings, consultancies, training programs, and websites. For a field dominated by actors from "above" and "below" the state, the entry of the state itself into the business of human rights represents a formidable development in world affairs.[5]

States began creating NHRIs late in the twentieth century, as human rights norms and discourse rose visibly to prominence.[6] The idea was that if international human rights standards were ever to take root, they had to be firmly implanted within countries—within domestic laws and administrative practices and even systems of education.[7] International laws and institutions would not suffice, just as social movements and committed activists would be unable on their own to carry the burden of human rights reform. NHRIs were instead viewed as uniquely positioned to implement human rights effectively.[8] They were located within the state but independent of it, so they could potentially imbue the state with both legitimacy and credibility. Situated between the state and society, they might also serve as able interlocutor; and ensconced between the state and international system, global coordination could be maximized. Added to this distinctiveness is a vast array of possible NHRI functions: advising governments, processing complaints, monitoring violations, conducting inquiries, preparing reports, sometimes investigating abuses and interacting with courts, training government officials, devising media campaigns, diffusing human rights materials nationwide, and shaping school curricula. Given this potentially broad, even exhaustive, array of activity, it is easy to see how expectations can quickly outpace performance. The result has been a world of markedly similar institutions with important local differences inflected into them, a juxtaposition that has made understanding NHRIs as fascinating as it is challenging.

In keeping apace with these developments, the research on NHRIs has quickly grown in volume and scope, as scholars and practitioners from around the world have looked to document the expansion and significance of these institutions.[9] This book joins this endeavor, contributing to existing work in several distinct ways. First, I offer a theoretically and politically grounded account of NHRIs, complementing most of the work in this area, which is richly descriptive and legalistic. Second, my analysis is historical and global in scale, rather than focused on a single NHRI or particular region, though I draw heavily on my own and others' empirical case studies. My objective is to provide a broad overview of NHRIs, appealing to both specialists immersed in the workings of these institutions and nonspecialists curious about the role of the state and human rights. Third, I view NHRIs through an institutionalist lens, focusing on related issues of institutional creation, design, and influence and on the path dependencies partially connecting these. In a sense, the story I tell of NHRIs is also a broader story of how the state as complex actor negotiates human rights claims among competing demands and moves to occupy rights discourse and space: in this account, for example, NHRIs are strategically deployed by state and nonstate actors as a new site of struggle, at the same time that NHRIs themselves reconstitute the state and society.[10] Fourth, my analysis is an explicit attempt to speak to an audience of academics and practitioners, an effort to bridge the divides between analytically informed research, the world of human rights practice, and the actuality of people's lives. This leads me to approach the research in somewhat pragmatic and eclectic ways, with room for normative conclusions.[11] Finally, to offer a broad-gauged and comprehensive overview of NHRIs, I examine questions of both institutional creation and influence: Why do states create NHRIs, and what is the impact of these institutions? Embedded within these central questions are related issues of global diffusion, institutional design, and perverse outcomes, also featured as key themes throughout the book.

For good or ill, mundanely or radically, NHRIs are now part of contemporary human rights struggles—a reality that human rights histories, theories, and strategies must be able to accommodate, in its full ambiguity and messiness. This chapter sets the stage for such an effort, introducing the basics of what NHRIs are and what they do. By way of framing, I present three key puzzles that structure the overall analysis, all linked broadly to the notion of a self-restraining state. A preliminary overview of the key arguments and animating themes, detailed over the course of the first few chapters, serves to orient and anchor subsequent discussions. Rather than demonizing the state or assuming the benevolence of human rights institutions, I intentionally privilege a nuanced view of the state and its complex reach. From this critically open premise, the book surveys the global rise of NHRIs and the place of these institutions in the state–human rights nexus.

Puzzles and Dilemmas

The emergence of NHRIs has been both highly celebrated and puzzling. Former UN secretary-general Kofi Annan observed in a well-known 2002 report on UN reform that "[b]uilding strong human rights institutions at the country level is what in the long run will ensure that human rights are protected and advanced in a sustained manner."[12] The Canadian government described NHRIs with similar conviction in the 1990s, as "the practical link between international standards and their concrete application, the bridge between the ideal and its implementation."[13] More recently, in a spring 2010 meeting in the Persian Gulf region, UN high commissioner for human rights Navi Pillay remarked enthusiastically that NHRIs "can have an immeasurably positive impact on the entire fabric of nations."[14] Even in the United States, which has resisted joining the NHRI bandwagon, a quiet movement has been afoot for the establishment of a national human rights commission; and in China, which still lacks an NHRI, the possibility has long been on the government's agenda and captured the attention of nonstate groups.[15] Every year, in region-wide conferences, dozens of NHRIs across Africa, the Asia Pacific, Europe, and the Americas reaffirm the idea that these institutions can advance the causes of human rights, peace and security, transitional justice, democracy, and good governance.[16] Despite this extraordinary range of support, three pivotal issues still are far from clear; these puzzles revolve around basic questions of institutional creation, design, and influence. Each puzzle in turn raises a set of secondary questions, sketched below to illustrate the scope of the debates surrounding NHRIs and the state of the field.

First, it is not at all self-evident why so many states around the world have bothered to create NHRIs. States already compliant with international human rights norms would have little incentive to do so, while it remains unclear why states with relatively poor human rights records would risk creating potentially destabilizing institutions. And yet NHRIs have proliferated around the world, across different regions, types of regimes, and development categories. How, if at all, can we account for the global diffusion of NHRIs? And why do individual states decide to create an NHRI at a particular time, while others have appeared to resist the trend? More broadly, what factors lead state actors to create an agency to monitor and regulate state activities? Do "regions" or questions of timing play an important part in these developments? These are some of the issues underlying the puzzle of institutional creation.

Second, what accounts for the forms and functions of an NHRI, or the details of institutional design? On the one hand, these institutions look remarkably similar across very different kinds of states. On the other hand, NHRIs do vary considerably in their design, and these national differences are not altogether obvious. Why does a state adopt a particular type of NHRI? Why are some institutions given more "teeth" than others, while some are made weak even in the face of substantial criticism? For example, some of the weakest NHRIs are found in the most long-standing democracies, while even egregious violators can design fairly strong institutions. Do institutions designed by a heavy international hand, including those originating in peace agreements, tend to follow an external template, or do local forces still leave their mark? Why are institutional reforms sometimes undertaken, and what role does international accreditation play? More fundamentally, do an NHRI's origins affect its design?

Third, once created, the actual influence of these institutions remains puzzling. For states seeking mostly to appease international audiences, can these institutions have an independent impact? Where respect for human rights is already strong, is there added value from having these institutions? Given their broad functions, moreover, how can we best conceptualize an NHRI's influence? How far within the state and society should we look for signs of an NHRI's influence? And what accounts for an NHRI's actual influence, or for why these institutions vary so much in their effects? How, for instance, should we address the legacies of institutional creation and design? And what other factors intervene to affect an NHRI's effectiveness? Does personality play an unusual role? In accommodating for the possibility of complex effects, do NHRIs have unintended and even perverse consequences? Is it at all possible to make general claims about an NHRI's impact, or is the puzzle of influence best addressed on a case-by-case basis?

This ensemble of questions strikes at the notion of a "self-restraining" state. Scholars of democratization have referred to a self-restraining state as one where "horizontal accountability" exists, or where a state agency is empowered to check the power of parallel state actors, that is, self-regulation by the state.[17] Clearly, an NHRI falls nominally under these rubrics of oversight, accountability, and self-restraint (alongside electoral commissions, constitutional courts, anticorruption bodies, and central banks, which also have proliferated worldwide).[18] Integral to these ideas is the view that the state is not simply a coherent whole, to be reified and treated as a unitary actor. On the contrary, the state is a complex set of actors that must be disaggregated into its various parts if it is to be understood adequately.[19] This notion of the disaggregated state provides an essential foundation upon which to begin thinking about NHRIs and the dilemmas they pose as state institutions.

If anything, an NHRI's location within a complex state makes it particularly difficult to assess the institution's creation, design, and influence. Some observers will be inclined to assume a close connection between NHRIs and notions of self-restraint and accountability, whereas others will be suspicious of these institutions as "pretenders" and "placebos" in democratic disguise.[20] In practice, these institutions have their supporters and detractors (within the state, in civil society, and internationally) who simultaneously react to an NHRI and inject their own political interests and agendas into the discussion. Evidence of real successes and failures across the globe, and even within the same institution over time, only complicates the picture. Yet the puzzles identified above require that we set aside our expectations of NHRIs—both effusive enthusiasm and cynical skepticism—and treat the state's self-restraint as an empirical question, open to critical investigation. They also require that we look below the surface, within the narrow interstices of state and society, to locate the multiple and contradictory meanings of an NHRI. NHRIs present us with a host of puzzling questions, ultimately related to the nature of the modern state and its peculiar interface with the discourse and practice of human rights.

A New Institutional Landscape

The global rise of NHRIs dates to the end of the twentieth century, although the idea emerged in the immediate aftermath of World War II, was developed more fully in the 1960s, and gradually evolved into a relatively coherent concept as of the early 1990s. In 1993, the "Paris Principles," which to this day remain the standard minimal guidelines for creating and strengthening NHRIs, were articulated; discussed at length in Chapter 3, the Paris Principles emphasize notions of institutional independence, representativeness, and pluralism. In this post–Cold War context, widespread diffusion of the institution quickly followed in the 1990s and beyond. The new millennium ushered in more institutions, as well as a system of international accreditation, overseen by sixteen leading NHRIs on the International Coordinating Committee, and the emergence of numerous regional and subregional networks of NHRIs.[21] By mid-2012, 115 states had created an NHRI, with over 60 more agreeing to establish the institution or taking concrete steps to this effect; only 15 states resisted the global trend.[22] Whether NHRIs are a passing historical fad, as skeptics might warn, remains to be seen; but their incorporation into contemporary human rights discourse and struggles, itself building on long-standing historical antecedents, cannot be ignored. Before moving to more in-depth examination of these issues, taken up in later chapters, it is worth surveying the basics contours of NHRIs: their definition, types, and functions.

What Is an NHRI?

A "national human rights institution" is a term of art. It refers to a very specific entity, not just any human rights institution at the national level. Despite the extensive attention given to NHRIs, a clear definition of the institution has proved elusive. The diversity of NHRI types, mandates, functions, and independence has made it difficult to settle on a core meaning. Yet absent a standard definition, it is altogether unclear what NHRIs have in common with one another and what exactly differentiates them from other institutions. In addressing these basic gaps, I adopt the following working definition: an NHRI is an administrative body responsible for protecting and promoting human rights domestically.

This definition serves, first, to highlight an NHRI's unique structural position within the state while differentiating it from other bodies. Being an administrative entity implies that this is a permanent agency created by the government. An NHRI, even one taking the form of a "human rights commission," should not be confused with a temporary or ad hoc body like a truth commission. Nor is an NHRI a nongovernmental organization (NGO); it is an official body, though admittedly some NGOs go by the name of "human rights commission" (e.g., in Hong Kong, Pakistan, and Kenya). The administrative nature of an

NHRI in turn distances it from judicial and lawmaking capacities. While some NHRIs have quasi-judicial functions, these are not the institution's central tasks.

The reference to both human rights protection and promotion addresses an NHRI's central purpose—the substance of its oversight. This dual mandate is central to and regularly highlighted in international standards.[23] In practice, of course, states interpret protection and promotion very differently; but at the level of conceptualization, these twin goals are the most commonly stated purposes of NHRIs. While there has been an attempt to define NHRIs in terms of what they actually *do*, institutional performance is an empirical, not definitional, matter.[24]

The broad definition provided here—an administrative body responsible for protecting and promoting human rights domestically—is also consistent with standard usage of the term by practitioners. In this regard, an institution can be an NHRI even if it is not accredited. It can share core institutional attributes, be labeled an NHRI, and participate in NHRI forums. While international accreditation standards and procedures have changed over time, as discussed in Chapter 3, accreditation still serves as a marker of NHRI compliance. Of the over one hundred NHRIs I identify here, sixty-nine are fully accredited (A-status bodies). The remaining institutions are partially accredited B-status NHRIs, with observer status (twenty-four NHRIs); C-status bodies deemed non-compliant with the Paris Principles (ten NHRIs); or institutions that have not yet applied for accreditation. Recognition by social peers is always crucial, whether the institution proves more or less effective.

Definitions do not have to be definitive, just reasonable starting points for analysis and debate. The definition I adopt here can accommodate the fact that an NHRI can take various forms. Moreover, given the institution's popularity, states and others seek to appropriate the term and infuse it with various meanings, either to pass off an existing body for an NHRI or to push a functioning NHRI to higher levels of effectiveness. In this sense, the concept of an NHRI must be viewed as socially constructed, open to contestation, necessarily in flux. It should be possible to recognize these flexible parameters while still defining an NHRI clearly and concisely.

Designing NHRIs

NHRIs can indeed take numerous forms, presenting states with a range of design options. States can choose among different types of NHRIs, just as NHRIs can vary in terms of their legal bases, jurisdiction and mandate, composition, representation, and independence. This openness in design has always been integral to the notion of NHRIs, which in principle can be tailored to meet local needs and circumstances while satisfying the baseline international requirements stipulated in the Paris Principles.

In terms of the basic building blocks, those working in the field widely recognize two primary types of NHRIs: national commissions and national ombudsmen. There are also hybrid institutions that combine features of both the commission and ombudsman models, just as there are specialized NHRIs focusing on vulnerable populations (e.g., children and indigenous peoples). To complicate matters, NHRIs often operate in a national environment with overlapping institutions, leading to redundancies and other challenges discussed later.

A few key differences exist between the ombudsman and commission models of NHRI. Just under 50 percent of NHRIs are human rights commissions, and their focus is primarily on human rights violations and discrimination, regardless of whether abuses are committed by state or nonstate agents.[25] National ombudsmen in turn emphasize questions of "fairness and legality in public administration"; and they investigate allegations of "maladministration" by public officials. Unlike their classic version, with origins in the nineteenth century, ombudsman agencies that are NHRIs should have an explicit human rights mandate.[26] These ombudsmen are also typically vested in a single individual, that is, monocratic institutions, in contrast to the "commissions" model. Ombudsman NHRIs are especially popular among Caribbean countries, originally influenced by Commonwealth ideas.

Hybrid institutions, a mixture of national ombudsmen and human rights commissions, reflect national ombudsmen that have had human rights responsibilities grafted onto their mandates. Examples of these hybrid institutions (sometimes called "quasi human rights commissions" or "human rights ombudsman") include Ghana's Commission on Human Rights and Administrative Justice, the Palestinian Citizens' Rights Commission, and Russia's Plenipotentiary for Human Rights. Hybrid human rights institutions have been especially prevalent in Latin America and Iberia, where they often carry the name of Defensores del Pueblo, or Defenders of the People, and throughout Central and Eastern Europe.

In designing the more specific features of an NHRI, independence is typically considered a top institutional priority.[27] In practice, an NHRI can have its legal bases in various sources, including executive decree or even a peace agreement (e.g., Bosnia, Guatemala, Northern Ireland, Sierra Leone, and Afghanistan), but the Paris Principles strongly recommend embedding NHRIs in a national constitution or legislative statute, making them less likely to be overturned.

Other issues, such as composition, the appointment of members, and funding sources, can also vary substantially and affect an NHRI's independence.

Another essential institutional axis is the scope of an NHRI's mandate or jurisdiction. Some NHRIs focus narrowly on issues of equal opportunity and nondiscrimination; examples of these institutions are found mostly in Commonwealth countries, including New Zealand, Canada, and Australia.[28] While a few institutions, such as the NHRI of the Philippines, address all internationally recognized human rights norms, others limit the scope of their activities in very specific ways (e.g., both the Canadian and Mexican national human rights commissions have excluded land disputes from their jurisdictions, while this issue features prominently in cases handled by Indonesia's NHRI; likewise, national security issues are expressly off-limits for India's NHRI). More specifically, NHRIs have traditionally focused on civil and political rights, but increasingly— spurred by a 1998 UN document outlining the evolving role of NHRIs—these institutions have also turned to economic, social, and cultural rights, tapping into broader global discourses.[29]

What NHRIs Do

In implementing human rights domestically, NHRIs can undertake a vast range of activities. These functions can generally be classified in terms of protecting or promoting human rights, or what I refer to respectively as the "regulative" and "constitutive" roles of an NHRI.[30] Regulative functions focus on eliciting state compliance with international norms and rules. Constitutive functions are intended to transform the identity of state or societal actors. Both sets of activities can overlap in practice, and not all NHRIs will undertake all functions; but the distinction still can be useful in organizing a large number of tasks. Even a partial list of NHRI functions, provided in Table 1, offers a glimpse into what these institutions do and suggests how they might have potentially far-reaching effects.

On the regulative side, NHRIs tend to target state compliance with human rights standards, interact with the judiciary, or undertake independent activities. As Table 1 shows, in eliciting government compliance, NHRIs can offer general advice on human rights issues, encourage treaty ratification, review proposed legislation, and assist governments in preparing state reports for treaty bodies. NHRIs can also work with governments in devising national human rights action plans.[31]

Table 1

Potential Functions of National Human Rights Institutions

Regulative functions	Constitutive functions
Government compliance	*Domestic socialization*
Counsel government on human rights matters	Promote human rights locally
Lobby for treaty ratification	Train professional groups (e.g., police)
Advise government on preparing state reports	Disseminate international instruments nationally
Issue recommendations on harmonization	Develop public awareness campaigns
Review proposed legislation	Coordinate educational/curricular reforms
Relations with the judiciary	Support and cooperate with NGOs
Assist victims in attaining legal redress	Conduct human rights research
Refer human rights cases to courts	*International cooperation*
Participate in legal proceedings, including litigation	Network with other NHRIs
Encourage human rights jurisprudence	Participate in regional/ international forums
Receive evidence on affidavits	Coordinate activities with the United Nations
Issue codes with statutory force	Promote NHRIs abroad
Submit amicus briefs in discrimination cases	Cooperate with treaty bodies
Independent activities	
Document wrongdoing	
Review national policies and practices	
Investigate complaints of abuse	
Conduct on-site inspections of detention or other facilities	
Compel production of documents and information	
Examine witnesses	
Issue reports on national situations	
Hold public inquiries	
Mediate between parties	
Issue (non)binding determinations	
Award compensation to victims of abuse	

Source: Adapted from *Global Governance: A Review of Multilateralism and International Organizations*: Sonia Cardenas, "Emerging Global Actors: The United Nations and National Human Rights Institutions," vol. 9, no. 1. © 2003 by Lynne Rienner Publishers, Inc. Reprinted by permission of the publisher.

A related and often vital task of NHRIs is to complement the role of the courts in protecting human rights norms. Accordingly, NHRIs can assist human rights victims in seeking legal redress, refer human rights cases to national tribunals, and contribute to the overall development of human rights jurisprudence. In some cases, NHRIs may receive evidence in affidavits and participate in legal proceedings, including litigation.

In addition to their relations with the government and the judiciary, NHRIs themselves can play an independent role in regulating compliance. Most national institutions review state practices and compile this information regularly in annual and other reports. Many NHRIs investigate complaints or allegations of human rights abuse. In the course of investigation, some NHRIs are empowered to inspect facilities, compel governments to turn over documents or information, and examine witnesses. When broader types of abuse, such as those involving economic and social rights, are at stake, NHRIs sometimes may initiate a general public inquiry in lieu of a specific investigation. Following an investigation, moreover, some NHRIs can mediate between parties in a human rights conflict or submit the dispute to arbitration. A few national institutions can even issue binding resolutions (e.g., Uganda's commission) and award victims compensation (in the case of Australia).[32]

On the constitutive side, NHRIs perform two fundamental sets of activities. The first set involves socialization, namely attempts to diffuse international human rights norms domestically by means of the media, grassroots campaigning, professional training, and educational reform. Socialization also consists of establishing and strengthening ties with domestic NGOs, an increasingly important but often challenging task for many NHRIs. A second set of constitutive activities moves beyond socialization to address issues of international cooperation. The objective in this area is to forge common interests with and links to other NHRIs around the world and to cooperate with treaty bodies. Both sets of constitutive functions are premised on the assumption that engendering a human rights culture is a prerequisite for sustainable human rights reform.

Guideposts, Methods, and Metaphors

Why NHRIs are created, how they operate, and what they signify on the world stage are all intricately connected. The remainder of this book is a comprehensive and systematic attempt to grapple with these complexities. I canvass a large volume of material about NHRIs, draw on cross-disciplinary tools, and rearrange existing data to reach novel conclusions. My goal is to offer new insights into the origins and influence of NHRIs and to provoke critical reflections about these still understudied institutions, while contributing to broader debates about human rights, global diffusion, and state institutions.

The logic of institutions indeed guides my analysis, anchoring it in a particular vision of political life.[33] My argument, detailed in Chapter 4, focuses on *strategic emulation*, taking into account both the strategic and social contexts in which actors operate. I proceed from the assumption that NHRIs are self-restraining, accountability mechanisms, and that creating such institutions is especially desirable under conditions of norm ambiguity, when an actor's commitments and authority are open to interpretation. Such conditions present leaders with "problems," or strategic incentives to adopt a self-restraining mechanism; and they open space for norm-diffusing agents to promote new ideas (or "solutions"). In the case of NHRIs, I focus on three situations of norm ambiguity that may stimulate institutional adoption: regulatory moments, including new constitutions or political transitions, when state leaders look to lock in commitments; external obligations, such as those resulting from treaty accession, which create incentives to localize authority; and organized, systemic patterns of abuse, which can lead to transnational pressures and efforts to appease. While the literature on diffusion in international relations has focused on the role of distinct pathways (e.g., coercion or emulation), I attempt to make sense of global diffusion by bridging the strategic-social divide and incorporating more fully the local context.[34] When assessing impact, an institutional lens encourages broad-gauged analysis, inviting us to look beyond the obvious, including checking for the possibility of "feedback" (when NHRIs transform the actors and contexts that shaped them) as well as unintended consequences.[35]

In exploring the world of NHRIs, I also rely on a mix of methods. In terms of the universe of cases, I take into account both states that have an NHRI, regardless of their accreditation status, and states that have not created an NHRI. With this full range of cases in view, I am better equipped to assess and illustrate the strength of my claims. Since a firm grasp on so many cases is obviously impossible, I rely heavily on the large volume of reports and case studies proffering intimate knowledge of particular cases. I also rely on extensive primary documentation, from a range of national and international institutions, including materials from the first full round of the Universal Periodic Review, completed in 2011 and covering all the countries in the world; this is, in fact, one of the first human rights studies to make use of this new stock of data.[36] In some instances, I deploy statistical methods to explore key propositions. At other times, I draw on diverse historical materials, from early twentieth-century newspapers to minutes of UN meetings from the 1940s and even foreign legal memoirs. In all cases, I work to triangulate sources, ensuring multiple pieces of evidence are in place before advancing my claims. Fundamental to these processes are my own assessments derived from over one hundred firsthand interviews and field research in several countries beginning in the mid-1990s, including India, Mexico, South Africa, Canada, France, and Denmark, and the UN offices in Geneva, as well as multiyear access to leading practitioners in the NHRI field.

Context and argument are presented in the next three chapters, beginning with a look at the historical backdrop in Chapter 2, especially the contradictory role of the state vis-à-vis rights issues and a set of more long-standing institutions that variously informed the idea of an NHRI. Chapter 3 turns to the question of global diffusion, offering evidence of diffusion over time and across regions. I also trace the evolution and gradual maturation of an international regime for NHRIs, one crucial aspect behind the global rise of NHRIs, which itself reflects the growth of these institutions. The argument for why NHRIs and accountability institutions are created as they are is presented in Chapter 4, developing my logic of strategic emulation. That chapter also includes the findings of a statistical probe into the argument's viability, as well as a look at how an NHRI's name can give us clues about key organizational features.

The next set of chapters turns to an empirical overview of the world's NHRIs, taking the form of concise narratives organized by time and place.[37] Chapter 5 examines the creation of the earliest, pre-1990 NHRIs, or the trendsetters and early adopters around the world. Chapters 6 through 9 survey the diffusion of NHRIs in particular regions: Africa, the Americas, the Asia Pacific, and Europe. Each chapter addresses region-wide developments, analyzes the creation and form of NHRIs in the region, and concludes with a discussion of latecomers and holdouts. I focus on institutional creation more than anything else. Despite existing research on this question, a definitive and comprehensive account of this political history has yet to be written. In covering so much ground geographically, I am following the lead of Linda Reif's expansive book on the ombudsman and the large-scale volume edited by Kamal Hossain and colleagues.[38] The focus of Chapter 10 shifts to the important question of impact, providing a new analytic framework and illustrating it through numerous examples of NHRIs in action around the world. The chapter also introduces a more dynamic dimension to the analysis, considering how an NHRI's performance can alter the broader context in both beneficial and perverse ways. In the concluding chapter, I review overarching and outstanding themes, including the implications for how we might understand state sovereignty in the twenty-first century and apply an ethics of justice in assessing human rights institutions.

The metaphor of the chain, evoked by Jahangir's seventeenth-century mechanism of justice, holds multiple meanings for NHRIs. Like Jahangir's chain, NHRIs can directly link state and society to one another, including by giving members of society access to the state. At the same time, NHRIs can signal a leader's attempt to control parts of the state and redirect social grievances, relying on an institutionalized mechanism that potentially channels opposition. The global rise of NHRIs, across so many countries, regions, and now formal networks, creates interconnections and linkages, parallel to other globalizing trends like the diffusion of democracy and markets. Yet chains that connect can also be shackles of oppression, depicted in archetypal images of prisoner or slave. NHRIs, too, can have perverse effects, whether acting as a cover to evade criticism of human rights abuse or in extreme cases as the mouthpiece of a repressive state. The notion of a self-restraining state thus sits uneasily between these simultaneously competing metaphors, just as NHRIs have inescapable dualities and ambiguities that must be confronted if their full significance is to be grasped. In this complex panorama, NHRIs feature as new and innovative institutions, even while they manifest the modern state's fundamental, seemingly contradictory drive to reproduce itself via coercion and consent.

2

Historical Linkages

Just as human rights is a modern and contested discourse, which cannot be read retroactively into every past struggle, not all government bodies that address human rights issues are NHRIs.[1] National human rights institutions are a formal designation, a term of art, referring to a specific type of state institution, first created in the late twentieth century and defined by a particular set of international standards. Yet it is also true that institutions always carry some baggage of the past with them, so understanding this contemporary phenomenon and its significance requires situating the institution in its broader historical context. Even if the institution is in many ways new, the dynamics propelling it may have deeper roots—reflecting past legacies and struggles.

Tracing the origins of an NHRI reminds us, first and foremost, that human rights issues are inextricably linked to the modern state.[2] Even those who emphasize the substantive contributions of social movements or who critique the deep inequalities of the state system agree that the state is bound up in the history and notion of human rights.[3] Conceptually, human rights are standards about the way the state should treat society. Even when the state does not directly harm individuals, human rights typically denote the state's duties to guarantee human rights. Yet despite the modern state's centrality for understanding human rights practices, most human rights scholarship has focused on challenges from below (societal responses to human rights abuse) and regulatory efforts from above (the evolution and impact of international human rights institutions). The state itself typically features only tangentially or in a taken-for-granted manner, assumed to be either the source of rights protection and the locus of reform or an abusive and exploitative power. Surprisingly little effort, however, has been made to grapple with the state's complex role vis-à-vis human rights.

The aim in drawing historical linkages—between today's NHRIs and past institutions—is to explore potential similarities and differences, not to establish clear causal connections. In this chapter, I therefore draw on history to set the stage for a fuller account of NHRIs. I do so by sketching, first, the state's complex relationship to human rights, focusing on a Janus-faced state that is both violator and regulator of rights. I then turn to a more specific set of institutional parallels to NHRIs: ombudsman agencies dating to the nineteenth century, government commissions also from the nineteenth century, interracial bodies in the United States created in the first half of the twentieth century, and national counterparts of postwar international organizations. Across these historical planes, it is evident that state actors created these various institutions partly in response to a perceived need to retain power (itself occasioned by other factors, including executive-parliamentary tensions, the rise of modern bureaucracy, racial tensions in the aftermath of war and a changing labor force, and the advent of international organizations). All of these institutions, moreover, share very specific characteristics with today's NHRIs, with evidence linking each to the development of specific NHRIs. Despite their recent emergence, NHRIs are no more ahistorical than the state itself or the discourse of human rights.

The Janus-Faced State

Images of a state variously playing the role of rights guarantor and violator are present in our most elemental conceptions of the modern state, and they remain integral to our understanding of NHRIs.[4] Across varying traditions, the Janus-faced state is amply on display. From a Hobbesian perspective, for example, individuals willingly trade some of their freedom and rights for state protection. The Weberian administrative state, in turn, is defined partly by its monopoly over the legitimate use of force; the tools of repression are squarely in the hands of state agents. And in liberal democracies the state's coercive powers are foundationally necessary for protecting the primacy of individual rights.[5] Marxist conceptions of the capitalist state characterize it as the handmaiden of economically powerful classes, inherently opposed to economic and social equality and predisposed to accept some rights violations in exchange for commercial gains.[6] Historical processes of state formation also reproduce contradictory human rights practices, as states forged through war and violence are empowered to violate rights under certain conditions.[7] These conditions, or exceptions, are frequently stipulated in modern constitutions, which traditionally have prioritized national security interests and state stability over the rights of individual citizens.[8]

These dynamics have persisted historically even as the relationship, or relative balance, between the state and rights concerns has evolved. Human rights standards have gradually broadened in scope, covering a wider spectrum of rights and groups deemed worthy of protection—but always against the backdrop of a conflicted state unwilling to provide full equality. These tensions are evident across historical periods, even before "human rights" emerged as an explicit discourse: absolutist states of the sixteenth and seventeenth centuries that embraced Enlightenment ideals, themselves intellectual predecessors of contemporary norms; liberal eighteenth- and nineteenth-century states that recognized selectively the rights of organized social groups; and mid-twentieth-century states that forged an ambitious postwar international human rights architecture often falling short of expectations.[9] Tellingly, even as the state has become more inclusive over time in guaranteeing some human rights, it has never desisted from violating other rights.

The state's interest in human rights and inclusiveness, in practice, has always been partly strategic. As social groups have reacted to the exclusionary policies of the state, demanding that equal treatment be extended to a broader array of people, the state has sometimes accepted human rights standards. In doing so, the state's embrace of human rights norms (or its change in methods of violence) has often been an attempt to control moral discourse, co-opt civil society, and maintain political legitimacy.[10] The state still seeks to retain its monopoly over the legitimate use of force, that is, its right or authority to resort to violence. By emphasizing the state's obligations to society, human rights standards permit the state to claim it is ruling by consent, in the process appeasing domestic and international critics.

Consequently, the historical expansion of human rights as legitimate state discourse has continued to occur alongside the exclusionary tendencies of the modern state. Using nationalism and citizenship to demarcate the boundaries of political community, states effectively exclude certain categories of people from rights protection, including foreigners and other outsiders.[11] Once groups are excluded domestically, it can become appropriate and even expedient to violate their internationally recognized rights. Ongoing human rights abuses are thus endemic to the modern state, which in its liberal and democratic (even multicultural) variants has always treated certain groups within its borders as less equal than others. Insofar as human rights standards are axiomatically inclusionary, entitling groups of people to protection, human rights violations are inherently exclusionary.[12] No state has yet to be free of human rights abuses, of one sort or another, to some degree or other.

The Janus-faced nature of the state becomes most blatant in the face of "organized hypocrisy"—when despite the state's capacity to comply, a gap exists between international standards and actual practices.[13] The conventional wisdom most often attributes hypocrisy to individual state characteristics. For example, nondemocracies are viewed as being much more prone to hypocrisy, eager to silence critics but unwilling to meet human rights demands. Likewise, powerful states that can afford to be exceptionalist can be hypocritical.[14] State hypocrisy, however, is by no means confined to illiberal or exceptionalist states. Rights violations and protection are part and parcel of the modern state's strategic use of force and morality to retain social control.

A basic point of departure, then, is to recognize that in the human rights domain, the state is inherently Janus-faced, in both a theoretical and a historical sense. Even if the discourse of human rights is relatively new, notions of rights, coercion, and welfare have been basic features in the state's evolution. While the scope of rights—in terms of both guarantees and beneficiaries—has expanded historically, the state's dual reliance on moral discourse and violence to exercise its rule has been a staple feature. Human rights has long fit this depiction, as the state alternates and negotiates its twin role of protector and violator. This basic tension also underlies the historical rise of NHRIs.

Institutional "Precursors"

Institutions rarely are created from scratch. Actors draw on existing structures and frameworks when building putatively new institutions. Old institutions can be resurrected, new agendas and functions grafted onto them. Institutional adaptation, however, is not always intentional, as actors in a particular context can also construct institutions more innately or organically, as they look for ways to solve problems, satisfy interests, and fulfill their identities. Still, adapting an old institution to a new context—institutional transformation—often makes sense: it can resonate socially and reduce the costs of institutional design.

These basic insights can be applied to understand the origins of NHRIs as a historical idea. When the notion of an NHRI was first articulated in the mid-twentieth century, what institutional models served to inform it? The question is significant in revealing underappreciated historical similarities between NHRIs and prior state institutions, or persistent dynamics that can be overlooked when NHRIs are treated as fundamentally new institutions. In subsequent chapters,

I consider how various historical legacies may have informed states' willingness to create particular types of NHRIs. The focus in this section, however, is on the historical emergence of NHRIs as a political and legal idea.

As noted, the concept of an NHRI is linked historically to four key sets of institutions: ombudsman agencies, government commissions, interracial bodies, and national counterparts of international bodies. Each institution, I show, is connected to contemporary NHRIs in various unique ways. Rather than tracing connections between prior institutions and particular NHRIs today, I am most interested in exploring the broader conceptual and historical parallels, including the contradictory logics so often embedded in state institutional projects.

Ombudsman Agencies

At first glance the most direct forerunner of today's NHRIs is the ombudsman. Many of today's NHRIs are themselves ombudsman or hybrid ombudsman, a variant of the classical ombudsman with a human rights mandate attached to it.[15] The original ombudsman dates to 1809 in Sweden, though these institutions did not begin diffusing globally until the 1960s. By the 1970s, as Chapter 5 recounts, leading Western ombudsmen served as models for emerging NHRIs and even participated in early NHRI forums. Pure ombudsman agencies are of course far broader institutions than NHRIs, concerned with administrative grievances of any nature: an ombudsman is an independent agent appointed to investigate grievances against an administration or bureaucracy. As modern governance has become more complex and demands for transparency and accountability have grown, the ombudsman offers any organization an appealing option. This may explain in part the institution's widespread appeal, across local and federal governments around the world and throughout the public and private sectors—from nonprofit organizations to corporations and universities.

The classical ombudsman is partly an institution of the state, and here the similarities with NHRIs are starkest. Structurally, for example, the ombudsman is an intermediary organization, mediating simultaneously between various parts of a complex state and between the state and society. Functionally, it is a complaints-handling body, collecting grievances against administrative acts committed by the state, investigating them, and reporting their findings. The agency's purported goals are typically twofold: to provide specific remedies to individual complainants and to promote administrative reform and good governance. Reforms can be undertaken directly as a result of the ombudsman's work or be irrelevant because the ombudsman's very existence deters administrative wrongdoing.

Viewed most favorably, ombudsman agencies are seen as a win-win arrangement, benefitting both society and the state. For example, the institution can offer members of society with an alternative recourse to the courts, which can be onerous, costly, and overly legalistic. Scholars also speak of the ombudsman's effects in "humanizing" and "personalizing" bureaucracy and in promoting democracy, human rights, justice, and good governance.[16] For the state, under the best of circumstances, the ombudsman can provide oversight and serve as a check on errant actions; complaints can bring to light both isolated and systemic wrongdoing. While ombudsman agencies differ a great deal, and not all NHRIs are complaints-handling bodies, NHRIs do share the central structural features of the ombudsman and its perceived benefits.

As quasi-state institutions, however, ombudsman agencies can also be viewed more critically. The word *ombudsman* is most often translated as "representative" or "agent" of the people, since the classical ombudsman is typically a parliamentary creation designed to check executive power; indeed, the institution's focus has shifted over time from official wrongdoing to the defense of citizens.[17] While ombudsman promoters emphasize the institution's independence, far less attention is paid to the fact that the office holder still is an appointed figure, that is, one state actor appoints—or delegates authority to—the ombudsman, to control another state actor. The history of the ombudsman, in fact, suggests that the figure originally was intended to represent a *ruler* ruling from afar.[18] This delegative role leaves open the possibility that whoever appoints the ombudsman can use the agency, and the information gathered from the complaints process, strategically. The strategic use of the institution can range from taking advantage innocently of the complaints process, in competition with political rivals, to extreme cases of selecting an ombudsman who will favor or do the bidding of the appointer. Even if these dynamics do not play out in practice, the ombudsman is ensconced within the state, and institutionally the office can reflect power struggles between different state actors. Like the classic ombudsman office, NHRIs face comparable structural (and political) challenges inhering in any *state* institution claiming to perform the delicate task of protecting social actors from state abuse.

Government Commissions

Another institution that has contributed historically to the idea of NHRIs is the government commission. Though many NHRIs take the form of "commissions," historical antecedents among other government commissions have received little attention. A few students of NHRIs have referred in passing to "commissions of inquiry," especially in the British context, as an evident historical influence.[19] Indeed, the first *human rights commissions* appeared in the Commonwealth countries of New Zealand and Canada. Consultative commissions, reflecting a French administrative tradition, are another long-standing set of institutions sharing certain institutional attributes with today's NHRIs; and perhaps not surprisingly, the world's first NHRI was a *consultative commission* in France. If the ombudsman typically is embodied in a single person and focuses on the handling of individual complaints, government commissions are bodies appointed to investigate a broader set of conditions and to advise leaders generally. While rulers have relied on commissions for centuries, government commissions proliferated in the nineteenth century, often resulting in polarized debates about their utility. Commissions, moreover, can be created by diverse state actors at any level of government, including royal commissions, military commissions, parliamentary-based commissions, and an array of local commissions.

Government commissions are created to deal with any matter of public policy. Indeed, they reflect the overall expansion of state bureaucracy, especially into areas requiring technocratic expertise, hence their popularity in nineteenth-century Western states. While many government commissions are ad hoc, unlike NHRIs, their focus on wrongdoing (especially in commissions of inquiry) and the advisory role they perform (consultative commissions) are also integral to the work of NHRIs. Government commissions, moreover, are producers of knowledge, presenting the state with copious reports and statistics to support a particular assessment of conditions, a range of options and recommendations, a version of the truth. Certainly, NHRIs can perform a wider array of functions, but the parallels with the general model of a governmental human rights commission— bodies appointed by the state to investigate wrongdoing, furnish supporting information, and offer advice—are indisputable.

In marked contrast to ombudsman agencies, government commissions have always faced extensive criticism. In a particularly scathing text from the 1840s about the "pernicious" effects of government commissions, a British political theorist excoriated "government by commissions."[20] The claim was that states were using appointed commissions as an alternative tool of governance, under the guise that such commissions were composed of independent experts. Consultative commissions have also been attacked by skeptics, with an especially flagrant example being Napoleon Bonaparte's Consultative Commission, composed of eighty to one hundred handpicked loyal nobles.[21] Historically, government commissions have had bad reputations as bureaucratic, undemocratic, unnecessary bodies appointed by self-serving leaders. NHRIs may not always conform to this stereotype, but on some level they confront similar critiques. Both long-standing government commissions and today's NHRIs can be perceived, fairly or not, as part of an ineffective state bureaucracy.

Interracial Bodies in America

The United States has been almost entirely absent from the international discussion of NHRIs. Only recently have some observers considered possible connections between NHRIs and local human rights commissions in the United States, which today are found in almost every state in the country and together form part of the International Association of Official Human Rights Agencies. The first of these local human rights commissions is often traced to Connecticut, with roots in an interracial committee created in 1943.[22] Despite similarities in nomenclature and functions, the connection between local human rights agencies in the United States and the global notion of an NHRI has been lost, partly perhaps because the discourse of human rights (versus civil rights) remains relatively exceptional in the country.

Yet the evidence, reviewed in subsequent chapters, suggests intriguing links between these institutions in the United States and the global context. Interracial bodies proliferated across American cities during World War II in the aftermath of race riots, influencing similar developments in Canada, where local rights bodies gradually set the stage for one of the earliest and most active NHRIs in the world (Chapter 5). Regardless of local government support for interracial bodies, in the immediate postwar period, the U.S. government resisted the idea of strengthening national human rights bodies at the United Nations, concerned that its own "race problem" would play out on a global stage (Chapter 7). By the 1960s, the United States reversed course, now moving to promote the notion of local rights bodies within the United Nations, this time pointing to its own rights agencies as a way of countering proposals to strengthen international mechanisms (Chapter 3). Despite brief rhetorical support and a long history of local rights agencies, U.S. officials have always resisted the idea of creating an NHRI— unwilling to "bring home" human rights standards that could be claimed in domestic courts.[23]

Interracial bodies, the forerunners of today's local human rights agencies in the United States, were direct responses to racial conflict following the two world wars. After African Americans were drafted into and fought in World War I, racialized mobilization followed. Fighting in the war raised awareness that

African Americans were citizens entitled to equal treatment, just as migration to the American North and labor shortages in the South exposed the potential "economic value" of African Americans and other minorities. In challenging the status quo, however, these very developments also exacerbated racial tensions, culminating in postwar race riots across numerous American cities.[24]

Against this backdrop, especially the outbreak of race riots after World War I, interracial bodies began emerging at both the municipal and state levels. These were initially nongovernmental groups, appearing first in Atlanta, Georgia, in 1919 with the creation of an interracial committee. Originally found mostly in southern states, these bodies focused on bottom-up, socially driven change and emphasized community relations.[25] They promoted local activism, interracial collaboration, and a willingness to cooperate with the government. By 1922, approximately eight hundred local interracial committees existed across thirteen southern states; they were complemented by state-level interracial committees (often in cooperation with governments) and overseen by an umbrella group, the Commission on Inter-Racial Cooperation, which facilitated extensive networking and information exchange.[26] Despite their real successes (e.g., producing pathbreaking research, building schools, preventing mob violence, using the press effectively, mediating local conflicts), and their imagined impact on "racial peace," membership in these bodies was dominated by white elites who often called for racial harmony over desegregation and equality.[27]

After World War II and the eruption of further race riots and violence across the United States, a new brand of interracial bodies formed: permanent bodies created by *governments* at both the municipal and state levels. These bodies could themselves be traced to similar temporary interracial bodies that local authorities had created in some American cities and states after the 1919 race riots; the Chicago mayor's Committee on Race Relations was the first of these, calling in its final report for a permanent interracial commission in Illinois.[28] But it was not until the race riots of summer 1943 in American cities like Beaumont, Detroit, Mobile, and New York that permanent, statutory interracial commissions were formed in over thirty American cities and more than ten states. Connecticut's state legislature enacted the first of these in late June 1943, followed by Illinois in July.[29]

In both its state and nonstate variants, interracial bodies in the United States became exceedingly popular during World War II. As a general matter, these were politically moderate bodies, dedicated more to improving the quality of life in segregated neighborhoods than challenging segregation. Historian Neil McMillen captures the mood:

Race relations suddenly became a cottage industry: interracial committees begat commissions against bigotry which begat councils for unity; there would be more than a thousand such groups dealing with tolerance for minorities by 1948. In return for not directly attacking racial discrimination and segregation, they had the support of such newly organized national groups as the Race Relations Division of the American Missionary Association, the American Friends Race Relations Committee, the American Jewish Congress Commission on Community Interrelations, and the American Council on Race Relations. Given the backing of such prestigious company and the official status many of the commissions had by virtue of being municipal agencies, as well as the endorsement of leading African Americans, promoting tolerance became voguish.[30]

Still, if interracial committees failed to challenge segregation in the American South, others may have been subtly influential. It was an agreement between Connecticut's Inter-Racial Commission and a movie projectionist in the town of Simsbury that permitted black tobacco workers to attend movie screenings and sit alongside a white audience. One of these young workers was a fifteen-year-old Martin Luther King, Jr., whose experiences as an African American in Simsbury in summer 1944 proved formative.[31]

With a host of permanent interracial commissions created by local governments during the war, a report commissioned by President Truman in 1946 called for the creation of a permanent, federal civil rights commission in the United States and the establishment of complementary state-level bodies. The body would not be created until the next decade, the focus would be exclusively on civil rights, and its structural criteria would not meet the requirements of today's NHRIs. Still, functional similarities between the federal civil rights commission and contemporary NHRIs exist, evident in the 1947 report's rationale and recommendation:

> Nowhere in the federal government is there an agency charged with the continuous appraisal of the status of civil rights, and the efficiency of the machinery with which we hope to improve that status. . . . A permanent Commission could perform an invaluable function by collecting data. It could also carry on technical research to improve the fact-gathering methods now in use. Ultimately, this would make possible a periodic audit of the extent to which our civil

rights are secure. If it did this and served as a clearing house and focus of coordination for the many private, state, and local agencies working in the civil rights field, it would be invaluable to them and to the federal government. A permanent Commission on Civil Rights should point all of its work towards regular reports which would include recommendations for action.[32]

Substitute "human rights" for "civil rights," and the description could apply to a contemporary NHRI.

In the next decades, local civil rights commissions at the state and municipal levels continued to be created in the United States, with clear links to prior inter-racial bodies. Various states' trajectories illustrate these linkages. For example, Connecticut's governmental Inter-Racial Commission, created in 1943, was re-named the Civil Rights Commission in 1951 and the Commission on Human Rights and Opportunities in 1967, its current name. In South Carolina, non-governmental committees functioned from 1919 until 1975 under various names; the original 1919 Committee on Interracial Cooperation became the Council on Human Relations in 1957 and the Council for Human Rights in 1963, until it was effectively replaced by a governmental commission in the early 1970s.[33] After the 1954 landmark ruling in *Brown v. Board of Education*, the Southern Regional Council (which in the mid-1940s had replaced the Commission on Interracial Cooperation) advocated explicitly that state human relations agencies be cre-ated.[34] By the early 1970s, most of the fifty states had governmental civil rights agencies, while only a handful of nongovernmental committees that could trace their lineage to the original interracial committees of the interwar period survived.[35]

Interracial bodies dating to the early and mid-twentieth century in the United States share important if surprising links with today's NHRIs. Histori-cally, interracial committees and commissions were the predecessors of civil rights agencies, national bodies that American officials promoted at the United Nations in the 1960s as an alternative to international human rights mechanisms. Substantively, these agencies sought to remedy wrongs and engaged in research and education, just as they networked extensively, all attributes of NHRIs. And though earlier bodies were not typically complaints-handling mechanisms, their later counterparts often were, generally working within a limited mandate of discrimination (e.g., housing, employment). As Gunnar Myrdal noted, more-over, these institutions "rendered interracial work socially respectable in the conservative South." Like the agenda-setting, legitimating effects of NHRIs, that was no small feat.[36] At the same time, the fact that leaders resorted to them in the aftermath of conflict, as a means of allaying social tensions and promoting a moderate human rights agenda that accepted inequality as part of the status quo, serves as a warning of the dualities often inherent in state institutions. It is stunning how official U.S. exceptionalism on the human rights front has virtually erased the history of these interracial committees; they are remembered in conjunction with local civil rights but in no way connected to broader global accounts of human rights institutions, including NHRIs.

National Counterparts of International Organizations

As international organizations emerged on the world stage, it became apparent that implementing their mandates would require active involvement by states. To this end, international organizations promoted the idea of national bodies, sometimes known as cooperating or implementing agencies. While NHRIs take various forms, on some level all NHRIs are counterparts to international human rights institutions.

When NHRIs are the starting point of analysis, it is tempting to overlook that these institutions are essentially the domestic counterpart of the UN Commission on Human Rights (CHR), now the Human Rights Council. It was the preparatory CHR, after all, that first mentioned the idea of an NHRI. In a 1946 resolution to the United Nations Economic and Social Council (ECOSOC), the nascent CHR recommended as part of its preparatory work that member states "establish information groups or local human rights committees within their countries who would transmit periodically information to the CHR on the observance of human rights in their countries, both in their legal systems and their jurisdictional and administrative practice."[37] Likewise, the twin functions of "promotion and protection," emphasized in the Paris Principles, have long been central framing devices in the work of almost all international human rights regimes, both at the United Nations and regionally.

The UNCHR had the example of at least two institutional forerunners: both the International Labor Organization and UNESCO had established national counterpart bodies. The ILO had created labor inspectorates in the interwar period, which had clear similarities with contemporary NHRIs. They were "composed of independent inspectors, who would be vested with the task of investigating, advising on, and informing about the protection of the workers. It was also recommended that the inspectors should report regularly on their findings to the central authority of the state, which would, in turn, publish the findings in the form of annual reports."[38] UNESCO also called, shortly after its creation in 1945, for national commissions to "advise the government . . . in matters relating to the parent-organisation."[39] Interestingly, there is evidence that commission members were aware of the UNESCO commissions, since René Cassin, who was France's representative to the CHR, was also a delegate to UNESCO conferences.[40] More important, as detailed below, records of CHR meetings confirm that Cassin himself, an ardent supporter of implementing human rights domestically, introduced and promoted the idea of local human rights committees within the commission.

National counterparts to international bodies may appear innocuous, but like NHRIs they raise a few critical questions. For one, the risk that international demands will overwhelm these domestic bodies is ever present. International and regional human rights mechanisms are governmental agencies, run by member states with political interests; even where independence and expertise are valued, politics can carry the day. This is amply evident in ECOSOC's 1946 resolution where the idea of a national human rights body was first mentioned officially: "The Members of the United Nations are invited to consider the desirability of establishing information groups or local human rights committees within their respective countries *to collaborate with them in furthering the work of the Commission on Human Rights*."[41] This resolution is emphasized in virtually every account of NHRIs as the initial spark behind today's NHRIs. Yet note the emphasis on international collaboration, in contrast to the preparatory CHR's actual proposal, quoted above, where the focus was on transmitting information about national human rights practices. It is no secret that UN member states, on both sides of the Cold War divide, wanted to advance human rights standards but not enforce them, since a strong human rights system might expose each of them to unwelcome pressures. These perverse interests seeped into the first official reference to a national human rights body, the 1946 ECOSOC resolution.

These dynamics were also evident in France, which claims the world's first NHRI. For Cassin, who was a law professor acutely interested in legalizing and implementing human rights and was committed to human rights activism (long before losing almost thirty relatives, including his sister, in the Holocaust), the idea was to create national bodies independent of their governments.[42] The primary goal of these bodies would be to serve as information transmitters, sending uncensored reports of domestic practices to the international body, thereby contributing to implementation and a stronger UN system. Unlike subsequent NHRIs, moreover, Cassin imagined these national bodies would include nonstate actors, who would act in their capacity as experts, much as Cassin had advocated for a CHR of independent experts rather than governmental representatives.[43] This is clearly not what the commission as a whole had in mind.

Within the CHR, Cassin advocated unsuccessfully for independent national human rights bodies, failing to re-place the issue on the CHR's agenda after the initial proposal to ECOSOC misfired. At the eighteenth meeting of the commission's first session in 1947, Cassin reminded his colleagues that an ECOSOC resolution had already called on member states to create "information groups."[44] Noting that France intended to establish such a body shortly, Cassin said he wanted to gauge other states' positions. Eleanor Roosevelt, as the CHR's chair, declared it was unnecessary to take any concrete steps regarding national bodies, which were already charged with transmitting information to the United Nations *through their governments*. The Soviet Union's representative successfully introduced a motion tabling the debate. A few meetings later, shortly before the close of the commission's first session, Cassin moved to amend the final report, hoping to remind member states to create national bodies that would provide the CHR *directly and regularly* with information about state practices—bypassing their national governments altogether.[45] The idea went nowhere, though a few months later in 1947 France created the first state institution for human rights, headed until 1960 by Cassin himself. But the French government and Cassin also had very different views of what this would entail. The CHR was a consultative or largely advisory body, tellingly housed within the French Foreign Ministry and focused almost entirely on international law. According to some accounts, Cassin himself may have used the national commission strategically as a counterweight or buffer to French government opponents, who resisted strong UN human rights mechanisms; they feared that, given the country's colonial context, French naturalized citizens might begin making formal human rights demands of their own state.[46]

The history of NHRIs is often traced to the 1946 UN resolution, two years before the Universal Declaration of Human Rights was even issued, just as France is known to have created the first governmental human rights institution. But an uncritical look at these developments offers an incomplete picture of the historical emergence of NHRIs. From the first time that the idea of governments creating an NHRI was raised in 1946, powerful states fought quickly to limit these bodies and ensure that they remained an extension of international mechanisms: state controlled and largely promotional. From the very outset, NHRIs were set up to be weak, subordinate to states' international interests.

Preliminary Lessons

In retelling the history of human rights, Samuel Moyn warns, there is a danger that the past will be distorted "to suit the present."[47] It is possible that the institutional parallels traced here were historical coincidences more than antecedents in any meaningful sense, or that the state in the past acted very differently from the state in today's globalized world. To justify linking NHRIs to long-standing state institutions and practices, one must demonstrate that substantive commonalities existed and there was a reasonable chance that actors were aware of past institutions and drew on them in designing NHRIs. Ideally, one should also clarify how past institutional persistencies or experiences might inform current institutions.

Each of the state institutions reviewed here has strong similarities with particular NHRI functions: both the ombudsman and NHRI can have mechanisms for handling complaints or social grievances; government commissions emphasize inquiries, information, and advising; interracial committees have a comparable educational and research role; and international cooperation is integral to all national counterpart bodies to international organizations. When the first NHRIs were created, they drew variously on prior institutional arrangements, including those discussed here, though the specific processes of selection and convergence by which this occurred varied.

Five preliminary lessons arise from this historical overview, preliminary because their full implications—and limitations—can become more apparent only after examining specific NHRIs in subsequent chapters. First, the contradictions embedded in the Janus-faced state are apparent in all of the historical precursors. On the one hand, these institutions were potentially beneficial, acting as democratic checks (ombudsman), furthering efficient and informed governance (government commissions), raising basic awareness and legitimizing rights claims (interracial committees), and implementing international norms domestically (national counterparts to international organizations). On the other hand, a closer look reveals a more critical side to these institutions: the challenging structural position occupied by the ombudsman, mediating between state and society from within the state; the possibility of undemocratic inefficiencies sometimes associated with government commissions; the narrow mandate and status-quo agenda characterizing interracial committees; and the weak, exclusionary, state-centric tendencies of national counterparts to international organizations.

Second, these state institutions exemplify vividly how the state is an organizationally complex actor. An NHRI is a single actor in a web of other state actors, marked by differentials of power and interests. Consequently, actors in and out of the state can use state institutions strategically to advance their own interests (as in the case of some government-appointed commissions). This playing field is potentially complicated in situations where the state institution is also supposed to be an interlocutor for society, as is the ombudsman. When civil society is itself divided about the desire to confront the state, violence is thrown into the mix, or multiple institutions operate locally as they do in a federal system of governance, identifying state authority becomes a more complicated task, evident in the role of interracial committees. Add an international dimension, so that the state institution is the domestic counterpart of an international organ, and the likelihood of contradictory demands and constituencies further rises.

Third, internationally, embryonic calls for NHRIs in the immediate postwar period revealed a somewhat sinister dynamic still evident today. Powerful states attempted to limit national human rights bodies, restricting them to a largely promotional and advisory role, attempting to ensure that they remain subsumed to their international counterparts, and blocking society's direct access to and representation on international human rights bodies. Stated bluntly, states with shared interests in avoiding criticism and pressure for their own human rights practices colluded in the UN Human Rights Commission to limit human rights enforcement, internationally and nationally. Likewise, interracial commissions in the United States allied with politically moderate but powerful actors, who supported the status quo and limited the human rights agenda, while political leaders creating these bodies may have been more interested in avoiding further violence than committed to equality. Despite the advance of human rights norms since the end of the Cold War, it pays to remain vigilant of state motives for institutionalizing human rights.

Fourth, the role of personalities can be essential in understanding any institution, evident here most starkly in the case of René Cassin, but also in the local personalities who led and energized the work of interracial committees. Individual leaders sometimes served as mediators, representing particular claims and interests and helping to define the terms of the debate. It may in fact be that individual personalities matter most when state institutions are weakly institutionalized or contested; like any organization, as institutionalization rises, the cult of personality may decline.

Fifth, all of the state institutions examined were important producers of knowledge, transmitting information and issuing reports. This function is often dismissed out of hand as empty rhetoric, far from the concrete changes required for rights violations to desist. Yet the historical evidence from these institutions suggests that information and knowledge played a valuable role. The ombudsman collected information about particular social grievances, government commissions recorded an official account of wrongdoing, interracial committees placed human rights issues on the political and social agendas via research and education, while national counterparts to international bodies transmitted information about local conditions. This informational and knowledge-producing role, addressed more fully in Chapter 10, remains an integral feature of NHRIs, significant for its potential to contribute to human rights reform and for its institutional power to shape and control (or "officialize") social discourse and "truth."

Designed to regulate human rights locally, NHRIs signal the entry of the modern-bureaucratic state into the domestic human rights arena. While some states have institutionalized human rights in their foreign policies, the state in general has not tended to regulate human rights practices at home. The "regulatory state" has been active in other areas of governance, but it is indeed a relative newcomer to the business of human rights domestically.[48] Consequently, the rise of NHRIs is significant and to some extent a novel departure, linked to the modern discourse of human rights. Yet despite their nascency, these institutions share crucial similarities with earlier agencies, in terms of both historical connectivity and substantive overlap in functions and design. Each of the institutions identified here does not constitute distinct strands that fit neatly into a coherent whole, a compact history or linear account of contemporary NHRIs. Each set of institutions varies considerably, as a category and when compared to other precursors and today's NHRIs. Still, one common theme emerges: when governing authorities create institutions to regulate their own actions, a strategic logic is partly on display.

3

Tracking Global Diffusion

Sometimes ideas spread rapidly, as if out of nowhere, adopted by very diverse groups and across disparate contexts. Diffusion occurs when these ideas are institutionalized across a wide range of countries, despite obvious national differences and local resistance.[1] In this manner, democracy, liberalism, markets, and human rights became common parlance in the late twentieth century, embraced by a broad segment of political elites and social groups. The same is true of NHRIs, which in a relatively short span of time have proliferated around the world and evolved significantly. This chapter zeroes in on the global rise of NHRIs, offering evidence of these institutions' diffusion—quantitatively, I present trends and patterns showing that NHRIs have spread over time and space; qualitatively, I describe an evolving global "regime" on NHRIs (characterized by an international normative framework, cross-cutting transgovernmental networks, and formal participatory rights and standing in international organizations). These developments, themselves the product of parallel global processes, set the stage for understanding why specific NHRIs are created.

When an idea diffuses globally, it does not mean that actors are committed wholly and unhypocritically to it, or that the ideas are in some way optimal or even largely beneficial to society. Diffusion describes, first and foremost, an idea's proliferation across different contexts; on its own, it tells us nothing of specific causes and consequences. And yet diffusion is remarkable in that it suggests a world of interconnectedness, where states do not make choices in isolation. These choices are all the more fascinating when they entail policy areas and domestic structures traditionally falling under national prerogative: Why would so many states undertake similar domestic structural changes, often highly controversial and sometimes costly, especially when the benefits of doing so are unclear?

The global rise of NHRIs refers, on the most basic level, to an increase in the number of NHRIs in the world. I review several of these trends below, tracing the number of NHRIs since the 1970s, and patterns of diffusion across regions. But diffusion is about more than numbers. When an idea diffuses, it can also mature, evolving in more concrete and complex ways, achieving greater depth and institutionalization. The diffusion of NHRIs, then, is also apparent in the emergence of an international regime devoted to the creation and strengthening of these human rights institutions. While students of NHRIs have described aspects of this development, and attention to other human rights regimes is extensive, the emergence of an overarching and coherent regime (consisting of "principles, norms, rules, and decision-making procedures around which actor expectations converge in a given issue-area") has yet to be recognized.[2] I outline below the evolution of this international regime, which has progressed through various phases and signals the institutionalization of NHRIs on an international level.

Just as the emerging international regime on NHRIs provides evidence that these institutions are diffusing, it also reinforces the very growth and strengthening of NHRIs. This evolving regime exerts influence by socializing states about the meaning and desirability of an NHRI, sometimes equipping them with the technical capacity to create these institutions. If the historical precursors discussed in Chapter 2 help to account for the *origins of the idea* of an NHRI, the international regime on NHRIs—itself embedded within a broader international context and historical moment—goes a long way toward explaining the *global diffusion* of these institutions, or how the idea of an NHRI has evolved over time and been transmitted across so many states.

The Proliferation of NHRIs: Trends and Patterns

Diffusion cannot be assumed; it requires evidence, confirmation that an idea really has spread across diverse contexts. Two closely related pieces of evidence are especially valuable. First, there needs to be evidence that the idea's acceptance has grown over time. When an idea diffuses, it will often occur in "waves," or stages, with each period evolving in somewhat distinct ways.[3] Second, just as the idea should diffuse over time, studies of diffusion suggest that there may be evidence of geographic clustering, including subregionally; this is because ideas often spread at a similar pace and in comparable ways within areas in close proximity

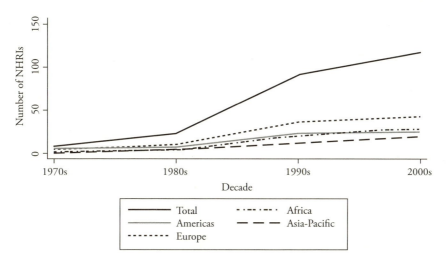

FIGURE 1. The global diffusion of NHRIs, 1970–2010.

to one another.[4] The rise of NHRIs shows strong evidence of diffusion both over time and across space.

Trends over time reveal a steady rise in the number of NHRIs since the 1970s (Figure 1). Like the diffusion of most innovations, the trend of the past four decades is a classic S-curve, marked by a few early adopters, a period of rapid proliferation, and then some leveling off. In 1980, there were only a dozen NHRIs in the world; these doubled in the next decade, growing by almost 300 percent to reach 95 NHRIs at the end of the millennium. By mid-2012, there were 115 such institutions, over two-thirds of which were created in the post–Cold War period; only 15 states had not yet committed to creating an NHRI.[5] The explosive growth of NHRIs in the 1990s reflects several global trends discussed below, including the end of the Cold War, a parallel rise in human rights institutions and activism, and a broader drive toward democratization. Alongside the diffusion of NHRIs, parliamentary human rights bodies and state institutions devoted to international humanitarian law have even proliferated worldwide.[6]

As with any innovation, there are also signs of clustering, in this case evident across regions. In absolute terms, Europe has the highest number of NHRIs in the world today (40), followed by Africa (28), the Americas (25), and the Asia Pacific (22). In relative terms, as a percentage of the overall number of countries in a region, the ranking varies somewhat. Europe still has the highest concentration of NHRIs (80 percent), followed by the Americas (68 percent), Africa (54 percent), and the Asia Pacific (38 percent).

Among the first generation of NHRIs pre-1980, the highest concentration of these institutions was found in the Americas and Europe, which each had five. The 1980s saw the largest rise in Europe and steady growth across other regions. It was not until the 1990s that NHRI creation across all regions spiked, especially pronounced in Africa (a 600 percent increase from the previous decade) and quintupling in other regions. Since 2000, NHRIs have continued to be created across all regions, with the highest growth occurring in the Asia Pacific.

While decades and regions are somewhat artificial demarcations, they can capture changes in an institution's diffusion. The summary trends and patterns presented here, including the growth of NHRIs over time and regional clustering, offer two crucial pieces of evidence that NHRIs have diffused globally. Yet the reasons for or significance of this institutional diffusion cannot be read off of these developments. A closer look at the evidence suggests a related qualitative shift: as the number of NHRIs around the world has risen, a global regime on NHRIs has evolved and reinforced states' willingness to create and strengthen these institutions. Once the number of these NHRIs crossed a certain threshold, a self-reinforcing logic took hold in the 1990s, with the number and scope of these institutions only growing exponentially.[7]

An Evolving Regime

International regimes can be difficult to spot because they are created in piecemeal fashion—a meeting here, a treaty there, a set of guidelines, informal meetings that transform into formal forums. Once recognized, however, international regimes can appear across disparate regulatory arenas and garner considerable attention, from international nonproliferation regimes to those focusing on trade or the environment. In the human rights field, regimes have been studied on three levels: the human rights regime within the United Nations, itself revolving around the Human Rights Council; regional human rights regimes in Europe, the Americas, and Africa; and treaty-specific (or issue-area) regimes, such as those on torture, women's rights, and racial discrimination.[8] Unlike transnational networks, which comprise a broad segment of actors, including NGOs, international regimes focus on rules, norms, and procedures, with states and international organizations playing a central role.[9] These features are fully on display for NHRIs. Indeed, the system of standards, networks, capacity building, international accreditation, and participation that revolves around NHRIs constitutes an evolving international regime, one both reflecting and shaping the global diffusion of NHRIs.

In a seminal study of human rights regimes, Jack Donnelly traced the evolution of the major human rights regimes, identifying stages of institutionalization: declarations, promotion, implementation, and enforcement.[10] The evolving international regime on NHRIs has also gone through comparable phases. Between the 1960s and 1980s, as elaborated below, the nascent regime focused almost exclusively on standard setting, with some attempts at promotion; it was mostly a declaratory regime. This culminated in the 1993 Paris Principles, an authoritative body of standards that set the stage for much greater institutionalization. Indeed, this next period consisted of far greater formalization of standards. The Paris Principles opened the way to more intense promotion of NHRIs, especially through technical assistance, and some implementation via formal networking and coordination. These implementation and networking efforts deepened in the new millennium and gave way after 2006 to partial enforcement, as the process of international accreditation and legal standing became increasingly formalized.

For decades now, a broad spectrum of international standards and activities surrounding NHRIs has evolved into a global regime. These developments should no longer be viewed as disparate mechanisms, arising in an ad hoc fashion or by coincidence. Rather, the evolution of this international regime reflects a gradual process of institutionalization, described in the remainder of this chapter, building on prior institutional developments and reflecting the broader global context. The evolving regime on NHRIs, moreover, has served both to regulate NHRIs and to help transform them into viable international and domestic actors.

Phase 1: Norm Emergence, 1940s–1980s

Fundamental to any international regime are its defining norms, rules, and guidelines. When the idea of an NHRI was first articulated in the immediate postwar period, it was initially framed in general, vague terms, as national information-generating bodies that would serve as domestic counterparts to the UN Human Rights Commission. As discussed in Chapter 2, the United Nations first addressed the topic of NHRIs in 1946, when the Economic and Social Council issued a resolution calling for their creation.[11] Silence followed. With the exception of a few resolutions in the 1960s, little attention was paid to enhancing the independent role of NHRIs. The ongoing assumption in these ECOSOC resolutions in the 1960s was that national human rights bodies were to supplement the work of the UN Human Rights Commission.[12] Beginning in the late 1970s, however, UN standard setting started to gain momentum at the same time that international human rights issues more generally began consolidating.

The reasons for this hiatus—for why UN activism vis-à-vis NHRIs, first articulated in the 1940s, did not increase notably until the 1970s—are most likely related to why human rights discourse itself did not take off during the same period. As some historians argue, it took the social mobilizations on behalf of rights and equality issues of the 1960s and early 1970s for "human rights" to gain traction as a global discourse.[13] And as international human rights mechanisms (including treaties) grew in the 1970s, the creation of parallel domestic bodies was a natural organizational complement. In particular, given that the activities of the UN Human Rights Commission were under strain, marked by heavy workload, creating national institutions may have seemed a viable long-term solution. Politically, and perhaps most importantly, human rights institutions generated a unique degree of international consensus, overcoming both East-West and North-South divisions. As domestic bodies, potentially under state control, they bypassed controversial sovereignty trade-offs associated with international human rights institutions.

The position of the United States is instructive in this regard. As human rights issues became increasingly politicized internationally, while civil rights in the United States came to the forefront and transnational activist networks formed, it became increasingly likely that any state (whether newly independent, Cold War proxy, or even hegemonic power) could come under assault for its human rights practices. Thus, in a reversal of its postwar stance, when it tried to limit the development of independent national human rights bodies (Chapter 2), the United States in the 1960s supported the creation of national advisory committees on human rights—even while resisting both UN pressure for its civil rights record and the creation of a UN commissioner for human rights. According to the U.S. representative to the UN Commission on Human Rights,

> Judging from the interest evoked in the Commission by the US report on its national advisory committees on human rights (national and state Civil Rights Committees . . .) and the comparative lack of government . . . committees on human rights in all other countries . . . our Government could profitably elucidate this point—especially for the benefit of African and Asian states.[14]

For any state that was subject to (or feared being subject to) international human rights pressure, national institutions may have offered a way of avoiding greater *international* institutionalization.

By the 1970s, then, promoting the idea of an NHRI within the United Nations generated consensus partly because it promised to shield state sovereignty, at the same time that it satisfied rising demands for human rights reform. The political climate of the time made it amply clear that states could hope, at best, to control but not to stop the institutionalization of human rights. Against this political backdrop, international norms for NHRIs were detailed in a seminar on National and Local Institutions for the Promotion and Protection of Human Rights held in Geneva in September 1978. This may also have been the first time reference was made to "national human rights institutions" as a term. Significantly, moreover, the name of this early seminar reflected NHRIs' dual functions of promotion and protection, standards that remained in place throughout the decade of the 1980s.[15] By the late 1980s, the United Nations began issuing annual resolutions, calling for concerted efforts to create and strengthen NHRIs.[16] As states enhanced their support for NHRIs within the United Nations, the idea of an NHRI began cohering around a minimal standard and became the subject of regular international resolutions. Decades of international standard setting and the experience of over a dozen NHRIs now paved the way for global diffusion.

Phase 2: Standard Setting and Promotion, the 1990s

The end of the Cold War gave fresh impetus to human rights, and NHRIs were no exception. Two documents were essential in taking the notion of an NHRI to a new level: the 1991 Paris Principles and the 1993 Vienna Declaration and Programme of Action. Building on the guidelines issued in Geneva in 1978, UN standard setting was transformed in the 1990s, as NHRIs went from relative obscurity to playing a leading role in the human rights program of the United Nations. This sea change was launched at a workshop in Paris in 1991, where a "common charter" for NHRIs emerged.[17] The Paris Principles, as they came to be called, developed into the touchstone of all NHRIs. They remain to this day the authoritative set of international standards or minimum requirements defining an NHRI.

While not differing significantly in content from the rules agreed to in earlier decades, the Paris Principles began to outline a more ambitious role for NHRIs as *autonomous* institutions. These guidelines called for institutions that were pluralistic and representative, adequately funded, and carrying stable mandates irrespective of the ruling government. Above all, NHRIs were to be independent of

Table 2

Evolving International Standards for NHRIs

Paris Principles (1993)	Emerging interpretations (2009)

Dual mandate
  Human rights promotion *and* protection
 	
Legal basis
  Constitution or legislation
 	
Functions
  ■ *Advisory role* (jurisdiction: any domestic human rights matter)
  ■ *Treaties:* promote ratification and ensure harmonization between domestic and international laws
  ■ *International cooperation* (UN bodies, regional institutions, and other NHRIs)
  ■ *Domestic cooperation:* governmental *and* nongovernmental bodies
  ■ *Human rights education*
 	
Independence
  ■ Governmental representatives can serve only in advisory role
  ■ Adequate capacities: infrastructure and funding
  ■ No arbitrary removal of members
  ■ Noninterference in work by higher authorities
  ■ May address public opinion directly or via the press
 	
Pluralism
  Socially representative (civil society forces "involved in the promotion and protection of human rights")
 	
Optional capacity
  Process complaints and petitions
    ■ May be brought by anyone
    ■ Must resolve (via conciliation, legally binding decision, or confidentially)
	Functions
	  ■ Emphasis on *international cooperation* with three types of body: the Human Rights Council and its mechanisms; UN human rights treaty bodies; NHRI networks (ICC and regional networks)
	  ■ *Follow-up:* government must consider NHRI recommendations in a timely manner
	  ■ Annual reports required
	
	Independence
	  ■ *Selection and appointment*: transparency, broad consultation, and recruitment
	  ■ *Staffing*
	    ○ Secondment: senior posts excluded; no more than 25% (and never over 50%) of staff can be seconded
	    ○ Some full-time members required
	  ■ *Funding*
	    ○ Comparable to public service salaries; adequate accommodation for head office and for communications system
	    ○ Foreign sources should *not* compose "core funding"
	    ○ Complete financial autonomy over budget
	
	Pluralism
	■ Emphasis on *diverse models,* including: members representing different social groups (Paris Principles); diversity in terms of appointment procedures; procedures facilitating ongoing input from social groups; diverse staff

(continued)

Table 2

(Continued)

Paris Principles (1993)	Emerging interpretations (2009)
■ Ensure complainant has access to remedies ■ Issue recommendations	■ Requires "meaningful participation of women" *Additional Issues* Special consideration given to NHRIs during a coup or state of emergency; limitations due to "national security" or operating in a "volatile context"

Sources: Paris Principles (1993); and International Coordinating Committee of National Human Rights Institutions for the Promotion and Protection of Human Rights, "General Observations" (November 2009).

executive power if they were to be functionally effective. These and other key provisions of the Paris Principles are outlined in Table 2.

This expanded agenda was echoed in the Vienna Declaration (1993), which confirmed the growing significance of NHRIs: "The World Conference on Human Rights reaffirms the important and constructive role played by national institutions for the promotion and protection of human rights."[18] The Vienna Declaration, accepted by 171 states, was the concluding document of the World Conference on Human Rights in 1993, a turning point for human rights governance.[19] The two-week conference was attended by approximately seven thousand participants, including over eight hundred NGOs. The emphasis was on the interdependence of various rights (i.e., civil, political, economic, and social); linkages among rights, democracy, and development; the rights of marginalized groups like women, children, and indigenous peoples; and the creation of mutually reinforcing mechanisms at the international, regional, and national levels. Conceptually, NHRIs thus complemented evolving notions of global rights governance articulated in Vienna: interdependence, comprehensiveness, social inclusion, and multilayered global governance.

The Vienna Declaration's attention to NHRIs was itself the outgrowth of a series of regional meetings following the Paris Principles. These meetings included regional preparatory meetings for the Vienna Conference (Africa in November 1992, Latin America in January 1993, and Asia in March and April 1993), a Commonwealth Workshop on NHRIs in 1992, and a human rights workshop for the Asia-Pacific region in 1993. These regional meetings, addressing human rights more generally, permitted state and nongovernmental representatives to collaborate and develop ideas about the structure and role of NHRIs.

International standards, moreover, still gave states freedom in choosing the particular kind of NHRI that best suited their needs. While on some level the idea of an NHRI necessitates accepting the universality of at least some basic human rights, international actors repeatedly recognized the importance of national differences. Hence, the Vienna World Conference noted that, as long as states abided by the Paris Principles, they were free to "to choose the framework . . . best suited to its particular needs at the national level."[20] Institutional design, at least in principle, consisted of balancing national preferences with international guidelines.

All of these efforts, from the workshop producing the Paris Principles to a host of regional meetings and then the World Conference in Vienna, culminated in a UN General Assembly resolution in December 1993 devoted exclusively to NHRIs. The resolution reasserted the messages set forth in Paris and Vienna, further legitimating the creation of these institutions. It called for follow-up meetings and greater technical assistance, committing the United Nations to an ongoing "catalytic" role in support of NHRIs. The stage was set for the proliferation of these institutions worldwide.

NORMATIVE EXPANSION

Once the Paris Principles were in place, and as the number of NHRIs grew, international activities surrounding these institutions duly expanded. One of the key developments was the formation of NHRI networks, with the International Coordinating Committee (ICC) at the helm. Composed of over a dozen leading NHRIs, the ICC was created in 1993 and proceeded to meet annually. Throughout the 1990s, the group's primary objective was to promote compliance with the Paris Principles.

Substantively, the Paris Principles continued the emphasis from earlier decades on independence and pluralism as guiding principles, while broadening its scope to include cooperation with NGOs, protection of marginalized groups, and attention to economic and social rights. These trends mirrored broader shifts in human rights discourse. Thus, the Paris Principles called on NHRIs to "develop relations with the non-governmental organizations devoted to promoting and protecting human rights, to economic and social development, to combating racism, to protecting particularly vulnerable groups (especially children, migrant workers, refugees, physically and mentally disabled persons) or to specialized areas."[21]

International guidelines had long recommended that NHRI membership be representative of society, but beginning in the 1990s these principles also became more socially *inclusive*: they paid closer attention to NGOs and otherwise-marginalized vulnerable groups.[22] First, there was stronger emphasis on NHRIs cooperating with domestic NGOs and treating them as partners in human rights implementation. This has not always worked out in practice, and NGOs remain among the most vocal critics of state human rights agencies. Still, the move to work alongside NGOs and sometimes include them in NHRI decision making is significant, reflecting post—Cold War dynamics where nonstate actors played a more prominent role.

International standards for NHRIs also became more inclusive in calling attention to vulnerable groups, including women, children, and disabled persons. In some cases, this meant creating specialized NHRIs devoted to these previously overlooked groups; in other cases, existing institutions targeted the treatment of these groups.[23] While the rights of some vulnerable groups had been recognized previously, these rights were eclipsed during the Cold War by rights violations that were more blatantly political, that is, deliberate acts committed by the state against its purported opponents. In contrast, once the Cold War ended, the status of vulnerable groups quickly rose on the rights agenda. This is illustrated vividly by the Convention on the Rights of the Child (CRC): whereas a 1959 declaration on the rights of the child had stalled for decades, the CRC opened for signature a little over a week after the Berlin Wall's fall and soon entered into force.[24]

The post–Cold War period also saw much greater attention to economic and social rights in NHRI mandates.[25] Both international actors and state institutions began emphasizing rights associated with health, housing, education, and employment. While the West had embraced civil and political rights almost exclusively during the Cold War, the end of superpower conflict made it possible for economic and social rights to lose their stigma as socialist or communist prerogatives. Systemic rights violations that had previously been all but neglected became visible and legitimate objects of reform. This growing attention to economic and social rights occurred in tandem with a more general inclination to recognize the interdependence of all rights, close linkages between human rights and development, and growing interest in how "structural violence" and human rights intersected.[26] Even if states merely found it less threatening to address economic and social rights, which could be realized only progressively, versus more traditional human rights, NHRI attention to these neglected rights no less signaled normative expansion.

These substantive trends (Table 2) were themselves part and parcel of a larger agenda linking human rights to notions of democracy and development. Whereas NHRI guidelines during the Cold War had operated more or less in isolation, the 1990s ushered in a period where the idea of an NHRI was grafted onto democracy and development programs more generally. These, in turn, were supported by Western governments and international financial institutions, signaling markers of "good governance" and credit worthiness.

CAPACITY BUILDING

The institutionalization of NHRIs in the 1990s occurred alongside a dramatic rise in technical assistance to NHRIs, by both international organizations and foreign governments. Technical assistance in the international realm consists of knowledge transfers intended to increase a state's capacity to implement an international goal. In the case of NHRIs, governments can initiate a request for technical assistance, for either creating or strengthening an institution. Since the 1990s, technical assistance for NHRIs has been closely interconnected with support for democracy enhancement (including in postconflict settings) as well as partnerships with civil society.

The United Nations, namely the Office of the High Commissioner for Human Rights (OHCHR), but also the United Nations Development Programme (UNDP), has been at the forefront of providing technical assistance for NHRIs.[27] This was itself part of a greater trend of UN human rights assistance offered since the mid-1950s. Initially consisting mostly of "advisory services" (especially provision of experts, funding of fellowships, and organizing of human rights seminars), over time UN advisory and technical support in the field of human rights came to include constitutional, electoral, and legislative reform assistance; the administration of justice; and support for NGOs and civil society.[28]

Human rights capacity building increased gradually over time, skyrocketing in the mid-1980s and especially the early 1990s. The creation of the Voluntary Fund for Technical Cooperation in the Field of Human Rights in 1987 propelled activities in this area. Most, though not all, future NHRI projects would be supported by this Voluntary Fund. A decade later, the UN General Assembly and the UN Commission on Human Rights tasked the nascent OHCHR with devoting a major component of its technical cooperation program to the creation and strengthening of NHRIs.[29] A special post within that office focusing exclusively on NHRIs reinforced these developments. International attention and assistance to NHRIs increased almost immediately. Under its Technical Cooperation

Programme, the OHCHR elaborated a comprehensive "programme of action" for providing technical assistance to NHRIs, fostering their creation, strengthening, and cooperation.[30]

In addition to international organizations, governments themselves, including those of Canada, Australia, and Denmark, have helped to diffuse NHRIs. Governments can provide foreign NHRIs with technical assistance through their own NHRIs, through cooperation agreements, or through other state bodies like development agencies. Government support of foreign NHRIs often is part of a broader strategy of promoting "sustainable development and good governance," whether out of a normative commitment to these principles, a strategic interest in strengthening foreign partners, or a more complicated mix of motives.[31]

Whether technical assistance to NHRIs is provided by international organizations or foreign governments, it can take a range of forms, including offering expertise and training, organizing workshops and seminars, sponsoring consultancies and exchanges, and helping to draft legislation. Among the most basic types of technical assistance to NHRIs is training or education.[32] Training often consists of developing educational materials or courses, as well as helping NHRIs create documentation centers. It can involve the transfer of specialized skills to diverse state actors, such as those investigating human rights complaints and members of the judiciary. Technical assistance can also take the form of consultations and advisory services, including assisting an NHRI in devising strategic plans or hosting an international conference. Sometimes exchanges occur, in which staff members of two or more NHRIs trade personnel, or when an NHRI "loans" senior personnel to its counterpart; other exchanges can take place between state agencies, including law enforcement, or via internships and study tours. While easy to dismiss as technical-bureaucratic mundanity, capacity-building efforts have been essential in transmitting the internationally sanctioned idea of an NHRI across borders.

Phase 3: Networking and Implementation, 2000–2005

The international regime on NHRIs reached a new level after 2000, as networking of NHRIs became far more institutionalized. Supported by the United Nations, NHRIs after the Cold War began regular information exchanges with each other. This occurred on multiple levels of governance: internationally, regionally, and even subregionally. Over a dozen networks of NHRIs gradually emerged around the world, with members meeting regularly, issuing statements, and placing issues on each other's agendas. Parallel to the rise of other transgovernmental networks (e.g., of judges, regulators, and central bankers), NHRI networks represent the extension of this post–Cold War organizational form to the human rights arena. And given the traditionally dominant role of nonstate actors as active promoters of human rights, the rise of NHRI networks signifies an especially significant development. This networking shift follows a broad trend toward multilateralism, as well as post–Cold War dynamics of globalization and regionalization.[33]

Networks of NHRIs have emerged across diverse regions of the world. These transgovernmental linkages set standards of state behavior, meet regularly, and exchange valuable information and services. These networks first appeared in the 1990s, though becoming far more institutionalized after 2000, as detailed below. The umbrella forum for the international network of NHRIs is the ICC, created in 1991. Since then, the ICC has held over ten international workshops or conferences in which dozens of NHRIs participate. Following the First International Workshop on National Institutions for the Promotion and Protection of Human Rights in Paris (1991), similar UN-sponsored international workshops have been held biannually.[34]

Regionally, networks of NHRIs also formed. In 1994, for example, the first European Workshop on National Institutions was hosted by France. Africa likewise held a series of regional workshops, beginning with one in Yaoundé, Cameroon, in 1995. The Asia-Pacific region also saw a significant increase in activities devoted to NHRIs since the mid-1990s, including several regional meetings and the creation of a permanent region-wide network, the Asia Pacific Forum of National Human Rights Institutions. Most recently, a network of NHRIs in the Americas has formed. Table 3 lists some of these emerging transgovernmental networks.

After 2000, a more formal and hierarchical structure of regional and international networks of NHRIs emerged.[35] Under the umbrella of the ICC, each of four regions would have a recognized network: the Asia-Pacific Forum, the Network of African NHRIs, the European Group of NHRIs, and the Network of NHRIs in the Americas. Only those NHRIs accredited by the ICC with "A" status could be full voting members of the regional network; and the chair of the network would be the region's representative on the ICC Bureau. In this manner, a system has emerged of regional networks structurally interconnected with the international network of NHRIs (or ICC), even while other regional and subregional networks continue to coexist.

As relatively coherent groupings, regional networks have been exceedingly active in promoting the creation and strengthening of NHRIs. They provide regular forums for exchanging information, whether annual meetings or thematic workshops, or training and staff exchanges. They are also standard-generating

Table 3
Transgovernmental Networks of NHRIs

NHRI network	Year created
International Coordinating Committee of NHRIs	1991
European Group of NHRIs*	1994
Asia-Pacific Forum of NHRIs*	1996
Ibero-American Federation of the Ombudsman	1996
Conference of Euro-Mediterranean National Institutions for the Promotion and Protection of Human Rights	1998
Network of NHRIs in the Americas*	2002
Arab NHRIs	2003
West African Network of NHRIs (previously West African Forum)	2006
Network of African NHRIs*	2007
Commonwealth Forum of NHRIs	2007
NHRIs in the East African Community	2009

*A regional network formally affiliated with the ICC.

bodies, as they issue resolutions, commission reports, and in some cases assist in developing region-specific jurisprudence. Within their region, they serve as pressuring mechanisms, encouraging states to create and reform NHRIs. They can transfer knowledge about international standards and technical capacities, or they can create incentives for states to join the regional club of NHRIs. The impact of these networks is thus both bilateral (in terms of individual NHRIs) and multilateral (on the world stage, interacting with other networks and international organizations).

Despite broad similarities, regional networks have evolved in somewhat different ways. The European Group of NHRIs was first to appear in 1994, assisted by the Council of Europe; it now consists of thirty-four NHRIs from thirty-two countries.[36] As informal exchanges intensified among NHRIs in the Council of Europe and international calls for coordination and accreditation intensified, ad hoc meetings hardened into a formal network. And unlike other regions, Europe has seen relatively little by way of subregional networking of NHRIs, with the partial exception of a Euro-Mediterranean partnership. In addition to the Council of Europe, the Organization for Security and Cooperation in Europe (OSCE) has been especially active in promoting NHRIs in the region.

In Africa, though a formal regional network was also created only after regularized meetings were in place, the African network reflected the growth of the region's broader human rights regime. In particular, the formation of the African Commission on Human and Peoples' Rights in the mid-1990s spurred regional human rights cooperation, including among NHRIs. A West African Human Rights Forum has further served to coordinate NHRIs in that subregion since 2006, with an East African counterpart forming more recently.

In the Asia Pacific region, a formal regional network has proven exceedingly active. Paradoxically, this activism has occurred in the only area in the world lacking a region-wide human rights regime. In no small measure, network activism in the region reflects the work of the Asia Pacific Forum (APF). The APF was created in 1996 and functioned until 2001 under the auspices of the Australian Human Rights Commission; beginning in 2002, it became fully independent, in the same manner that the ICC is an independently incorporated body with its own statute.[37] Given the region's broad diversity, moreover, subregional networking has emerged (e.g., a Declaration of Cooperation finalized in 2007 among NHRIs in Thailand, Indonesia, Malaysia, and the Philippines).

In contrast, network dynamics in the Americas have reflected international competition and shown extensive subregionalism. The Network of the Americas, formally linked to the ICC, was created in 2000, though the Ibero-American Federation of the Ombudsman (FIO) has existed since 1995. Very active in the region, the FIO includes non-Latin American states, including Spain. By some accounts, the formation of the Network of NHRIs in the Americas was partly delayed, compared to those in other regions, precisely because the FIO had overshadowed regional network activities. According to some experts, foreign governments like those of Canada and Denmark were strong proponents of an alternative network of NHRIs that would offset Spanish influence in the region.[38] Overlaying these apparent international tensions, subregional networks of NHRIs have also formed in the Caribbean, Central America, and among Andean countries.

It is true that networks not only have emerged from the inside out, but also have been actively encouraged by foreign states and international organizations. Former colonial powers, in particular, have fostered NHRI network growth as an ongoing extension of their influence. Thus, Spain has been active in Latin America, and France has supported NHRIs in North and East Africa. Straddling the role of former colonial power and international organization, the British Commonwealth has also been at the forefront of promoting the creation and strengthening of NHRIs. States with leading NHRIs (and typically active human rights dimensions to their foreign policies) have also played an active role, evident in the cases of Canada, Australia, and Denmark. For example, as part of a cooperation agreement with Cameroon's NHRI, Canada's Human Rights Commission helped organize the first African Conference on NHRIs in Yaoundé in 1996 and sent a delegation to participate in the landmark conference.[39]

The formation of NHRI networks can be variously interpreted. On the one hand, networks of NHRIs may be seen as uniquely positioned to promote human rights. These networks potentially bypass charges of intervention or cultural relativism, since they are composed of state agencies from among regional or social peers. In this sense, NHRI networks would seem to be both more efficient and more legitimate modes of global human rights governance. On the other hand, network formation signals a pooling of resources and power, potentially an entrenchment of state control over the human rights agenda. While reality may fall somewhere between the two depictions, the full implications of NHRI networks still need to be considered.

Networks of NHRIs emerged partly in response to the Paris Principles' calls for international collaboration of these state institutions; and once created, they have exerted autonomous influence as actors in their own right. The development of these networks, moreover, reflects several reinforcing factors, including broader regional and postcolonial networks; the role of international organizations (especially the OHCHR and, more recently, the UNDP); and leading NHRIs, themselves embedded in more general international political dynamics and serving as important network "hubs" or "nodes."

In terms of their effects, NHRI networks have been central mechanisms for diffusing NHRI standards and transmitting technical expertise, as well as gatekeepers of membership and participation in international forums—at once, reinforcing the participation of these networks in global human rights governance while promoting and strengthening a particular notion of what constitutes an effective NHRI. Put simply, NHRI networks have shaped the idea of an NHRI and enhanced its legitimacy. Whether these networks serve to protect more than transform state interests remains to be seen.

Phase 4: Enforcement and International Standing, Post-2005

Since the mid-2000s, the international regime on NHRIs has become more deeply institutionalized in terms of accreditation and standing. Accreditation refers here to the process by which membership in an organization is granted on the basis of having met specific standards or criteria. Accreditation is significant because it elicits conformance on the part of prospective members, since certain rights are conferred only on members and all others are excluded from the benefits. In this manner, accreditation is integral to constructing notions of what constitutes an effective NHRI. It defines what an NHRI is and which institutions merit approval as one, pushing states toward institutional convergence.

NHRI accreditation is conferred by the ICC, so that leading (A-status) NHRIs serve as the gatekeepers of membership. While the ICC has long had procedures in place regulating its activities, these had been largely informal processes. Procedural rules governing the work of both the ICC and its Subcommittee on Accreditation (SAC) were formalized, respectively, in 2000 and 2004.[40] And in 2002, the accreditation process reached a new level of maturation, as a working group was created to revisit the accreditation process and implement important reforms. These reforms included reaccrediting A-status institutions every five years, which in turn promised more systematic and ongoing monitoring of—and leverage over—NHRIs.

Quite significantly, moreover, as of October 2006, SAC started issuing "general observations," which amounted to a body of evolving jurisprudence, or authoritative interpretations of the criteria of membership and the precise functions and design requirements of NHRIs. This kind of self-reflection and explicit standard setting is intended to guide NHRIs as to the meaning and implications of the Paris Principles, to pressure states to conform more closely to internationally accepted practices for their NHRIs, and to set a systematic touchstone for ongoing evaluation of NHRIs. By October 2007, measures recommended by the working group's proposals for improving the accreditation process were adopted, intended to enhance transparency, introduce more rigorous reviews, offer more focused recommendations, and disseminate findings more broadly. This period of reform culminated in October 2008, in a new statute for the ICC and in amended rules of procedure for the SAC.

The international standing of NHRIs, as a category of actors, has also changed dramatically in recent years. International standing refers to the accorded status that a set of actors has, which can translate into formal recognition and participatory rights. These formal rights to participate in international forums and organizations reflect growing recognition that NHRIs appear to be autonomous and enduring actors, independent of states and nonstate actors. At the same time, formal standing can be essential in enhancing the collective power of NHRIs, especially in influencing international developments (e.g., treaty negotiations and procedures) and even the everyday work of international organizations. Significantly, standing and participation relate directly to accreditation: international organizations typically are willing to allow only accredited NHRIs to play a formal role in international-level proceedings.

International participation by NHRIs has been most intense within the UN system, especially within three settings: the Human Rights Council, treaty bodies, and broader standard-setting forums. In each venue, NHRI participation has been increasingly formalized and has accelerated rapidly since the mid-2000s, building on a decade of more limited—though not insignificant—participation. For example, NHRIs were present as a group in major world human rights conferences, including at Vienna (1993), Beijing (1995), and Durban (2001). And within the United Nations, in 1999, the UN Commission on Human Rights granted NHRIs limited rights to participate in relevant meetings from a special section of the floor devoted to "national institutions"; prior to that, NHRIs had to be seated with their states. Members of the ICC were even given seven minutes of speaking time on items concerning NHRIs.[41] Yet throughout the 1990s and early 2000s, the exact nature of NHRI participation remained in flux, with debates over whether and how these institutions should be participating in international bodies—directly, as observers, or akin to UN specialized agencies.[42]

Crucial to the evolving international regime on NHRIs was the decision by the newly established Human Rights Council in 2006 to continue its predecessor's policy (approved but never used) of permitting NHRI participation. This allowed NHRIs to participate broadly in the council's deliberations, both through oral and written contributions. More recently, under the Human Rights Council's new Universal Periodic Review system (whereby the council periodically reviews the human rights practices of all states), NHRIs have an additional opportunity to influence deliberations and recommendations as "relevant stakeholders"—in principle, reinforcing their independence from the government.[43] They can submit information for the review, comment on the draft of the report, and respond to the council's specific recommendations. Remarkably, NHRIs now have unimpeded and direct access to influence an international body's assessments and suggestions of its own state's practices. Just as international participation elevates the standing of NHRIs, then, it potentially maximizes the institution's domestic leverage.

In addition to the Human Rights Council, NHRIs play an extensive role within treaty bodies, especially in contributing to state reports and special procedures—two of the principal mechanisms treaty bodies use in carrying out their work. State reports are prepared by state parties to a treaty, ideally at regular intervals and detailing the degree of implementation and compliance with the treaty's requisites; treaty bodies then review these reports, and an exchange of communications can ensue, with the aim of pressuring the state to reach higher levels of compliance. NHRIs participate in this process in various ways, including

by serving as an additional source of information and contributing to the formu-
lation of General Comments and Concluding Observations; to this end, they can
attend relevant informal meetings and official sessions, shaping treaty bodies' assessments of state reports. Significantly, moreover, since the adoption of the Op-
tional Protocol of the Convention Against Torture (OPCAT) in 2002, many
states have designated an NHRI as their National Preventive Mechanism, task-
ing the institution with primary responsibility for implementing OPCAT.[44]

Beyond treaty bodies, NHRIs have been quite active in other international
forums.[45] For example, they have been instrumental in international pretreaty
negotiations, most notably the Convention on the Rights of Persons with Disabilities, which opened for signature in 2007. Despite earlier contributions to the
Convention on the Rights of the Child in the late 1980s, not until the disabilities
treaty and the Declaration on the Rights of Indigenous Peoples (approved in
2007) did the scope and intensity of this mode of NHRI participation increase
notably. As an astute observer of the international workings of NHRIs notes, it
was in the negotiations for this major treaty that these national institutions came
of age as "international contributors."[46] Furthermore, NHRIs have continued
participating in human rights "special procedures," key mechanisms created
by the UN Charter (examples include rapporteurs and working groups, revolving around a country or issue). They are permitted to present their own briefs as
part of the special procedures, and they are among the main actors that meet
with official representatives conducting human rights visits in their home state.

Accreditation and standing represent a new and deeper stage of institutionalization for the international regime on NHRIs. With accreditation, a formal system is in place that enforces who is and is not a recognized member of the NHRI
club. Such recognition, moreover, carries with it new privileges and rights, including formal participation in international forums. In the process, as networks
of NHRIs have become more coherent, designated regional networks enjoy representation in the overarching ICC. This type of "nesting" and complexity is a char-
acteristic of deepening institutionalization, signaling the rise of autonomous, active,
and socially recognized actors.[47]

Making Sense of Diffusion

Little question exists that NHRIs have diffused globally. We see both quantitative and qualitative evidence of this. Quantitatively, the number of NHRIs has
expanded predictably, in a classic S-curve, and regional clustering is evident.
Qualitatively, we see an evolving regime of NHRIs, which has progressed through

various stages of institutionalization: from gradual norm emergence over the course of four decades to a more rapid period of standard setting and norm promotion in the 1990s, including normative expansion and capacity building, followed by a period of more intense networking and implementation and more recently entering a phase of partial enforcement and legal standing—as a formal system of accreditation defines membership in the "club" of NHRIs, and accredited NHRIs are permitted to participate as freestanding agents within international forums.[48] Throughout these six decades, international standards defining NHRIs have become more precise, spelling out institutional functions and criteria of independence; and they have become inclusive of a fuller range of rights, marginalized populations, and even hot-button issues like national security emergencies.

A transnational network of actors has both reflected and shaped the global diffusion of NHRIs. This network has been influential in three key ways: socializing domestic actors to want to create an NHRIs, by defining the institution's *appropriateness*; shaping states' *capacities* to create an NHRI; and altering leaders' *calculations* about the advantages of an NHRI. This influence has been evident in the confluence of activities undertaken by a broad range of actors responsible for crafting the international regime on NHRIs. The OHCHR, and its NHRI unit, have in many ways been at the helm of these activities; but the network also includes a wide range of other actors, such as the OSCE, UNDP, World Bank, national development agencies and foreign ministries, as well as NGOs. In recent years, the International Coordinating Committee of NHRIs and numerous regional and subregional networks of NHRIs have also played pivotal roles.

The broad-gauged role of transnational activism in influencing states' interests, capacities, and calculations is evident in the specific work undertaken by the international regime on NHRIs. For example, as NHRIs have become recognizable and independent actors with rights of participation and membership, socialization has taken place by various mechanisms, including standard setting and authoritative interpretation of evolving standards. Knowledge and resource transfers, much of it falling under the rubric of capacity building, have also equipped states to create NHRIs. Some states, after all, may wish to create an NHRI but lack the means to do so; and even relatively capacious states may be short on technical know-how or reluctant to divert resources. International and regional networking forums, offering opportunities for interaction and exchange among social peers, have facilitated and reinforced these processes.

If other factors were important and even necessary in the proliferation of NHRIs, they alone were insufficient. The end of the Cold War may have provided the structural context in which human rights norms were able to advance. Yet the initial impetus for the global rise of these institutions came from the United Nations, which devised the concept of an NHRI as part of its human rights foundations as far back as the 1940s. As NHRIs diffused, a broad transnational network also grew in its wake. This web of activity not only has accumulated over time but also has cohered around an evolving international regime on NHRIs—increasingly institutionalized and autonomous.

These developments remind us that, though NHRIs are state institutions, their proliferation is partly a global phenomenon. These institutions have diffused worldwide, across all regions of the world and highly diverse states. International standards define them and transnational networks of actors actively promote them, while NHRIs have formed international and regional groupings and acquired legal standing and rights to participate in international bodies. The global dimension of NHRIs does not signify that individual states create NHRIs only or even largely for international reasons. It highlights that without the active engagement of a transnational network of actors promoting the idea of an NHRI, it is unlikely that so many states would have created these institutions. Their diffusion is not a coincidence, or a natural convergence of domestic preferences.[49] As Chris Sidoti so ably reviews, the rise of NHRIs is deeply implicated in the international system.[50]

If we can locate traces of today's NHRIs in long-standing state institutions, the contemporary idea of an NHRI can be seen as having gradually evolved internationally since World War II. Global efforts aside, normatively, the idea of an NHRI resonated with current trends. Modern states, for all their differences, are products of their time. Retaining sovereign authority, internally and externally, requires tapping into the norms of the day—whether rejecting them, adopting them, feigning commitment, or offering a symbolic nod. Contemporary notions of an NHRI have been framed broadly, cast multifariously as a democratic institution, a sign of adherence to international norms, and the emblem of membership in a community of liberal states. NHRIs may have become so popular precisely because they are bundled alongside the hegemonic ideas of the day.

4

The Logic of Strategic Emulation

*The manager of a fruit and vegetable shop places in his window
among the onions and carrots, the slogan: "Workers of the World,
Unite!" Why does he do it? What is he trying to communicate to
the world? Is he genuinely enthusiastic about the idea of unity
among the workers of the world? . . . That poster was delivered to
our greengrocer from the enterprise headquarters along with the
onions and carrots. He put them all into the window simply
because it has been done that way for years, because everyone
does it, and because that is the way it has to be. If he were
to refuse . . . [h]e could be reproached for not having the proper
"decoration" in his window. . . . He does it because these things
must be done if one is to get along in life.*

—Václav Havel et al., *The Power of the Powerless*[1]

When institutions diffuse widely, resistance can be difficult to decipher. Like Havel's green grocer, states can face system-wide pressures to embrace popular international symbols and practices. Adopting popular policies does not, of course, mean that state commitments are superficial or that the policies are inconsequential. Still, the rapid diffusion of an institution across highly diverse contexts invites caution—to look carefully for the subtle (and not-so-subtle) ways in which local actors may resist and transform international templates.[2] Doing so detracts from easy assumptions that global diffusion is largely good or mostly bad. The reality is that local actors appropriate international forms, and these appropriations can have important repercussions for domestic practices, sometimes with multiple and contradictory meanings.

The proliferation of NHRIs merits similar critical scrutiny. I begin by focusing on the question of institutional creation, searching for the various pathways by which NHRIs have diffused. I assume that NHRIs are in principle self-restraining mechanisms, which is precisely what makes their creation puzzling. As mentioned in Chapter 1, it is not altogether clear why egregious human rights violators create self-restraining mechanisms given the potential costs and risks of doing so. Establishing an NHRI, even a relatively toothless one, still can entail substantial setup costs, including the provision of facilities, professional staff, and ongoing resources.[3] Once created, moreover, an NHRI could bring abuses to light and generate greater human rights demands. Nor is it clear why states with relatively strong human rights records, whose broader domestic institutions already facilitate human rights implementation, would bother erecting an NHRI. Indeed, both democratic and nondemocratic states, economically wealthy and poor countries, have created these self-restraining institutions.

Thinking about NHRIs as self-restraining mechanisms, I provide an argument for why states may choose to "join the club" of NHRIs.[4] I focus on the logic of strategic emulation, as states seek *to retain regulatory authority by identifying socially appropriate mechanisms.* The particular pathway by which diffusion occurs will depend on a state's specific strategic circumstances and broader social environment. Actual outcomes can also be contingent on the personalities at play, who help to interpret and mediate structural conditions, and sometimes account for seeming anomalies. If the human rights institutions states create and the discourses they adopt sometimes appear contradictory, it is partly because of this logic of strategic emulation. Despite enormous variance at the margins, most NHRIs reflect this core dualism.

Institutional creation itself has multiple dimensions. For NHRIs, I focus on the timing, type, and strength of the institution. Why were some states among the first to create an NHRI, while others joined the bandwagon in the 1990s, others joined still more recently, and yet some have resisted the global trend for decades? And once the decision to create an NHRI is taken, what accounts for why a state forms a commission, a hybrid ombudsman, or an alternative institution? Finally, why are some NHRIs created to conform more closely than others to internationally recognized standards? In answering these questions, I probe how states' willingness to create an NHRI depends largely on their strategic and social circumstances, thus accounting for the rich variance we see in NHRIs around the world.

The global rise of NHRIs strongly suggests that the diffusion of ideas and institutions can reflect strategic emulation, as states latch onto socially appropriate mechanisms to retain power and authority. Accordingly, when states adopt human rights policies, the goal is never only to promote human rights, even if that is one of the outcomes. On a fundamental level, states are looking to reinforce their power. Strategic emulation is a fact of international and political life, no more and no less. Understanding why state institutions like NHRIs are created requires grasping this fundamental, driving force.

Pathways of Diffusion

Combining the research on global diffusion with studies of NHRIs takes us part of the way in understanding the creation of NHRIs by so many states around the world. The research on global diffusion has emphasized for its part the role of four general pathways: coercion, competition, learning, and emulation.[5] While competition, for example, has been closely linked to the diffusion of economic institutions like markets, emulation—and its emphasis on socialization—has been associated more so with the diffusion of human rights norms.[6] NHRI scholarship, with some exceptions, has tended to focus instead on agents more than processes of diffusion, especially the role of international organizations and networks of NHRIs. And though infrequently theorized, the creation of NHRIs has been most often depicted in terms of organizational emulation and socialization, with a few studies also suggesting that states can create an NHRI to appease international actors. While some scholars have pointed to the variability of the domestic context, they have done so mostly as a means of describing more than theorizing why particular NHRIs are established.[7] Rich in many ways, the literature has been unable to resolve the tension between the strategic and social pathways of NHRI diffusion, nor to accommodate adequately the role of domestic factors. The logic of strategic emulation, presented here, addresses precisely these gaps.

Fundamentally, the creation of NHRIs and other accountability mechanisms connects to the basic nature of governance, regulation, and authority. This is the starting point: all governing authorities seek to regulate activities. Regulation itself entails, among other things, drafting rules, monitoring compliance, and promoting and ensuring rule-abiding behavior. We tend to assume that regulation occurs because of either the interventionist proclivities of authority or the functional need to regulate things like public goods, services, and spaces. But regulation can also be self-serving, offering authorities a way to reproduce their own power. When subjects conform to rules, internal order and stability are more likely; and it becomes more possible to isolate dissenters, or address challenges to authority before they become threatening. Regulation, moreover, is imbued in modern society with an aura of greater legitimacy than the use of force or raw coercion as forms of social control. In this sense, regulation is not just a mode of improving individual and social welfare, but a means of constituting and controlling subjects (and onlookers) while extending a governing authority's very reach and existence.[8]

The same dynamics hold true when regulation takes the form of self-restraining mechanisms, that is, when self-regulation is at stake.[9] Self-restraining institutions are a form of regulation, a horizontal mechanism deployed by the state or other organization to regulate itself internally. Governing authorities are willing to relinquish nominal control over an issue in order to secure their power in the longer term. The amount of actual control they are willing to sacrifice depends on the extent to which leaders perceive their authority is at stake; and this is reflected in the strength of the self-restraining institution they are willing to adopt. Despite huge variance, then, all self-restraining mechanisms are partly an attempt to retain authority. The attempt may not be deliberate or premeditated, but it is no less real. Paradoxically, self-restraining mechanisms are intended partly to maintain or enhance control over a given regulatory arena—to extend and localize, not limit, authority.

Regardless of actual motives or performance, self-restraining institutions promise to be effective strategies for maintaining authority. Within complex organizations (including the state), creating a self-restraining mechanism signals a commitment to rule-abiding behavior and fairness. After all, the organization has sunk costs into the institution, and it is signaling its openness to critical scrutiny and to potential complainants. This surely portrays concrete evidence of good faith, of being committed to a set of socially recognized standards. Implicitly, moreover, the act of creating a self-restraining mechanism conveys another set of messages. In tacit exchange for creating such a mechanism, external criticism becomes less necessary; so does radicalizing the agenda. And if leaders themselves are willing to be held accountable, any other rule breaker should expect the same. Likewise, since potential complainants can access the organization directly, little need exists to resort to other dispute-resolution mechanisms, internally or externally. Self-restraining institutions, though hailed conventionally as limitations on authority, can also be a means of reasserting control.

Creating a self-restraining mechanism is especially desirable during periods of norm ambiguity, when an actor's normative commitments (and possibly authority) are open to interpretation.[10] Unlike situations of uncertainty, where probabilities are in question, situations of ambiguity involve differences over meaning, which is why norm-diffusing agents and processes of socialization matter so much. More specifically, situations of ambiguity shape the social and strategic contexts in important ways. On the one hand, norm ambiguity creates strategic incentives for leaders to adopt self-restraining mechanisms, thereby signaling their normative commitments. On the other hand, norm ambiguity opens space for norm-diffusing agents to promote new ideas. These processes—the strategic and social—work hand in hand. Strategic incentives present authorities with a political "problem," while norm-diffusing agents provide the "solution." When norm-diffusing agents apply pressure during a period of norm ambiguity, states are quite likely to adopt an NHRI.

In the case of human rights accountability mechanisms, three instances of norm ambiguity signal a potential loss of regulatory control for state leaders, providing them with an incentive to reassert authority: regulatory moments (like the drafting of constitutions or postconflict peace agreements), during which new norms and standards can be locked in; external obligations, including treaty commitments, which can push states to localize authority; and organized abuse, which makes appeasing critics highly desirable. Each situation (Table 4) presents leaders with a particular political problem, over *how* to resolve ambiguity: regulatory moments present a problem of imagination and selection, as actors face alternative institutional scenarios, potentially breaking from the past: which norms will they lock in? External obligations introduce a problem of delegation, as actors seek to localize authority and thus avoid external scrutiny and enforcement: how will they delegate internal regulatory authority? Finally, organized abuse exposes a problem of reputation, as actors systematically violate a norm and criticism is all too possible: how can critics of norm violation be appeased? The decision to create an NHRI often arises at these particular junctures, with each situation both serving as a strategic incentive to reduce ambiguity and opening space for norm-diffusing agents to exert influence.

Regulatory moments consist of periods when basic rules and principles of governance are open to reinvention or revision. These "moments" act as institutional junctures, offering actors a conspicuous opportunity to formalize expectations and standards. While obviously forward-looking, regulatory moments (like constitutional ones) represent a crucial transition or potential turning point.[11] Ambiguity is present because there may be different perspectives about which norms exactly should be adopted and the extent to which new standards will represent a break from the past. During regulatory moments, then, leaders lock in commitments to

Table 4
Norm Ambiguity and Self-Restraining Mechanisms:
Pathways of Diffusion

Type of norm ambiguity	"Problem"	Form of strategic emulation
Regulatory moment	Selection	Lock in
External obligations	Delegation	Localization
Organized abuse	Reputation	Appeasement

extend their rule and bind would-be recidivists.[12] For today's states, regime transitions (often in the context of democratization) serve as broad regulatory moments, where a wide range of basic organizing principles are open to design and selection, even as international actors attempt to transfer templates and communicate preferences. New constitutions or periods of constitutional reform also offer leaders an opportunity to lock in commitments, including by creating self-restraining mechanisms like NHRIs. Constitutions are uniquely positioned to shape foundationally who participates and other basic rules of governance. Another regulatory moment occurs after conflict situations, when peace agreements stipulate an entire package of rules and reforms. Peace agreements demarcate the boundaries of political life, including pressing accountability issues, following social upheaval.[13] In general, we should expect some states to create NHRIs partly as a result of regulatory moments—namely, in the context of political transitions, constitutional revamping, and postconflict peace agreements. While regulatory moments provide political leaders with an incentive to lock in normative preferences, specific actors—from legal consultants to peace negotiators—transmit and promote the idea of an NHRI. Their substantive intervention is crucial in defining institutional options.

Self-restraining institutions can also be created in response to *external obligations.* Even when states accept treaty obligations willingly, political leaders can have an interest in delegating authority to internal actors. Like other instances of delegation, such localization can signal credibly one's commitment to international standards. It can also help bypass external scrutiny and enforcement, by ensuring that norm violations are kept in check and accountability is dealt with at home.[14] Delegation, moreover, can serve to relocalize authority domestically, especially in situations where the political executive wishes to shift control away from institutions like the courts or parliament. For example, in countries with a strong rule of law, where treaty obligations are most justiciable, leaders may find a self-restraining mechanism an appealing complement to the courts, one promising to be more flexible, specialized, and efficient. In some instances, treaties themselves may call explicitly on states to delegate authority to a self-restraining mechanism. Here too, states with a stronger rule of law, already more attuned to complying with external obligations, may be the most likely takers.[15] Overall, external obligations provide state leaders with an incentive to delegate authority over treaty obligations to domestic actors. But it is international actors, including treaty bodies, that define and communicate actively the idea of delegating authority to a self-restraining institution per se.

Another incentive to create a self-restraining mechanism occurs in the face of *organized abuse*, or systematic norm violations.[16] Norm violations create ambiguity because they lead to opposition and challenge, questioning rulers' commitments and authority. When states violate international norms, moreover, opposition can be transnational and include powerful international actors. To minimize these risks and appease critics, human rights violators can establish self-restraining mechanisms, adopting institutional forms that will satisfy international standards. In some cases, therefore, NHRIs will be created by states that violate international human rights norms to appease critics. Sometimes local norm promoters themselves will call for a self-restraining mechanism as a way of undermining the power of those propagating abuse. Regardless of the particular circumstances, insofar as organized abuse presents a regime with potential problems, the creation of an NHRI can be a strategic solution, targeting either an international or domestic audience or both.

To summarize, three sets of strategic circumstances increase norm ambiguity and help to explain why states create a self-restraining mechanism like an NHRI: regulatory moments, which encourage leaders to lock in commitments; external obligations, which move state actors to localize authority; and organized abuse, which pushes states to appease critics.[17] In practice, states that create an NHRI may face just one of these conditions or all three. On their own, though, these strategic processes do not tell us why states chose an NHRI rather than another option. They reveal only why, given the circumstances at hand, an NHRI can make strategic sense. They also help to account for the timing of NHRI creation (at least one of these incentives is likely to be in place) and issues of design (depending on the incentives at play, institutional capacities may vary).

Without considering the broader social context (international and domestic), however, strategic incentives provide only a partial picture of NHRI creation. Even before a particular type of mechanism is selected, state leaders have to identify socially appropriate institutions. This is required if they are to succeed in locking in standards, localizing authority, and appeasing critics effectively. Accordingly, a wide range of actors serve as norm-diffusing agents, vigorously promoting the idea of an NHRI, including by defining institutional benefits, providing design templates, identifying criteria of success, and offering technical know-how and support. This assembly of actors is composed of UN groups (from the Human Rights Council to the OHCHR to specific treaty bodies), regional organizations, human rights NGOs, foreign governments, local social groups and political leaders, as well as NHRI networks, among others. These norm-diffusing agents, as reviewed in Chapter 3, promote international standards about NHRIs, including basic principles and rules, and help equip states with the capacity to build and strengthen these institutions. Diffusion thus becomes cause as much as effect.[18]

Often, moreover, the social context shapes the type of NHRI created, with different institutional forms (e.g., ombudsman versus commission model) depending largely on what social peers in the global environment have selected. The domestic social context can also be quite significant, especially in terms of prior institutional forms that sometimes substitute for or morph into an internationally accredited NHRI.[19] In general, states will create an NHRI or accountability mechanism when it is socially appropriate *and* beneficial to do so. Emulation is important, but so is the strategic context.

Empirical Evidence

Activists and scholars in the human rights field are always searching for evidence. No one claims to be against human rights, but few are willing to take action absent a sense of urgency and concrete evidence of egregious wrongdoing. Human rights activists have long deployed two powerful methods to mobilize support and jolt onlookers into taking action. On the one hand, they have packaged careful narratives and images to produce campaigns that will generate sympathy. On the other hand, they have collected meticulous statistics and data detailing abuse, which might serve as concrete evidence and spark outrage. These methods have their counterparts among human rights researchers, who have alternated between conducting in-depth studies of a single or small number of cases and large-scale quantitative analysis of hundreds if not thousands of data points. The dilemmas are similar, as numbers on their own can fail to capture the human side of the story while rich detail often raises questions about the pervasiveness and magnitude of the claims. Not surprisingly, in both the activist and academic worlds, attempts to join the two methods are increasingly apparent.[20]

I follow this trend here, bridging quantitative and qualitative analysis to offer empirical evidence of the various pathways by which NHRIs have diffused globally. I begin with a statistical analysis, providing broad if incomplete cross-national evidence of the mechanisms by which NHRIs are created. Equipped with a sense that these pathways of diffusion are at the very least plausible, I proceed in subsequent chapters to examine via brief narrative accounts the creation of NHRIs around the world. That analysis is divided by region and time period, both of which are part of the diffusion story I tell. Significantly, I show that while the general argument holds, the particular interplay of factors is context-specific. For example, the forces that motivated early adopters in the 1970s to create an NHRI are different from those that moved the bandwagoners of the 1990s. And even within one period, the motive forces among Eastern European democratizing states, for instance, were different than the dynamics evident among Latin America's new democracies during the same period, where regional diffusion took on its own forms.[21] Of course, each country might face its peculiar circumstances that do not form part of a broader, more general trend; I highlight these conditions as relevant, while still finding merit in a more coherent accounting of institutional creation and design.

I begin by examining whether some factors have seemed to enhance the likelihood that a state will create an NHRI. I include all of the countries in the world in the analysis, noting whether or not they have created an NHRI. For those with an NHRI, I record the year of institutional creation (see Table 5).[22] I tested the significance of thirteen variables in this model: human rights abuses, regional diffusion of NHRIs, global diffusion of NHRIs, regulatory moment, rule of law, human rights treaty commitments, an interaction term created by combining rule of law and treaty commitments, regime type, domestic NGOs, economic development, population size, and common-law system. Table 6 elaborates how each factor is measured and a brief rationale for its inclusion. Unless otherwise stated, these sources are used consistently throughout the book, informing all country cases presented in subsequent chapters.

Consistent with my theoretical claims, only four factors were statistically significant: the level of human rights abuse, regional diffusion, regulatory moments, and whether a state had *both* accepted external treaty commitments and enjoyed a relatively strong rule of law system. That states with worse human rights records (i.e., organized abuse) are generally more likely to create an NHRI suggests that an appeasement mechanism may be at work for many

Table 5
Likelihood of Creating a National Human
Rights Institution: Logit Analysis

Explanatory variable	Coefficient (robust standard error)	
	Institutional creation	Institutional design
Physical integrity violations[a]	0.04 (.01)*	.01 (.02)
Regional diffusion	0.03 (.02)*	.00 (.01)
Global diffusion	−0.30 (.08)	−.05 (.02)
Regulatory moment	4.90 (1.21)*	1.70 (.53)*
Rule of law	1.40 (1.08)	1.32 (.61)*
Treaty commitments	−7.61 (3.28)	.86 (1.69)
Rule of law x treaty commitments	2.73 (1.11)*	−.17 (.70)
Regime type[a]	0.01 (.06)	.02 (.04)
Human rights NGOs	−0.00 (.00)	−.00 (.00)
Economic development (GNP per capita)[a]	0.09 (.45)	−.25 (.26)
Population size (logged)[a]	0.10 (.22)	.58 (.18)*
Common law legal system	−.01 (.89)	−.45 (.77)
Constant	18.26 (5.26)	−1.44 (2.22)
Number of observations	143	142
Pseudo R^2	.67	.32
Prob > chi^2	0.00	0.00
Log pseudolikelihood	−29.94	−67.24

[a] A two-tailed test of significance was performed for this variable.
*Significant at the 0.1 level of significance.

states establishing NHRIs. While human rights abuses are measured here in terms of physical integrity rights, this is standard in the field and reflects the reality that these are the abuses most likely to generate international criticism.

NHRIs also seem to spread more rapidly within regions; that is, the percentage of countries with an NHRI in a region shapes the likelihood that any given country within that region will create an NHRI. From this analysis, however, the underlying dynamics are unclear. Leaders may calculate that the costs of not creating an institution adopted by many neighboring peers are too high. At the same time, regional forums provide state leaders with opportunities to exchange information about NHRIs and become persuaded of their value. Strikingly, however, *global* diffusion was insignificant. This suggests that while these domestic institutions form in clusters, this occurs only in relatively close proximity; the worldwide diffusion of NHRIs does not in and of itself affect the likelihood that any given country will create a state human rights institution.

The strongest incentive to create an NHRI nonetheless arose internally, among states experiencing a regulatory moment. Countries that underwent a political transition, drafted a new constitution, or signed a peace agreement faced an opportunity to lock in rules and mechanisms. Why they chose to create an NHRI per se has to do with a broader set of dynamics, including regional diffusion, but there is strong evidence that regulatory moments were significant. In contrast, the degree of democracy did not seem to be significant for explaining NHRI creation. It is not the extent of democracy, therefore, that matters as much as the act of transitioning to a new type of political or regulatory regime.

Interestingly, the combination of treaty commitments *and* rule of law also influenced the likelihood that a country would create an NHRI. The fact that neither of these factors on its own is significant is itself noteworthy. Since NHRIs are intended to implement international standards, one might assume that treaty ratification alone motivates states to create an NHRI. In and of itself, however, ratifying the most important human rights treaties (in this case, one of the two international covenants) is not associated with a greater likelihood of having an NHRI. Likewise, whether a country has a relatively strong rule of law does not appear to be significant; in fact, countries with a weaker rule of law system seem more inclined to establish an NHRI, though this finding was not statistically significant. What does matter is the combined effects of these factors: ratifying a major human rights treaty is associated with a greater likelihood that a country will also have an NHRI, but only for those countries already under a relatively strong rule of law. In other words, the obligation to implement treaty standards domestically, including by creating implementing institutions, is taken most seriously by countries whose legal systems are most inclined to enforce treaty obligations. In this sense, regulatory moments seem to give states with a strong rule of law an incentive to localize authority, whether to avoid external third-party enforcement or shift domestic regulatory authority, as discussed above.

Tellingly, other factors were not found to be significant: the number of NGOs, the level of economic development, population size, or whether a country had a common or civil law system. These findings are significant, since they may run counter to common assumptions. For example, one might assume that poor countries cannot afford to establish domestic implementing institutions, but there is no widespread evidence for that here. Likewise, while countries under common-law systems seem more likely to enforce some human rights treaties, the same does not hold for the likelihood that they will create an NHRI. Nor does the creation of an NHRI depend on the number of human rights NGOs in the country, even when the size of the national population is taken into account; though subsequent case studies show evidence of bottom-up NHRI creation, on a global scale, this analysis suggests that this is not generally the driving force.

In another round of tests, focusing on institutional design (Table 6), I examined how the same factors were related to whether or not an institution was accredited internationally as an NHRI. What were the characteristics associated with having an internationally accredited NHRI? In coding institutions, I deemed those with an "A" or "B" rating stronger and all others weaker.[23] Given the challenges of relying on international accreditation as a measure of institutional strength, I treat accreditation as an indicator of design rather than impact. In contrast to institutional creation, the analysis of institutional design revealed the role of three key factors: regulatory moments, a strong rule of law, and large population size. Put differently, institutional origins and national capacities seem to shape design features most closely. We know that among countries lacking an NHRI, small states often figure. Yet the findings here further indicate that national capacities may matter more for explaining an accountability institution's strength than the likelihood that it will be created. Likewise, countries under a secure rule of law may have greater institutional capacities to create accountability mechanisms that can meet international standards. Regarding institutional legacies, it seems that regulatory moments have tended to result in the "strongest" NHRIs, or at least those most likely to attain a higher accreditation rating. This does not mean that NHRIs established mostly to appease critics or localize external obligations are not accredited or influential, as many examples in subsequent chapters demonstrate, only that they are not generally as strong as NHRIs created to lock in commitments during regulatory moments of ambiguity.

The analysis presented here is highly suggestive but limited. These models account only for a percentage of the variance we observe; in fact, the factors examined take us further in accounting for institutional creation than design (the models for creation and design explain, respectively, about two-thirds and one-third of the overall variance). Nor does this quantitative analysis tell us how institutions that are initially created weak can evolve, sometimes as a result of international regime pressures—including the new system of Universal Periodic

Table 6

Factors Potentially Associated with NHRI Creation and Design

Factor	Description	Source	Other notes
Human rights abuse	The extent to which a country engages in violations of personal integrity: torture, political imprisonment, extrajudicial executions, and disappearances	Political Terror Scale	Range: 1–5 (5 = highest level of abuse); lagged by one year Since it is unclear whether NHRIs are more likely to be created in countries with a high or low level of abuse, I conduct a "two-tailed" test of significance
Regional diffusion	The percentage of countries in a region that have an NHRI	Data on NHRIs from various sources. Regions are defined by official UN categories (http://nhri .ohchr.org)	More regional diffusion should be associated with a higher likelihood of NHRI creation
Global diffusion	The percentage of countries in the world with an NHRI	Same as regional diffusion	More global diffusion should be associated with a higher likelihood of NHRI creation

(continued)

Table 6

(Continued)

Factor	Description	Source	Other notes
Regulatory moment	Whether a country underwent a political transition, adopted a new constitution, or entered into a peace agreement, just prior to creating an NHRI	Data on national constitutions are from the World Constitutions Database. Data on political transitions are from Polity. Data on peace agreements are from the Peace Agreements Database (Transitional Justice Institute, University of Ulster)	For countries without an NHRI, the most recent regulatory moments are recorded
Rule of law	The extent to which a country respects the "rule of law"	Beth A. Simmons, *Mobilizing for Human Rights: International Law in Domestic Politics* (Cambridge: Cambridge University Press, 2009), 396–99, based on World Bank data	A higher rule of law should be associated positively with NHRI creation
Treaty commitments	Whether a country has ratified either the ICCPR or the ICESCR; for countries with an NHRI, the variable is coded one year prior to the institution's creation	UN Treaty Database	Countries with treaty commitments may be more willing to create an implementing institution like an NHRI

Table 6

(Continued)

Factor	Description	Source	Other notes
Regime type	The extent to which a country is democratic or autocratic	Polity IV data (20-point scale)	Is NHRI creation associated with higher degrees of democratic rule? (two-tailed test of significance)
Domestic NGOs	Number of "human rights" NGOs operating in a country	Human Rights Internet, Human Rights Organizations Database (www.hri.ca)	More NGOs should lead to a greater likelihood of an NHRI.
Economic development	GNP per capita	World Bank data	Poorer countries may have a lower capacity to create an NHRI, though they may also be less able to resist pressures for doing so (two-tailed test of significance)
Population size	Number of inhabitants in a country (logged to account for effects of skewing)	World Bank data	Larger countries may be both more capable of resistance and more capacious in creating an institution
Common or civil law system	Whether a country is under a common law system	Multiple sources	Common law systems are less likely to ratify human rights treaties, so this could extend to an implementing institution

Review—to outstrip initial expectations. Subsequent cases reveal these hidden dynamics, but the general patterns identified here show this: NHRIs have arisen mostly under conditions of regional diffusion and norm ambiguity (as leaders have looked to lock in commitments, localize authority, and appease critics); NHRIs with origins in regulatory moments, moreover, have been most likely to conform to international standards, as have those that are part of large and legally capacious states. Beyond these parameters of institutional creation and design, examined historically and cross-regionally in the next few chapters, lies the issue of institutional influence (Chapter 10), a touchstone for evaluating these NHRIs in practice and understanding how they might be improved.

What Is in a Name?

When institutions diffuse, they do not just spread from one place to another. They must be *recognized* as fitting a broader pattern of similar institutions. In this sense, an institution's name often shapes first impressions. It can give onlookers a split-second snapshot into what the institution does, what form it takes, and what it stands for as an entity. The name identifies and differentiates the institution in relation to others. This is why businesses and nonprofit organizations invest heavily in branding themselves with names that will resonate and appeal to their intended social audiences. The names of state institutions and international organizations tend to receive far less attention, though they too can be consequential, serving as simplified forms of representation—concise ways of summarizing an organization's essence and presenting itself to the world. An institution's name always carries meaning, even if the meaning depends on the observer, is vague and contested, or changes over time. In this sense, an institution's name is akin to a "speech" or "performative" act, where language cannot be separated from the broader give-and-take of social interaction.[24]

In cases of diffusion, an institution's name is partly borrowed—a form of mimicry—and then possibly tailored to accommodate local preferences, to express uniqueness or give emphasis. For complex organizations, one cannot assume that an institution's name reflects an entirely deliberate and measured act; in other words, one should not read too much into a name that might have been selected somewhat by accident, by happenstance, cobbled together either as political compromise or haphazardly. Still, whatever its exact genesis, an institution's name conveys various meanings, often subtle and complex. And more so than institutions themselves, names can recede into the background and acquire a taken-for-granted quality, even while shaping impressions and expectations.

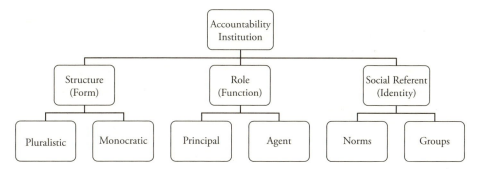

FIGURE 2. Parsing accountability institutions.

Accountability institutions, like other categories of institutions, have their own nomenclature. Partly products of global diffusion, they replicate names elsewhere. What they replicate is itself important: From whom do they borrow? What exactly do they borrow, and what do they omit? Is anything changed or lost in translation? How is the global discourse altered to represent local needs? While studies of NHRIs often categorize these institutions by type (i.e., commissions, ombudsman or hybrid models, and institutes) as well as geographic or cultural zones (e.g., the Iberian or Commonwealth models), NHRI names have not yet been diagrammed according to general organizational features. For example, NHRIs can vary in the structural form they take, including whether they are pluralistic or monocratic bodies. In treating NHRIs as accountability institutions, the framework outlined here could be adapted to other accountability institutions (see Figure 2).

In addition, an institution's name can convey some information about the organization's central role, or its functions. Since accountability institutions mediate between different sets of actors, including the state and society, their role can be thought of in terms of whether an institution situates itself mostly as principal or agent. An NHRI acts as an agent when it is a consultative, advisory, or observing body (relative to the state) and as a principal when it stands as a provider, protector, defender, or advocate of society.

Beyond its form and function, an accountability institution's name can tell us something about the organization's identity. In particular, an institution's name can convey some information about the organization's key social referent, or its principal source of identification: who does the institution claim to serve, social norms or groups? In the case of social groups, the institution's referents are its subjects, and the institution derives its identity primarily from promoting its subjects' well-being. For NHRIs, for instance, this is the case when the name includes reference to citizens or people. When the referent is an abstract idea, the institution's identity revolves mostly around advancing this object, whether it be in the case of NHRIs "human rights," "freedom," "justice," or "equality."

Accountability institutions have other design features beyond those described here, and a name can reveal only so much. Still, the characteristics reviewed here illustrate an accountability institution's distinctive organizational structures. Differences in name, at the very least, communicate differences in an institution's image. The label of a "human rights commission"—the most popular type of NHRI—conveys an image of pluralism, the institution as principal, and social norms as the key referent. A defensor del pueblo in turn represents a purposive, agent-centered, group-oriented institution. Are these differences actually manifest in an institution's design, or do they translate into concrete differences in terms of institutional practice? I return to these questions in passing, especially when an NHRI's name changes or the name is translated inconsistently across languages. Those instances of linguistic shift and deviation can be evidence of strategic emulation, as state actors realign their institution's name (and image) vis-à-vis particular organizational models.

Conclusions: Strategic Emulation and State Accountability

The diffusion of NHRIs, or self-restraining accountability mechanisms, can be understood as a process of strategic emulation. On the one hand, states face incentives to create such institutions, especially during periods of norm ambiguity, including regulatory moments, external obligations, and organized abuse. All of these circumstances present states with a political problem they must address. On the other hand, episodes of norm ambiguity open spaces for norm-diffusing agents to introduce and promote new ideas. The networks associated with the international regime on NHRIs are at the forefront of these efforts, helping to explain the widespread adoption of NHRIs.

The research on diffusion in international relations has identified various mechanisms, from coercion and competition to learning and emulation. In focusing on norm ambiguity and strategic emulation—when state leaders have an incentive to adopt socially appropriate ideas or institutions—I combine rationalist and constructivist accounts. I also take this a step further to explore more specific mechanisms of diffusion. Rather than focusing on the issue of uncertainty, so prevalent in the social sciences, I consider the role of ambiguity. While the two concepts are closely related, ambiguity occurs when meanings are contestable; under such circumstances, actors look to signal their commitments. And just as they get cues from the strategic context in which they operate that they should adjust their practices, they also draw on their social environment for defining *what* exactly they might do. Thus, new ideas promoted by norm-diffusing agents can get locked in during regulatory moments, localized as a result of external obligations, and deployed by leaders looking to appease critics.

The findings of a large-N quantitative analysis, examining the creation and accreditation of NHRIs, offer compelling if preliminary support. Consistent with the theoretical claims, for example, there is strong evidence that states have been more likely to create an NHRI as a result of regional diffusion, as well as regulatory moments, external obligations (for states with a relatively strong rule of law system), and norm violations. In terms of design, accreditation seems to be most closely related to institutional origins (viz., regulatory moments) and national capacities. Since institutions can be studied and approached from a multiplicity of methods and perspectives, I also included here a brief look at—really, an exploratory reflection on—how an NHRI's name can convey meaning about the institution's intended form, function, and identity.

The action, of course, is in the details; and an account of why NHRIs are created must look more closely at what was happening on the ground. A version of that account, of how so many states around the world moved to create an NHRI and why they varied as they did, across diverse regions and circumstances, is told in the next four chapters. The findings reported here are sustained, with new details, nuances, and supplements emerging along the way.

5

Trendsetters and Early Adopters, pre-1990

The story of how NHRIs have diffused around the world is one of multiple contingencies, of diverse but partially converging pathways. It is a story about the power of institutional models to spread, especially when they are promoted actively and adopted by others similarly situated. In this sense, no single NHRI can be understood in isolation or separated from its broader context. NHRIs created during similar periods are partially connected to one another, even if they are found halfway around the world.

The global rise of NHRIs has occurred in waves, corresponding roughly to three periods: pre-1990s, when just over two dozen NHRIs existed; the 1990s, marking the most rapid period of expansion; and post-2000, when states continue joining the global trend. Significantly, each period corresponds to the rising evolution of the international regime on NHRIs, subjecting states to distinct sets of global pressures. Within each period, diverse patterns of institutional diffusion are nonetheless apparent, reflecting particular domestic contexts and trajectories no less than broader historical developments.

The first group of countries to create NHRIs was as varied as the national institutions they would establish. These "trendsetters," numbering about two dozen, did not appear all at once. Rather, they were created in different parts of the world, for different reasons, over the course of four decades, from 1947 through the end of the 1980s. Yet these early NHRIs were all first-of-a-kind trendsetters in their own way, whether in the type of NHRI established, the circumstances leading to the institution's creation, or an institution's initial appearance in a given region. This early set of adopters paved the way for others to follow suit.

External Attachments and Global Interlocutors

Among the earliest trendsetters, the role of global interlocutors proved crucial, despite important national differences. Global interlocutors refer to individuals and groups who bridge the national and international contexts, promoting international standards locally, and communicating local needs to international actors.[1] In this context they all happened to be jurists, interested in the linkages between international human rights norms and domestic rule of law; their activism confirms long-standing connections between NHRIs and the legal sphere. Yet despite their best aspirations for a global system of justice, where national and international-regional mechanisms would complement one another, state interests carried the day. In this sense, a (post)colonial theme permeates these early experiences, showing how the original visions that led to these institutions were constrained from the outset. These dynamics are evident in the creation of the first NHRIs, in France (1947), Guyana (1966), and Senegal (1970)—all before the term "national human rights institution" was even coined.

The World's First NHRI: Droits Humains or Raison D'état?

That France was the first country to create an NHRI can be traced directly to René Cassin and his close participation in the twentieth century's key international organizations. The prominent jurist seemed convinced that international organizations required domestic bodies to implement their standards and transmit their practices to a national context, where they could be given concrete meaning. Cassin may have seen this as intrinsic to international bodies operating in a world of states; indeed, as the French delegate to the League of Nations, Cassin was already deeply immersed in international governance in the first half of the twentieth century. He picked up on the idea of national complementing institutions from his own experience working with international organizations like the ILO and UNESCO, which had national counterparts.[2] Then, within the United Nations, he was the leading voice behind the 1946 resolution on national human rights bodies. France's decision to create a national consultative commission in 1947 was a clear outgrowth of these developments.

While Cassin was unable to convince either his fellow UN Human Rights Commission members or the French government that national bodies should collect and transmit information about domestic human rights practices, as recounted in Chapter 2, he was able to place the notion of an NHRI on both the international and national agendas. This meant that when the French agency was established in 1947, it was overwhelmingly oriented toward international law, with the goal of shaping nascent international human rights laws. This is reflected in the institution's first name: la Commission consultative pour la codification du droit international et la définition des droits et devoirs des états et des droits de l'homme (Consultative Commission for Codifying International Law and Defining the Rights and Duties of States and Human Rights). And it was evident in the institution's first assigned task, which was to study and comment on the proposal for a universal declaration of human rights. In fact, the commission was originally a body of independent experts, or respected jurists, a vehicle for France to shape the early human rights machinery at the United Nations. It had no budget and no dedicated physical space, tellingly ensconced within the foreign ministry.[3]

Beginning in 1948, with the work of the Universal Declaration of Human Rights coming to fruition, the commission began acquiring tentacles within the French government, attaching itself to various ministries. In today's parlance, the commission worked to mainstream human rights throughout the French government. But it met with some resistance, and both the commission's organization and functions were much debated. One faction called for expansive powers, while others wanted to dismantle the institution entirely. These tensions were evident in the institution's first couple of years, as the commission underwent two reforms, including changes to its structure and name. In acquiring its current name, the focus settled more squarely on human rights. While Cassin himself was committed to the idea of international human rights institutionalization, he was enough of a diplomat to be willing to compromise pragmatically and accept the French government's vision for the commission: a body asserting itself only on the international scene.[4]

As opposition to French colonial rule mounted, exposing glaring human rights contradictions, the human rights institution experienced virtual paralysis. The commission continued holding meetings and working quietly almost confidentially, with little public awareness of its inner workings. When Cassin, as the commission's long-standing president, died in 1976, the commission also disappeared. If it had not been for the personal drive of Cassin and a few others sustaining the commission, it is all but certain that it would have ceased to exist even before then. As the Algerian war and social protest intensified after 1960, there appears to have been strong support for eliminating an institution that could prove threatening to the state's image as the eighteenth-century revolutionary cradle of human rights.[5]

The institution's reappearance in 1984 coincided with an emerging global trend, as NHRIs slowly began growing in number, including among Commonwealth and South European countries. Domestically, a relatively new socialist administration was open to international human rights commitments; and France had just ratified in 1980 the two international covenants.[6] The French commission's second coming in the 1980s thus reflected the state's external obligations, but this time less so because of the role of global interlocutors and more the result of recent treaty commitments and the institution's early diffusion. As a global leader of human rights, France played the role of innovator in 1947 and early adopter in 1984, while retaining its previous institutional model of a "consultative commission."

Indeed, it is significant that when the commission was resurrected in 1984, it kept its name, perhaps in recognition of the commission's historical significance and Cassin's own contributions. It is also telling, as one French scholar has recognized, that despite paralysis and upheaval, the *consultative* nature of the institution always remained front and center—in its name and mission.[7] There was no question that this body was a recommending institution, an agent more than principal. France's decision to create a "consultative commission" also reflected this bureaucratic form's long pedigree, used often since the nineteenth century, from Great Britain to Japan, and usually reflecting the state's interest in creating an oversight agency that it could ultimately control (see Chapter 2).[8]

The world's first NHRI thus arose at the intersection of new international organizations and traditional state bureaucracy. It was a contradictory project from the start, one designed to project France's *international* role as defender of human rights while the country fought fiercely against abandoning its own position as a colonial power, one that stifled self-determination and engaged in egregious human rights abuses including torture.[9] Indeed, the divergence between the country's stated commitments to human rights and its role as colonial power crippled the institution. These fundamental tensions were debated by local jurists, ultimately reflected in the institution's narrowly confined mandate and accounting for the organization's decades-long paralysis. While external obligations were the impetus for creating France's NHRI, they also proved its Achilles' heel. The overriding interest was to promote international human rights norms abroad rather than constrain the state's internal practices. It was, ironically, in 1976, the same year that the two international human rights covenants entered into force, that the commission disappeared with Cassin's death.

Yet in simply borrowing in 1984 from its own historical model, the institution was again endemically weak from the start, and its orientation remained largely international. Institutional reform would depend largely on evolving international standards and ongoing international regime pressures. Gradual changes were indeed made. Two years after it reemerged, the commission was moved in 1986 from the Foreign Ministry to an agency under the prime minister. In 1990, national legislation refocused its mandate to emphasize racism, anti-Semitism, and xenophobia, requiring an annual report on issues that especially plagued the country. In direct response to the Paris Principles—elaborated, after all, at a meeting in the French capital—reforms in 1993 were intended to align the commission with international standards. And in anticipation of the reaccreditation process by the International Coordinating Committee of NHRIs, another set of reforms was enacted in 2007.[10] As a leader among NHRIs, the symbolic site of the world's first NHRI and the first international meeting of NHRIs that produced the foundational document anchoring these institutions, France had to strengthen its NHRI if it was to continue playing a global role. That said, it has never been entirely able to escape its origins and trajectory as a consultative body embedded within a historically strong state, inclined to overshadow it.

The Rise of the Caribbean Ombudsman

If a colonial power's human rights contradictions drove the world's first NHRI, the racial tensions that ensued from colonialism led to the developing world's first NHRI—albeit an unaccredited one. Newly independent Guyana created an ombudsman in 1966, in the context of drafting a national constitution. Despite this "regulatory moment," global interlocutors proved crucial. In this case, the International Commission of Jurists (ICJ)—an international NGO promoting human rights via the rule of law—visited British Guyana in 1965 as part of a racial inquiry into public administration, including the police forces; in its report, it recommended the creation of an ombudsman.[11] The institution was based mostly on the model of New Zealand's ombudsman, created only a few years earlier in 1962, although in practice it continued the work of the local attorney general's office.[12]

In Guyana, the creation of the ombudsman reflected the role of an international actor (the ICJ) serving as interlocutor and responding to domestic tensions, as well as a shifting domestic regulatory context that permitted locking in new commitments. The idea of creating an ombudsman was introduced by an external actor prior to political independence. It was an externally derived idea, partly reflecting the country's membership in the Commonwealth. Guyana's ombudsman thus emerged in the midst of a regulatory moment.

A closer look at the period's history also reveals that, from the perspective of international actors, the ombudsman was partly a political tool. The ICJ report that recommended creating an ombudsman in Guyana may itself have been politicized. Only a year after Guyana gained independence, the CIA's role in funding the ICJ was made public; and while the three jurists who visited Guyana for two weeks in 1965 may have been well-intentioned, their report gave the British government a way of leaving the colony while seemingly paving the way for racial progress.[13] They left Guyana, moreover, in the hands of a U.S. supporter who accepted the terms of the ICJ's report and who counterbalanced an Indian Marxist-Leninist candidate. In the context of the Cold War, the ICJ's report—including the call for building an ombudsman—gave Britain's political transition a veneer of social progress, suiting both Britain and the United States' interests in the region. Whether the ICJ was a willing or unwitting accomplice is less important than the reality of this broader political context. Not surprisingly, then, when the ombudsman was created and included in the country's constitution, some observers have pointed out that more attention was paid to what the office of the ombudsman should *not* do than to what it should do.[14] This illustrates how state leaders often want the gains from appearing accountable while still retaining a way out when it is politically expedient, resulting in accountability mechanisms that are relatively weak.

The ombudsman in Guyana like all of those that followed in the Caribbean was never formally accredited as an NHRI, and yet for many international actors and scholars it is treated as a national human rights body—appearing on the International Coordinating Committee's database of NHRIs and participating in relevant meetings. This lapse may reflect weak state capacities. Indeed, in small developing countries, the capacity to build separate institutions devoted to promoting and protecting human rights can be quite limited; subsequent chapters show that many of the world's smallest states lack an accredited NHRI.[15] Also, the fact that the institution was essentially imported and a product of the country's colonial ties may have limited its significance. As with France, a strong international impetus partly weakened the institution's domestic reach.

Once the institution of the ombudsman was created in the Caribbean, the region was targeted by international actors as a place ripe for creating similar bodies. Thus, in 1967, the United Nations held an international seminar in Jamaica promoting the creation of NHRIs, while the Commonwealth also pushed the idea of national ombudsmen offices.[16] Gradually, the ombudsman diffused to other Caribbean countries. Within this early period, similar institutions would form in Trinidad and Tobago (1976), Saint Lucia (1978), Puerto Rico (1977), Jamaica (1978), Barbados (1981), and Haiti (1987). Reflecting somewhat different circumstances, the role of subregional diffusion was nonetheless an overarching similarity. Both Trinidad and Tobago and Saint Lucia created their ombudsmen in the context of regulatory moments: independence and the drafting of new constitutions in the mid-1970s. While Jamaica and Barbados did not face similar regulatory changes during the period, they had taken on external human rights obligations. But it was the context of ongoing support for NHRIs around the world and for the ombudsman in this region, including that key meeting in Jamaica, that defined this institutional option in the first place. If the small states of the Caribbean represented one of the first regional clusters of NHRIs, after Europe, it was partly because international bodies (e.g., the United Nations, ICJ, and British Commonwealth) actively promoted NHRIs throughout the region.

In all cases, these institutions were not accredited even after more than three decades, making them among the most formally weak NHRIs in the world. Though this weakness may be attributed to their international origins and weak national capacities, this may be changing. For instance, when Human Rights Council members called on Guyana to create an independent NHRI during its Universal Periodic Review, state representatives agreed to do so.[17] As part of their own institutional evolution, and with heightened international support, ombudsmen in the Caribbean may yet transform into accredited NHRIs.

Globalizing the Rule of Law in Senegal

The idea of creating a national human rights committee in Senegal in 1970—the Comité sénégalais des droits de l'homme—was promoted most closely by Kéba Mbaye, a respected Senegalese judge who headed the country's supreme court and would go on to chair the International Commission of Jurists. Mbaye was an accomplished jurist, and he was one of the most important voices from the Global South when it came to human rights discourse, championing like no one else the formation of a region-wide African human rights system, helping to draft the African Charter on Human and Peoples' Rights, and first articulating the "human right to development."[18]

Mbaye was a leading advocate of creating a national human rights committee, but his proposal resonated given the country's external obligations and status. Senegal had already ratified the two international human rights covenants by 1970, one of the first countries in the world to do so. A few years earlier, it had hosted the first meeting in Africa of judges from the region, partly under the auspices of the International Commission of Jurists. In addition to focusing on the linkages between human rights and the rule of law, the meeting was a crucial precursor to the formation of a region-wide human rights commission. The Senegalese Human Rights Committee itself, moreover, emphasized early international calls for NHRIs, referring explicitly to both the 1946 and 1960 UN resolutions on national human rights bodies as motive driving forces for its own institution. Even the name of a "committee" is the same language used in the UN resolutions. Still, the body created in 1970 was most concerned with raising national awareness of internationally recognized human rights standards. It did not appear to exert much authority beyond this, and it remained largely under the discretion of the executive.[19]

With Mbaye playing the role of global interlocutor, the Senegalese committee was following the template outlined in UN resolutions for national human rights bodies. In this sense, it was more explicitly and self-consciously an NHRI, somewhat like the French commission. Senegal's role as a regional leader and innovator in the human rights field also helps to explain why this country was the first site of an NHRI in Africa. The national committee, moreover, was highly legalized and bound up in the notion of the rule of law. It was intended to complement legal institutions, and the country's chief justice would also be its designated leader. This legalism reflected Mbaye's own professional identity and the local presence of the International Commission of Jurists. It also reflected Mbaye's belief that the law could act as a necessary sanction: for him, protecting human rights ultimately required a system of legal accountability.[20] The Senegalese institution took the idea of a national human rights committee promoted in UN resolutions and linked it to the rule of law, even while the country operated undemocratically under one-party rule.[21]

In the history of NHRIs, Senegal's human rights committee created in 1970 is essential, even though it has been largely forgotten. If it maintained a relatively low profile and undertook mostly promotional work, it was perhaps because it operated in a relatively closed political system. While Senegal's NHRI is often dated to later, after the institution became an independent body and accepted the Paris Principles in 1997, the committee never fully stopped functioning or changed its name since 1970; and its origins do reveal close awareness of early NHRI resolutions by the United Nations. Despite being fully accredited since 2000, the NHRI was demoted to partially compliant a decade later. Long before a system of accreditation, however, Senegal's human rights committee operated as an NHRI, created in response to the first UN resolutions on the subject and led by one of the most prominent jurists of the twentieth century.

Innovators from the Inside Out

The mid-1970s saw the arrival of the hybrid ombudsman (in the Iberian context) and the "human rights commission" model (in British Commonwealth countries). These NHRIs appeared in states that were either long-standing or emerging democracies. In all cases, albeit in different ways, creating an NHRI permitted them to lock in commitments or, faced with new external obligations, to shift domestic regulatory control over rights issues. The idea for a self-restraining institution was nonetheless borrowed largely from the international context. Though it was a period of high institutional innovation, it was one marked by broader processes of transculturation. A few other institutions, considered NHRIs only in retrospect, also appeared during this period, all in Europe.[22]

Democratic Regulatory Moments and Iberian Hybrids

The first two countries to create hybrid ombudsman—a combination of the classic ombudsman with an explicit human rights mandate—were Portugal and Spain. In both instances, the creation of the ombudsman was part of a broader democratic transition and new constitutions. Even if the idea originated with local actors, they were still borrowing from the global context, in terms of both the recent diffusion of the ombudsman and the rising popularity of human rights discourse. While Portugal and Spain were partially inventing how to craft a modern Western and European democratic country, following decades of authoritarian rule and abuse, they also were drawn to historically relevant institutions.

Portugal's Provedor de Justiça was created by legal decree in 1975 and incorporated into the country's 1976 constitution, though the institution had been proposed a few years earlier. José Magalhães Godinho, a lawyer in the democratic opposition introduced the idea of a national human rights council, closely resembling an ombudsman, in 1971; he would go on to become the country's first ombudsman in 1976.[23] At the time of Magalhães Godinho's proposal in 1971, the European Parliament in Vienna also encouraged all member states to create an ombudsman. And at a national lawyer's conference in 1972, the idea of an ombudsman for Portugal also was introduced. Likewise, at the Third Congress of Democratic Opposition in 1973, the notion of an ombudsman was promoted, referencing antecedents across Western Europe, New Zealand, Canada, and Mauritius.[24] Included within a package of judicial reforms, the ombudsman was finally created in 1975 as the world's first hybrid NHRI, or human rights ombudsman. In addition to monitoring public authorities, the domain of a traditional ombudsman, Portugal's ombudsman was charged with protecting and promoting citizens' rights, an acknowledgment that the institution was part and parcel of the democratic transition.

In neighboring Spain, when seven men sat together to draft the country's new democratic constitution, they looked to precursors, including Portugal's recent constitution, especially when enumerating rights and freedoms.[25] Like Portugal, Spain opted for a hybrid ombudsman, combining the features of a traditional ombudsman with the protection of human rights. The Defensor del Pueblo was first included in Spain's 1978 constitution, though it would not be up and running until 1982.[26] The notion of the ombudsman must have seemed appropriate for a new democratic regime, especially given the preferred Spanish translation: literally, defender of the people—an accountability mechanism within the state, allowing ordinary people to appeal wrongdoing. The Portuguese Provedor de Justiça in turn has a somewhat different connotation: provider of justice. While the Portuguese institution acts as "principal" in making sure the state abides by its legal obligations, the Spanish defensor casts the institution primarily as an "agent" of the people. In both cases, this was the antithesis of everyday political life under authoritarian rule. Given Portugal's adoption of the institution and its growing popularity among Western democracies, it must have seemed an obvious choice for the Spanish politicians looking to forge an institutional compromise. That the Spanish province of Aragón features in the folklore of the traditional ombudsman may have also resonated with some of them.[27] In fact, beginning in the 1980s, a system of provincial and local defensores grew in Spain, alongside the national-level ombudsman.[28]

For both countries, the transition to democracy was about locking in commitments so as not to return to an all-too-familiar recent past. In this view, the creation of an ombudsman appealed because it both struck a clear democratic chord and served to channel social discontent. These Iberian countries may have been first and foremost following a Western democratic script when they incorporated the office of the ombudsman into their new constitutions, but the fact that they imbued it with authority over fundamental rights and freedoms suggests they were also looking to "lock out" a return to abuse. That they embraced the language of rights and freedoms as a means of doing so reflects the emerging discourse of the times. Spain even referenced the Universal Declaration of Human Rights explicitly in its new constitution, going further than its neighbor in embracing "human rights" as a framing device.[29]

Regulatory moments are not all the same, but the Iberian model paved the way for other regimes undergoing democratic transitions to adopt accountability institutions. The ICJ again played an important role, linking the notion of the ombudsman and the rule of law. In fact, the ICJ's greater role in Portugal may help to account for why the Provedor de Justiça took on a more legalistic veneer than Spain's ombudsman. While the Iberian countries added a rights dimension to the traditional ombudsman, in both contexts they followed the ombudsman model and created monocratic bodies, that is, an office composed of a single individual. In contrast to the Caribbean, however, where the office remained captive to the individual overseeing it, in the Iberian context the ombudsman evolved into an institution into its own right. This key difference reflected distinct origins and political contexts: on the one hand, an externally imposed institution whose power and resources were severely constrained from the start, and on the other hand, a body selected by local actors in the midst of negotiating a political transition. In so doing, Iberian leaders were adapting an institution promoted by Western democracies, whose ranks they aspired to join.

The New Commissions Model

Among the most significant of the early NHRIs were those created in the British Commonwealth countries of New Zealand and Canada. These NHRIs reflected a convergence of external obligations and a strong domestic rule of law system, with incentives to localize international standards. NHRIs created in New Zealand and Canada in 1977 also represented the first "human rights commissions" model in the world. In both cases, significantly, these institutions were antidiscrimination bodies, connected to broader global struggles against racial injustice. And for both countries, accession to human rights treaties proved crucial.

The decision to create a human rights commission in *New Zealand* was linked directly to the country's external obligations, namely its upcoming ratification of the International Covenant for Civil and Political Rights. Thus, the Human Rights Commission Act was passed in 1977. As a common-law country with a dualist system, requiring that international law be incorporated explicitly into national legislation before taking effect, New Zealand's human rights commission flowed out of its international obligation to implement the International Covenant on Civil and Political Rights (ICCPR) domestically. In the same way, the country had passed a Race Relations Act and instituted the office of Race Conciliator in 1971, in anticipation of its ratification a year later of the Convention on the Elimination of All Forms of Racial Discrimination (CERD); like other human rights treaties, CERD calls on member states to designate a national body that can accept complaints involving treaty violations. After passage of a statutory bill of rights in New Zealand in 1990, the new Human Rights Act of 1993 folded the Race Relations Act into the broader Human Rights Commission.[30] In 2001, the Human Rights Act was itself amended giving its tribunal proceedings greater independence, partly in response to issues raised as part of the review for NHRI accreditation.[31]

Nor is there any question that the creation of *Canada's* Commission on Human Rights was partly linked to ratification a year earlier of the two international human rights covenants.[32] Though the Human Rights Act laid the foundations, the act did not explicitly mention international human rights instruments, and domestic actors were not legally obligated to protect the full range of internationally recognized human rights, unlike the case with New Zealand's commission. Still, informal connections existed in practice, linking treaty obligations to domestic implementation of human rights standards.

In the Canadian case, moreover, the federal commission followed the lead of local human rights commissions that had existed for over a decade, established to administer related legislation. These legislative statutes had their roots in postwar antidiscrimination legislation (usually focusing on race) and "fair practices" legislation (typically addressing employment and housing considerations). These cases, in turn, were influenced by the experience of U.S. cities, with one careful study documenting how institutional development in New York in the 1940s influenced developments in Canada.[33] Ontario, which had enacted the country's first Racial Discrimination Act in 1944, also created the first local human rights commission in Canada, intended mostly to implement a new human rights code. Thus, in the 1960s, four provinces had created human rights commissions: Ontario (1961), Nova Scotia (1967), British Columbia (1969), and Newfoundland (1969). By 1977, when the Canadian Human Rights Commission was created, human rights commissions already existed in every province in the country.

Other factors also made the creation of human rights commissions appealing in Canada. In particular, a broad critique of the courts made the formation of an alternative administrative entity desirable. Not only could the courts be sluggish, fairly expensive, and insufficiently progressive, according to this view, but their adversarial approach (and the high burden of proof that the prosecution needed to meet) did not always seem appropriate for addressing human rights problems.[34]

Human rights commissions, in contrast, were viewed as bodies that could provide social actors with greater access to the state, potentially even "socializing" state agents. Yet despite these promises, the rise of human rights commissions and complementary tribunals had the unintended effect of subjecting human rights cases to a civil standard, appearing to favor complainants disproportionately while stripping away the due process rights of defendants. Though these administrative, regulatory agencies were initially favored partly because they served as an alternative to the courts, their own legalization and quasi-judicial aspects later eroded support for them, sparking much of the contentiousness surrounding Canada's human rights commissions at the turn of the millennium.[35]

In general, the commission model adopted by both New Zealand and Canada has had a few implications. First, as antidiscrimination bodies, their focus has been largely on civil and political rights.[36] While the commissions could promote compliance with the full range of international human rights treaties that these countries have ratified, they remain first and foremost antidiscriminatory agencies. Second, the choice of a "commission" structure reflected more than anything a historical antecedent inherited from the British tradition. (See Chapter 2, for a discussion of commissions of inquiry.) Third, unlike states that created accountability institutions during a regulatory moment, these states were making good on new international and domestic legal obligations. Yet they were no less strategic: even if memories of the past were not haunting leaders or giving them an incentive to erect self-correcting measures, they may still have been mindful of the strategic uses of such an institution in channeling social demands. As an observer noted of New Zealand's original ombudsman, created in the 1960s, it was a case of "rather unspectacular legislative history," revealing "how little the Ombudsman was a response to excited clamor. . . . The Ombudsman was created not to clean up a mess, but, rather, simply to provide insurance against future messes."[37]

Despite their differences, then, the first two human rights commissions share important similarities. Like countries under the Iberian model, these countries were subject to the human rights discourse that had emerged on the international scene by the 1970s, reflected in the entry into force of the two international covenants and rising social activism, as well as injected into Cold War relations and the new language of détente. For both countries, these commissions served to localize authority over human rights issues. New Zealand's commission offered a straightforward mode of implementing the ICCPR, while human rights commissions in Canada also sought to shift the locus of local control away from the courts. Both NHRIs, moreover, were originally erected to deal with racial inequality; they were mostly antidiscriminatory and equal opportunity bodies. Like those in the United States, authorities in these countries have preferred approaching problems of race by focusing on civil and political rights. This has permitted them to address overt discrimination, without framing the issues in terms of internationally recognized economic and social rights. The latter, after all, would require confronting poverty and other systemic conditions, which could upset the ongoing inequality of Maori and Aboriginal peoples, among others.

Labeling NHRIs, Retroactively

Many of the institutions created before the mid-1980s did not refer to themselves as "national human rights institutions." They were not necessarily referencing UN resolutions (1947 and 1960) or UN workshops on the topic (1967 and 1978), with the exception of the French and Senegalese commissions. In the case of the Caribbean and Iberian institutions, these represented first and foremost the creation of ombudsman offices, regardless of whether a human rights mandate was included. Even when leaders were mindful of international obligations and rising human discourse, as they were in New Zealand and Canada, the notion of an NHRI had not picked up traction during this period; they were simply implementing new treaty obligations domestically. Four other institutions—created during this early period in Europe— have come to be recognized today as NHRIs, although that was not at all the intent when they were first created: institutions in Switzerland, Austria, Sweden, and Italy.

Switzerland's Commission fédérale pour les questions féminines counts as one of the country's NHRIs today. That commission was created in 1976 by an internal ministry decision to focus on women's issues, a move that reflected feminist mobilization within the country and growing transnational consciousness more than anything else.[38] At the time, the country was not facing a regulatory moment and had not undertaken any significant international human rights obligations. Though the institution's creation is considered a milestone in the Swiss women's movement, one preceding the inclusion of gender equality in the national constitution in 1981, its strong emphasis on research and its narrow mandate on women's issues, led the ICC to give it a C rating among NHRIs—in noncompliance with the Paris Principles. In recent years, a debate has ensued over the desirability of creating a standard NHRI in Switzerland. Pressured by a range of countries to do so, the Swiss government has nonetheless rejected the proposal.[39] And despite the government's insistence on holding up the women's commission as an NHRI, no one seems to buy it; even human rights activists within the country are unaware that Switzerland has an NHRI.[40] Regardless of Swiss intransigence today, in the 1970s, when the women's commission was formed, it was unrelated to the notion of an NHRI, only presented later for accreditation.

While *Austria's* Ombudsman Board, created in 1977, was eventually incorporated into the constitution (in 1981) and revised via constitutional amendments (1986 and 1988), at the time of its creation it was intended only as a temporary body. First proposed in 1970 as a "public law attorney," it took a few years for the ombudsman to take off, and it was never viewed as an NHRI. Just as Austria's constitution does not include human rights, the Ombudsman Board is not explicitly tasked with a human rights mandate, though in practice acts of maladministration sometimes become intertwined with human rights violations. These limitations notwithstanding, the ombudsman was accredited internationally as an NHRI in 2000, after which it started adding a chapter on basic rights to its annual report. In more recent years, the government has raised the issue of incorporating the Advisory Council on Human Rights (Menschenrechtsbeirat) into the Ombudsman Board, presumably attempting to add a human rights dimension to the NHRI.[41] The Advisory Council was itself created in 1999, first proposed by the Council of Europe's Committee on the Prevention of Torture. The impetus for that recommendation was the death of a Nigerian asylum seeker that prompted widespread pressure from NGOs.[42] The Advisory Council has nonetheless been critiqued for lacking independence, and a fully functioning human rights ombudsman has not yet been created in Austria. The existing ombudsman institution, originally intended as a temporary body, has itself turned to human rights issues only sporadically.

As the birthplace of the modern ombudsman, it is perhaps fitting that *Sweden* would be the country that at one time had the most number of recognized NHRIs. After the Equal Opportunities Act was adopted in 1979, an Equal Opportunities Ombudsman was created, along with a few specialized antidiscrimination ombudsman offices. Four of these would come to be fully accredited NHRIs: the Children's Ombudsman (1993), the Swedish Ombudsman against Ethnic Discrimination (1986), the Swedish Disability Ombudsman (1994), and the Ombudsman for Equal Rights (1980). In 2009, a new Discrimination Act led to the formation of the Equality Ombudsman, with the previous antidiscrimination ombudsman being phased out (except for the Children's Ombudsman, which continues to function independently). Only the new Equality Ombudsman would apply for international accreditation as an NHRI, dropping to B status in 2011.[43] Throughout this complex trajectory, the formation of antidiscrimination ombudsman agencies in Sweden reflected the country's long-standing history with the institution and broad global attention to issues of discrimination. While technically considered human rights ombudsmen, or hybrid institutions, these bodies did not formally or centrally draw on "human rights" as a point of reference.[44] And despite the country's historic leadership among the world's traditional ombudsman, it has not played a similar role in the field of NHRIs.

In *Italy*, a national human rights commission—Commissione per i diritti umani—was established in 1984, but only as part of the Council of Ministers. The institution seems to have been partly a response to mounting international human rights discourse, as Italy ratified the international covenants in 1978 (and created an interministerial body, designed mostly to advise the Foreign Ministry).[45] In the early 1980s, moreover, the country was subject to intense charges of human rights abuses resulting from preventive detention and mounting torture, some of it in response to a domestic terrorist threat. A transnational array of actors, including Amnesty International and domestic groups, applied pressure.[46] As the Council of Ministers proposed legal improvements in response, and Southern European neighbors were creating NHRIs, the government may have deemed it wise to create the human rights commission. Unlike the human rights commissions model adopted in Canada and New Zealand, the Italian name may have been mirroring the UN Human Rights Commission. It should also be noted that local ombudsman and human rights bodies had existed in Italy since the early 1980s (though the country lacks a national-level ombudsman).[47]

Since the Italian commission's formation, international and domestic groups have pressured the government to create a functioning NHRI that can be accredited. A domestic group of NGOs, formed in the new millennium, mounted a campaign for an NHRI that went as far as drafting a proposed bill.[48] Pressure intensified on the eve of Italy's bid to win a spot on the UN Human Rights Council in 2010; but despite general assurances, a new institution was not formed.[49] While the creation of the current commission was not conceived as an NHRI, its existence has permitted international and domestic actors to call for an independent NHRI, building rhetorically on the commission's inadequacy. The evolution of the international NHRI regime and the institution's diffusion worldwide has undoubtedly propelled calls for a "real" NHRI in Italy.

Early Adopters

Starting in the mid-1980s, two trends became apparent in the nascent world of NHRIs. First, this was the beginning of actual diffusion, as institutional models began to be replicated. In labeling this an instance of diffusion, it is important to establish both institutional similarities and mechanisms of transfer. While there was one innovator during this period—Denmark—most other new institutions reflected straightforward diffusion. Second, this was the first time that the creation of NHRIs was linked to organized abuse: states with widespread human rights abuses, and subject to international and domestic criticism, began creating NHRIs in the 1980s. In a sense, this was evidence that the notion of an NHRI was now beginning to acquire the characteristics of a social marker or emblem, a sign of commitment to international human rights norms, worth emulating.

Domestic Politics and the Australian Commission

Australia's human rights body followed the commission model already adopted by Commonwealth peers New Zealand and Canada. Initially, it established a part-time antidiscrimination body in 1981, named the Human Rights Commission. The most immediate rationale was to implement the Human Rights Commission Act of that year, itself a vehicle for ensuring compliance with international human rights instruments.[50] Indeed, the act's preamble referred to the ICCPR—ratified by Australia a year earlier, in 1980—and to several other declarations (e.g., the rights of the child and disabled persons, as well as "other international instruments relating to human rights and freedoms"). But it would take a new Labor government, more committed to human rights institutionalization, to establish a permanent human rights agency in 1986, when the new Human Rights Equal Opportunity Commission Act also went into effect.[51]

A string of important institutional precedents nonetheless existed. For example, the Racial Discrimination Act, passed in 1975 to implement the Convention on the Elimination of Racial Discrimination, created the related post of Commission for Community Relations, a complaints-handling body. Going further back, other institutional precursors existed. In 1973 the federal parliament had passed a Discriminatory Laws Act, applicable only to the state of Queensland, which had the largest population of Aboriginal peoples. And beginning in 1966, state laws had enacted antidiscrimination statutes and bodies.[52] As the first state to pass antidiscrimination legislation in 1966, South Australia was apparently pushing the government to accede to CERD.[53] A series of national and state committees on discrimination in employment were also created starting in 1983, to implement a 1958 International Labor Organization Convention (No. 111); these would be subsumed under the new human rights commission in 1986.[54] Finally, a Human Rights Bureau, created as a temporary body within the attorney general's office in 1980, was another precursor; its head was later moved to serve as deputy chair of the newly established commission. Like a Special Adviser on Human Rights dating to the 1970s, the Human Rights Bureau was created during a time when human rights issues were becoming more globally prominent.[55]

Over the years, the institution has gone through various permutations, reflected in a series of name changes—from the Human Rights Commission to the Human Rights and Equal Opportunity Commission to the latest, the Australian Human Rights Commission—as well as steady expansion into new rights issues.[56] While new governments have attempted to dilute the watchdog's resources and power, the commission has remained on solid footing as a statutory body, fully accredited and a global leader among NHRIs. In 1996, Australia in fact hosted the first meeting of the Asia Pacific Forum of NHRIs. Domestically, it reports directly to Parliament, handling complaints, intervening in litigation, conducting research, and engaging in human rights education. And since its early years, it has shown a notable capacity to adapt and reform. In 2000, for example, its complaints-handling function was transferred to the courts system, though it can still intervene in legal cases by acting as amicus curiae. The decision to change its name in 2008, just after its twenty-year anniversary—a move the commission describes as a realignment of its "corporate identity"—may also reflect a stronger embrace of human rights discourse beyond the traditional antidiscrimination focus.[57]

However, if Australia did not create an NHRI in the 1970s, as did New Zealand and Canada, it was partly because it had not yet ratified both international human rights covenants, itself a sign of political infighting; Australia ratified the International Covenant on Economic, Social and Cultural Rights (ICESCR) in the 1970s but signed only the ICCPR. Despite important precursors, the government's ideological commitments, partisan disagreements, and a constitutional crisis mid-decade in the 1970s blocked any move to ratify the ICCPR.[58] Though treaty commitments can readily be interpreted from the outside looking in as representing a state's coherent interests, in practice internal disagreements over acceding to a human rights treaty can run rampant. As early as 1966, when voting for the international covenants was on the table at the United Nations, Australian officials at the Department of External Affairs noted that the country would have to agree to the conventions regardless of domestic divergences for the sake of "international political consideration."[59] In the end, the country acceded to international human rights treaties, but only after issuing reservations and always remaining leery—often reflecting a bipartisan dissensus—over issues like immigration, indigenous peoples, and national security.[60]

Australia illustrates how for countries with a strong rule of law, NHRIs can be primarily a means of implementing treaty obligations; but treaties themselves reflect domestic compromises. Domestic conditions, including the government in office, must be supportive of treaty accession. The Australian case likewise suggests that local institutions created at one point in time can "accumulate," acting as precedents and serving as organizational forms ready to be adopted or remolded. There is some evidence that Australia ratified the IC-ESCR in 1975 but not the ICCPR because leaders viewed the former as "progressive" in nature, and therefore less subject to implementation, while the ICCPR triggered immediate obligations.[61] When Australia did ratify the IC-CPR in 1980 it was partly because of the mounting global context and a domestic buildup of similar institutions. That the government's interests remained halfhearted is evident in the fact that they only built a part-time body to implement the Human Rights Commission Act. Perhaps that was fortuitous from the standpoint of institutional development: rather than the subsequent administration inheriting a weakly capacitated body, it was able in 1986 to erect a more solid permanent organization, capable of withstanding political attacks over time.

Strategic Liberalization in Poland

The first NHRI in Eastern Europe appeared in Poland in 1987 (the Commissioner for Civil Rights Protection). Focusing only on civil rights, the government faced seemingly competing incentives, having accepted international human rights obligations but continuing to practice widespread abuse. Interestingly, this human rights institution was created before the country embarked on a democratic transition, as part of a set of political and legal institutional reforms meant to appease the public during a severe economic crisis. The same year the NHRI was created a referendum led to limited liberalization, including a revival of Solidarity and some press freedom. Part of these nominal reforms, the commissioner's office also reflected the country's relatively strong legalist tradition, especially its Catholic variant, which was permitted to exist during the Cold War. This commitment to legalism translated into Poland being the first European country in the 1980s to create judicial accountability mechanisms. When the Commissioner for Civil Rights Protection was formed, it too followed a very legalist approach, including a tendency to install commissioners with a strong juridical background.[62]

Most fascinating is that the proposal for an ombudsman, or civil rights spokesperson, had already been made by a Solidarity-related organization (Experience and Future Group) in 1981, only to be ignored. The idea all but disappeared until the government's announcement in 1986 that it would be creating the body. As David Ost describes it, "The Ombudsman would bring state abuses to the public eye and provide the citizen with an avenue of protest less costly and less arduous than the court system. Based on the Swedish model, . . . the Ombudsman would be a kind of special prosecutor acting for society against abuses by the state."[63]

While the 1987 institution was not at all what the opposition had envisioned, it was relatively strong and quickly surpassed expectations, especially given its resources. In 1989, the institution was incorporated into the constitution and later strengthened in the 1997 constitution. Though in the late 1980s the regime was attempting to retain control by liberalizing, the turn to legalism—of which the NHRI was one key instance—also served other ends beyond checking the power of the party and the state. According to Kazimierz Poznański, "[T]hese agencies reduced the need for the independent unions as representatives of diverse societal interests."[64] Accountability mechanisms were strategic, therefore, in the sense that they permitted the regime to rechannel social demands in less seemingly threatening ways.

Comparatively, the Polish institution represents the diffusion of the hybrid ombudsman for the first time to Eastern Europe. Democratizing countries adopting an ombudsman in the region might now be inclined—in the context of ongoing or past abuses—to add a human rights mandate. While the regime may have been aware of broader global developments, the most immediate reason for introducing this particular institutional reform was Solidarity's proposal in 1981 for creating a civil rights spokesperson, itself reflecting an awareness of the ombudsman's worldwide diffusion. For the government, the institution had the added advantage of appearing to meet social demands while channeling, and thereby potentially controlling more effectively, those very demands. A strong legalist trend in the country merely facilitated these developments.

One interesting side note concerns a question of translation: though the institution refers literally to "civil rights spokesperson," it has been translated most commonly as Commissioner for Civil Rights Protection.[65] As of 2009, however, the institution began changing its *English*-language translation to Human Rights Defender, joining Armenia and Georgia, which share the same name, and thereby embracing a broader notion of rights.[66] The discrepancy in translation appears to represent more of a shift in the institution's external versus internal identity, wishing to project an image of itself more fully aligned with internationally recognized human rights norms.

Denmark Introduces the "Institute" Model

Another NHRI appeared in Europe in 1987, the Danish Centre for Human Rights. From the start, Danish interest in an NHRI was a matter of foreign affairs—a way of promoting human rights abroad and projecting its identity as an exporter of liberal, egalitarian values. It was the creation of an ombudsman in Denmark in the 1950s, after all, that set off the diffusion of that institution elsewhere in the world. Interestingly, the Danish ombudsman in the 1960s had participated in seminars of the UN Division of Human Rights, including the 1967 meeting in Jamaica and in ICJ conferences promoting NHRIs.[67] The Danish Centre's creation itself followed on the heels of an important UN resolution on NHRIs in 1986. It was not surprising, then, that this leader among national ombudsmen would create an NHRI in this early period of institutional adoption.

Especially once NHRIs appeared in Commonwealth countries, which borrowed their own classic ombudsmen agencies partly from the Swedish model, it is likely that the Danish government may have felt some pressure to establish a human rights body. The Danish institution was framed explicitly in terms of human rights, but it parted ways with existing models of NHRIs to create what was mostly a research center, oriented toward human rights in *other* countries. As a traditionally homogenous society embracing values of egalitarianism and solidarity, the Danish social welfare state has deemed it unnecessary to incorporate international human rights laws into domestic laws or daily discourse. Not surprisingly, the NHRI's first application for international accreditation in 1999 earned it a B, only partially compliant with the Paris Principles that Danish representatives had helped draft.[68]

The situation changed after 2001, when the political right in Denmark made significant electoral gains. Almost immediately, the Human Rights Centre was targeted, with the intent of merging it with other bodies and placing it under the Foreign Ministry. A vigorous international campaign was launched by organizations and academics to save the center from closure, proving successful against a government that was about to take over the presidency of the European Union. In the end, the center was renamed the Danish Institute for Human Rights (DIHR) and merged, somewhat awkwardly, with the academic Danish Center for International Studies and Human Rights. Most important, however, the institution was embedded in legislation in 2002, placing it on more solid footing than its prior basis in a decree. Internally, the crisis had fueled a strategic reevaluation of activities.[69]

After the crisis, and partly related to Denmark's leadership at the EU during this period, the institution was designated an equal treatment body, as called for in various region-wide directives. In 2003, the DIHR thus became the national equal treatment or antidiscrimination body for issues of race and ethnicity envisioned in a European Council directive, known as Article 13; a complaints-handling body was also created for this purpose, though its activities were later assigned to another agency. In 2011, the DIHR also became the antidiscrimination body for gender (following a European Council directive from 2004) and for disabilities (based on the UN Convention on the Rights of the Child).[70] Overall, the postcrisis period introduced an antidiscrimination aspect to the institution's mandate, responding to regional standards and criticisms that the body was overly focused on research.

The establishment of an NHRI in Denmark in 1987 reflected external obligations more than anything else. Unlike other Western democracies, external obligations were not entirely related to attempts at localizing authority; in a manner somewhat reminiscent of France in the 1940s, the institution offered above all a way to maintain a consistent image of itself in the world. Historical precursors played a role, given the NHRI's links to the institution of the ombudsman, closely related to its own history and global leadership. In fact, its global promotion of the ombudsman led the country to participate in early international forums devoted to NHRIs. By the mid-1980s, especially as more Western democracies created human rights institutions, Denmark itself moved to create a similar institution.

Foreign policy has been the Achilles' heel of Denmark's NHRI, though there are signs of change. Both the NHRI's form and mandate reveal the externally oriented nature of the body, and the concern with foreign policy has overwhelmed the institution in many ways; but it also proved useful when the institute was threatened by a hostile government. As Julie Mertus aptly notes, "[F]oreign policy commitment provided the impetus for the DIHR to be established in the first place and supplied the strength to shield the institute from threats of closure."[71] While the institution still focuses heavily on research, a broader antidiscrimination mandate has turned it into a fully accredited NHRI, and the institute regularly continues to act as a leader in regional and international forums.

Diffusion across the Global South

This early period also saw the heightened spread of NHRIs to developing countries, across three world regions; this often occurred in the context of regime liberalization or a more dramatic regulatory moment and in the midst of ongoing abuse. The development also coincided with a rise in UN technical assistance for human rights capacity building, namely for creating and strengthening NHRIs. In other words, as international standards like the UN resolution in 1986 promoted the notion of NHRIS, international actors enhanced the concrete resources that would make diffusion possible. Internationally relevant social peers, sometimes including former colonial powers, served as important models, often accounting for the type of NHRI adopted.

Guatemala's Military in Search of Legitimacy

The first NHRI in Latin America appeared in 1985 in Guatemala, the Procuraduría de los Derechos Humanos. Like the countries home to the Iberian counterparts on which it was modeled, Guatemala was undergoing apparent democratization, though violations persisted in the Central American country. Despite steps toward constitutional rule, including the Procuraduría's creation, the military held on to power and armed conflict continued for another decade. The NHRI was arguably part of a broader strategy on the part of the regime to imbue itself with legitimacy and hang on to power.[72] It arose at the nexus of a regulatory moment and organized abuse.

Following the brutality of Efraín Ríos Montt's rule, and growing international pressure, including the appointment of a special UN rapporteur for the country in 1983, Guatemala's 1985 constitution featured human rights centrally. While the country had already acceded to the American Convention on Human Rights, it had not yet ratified the international human rights covenants. And in a move some observers have described as puzzling, the Guatemalan military turned to constitutionalism to stay in power.[73] Part of this reflected a historically engrained tendency, broadly evident in the region's early nineteenth-century dictators who ruled under the guise of liberal constitutions. It also spoke to a "third wave of democratization," and rising global human rights discourse, most recently and vocally articulated in Argentina, as that country emerged from its dirty war and turned to democratization. Guatemala's constitutionalist turn also followed in the footsteps of a broader diffusion of constitutional democracies that, as Frederick Drake has described, "rolled through Central America" in the 1980s.[74]

The regime's embrace of constitutionalism was intended to appease critics and retain power. To this end, the human rights ombudsman was one of the institutions included in the 1985 constitution, along with a constitutional court and a supreme electoral tribunal. The idea for an NHRI was reportedly proposed by the Colegio de Abogados y Notarios, the equivalent of a national legal bar association, composed of the country's top lawyers, who certainly were aware of the Spanish human rights ombudsman.[75] While Guatemalans adopted the hybrid ombudsman, imported from the Iberian context, they opted for a different name more closely associated with existing legal institutions: the term "procuraduría" was more akin to the office of attorney (or solicitor) general.

Overall, the regime sought to enhance its international image by adopting legitimate structures, borrowed from the external context to extend its rule. This fit into the contradictory logics embedded in the constitution, which shifted the country from "a state of siege to a country of laws," or more specifically a "counterinsurgent constitutional order."[76] Thus, Article 30 of the constitution limited the NHRI's access to information in cases of national security. As one scholar describes, it was "a structure by which to regulate the governed while the governors act with impunity."[77] This interpretation is further consistent with the fact that the Procuraduría was structured relatively well on paper and then insufficiently funded. A system of organized abuse had pushed Guatemala's military regime to search for legitimacy in constitutional rule, including a state-controlled human rights agency.

The human rights ombudsman continued to figure over time in democratic institution building. It was included in the 1996 peace agreement, and given the particular domestic context, it has focused its work on vulnerable populations.[78] Deemed a partially compliant NHRI in 1999 (a B-status institution), the NHRI seemed to implement necessary changes and it was soon accredited fully.[79] Guatemala's NHRI had come a long way, created at the initiative of an abusive military regime that was searching for legitimacy in nominal democratization and constitutional rule. A history of legalism proved significant, including when a national professional association of lawyers introduced the idea based on the Spanish model. It would nonetheless take resolution of the armed conflict and international accreditation pressures to push the state to reform and strengthen the institution, even if on some level it has never managed to escape its origins as a halfhearted state agency.

Co-optation and Vilification in the Philippines

Following the example of Australia and New Zealand, the Philippines created a human rights *commission* in 1987, third in the Asia-Pacific region to do so. It was, significantly, the first country in the world to face an overwhelming round of incentives to create an NHRI: a regulatory moment, external obligations, and organized abuse. The country was just emerging from a period of authoritarian rule and undergoing democratization, a transition formally begun in 1986 and in the context of large-scale social protests that came to be known as the People Power Revolution. The Philippines also ratified the ICCPR in 1986, having already acceded to the ICESCR in 1974. In this context, a new constitution was introduced in 1987, incorporating the Human Rights Commission.

The immediate precursor for the commission was the Presidential Committee on Human Rights, created shortly after President Corazon Aquino took office in 1986. While human rights issues had been central to the president's campaign platform, given the large amount of human rights abuses in the country's recent past, the idea for a national human rights body appears to have been borrowed directly from the international context. According to former Supreme Court Justice Abraham Sarmiento, Executive Order No. 8, which created the president's committee, "itself was a response to the resolution of the United Nations General Assembly of December 14, 1984, encouraging 'all member states to take steps for the establishment or, where they already exist, the strengthening of national institutions for the protection and promotion of human rights.'"[80] Yet if the UN resolution planted the seed for creating a national human rights body, its specific form was likely emulated from regional peers. After all, only a handful of countries in the world, including Australia and New Zealand, had adopted the "commission" model.

With a UN resolution defining the option of an NHRI and regional peers setting an example, the creation of a human rights body portrayed internationally an image of a democratic country committed to human rights. Even economically, there were diffuse pressures to project such an image. In the 1980s, the new Aquino regime depended on both the United States and international actors for legitimacy and funds, while negotiating with international financial institutions like the International Monetary Fund.[81] Creating a human rights commission would convey an appropriate image to the country's Western partners and donors during a period of transition.

The body was in fact noteworthy for recognizing the full range of human rights, both civil-political and economic-social. In its form and functions, the commission closely mirrored emerging international standards for NHRIs. Perhaps most significantly, at the time it was created, it was the only national human rights commission anywhere in the world to be constitutionally mandated. No wonder that it was widely viewed as ushering in "a new phase in the growth of national institutions in developing countries."[82]

Domestically, the reality was somewhat more complex, as the human rights institution straddled various social divisions. In the aftermath of human rights atrocities committed under the Marcos government, human rights issues served as the coalitional glue holding Aquino's regime together.[83] But just as the government was appeasing international actors, it was also negotiating various interests on the domestic front, especially between civil society and a military wanting to avoid accountability for past abuses. In terms of civil society groups, which had been quite active during the Marcos dictatorship, they welcomed the political transition no less than the human rights structures erected by the new regime. Relatively heavy support from international donors, nonetheless, may have made at least some local activists amenable to being co-opted by the new government.[84] As for the armed forces, they reportedly approved of the new president's human rights committee, though apparently in exchange for an agreement that the body would investigate abuses by insurgents.[85]

The result of this balancing act was that the commission emphasized promotional activities more than anything else. It exposed violations by insurgents but seemed to give the armed forces a free pass. Over time, as the initial enthusiasm wore off, local human rights activists often became alienated and disillusioned, accusing the commission of a lack of independence and ineffectiveness. Perhaps in trying to appease too many actors, the NHRI became "hamstrung."[86]

The state still has managed to reform the institution incrementally in response to pressure. This was evident, for example, as early as 1998. Two years prior, Amnesty International had issued a critical report detailing the NHRI's inadequacy, especially on the issue of disappearances.[87] Significantly, the substance of the 1998 reform mirrored closely the specific criticisms raised by Amnesty International and other international actors. Just as Amnesty International emphasized the failure of the commission's "quasi-judicial functions," a 1998 bill extended the commission's powers to "give teeth to its quasi-judicial functions."[88] To be sure, the reform coincided with a change in government, and occurred only after a substantial reduction in armed conflict earlier in the decade, but the particular content of the reform matched international recommendations too closely to be coincidental. Pressure induced at least some institutional reform.

Despite being internationally accredited and relatively active among NHRIs, the commission still has been the subject of harsh criticism, in a country where the state has responded to armed insurgency with violence and coercion. Even in conflict situations, an NHRI can be strategically deployed by the state to co-opt potential critics (international and domestic) and condemn enemies. In the words of Filipino Justice Abraham Sarmiento, "human rights commissions . . . do have their use to State propagandists, not only as the State's means to deodorize State terror, but just as important—and sinister—as their own medium to vilify 'the other side.' "[89]

Africa's Earliest Commissions

After Senegal led the way in creating an NHRI, the institution began spreading in Africa. The first wave of NHRIs after Senegal appeared in three French-speaking countries in West Africa: Togo (1987), Benin (1989), and Mali (1989), all of which had ongoing human rights abuses. In addition, the Libyan government created a body resembling an NHRI during this period. In all cases, the formation of a regional human rights regime in Africa during this period played a fundamental role.

Even though organized abuse featured centrally in the decision to create early NHRIs in Africa, the significance of region-wide standards cannot be discounted. The notion of an NHRI had already become part of formal regional standards in the early 1980s. In particular, the African Charter on Human and Peoples' Rights, adopted in 1981 by the Organization of African Unity, included a specific reference to NHRIs: "States parties to the present Charter shall have the duty to guarantee the independence of the Courts and shall allow the establishment and improvement of appropriate national institutions entrusted with the promotion and protection of the rights and freedoms guaranteed by the present Charter."[90] The African Charter went into effect in 1986; and when the related African Commission on Human and Peoples' Rights started functioning in 1987, it further called on state parties to report on their human rights practices and enter into a regularized exchange with the regional body. It was in this setting of regional human rights institutionalization that national human rights bodies were defined as appropriate and sometimes necessary institutions in Africa.

Togo was the first country in Africa in the 1980s to take up the African Charter's call for NHRIs, establishing the Commission nationale des droits de l'homme in 1987. It was also among the region's first ratifiers of international human rights instruments, acceding to the ICCPR in 1984 and to the Convention against Torture in 1987. Interestingly, this was a case of an NHRI being created by a dictatorial regime to appease critics, even if once created, the institution exerted pressure on the regime and itself became a player in the country's subsequent democratic opening. Indeed, President Gnassingbé Eyadéma appears to have created the body mostly to "overcome criticisms by Amnesty International and the Togolese opposition in France."[91] According to one commentator, a "mountain of allegations" by Amnesty International had built up against the regime.[92] Many of these charges revolved around the alleged torture of political prisoners, suggesting that the commission may have been intended as a temporary commission of inquiry to look into a very specific category of charges. The broader context just before the institution's creation is also significant; it included an attempted coup in 1986 and the onset of social protests, coinciding with the regime's twenty-year anniversary. Establishing the NHRI was a clear attempt by the regime to make conciliatory concessions that might fend off mounting international criticism—just as a year later, the regime released three hundred political prisoners. On some level, the regime's agenda was "to maintain itself in power by appearing to unite the country, and the strategy through which to accomplish this was to seek international legitimacy while continuing to limit political participation domestically."[93]

Two years after Togo's NHRI was created, neighboring *Benin* established its own human rights institution in 1989 (Commission béninoise des droits de l'homme), under somewhat different dynamics. Externally, pressures for NHRI diffusion mounted, after Togo created its NHRI and UN workshops in the sub-region promoted the idea of national human rights bodies.[94] The regime was also certainly motivated by the changing Cold War context and a desire to retain foreign aid, as international actors called for democratic and human rights reforms. Internally, and after a series of pressures for reform, Benin had dropped its long-standing Marxist-Leninist state ideology and turned to constitutional reform. In this context of reform, a group of Beninoise human rights lawyers proposed the institution, just as the country had created a strong Constitutional Court that gave victims direct access and was constitutionally empowered to protect human rights and fundamental freedoms. According to some accounts, the extensive powers given to the constitutional court in the end overshadowed the country's NHRI, which has languished in relative obscurity.[95]

It is perhaps surprising that an institution that was created in the context of democratization has become "lethargic" or largely irrelevant (Benin) while one established by a dictatorship ultimately gained acceptance and accreditation (Togo). In some sense, the comparison illustrates the limits of formal institutionalization and democratization. As a report by Human Rights Watch remarked about Benin's NHRI, "Despite the strongest guarantees of formal and actual independence, the CBDH has one of the poorest records of human rights promotion and protection in the region."[96] Togo's commission, in turn, had a very mixed record over time: initially, it helped challenge the regime and bring about democratization; then, it fell "victim to its own success" only to recede into oblivion when NGOs appeared on the domestic scene; and after Eyadéma's rule ended in 2006, it began to recalibrate.[97] The lesson is that institutional development cannot entirely be read off of an NHRI's origins.

Mali is another Francophone country that created an NHRI at the end of the decade, albeit one never accredited, until 2012, when it was found to be partially compliant. In 1989, the government established a national human rights commission by decree, placing it within the Ministry of Justice, apparently in direct response to the 1986 UN General Assembly resolution calling for the creation of NHRIs. While a democratically weak transitional government and new constitution, along with a multiparty system, were introduced in 1992, it was not until 1996—coinciding with an end to the war between the government and Tuareg resistance groups, which had generated international criticism—that a decree reconfigured the NHRI. The new Commision nationale consultative des droits de l'homme, adopting the name of France's NHRI, was placed under the prime minister's authority and mandated to focus on the question of torture. Ten years later, in 2006, a National Human Rights Commission replaced the decade-long NHRI, returning it to its original home within the Ministry of Justice. While observers note that the institution has evolved over time, one constant has been the government's unwillingness to equip it with sufficient resources and independence. The NHRI has existed for over two decades mostly on paper but remained largely inactive in practice. Only in very recent years have there been calls for more meaningful reform.[98]

Significantly, at the end of the 1980s, Libya features in a lost episode of NHRI history. The African Commission on Human and Peoples' Rights, meeting in Benghazi, Libya in April 1989, called on the Organization of African Unity's secretary general to submit "a detailed report on national [human rights] institutions."[99] One month later, the Libyan government announced the formation of the Libyan Arab Human Rights Committee (LAHRC), presumably to implement reforms initiated the previous year—the reforms were announced by Gaddafi himself in a series of speeches in March 1988; and they included prisoner releases, death-sentence commutations, legal reforms affecting detention, the abolition of extraordinary courts, and accession to international human rights agreements.[100] According to Gaddafi, the reforms would transform Libya into a country where "human rights are respected."[101] Beyond ongoing international human rights pressure, the regime was also under intense scrutiny in early 1988 for its chemical weapons program. Regardless of the precise motives, the regime chose to create—one month after the African Commission meeting in Benghazi, calling for progress on human rights *committees*—a human rights committee that, in terms of its assigned tasks, closely resembled an NHRI. Despite these similarities, which some scholars from the region took to be an NHRI, the government described the body as an NGO that received complaints and channeled them to the appropriate state bodies.[102] Largely inactive and "cosmetic," the institution was given observer status as an NGO at the African Commission's eleventh session.[103] The LAHRC was, ironically, a state institution, created in an intriguing institutional twist, to pass off for a human rights NGO in a country where the state did not permit nonstate organizations to function. The institution has been all but forgotten in the world of NHRIs, but it demonstrates the extent to which the idea of an NHRI was already on the regional agenda in the 1980s.

Setting the Stage: Institutional Innovation and Adaptation

As the Cold War drew to a close, NHRIs had appeared on every continent, numbering about two dozen. To be sure, they varied in terms of their strength and even the extent to which they self-identified as an NHRI. Yet the net effect was powerful, as these institutions participated in international forums, began networking, and made their replication all the more likely. The dynamics undergirding the diffusion of NHRIs before 1990 varied as much as the countries across which they proliferated. And it is true that the spread of these institutions can be considered a story of *NHRI* diffusion only in retrospect. In some cases states were willingly creating national human rights bodies to implement newly acquired international obligations. In other cases, they were adopting a traditional ombudsman, perhaps grafting onto it a human rights mandate to accommodate past abuses or respond to international critics. Still other times, the rise of an institution we now recognize and label an NHRI was then viewed as something very different—an instance of re-creating at the national level a body that existed locally; or in some cases, state leaders pursuing narrow interests were unaware that the body was related to human rights at all let alone to a globally diffusing institutional form. So diffusion is partly and necessarily an interpretive story, where we trace the rise and spread of institutions—looking for interconnections—in retrospect. Once created and labeled, even local actors themselves can reinvent the origins of these institutions, tapping into a broader and more coherent transnational narrative that may not have been present at the creation.

The trendsetters or innovators among NHRIs were those countries that created a human rights body before 1980, usually introducing a particular variant of an NHRI into a given regional setting. Early adopters were more generally those countries that were among the first group in a region to create the institution. The fact that together they represented about 16 percent of the world's states is consistent with models of institutional diffusion.

Overall, this early period suggests the importance of several factors. First, the significance of the ombudsman as an institution cannot be exaggerated, even though it was often divorced from the notion of an NHRI in practice. The ombudsman's significance was most evident during this period in the invention of the hybrid ombudsman and in the institution's spread across Eastern Europe and Latin America. Second, most of these early NHRIs were strongly connected to the rule of law, constitutional rule, and legal professionals. That the institution has been studied most closely by students of the law should make sense given these origins. Third, in some cases, the institution was shaped (and constrained) by the abuses of the past, especially relevant in the case of democratizing countries. In virtually every case, the institution's creation can be seen as partly strategic: whether to project an international image, deflect attention from abuses and appease critics, lock in commitments while avoiding a return to the past, or legitimizing an abusive regime.

Diffusion itself occurred through various pathways. While the timing of institutional creation typically coincided with episodes of norm ambiguity (regulatory moments, external obligations, and organized abuse), reflecting a combination of international and domestic pressures, the type of institution selected tended to mirror institutional precursors and social peers. Ultimately, among this early group, the strength of the institution was a product of the diffusion mechanism. The most weakly designed institutions, as defined by international standards, were found where "externalization" (or the projection of interests and identities abroad) drove institutional creation (France and Denmark) or where external obligations were not locally embedded and no other incentives to create an accountability institution existed (the Caribbean).

The international context was shifting decisively for NHRIs at the end of the 1980s. The Cold War's last days ushered in a period when international actors emphasized the importance of democratic, constitutional rule and human rights discourse proved to be a powerful framing device. Human rights institutions themselves were growing at the international and regional levels, and these were being diffused by means of technical assistance and other knowledge transfers outlined in Chapter 3. More specifically, the international regime on NHRIs was developing increasingly detailed standards, as UN resolutions and workshops spread the notion that national bodies for promoting and protecting human rights should be created. Two dozen institutions, even if they were not all labeled NHRIs or meaningfully interconnected, constituted a critical mass for subsequent diffusion. These early innovators and adopters set the stage for the unprecedented proliferation of NHRIs soon to follow.

6

Democratization Scripts and Bandwagoning in Africa

Dozens of countries joined the NHRI bandwagon after 1990, showcasing the role of international diffusion. Especially at the regional level, neighboring countries emulated each other, while international organizations and regional networks actively fostered the creation of these institutions. If earlier decades had set the normative foundations for the concept of an NHRI, the 1990s saw rising institutionalization. Beginning with the drafting of the seminal Paris Principles in 1991 and the promotion of NHRIs at the Vienna World Conference two years later, the notion of an NHRI was championed and popularized. Even before Vienna, however, resolutions within the United Nations focusing on NHRIs had picked up momentum after 1987, appearing biannually until the Paris Principles were issued. As standard setting rose, capacity building and technical assistance followed in its wake.

Two other global and coacting forces acted as transmission belts for the proliferation of these institutions. First, the end of the Cold War did not only elevate the place of human rights discourse globally; it led also to the independence of numerous Eastern European countries. Second, and closely related, a wave of democratization seemed to spread worldwide, with many authoritarian regimes collapsing. Both trends created conditions of norm ambiguity, as regimes looked to create new institutions and constitutions; and in a globally sanctioned democratizing context, an emphasis on human rights seemed natural. With the Paris Principles in place, NHRIs became a fairly standardized model to be borrowed, adapted, and transported across borders.

Africa was no exception, and NHRIs diffused across the continent after 1990. By the end of the 1990s, almost the majority of countries, over two dozen, had created human rights bodies. As Dejo Olowu notes, "Whether as a result of genuine concern for effective human rights monitoring, promotion and protection, or for the purposes of appeasing the curious international community, all that is certain is that the establishment of human rights commissions became a vogue in African countries in the 1990s."[1] By the end of 2011, moreover, when the first round of the UN system of Universal Periodic Review (UPR) was completed, virtually all states in Africa had agreed to create an NHRI.

A few factors are immediately striking about the proliferation of NHRIs across Africa. First, many of these NHRIs were created in the context of regulatory moments or in the face of transnational human rights pressures. In other words, NHRIs were one institution in a larger bundle of broader reforms undertaken by states that were following a script for what it was to be a democratizing, liberalizing regime, one that would appeal to (and appease) Western states in a post–Cold War context. Second, the role of former colonial powers was significant, as both France and the British Commonwealth promoted the creation and reform of these institutions, including via technical assistance. In this regard, former British colonies were more likely to adopt a complaints-handling body, while former French colonies borrowed the model of a consultative agency. Despite these and other differences, the dominant preference in the region was to label the institution a "commission," reflecting a localized dynamic of emulation.

A tipping point in the region was reached when the first continental meeting of NHRIs was held in Yaoundé, Cameroon, in 1996; the second would be in Durban, South Africa, in 1998, both convened by the Organization of African Unity.[2] The African Commission on Human and People's Rights, moreover, called on all governments in 1996 to create or strengthen NHRIs.[3] And in 1998, the commission granted NHRIs observer status, giving states an additional incentive to create these ever popular bodies.[4]

Two broad pathways are evident in the diffusion of NHRIs in Africa in the 1990s. On the one hand, NHRIs in some countries have accompanied the drafting of new constitutions and larger scale political transitions, or regulatory moments. In many cases, these were member states of the British Commonwealth. On the other hand, some countries have created NHRIs in the context of more limited liberalization, itself in response to transnational criticism of ongoing abuses, especially in Francophone Africa.[5] The first pathway has been related to nominally stronger NHRIs, at least at the level of institutional design, whereas the second pathway tended to result in weaker bodies.

Diffusion across Commonwealth States in the 1990s

Even before the Cold War ended, the Commonwealth had been promoting human rights in general and NHRIs in particular. A series of declarations highlighted the central importance of human rights, including the 1971 Declaration of Commonwealth Principles, the 1979 Lusaka Declaration on Racism and Racial Prejudice, the 1981 Melbourne Declaration, and especially the 1991 Harare Declaration. And in 1992, in the lead-up to the World Conference on Human Rights in Vienna, the Commonwealth held a workshop on national institutions in Ottawa.[6] Throughout the 1990s, in conjunction with the United Nations and some foreign governments, the Commonwealth also provided technical assistance for creating and strengthening NHRIs.

For African states that belonged to the Commonwealth in the 1990s, diffusion happened in two waves. A first group, coinciding with the first half of the decade, adopted NHRIs mostly as a result of a regulatory moment. This included Namibia, Ghana, South Africa, Malawi, and Uganda. The second group formed NHRIs in the latter part of the decade, driven mostly by attempts to appease critics for ongoing abuse. This group consisted of Nigeria, Ethiopia, Zambia, and Kenya. Despite these differences, these institutions were subject to pressures from the Commonwealth to create an NHRI and most of the resulting institutions have been accredited internationally. The chronology suggests that states undergoing regulatory moments are more likely to jump on an institutional bandwagon, while there is some delay among states merely looking to appease critics for ongoing violence. In all of these cases, NHRIs were created as a result of regional diffusion and strategic emulation.

The Regulatory Moment

Namibia was one of Africa's first countries to create an NHRI in the 1990s. It did so in the context of democratization and strong international influences. The creation of the Office of the Ombudsman in 1990 coincided with a dramatic regulatory moment—national independence and a protracted, negotiated process of constitutional drafting.[7] The constitutional committee worked behind closed doors, so it is unclear who exactly proposed the ombudsman, but the group was subject to two relevant influences: many of its members were heavily internationalized, with advanced degrees from Western countries; more broadly, they were drawing on and obligated to consider a 1982 Western-forged set of principles, itself part of an ongoing negotiated settlement, which required that strong human rights standards be included in an eventual constitution. The decision to include an office of the ombudsman in the constitution further represented an attempt to supplement the courts as places of human rights enforcement, since an ombudsman's office might be more accessible and efficient to individuals seeking remedies for rights abuses.[8] With Namibia joining the Commonwealth in 1990, it is perhaps unsurprising that an ombudsman was selected as the national agency to implement international human rights standards, especially given the recent, if short-lived experience of a national "ombudsman" created in 1986. At the same time, given the constitution's strong emphasis on human rights—arguably, the strongest on the continent and among the most vibrant documents anywhere in the world—it is understandable that the ombudsman would be a hybrid body, combining elements of the traditional ombudsman with an explicit focus on human rights. The importance of the rule of law was evident in the requirement that the ombudsperson belong to the legal profession. Hand in hand with a global script about the importance of good governance, the rule of law, and democratization, the ombudsman was designated an anticorruption body, tapping into a related international value.[9]

If Namibia was the first Commonwealth African country to create an NHRI in the decade, *Ghana* was the first one to do so after the Paris Principles were drafted in 1991. The West African country also did so as part of a regulatory moment, both a democratic transition and new constitution. Ghana's 1992 constitution called for the Commission on Human Rights and Administrative Justice, a body incorporated into legislation in 1993. As one commentator notes, "The Fourth Republican Constitution was drafted and adopted in a drastically changed national and global political context. The discourse of the early 1990s advocated respect for human rights and democratic pluralism instead of authoritarianism. The triumph of liberal ideology in the wake of the collapse of the Soviet variant of socialism . . . influenced the drafting of the 1992 Constitution."[10] During the period, Ghana also acceded to the African Charter on Human and Peoples' Rights, even though it was not to ratify the international human rights covenants until later. These developments occurred during a time when government leaders were becoming more fearful of human rights criticisms, themselves steadily mounting since a 1981 coup. In 1991, for example, the government permitted an Amnesty International delegation to visit the country, though it had previously resisted such a visit, just as the nongovernmental Ghana Committee on Human and Peoples' Rights also was permitted to form that year.[11]

It is especially noteworthy that Ghana's Commission absorbed the country's ombudsman office, which had been created by the 1979 constitution but had had a volatile history. Though the argument for combining the two institutions was apparently more financial than structural, the model is often depicted as a "holistic" approach to NHRIs, where various bodies and mandates are combined together in a single institution.[12] This integrated approach encompassed the related idea that all human rights are interdependent and development cannot be separated from human rights, a view articulated by the country's representative to the World Conference in Vienna in 1993.[13]

Though Ghana's commission has faced resource challenges, it was established as a relatively strong independent body with a broad mandate, including anticorruption functions and unique powers of enforcement.[14] It is widely considered to be one of Africa's strongest NHRIs. And its creation served as somewhat of a watershed: all subsequent African members of the Commonwealth would adopt some variant of a "human rights commission."

While Namibia resurrected its ombudsman agency and converted it to a hybrid human rights institution and Ghana absorbed its existing ombudsman into a hybrid human rights commission, *South Africa* created distinct if overlapping bodies. First mentioned in the 1993 interim constitution, the new postapartheid regime created the South African Human Rights Commission (SAHRC), part of a broad-scale political transition. The SAHRC, which began operating in 1995, was established through the Human Rights Commission Act signed by President Nelson Mandela in 1994. It was also included in the final 1996 constitution, under the rubric of "State Institutions Supporting Constitutional Democracy." These "Chapter 9" institutions, as they are known, include the Public Protector (more akin to an ombudsman), the Human Rights Commission, and the Commission for Gender Equality. In this sense, South Africa's approach differs markedly from Ghana's holism, or the decision to centralize human rights institutions in a single body. While the SAHRC has been one of the leading fully accredited NHRIs in Africa and the world, the creation of multiple somewhat overlapping bodies has subjected it to criticism.

The establishment of a human rights commission for a new South Africa was in many ways unsurprising. Given the deep violence of apartheid, combined with the particular international climate of the early 1990s, the political transition no doubt was to attend explicitly to human rights. In the negotiations over a new constitution, members of the African National Congress who had fought hard against the apartheid regime were strong proponents of human rights protections. A keen interest in including human rights within *state* institutions was also evident, since the apartheid state itself had been so fully discredited. A new transparent, self-restraining state that monitored itself and promoted accountability was both domestically sensible and consistent with international prescriptions of democratic governance. All of those involved in the drafting process, moreover, were acutely aware of the importance of conforming to international human rights standards.[15] The choice of a human rights commission may have been even more obvious, following on the heels of the Paris Principles and the creation of other NHRIs in Africa.

Why South Africa decided to create multiple state human rights agencies, however, remains unclear. On the one hand, it may have reflected a "more is better" view in a moment of democratic and constitutional effusiveness. Another, more likely, possibility is that there was too much disagreement over specifics to achieve consensus over a single unified body. The ombudsman, for example, had been a preexisting body, essentially relabeled the "public protector." The model of a human rights commission was borrowed from the international context but resonated domestically given the country's recent history; it was tailored to local circumstances, including strong attention to human rights education and economic-social rights. Yet the institution was also the subject of intense debate within a constitutional subcommittee, just as the campaign to include women's rights in a gender commission had met with a great deal of resistance.[16] That the creation of multiple state institutions for human rights reflected more disagreement than consensus is also consistent with the constraints on independence and funding that were placed on the commission. Despite its international and domestic activism, South Africa's NHRI has reflected the state's lingering, unresolved contradictions in a postapartheid era.

During this same period, a new constitution in *Malawi* in 1994 included a human rights commission, though it did not become fully operational until 1999. The NHRI was not provided with any funding until 1996, when a staff of two dedicated lawyers laid the groundwork for enabling legislation.[17] Two years later, in 1998 the Human Rights Commission Act set in place a relatively strong institution, armed with investigatory powers and a broad mandate, extending to new issues like HIV/AIDS. One important aspect of the commission was that "reputable organizations representative of Malawian society," whose activities had been legalized only during the recent transition, would be involved in nominating the institution's members.[18] Malawi's NHRI was therefore established in the context of a political transition, including a new constitution, after the country had already acceded to the two international human rights covenants and the African Charter. By some accounts, in fact, human rights discourse in Malawi in

the early 1990s was framed in terms of the broader transition and a new constitutional order. The incoming president himself emphasized themes of human
rights and rule of law before taking office.[19]

Despite the NHRI's formal organizational strengths, Malawi's government
has withheld funding and intervened politically in the commission. Indeed, all
accountability institutions in the country have apparently suffered similar constraints. As one observer notes, Malawi's "constitution provides a strong legal and
institutional framework that protects citizens' rights and establishes a sophisticated
system of horizontal accountability bodies. . . . Not surprisingly, for a young and
poor democracy, however, these accountability institutions, as well as the whole
democratic framework, have yet to be consolidated."[20] In general, Malawi's government created a relatively well-designed NHRI in the midst of a regulatory
moment, largely following a democratic script, but the institution's subsequent role
has been woefully constrained by the domestic political context.

While *Uganda's* Human Rights Commission was included in the 1995 constitution, its roots dated to the political transition initiated in the mid-1980s. A
commission of inquiry created in 1986, and charged with examining past human
rights abuses (committed between 1962 and 1986), pushed the constitution's
drafters as early as 1988 to include a human rights commission.[21] When the commission of inquiry issued its seven-hundred-page report in 1994, it called again for
the creation of an NHRI. By then, the Constitutional Commission had already
outlined in detail the contours of a permanent human rights body.[22] The origins of
Uganda's commission thus lie partly in a truth commission, which in the context
of constitution making recommended a permanent body to redress and prevent
future violations.

In some respects, however, the commission also reflected a prior set of institutional alternatives. In particular, the inadequacies of the Inspector-General of
Government (IGG), a hybrid body created in 1986 (combining a traditional ombudsman with human rights duties), featured as a central internal rationale for establishing the freestanding NHRI. Given critiques of the IGG's inactivity, itself
reflecting an overly broad mandate and poor funding, the human rights functions
of the IGG were essentially transferred in the new constitution to the commission,
while the IGG was left as a traditional ombudsman with a related anticorruption
mandate.[23] The new NHRI was also viewed as an alternative to the courts, "when
redress and remedies are needed quickly," even if in practice the HRC experiences
its own delays.[24] Overall, the NHRI's creation reflected a larger process of domestic institutional learning and globally oriented democratic constitutionalism,
even while the idea for a commission per se was directly influenced by regional

diffusion. This combination of a domestic regulatory moment and external obligations resulted in the design of a strong body, leading the NHRI to play a leadership role among similar bodies in the region and beyond.[25]

Appeasement as Driving Force

Compared to the five NHRIs created in Commonwealth Africa in the first half of the 1990s, those formed in the second half were relatively weaker, at least at the outset. Though all had accepted human rights treaty obligations, this group—Nigeria, Ethiopia, Zambia, and Kenya—did not experience a full regulatory moment. Organized abuse, met by an interest in appeasing regime critics, was the primary motive force. These institutional origins notwithstanding, all except Ethiopia enjoyed full NHRI accreditation.

Nigeria's military government undertook a series of transitional measures in the mid-1990s, largely in response to international criticism of the regime and its practices. The creation of the NHRI (National Human Rights Commission of Nigeria) in 1995, by military decree, was one of these measures.[26] Given that the regime, led by General Sani Abacha, was known as being "perhaps the most rapacious and oppressive in Nigeria's short but checkered national history," it is no surprise that the institution was cynically labeled a "red herring" and a propaganda tool by locals.[27] For one observer, its creation was purely "a product of pretentious foundation."[28] Its creation came at the same time that the regime was under intense pressure for its arbitrary detention and trial of Ogoni activists. In fact, in the same month that the NHRI was created, Amnesty International released a report titled *Nigeria: The Ogoni Trials and Detentions*.[29] Western governments were threatening sanctions if the Ogoni activists were killed; when they were killed two months later, economic sanctions followed and Nigeria was suspended from the Commonwealth until the return of civilian rule in 1999.[30]

Not surprisingly, given the overwhelming drive to appease external actors, the institution itself was generally limited, with the regime playing a heavy-handed role in appointments, paying staff salaries, and withholding funding. Despite ongoing problems, the commission cooperated well with local NGOs and was internationally accredited in 1999, coinciding with the transition to civilian rule, a new constitution, and an improved human rights climate. Even then, however, the institution's independence would remain compromised so that criticism of the regime led to negative consequences, epitomized in the removal of two executive secretaries and the entire governing council in 2006 and 2009.[31] The International Coordinating Committee of NHRIs responded to the first of these incidents in 2007 by downgrading the institution's accreditation status to a B— only partially compliant with international standards. Consequently, on March 2011, Nigeria's government approved a bill that had circulated since 2004, which would give the institution more meaningful autonomy.[32] The ICC responded in kind in May 2011, reinstating full accreditation status to the body. Nigeria's NHRI shows how even an institution created in the context of organized abuse, and almost entirely to appease critics, can be strengthened as a result of a political transition and ongoing socialization efforts by international actors.

Ethiopia also created a human rights commission in 1995, as part of a political transition begun a couple of years earlier; the Ethiopian Human Rights Commission, however, did not start functioning until a decade later in 2005. The internationally approved 1995 constitution called for the creation of both a human rights commission and an ombudsman.[33] When war broke out with Eritrea in 1998, the commission was nonetheless suspended, until a parliamentary law in 2000 resurrected it.[34] In the interim, the government held a widely publicized conference, inviting government representatives from over sixty countries, but excluding international and domestic NGOs, to discuss the creation of a human rights commission and ombudsman office in Ethiopia. Government support for the commission was met skeptically by nonstate actors, who called the institution window dressing and a potential "propaganda vehicle." The opposition newspaper *The Reporter* talked of NHRIs in the context of "sterilised independence": "the one thing the Human Rights Commission and the Ombudsman have in common with the courts is that they don't have an army or a police force of their own to enforce their rulings or recommendations."[35]

Years after its formation in 2005, Ethiopia's Human Rights Commission still was not independent, though the government attempted to have it accredited. International actors criticized both the government and the commission itself. For instance, in the aftermath of a clampdown on human rights NGOs in 2010, Human Rights Watch noted, "The government is encouraging a variety of ruling party-affiliated organizations to fill the vacuum, including the Ethiopian Human Rights Commission, a national human rights institution with no semblance of independence."[36] Despite its formal creation during a regulatory moment, war and ongoing authoritarianism curtailed the institution's development—just as it resulted in an aborted political transition, marked only by formal constitutionalism. The regime had bothered to create the NHRI, in the context of international pressures, but then merely deployed it strategically to control the human rights agenda.

Shortly after Nigeria and Ethiopia created NHRIs, *Zambia* established the Permanent Human Rights Commission in 1996. Like Uganda, the permanent body had been recommended by an ad hoc commission of inquiry created in 1993 to look into past human rights violations—the Munyama Commission, named after the well-known lawyer and its chair, Bruce Munyama. The NHRI was incorporated into the constitution by amendment, and then into the 1997 Human Rights Commission Act.[37] It reflected a broad regulatory moment, namely a transition from one-party rule in 1991 to greater pluralism, moving away from a period of human rights abuse and weak state institutions.

But the particular timing of the institution's creation also seemed to be driven by international considerations. After antidemocratic clauses embedded in the new constitution of 1996 threatened to interfere with upcoming national elections, Western democratic governments suspended aid.[38] The appointment of commissioners themselves seems to have been rushed to predate an international donor meeting in 1997, where foreign aid was linked to human rights performance. Also tellingly, documents and other materials about the commission were initially circulated abroad but not at all domestically. Despite a broad mandate, the commission's weak powers and resources threw into question the government's stated commitment to the institution.[39] It is little wonder that local skepticism abounded. One newspaper described the nascent NHRI as a "toothless bulldog tamely wagging its tail to the executive and instituted purely to assuage donor options."[40]

These roadblocks aside, international efforts to provide technical assistance to the NHRI and its staff persisted. By 1999, the commission had managed, on its own merits, to attain some measure of credibility with the public, especially for its work on prison conditions. And in 2003, the institution was fully accredited as an NHRI. With the institution still lacking resources, international actors (including the UN Human Rights Council and treaty bodies) have called on the government to strengthen it.[41] In submitting information for the country's UPR in 2008, societal actors detailed the institution's weaknesses, including staff shortages, a significant backlog, and lack of full independence. The Human Rights Council called on the Zambian government to strengthen the commission and align it with the Paris Principles.

Kenya's National Human Rights Commission, in turn, has its origins in the Human Rights Standing Committee created in 1996. The initial body was exceedingly weak, driven largely by international considerations and apparently formed in anticipation of a donor meeting where ongoing aid was partly conditioned on human rights.[42] More broadly, it was a response to intense international and domestic human rights pressure against Kenya in the mid-1990s, including an Amnesty International report released in December 1995 asserting that the security forces were systematically torturing opponents.[43] The committee, created in June 1996 to investigate human rights abuses, was placed entirely under the president's discretion and proved largely inactive. NGOs that had begun organizing in the early 1990s, including the Kenyan Human Rights Commission, distanced themselves from the state body, which was described as a "bogus institution."[44]

While some observers do not consider the standing committee to have been an NHRI, it was in fact a governmental human rights body. Its head and members attended international seminars on NHRIs during the late 1990s, suggesting an explicit interface with the notion of an NHRI.[45] Most significantly, the new governmental Kenyan National Human Rights Commission created in 2002 was described at the time as "the successor entity" to the standing committee.[46]

The new Kenyan National Human Rights Commission, formed by a legislative act in 2002, was part of the country's electoral transformation that same year, marked by the end of Daneil arap Moi's brutal rule. Even so, in the parliamentary debates surrounding the proposed bill, supporters of the NHRI pushed the government to move beyond "image" and a "public relations exercise."[47] They were under no illusion about political motives, accusing the government of wanting to "upgrade" from the state committee to the new commission "not because of any genuine commitment, but, only to impress the donor community that Kenya is among the countries which protect human rights and have good governance records and, therefore, qualify for foreign aid."[48] The debates themselves are instructive, referencing the Paris Principles and the example of national human rights commissions in South Africa and India, while contesting the general concept of human rights and how it might and should apply in Kenya.

The NHRI soon received full international accreditation, given a broad mandate that draws on international human rights instruments and highlights the interdependence of all human rights. The transformation of Kenya's state body shows an interesting trajectory, somewhat similar to Nigeria's: a weak institution created for purposes of appeasement can transform into a stronger institution during crucial political turning points. So while Kenya did not experience a full-blown regulatory moment, the change in political circumstances proved crucial. The 1996 body, which was the precursor to the 2002 NHRI, was itself created in the context of organized abuse and external commitments. Hans Peter Schmitz has described the "spiral of influence":

the seemingly empty rhetoric used by the Kenyan government to appease mainly international human rights criticism gradually took on a life of its own. In a situation where a non-governmental human rights network defines what constitutes a human rights abuse, any however instrumental acceptance of the norm on the part of a government opens a number of new windows for further mobilization, consciousness-raising, and persuasion.[49]

If the NHRI's introduction in 2002 seems like the product of external obligations alone, this is not the case when looked at more closely.[50] Shifting political circumstances facilitated the institution's evolution, so that a weak body designed only to appease critics morphed into an institution that conformed to international standards and still met the regime's strategic goals. That regional (and global) diffusion was also at play is evident not just in the references to international norms and other NHRIs, but to the institution's name change: even at the risk of being confused with one of the country's main human rights NGOs, the government adopted the "human rights commission" nomenclature prevalent across Africa.

Transnational Pressure and Mimicry in Francophone Countries

The 1990s also saw the rise of NHRIs across French-speaking African states. These states did not experience full political transitions, undertaking instead a package of liberalizing steps, often in the context of ongoing abuse and transnational pressures. Of the ten NHRIs created in Francophone Africa in the 1990s, half of them are still not fully accredited. Yet even in cases of high political volatility, NHRIs have tended to persist and evolve, mostly due to international regime pressures. In general, these states have created largely promotional institutions.

The first set of states reviewed here created NHRIs as part of nominal liberalization measures in the early 1990s: Cameroon, Morocco, Tunisia, and Algeria. As such, the institutions were typically created by presidential decree and remained largely weak. Since liberalization was often a response to rising social opposition and other transnational pressures, in the face of ongoing abuse, these NHRIs sometimes were ineffective in meeting international standards but succeeded in co-opting human rights discourse domestically (or even securing international accreditation). The second, more geographically dispersed group consisted of Chad, Niger, Madagascar, Mauritius, and Mauritania. These countries, with the exception of Mauritius, created even weaker NHRIs beginning in the mid-1990s.

Symbolic Institution Building

In *Cameroon*, the government followed its West African neighbors and created the National Committee on Human Rights and Freedoms in 1990, marking the end of one-party rule and a move toward multiple political parties. While not a period of constitutionalism or political transition, the regime responded to rising social opposition with limited democratization, just as the country had already acceded to international and regional human rights instruments.[51] The NHRI was established by presidential decree and remained weak, failing to engage civil society effectively.[52] This fed into skeptics' assumptions that the NHRI was merely a presidential ploy to appease critics. As one commentator remarked, "It didn't seem logical that a highly repressive regime would voluntarily create a genuine Human Rights Commission to check its own abuses."[53] Other observers emphasized how the commission represented an attempt to "retain tight executive control over all state institutions."[54] Despite these criticisms, in 1996 Yaoundé was the symbolic site of the first regional meeting of African NHRIs.

The formal strength of Cameroon's body shifted over time, mostly in response to transnational pressures. In the course of its first decade, it managed to remain largely under the domestic radar while becoming fully accredited internationally. Anticipating its first accreditation review in 1999, the institution made its reports public and undertook other limited reforms, earning the rank of A-status institution. And when transnational criticism of rising human rights violations mounted in 2003 and 2004, the government passed new legislation in 2004 intended to strengthen the human rights body, whose name was changed to the National Commission on Human Rights and Freedoms.[55] The new name aligned the institution with other NHRIs in the region and was showcased—in the context of rising human rights pressures, an upcoming national election, and the next round of reaccreditation—as a move to conform more closely to international standards and with the African Charter's call for a national human rights body. While a welcome move, the NHRI's accreditation status still was downgraded to a B amid rising concerns over its lack of meaningful autonomy.[56] In response, an amendment in 2010 promised greater independence and led to the NHRI's accreditation status being fully reinstated.[57] The experience of Cameroon's NHRI shows how, even absent democratic governance (indeed, the same ruler has been in power for almost three decades), a state human rights agency can still become formally strong as a result of international accreditation pressure and the drive to appease critics.

When *Equatorial Guinea* also created a National Human Rights Commission in 1990, it faced overwhelming incentives to do so. Since a coup in 1979, a high level of human rights violations was met by transnational pressure, including ongoing monitoring by the UN Human Rights Commission. Yet a more immediate impetus for establishing the NHRI in 1990 seems to have been a critical Amnesty International report issued earlier that year on torture in the country.[58] The NHRI's formation also coincided with a general shift in repression, as smaller groups of people were being arrested, albeit with growing frequency, apparently to deflect international criticism.[59] The country had also relatively recently accepted new international human rights obligations, including acceding to the human rights covenants in 1987. And, significantly, the government was in the process of drafting a new constitution in 1991.

Equatorial Guinea nonetheless created a relatively weak institution, never seeking international accreditation for it. International regime pressures intensified against the small, oil-rich country after 2000. For example, in 2003, a UN special rapporteur called for an independent NHRI, compliant with the Paris Principles; and in 2009, the Working Group on Arbitrary Detention recommended strengthening the existing NHRI.[60] When Human Rights Council members urged the country during its UPR in 2009 to create an accredited NHRI, the government conceded. That a state human rights institution existed for over two decades without major reform reflects the broader political climate, marked by an entrenched autocracy, executive control, and closure to independent social organizations.

Reflecting a similar dynamic to Cameroon's—nominal liberalization in the face of ongoing abuse and transnational criticism—NHRIs were created in quick succession in North Africa: Morocco (1990), Tunisia (1991), and Algeria (1992). There is no question that geographic and cultural proximity, as well as French pressure and example, facilitated the diffusion of NHRIs in this subregion. Rather than being created in the context of a new constitution or regime transition, all were formed in response to transnational criticism of rights abuses, by regimes that had already accepted human rights obligations. Not surprisingly, in view of these dynamics, all three were formed under the auspices of executive power: a royal decree in Morocco and presidential decrees in Algeria and Tunisia. They all modeled themselves, moreover, after France's human rights commission.

Morocco's institution—the Human Rights Advisory Council, or Conseil consultatif des droits de l'homme—was established in May 1990 in response to transnational human rights criticism. Beginning in the late 1980s, Morocco faced growing criticism for various reasons: its entrenched control of the Western Sahara, despite UN involvement in the conflict; a widely perceived failure to account for its past human rights violations; and rising repression of Islamist opponents. Energized by French-led international criticism, threats of economic sanctions, and a growing national discourse of democratic reform, Morocco's nascent domestic human rights movement was becoming increasingly visible but less easily controlled by simple state repression. Indeed, the NHRI's creation followed closely a rise in domestic activism, which had put human rights issues on the national agenda. In particular, the Moroccan Human Rights Organization had formed in 1988 and become a key regime opponent, just as the Moroccan Human Rights Association (founded in 1979) was reinvigorated. In short, the NHRI was created just as the monarchy attempted to co-opt the human rights agenda advanced by regime critics.[61] The late King Hassan II himself stated that the NHRI's creation "once and for all puts an end to hearsay about human rights. We would like to settle this issue."[62]

Further liberalization came to Morocco with the new monarchy in 1999, the same year that the country's NHRI was first reviewed for accreditation and deemed fully compliant with the Paris Principles. Almost immediately after Mohammed VI took over his father's reign, he initiated a series of reforms bearing on human rights, including judicial and prison conditions, creation of an arbitration panel, introduction of human rights education into public schools, and restructuring of the NHRI—giving the body more independence and requiring annual reports.[63] Though the commission still remained a largely advisory body, and could not accept individual petitions, it is considered relatively strong and was reaccredited in 2001 (and again in 2007 and 2010).[64]

Just a year after Morocco's NHRI was created, *Tunisia* established its own: the Higher Committee on Human Rights and Fundamental Freedoms (or Higher Committee).[65] With criticism of the regime mounting, itself reflecting a spike in serious rights violations, President Zine al-Abidine Ben Ali established the Higher Committee via presidential decree in 1991, mostly as a means of defending the country's image with multiple audiences. Domestically, the Tunisian League of Human Rights (Ligue tunisienne des droits de l'homme) helped generate human rights pressure by foreign actors, including Amnesty International, the United States, and France—at the same time that the country was attempting to maintain neutrality in the Gulf conflict. In a speech marking the formation of the Higher Committee, Ben Ali traced the Committee's origins to "our principled choices," and the "United Nations' call for the foundation of a body such as this one."[66] In practice, most non-state observers agreed it was "nothing more than a mouthpiece to defend government abuses."[67]

Nor can Tunisia's decision to establish an NHRI be viewed in isolation from the regime's broader attempts to engage in cosmetic liberalization and reform, including by means of human rights discourse. When Ben Ali seized power in a November 1987 coup, he had promised to protect human rights and promote liberalization in a post-Bourguiba era. After some political reforms in his first year in power, Ben Ali refused to legalize the Islamist opposition and rigged the 1989 electoral code, soon moving to abort Tunisia's democratic opening. With rising political opposition, including a growing human rights community, criticism of the regime only intensified, and the government responded with a series of human rights initiatives. In 1988, for example, it ratified the UN Convention against Torture, at the same time that it sponsored international symposia on human rights; and in 1989, the Arab Institute for Human Rights established its headquarters in Tunis. More concretely, the government granted a general amnesty to those accused of political crimes in the Bourguiba era, and it authorized the formation of domestic civil groups. The Higher Committee's creation was therefore one of several strategies by which to appease transnational criticism of ongoing human rights abuse, and some critics assert that it actually served its unstated purpose of weakening the human rights movement domestically.[68]

Not surprisingly, when Tunisia's NHRI went up for international accreditation in 2009, it was found to be only partially compliant. Perhaps in anticipation of its candidacy for a seat on the Human Rights Council, the government nominally reformed the institution. More substantially, in January 2008, President Ben 'Ali announced reforms to the institution's composition and its ties to civil society:

> we will ensure the further evolution of the Higher Committee for Human Rights and Fundamental Freedoms by elevating the provisions organizing it to the level of law, by endowing it, as a national human rights institution, with its administrative and financial autonomy, by reviewing its composition in such a way as to strengthen communication between the state and civil society components, and by consolidating its prerogatives in order to emphasize its role in the promotion and protection of human rights.[69]

That he did so with much fanfare before the diplomatic corps and that Tunisia's first UPR was set for April 2008 left many skeptical.[70] During the UPR, governments called on Tunisia to strengthen its NHRI and align it with the Paris

Principles. Shortly thereafter, the Tunisian government at last applied for accreditation. According to the head of the NHRI, B-status designation was an embarrassment for an institution that had participated in creating the Paris Principles.[71]

Indeed, the Arab Spring of 2011 may have injected renewed momentum into longstanding calls for embedding the NHRI in legislation. Farhat Rajhi, a jurist who was minister of the interior during the first few months of 2011 and then appointed head of the NHRI, called the moment propitious for strengthening, the institution and bringing it in compliance with the Paris Principles. On May 3, 2011, he announced that consultations with the United Nations and civil society groups (almost one hundred human rights organizations were legalized after Ben 'Ali's ouster) would lead to a concrete set of reforms. Four days later, following controversial comments he made on Facebook, in which Rajhi apparently declared that Islamist rule would result in a coup, he was removed from his post. Tunisia's NHRI could never entirely overcome its origins as long as authoritarian rule persisted.[72] However, in a new political context, and given the positive steps taken in 2011, the institution may well follow a conventional democratization script and create an NHRI more closely meeting international standards.

In neighboring *Algeria*, the military government established the National Human Rights Observatory, or Observatoire national des droits de l'homme (ONDH), in 1992. As the name implies, the main function was one of monitoring. Yet the primary purpose may have been to pacify those critical of widespread torture; not surprisingly, the body soon devolved into an apologist of state practices. Though the government had created a Human Rights Ministry in 1991, it still opted for the NHRI in February 1992, one month after a broadly criticized and bloody coup.[73] Members of the opposition at once viewed the institution critically, calling it an "institutional monstrosity."[74]

Nominal institutional change did not come until 2001, when following intense pressure over the issue of disappearances, another presidential decree created the National Advisory Commission for the Promotion and Protection of Human Rights, replacing the original NHRI and presumably focusing more on the issue of disappearances.[75] Though President 'Abdelaziz Bouteflika cast it as a renewed effort to strengthen the image of the state's human rights machinery, in practice, there was substantial continuity between the two institutions, including the sharing of files.[76]

It seems that in both attempts at creating an NHRI, the Algerian government was largely attempting to silence critics. As one commentator said, "The establishment of a symbolic mechanism, devoid of prosecution or clear investigatory powers is in line with the President's efforts to further bury the grievances of those affected by the phenomenon of disappearances in Algeria."[77] The audience was still an international one, insofar as the institution was "intended to provide a 'human' face to the ruling junta and to parry attacks from human rights organizations from abroad, especially Amnesty International."[78] And in the end, the NHRI may also have succeeded in weakening an already fragmented human rights movement.[79]

Even before the new NHRI was formally established in 2001, Algeria applied for international accreditation.[80] The ICC approved the new body but with reservations, criticizing government representatives on the institution and the absence of annual reports. The government addressed these concerns in 2003, and the NHRI was fully accredited—until 2009, when the NHRI's standing was downgraded to B, and a stricter ICC moved to demand full independence and either statutory or constitutional standing. The government responded by issuing vague assurances that a bill was forthcoming.[81]

For two decades, the Algerian government's strategic response to international human rights pressure has been the same: attempting to pass off nominal institutional changes for more significant reform, and co-opting the human rights agenda through the creation of state institutions. But the Algerian case also suggests a novel trend. An institution created purely to appease critics was able to gain international accreditation during an earlier stage of the international regime on NHRIs; as the accreditation process became more institutionalized and stringent, however, international actors no longer accepted so readily an institution operating in a repressive context. Ongoing reforms will necessarily depend on international regime pressures and, especially, domestic political liberalization.

The Political Context of NHRIs

A couple of years after Algeria created its NHRI, *Chad* also established in 1994 the Commission nationale des droits de l'homme. The commission was based on the French model and created by a parliamentary act.[82] The idea had first been promoted by an NGO with strong transnational ties, the Ligue tchadienne de droits de l'homme (Chadian Human Rights League); the Ligue had introduced the proposal within the Sovereign National Conference in 1993, a group of state and civil society representatives charting a democratic course. The National Conference, in turn, recommended that human rights protection be centralized in one national commission. Likewise, the country's truth commission final report of 1992 called for the creation of a permanent human rights commission.[83]

Chad's NHRI has had a somewhat unexpected trajectory. Despite a promisingly strong start, during which the institution showed some initiative vis-à-vis a recalcitrant state, over time it became largely inactive. In 1997, after the commission openly criticized a policy of extrajudicial executions, the government blocked its funding. The commission then made a strategic and perhaps fateful decision, opting for quiet diplomacy and a focus on seemingly nonthreatening promotional activities. This nonetheless backfired when nonstate actors rejected the commission.[84] The NHRI's reaction led to "deep mistrust by the NGO community," who believed the government had effectively co-opted the institution's leaders.[85] From an organizational standpoint, however, it is significant that the Commission adopted promotional functions that were outside its formal scope.

Though Chad's commission was accredited as an NHRI, with reservations in the early 2000s, the weaknesses proved unsustainable; and it was downgraded to a B status NHRI in November 2009, shortly after the country's UPR review that year.[86] Chad's human rights institution indeed reveals the dilemmas that NHRIs operating in exceedingly weak states face (and, technically, Chad is deemed a "failed state"): they can challenge the state openly and risk a cutoff in funding; or they can turn to unobtrusive promotional activities and perhaps alienate civil society. Absent strong leadership willing to navigate this fine line skillfully, the trade-offs can be institutionally debilitating. For the foreseeable future, Chad's NHRI will be hostage to the country's broader political context.

Even before Mobuto's fall in 1997, *Zaire* had created an NHRI and it had done so at least partly to satisfy an international audience. Following the creation of a UN Special Rapporteur on Human Rights in 1994 and a March 1995 UN resolution on the situation of human rights in Zaire, the government issued a decree in mid-1995 creating the National Commission for the Protection and Promotion of Human Rights (CNPPDH according to its French acronym).[87] The institution was not established until May 1996, and the public seemed to be completely unaware of its existence while NGOs were only selectively invited to participate. In contrast, both the prime minister and foreign affairs minister mentioned the NHRI, asserting the institution's independence and compliance with UN standards. This was contradicted when the institution's staff complained to the UN special rapporteur in 1996 that they lacked resources, their premises were limited to space "donated by a European embassy," and their access to conflict zones was barred.[88] Though the government intended the commission to be a "national institution for promotion and protection," the United Nations OHCHR remarked sharply, "Nothing is achieved by establishing a national institution which does not rely on the participation of civil society. The interest of Government in establishing this Commission, with a pluralist and transparent character, must be manifest from the start, must protect the possibility of giving a public character to its reports and recommendations, the freedom to have recourse to it and in general respect for the Principles approved by the General Assembly of the United Nations."[89]

The post-Mobuto transition would represent in some ways a dramatic turning point, vividly symbolized in the country's name change; but the history of NHRIs in the country, as detailed below, would prove to be no less volatile. A Ministry of Human Rights was established in June 1998, as part of a cabinet reshuffling and new draft constitution and amid rising transnational human rights pressure, all shortly before the outbreak of another war in mid-1998.[90] The new government in Kinshasha was again following a two-pronged strategy of rejecting international accusations and violating human rights, while offering symbolic gestures of its commitment to democratic rule and its break from an abusive past, including taking steps to institutionalize human rights in state structures.

In nearby *Niger*, too, NHRIs have depended on the broader political context for their survival. Reflecting a political opening dating to the early 1990s, during which rising social demands led to multiparty elections and constitutionalism, the National Conference charged with drafting the new constitution called for the creation of a permanent human rights commission. In a post–Paris Principles era, the new constitution of 1996 included a national human rights commission, and enabling legislation established the Commission nationale des droits de l'homme et des libertés fondamentales in 1998.[91] Significantly, despite coups in 1996 and 1999, the new constitution of 1999 retained the national human rights commission. While another coup in February 2010 led to the NHRI's official dissolution, which had already been fully accredited internationally, almost immediately another NHRI—l'Observatoire national des droits de l'homme et des libertés fondamentales—appeared, on an interim basis and coinciding with Niger's UPR at the UN Human Rights Council.[92] Discussions facilitated by the interim NHRI, with the support of the United Nations, soon called for a new national human rights commission in full compliance with the Paris Principles. This was included in the final recommendations from the UPR, released in June 2011.[93]

In 1996, *Madagascar's* government also issued a decree creating an NHRI, the Commission nationale des droits de l'homme de Madagascar. The idea for establishing an NHRI, however, had already been included in the country's 1992 constitution: "The States shall be committed to instituting an independent agency responsible for the promotion and protection of human rights."[94] The language of "promotion and protection" matched closely the notion of NHRIs.

Though Parliament delegated the role of an independent human rights body to the Mediator's Office, which was an ombudsman agency formed a few years earlier, by 1996 the decision was taken to create a separate body.[95] New government leaders may have thought that introducing a state human rights agency would appease critics, just as it was in the process of negotiating a reform package with international financial institutions. Despite international and domestic calls for its implementation, the institution did not begin functioning until 2000; it was accredited internationally, with reservations, between 2000 and 2003. After falling inactive a couple of years later, when its members' terms expired during a national political crisis, international reviews in 2006 dropped Madagascar's NHRI to a C rating.[96] In 2008, and following pressure from treaty bodies like CERD and the Convention on the Elimination of All Forms of Discrimination Against Women (CEDAW) as well as an upcoming UPR, a brand new NHRI was created: the National Human Rights Council, though a coup in 2009 delayed the institution's actual formation.

In an environment of regional diffusion, Madagascar's democratization movement of the 1990s and a related process of constitution making led to the creation of an NHRI. Though the initial choice was for a traditional French-style ombudsman, a human rights commission was introduced in late 1996, by a new government that was autocratic in style but willing to adopt the language of human rights, especially on the eve of a structural reform package negotiated with international financial institutions. Once created, an unsupportive environment, marked by political volatility and fragility, led to the institution losing its international accreditation, even while domestic institutional precedents, regional diffusion, and international regime pressures kept the notion of an NHRI alive and on the national agenda.

Mauritius presents a somewhat different case, of a small island state in Africa with a relatively well consolidated if imperfect democracy—a "social-democratic developmental state," itself the product of unique historical-structural circumstances.[97] Though it had ratified the two international human rights covenants in 1973 and the African Charter in 1992, an NHRI was not created until 1998, accredited one year later. The government also created complementary bodies in an ombudsman and a specialized ombudsman for children.[98]

While Mauritius did not create its NHRI in the midst of a regulatory moment or to counter organized abuse, external obligations alone cannot account for the timing of the Commission's appearance in the latter part of the 1990s. This member of the both the British Commonwealth and the Francophonie, with a relatively strong rule of law system, appears to have created the NHRI as a result of international regime pressures. In 1996, Mauritius hosted a regular session of the African Commission on Human and Peoples' Rights, which resulted in the so-called Mauritius Plan of Action, a five year region-wide human rights action plan. One of the items prioritized for regional workshops, seminars, and training was support for "national structures for protection and promotion of human and peoples' rights"; in addition, NHRIs and their role in collaborating with the commission were highlighted.[99] Mauritius thus created an NHRI largely as a result of regional diffusion pressures combined with its prior external obligations. The fact that it did not experience a regulatory moment in the 1990s or high levels of abuse explains why the NHRI did not surface until later in the decade. When a regional meeting held in its territory promoted the idea of NHRIs, it quickly conformed to regional expectations and agreed to establish the institution.

Mauritania also created an NHRI in 1998, the Commissariat aux droits de l'homme, à la lutte contre la pauvreté et à l'insertion (Commission on Human Rights, Poverty Reduction, and Integration). A commission that emphasized poverty and development as integral to notions of human rights appeared to be an innovative breakthrough, but the institution proved weak from the outset. It lacked independence, was accused of corruption, and cooperated too closely with the World Bank without sufficiently focusing on issues of discrimination. Despite the inflated promise of its rhetoric, as one observer said, it was "destined for stillbirth."[100] Created one year after the African Commission on Human and Peoples' Rights held its ordinary session in Nouakchott, the institution was widely portrayed as an NHRI though the government never applied to have it accredited, perhaps aware of its perceived weaknesses. Despite attempts to reorganize it in the early 2000s, the commission became moribund a few years later.[101]

In 2006, following a coup, the government nonetheless moved to create the National Human Rights Commission via executive decree, referring to the 2000 Declaration of Bamako issued by the Francophonie and conforming to the more conventional model of an NHRI.[102] In November 2009, the NHRI was found to be only partially compliant with international standards (B status), but an amendment one year later permitting unscheduled visits to detention centers helped the institution earn full accreditation in mid-2011, a few months after its UPR. It is noteworthy that the government also created several other human rights institutions during this period, including a Commission on Human Rights, Humanitarian Action and Relations with Civil Society and a Ministry of Human Rights and Reintegration.[103]

Despite nominal liberalization in the early 1990s, Mauritania has experienced a great deal of political volatility. Even its liberalizing efforts, moreover, appeared closely tied to an interest in reestablishing ties with Western countries, especially following its support for Iraq in the Persian Gulf War in 1991. A pattern also emerged of repressing the opposition in the run-up to elections, which were marred by fraud and widely denounced. It was in this context, and at the same time that Mauritania was undergoing a foreign-policy realignment, that it created a rhetorically strong but practically weak NHRI in 1998. The 2006 institution, much more in line with international standards, came as a result of changes in domestic governance (after a 2005 coup promising democratization) and ongoing regional diffusion (including via the Francophonie and United Nations). Reforms to the institution have reflected international regime pressures, especially through the UPR and the process of accreditation, as well as an attempt to appease critics after rising human rights abuses and transnational pressures.

Peace Agreements in Sub-Saharan Africa

As the decade ended, NHRIs also appeared in the region's postconflict states. A human rights commission was first created in Rwanda in 1999, having been envisioned in the Arusha peace process begun earlier in the decade. That same year a national human rights commission was included in Sierra Leone's Lomé Peace Accord of 1999, followed in the new millennium by NHRIs in postconflict Côte d'Ivoire, Liberia, and Sudan. Though an NHRI was not created in Sierra Leone until 2004, after the civil war had ended, it is noteworthy that the earlier peace accord referenced it: "The Parties pledge to strengthen the existing machinery for addressing grievances of the people in respect of alleged violations of their basic human rights by the creation, as a matter of urgency and not later than 90 days after the signing of the present Agreement, of an autonomous quasi-judicial national Human Rights Commission."[104]

Rwanda's Commission Nationale des Droits de l'Homme, the last bandwagoner of the decade in Africa, could trace its roots to the second protocol signed between the Rwandan government and the Rwandan Patriotic Front in 1992 during the Arusha talks and focusing on the rule of law. The Arusha Accord itself stated, in Article 15, that "the two parties agree that a National Commission on Human Rights shall be established. This institution shall be independent and shall investigate human rights violations committed by anyone on Rwandese territory, in part, by organs of the State and individuals in their capacity as agents of the State or of various organizations." Tellingly, in the accords, the human right to democracy was linked to the notion of the rule of law. This emphasis was apparently added in an effort to appease Western governments, including the French.[105] The postgenocide Rwandan government's first reaction was to create the commission envisaged in the Arusha Peace Accord by presidential decree. However, the United Nations applied pressure until a parliamentary debate took place and the Commission was established by law.[106] Despite a broad mandate, which stretched to investigate past abuses, and an injection of international assistance and foreign funding, the Rwandan Commission was initially given limited powers. By 2001, however, it was deemed sufficiently strong to gain international accreditation. And in an interesting extension of its activities, the commission was charged with (and provided foreign funding for) monitoring local justice by the *gacaca* system. Still, in its reaccreditation bid in 2012, the ICC put Rwanda's NHRI on notice, threatening to reduce its status if it did not become more fully independent and compliant with the Paris Principles.[107]

The Accra Peace Agreement of 2003 similarly called for an independent national human rights commission in *Liberia*. The government soon established it through the 2005 Independent National Human Rights Act. Despite formally creating the body, the government seemed to stall when it came to equipping it. By 2010, the government came under pressure to strengthen and accelerate the institution's reform; critics included the Human Rights Council during the UPR and a joint statement by Human Rights Watch and Amnesty International.[108]

In West Africa, *Côte d'Ivoire* also created a National Human Rights Commission amid armed conflict, though the idea was first mentioned in the peace accord of 2003. The Linas-Marcoussis accord, completed in France, called explicitly on the government of reconciliation to establish a "national human rights commission." The Roundtable leading to the accord was heavily internationalized; it was co-chaired by a French jurist and by Senegalese Judge Kéba Mbaye, the founder of Africa's first NHRI (Chapter 5), and it included representatives from the United Nations and the African Union. Along with an ombudsman and Human Rights Ministry, the government agreed to create the NHRI in the aftermath of the peace accords, and following the UN Security Council's call in May 2004 for the immediate establishment of the NHRI. The commission was formed both via legislation (2004) and a presidential decree (2005), becoming operational in 2007.[109] At least one study asserts that the NHRI's law "in many aspects seems to live up to the Paris Principles."[110]

During the country's UPR in 2009, the fact that the institution still had not been accredited was the subject of numerous recommendations.[111] In general, member states of the Human Rights Council called on the Ivoirese government to amend the law and endow the NHRI with greater pluralism and independence. The government accepted these recommendations, and there is some chance that structural changes will lead to a more active institutional player.

The incentives to create an NHRI in Côte d'Ivoire were initially overwhelming: a regulatory moment, external obligations, and organized abuse. However, ongoing conflict, marked by the failure to disarm after another peace accord in 2003, the presence of a UN peacekeeping mission since 2004, and the outbreak of a second war in 2010 made it nearly impossible for the institution to overcome its circumstances. In a postconflict setting, it will also be difficult for the institution to promote accountability for past human rights crimes committed by all sides. Despite these challenges, the experience of Côte d'Ivoire shows how in the midst of war, an NHRI can exist and even undergo reform. Whether this reflects the power of institutions to persist, the determination of international actors to support Western institutions, or both, remains unclear.

Finally, *Sudan's* Comprehensive Peace Agreement in 2005 also called for a national human rights commission, though ensuing progress has proved slow. In 2009, the National Human Rights Commission Act was passed, but the institution had not become operational by the time of the UPR in 2011. The incentives for an NHRI were strong and included human rights obligations dating to the mid-1980s as well as ongoing transnational pressure. In the end, however, an ongoing conflict undermined the NHRI's functioning.

NHRIs that are envisioned in peace agreements tend to appear once a country is past conflict and embarking on democratization reforms; most are adopting a borrowed script. Even in cases like Rwanda where a parliamentary debate took place over the legal foundations of a human rights commission, such cases are broadly speaking instances of diffusion by coercion.[112] At the same time, peace agreements themselves constitute regulatory moments, where participants must necessarily confront the past to construct the future. NHRIs in this context tend to receive high levels of external support, leading to relatively strong institutions—at least formally so.

Since the Paris Principles, peace agreements have incorporated the notion of NHRIs. On one level, this reflects the view that peace and human rights are inextricably linked.[113] On another it reveals how human rights are part of a "bundle" of good-governance principles that states reconstructing in the aftermath of atrocities and violent conflict are expected to embrace. This bundle includes notions of human rights, democracy, rule of law, pluralism, and national unity. These principles have been defined and promoted, sometimes aggressively so, by

Western powers who often have conditioned their aid on nominal acceptance of these institutions.

Millennial Leaders

Following the initial wave of the 1990s, other countries in Africa created NHRIs after 2000. Among all the African countries that established NHRIs in the new millennium, only four have been accredited (either fully or partially): Tanzania, Burkina Faso, Egypt, and the Congo. If these countries did not jump on the NHRI bandwagon sooner, it was because they faced political obstacles or relatively weak incentives in the 1990s. Tanzania spent a good part of the decade debating the merits of an NHRI replacing a long-standing institution. Burkina Faso enjoyed relative stability; ironically, only in the context of a domestic crisis did the option of an NHRI make it onto the political agenda. In Egypt, it was only after 2000 that domestic and international incentives converged to make an NHRI desirable. And the Congo had to come out of a protracted conflict before it established its NHRI. Domestic political conditions, therefore, kept these countries from creating an NHRI in the 1990s, despite regional and global diffusion pressures to do so.

Tanzania's Donor-Driven Institutions

The Commission for Human Rights and Good Governance (CHRGG) was created in *Tanzania* in 2000, by means of a constitutional amendment. Implementing legislation followed one year later, when the NHRI opened its doors and replaced the long-standing Permanent Commission of Inquiry (PCI), created in 1965 as Africa's first ombudsman office, second in the British Commonwealth after New Zealand's. In this sense, the CHRGG absorbed the ombudsman function while moving to adopt a much fuller human rights mandate.[114]

Establishing the commission reflected a few interrelated factors, including popular discontent with the PCI. Though the PCI was originally envisaged as an independent ombudsman-type figure, following the Scandinavian model, in practice the institution had evolved into an extension of the presidency.[115] Initially intended as a compromise measure, after transnational calls for a postindependence bill of rights went unheeded, the institution's ineffectiveness became most apparent when a bill of rights was finally enacted in 1984 and the language of human rights was increasingly on the agenda.[116] Criticism of the commission was compounded by the broader domestic climate in the early 1990s, one in which social demands for public accountability rose in the face of rampant corruption and increasingly well-organized civil society groups.[117]

The final blow to the PCI came when the institution became caught up in the government's anticorruption campaign, itself encouraged by international lending agencies. To counter critiques of political party corruption and appease foreign donors, newly elected President Benjamin Mkapa established in 1996 a commission to examine corruption. Known as the Warioba Commission, the group issued a five-hundred-plus-page report in 1997, detailing corruption in Tanzania and making relevant recommendations; the World Bank apparently supported and funded the report's release.[118] The report traced corruption to several factors, including weak oversight and watchdog institutions, naming the PCI specifically.[119]

At the same time as the PCI's death knell was sounded, civil society, including members of the legal profession, came to support the idea of a human rights commission. For example, in a workshop in November 1996 on constitutional and legal changes under democratization, sponsored by Tanzania's bar association (the Tanganyika Law Society) a constitutionally incorporated human rights commission was discussed.[120] As 1998 approached, a decade after the bill of rights had entered into force and on the fiftieth anniversary of the UDHR, civil society groups supported the idea of transforming the PCI into a human rights commission. From the perspective of Tanzanian society, "The decision to form a Human Rights Commission was partly an answer to a long outcry about the ineffectiveness of the previous commission and the need for a human rights watchdog."[121]

With mounting social pressure for a new constitution, one that would address the issues raised in the Warioba Commission report, the government issued a white paper to preempt the debate. The government elaborated in the paper various positions and staked out its own ground. In discussing critiques of the PCI, the government stated that it had endorsed establishing a Human Rights Commission, which would now perform the functions of the PCI. A follow-up committee purportedly created to gauge public reactions to and support for the white paper endorsed in its final report of 1999 the government's proposal to dismantle the PCI and establish an NHRI. That committee was chaired by Justice Kisanga, who would go on to be appointed the NHRI's first head.[122]

The idea for a human rights commission, then, was closely related to international donor interest in fighting corruption through accountability institutions—corruption, after all, hinders investment. In a 1998 report supporting the findings of the Warioba Commission report, the World Bank explicitly recommended reconstituting the PCI as a human rights commission, labeling this a "high priority" to be achieved in the short to medium term.[123] The very inclusion of "good governance" in the NHRI's name reveals these close linkages with international financial agencies, favoring Western democratic political institutions. As one local skeptic said, "In Tanzania, we had first a ministry, headed by a full-fledged minister of good governance. Then, though donor pressure, the government was obliged to establish a Commission for Human Rights and Good Governance with aid from the Danish government. Among the first tasks was to build a gargantuan structure to house the commission and establish its infrastructure."[124]

Given the interconnections with the PCI, some critics have asserted that similar weaknesses befuddled the new NHRI. Rather than having parliament appoint the head of the commission, the president initially did so. After this problem was addressed as part of international accreditation, a contingent A status (assigned in 2003 and 2005) was changed to fully compliant by 2006.[125] Still, treaty bodies (e.g., the UN Committee Against Torture, CRC, and CERD) critiqued government funding cuts to the NHRI and poor access in rural areas, while the OHCHR offered the institution advice and assistance. During the UPR process in 2011, Tanzania was pressured to continue strengthening the institution.

By the late 1990s, the timing was right for Tanzania to create an NHRI. Beyond rising global attention to the institution, the government faced overwhelming incentives. Not only had popular discontent over the inadequacy of the PCI risen, but the Tanzanian government had both accepted external obligations even while continuing to violate human rights. In this context, World Bank support for transforming the PCI into a human rights commission carried a great deal of weight for a government ruling over one of the poorest countries in the world while in the process of implementing an IMF structural adjustment program and reliant on foreign loans. The debate over amending (or rewriting) the constitution between 1998 and 2000 offered just the opportunity to undertake socially appropriate institution building.

Postcrisis Reforms in Burkina Faso

Burkina Faso's relative stability in the first part of the 1990s may have kept an NHRI off the agenda. The establishment of the National Human Rights Commission in 2001 can be traced instead to a national crisis dating to 1998, including rising social opposition. The government of the West African country responded by initiating broad democratic reforms and granting civil society a more participatory role in governance. The NHRI grew out of this evolving domestic context, though the idea for it had originated from and was supported by a confluence of actors that included newly appointed government bureaucrats charged with promoting human rights, civil society representatives, and international actors like the Francophonie.

The creation of an NHRI in Burkina Faso was part of a series of reforms undertaken in the aftermath of an unprecedented political crisis. Soon after a national election in 1998, the murder of journalist Norbert Zongo in December set off a violent conflict. But it also served to galvanize opposition against the nondemocratic aspects of the regime. A national unity government created to defuse the conflict opened what some described as a "new political context." An independent commission of inquiry was formed, chaired by a member of an important human rights NGO (Burkina Faso Human Rights Movement), and the government turned to institutional solutions to move past the conflict, including a consultative commission on political reforms and a National Reconciliation Commission to facilitate a political dialogue; broad alliance governments were also formed in 1999 and 2000. The momentum of change did not stop there, as postcrisis reforms broadened to address constitutional questions, electoral processes, decentralization, and human rights governance.[126]

Rising social demands, often articulated as claims for rights protections, led in 2000 to the creation within the Ministry of Justice of a State Secretariat for the Promotion of Human Rights, which would prove influential in establishing the NHRI. Significantly, the same month the secretariat was created, members of the Francophonie, including Burkina Faso, had issued the Bamako Declaration, agreeing "[t]o create, generalize and strengthen national institutions, advisory or otherwise, for promoting human rights and to support the creation of structures within national administration, devoted specifically to human rights."[127] Though Burkina Faso's new human rights secretariat was initially understaffed, the symbolic effects of the office were soon evident and drew on international discourse related to NHRIs. For example, in a policy document about the importance of promoting and protecting human rights, the department emphasized a "major role for the state." A day of consultation with civil society groups in April 2001 led to participants supporting explicitly the idea of an NHRI, cast as a permanent dialogue framework. This informal agreement itself followed a groundbreaking National Day of Forgiveness on March 30, 2001, when before a stadium filled with thousands of people, the president asked the country's forgiveness for any abuses committed by the state since independence in 1960.[128]

In this context of postcrisis reform and dialogue, the NHRI was established by decree in November 2001, adopting the popular "national human rights commissions" model in Africa. In the initial applications for accreditation, the ICC raised problems with the institution's independence, including its appointment procedures and funding (e.g., the commissioners were unpaid), leading the NHRI to be accredited only partially as a B-status institution. To some extent, of course, the NHRI's limitations may have reflected a situation of immense poverty, but it also may have signaled that "[i]n Burkina Faso, the human rights situation is rather paradoxical in the sense that the abundance of human rights problems is in stark contrast to their effectiveness."[129] That is, the government—in power for almost a quarter of a century—had become quite adept at institutionalizing human rights in a formal sense (including the transformation of the human rights secretariat into a freestanding ministry in 2002, which the prime minister described as a "sign of strong commitment to human rights protection"), without noticeable consequences.[130] It was only with the UPR process in 2008, and the formation that year of a Network of African NHRIs, that the government committed to strengthening the NHRI. Indeed, in 2009 and 2010, Burkina Faso made several key reforms, including legally incorporating the NHRI. Yet caught up in broader domestic protests and violence in 2011, the government somehow did not submit its materials to the ICC, losing its NHRI's accreditation in March 2012.[131]

Burkina Faso's NHRI thus arose during a postcrisis regulatory moment and in the context of its external obligations. The constitutional amendment of 2001 reflected a broader series of reforms undertaken in the aftermath of conflict. While human rights abuses had been relatively high when the NHRI was created, they leveled off to precrisis levels that did not generate strong international pressure. Reforms that involved creating governmental human rights structures, of which the NHRI was one example, appeared to mirror international support for NHRIs, especially the Bamako Declaration of 2000. Despite having created an initially weak institution, Burkina Faso undertook reforms in direct response to the UPR process, during which several countries called on it to strengthen the NHRI and make it fully compliant with the Paris Principles. International regime pressures and a regulatory moment brought on by domestic crisis worked in tandem to produce and strengthen the NHRI, only to succumb again to domestic unrest and have its accreditation status lapse.

Egypt Performing Human Rights

Among the most prominent latecomers in Africa was Egypt's National Council for Human Rights, formed in 2003 by a legislative act. The NHRI's establishment was proposed in mid-2000 by the Ministry of Justice, which also drafted the initial legislation. The minister of justice at the time described the idea of an NHRI as "a striking example of democratic reform in the Arab world."[132] Though the institution was initially accredited only partially in April 2006, in the course of a few months it made the requisite changes and was elevated to an A-status body.[133]

The role of international and regional diffusion was paramount. Following the Paris Principles, NHRIs had begun networking within the African and Mediterranean contexts, holding key meetings in Durban and Marrakesh, just as the United Nations was promoting the idea actively and the institution was starting to diffuse throughout the Arab world. Moreover, domestically, a Permanent Commission on Human Rights had been created as an interministerial body in 1997. That body brought together representatives from various ministries including Justice and the Interior, with the task of following up on UN-related human rights work. This itself complemented the Department of Human Rights, which earlier in the decade had been created as part of the Foreign Ministry.[134] More broadly, European human rights pressures had begun rising in 1999. In anticipation of the fourth meeting of Euro-Mediterranean foreign ministers that year, the European Community called on states to sign association agreements (Egypt would do so in 2001) and to place "greater emphasis on human rights issues," as economic assistance would become "more dependent on substantial progress in these areas."[135]

Likewise, by 2000 other domestic incentives existed for creating national human rights structures. The government had hardened its line against civil society organizations, passing a highly controversial law on civil society associations in 1999. Though that was subsequently overturned by the courts, the negative attention the law attracted both within and outside of Egypt may have shifted government tactics in controlling civil society. Apparently, a couple of months after the Ministry of Justice mentioned the possibility of a human rights council, the head of the Egyptian Organization for Human Rights—an influential domestic NGO—also raised the idea directly with the president's chief of staff, part of a more general proposal for a dialogue between the government and civil society groups.[136] Even if the Ministry of Justice had already considered the idea of a human rights council, the support signaled by a key human rights activist may have convinced the government of such an institution's capacity to appease critics.

The idea for an NHRI, first announced in 2000, was temporarily shelved until 2002, when the influential Policies Committee picked it up as part of a package of liberalizing reforms. The Policies Committee was part of the ruling National Democratic Party, and it was spearheaded by Gamal Mubarak, the president's son. The notion of a human rights council certainly promised to enhance Egypt's international image; and it fit the reformist, democratic agenda that the government was intent on crafting, including eliminating state security courts and hard-labor penalties. It also matched the proliferation of more human rights structures within the government during this period (e.g., the Higher Committee for Human Rights within the Ministry of the Interior, 2001; the General Department for Human Rights in the Ministry of Justice, 2002; and the Human Rights Committee of the Ministry of Social Affairs, 2004), as well as a National Council for Women. As one analyst describes it, these liberalizing reforms all represented the regime's "soft adaptation technique" to rising international pressures in the aftermath of September 11.[137] Given Egypt's strategic value, human rights pressures had always been relatively weak; yet after the U.S.-led "war on terror," Egypt like other states in the region became subject to competing international forces. U.S. pressure to combat terrorism by any means necessary was countered by growing opposition within Egypt and rising demands from international human rights groups to protect human rights, with the state caught somewhere in the middle.

The government's real intentions were perhaps most apparent in the institution's design. The council's members were not appointed for six months, and the first council meeting was not held until February 2004. Despite its legislative stamp, the NHRI's creation only required the approval of Egypt's consultative upper house of parliament, the Shura Council, while NGOs were not consulted. The council's members included internationally renowned individuals, though with very limited legal reach. Most notably, former UN secretary-general Boutros Boutros-Ghali served at its helm. Boutros-Ghali, in an interesting twist, had been the executive secretary of the Francophonie when the Bamako Declaration was issued in 2000. Many of the council's members were also ruling party insiders, and the body remained virtually silent in the face of egregious human rights abuses. All told, the NHRI seemed to be designed to signal Egypt's commitment to democratic reform and human rights, mostly with an eye to the country's international image, while retaining firm state control over the institution's actual shape and direction.[138]

The NHRI's weak initial design, reflecting the government's attempts to appease critics and co-opt the human rights agenda, has left its imprint. The council remains cautious, and the government has stepped in at critical moments and signaled its control, for instance replacing an outspoken vice president in 2010.[139]

At the same time, joining the world of NHRIs has led to institutional reforms resulting from international accreditation and review procedures, including the decision to establish a complaints committee within the council in 2008. In the country's UPR in 2010, the institution received relatively little attention—quietly and effectively recognized for doing its work, but remaining in the background.[140] This is what the NHRI is like at home. In a post-Mubarak dramatically changing domestic context, the institution may yet have an opportunity to distance itself from its early performance and be a force for social and political change.

Brazzaville under Conflict

The same year in which Egypt created its National Council for Human Rights, the Republic of the Congo (Brazzaville) established a National Human Rights Commission. The institution, along with an ombudsman, had been envisioned in a new constitution in 2002.[141] Adopting international language, the constitution called for the establishment of a "national human rights commission" for the "promotion and protection of human rights." The country indeed faced overwhelming incentives to create an accountability mechanism following a war dating to 1997, while engaged in constitution making and already having accepted human rights obligations.

The Congo's NHRI arose in a postconflict situation. The introduction of multiparty democracy in 1991 was met with ongoing violence for most of the decade, though a National Forum for Reconciliation in 1998 called for elections, a constitution, and overall reform; and a peace accord in 1999 (one of others that would follow) led to a national dialogue. In general, however, the period since 1998 was one of difficult negotiations intermixed with violence. The 2002 constitution embodied these contradictions: democratic reforms and rights protections alongside an inordinately strong presidency. Interestingly, the chair of the constitutional commission was Aimé Emmanuel Yoka, a lawyer also serving as ambassador to Morocco (which had a prominent NHRI); he would later be appointed minister of state for justice and human rights.[142]

The NHRI was relatively weak from the start and lacked clarity in many respects, failing for example to specify how representatives from civil society were to be selected.[143] Symbolically, it also lacked adequate facilities at the outset, though this changed later in the decade. By the time of the UPR process in 2009, then, the institution had never applied for NHRI accreditation, though it assured the international committee that bilateral and multilateral partners were assisting it in this regard. When it did apply in 2010, it was found to be only partially compliant with the Paris Principles.[144] Strong incentives had led the government to create an NHRI, but a domestic context of ongoing violence proved overwhelming and perpetuated a structurally weak institution.

NHRI Latecomers

Another set of countries created NHRIs after 2000, though they had yet to attain international accreditation by the end of the decade. In many cases, the failure to apply for accreditation reflected an awareness of the institution's limitations; from a certain perspective, it can be better to have an unaccredited NHRI than to have one's NHRI rejected for accreditation. And to the extent that these institutions were relatively weak, this reflected a whole range of factors, including closed political systems, small states, climates of high violence, and weak strategic incentives. That these institutions were created at all reflects the power of international regime pressures to place NHRIs on the political agenda.

Djibouti from the Outside In

Djibouti followed a similar trajectory to other countries in the region, permitting some opposition parties in the 1990s while persisting as a single-party state. It was not until 2000, however, that it took tepid steps to create a body resembling an NHRI. An actual National Human Rights Commission was eventually established in 2008, with international actors playing an essential role.

The turn of the millennium seemed a propitious time to take steps toward creating an NHRI. In addition to global developments surrounding NHRIs, Djibouti's second president since independence was elected in 1999. He soon adopted numerous reforms, including moving to create an ombudsman's office that year via a presidential decree and ratifying CEDAW. A peace agreement concluding a ten-year civil war also was concluded in 2000–2001. And the period of transition that had been envisioned in the constitution of 1992 ended in 2002, permitting a fuller multiparty system. As part of these changes, the government issued a law on judicial organization in mid-2000 that included creating a National Committee for the Promotion and Protection of Human Rights. Opposition groups refused to cooperate, protesting the government's ongoing unwillingness to respond to abuses. The committee thus whittled away, though the government continued paying lip service to human rights. For example, before the presidential election in 2005, the government organized a national forum for human rights dialogue, but it later failed to release the report. Significantly,

Djibouti was elected onto the Human Rights Council in 2006; in its official statement, it affirmed its general commitment to human rights and agreed to ratify a few treaties, without mentioning the possibility of a human rights commission.[145]

International momentum for a human rights commission nonetheless grew. In particular, the East Africa regional office of the OHCHR claims to have lobbied successfully for an NHRI. And at last, in April 2008, a presidential decree created the NHRI: "In order to enhance the promotion and protection of human rights and to address the failure to submit the reports required under the international and regional human rights instruments ratified by Djibouti, a National Human Rights Commission was established in April 2008, bringing together representatives of the State and civil society involved in human rights issues and in action to eliminate all forms of discrimination."[146] One month later, a consultative workshop co-organized by the regional office of the OHCHR and Djibouti's Ministry of Justice recommended that the country devise a national action plan for human rights, which necessitated that the NHRI be functional. It is noteworthy that the OHCHR regional office strongly recommended the NHRI, in an attempt to institutionalize human rights within the state. This all occurred against a backdrop of human rights violations and intolerance for independent NGOs.[147]

If Djibouti was relatively late in erecting an NHRI, it was also rather late in gaining independence and accepting human rights obligations; unlike most of its peers, France ruled Djibouti until 1977; and the country ratified the two international covenants only in 2002. While a regulatory moment led briefly to a superficial NHRI in 2000, the peace accord did not address human rights issues explicitly.[148] In 2000, then, international diffusion may have led to the announcement that a national human rights body would be created; but in a context where the political transition itself was largely symbolic and NGOs were not allowed to function, human rights abuses did not translate into strong transnational pressures. By 2008, however, Djibouti's participation in the Human Rights Council served as an additional impetus to institutionalize human rights within the state apparatus.

Gabon's Regional Outlook

The small, middle-income, oil-producing country of *Gabon* in west-central Africa also created a National Human Rights Commission in 2000. Established by decree, the institution was gradually strengthened, though even more than ten years after its formation it still had not applied for accreditation.[149] The commission was established during a weak regulatory moment amid limited constitutional reforms, by a country that had already accepted human rights treaty obligations.

While standard transnational human rights pressures were minimal, Gabon's government may well have been influenced by international diffusion. A relatively low level of recorded human rights violations, and the country's presence in the volatile Great Lakes region, meant weak transnational pressures for this close French ally. Nor did Gabon have independent, functioning NGOs. Though opposition parties were nominally permitted after 1990, the regime remained a single-party state, ruled by Omar Bongo from 1967 until his death in 2009.[150] The regime faced few structural incentives to create an NHRI.

International regime pressures, in turn, help to explain the creation and evolution of the unaccredited NHRI, evident at every major junction of the institution's development. The government announced the decision to create an NHRI in October 1999, one month after a milestone meeting of ministers of the Francophonie, where human rights were emphasized. Somewhat earlier, in 1998, not only had the second meeting of African NHRIs been held, but NHRIs were given observer status within the African Commission on Human and Peoples' Rights. And when the government had created a Ministry of Justice and Human Rights in 1987, it did so just after having ratified the African Charter on Human and Peoples' Rights.[151]

The government responded to critiques of the NHRI by undertaking some reforms. In 2005, it gave the NHRI legal standing; and leading up to the country's first UPR in 2008, the government issued a decree detailing the appointment process for commissioners. In November 2010, moreover, the government reported it would align the existing NHRI with the Paris Principles. Despite these steps, after the president appointed one of his closest advisers to lead the NHRI in 2011, critics in Gabon and France labeled the institution "cosmetic" and "decorative."[152] Weak pressures had led a government noted for its support of regional integration efforts to respond to region-wide diffusion pressures by creating an NHRI, but the institution's weaknesses attest to the primacy of the broader domestic political environment.

Weak Incentives, from Cape Verde to Swaziland

Across widely varying landscapes, NHRIs were created in Cape Verde, the Central African Republic, and Swaziland. Despite the divergent contexts, all had faced weak incentives to establish a human rights institution in the 1990s. *Cape Verde* created a National Human Rights Committee in 2001, following an ombudsman two years earlier.[153] It did so as part of constitutional revisions. Though its human rights treaty obligations dated to the early 1990s, a relatively strong human rights record and its ties to Portugal meant that international regime pressure was more indirect and weak—until the UPR in 2008, when the Human Rights Council called for strengthening the NHRI.

Almost three thousand miles away, the *Central African Republic* created a High Commission for Human Rights and Good Governance in 2003. Though attached to the office of the presidency, its creation coincided with the government's overthrow that year and an ensuing constitution; the country had ratified the human rights covenants as far back as 1981.[154] A regulatory moment and ongoing violations represented an opportunity for a new government to appease critics by appearing to lock in a set of human rights commitments (while placing the NHRI under the president's purview). With political violence at very high levels, it is perhaps unsurprising that recommendations to strengthen the NHRI, made as part of the UPR process in 2009, were met with no immediate response. After long-delayed elections were held in 2011, amid a strong contingent of international aid workers and peacekeepers, it remained unclear if and when the political context might change more substantially so that the existing NHRI could be reformed.

Swaziland included in its constitution of 2005 a Commission on Human Rights and Public Administration, which was partly conceived as an "integrity" body to combat corruption in public life, though implementing legislation was not passed until 2009.[155] The country had ratified the international human rights covenants in 2004, the year before the new constitution; and with human rights violations running high, the government faced strong incentives to institutionalize human rights. A constitutional committee, in fact, had been mandated to incorporate human rights treaty standards. In practice, however, an absolute monarchy limited the influence of human rights norm promoters and constitutionalism, leading to a weak NHRI. The government requested technical assistance in 2011 to strengthen the NHRI, as Human Rights Council members called during the UPR process for the commission to comply with the Paris Principles.[156] Swaziland stands as yet another autocratic state that created a weak NHRI in the face of strong incentives, moving warily to strengthen the institution only in the context of international regime pressures.

From Zaire to the DRC: "Plus ça change . . ."

The *Democratic Republic of the Congo* (DRC) created its Observatoire national des droits de l'homme (National Human Rights Observatory) in 2004, following war and a transitional government that had already issued an interim constitution. Despite facing overwhelming incentives to create an NHRI, the volatility of the transition translated into a very brief institutional life, and this NHRI essentially disappeared in 2006. Regardless, in anticipation of the upcoming UPR in 2009, the government took steps to create another Human Rights Commission.

The conclusion of a peace agreement in 1999 returned the United Nations to the country, including a field office of the OHCHR.[157] As part of that office's mandate, they worked with local officials to devise a "national plan for the promotion and protection of human rights." That plan focused on strengthening relevant national institutions, including support for nongovernmental ones and for a Human Rights Ministry, as well as the establishment of a *national human rights commission*.[158]

When Joseph Kabila then met with senior officials in the United States during a visit to Washington, D.C., part of a Euro-American tour in February 2001, he faced strong incentives to communicate his support for human rights. Kabila had just taken over as president in January, when his father was assassinated. With UN peacekeepers on the ground in his country, he was being pressured to move quickly toward peace and full democratic transition. Thus, on February 1, in Washington, D.C., the idea of a national human rights conference for the DRC was first raised. Later that month, a presidential decree was issued in preparation for the upcoming conference, which the president confirmed in an important address on March 30 at the UNHRC in Geneva.[159] The conference that June was attended by almost five hundred people, and it produced a Congolese Charter on Human and People's Rights. One of its official recommendations was to set up a "totally independent, autonomous and permanent National Human Rights Commission."[160]

The first NHRI created in 2001, the National Observatory for Human Rights, clearly illustrates the challenges of postconflict human rights institutions. The NHRI had its legal bases in the transitional constitution's attention to democracy-supporting institutions. Around the same time, the government had merged two freestanding ministries to create the Ministry of Justice and Human Rights, raising questions about the extent to which the state was in fact prioritizing or controlling human rights. Yet not long after the observatory was provisionally accredited as an NHRI in 2005, in July 2006 members of the antigovernment Movement for the Liberation of the Congo apparently looted its offices and destroyed its records.[161] The government, whose commitment to human rights institutions may have been directed mostly at an external audience, allowed the institution to cease functioning.

More contradictory actions followed in the run-up to the UPR process scheduled for 2009. Though the Senate passed in mid-2008 a bill creating yet another National Human Rights Commission, the bill stalled in the national assembly. By the time of the UPR, the government declared that "the process of establishing the National Human Rights Commission is on track."[162] Other African countries recommended that the government expedite the process, though Western powers did not mention the issue in their recommendations. In late 2008, the government again made the Ministry of Human Rights a freestanding body, only to merge it again with the Ministry of Justice in 2010, raising concerns that human rights were being subsumed under more pressing state interests.[163] A second national conference on human rights and the rule of law was held in mid-2009, supported by the UN human rights field office, the EU, and the Open Society Institute for Southern Africa.[164]

While the DRC's NHRI has gone mostly undetected by students of these institutions, it reveals an interesting trajectory, created in the face of both high violations and treaty obligations. A dramatic change in regime in the 1990s led to a rejection of past institutions, though in practice this meant adopting new names and institutional forms more than anything else. When the proposal for creating an NHRI was itself resurrected, it was under the aegis of a regulatory moment and international regime pressures, mostly via the UN OHCHR's field presence in the country and its promotion of human rights institutionalization. The National Observatory nonetheless proved short-lived, having been created during a volatile transition and directed mostly at an international audience. Even if ongoing pressures for an NHRI lead to a stronger NHRI in the future, any NHRI's fate in the country will be bound up in the nation's sociopolitical struggles.

Angola's War Legacies

Angola's Provedor de Justiça, or ombudsman, began functioning in 2005, despite having been included in the 1992 national constitution.[165] While by 2012 the institution still did not have a strong human rights mandate and had not applied for international accreditation, it participated in NHRI networks. Almost forty years of armed conflict, including extensive destruction of the country's physical infrastructure, has taken its toll on all aspects of governance in Angola, fundamentally limiting the prospects for a fully functioning human rights ombudsman.[166]

When the office of the ombudsman was included in the 1992 constitution, it was in the context of a postwar transition. The institution was borrowed directly from Portugal, the former colonial power. Though Angola went on to ratify international human rights treaties, the return to war derailed the institution and the institutionalization of human rights more generally. The Ministry of Justice supported the creation of provincial human rights committees in 1998; but these functioned very briefly, collapsing with the end of the peace talks. In fact, the initial push for these committees seems to have come from the UN office in Angola, which favored peace over human rights and pressured the government accordingly.[167] However, with the peace process in obvious jeopardy in mid-1998, the United Nations seemed to shift its approach on the ground, moving to highlight human rights and to support and ally closely with the Ministry of Justice.[168]

The next crucial turn came in 2002, as a postwar settlement seemed to take hold after Jonas Savimbi's death that year and UNITA's decision to disarm and participate in governance rather than suffer intense international isolation. Indeed, after the war ended, Angola faced strong international pressure to adopt democratic institutions, which it did, though quite superficially. It was in this apparently democratizing context that the ombudsman was at last put in place, just as the government would create a Ministry of Human Rights in 2008. But the ombudsman's connections to human rights seemed at best tenuous. The institution was not given adequate resources, and the language of *direitos humanos* did not feature explicitly anywhere.[169] While international documents refer to the NHRI as a "justice and rights" ombudsman, the constitution, implementing legislation, and even the ombudsman's website include only the word "justice" in the institution's title, revealing a possible gap between the institution's external image and its internal identity.

International actors have worked to support the institution, but always operating within broader political constraints. For example, Portugal's NHRI co-sponsored a workshop in 2006 with the OHCHR to support Angola's new ombudsman.[170] The UN country team has also called on the government to strengthen the ombudsman's human rights mandate.[171] And during the UPR in 2010, a few governments recommended that Angola establish an NHRI in full compliance with the Paris Principles. The government agreed, though its new constitution was widely perceived as being nondemocratic and authoritarian.[172] The ombudsman's incorporation in the 1992 constitution and its establishment by law in 2005 occurred in the face of overwhelming incentives, but war and ongoing authoritarianism have crippled the institution's basic capacities. The road ahead is likely to be uncertain, as the country reaches toward peace and national reconciliation.

International Diffusion Catches Up

Late in the decade, a few states created NHRIs largely as a result of international regime pressures. *Burundi*, for instance, provides an interesting example of an NHRI with origins in a UN Human Rights Council resolution. In the context of a highly fragmented and fragile state, the Human Rights Council recommended in 2008 that an independent expert be appointed until the time a national human rights commission was formed. That same year during the country's UPR, members of the Human Rights Council supported the idea of an NHRI, with the government assenting.[173] In 2011, Burundi and other African countries opposed extending the independent expert's mandate, since a National Independent Human Rights Commission had already been established that year. Debate ensued over whether nominal creation of the institution was sufficient or whether the institution needed to comply first with the Paris Principles and be accredited, all in the context of ongoing violations.[174] Human rights treaty obligations dated to 1990, but a weak rule of law system did not encourage localization. International regime pressures therefore combined with an attempt to appease transnational critics, resulting in this NHRI's late arrival—accredited as fully compliant in November 2012.

Likewise, the *Seychelles* did not create an NHRI until 2009, when the Protection of Human Rights Act established a national human rights commission. In 2011, the government accepted the recommendation made as part of the UPR process to seek international accreditation. With long-standing treaty ratifications dating to the early 1990s, a constitution from 2001, and minor violations, the Commonwealth member did not face especially strong incentives to create an NHRI until relatively late. International regime pressures at last converged with treaty obligations to establish a long-awaited NHRI.

Following years of instability and fragile rule, *Zimbabwe's* government finally moved to create a human rights commission via constitutional amendment in 2009. The Zimbabwe Human Rights Commission began operating a year later; though by the time of the UPR in 2011, enacting legislation was still pending. Human Rights Council members expressed concerns over the institution's funding, while some treaty bodies recommended that the NHRI better complement existing commissions dedicated to anticorruption and the media. Significantly, during the UPR, the NHRI acted as a stakeholder, pleading for the government to ensure its statutory independence and comply with the Paris Principles. The decision to create the Commission in 2009 was partly the result of a power-sharing deal in 2008, following a post-transition crisis. With external human rights obligations in place since the early 1990s, along with ongoing violations, a regulatory moment at last permitted international diffusion to take effect.

Guinea's constitution of 2010, passed by presidential decree, recognized a National Human Rights Institution. The NHRI had been recommended as a result of the country's UPR process; and in July of that year, a parliamentary law established a national human rights commission, though most observers contend that there was insufficient consultation, and the process was marked by top-down institutionalization.[175] In a context of ongoing violations and long-standing treaty obligations, Guinea's NHRI reflected a regulatory moment converging with international regime pressures.

The Holdouts

By the time of their UPRs, about ten states in Africa had not yet established an NHRI. Most, however, had agreed to do so in principle and had even taken some concrete steps. The "holdout" states tended to face weak incentives, to be small in size, or to have had an institutional alternative, that is, an institution that resembled the notion of an NHRI and therefore could essentially stand in for it. Only with the accumulating pressures of diffusion, regionally and internationally, did these states move in the direction of creating an NHRI.

Landlocked *Lesotho* had created a human rights unit within the Ministry of Justice as early as 1995; and one year later an ombudsman was established both via legislation and a constitutional amendment. These steps seemed to be taken just as a new government—replacing the long-standing monarch, killed in an automobile accident—attempted to signal its acceptance of international standards. In 2005, the Ministry of Justice, supported by the UNDP and Ireland, embarked on a plan to create a national human rights commission. This reflected both rising international diffusion as well as growing domestic openness stemming from social mobilization during this period. International actors offered assistance, resulting in draft legislation, described by the government as a work in progress by the time of the country's UPR in 2010.[176] A regulatory moment, combined with long-standing external obligations and international regime pressures, resulted in gradual if incomplete institutionalization.

Despite an earlier aborted attempt to create an institution resembling an NHRI (Chapter 5), *Libya* had not yet established an NHRI by the time of its

UPR. It had created, however, a National Human Rights Committee within parliament in 2007, a body the government portrayed explicitly as an independent NHRI conforming to the Paris Principles.[177] In the UPR process, Human Rights Council members were not satisfied and called for an independent NHRI in Libya, or for the government at least to seek accreditation for the national committee.[178] Treaty bodies, including the CESCR, CEDAW, and CRC, also called for an NHRI. Gaddafi's ouster in 2011 and a new constitution raise the likelihood that an accredited NHRI will be formed. Significantly, regional peers have reinforced the notion. For example, in January 2012, the head of Qatar's NHRI met with Libya's minister of justice and human rights, promoting greater cooperation and closer linkages between NHRIs.

The Libyan government's move to create a human rights commission in 2007 may have reflected its efforts to play an international leadership role. In 2010, Libya had been elected to a seat on the Human Rights Council. Before then, international pressure for ongoing violations had not resulted in an NHRI, since independent human rights organizations were forbidden. And while the government's human rights obligations were long-standing, dating to the mid-1970s, Libya's legal system was too weak to create incentives for localization. In this sense, Libya's institutionalization of human rights was also a top-down initiative, ultimately geared at deflecting international human rights criticism.

Following recommendations by the UN Human Rights Committee and CERD that *Botswana* create an NHRI, Human Rights Council members reiterated the idea as part of the UPR process in 2008. Though Botswana accepted the recommendation, it also noted in response to the UN Human Rights Committee that year that an NHRI is "not an inexpensive institution to run," and it may not be the right time to establish it.[179] Botswana's government accepted the idea of creating an NHRI halfheartedly. Absent a regulatory moment or organized abuse, and having ratified the ICCPR only in 2000, the incentives were weak and international regime pressures were met with ambivalence.

Eritrea's government accepted the Human Rights Council's recommendations in 2009 that it establish an NHRI. Even before the UPR, some international actors had pressured the government to create an NHRI, including the CRC and even a U.S. commission.[180] Significantly, the country had not ratified the human rights covenants until 2001 and 2002. But it was not until the UPR process that the government agreed at least rhetorically to create an NHRI. Its holding out for so long may reflect one-party autocratic rule, which prohibited a strong opposition from forming and blocked the promise of political transition.

Comoros also agreed to establish an NHRI as a result of its UPR in 2009. It was a late ratifier as well, having acceded to the human rights covenants only in 2008. Its most recent constitution was also relatively new, dating to 2001. International regime pressures, mostly associated with the UPR, shaped the government's willingness to create an NHRI just as it may have influenced treaty acceptance. The strength of any NHRI, however, is likely to be somewhat constrained by the weak rule of law.

Despite being the seat of the African Commission on Human and People's Rights (ACHPR), and having ratified the human rights covenants as early as 1979, *Gambia* still did not have an accredited NHRI by 2012, though an ombudsman had been included in the 1997 constitution; and at least as early as 1993, a group of experts had advised the government on the creation of a national human rights commission.[181] It was not until after 2000 that pressure for an NHRI actually intensified. Within the subregion, the 2001 Economic Community of West African States (ECOWAS) Supplementary Protocol on Democracy and Good Governance encouraged member states to create independent NHRIs in West Africa, while a consultative meeting of NHRIs (sponsored by ECOWAS and ACHPR and attended by UN representatives) was held in Banjul in 2006. For states like Gambia that did not have an NHRI, representatives from their ministries of justice attended.[182]

Despite the rising pressures, by the time of the country's UPR in 2010, Gambia had still not created an NHRI nor responded to recommendations that it do so. With support from the EU and the OHCHR, and calls from civil society for a human rights commission, the government announced in February 2011, after a visit of senior OHCHR officers, that it was in the final stages of creating a unit that would transform into a human rights commission.[183] Gambia's somewhat puzzlingly long delay in creating an NHRI partly reflects the decision to establish an ombudsman in 1997, which may have served as an institutional alternative to a human rights commission.

While *Guinea-Bissau* also had not created an NHRI by the time of its UPR, it agreed to continue receiving technical assistance toward this end, including from the OHCHR. Indeed, the country did not ratify the ICCPR until 2010. Without a regulatory moment and given weak external obligations, transnational pressure alone did not translate into an NHRI. Ongoing violations and military instability, marked in recent years by high-level political assassinations and a burgeoning drug trade, also called into question the political viability of any future NHRI.

Yet another state that had not created an NHRI by the time of its UPR was *Somalia*, though the government agreed to do so in its formal responses to the Human Rights Council, while the prime minister offered similar assurances. The Independent Expert on the Situation of Human Rights in Somalia had already called in 2007 for an NHRI to be established.[184] Despite a heavily internationalized regulatory moment in 2004, evident in the Transitional Federal Institutions, long-standing human rights obligations dating to 1990, and transnational human rights pressures, an NHRI was long delayed in Somalia. Local conditions were simply not conducive to establishing an NHRI: the virtual collapse of state institutions, weak rule of law, and diminished civil society amid ongoing violence.

Neither had *São Tomé*, Africa's smallest country, established an NHRI by 2011, though the government accepted numerous recommendations to this effect.[185] The tiny country had managed to bypass international diffusion, given a high degree of stability, treaty obligations dating to the early 1990s, and minor violations. Only in the context of the UPR was the idea of an NHRI placed on the political agenda.

Mozambique's government was also urged during its UPR in 2011 to finalize creating an NHRI, a recommendation the government accepted. A bill had been introduced in 2008, with members of the NHRI to be appointed in 2011. Years earlier, in 2004, a justice ombudsman had already been formed. The former Portuguese colony had liberalized politically in the 1990s, but the ongoing dominance of FRELIMO and related social tensions may have hampered efforts to strengthen democratic and human rights institutions; for instance, the country had ratified one of the international human rights covenants, the ICCPR, only in 1993.[186] Around 2005, the Ministry of Justice did explore the possibility of creating an NHRI, a proposal that continued to be lobbied about. Overall, a regulatory moment in the mid-2000s led to the ombudsman and shortly thereafter, partly as a result of international regime pressures and ongoing violations, a move to create a human rights commission. The delay in doing so has reflected a convergence of weak domestic and international incentives.

Conclusions: Institutionalism as Resistance

In *Domination and the Arts of Resistance*, James Scott notes that "[t]he script and stage directions for subordinate groups are generally far more confining than for the dominant."[187] African states were no doubt following a global democratization script when they created NHRIs. That leaders did so, and felt compelled to do so, reflects the role of NHRI-diffusing agents in and out of the region: including the United Nations, international NGOs like Amnesty International, as well as the World Bank, the African Union, and regional or subregional networks of NHRIs. These actors transmitted the idea and the templates, convincing local leaders of the institution's social appropriateness—and strategic value. In this sense, when African leaders adopted NHRIs, they were following a democratization script; but they were usually doing so from a position of global dependence and vulnerability. That they often used and controlled the institution, attempting to tailor it to their advantage and political interests, reflects acts of international resistance. While the diffusion of this Western institution across a postcolonial context may seem like a supreme example of convergence and normative transfer, there was much more at work here. The patterns of diffusion I have traced consistently confirm a logic of strategic emulation.

The impressive spread of NHRIs across Africa, moreover, shows as much variance as the diversity of states in the region. Yet remarkably, the timing of institutional creation seems more often than not to coincide with a regulatory moment (like constitutional drafting or a postconflict peace agreement), new external obligations, and organized abuse. These circumstances gave NHRI proponents an opportunity to promote the idea of an NHRI and leaders an incentive to adopt a socially appropriate mechanism, or permanent accountability institution. Even when incentives were low, often accounting for those NHRIs established after 2000, the role of international socialization and regional diffusion proved influential. Even relatively weak NHRIs demonstrated how the inherent tensions of strategic emulation were indeed at play.

The form and strength of any given NHRI also varied significantly across the region. In this regard, the role of cultural peer networks, notably the Commonwealth and the Francophonie, were influential in the precise forms an NHRI took. That the "national human rights commission" was most popular across so many different states, for example, suggests the power of *regional* diffusion. In terms of organizational design, as indicated by international accreditation, those institutions that most closely mirrored international standards tended to be those that had faced the strongest incentives, or the most international regime pressures. External obligations alone did not tend to play such a significant role in the region, given the relative weakness of the rule of law; but regulatory moments and organized abuse often led to NHRIs sufficiently strong to pass international accreditation. International regime pressures always were significant, becoming even more so in the context of a new UN system of periodic review; in fact, the most recent states to accept establishing an NHRI have done so in direct response to pressures during the UPR process. Absent conditions of norm ambiguity, however, even strong international regime pressures tended to result in fairly weak institutions.

Though leaders of African states were both emulating socially appropriate practices and acting strategically, the broader political context has always constrained the realm of possibilities. Thus, despite the efforts of NHRI-diffusing agents, the institution's adoption and strengthening have always remained constrained by partially exogenous factors, especially the occurrence of regulatory moments, the strength of the domestic rule of law (refracting external obligations), and the application of transnational pressures for ongoing abuses. The historical trajectory of NHRIs in Africa necessarily reflects the broader course of political life, intertwined in colonial legacies and global dependencies. The irony of NHRI growth is partly this: in a context of global subordination, NHRIs have proliferated widely across Africa, following a Western script; but this institutional diffusion is not entirely what it appears, as local leaders have deployed NHRIs strategically to resist incursions into their rule.

7

Transitional Myths and Everyday Politics in the Americas

I f Africa has more NHRIs than any region, Latin America and the Caribbean is the region of the world with the highest relative concentration of NHRIs. It is also the place with the greatest number of fully accredited NHRIs. These trends partly reflected a democratization wave that swept the region in the decade after the Cold War ended, combined with long-standing tendencies toward legalism and institutionalization in many of the region's countries. Internationally, the 1990s marked a watershed period for NHRI growth, and numerous international actors (including foreign governments, the EU, and UNDP) provided Latin American governments creating human rights institutions sizeable funds.[1] It is striking that despite important domestic and international differences, so many countries across Latin America created NHRIs after 1990.

Though the Spanish model was explicitly adopted (and amended) throughout the region, and despite the fact that the institution was diffusing at the same time in other parts of the world, there was still something distinctive about the ombudsman's transplantation to this region, what the head of Mexico's NHRC, called the *ombudsman criollo* and what an Argentine ombudsman described as a unique stage in the historical development of the ombudsman.[2] Honduras's first ombudsman, Leo Valladares Lanza, elaborated what this meant in practice:

> [The] *ombudsman criollo* is placed before a state whose institutions are weak and inefficient, and which lack the confidence and credibility of citizens. In some cases, it finds unhealed scars of massive

violations of human rights committed by the authoritarian governments, cases of torture and disappeared people which have not been
investigated deeply enough yet. It has to face complaints against the
slowness of legal procedures and the growing impunity arising from
the lack of adequate activity of the investigative organs. It faces a crucial situation: there exist thousands of homeless people; people without food, access to health services and education; and large groups of
the population, boys and girls, women, old people, aboriginal groups,
etc. suffer marginalization.[3]

Fredrik Uggla has further pointed out that the ombudsman in the region has
been especially vulnerable to its broader political context, in an ongoing "tug-
of-war between the institution itself, public opinion, state agencies and international actors."[4] This dependence on context is of course present elsewhere in
the world, but the overall dynamic of this historical moment had its own sensibility in the region, given broad similarities in colonial experience, geostrategic significance, political economic development, and sociocultural bonds.
Latin America and the Caribbean, after 1990, presented a particular set of human rights problems, which taken together offered a somewhat coherent picture, when compared to other parts of the world: the transitional moment was
an overriding political theme, often simplistically if understandably depicted
as a stark break with the confrontational human struggles of the past to an
embrace of the more mundane business of everyday living. The human rights
issues before many NHRIs reflected just how this myth played out in each
country.

Mexico's Strategic Emulation

Perhaps not surprisingly given its role as a regional leader, Mexico led the way in
1990 and created a National Human Rights Commission (Comisión Nacional
de Derechos Humanos, CNDH), soon becoming one of the world's most visible
NHRIs. Since then, it has grown into one of the largest systems of state human
rights institutions in the world, with over thirty state commissions, hundreds of
staff members, and a sizeable budget. Significantly, it was also the region's first
"human rights commissions" model. Rather than following the Iberian path,
Mexico borrowed its name from the international context, revealing its willingness to use the institution to enhance its global standing.

Mexico's image as a global leader was contradicted on the human rights front by a gap between its external obligations and actual practices, yet it somehow had managed to escape intense transnational pressure. The massacre of students in 1968 in a central square in Mexico City had not garnered much world attention in a Cold War context, whereas in the 1970s and 1980s the world was too focused on the human rights abuses of military regimes in the Southern Cone and elsewhere in the hemisphere. Only when its systematic policy of abuse began to generate potential transnational consequences for the first time, Mexico's government responded by attempting to appease critics, including adopting institutions that were considered internationally legitimate.

Human rights issues had become salient in Mexico in the mid-1980s, as abuses by political authorities came to light and social mobilization rose. In 1984, for example, the Mexican Academy for Human Rights, a nongovernmental and academic organization that projected human rights issues into national debates, was formed. Nonstate actors organized more broadly in the aftermath of the 1985 earthquake in Mexico City, when the government failed to respond adequately to the disaster and bodies of prisoners who had been tortured were discovered in the ruins of the Federal District Attorney General's office. Human rights issues gained further attention in 1987 with the widely publicized murder of the president of a human rights organization in the state of Sinaloa. And finally, the split that occurred within the dominant Institutional Revolutionary Party (Partido Revolucionario Institucional, PRI) on the eve of the 1988 presidential elections served only to strengthen the opposition's position.[5]

In response to this confluence of developments, the Mexican state in the late 1980s took a series of concrete steps. A government office for human rights, the most direct institutional antecedent to the CNDH, was created in 1988, though the state of Nueva León had an office for the defense of human rights as early as 1979.[6] Then, in May 1990, the vocal response of human rights groups to the murder of Norma Corona Sapién, the human rights lawyer and activist heading the same organization in Sinaloa whose leader had been killed a few years earlier, served as a catalyst for immediate change.

At the international level in the late 1980s, human rights issues threatened for the first time to interfere in Mexico's foreign relations, while plans for a free trade agreement with the United States and Canada enhanced the importance for state elites of the country's international image. Consequently, a rise in reports by nongovernmental and intergovernmental organizations on repression by the Mexican state was potentially damaging to the country. Two instances of international publicity regarding Mexico's human rights practices in 1990 stand out: the Inter-American Commission on Human Rights' first decision finding Mexico in violation of the American Convention of Human Rights, and a June 1990 publication by Americas Watch devoted to the Mexican situation.[7]

In view of this domestic and international context, it is unsurprising that President Carlos Salinas de Gortari responded to human rights pressure in 1990 with a strategy of appeasement. In June of that year, the CNDH was established by executive decree, without any real debate, only a few days before Presidents Salinas and Bush announced plans for a free trade agreement. It replaced the General Human Rights Department, an entity created in February 1989 as part of the Interior Ministry.

Yet the creation of the CNDH did not stop international human rights pressure. In September 1990, the first hearings ever on human rights in Mexico were held in two U.S. congressional subcommittees. And one year after the commission was established, Americas Watch issued a report on the persistence of human rights abuses.[8] The CNDH was widely characterized as an obvious attempt by the government to improve the country's image abroad.

Partly in reaction to these criticisms, the government reformed the CNDH. In an important step in January 1992, a constitutional decree required national and state legislatures to establish human rights commissions. The CNDH was then assigned its own regulatory structure with the National Commission on Human Rights Law of June 1992. Even then, however, the CNDH remained under executive control. The 1992 reform did not explicitly grant the commission independence from other branches of government, while it did limit its range of competence. The CNDH's power was restricted in areas relating to electoral issues, labor conflicts, and jurisdictional matters, in spite of the extent to which these areas can involve human rights violations. Still, introducing a federal system of NHRIs was crucial, with some of the local-level commissions (e.g., Mexico City's) thriving on their own as NHRIs.[9]

Only in the context of an important domestic political realignment did more dramatic changes follow in 1999. The CNDH was at last given autonomy from the executive, opening the way for still greater influence—although complaints against the judiciary on electoral matters remained off-limits. With reforms in place, Mexico's NHRI won full international accreditation after 1999. Its record of influence since then is mentioned in Chapter 10. Mexico's NHRI reflects a body created by a state that had accepted international human rights commitments, largely to appease international critics. Absent a regulatory moment, the commission was quite weak and was strengthened only gradually, especially as domestic political circumstances changed.

Violence in Peace: El Salvador and Colombia

After Mexico, the first NHRIs of the decade were created in El Salvador and Colombia, on the eve of the Paris Principles. Both of these institutions were established during regulatory moments: a peace accord in El Salvador and a new constitution in Colombia. Given that both states had already ratified international human rights agreements, the incentives to create NHRIs were quite strong. Since violent conflicts entail, almost by definition, human rights abuses, it is unsurprising that among the themes addressed during El Salvador's peace negotiations and in the course of constitution making in Colombia were human rights and accountability. In both El Salvador and Colombia, moreover, hybrid institutions, or human rights ombudsmen, were created, following the Spanish model rather than the "commissions" model adopted in Mexico. While international actors were important in both cases, one development that differentiated these institutions from others resulting from peace agreements or during conflict was that these NHRIs were run by locals, not temporarily staffed by international actors.

El Salvador's Procuraduría para la Defensa de los Derechos Humanos adopted a similar name to its counterpart in Guatemala, and it was created by a constitutional amendment in 1991 and legislation in 1992.[10] The ombudsman-like figure nonetheless had a long history in the country, traceable to a spokesperson for the poor in the nineteenth century.[11] In the actual peace accords, the human rights ombudsman's role was included under "judicial reform," and the institution itself was placed in the Justice Department (Ministério Público).[12] Both ONUSAL's Human Rights Division and the UNDP were significant in supporting the Procuraduría's creation, offering technical and financial assistance. Though the institution was assigned a broad mandate, it also had structural weaknesses and lacked autonomy, as manifest in the executive's control over funding. Some of these weaknesses, of course, reflected the inevitable political compromises associated with peace negotiations.

Despite these problems, the NHRI took a more activist role with the election of a new ombudsman in 1995. Victoria Velásquez de Avilés elevated the profile of human rights complaints, issued reports accusing state officials of human rights crimes, brought cases to the Inter-American Court of Human Rights, and established strong ties with human rights groups.[13] Much to the surprise of the governing party, public acceptance of the ombudsman rose substantially, outstripping the reputation of traditional bodies like the courts in public opinion polls.[14] This all may have proved too threatening, and the ombudsman herself began receiving serious threats, a pattern of violence that would persist for years.

When the ombudsman's term expired in 1998, the election for the post turned into what has been described as "a deliberate move to wreck the institution."[15] The controversial election of Eduardo Peñate Polanco fulfilled the ruling party's agenda, as the new ombudsman quickly tried to remove staff and dismantle institutional initiatives. Charges of misusing Swedish funds eventually led to his removal. The period between 1998 and 2001 was therefore one of institutional crisis, as the ombudsman lost its credibility and foreign funding was withdrawn.

The election of yet another ombudsperson in 2001 opened a semblance of stability; and in 2006, the institution was internationally accredited.[16] Despite this international stamp of approval, the institution continues to be threatened. For example, in 2010, Ombudsman Oscar Luna received a series of death threats for challenging the government's *mano dura* (i.e., iron fist) approach to fighting crime. Even as the domestic context has shifted in the past twenty years, then, partisan players constrain the institution: whether by restricting funds, using the appointments process to undermine the institution, or violently threatening the institution's staff. International actors have not always been able to shield the institution, including during the institution's 1998–2001 crisis; but pressures associated with accreditation in more recent years could lend the ombudsman some legitimacy and help empower it. The overwhelming incentives that were present in the early 1990s led to a strong institutional design, but broader domestic divisions over accountability—in a country whose truth commission's recommendations were met by a general amnesty and dismally implemented—ultimately shackled the ombudsman.

Like El Salvador, Colombia faced strong incentives to create an NHRI during this period, including a regulatory moment, external obligations, and high levels of organized abuse. Colombia's Defensoría del Pueblo, also created in 1991, was included in the country's new constitution and in legislation, apparently after "careful study of the Spanish *Defensoría*."[17] A presidential human rights adviser, a cabinet-level post created in 1987, had paved the way for the NHRI; and local ombudsmen (*personeros*) at the municipal level also began acquiring human rights mandates.[18] In fact, in response to rising transnational pressures, the Colombian state proceeded to create a series of overlapping and redundant state human rights agencies, intended mostly to appease and co-opt critics: in addition to the Defensoría, human rights units were established in the Interior Ministry, Foreign Ministry, Ministry of Defense, Fiscalía, and Procuraduría.[19] By 1994, a National Human Rights Network was even envisaged to coordinate all these various bodies; though despite millions of dollars in funding from the Dutch government, the network never became operational.[20] Today human rights policies are coordinated by the Human Rights Observatory, an office run out of the vice presidency.[21]

The state's institutionalization of human rights appeared to be in many ways strategic. One facet of the Colombian government's insertion into the business of human rights was that it attempted to shift rhetorical responsibility for abuse to nonstate guerrillas, substituting an "official bureaucratic human rights narrative," delinking paramilitary groups from the state.[22] Interestingly, the array of official human rights bodies proliferated even within the military. Faced with accusations of military involvement in human rights abuses, Winifred Tate observes that "over the course of the 1990s the Colombian military established a network of human rights institutions in order to influence the human rights debates at home and abroad."[23] As evidence of the vacuity of government rhetoric, human rights state agencies remain "chronically underfunded" and marked by significant state interference. In 1997, for example, the ombudsman apparently requested a $6 million budget but was given $400,000.[24] On a deeper, more problematic level, the creation of state human rights bodies detracted from the traditional work of human rights NGOs: "[T]hese agencies demonstrate an area where state functions are expanded, albeit often in contradictory ways. Through the appropriation of human rights education and documentation efforts that had previously been conducted by NGOs, these new institutions involved the conspicuous redeployment of the state as able to police its own efforts to implement a broad range of citizen rights."[25]

Even if it has been deployed strategically by the state, its autonomy hampered and staff threatened, Colombia's NHRI has been fully accredited internationally since 2001. The NHRI was created in the context of a regulatory moment by a state that had acceded to human rights treaties but was also embroiled in high levels of abuse and therefore subject to strong transnational influence. The Colombian state responded by creating and adapting multiple overlapping institutions. Obvious as the inefficiencies were to most participants and onlookers, different governments still opted for this strategy of institutionalizing human rights. Appropriating human rights discourse and information was an astute means of stealing the thunder from (and in some cases foreign funding of) human rights NGOs. The goal was to control human rights debates, minimizing the consequences of its own actions in a violent armed conflict.

Honduras's About-Face

Honduras followed suit and created an NHRI in 1992. The creation of an NHRI in Honduras served initially as somewhat of a substitute for a traditional truth commission. Though the country had embarked on a political transition ten years earlier, it was not until the end of the Cold War (and rising pressure from the United States, alongside declining military assistance and ongoing violations) that human rights became a prominent demand. At the forefront of this pressure, at least symbolically, were unprecedented rulings by the Inter-American Court of Human Rights in the *Velásquez-Rodríguez* case in 1988 and 1989, which found the Honduran government responsible for forced disappearances and demanded compensation for victims. Then, on the eve of the NHRI's formation in 1992, an Amnesty International report was released, titled "Honduras: Persistence of Human Rights Violations," followed a few months later by " 'Disappearances' in Honduras: A Well of Silence and Inefficiency."

The commission was established by presidential decree in 1992 (as the Comisionado Nacional de Protección de los Derechos Humanos, or Office of the National Commissioner for the Protection of Human Rights), attached to the president's office. In 1995, it became operational and was incorporated into the constitution via amendment; its name was then changed to Comisionado Nacional de Derechos Humanos (CONADEH). Yet the institution had somewhat earlier origins, dating to the Esquipulas Peace Accords that called for the creation of National Reconciliation Commissions (CNR). The CNR, formed in 1987, had recommended establishing a Commission to Modernize the State, which the government adopted in 1990. That commission, in turn, encouraged the president to create a commissioner for human rights, or ombudsman.[26] No wonder that the 1992 decree setting up CONADEH called for close collaboration between the human rights ombudsman and the CNR.

The first ten years of the CONADEH's life were quite promising. The commissioner was given broad competence, including in nontraditional areas like domestic violence, and authorized to demand compliance from the military and to compel confidential information. In a sense, the commission was part of an ongoing attempt to consolidate democracy while simultaneously demilitarizing the state. Even if resources and capabilities were never adequately matched to meet the mandate's ambitious breadth, the institution gained a great deal of credibility, due in large part to the first commissioner, Dr. Leo Valladares Lanza. Valladares had founded a human rights NGO in 1991 and had served two five-year terms. He proved a capable leader, immediately raising the NHRI's profile by addressing the problem of disappearances that had plagued the country in the 1980s and issuing what was described as an "electrifying report" on the topic. He followed up with specific cases and continued pressuring the government on several fronts. For example, another powerful report in April 2000, this one focusing on the politicized nature of the judiciary, led the U.S. Agency for International Development (USAID) to make its funding contingent on judicial reform. And following Hurricane Mitch's devastation in 1999, Valladares moved to document corruption involving international relief aid. Honduras's Congress attempted to retaliate by curtailing the NHRI's powers and removing its head, but it backed off in the aftermath of an intense transnational reaction.[27] And in 2000, CONADEH was internationally accredited as a fully compliant NHRI.

How this institution, which for years was deemed one of the region's strongest, was so compromised after the 2009 coup is a puzzling story intimately tied up in its leader. Ramón Custodio López, a medical doctor who founded in 1981 one of the country's most well-regarded human rights organizations, was elected head of the Comisionado in 2002 to replace Valladares. For most of his tenure, he headed the institution ably, assuming a leadership role among Central American NHRIs and overseeing the commission's reaccreditation in 2007. All of this changed with the coup on June 28, 2009. In a volte-face that made NGOs claim deep betrayal, Custodio López sided openly and unabashedly with the military regime, so much so that his entry into the United States was blocked and the Inter-American Commission on Human Rights singled him out in their report following their visit: "The Commission is concerned by the news regarding the role played by National Commissioner of Human Rights, Ramón Custodio López. By denying the existence of the *coup d'état* he prevented the inhabitants of Honduras from gaining access to an independent mechanism for the protection of their human rights."[28] This presidential hopeful, who had stood on the side of common people against a repressive state, now underwent what one critic referred to as a "Kafkaesque metamorphosis."[29] When the country's NHRI was reviewed for international reaccreditation in 2010, the ICC recommended downgrading the institution to B status. Most of the criticisms revolved around the institution's *actions* rather than design.

The Honduran commission's trajectory offers important insights into the role of leadership in state accountability institutions. The institution was originally created in response to transnational pressure, by a country that had willingly accepted human rights treaty obligations and yet was engaged in human rights abuse. The idea itself arose out of two existing ad hoc bodies (the National Reconciliation Commission and the Commission to Modernize the State) set up to address accountability and state building, themselves borrowing from the regional and international contexts. Reflecting these external influences, the commission was initially created by decree and then strengthened. Like other NHRIs in the region, its broad mandate outstripped its capacity; but activist, credible leadership in the person of the ombudsman ensured the institution thrived despite insufficient resources. And in 1999, transnational pressure effectively prevented a retaliatory congress from undermining the institution. The turnaround in 2009 is perhaps as surprising as the coup itself, but it does reveal the extent to which monocratic NHRIs can depend not just on the broader domestic political context but also on the leader to make or break the institution. Of course, the story is far from over, and the Honduran commission's future is bound up in the country's political course, including its foreign relations, and ongoing international regime pressures to retool what was once one of the region's strongest NHRIs.

Perverse Incentives in Costa Rica and Paraguay

Proposals for creating a state human rights agency in Costa Rica had been floated about since the late 1970s, perhaps not surprising given Costa Rica's standing as the first country in the world to accede to both international human rights covenants. A Defender of Human Rights had been proposed in 1979, while an Office for the Defense of Human Rights was discussed in 1982. An ombudsman for children (Defensoría de la Infancia) was created in 1987—second in the world, after Norway's—and one for women (Defensoría de la Mujer) in 1990 under the Justice Ministry; both were absorbed into the country's NHRI three years later.[30] But the NHRI itself—La Defensoría de los Habitantes—was not created until 1992; once it was, it was designed weakly, figuring as one of the only institutions in the region without constitutional standing.[31] As a global human rights advocate, Costa Rica moved to create an NHRI, but a weak set of incentives (i.e., no regulatory moment or organized abuse) led to a largely promotive body.

Paraguay in 1992 also included a Defensoría del Pueblo in its constitution, though the NHRI itself did not become operational until 2002.[32] The official reason given for the delay is that the institution faced crippling funding challenges from the outset, but the political context cannot be ignored. The country's democratic transition began after General Alfredo Stroessner's overthrow in 1989;

and given the timing of its constitution (in 1990), it is unsurprising that the document included a human rights ombudsman, albeit one claiming connections to colonial-era institutions.[33] The broader transition itself was marked by political infighting, largely revolving around the process of human rights accountability. Partisan conflicts were so intense that political leaders were unable to agree to a truth commission until 2003.

In the case of Paraguay's ombudsman, the Inter-American Commission on Human Rights (IACHR) seems to have played a crucial role. In its 1998 country report and in a subsequent press communiqué in mid-1999, it called on Paraguay's government to fulfill its constitutional mandate to establish the office of the ombudsman, deemed crucial for the protection of human rights. Paraguay's permanent minister to the OAS responded in March 2000, ensuring that the Senate had sent a slate of candidates and a decision was pending before the Chamber of Deputies. The IACHR's report on Paraguay in March 2001 referenced these full exchanges and called "urgently and immediately" for appointing an ombudsman, which the government finally did in October.[34] By 2003, five years after the initial IACHR report, the institution was fully accredited internationally.

Paraguay's NHRI signals an institution that was formally created on paper during a regulatory moment because it was "the thing to do." However, deep political and social divisions precluded broader efforts to address human rights accountability, including the formation of a truth commission—commonly adopted throughout the region during this period. The relatively low level of human rights abuses and a moderately weak rule of law system meant that the country did not face strong pressures for implementing the human rights agreements it had accepted. Including the institution in the constitution nonetheless proved essential, as the IACHR was then able to apply pressure for ongoing institution building.

Path Dependence after Transitions: Argentina and Peru

Despite very different human rights conditions in Argentina and Peru, regulatory moments led to creating relatively strong NHRIs. The creation of the Defensoría del Pueblo de la Nación Argentína was set by decree in 1993 and then included in the amended constitution of 1994, a period of relatively minor violations.[35] Though constitutional revisions were negotiated between the governing party and the opposition, the country had embarked on a democratic transition a decade earlier.[36] The amended constitution in 1994 was important in elevating the standing of human rights and creating new accountability mechanisms like the ombudsman and an anticorruption office. The period also corresponded to what Enrique Peruzzotti describes as a "new civic sensibility" revolving around social accountability. The Defensoría, according to Peruzzotti, marks a new type of initiative, calling for cooperation by both civil society and state agencies—combining vertical and horizontal accountability.[37] It has been internationally accredited since 1999.

Pressure to create an NHRI in Argentina dated to the transition itself, though the idea did not take off until the constitutional revisions of the early 1990s. The Defensoría had its origins in a proposal by two senators in 1984, just as the national institution was preceded by local human rights ombudsmen formed after 1986.[38] The national institution created in 1993, though solidly designed, was also constrained in important ways; for example, the NHRI was forbidden from addressing issues concerning defense and national security. And to a greater extent than other NHRIs in the region, the majority of complaints have concerned public administrative issues relating to economic and social rights.

In fact, Argentina's NHRI sets an important marker as an NHRI focusing largely on economic and social rights, even though it also addressed more traditional concerns like prison conditions. As former defensor Jorge Luis Maiorano explains the broader historical context, the institution of the ombudsman arose in Latin America at the same time as the "entrepreneurial state" was in decline.[39] Had Argentina's ombudsman been created in the 1980s, as originally envisioned by a few senators, its activities surely would have revolved around accountability for human rights abuses. In the 1980s in Argentina, human rights concerns revolved centrally around the democratic transition itself, including the truth commission established in 1984 and the harsh reality of an amnesty declared in 1986. Carlos Menem's presidency in the 1990s was in turn dominated by economic liberalization, from privatization and deregulation to decentralization. Against this socioeconomic backdrop, the constitutional amendments of 1994 represented an agreement to enhance rights protections via institutions like the ombudsman. The opposition was looking to check the government, while the government was willing to have a rights-protective democratic stamp of approval before international financial audiences.

The first ombudsman thus viewed the institution's role as one of *transforming* the state, in much the same way as economic and social rights are assumed to require progressive realization. This was a different kind of NHRI in the sense that the institution could do things like mediate between individual consumers and firms, shifting markedly the terms of the human rights debate and the state's role in it.[40] The shift is typically portrayed as a positive move, away from traditional individual rights to collective second-generation rights. What remains unclear is whether the shift has masked ongoing problems of human rights impunity—or whether for the state apparatus, defining human rights in economic-social terms seems relatively innocuous compared to more traditional denunciations.

Though Peru's democratic opening began in the late 1970s, it did not establish its NHRI until 1993, in the context of ongoing armed conflict. The institution was created as part of a process of constitutional overhaul, with a new national constitution drafted in 1993 after President Alberto Fujimori dissolved the Peruvian Congress and a crisis ensued. The incentives were therefore high: Peru was undergoing a regulatory moment, had ratified international human rights agreements, and was engaged in serious rights violations. The timing also made it quite likely that a new constitution would include the ombudsman, a period when the institution was diffusing throughout the region. The 1993 constitution was especially noteworthy for its contradictions, setting back the place of human rights in some respects while institutionalizing human rights in the Defensoría. Though the hybrid ombudsman was given broad powers, the first defensor was not appointed until 1996.[41]

Despite its origins in a constitutional crisis and armed conflict, the Peruvian Defensoría del Pueblo in the end proved quite strong. It managed to challenge the regime and withstand budgetary problems and other threats, often relying on "the shield of international support," as a former ombudsman referred to it, to protect the institution from state recrimination.[42] In opinion surveys, the NHRI has been placed at the top of the list in terms of generating public confidence.[43] While complaints have spanned the full range of rights abuses, most have concerned social welfare claims.[44] And given both its design and functioning, the institution has enjoyed a strong reputation and been fully accredited internationally since 1999. The NHRI even outlasted the Fujimori regime and proved influential in the subsequent transition in 2000–2001. One commentator notes, "Having thus grown strong during Fujimori's decline, the institution today appears to hold a solid political position not only in public life in general, but also with regard to the respect that it commands from other state institutions."[45]

According to Charles Kenney, Peru's ombudsman was "an island in a truncated network of horizontal accountability."[46] This meant that, in the end, it was still the attorney general's office and the judiciary that had the power to investigate and act on the ombudsman's findings and recommendations; and often they did not do so. Still, Peru's Defensoría confirms once again that an institution created during a period of overwhelming incentives can be designed strongly, since the government must appease critics and do so convincingly. Once created, if the institution fulfills its mandate, international actors can protect it from state incursions, setting in motion a self-reinforcing logic and leading to an even stronger institution over time.

Caribbean NHRIs

The small states of Antigua and Barbuda as well as Belize created traditional ombudsman offices in 1994, just after the World Conference on Human Rights in Vienna and the enactment of the Paris Principles. Antigua and Barbuda's institution dated to the 1981 constitution, which coincided with the Commonwealth country's formal independence from Britain, though implementing legislation was not passed until 1994 and the first ombudsman was not appointed until 1995, following a crucial transfer of power.[47] While this Caribbean Commonwealth member's institution was part of the drafting of a new constitution, and despite the fact that several international actors attempted to strengthen the NHRI over time, the Office of the Ombudsman has remained quite weak. Recommendations to create a hybrid institution, with an explicit human rights mandate—have also been disregarded.[48] This was raised, for example, during a workshop in 1998, jointly hosted by Antigua's ombudsman and the Commonwealth on human rights institutions in the Caribbean. The institution's weaknesses have proven overwhelming; and in 2001, the ombudsman was found noncompliant with international standards and designated a C-status institution. International calls for creating a fully functioning NHRI (including from CERD in 2007) have continued over the years, to no avail.[49]

A regulatory moment combined with international regime pressures proved insufficient for creating a strong accountability mechanism in Antigua and Barbuda. Limited resources and a political regime dominated by a single political party/family rife with corruption scandals, denoted by one scholar a liberal autocracy, impeded the institution's functioning. The ombudsman did not begin operating until after the 1994 election, when power was transferred and international pressures mounted to create accountability mechanisms and strengthen democratic governance.[50] Other factors during this period may have weighed in the decision to build democratic institutions, including the country's attempt to diversify its tourism industry by creating a free-trade zone as well as fears of political unrest in nearby Haiti. The ongoing failure to strengthen the institution, however, is wrapped in broader political and economic constraints. With persistent pressures from treaty bodies, as well as the Human Rights Council and ICC, the institution may evolve, though no less dependent on the domestic political context.

Belize's Parliamentary Commissioner, or office of the ombudsman, has also proved exceedingly weak; and the government has never applied for NHRI accreditation. Though Belize gained independence in 1981 and drafted a constitution that year, the Central American country's founding document did not include an ombudsman. Rather, the institution was created by law in 1994, the same year that British troops withdrew formally from the country and only three years after becoming a member of the OAS. Even so, the ombudsman did not begin functioning until 1999. While the more immediate impetus was a Commonwealth Secretariat Advisory Mission, the delay is not inconsistent with Belize's overall stance toward international human rights law: unlike most of its peers in the region, Belize has not signed the American Convention on Human Rights; and it was a relative latecomer to major international human rights agreements, not acceding to the ICCPR until 1996.[51] Despite being given relatively broad powers, including an anticorruption function, the institution does not have a human rights mandate, and it has been poorly funded. International actors, including the Commonwealth, CRC, and Human Rights Council have called for creating an NHRI from scratch, rather than strengthening the Parliamentary Commissioner.[52]

Belize represents the curious case of a state with very few incentives to create an NHRI, other than international regime pressures. Its small size and serious border dispute with Guatemala have constrained it in important ways; and while the country is formally a democracy, the rule of law remains weak in a context of serious poverty. State excuses for the ombudsman's weaknesses all point to resource issues, but some analysts have pointed out that political will is perhaps even more significant. Local critics have called the institution "a political gambit and rear guard action by political parties to defend their turf against complaints from citizens."[53] In recent years, government voices (including the ombudsman who took office in 2009) have assured that the country will cooperate with the OHCHR to create an internationally compliant NHRI. Now that the country has acceded to some international human rights agreements, and international regime pressures are on the rise, the structure of incentives may begin to shift.

Bolivian Contradictions

The Bolivian state created its NHRI in 1994, following a broad democratization agenda that promoted the notion of accountability bodies, including constitutional courts and hybrid ombudsmen. These reforms, significantly, went hand in hand with the adoption of neoliberal economic measures and (foreign-sponsored) militarized opposition to coca producers. Rising regional and global diffusion reinforced the appeal of a defensoría per se, as did a new government in 1997 looking to break from the past and move forward with nominal reforms; but the broader impetus was a regulatory moment framed in terms of democratization, neoliberalism, and human rights.

Indeed, Bolivia's Defensoría del Pueblo is a hybrid NHRI formed in the midst of constitutional reform, human rights obligations, and a climate of minor violations. Included in the constitutional reforms of 1994, under the rubric of institutions "defending society," implementing legislation was passed in 1997 and the body began functioning in 1998. Even with a dramatic new constitution in 2009, which had been a key project for Evo Morales since becoming president in 2005, the institution was retained. Since 2000, moreover, it has been fully accredited internationally, and it is widely considered one of the region's strongest NHRIs.[54]

The appointment of a well-regarded human rights activist proved crucial in the NHRI's development. Under the leadership of Ana María Romero, the Defensoría was active in mediating sociopolitical conflicts, challenging the government forcefully when necessary, as well as collaborating with the country's leading NGOs, especially after political protests rocked Bolivia after 2000, in response to the unequal effects of economic liberalization. All told, the ombudsman rose through the ranks of national institutions to become one of the country's most prominent political actors.

The ombudsman's prominence and strength, however, should not be mistaken for a simple convergence of interests. When it came time to elect the first ombudswoman's predecessor, partisan infighting nearly derailed the process. And it is noteworthy that a large volume of the institution's financial support comes from foreign sources, amounting during certain periods to half of the Defensoría's budget. International actors themselves no doubt have had mixed goals; in addition to strengthening an NHRI, there has been some interest in using accountability mechanisms to channel social discontent—off the streets and into institutionalized forums—thereby ensuring desired stability.

If in the 1990s, the Bolivian government moved to deepen the democratization project begun in the 1980s, after 2000 the contradictions inhering in that project were exposed to a society that included the region's largest indigenous population (over 50 percent of the overall population) and marked by the region's highest income inequality. It was perhaps inevitable that social actors would draw on human rights rhetoric to challenge a state that had embraced the same rhetoric.

As Mark Goodale has insightfully noted, both state and society adopted the discourse of human rights (and by extension, support for the country's NHRI), though for different reasons.[55] Human rights rhetoric and institutions were somewhat co-opted by the state, just as society was often implicated in the same contests for foreign funds. It is true that the rhetoric of human rights sometimes served broader, even global, interests that in principle were antithetical to human rights norms. But this merely meant that human rights became a touchstone of legitimacy, with neither state nor society having a monopoly over rights discourse.

In this complex field of mixed motives, overlapping identities, and institutionalized contradictions, Bolivia's NHRI has managed to carve out a valuable niche for itself. Some of this has to do with institutional origins: a move to localize authority during a regulatory moment, which led the government to appoint a credible first defensora who in turn served to reinforce the institution's standing. The country's potential volatility, especially its links to the global drug trade, and strong social activism led to an influx of foreign funds for democratic governance, including the popular ombudsman. And given the government's own transnational ties, it had to concede the institution's independence—though partisan debates in 2003 revealed an interest in potentially weakening the body. Regime change after 2005, despite involving seemingly dramatic state transformations, including a new constitution in 2009, did not threaten Bolivia's NHRI, which had already acquired substantial legitimacy and foreign backing. For a government claiming to be driven by historical inequality and the rights of indigenous, dehumanized people, the discourse of human rights could not be rejected—contradictions and all.

Defending Rights in Ecuador

Ecuador's Defensor del Pueblo arose out of constitutional reform initiatives undertaken in 1996. The human rights ombudsman was initially introduced as part of a constitutional reform package, which also established a Constitutional Court and followed a period of democratization begun in the 1980s. The ombudsman was given legal standing in 1997, and the office was later incorporated into both the 1998 and 2008 constitutions.[56] According to an institutional account of its own history, the example of existing NHRIs in Mexico and Argentina, two regional leaders, influenced the decision to establish a similar body in Ecuador.[57] That neighboring Andean countries (i.e., Colombia, Peru, and Bolivia) had already adopted the institution, in the broader context of regional diffusion and external treaty obligations, also may have factored into the decision.

Domestically, the constitutional reforms that led to the ombudsman occurred at a particular political juncture marked by high volatility.[58] Armed conflict along the border with Peru had just ended, political mobilization by indigenous groups was on the rise, and negotiations with international financial institutions continued in a context of extreme poverty and foreign debt. At the same time as social demands were increasing, access to justice remained limited, with an obvious need for alternative dispute resolution mechanisms.[59] As in Bolivia, creating a human rights ombudsman was part of a broader template, incorporating accountability mechanisms into democratic governance. For international funding agencies, the institution of the ombudsman and other accountability agencies were markers of democratic institution-building, channeling social discontent in ways that might enhance stability. That the 1996 constitutional reforms strengthened human rights protections on paper is therefore unsurprising, especially at a time when social demands for responsive governance were becoming more vocal—and potentially threatened a regime wanting to retain power.

Ecuador's Defensoría in the end survived the political volatility, including multiple presidencies in quick succession and sustained social protest. Yet the government's commitment to the institution was not unequivocal. The ambivalence of different governments toward general accountability was evident, for example, in the establishment of the truth and justice commission, which was not created until 1996 and disappeared when a new president came to power the following year. A new president in 1997 was pressured by international actors like Amnesty International to implement human rights protections and establish a National Plan of Action for Human Rights, as called for at the Vienna World Conference. When the first ombudsman was finally appointed, he ended up resigning after Congress withheld funds and arbitrarily limited his term in office.[60] Despite ongoing uncertainty, rhetorical support for human rights and the institutionalization of accountability continued apace. As the case of Ecuador shows, states operating on a world stage, generally tend to retain human rights institutions once these are created; governments assume they can control these bodies, just as they are aware of the potential political costs of dismantling them.

Internationally accredited since 1999, Ecuador's NHRI has a broad mandate though its structural position among other state institutions has shifted subtly over time. Reflecting the country's unique features, the ombudsman's mandate extends to private actors and the environment, and it includes a special unit devoted to indigenous rights.[61] In the new constitution of 2008, the ombudsman was linked to other accountability institutions, part of a set of "transparency and social control" functions; in contrast, the Procurador General, the Fiscal General, and the Constitutional Court were established as freestanding, independent bodies.[62]

Even with frequent changes in government and democracy strained, political leaders in Ecuador have sought periodically to limit but not eliminate the NHRI, especially by controlling its purse strings and the appointment process. Formed during a regulatory moment, Ecuador's NHRI was established long after the process of democratization had begun in the country. One of the things this meant is that, in terms of sheer volume, economic and social rights were abused most frequently. And these were violations for which responsibility could not be traced as readily and that, in any event, did not threaten key state actors like the security forces. In a region where impunity remains a dominant challenge, even accountability institutions with weak enforcement powers can prove a useful palliative in the face of ongoing criticism.

The Ombudsman in Democratic Panama

Panama's Defensoría, created in 1996, is most commonly portrayed as an initiative by a discredited executive, but broad evidence of social support for the institution dates to the early 1980s.[63] For example, citizen proposals for an ombudsman were made as part of the constitutional reform process begun in 1983. The executive itself first proposed the institution in 1991, in the context of dozens of constitutional amendments, with the purported goal of promoting democratic institutions. The fact that neighboring Colombia also created an NHRI that year may also have influenced Panama. Yet despite having been a civil-society initiative in 1992, the majority of Panamanian voters rejected the overall package of reform, which included dismantling the armed forces.[64] The vote may have reflected that the political opposition's call for a constituent assembly had gone unheeded, no less than rejection of a government essentially installed by the United States, after the latter invaded the strategically situated country in 1988. When constitutional reforms were approved in 1994, after the pivotal election of a new president, the ombudsman was not included in the constitution (though the armed forces were dissolved).[65] A few months later, a group of legislators influenced by the Panamanian Committee for Human Rights, an NGO formed in 1978, again proposed creating the institution.[66]

Building on these forces, in mid-1995, an ad hoc presidential committee was created to explore and promote the idea of an ombudsman in Panama, including preparing a draft law, with an eye to the country's democratic consolidation.[67] Various international actors shaped the process at different stages, from UNDP,

UNESCO, and the Inter-American Institute of Human Rights (IIDH), to the ombudsmen from Mexico, Argentina, Spain, and Central American countries that already had the institution. In addition, broad consultation took place with societal groups, including women and indigenous organizations and human rights NGOs, including in open meetings; if anything, the figure of the ombudsman appears to have been idealized in these settings. Spain's ombudsman at the time, Fernando Álvarez de Miranda, described it as an exemplary process of participatory democracy, to be modeled elsewhere in the world.[68] Likewise, the first inter-American course on ombudsmen and human rights, held in Costa Rica and attended by about one hundred staff from the region's ombudsmen, issued a resolution supporting the momentum gathering in Panama and calling for the speedy creation of the institution.[69]

Transnational pressures combined with the institution's inherent democratic appeal, convincing a president who claimed to support human rights; and at the end of 1996, a law was passed creating the ombudsman.[70] Though in principle it was intended to be "the critical conscience of the State," in practice the fact that the ombudsman was to be elected by the majority of the legislature undermined its legitimacy as an autonomous body in the eyes of some Panamanians, who viewed it as being politicized.[71] From the beginning, moreover, funding was an issue; in fact, initially the government did not even approve the budget required for the ombudsman to function. The FIO, which had also been created in 1996, had to visit Panamanian government officials and urge them to fund the institution.[72] Despite these setbacks, Panama's defensor was fully accredited internationally in 1999. And in a set of amendments in 2004, the institution was incorporated into the constitution, shortly before its international accreditation status was to be reevaluated.[73]

Diffusion in Nicaragua and Venezuela

Whereas many of the countries in the region that created an NHRI in the 1990s were not experiencing high levels of human rights abuse, Nicaragua and Venezuela were partial exceptions. Nicaragua's Procuraduría para la Defensa de los Derechos Humanos was created in 1995, in the context of constitutional reforms and transnational pressures, though the first ombudsman was not appointed until 1999.[74] While the institution fit broader processes of democratization and economic liberalization, begun in the postconflict period of the early 1990s, the role of international actors and commitments may have been paramount, especially talks held between Central American governments and the European Community.[75] As the institution portrays it, its creation occurred through the back door, as a "condition of international cooperation," rather than being driven by local demands.[76] Regional diffusion also played an important role. For example, in support of passing the 1995 bill, the IIDH visited the country, with a team that included the ombudsmen of Costa Rica, Guatemala, Mexico, and Argentina.

Buried in the history of NHRIs, however, is the fact that Nicaragua had created a National Commission for the Promotion and Protection of Human Rights as early as 1980.[77] It was created by the leftist Sandinista government, primarily in response to two developments. The first was the creation three years earlier of the Permanent Commission on Human Rights, a Nicaraguan NGO critical of the government (and apparently receiving funding from the U.S. government), which continues to exist. But the idea for the institution itself also emanated from evolving international standards about NHRIs. As the preamble to the decree creating the commission stated, it was a response to a set of UN resolutions in 1978 and 1979. While the commission operated under the Sandinista regime and was politicized, there is evidence that it attempted to exert its independence, cooperated with international bodies, and defended human rights.[78] In fact, in somewhat of a minor scandal in 1985, the institution's executive director, Mateo Guerrero Flores, defected and accused the government of controlling the body, charging the Interior Ministry with passing off reports as commission documents.[79]

The current ombudsman was itself accredited internationally in 2006, after surviving various crises of governance and strains on its resources. According to a revealing self-assessment, the ombudsman's international origins left the institution with a triple legacy that it was not entirely able to shake off. First, the institution found it difficult to connect to society, which remains largely unfamiliar with the institution. Second, given the politicized nature of society, the institution's monitoring of public administration is often confused with a general hostility toward the state. Third, state agents themselves are politicized and do not entirely understand the role of human rights in society. Despite these challenges, which explain why the ombudsman was not appointed until 1999 and why its budget was cut, the institution has been able to carve out "spaces of recognition" for itself.[80]

Venezuela's Defensoría del Pueblo was created in 1999, at the same time as a new constitution was enacted and following the election of Hugo Chávez as president in 1998. The new constitution was portrayed as a deep transformation of the state, one in which human rights (especially the rights of women and indigenous people) would be highlighted.[81] The human rights ombudsman, placed within the "citizen" branch of government, was to support good governance and implement human rights standards.[82]

Less attention has been paid to the fact that President Rafael Caldera had already created by decree a National Human Rights Commission in 1996, amended in 1998.[83] Part of the impetus may have been transnational criticism of the regime's human rights practices, including a 1996 report by Human Rights Watch labeling the country's prison systems one of the worst in the hemisphere. The human rights commission, whose name clearly resembled that of Mexico's, was intended to establish links with NGOs. In fact, a large meeting organized by the commission with NGO representatives in mid-1997, which Caldera had denoted the "Year of Human Rights," led to the country's National Human Rights Action Plan.

A regulatory moment, opened by the election of a new leader in 1998, pushed the country toward more dramatic institutional overhaul. The creation of the ombudsman fit with a rhetorical embrace of rights; but it also reflected a process of (sub)regional diffusion. According to the institution, the name of Defensoría is not an accident; it reflects a common link with other Andean countries, which seek to *defend* citizens against the abuses of the state and protect human rights.[84] In this sense, the shift from Caldera's commission model to the ombudsman reflected regional realignment, turning toward its culturally proximate Andean neighbors, even while the institution (like other ombudsmen in the region) also traces its lineage to the 1809 Swedish ombudsman and the European context. Formally, the ombudsman met the criteria for international accreditation in 2002, though its budget remained linked to the executive and its efforts were still mostly promotive.

Regional Latecomers

The new millennium saw NHRIs created in a few states, with several other countries in the region either accepting recommendations or taking concrete steps to establish the institution. These states included Bermuda, Chile, Brazil, Uruguay, and a few Caribbean states. That these countries were all relative latecomers to the NHRI trend may seem surprising in some cases. But it really reflected particularities of time and place, or the strategic incentives that existed for creating an accountability mechanism. By 2010, the Americas was replete with NHRIs, accredited or not, with only a few pockets of resistance left on the continent.

Race and Colonialism in Bermuda

The only territory in the Americas that actually created an NHRI after 2000 was *Bermuda*. This member of the Commonwealth, and British overseas territory, followed the lead of other small states and established in 2001 an office of the

Ombudsman, part of broader constitutional reforms. The institution did not begin functioning until 2005, and it was not reviewed for international accreditation until 2012.[85]

Constitutional reforms in 2001 occurred during a dramatic political moment, as the Progressive Labour Party won national elections in 1998. It marked the first transfer of political power in the territory's history, ushering in what the party described as "A New Bermuda." At the heart of this transformation were questions of electoral reform and race, an effort to move away from a system that favored parishes with small, predominately white populations. The same constitutional reforms that minimized the role of race in the electoral system introduced the office of the ombudsman in 2001. That year also saw reform of the criminal code, following the 2000 abolition of the death penalty and of legalized corporal punishment. In general, the political transition of the late 1990s led to crucial political reforms and the adoption of international good-governance markers.[86]

Interestingly, the ombudsman was adopted even though a Human Rights Commission had existed since 1981 and been amended various times. The commission had been created to implement Bermuda's Human Rights Act of that year, replacing the Race Relations Act of 1969 and the Race Relations Commission of 1970 and described as "a milestone in the history of human rights legislation."[87] Both bodies had been established in response to racist incidents, including riots, and generalized social unrest. Despite the commission's existence, two factors may have shaped the decision to create an ombudsman in 2001. First, the human rights commission was viewed as an institution belonging to the past, and the new government may have wanted to mark the political transition with new institutional arrangements. Second, regional diffusion pressures from the Commonwealth and the Caribbean were quite strong during this period. Though two human rights institutions coexisted, the government opted to seek accreditation for the ombudsman.

The ombudsman's creation reflected a regulatory moment, itself the result of a more general political shift in governance. This political shift, along with the territory's connections to the British Commonwealth and a subregional network of ombudsman NHRIs, help to explain why an ombudsman (and not the more long-standing human rights commission) was designated an NHRI. If Bermuda's Human Rights Commission was a response to local race problems, the ombudsman was a complementary body meant to align the territory (some of whose politicians favored eventual independence from Britain) with global standards and the practices of cultural peers in the Caribbean. From the British perspective, an ombudsman matched the Commonwealth's historical preference for that office, whose traditional focus on maladministration may not have seemed as potentially destabilizing for its dependencies as the more contentious frame of human rights, with its inevitable linkages to self-determination claims.

The Chilean Puzzle

Despite long-standing calls for an ombudsman in Chile, the government was slow to meet these demands. A domestic campaign for a national ombudsman began as early as 1985, rooted in civil society and broader calls for democratization, but momentum rose only after 2000 and reached a high point with the country's UPR in 2009. Members of the Human Rights Council called on the government to speed up its efforts in establishing a fully compliant NHRI, a recommendation that the Chilean government formally accepted. The Instituto Nacional de Derechos Humanos was fully accredited in November 2012.

When the Chilean Chapter of the Ombudsman ("Ombudsman Chapter") was formed in 1985, it was in the context of calls for democratization. The chapter's origins were to be found in the Constitutional Studies Group, formed at the end of the 1970s by two dozen experts thinking ahead to what a democratic constitution might look like. After Pinochet pushed through his own constitution in 1980, the group became only more energized. And in the aftermath of social protests in the early 1980s, they began more fully imagining how governance institutions could protect human rights in a post-Pinochet era. In this context and given the rising popularity of the ombudsman in the region, a Chilean academic who had been part of the Group for Constitutional Studies promoted the idea of an ombudsman for Chile.[88] This is how the Ombudsman Chapter came to be formed in 1985; and although foreign observers have often mistaken it for an ombudsman, it is actually the local branch of the Latin American Ombudsman Institute. The Ombudsman Chapter had campaigned unsuccessfully for an ombudsman for at least twenty-five years, though mobilizing valuable support along the way.

In view of the inadequacies of the 1980 constitution for a democratic context, Chile underwent numerous constitutional reforms after Pinochet stepped down in 1989. As a result of the groundwork laid by the Ombudsman Chapter, an ombudsman institution was proposed at each of the various junctures throughout democratization. The Concertación, an important coalition of leftist parties, included the notion of an ombudsman in its platform in 1989; even Sweden's ombudsman visited Chile that year in solidarity. President Patricio Aylwin (who himself had been part of the Constitutional Studies Group) proposed a Defensor del Pueblo as part of the 1991 constitutional reforms, with the Ombudsman Chapter drafting the proposal. The Rettig Truth Commission that year also recommended that Chile have a national ombudsman. President Eduardo Frei later proposed in 1997 a Defensor del Usuario, and President Ricardo Lagos proposed in 2003 a Defensor del Ciudadano.[89] Despite the various names and proposed variants, recognition of the ombudsman's legitimacy as an institution was evident.

The political climate had indeed shifted after 2000, more open to notions of executive accountability. In mid-2000, for example, a set of constitutional reforms was introduced in the Senate, potentially providing for parliamentary oversight of the executive. The bill was debated for five years and finally passed in 2005, but it did not include an ombudsman. This is partly because President Lagos in the interim had created a Comisión Defensora Ciudadana in 2001, intended as a temporary pilot project. It nonetheless continued operating out of the executive, essentially substituting for an ombudsman. Significantly, this was also a period of renewed pressures for human rights accountability, including the Santiago Court of Appeal's decision to strip Pinochet of his immunity and a 1,200-page report issued by the National Commission on Political Imprisonment and Torture in 2005. With these important steps, Chile's democracy at last appeared to be consolidating more fully as members of the military regime were formally discredited.[90]

Progress seemed imminent when a law for a National Human Rights Institute was introduced in Congress in mid-2005. UN treaty bodies and other actors (e.g., the Human Rights Committee, Committee on Economic, Social and Cultural Rights, CRC, and the special rapporteur on indigenous matters) were in fact calling on Chile during this period to establish an NHRI. And by the time of the UPR, the government asserted that it was "committed to the establishment of a national human rights institution, in line with the Paris Principles"; and it declared that both a bill for the national human rights institute and a proposal for an ombudsman via constitutional amendment were on the table. The bill creating the human rights institute took four years to approve, a few months after the country's UPR in 2009 (the Senate vote was divided, 16 in favor and 13 opposed). The institute, charged with promoting and protecting human rights, opened its doors in 2010, focusing largely on human rights education.[91] Its first head was Roberto Garretón, an internationally renowned human rights expert, who among other things had served as the OHCHR's Latin American representative.

The institute's establishment did not stop ongoing calls for the creation of an ombudsman, the most likely model for an NHRI given the regional context and long-standing social demands for the institution. When Chile's Ombudsman Chapter welcomed the institute's creation, it noted critically that it did not meet the Paris Principles.[92] In July 2010, the OHCHR's regional representative emphasized again the importance of creating the ombudsman. A group of senators issued a statement in March 2011, calling for the Human Rights Council's recommendations to be implemented, singling out the notion of an NHRI. A few months later, in August, a citizens forum was held, sponsored by the Ombudsman Chapter and Amnesty International in Chile, arguing for the need for an ombudsman—"now more than ever."[93] As close observers have noted, the problem with creating an ombudsman in Chile was partly that the national debate was forestalled and the issue was never categorized as urgent on the legislative agenda; political leaders, it seems, were either ignorant or fearful of the institution.

Official willingness to create a national NHRI in Chile has arisen mostly during regulatory moments, when broader constitutional revisions were on the agenda, and in the context of external treaty commitments. The key actors were from civil society, a local chapter of the regional ombudsman organization, motivated by constitution building for a democratic Chile, which in turn influenced the recommendations of the first truth commission and the willingness of various presidents under democratization to propose different versions of the body. These reforms, in turn, were constrained by the ongoing power of members of the former regime, who at last were somewhat discredited by the second (Valech) truth commission report and Pinochet's loss of legal immunity. The notion of an ombudsman in Chile has therefore gone hand in hand with domestic debates over human rights accountability—from the truth commission to the Pinochet case—which in turn have shaped constitutional reforms under democratization.

Unlike other countries in the region that have democratized, postdemocratic Chile inherited a constitution from the Pinochet era, itself created partly in response to transnational pressures. Its political transition was never marked by a clear regulatory break, explaining the piecemeal and sometimes contradictory nature of reforms. The creation by executive decree of a temporary ombudsman in 2001 served as an institutional substitute, though also potentially as a precursor to a congressionally mandated, independent body. A transnational campaign for creating an ombudsman and NHRI, capitalizing on international regime pressures, including the UPR, pushed for the body's creation. In general, the seemingly puzzling delay in creating an accountability mechanism in Chile is perhaps best explained by the fact that strategic incentives predated the transition to democracy: the constitution is from 1980, Chile ratified the major human rights treaties in the 1970s, and organized abuse has been low under democracy. Yet when the idea was first introduced in the 1980s, international diffusion was also far weaker. The question remains of whether institutional substitutes (the ad hoc commission as much as the more recent institute) sometimes contribute to delays in reform, undermining a sense of urgency or perceived need. Constitutional reforms and civil society pressures have been insufficient to counter political indifference and fear; but broad progress on human rights accountability combined with international regime pressures moved this holdout state in Latin America to create at long last an accredited NHRI.

Delayed Convergence in Brazil

Human rights institutionalization in *Brazil* took off in the mid-1990s, though an official body devoted to protecting the rights of the person had existed since the 1960s. Human rights issues gained prominence on the state's agenda in the context of democratization and civil society activism, as well as the state's related interest in playing an international role in multilateral forums. Like other cases where the appearance of an NHRI has been delayed, the relative absence of strategic incentives impeded the formation of an NHRI.

Strategic incentives for creating an accountability institution can be traced to the 1985 transition, marking the end of over twenty years of military rule. The country's constitution dates to 1988, though it has been amended numerous times, while the major human rights treaties were accepted in 1992. Though a relatively high level of human rights abuses existed even under democracy, the federal country's large size (and the regime's own efforts to counter the image of an abusive state) meant that transnational pressure remained disproportionately low during the early transition period.

One long-standing institution, labeled by some local experts as the country's first NHRI, played a significant if overlooked role in contemporary debates about creating an NHRI. In 1964, fifteen days before the country's infamous coup, the Conselho de Defesa dos Direitos da Pessoa Humana (CDDPH, or Council for the Protection of the Rights of the Person) was created by legislation, placed within the Ministry of Justice. The institution has survived into the present, with some of its members raising human rights concerns both during various phases of military and democratic rule; half of its members are from civil society and half from the state. The idea for the council had been Olavo Bilac Pinto's, a lawyer and member of congress, who introduced it in 1956. A member of the opposition National Democratic Union, Bilac Pinto was apparently inspired by resistance to the Getúlio Vargas dictatorship and sought to ensure that opposition legislators and civil society enjoyed representation on an official body; his hope was that it would always be possible to denounce political persecution.[94]

Despite ongoing representation on the Rights Council, civil society itself was not especially active on the human rights front until the later years of the dictatorship. An important group, the Human Rights Movement, formed in 1982, but it was not until the early 1990s that civil society activism around human rights took flight. On the one hand, Brazil's government was keen to improve its international human rights image, more specifically to convert domestic progress regarding democratization and human rights into international social capital. In the lead-up to the Vienna World Conference in 1994, for example, an unprecedented meeting took place between the state and civil society, opening space for cooperation and a more unified platform. One of the things proposed precisely at that meeting was reform of the CDDPH.[95]

Human rights institutionalization continued for the next decade and a half. For instance, it was during this period that Brazil's House of Representatives formed a Commission on Human Rights and Minorities in 1995, and the Department of Human Rights and Social Issues was also created that year within the Foreign Affairs Ministry. That was also the year that the government established the Special Commission of the Political Dead and Disappeared, though the commission's report was not released for over a decade.[96] The government launched in 1996 the first National Human Rights Program, a multiyear initiative in consultation with civil society. Impressively, it completed in 1996 a National Action Plan for Human Rights, the first in Latin America and third in the world.[97] In 1998, Brazil even accepted the American Court of Human Rights' jurisdiction.

Similar developments continued after 2000. By 2003, the president's office decided to create a Human Rights Secretariat, along with two other offices devoted respectively to racial equality and women's issues. At the ninth National Human Rights Conference in 2004, participants voted to reform the CDDPH and convert it into a National Human Rights Council, submitting draft legislation to that effect. And in 2005, the Senate took steps to establish a human rights committee.[98] On the international front, the CRC and the special rapporteur on racism and xenophobia called on Brazil to create an NHRI.[99] No wonder that by the time of the country's UPR in 2008, the government was prepared to accept recommendations that it establish an NHRI. A second national action plan for human rights in 2009 also called for the creation of a statutory national human rights commission in compliance with the Paris Principles.[100] The recommendation was framed in terms of the need to strengthen relations between the state and civil society, especially through participation and dialogue, and social control. However, when the second UPR cycle occurred in 2011, as relevant stakeholders noted, an NHRI still had not been established.[101]

The Brazilian state's embrace of human rights institutions in the mid-1990s, from treaties to a series of governmental bodies, reflected an attempt to improve the country's international image and a response to rising civil society activism on behalf of human rights. The country's 1988 constitution predated these developments, while an interest in implementing treaty obligations was mediated by a moderately weak rule of law. The argument that federalism may have made establishing a national human rights body more challenging is certainly plausible, though other large federal states have had long-standing NHRIs.[102] Even in Brazil, some states have formed human rights commissions, including São Paulo and Paraíba, while offices of the ombudsman are present in several state governments.[103] It is likewise true that despite formal institutional advances, the gap between international pronouncements and domestic practices continued to be large for a state that is a font of contradictions: among the wealthiest and most unequal countries in the world, with entrenched problems of racism, land conflicts, and indigenous claims. But the impact of violations, too, was mediated by the country's size and international power, resulting in modest transnational pressures.

The idea of an NHRI in Brazil did not pick up steam until after 2000, building on rising human rights activism and institutionalization in the latter part of the 1990s. The role of the longstanding CDDPH, a human rights body dating to the 1960s, was essential, as civil society called for necessary reforms of this body, which served as a kind of institutional precedent even though it did not conform to the Paris Principles. When the government agreed to create an NHRI in 2008, including it in its new national human rights action plan one year later, it was largely the result of accumulating international regime pressures by the United Nations with important allies from domestic civil society. Regulatory moments, external obligations, and organized abuse all existed in Brazil for years, but diffusion mechanisms themselves remained weak. Only when international regime pressures rose did Brazil formally accept establishing an NHRI, just as it agreed to confront past issues of human rights accountability.

Top-Down Institution Building in Uruguay

Like Chile and Brazil, Uruguay was one of the last governments in Latin America to agree to create an NHRI. Viewed in isolation, this may seem surprising, given the country's relatively strong human rights record since its transition to democratic rule in 1985. But the structural conditions for creating a human rights accountability agency were not strong until after 2005. For one thing, since the country's democratic transition, Uruguay had maintained a strong human rights record, subjecting it to almost no transnational pressure. While Uruguay had ratified the human rights covenants in 1976, norm-diffusing conditions were not strong until human rights issues themselves became institutionalized at the sub-regional level in Mercosur. The establishment of an NHRI in Uruguay has therefore reflected a combination of external obligations and international regime pressures, in what has been mostly a case of institutional creation from above.

Regulatory moments in Uruguay were virtually absent under democracy. With the 1967 constitution still in place, there was little constitutional revision.[104] A new government in 2005 even strengthened the power of the presidency. And while a truth commission operated between 2000 and 2002, seemingly challenging the iron hold of a 1989 amnesty, its mandate was focused only on disappearances. Likewise, during the first phase of democratization, domestic norm promoters remained weak. Unlike in neighboring states, such a high proportion of the population had been imprisoned during the dictatorship that social organizations only formed in the very last years of the regime. Yet even during this early period, the CRC had called on Uruguay's government in 1996 to create an NHRI, an act invoked a decade later as evidence of longstanding support for a national human rights body.[105]

Things began shifting only after 2005, when a new government committed to human rights took office and Mercosur's human rights focus also grew. With the election of a new government embracing both social justice reforms and foreign investment, human rights was deemed a priority. In 2005, for example, a Human Rights Unit was created within the Ministry of Education and Culture, elevated to a department in 2006. The Asunción Protocol of 2005 also institutionalized the commitment of Mercosur's member states to promoting and protecting human rights. The creation of a subregional parliament, including a Commission on Citizenship and Human Rights, in 2008 further reinforced this commitment.

International actors, from the United Nations to Spain's international development agency, actively supported the creation of an NHRI in Uruguay. The OHCHR, in 2005 and 2006, assisted in preparing a draft law on an NHRI, which was introduced formally in 2007 and referred explicitly to the Paris Principles; and in September 2008, the UNDP and the OHCHR held a workshop on NHRIs, complementing congressional deliberations on the draft law. The debate continued for two years, while international actors, including the Network of NHRIs in the Americas, applied ongoing pressure.

During this period, Uruguay's election to the Human Rights Council in 2006 and 2009, its tenure as chair of this body in 2011, as well as the UPR more generally, all pushed the government toward domestic implementation. While the government did not list an NHRI among its voluntary election pledges in 2006, by 2009 it reported in the context of the UPR and in its election to the council that a bill to create an NHRI was under consideration. Council members urged Uruguay to proceed promptly with its plans of establishing an NHRI, a recommendation that the government finally accepted.

If Uruguay waited so long after embarking on democratization to create an NHRI, it was mostly because regulatory moments were absent (given the long-standing constitution) and treaties acceded to so long ago that they did not generate pressures for implementation. It was also because the level of abuses in Uruguay was fairly low under democracy at the same time that human rights organizations remained relatively weak. Only when external commitments began shifting after 2000, partly the result of Mercosur's growing embrace of human rights and a government that wished to enhance the country's international role, did international regime pressures push more actively for establishing human rights bodies within the state apparatus.

Caribbean Holdouts

Despite the early presence of the ombudsman in the Caribbean, some countries in this region were quite late in creating an NHRI (the Dominican Republic, Saint Kitts and Nevis, and Grenada); others had merely agreed to create an NHRI or taken a few steps in this direction (Dominica and Suriname). Their trajectory at the turn of the millennium was similar to other small states in the world. In most cases, moreover, the UPR process proved crucial.

In the *Dominican Republic*, the ombudsman, or Defensor del Pueblo, was created by law in 2001, though it did not begin functioning until later in the decade. While regulatory moments were present before then, there was also a great deal of constitutional volatility. The country had accepted international human rights obligations as early as the 1970s, but a weak rule of law hindered norm implementation, while violations also remained high. Amid broader reforms, the senate took up the issue in 2008, the same year that CERD called on the government to create an NHRI. Similar appeals were made by the Special Rapporteur on Racism and by Human Rights Council members during the UPR process in

2009, a recommendation the government accepted. At last, the government incorporated the institution into the 2010 constitution, which was nonetheless considered a regressive instrument. The willingness to do so reflected a combination of factors, especially a regulatory moment and ongoing abuses, along with international regime pressures.[106]

The small federal island state of *Saint Kitts and Nevis*, a Commonwealth Caribbean member, passed the Ombudsman Act in 2006, with the institution becoming operational in 2009.[107] Interestingly, Saint Kitts and Nevis has not ratified the American Convention on Human Rights or either international human rights covenant. With a constitution in place since the early 1980s, no external human rights obligations, and no egregious violations that would translate into transnational pressure, the reluctance and delay in creating an NHRI was to be expected. The ombudsman formed in 2006 seems instead to have been the result of international regime pressures. For example, a Commonwealth seminar held in the island state in January 2004 on the theme of the role of the ombudsman in fostering good governance and democracy may have been influential, especially as the prospect of the UPR loomed.[108]

The case of *Dominica* reveals just how influential the UPR process has been. The country's independence constitution from 1978 called for an ombudsman (in the form of a parliamentary commissioner); but the institution was debated and remained under consideration for decades, despite the country's membership in the British Commonwealth and having acceded to human rights treaties. Though constitutional reforms were undertaken in the early 1980s, it was only in the context of the UPR in 2009 that the government at last agreed to establish an NHRI.

The idea of an ombudsman was first introduced during a constitutional regulatory moment, drawing on an institution common among its peers. As a small island state with no major human rights groups operating domestically, Dominica usually escaped reporting by major human rights organizations, so transnational pressure was quite low. The experience of a related Public Office Act passed in 2003 is instructive. That office also was delayed, which some attributed to corrupt officials who feared being exposed. As one critical voice observed in 2008, "all Dominicans are aware that although our Constitution mandates the appointment of such a public officer no government since 1978 has had the commitment and courage to appoint one."[109] Early international diffusion by Commonwealth states therefore helps to account for the parliamentary commissioner's insertion into the 1978 constitution. Over three decades later the delay in establishing the body seems to have depended on the domestic and international contexts: domestically, a fragmented parliamentary system that could not agree on the appointment of an ombudsman given widespread corruption and, transnationally, a small state subject to weak human rights activism and pressure.

Grenada in turn created an ombudsman in 2007, in the context of constitutional reforms and existing human rights obligations. The ombudsman was established via a legislative act, with the first ombudsman being appointed in 2009. During the country's UPR in 2010, members of the Human Rights Council called on Grenada to establish an accredited NHRI or to harmonize the existing ombudsman to conform to the Paris Principles.[110]

Since the small island country's constitution had been written in 1973, a year before actual independence, and was never approved by the parliament, constitutional review commissions were established in 1986 and 2006. Though the 1986 commission expressed reservations about the role of ombudsman bodies in small developing countries, by the time of the second constitutional review, the broader context had changed significantly. Whereas the 1980s were dominated by the U.S. invasion of the island in 1983, over time issues of accountability, good governance, and anticorruption gained traction. The two international covenants were also accepted in 1991. A truth commission later established in 2001 to investigate past abuses (1976–91) issued its final report in 2006, calling for public accountability. The UN Human Rights Committee that year also called for an NHRI, as did the constitutional review commission. When the government introduced the ombudsman bill, it enjoyed broad political support. Despite these developments, the release in 2010 of a working draft for a new constitution did not include an ombudsman; the rationale was that the institution (like a related integrity commission) was better left to legislation than to a foundational document. Regulatory moments and international regime pressures, combined with existing obligations, to create an ombudsman, albeit a weak one.[111]

The former Dutch colony of *Suriname* finally committed to establishing an ombudsman as part of the UPR process, though the institution had been proposed for at least a decade, including by regional and international actors. Despite independence in 1975, a coup in 1980 and a war between the army and the Maroon people over land rights had delayed democratic institution building. A political transition was initiated in the 1990s, marked by multiparty elections in 1991, peace negotiations with the Maroons in 1991 and 1992, and general constitutional reform. Yet calls for an ombudsman became most vocal after 2000, culminating when several members of the Human Rights Council called in 2011 for an NHRI and the government at long last accepted the recommendation.[112]

Following a Caribbean Community (CARICOM) heads of state meeting in late 1999, which urged states to cooperate more closely with civil society, a meeting was held in Suriname in 2000, called Forward Together Suriname Consultation: Involving Civil Society in Caribbean Development. The final report of that meeting recommended the creation of an ombudsman, also consistent with the Charter of Civil Society for the Caribbean Community concluded at the 1999 CARICOM meeting.[113] It should be noted that CARICOM, supported by the Inter-American Development Bank, was promoting international standards linking development and democratic governance. With the support of UNDP, Suriname thus adopted a five-year development plan (2006–11), where human rights was treated as a "cross-cutting issue." The UNDP's support was itself part of a program on legal protection, human rights, and anticorruption institution building. The notion of creating an ombudsman was reinforced in 2007, when the CRC called on Suriname to establish an NHRI; and by 2010, plans for a children's ombudsman were in fact under way. In this context, the government's acceptance of recommendations made during the country's UPR in 2011 was not all that surprising. An ombudsman fit in with decade-long calls for supporting the twin goals of development and democratization.[114]

Resistor States

In contrast to states that had agreed to create an NHRI, a few states seemed to resist the regional trend. This was true for both the Bahamas and Cuba, which faced weak strategic incentives to establish accountability institutions and were ambivalent in responding to international suggestions that they do so. Only two countries' governments explicitly rejected the notion that they create an NHRI: Saint Vincent and the Grenadines as well as the United States. In one case, the rejection reflected the smallness of the state and a broader lack of engagement with international human rights instruments. In the other case, rejection derived from more deeply rooted hegemonic exceptionalism.

Resistance to an NHRI by the *Bahamas* fit into a broader pattern of not acceding to human rights treaties. Never having accepted the American Convention on Human Rights, the Bahamas ratified the international covenants only in 2008, the same year as its UPR. With a constitution dating to 1973 and a low level of violations, the state had few reasons to create an NHRI. This could still change with ongoing international regime pressures, including from the UPR, especially now that the country, which has a strong rule of law system, has ratified major human rights treaties. Though the government's response to recommendations about creating an NHRI have been unclear, pressure for an ombudsman is only likely to intensify.

In responding to international calls for an NHRI, raised during its UPR process, the *Cuban* government's response also was unclear. When pressed by Mexico during that process to create an NHRI, government representatives issued only a general response—neither straightforward rejection nor acceptance. Perhaps in anticipation of its UPR in 2009, the country signed the human rights covenants, without acceding to the American Convention on Human Rights. Despite transnational pressures, little international regime pressures have taken place, given the political system's closure. Since organized abuse rarely is sufficient on its own to lead to norm implementation, an NHRI's creation in Cuba hinges on broader political changes, the kinds of change that will produce meaningful regulatory moments and a willingness to accept external obligations.[115]

Only a couple of states in the hemisphere explicitly rejected the notion of creating an NHRI. Saint Vincent and the Grenadines rejected recommendations made as part of its UPR in 2011 that it create an NHRI, though it had included an ombudsman in a 2009 draft constitution, later defeated in a referendum. With minor violations, alongside long-standing treaty obligations and a constitution from the late 1970s, the country's incentives to create an NHRI remained relatively weak. This was exacerbated by the fact that the island state had not acceded to the American Convention on Human Rights. For a small island with a low- to middle-income economy, the costs of an NHRI may have seemed high relative to its perceived need or benefits. U.S. rejection of an NHRI is another matter.

U.S. Exceptionalism

The case for an NHRI in the United States is in many ways intriguing. The United States does not have an NHRI, though there are comparable agencies at the national and local levels. The U.S. Civil Rights Commission, created in 1957, is in principle an independent commission, but the system of appointment (even after important restructuring in the 1980s) and the narrow focus on civil rights would fail to meet international standards for NHRIs. Locally, over one hundred state and municipal human rights commissions and related bodies also exist in the United States. Since 1949, they have met as a group and growing network, the International Association of Official Human Rights Agencies; this umbrella organization, interestingly, includes Canadian human rights commissions and Bermuda's ombudsman, suggesting strong similarities to NHRIs. Until recently, moreover, NHRIs around the world have known very little, if anything, about the existence of these official human rights bodies in the United States.[116]

The historical trajectory of these bodies in the United States is nonetheless essential in understanding why there is no overarching NHRI. As Chapter 2 recounts, state-level human rights commissions grew out of interracial bodies, themselves the product of race riots and the rising power of a black labor force in the context of wartime economies. Interracial bodies in the United States included well-meaning individuals, often religious and socially progressive; but they also consisted of largely unrepresentative bodies, moderate voices that unwittingly colluded with the government to permit highly circumscribed change. In a parallel development, the country became increasingly subject to international attention for its "race problem," especially as the United States in a post-WWII world itself promoted human rights abroad. Significantly, the country's very commitment to international human rights standards and institutions was partly an attempt to fight communism and therefore enhance its geostrategic and economic primacy. The report of the President's Committee on Civil Rights, "To Secure These Rights," in turn emphasized in 1947 that addressing discrimination in the United States was essential for the country's foreign affairs and global standing. One of the key recommendations made in the report was for the creation of a national civil rights commission. In this manner, institutionalizing rights issues domestically served the country's international interests.

After the landmark *Brown v. Board of Education* ruling in 1954, calls grew for local, state, and federal human rights bodies. The U.S. Civil Rights Commission was at last created in 1957, just as local and state bodies continued to proliferate. Whether a body carried "human rights" in its name had more to do with the decade in which it was created or substantially revised: most of the local commissions that are framed in terms of "human rights" were created in the 1960s, when international human rights discourse was explicitly adopted by civil rights activists in the United States. Almost without exception, these bodies today are equal opportunity, antidiscrimination bodies, rarely using the language of human rights or appealing to international standards in their everyday work—even when they are designated a "human rights commission."

In interacting with the United Nations, moreover, the U.S. government has long used the existence of domestic human rights institutions to deflect focus away from and to resist human rights concerns. At the United Nations in the 1940s, the United States promoted a weak version of national human rights bodies—pure supplements to the UN Human Rights Commission—with limited independence and access to the United Nations, undermining international human rights mechanisms by not providing them with direct institutional channels within states. And as Chapter 3 mentions, the United States held up its own institutions and promoted the creation of national human rights bodies at the United Nations in the 1960s as a way of again maintaining weak international mechanisms, which could have been redirected against itself and its allies. In this same way, it created a limited civil rights commission partly to appease international critics but without having to meet human rights demands at home that would have required subverting the status quo.

To this day, the United States maintains an exceptionalist, hypocritical stance when it comes to human rights domestically. For all the embrace of civil rights discourse, there is ongoing reluctance to bring the language of human rights more fully to the United States. With the election of President Barack Obama and in the aftermath of Hurricane Katrina, increasing attention turned to applying human rights standards and discourse domestically. A small but growing movement, composed mostly of lawyers, academics, and activists, has pushed quietly for a human rights framework in the United States, including the creation of an NHRI.[117] Whether there would be value added from such an institution is discussed in the concluding chapter.

Regulatory moments for creating an NHRI have been weak in the United States, with a long-standing constitution in place, few external human rights obligations, and little transnational pressure against the powerful country. While the United States ratified the ICCPR in 1992, it has not acceded to the ICESCR or to the American Convention. A range of international actors have promoted the idea of an NHRI for the United States, including Human Rights Council members during the UPR in 2010, as well as CERD, CRC, and the Working Group on the Experience of People of African Descent. The United States rejected these suggestions, presumably because the U.S. Civil Rights Commission is so well entrenched. Given U.S. power, international regime pressures have not targeted the country, which has remained largely resistant to human rights discourse and the idea of an NHRI.

Conclusions: The Power of Myth Making

The so-called third wave of democratization swept across Latin America, bringing an end to military rule and repressive regimes throughout the continent. The historical moment evokes a scene from one of Isabel Allende's novels, *Eva Luna*, published in 1985, at the same time that social protests were mounting against the Pinochet regime in the author's native Chile, and neighboring Argentina had already crossed the threshold into a post–dirty war world of democratic rule:

> When they saw that various dignitaries of the Church in their finest ceremonial robes were presiding over the pomp of the funeral, the populace were finally assured that the tyrant's immortality was only a myth, and came out to celebrate. The country awakened from its long siesta, and in a matter of hours the cloud of depression and fatigue that had weighed over it dissipated. People began to dream of a timid liberty. They shouted, danced, threw stones, broke windows, and even sacked some of the mansions of the favorites of the regime; and then burned the long black Packard in which El Benefactor always rode, its unmistakable klaxon spreading fear as it passed.[118]

For those caught in the middle of repressive rule, marked by disappearances and clandestine detention centers, political freedom must have seemed distant and elusive. Authoritarian regimes in the region ruled based on elaborate nationalist myths conveyed through complex lexicons of "enemies," "subversives," "fear," and "terror."[119] When political change at last came, the breaking point seemed dramatic and the notion of *la transición* could take epic proportions. "Then" and "now" represented two starkly different worlds of possibilities: the past was filtered through complex historical memories and narratives, while the future was imagined inescapably in relation to what had preceded it. In contesting today's policies, social groups have tended to situate themselves in reference either to a past they wanted to remember or one they hoped to transcend and sometimes forget. In this sense, the political transitions that swept the region—and seemed to unify it across national borders—became myths in their own right, variously interpreted and gaining a social currency and momentum all of their own.

The figure of the ombudsman, or defensor, acquired its meaning in the Americas in this context of mythmaking. It came to mark the transition to democratic governance late in the twentieth century, despite the institution's ties to European (neo)colonial bodies. It symbolized a new system, one promising to transform the state itself, where the ruler was to be held accountable before a figurative representative of the people. At the same time, the democratic transition coincided historically with the entry of economic neoliberalism into the region, bringing its own share of contradictions and vicissitudes. On some level, in fact, the complaints before the ombudsman in a democratizing context, revolving around economic and social rights, have seemed mundane compared to the dramatic violations of the past. On another level, this has served to perpetuate the transitional myth itself, obscuring somewhat from view certain abuses under democratization—especially those disproportionately affecting marginalized, near invisible populations, as discussed in Chapter 10.

The extent of NHRI diffusion in Latin America, and to a lesser extent the Caribbean, has been nothing short of remarkable. Regional and subregional diffusion and socialization have been essential for this institutional proliferation. And because the human rights ombudsman has been the most popular NHRI adopted throughout the region, the importance of individual leadership has been vivid. This helps to explain, for example, why an organizationally and historically strong institution like Honduras's NHRI experienced a voltc-face in 2009, siding with coup plotters rather than social activists and a disenfranchised populace. The depth of democratic transitions and the rule of law as well as ongoing violence and corruption have sometimes limited the NHRI's reach. Yet in many instances, NHRIs created purely to appease transnational critics have evolved over time into stronger institutions, due partly to international regime pressures. Myths can prove powerful, and the NHRI in the Americas illustrates both the transformation and limitations of the state as political actor in everyday life.

8

Appeasement via Localization in the Asia Pacific

Of all the regions in the world, the Asia Pacific has had the lowest concentration of NHRIs since the 1990s. Following the lead of New Zealand, Australia, and the Philippines in the 1970s and 1980s, nine countries in the Asia Pacific created an NHRI in the 1990s: India, Indonesia, and Palestine in 1993; Iran in 1995; Sri Lanka in 1996; Fiji, Nepal, and Thailand in 1997; and Malaysia in 1999. The fact that, unlike other regions, the vast area of the Asia Pacific (defined here by UN categories) did not have a region-wide system of human rights protection or undergo widespread democratization may account for the slower rate of diffusion. Still, as early as 1993, the Bangkok Declaration called for the creation of NHRIs, even before the World Conference in Vienna. The establishment in 1996 of the Asia Pacific Forum, an organization composed of NHRIs and dedicated to promoting the spread and strengthening of NHRIs, changed this dynamic markedly, though its effects would not become fully evident until the new millennium. Indeed, after 2000, numerous other states in the region joined the global trend of human rights institution building.

For a region that had put off the possibility of creating a regional enforcement mechanism and had leaders who rejected rhetorically the primacy of human rights (i.e., the Asian values debate), establishing NHRIs permitted regimes to do two things: appease transnational critics of local rights practices while retaining sovereign control over human rights issues. The creation of NHRIs in the Asia Pacific also reflected the influence of a regional NHRI network, led by the Asia Pacific Forum, and a more general logic of diffusion, as states followed the examples of social peers, often those in close subregional proximity. And in some cases, the idea of establishing an NHRI was placed on the political agenda by NGOs, to be adopted when egregious human rights abuses garnered intense transnational reaction. As the South Asia Human Rights Documentation Center noted in a March 1998 publication, "If in the 1950s, the status symbol of a developing country was a steel mill, in the 1990s, apparently, it was a human rights commission."[1]

The Transnational Reach of NHRIs in the Early 1990s

Influenced by the Paris Principles and the gradual spread of NHRIs, a core set of countries in the Asia Pacific opted for "human rights commissions" in the early 1990s. Between 1993 and 1995, four countries in the region established NHRIs: India, Indonesia, the Palestinian Authority, and Iran. All of them did so in the context of organized abuse and transnational pressure; only in the case of the Palestinian Authority was the institution created during a regulatory moment. And in all cases, except Iran, these NHRIs have been fully accredited internationally. Notwithstanding accreditation, all of the institutions have also been constrained by the broader political context, including ongoing violence and conflict. Likewise, the creation of these NHRIs was deeply implicated in the institution's global diffusion and the active efforts of NHRI-diffusing agents to promote the institution throughout the region.

India's Human Rights Commission

When India created its National Human Rights Commission in 1993, it did so largely to appease transnational critics. The formally democratic country was not in the midst of a regulatory moment; rather, a combination of organized abuse and external obligations made an institutional solution to its human rights problems seem especially appealing. In this regard, the early 1990s reflected a strong convergence of rising international pressures and, internally, a renewed campaign of state violence that mobilized social opponents.

Though the NHRI's establishment was part of a process that had gained momentum (and even urgency) in the early 1990s, as transnational pressure intensified, it also had deeper roots in a domestic dynamic that had started after the emergency period of the mid-1970s: social activism met by state violence only mobilized more human rights activism. The first mention of a human rights commission appears to have been made by the Junata Party, which became active after the mid-1970s emergency period. In their election manifesto in 1977, they promoted the idea of creating a human rights commission, to be led by a person with the stature of a Supreme Court judge—an idea that would survive into the 1990s. The suggestion, interestingly, seemed linked to the perceived weaknesses of two existing bodies: the Commissioner of Scheduled Castes and Tribes and the Commissioner for Linguistic Minorities. The Minorities Commission itself called in 1981 for a comprehensive human rights commission with constitutional standing.[2]

Against this backdrop, in 1985 Chief Justice P. N. Bhagwati promoted the idea of a "national human rights commission."[3] His own motivation may have reflected a convergence of factors, including an awareness of similar institutions worldwide; for example, he had traveled to Australia in 1984, where he met with other jurists and perhaps noticed the country's recent (albeit temporary) human rights commission. Within India, he recognized the courts could be slow and cumbersome, just as he was passionate about the idea of public interest litigation and deeply interested in how one might implement international law in common-law systems. The idea of a human rights commission tapped into all of these facets of his thinking, while building on domestic support in some quarters for an overarching human rights institution. Justice Bhagwati's proposal was echoed by L. M. Singvi, a leading jurist, who also called in 1988 for creating state and national human rights commissions.[4]

These early proposals for an official human rights commission intersected intriguingly with parallel efforts on the popular level. Perhaps most notably, a systematic massacre of Sikhs and a state-sponsored counterinsurgency campaign in contested zones of the country had led to fierce violence, especially after Indira Gandhi's assassination by her Sikh bodyguards. Some civil liberty and rights groups responded to this intensifying abuse by forming the Indian People's Human Rights Commission (IPHRC) in January 1987. The commission initiated a series of public inquiries and tribunals into serious human rights violations, including the Arwal massacre in 1986.[5] At the same time that proposals for an official human rights commission were being made, then, a *people's* human rights commission filled the gap by investigating abuse and demanding accountability.

Yet it was not until the early 1990s that the notion of creating a national human rights commission in India entered mainstream political debates. The government began discussing the desirability of a national commission, and major political parties took up the issue in their bid for parliamentary elections. The Congress Party promised in its 1991 election manifesto to create a human rights commission; and it called for a national debate in April 1992, since "the question of human rights has now climbed to the top of the international agenda. The best way to face the reality is to establish a Human Rights Commission. It can play a useful role in furthering human rights standards in the country. Its findings will act as correctives to the biased and one-sided report of some of the NGOs. It will be an effective answer to the politically motivated international criticism."[6] Prime Minister P. V. Narasimha Rao confirmed that "we must send a clear message that we do not tolerate human rights violations." The consensus, moreover, was that legislation creating a human rights commission was to be drafted only after studying similar institutions in other countries. By September 1992, the Home Ministry called a meeting of chief ministers, where they officially decided to create a human rights commission. The debate that ensued was predictable, with critics noting that human rights were already protected in the constitution and existing commissions would be redundant.[7]

International pressures against India during this period mounted. This reflected partly the growing appeal of human rights in international politics after the Cold War, as foreign trade partners drew close links between democracy, development, and human rights; and economic relations became increasingly contingent on human rights performance. For example, in 1991, the European Community tied development assistance to human rights conditions, while the European Parliament issued a resolution in 1992 targeting tensions in Jammu and Kashmir. The Kashmir issue was in fact slated to be addressed at the upcoming World Conference on Human Rights in Vienna. In addition to the United Kingdom and the United States, France, Norway, Sweden and Switzerland, as well as Amnesty International, Asia Watch, and the International Committee of the Red Cross, had all raised the issue of human rights in India.[8] In his exhaustive study of the country's NHRI, Arun Ray concludes that "the government decided to set up a native agency to examine its own human rights record" largely to avoid criticisms and reports made by human rights organizations.[9]

International pressure presented India's regime with a problem of how to improve its human rights image (necessitated by its rampant abuses in Jammu and Kashmir, Punjab, and Assam), just as a national body promised to localize authority over the issue and take it away from transnational critics. As one observer noted, India has long pursued institutional solutions to its human rights problems.[10] Yet another commentator remarked at the time, "It is incumbent upon us to uphold India's image at home and abroad by establishing an independent and investigating watchdog body on human rights."[11]

Both social advocates and government opponents in India have viewed the NHRC's origins as internationally inspired. Prominent human rights advocate Ravi Nair portrayed the government's motive in creating the commission as an effort "to circumvent international scrutiny by stating that they have adequate national institutions to investigate these charges."[12] Likewise, a Tamil-based lawyer, Rajeev Dhavan, emphasized the "threat that international economic decisions will carry human rights conditionalities."[13] India, after all, was considering creating a national commission at the same time that it was negotiating an agreement with the IMF. India's home minister, S. B. Chavan, similarly declared in March 1992 that the proposed commission would "counter the false and politically motivated propaganda by foreign and civil rights agencies."[14] Along the same lines, the Congress Party described the commission's potential findings as "a corrective to the biased and one-sided reports of the NGOs" as well as "an effective answer to politically motivated international criticism."[15] More colorfully, in a seminar organized by India's Bar Council to debate the commission's creation, Justice V. R. Krishna Iyer described the instrumental nature of the commission as "an optical illusion, cosmetic coloration, opium for the people at home and brown sugar for countries abroad, a legislative camouflage, a verbal wonder which conceals more than it reveals."[16]

India's NHRI was therefore the product of transnational pressure, as human rights abuses rose, committed by a state that was formally democratic and had accepted external human rights obligations. In this sense, the establishment of the NHRI was part of a broader attempt by the Indian state to institutionalize rights concerns, including giving statutory authority to existing commissions, such as the National Commission for Women, created in 1990.[17] Even before the Protection of Human Rights Act established the NHRI in October 1993, the state of Madhya Pradesh had already erected a human rights commission in 1992.[18] And a few months before the NHRI's emergence, tellingly, the Indian People's Human Rights Commission had released a report about human rights violations, following deadly riots in Bombay in December 1992 and January 1993. In addition, the form the commission took mirrored in large part recommendations by both the United Nations and Amnesty International, actors at the forefront of promoting NHRIs.[19] This was the period, after all, when the Paris Principles had recently been released; and as a regional leader, India would have an interest in joining the global bandwagon. The democratic and legalistic foundations of the Indian state helped to stack the commission with a committed and independent set of members, the majority of whom came from the judiciary. Yet in the absence of full governmental commitment, but ongoing armed conflict,

India's commission has always remained somewhat weak, even in a country with a long tradition of legalism and democratic rule.

Indonesia's Komnas HAM

In Indonesia, the National Commission on Human Rights (or Komnas HAM, Komisi Nasional Hak Asasi Manusia) was also established in the context of transnational pressures following egregious rights abuses. Significantly, the government announced the creation of Komnas HAM after the November 1991 massacre in Dili, East Timor, and an ensuing wave of international human rights pressure that included threats by major aid donors. When the massacre presented the regime with an international human rights image problem, the response was to draw on the options that international actors had defined beforehand. Komnas HAM, in fact, was announced at a UN-sponsored human rights workshop in Jakarta in June 1993, exactly one week before the government expected to face criticism at the upcoming World Conference on Human Rights in Vienna. The announcement also came on the heels of the first UN Human Rights Commission resolution targeting Indonesia and supported by the United States, as well as following a well-publicized and critical report by the Lawyers Committee for Human Rights. Furthermore, it was the minister of *foreign* affairs who convened the committee establishing Komnas HAM.[20] As one researcher commented, "In response to the increasing pressure from 'above and below,' tactical concessions and instrumental adaptation as response began to dominate the action repertoire of the Indonesian government in 1992 to 1993 which restricted its available options for action."[21]

Neither diffusion pressures nor the domestic context, however, can be ignored. Representatives of the United Nations had begun calling for the creation of a national commission at a human rights workshop held jointly by Indonesia's Department of Foreign Affairs and the United Nations in January 1991, almost eleven months before the Dili massacre in November.[22] Like a National Commission of Inquiry (Komisi Penyelidikan Nasional) that Suharto had set up to investigate the Dili massacre, Komnas HAM may also have been intended partly to fight factionalism within the military. Not only did the model of an NHRI promise to satisfy international critics, but it potentially held an added advantage domestically: an NHRI's specter of accountability would act as a check on errant state agents. At the same time, the nondemocratic nature of Indonesia's regime constrained the commission's role, helping to explain its principal weaknesses, including the conspicuous lack of pluralism, weak networking, and attachment to a state ideology (Pancasila) that in some respects is antithetical to international human rights norms.[23]

International actors proved essential in efforts to reform Indonesia's Human Rights Commission. The regime responded in 1999 to international pressure, including a UN peacekeeping force, by issuing a presidential decree to reform the commission, which also coincided with continued efforts to rebound from financial crisis. While Indonesia's parliament later rejected the decree in favor of more comprehensive reform, it is noteworthy that the government announced the NHRI's reform only after the regime attracted widespread international condemnation. It is also significant that reform efforts reflected measures that international groups like Amnesty International had advanced, including reconstituting the commission according to legislative statute rather than presidential decree and providing the commission with stronger powers of investigation.[24]

Over time, the Indonesian commission received substantial international assistance, aimed at strengthening the institution. For example, Australia's Department of Foreign Affairs and Trade assisted the commission, especially its awareness-raising capacity. Likewise, the Canadian Human Rights Foundation (an NGO) teamed up with Canada's own Human Rights Commission, to implement a capacity-building project in Indonesia, also targeting the commission's promotional functions. More broadly, the commission benefited from formal contacts with other human rights commissions, including India's, and UN representatives.[25] All told, international standards and assistance left an indelible mark on the creation and strengthening of Indonesia's human rights commission. And in 2000, Komnas HAM was fully accredited internationally.

Despite their differences, Indonesia and India both created NHRIs at the same time. In both instances, the regimes faced overwhelming incentives to establish an NHRI, while the domestic context shaped subsequent institutional strengths and capacities. If appeasement was initially a key driving force, an NHRI was appealing precisely because it permitted these regimes—embroiled in violent if targeted campaigns to localize authority over human rights tensions. It was better to control the agenda oneself than to let others do so.

The Palestinian Commission: "A Marker for Our Future"

Though not formally recognized as an independent state, the Palestinian Authority created an NHRI in 1993, the first in the Arab world to do so outside of North Africa. The Palestinian Independent Commission for Human Rights (PICHR) was a product of the Oslo peace process and served as an important example of a hybrid institution operating in a climate of ongoing violence.[26] The commission was created in September 1993 by a presidential decree issued by

Yasser Arafat. It was later institutionalized in the Basic Law of 1997 (ratified in 2002 and amended in 2003).[27] In 2005, it was internationally accredited as an A-status institution, though with the reservation that implementing legislation still was needed to ensure the commission's independence and authority; in 2009, it attained full accreditation.[28] Though originally called the Palestinian Independent Commission for *Citizens'* Rights, its current name—showcasing *human* rights—dates to 2008.[29]

The initial impetus for the commission was closely linked to international pressure. The decree, signed on September 30, 1993, took place in the context of a five-day visit by an Amnesty International delegation to the Palestinian leadership in Tunis. The Palestinians invoked the UN Human Rights Commission's Resolution 1992/54 on NHRIs, as having shaped their commitment to establish a National High Institution for Human Rights. Arafat himself expressed, "I am very much concerned that this institution be independent and protected from any interference."[30] Not only was Arafat surrounded by Palestinian advisors who were strong human rights advocates, but the PLO may have been drawing from the example of its home base at the time—Tunisia, which had created two years earlier an NHRI (or "Higher Committee") by presidential decree.

Once Arafat issued the human rights decree, Palestinian activist and scholar Hanan Ashrawi ran with it. Ashrawi's commitment to creating a human rights institution—"a marker for our future"—seemed a matter of conviction. In her memoir, she offers the intellectual rationale, linked closely to the notion of state building and democratic reform. Even as the Palestinian leadership gained international recognition, she said, they were not and could not be immune from "internal criticism and accountability. The transition from the glamour of a national liberation movement to the mundane tasks of building and running a state had begun. When symbols take on substance and become accessible, they turn into the stuff of daily life." Ashrawi captured the transformative potential of the state institution:

> Having been on the receiving end of a complex and systematic policy of abuse and repression, it was our turn to demonstrate that the victim would not turn oppressor and that the same stringent standards that we had applied to the Israelis would be applied to our system and authority. Besides, the practices of a national liberation movement and its exercise of "revolutionary justice" in exile would have to undergo a drastic transformation into a system of government and governance firmly embedded in the principles and rights of a

people on their own land. It was a new social contract. Such a transition, it seemed, would be the most difficult and painful passage.[31]

Ashrawi drew up the first concrete proposal for the PICHR with attorney Raja
Shehadeh in late November 1993, presenting it to Arafat a few days later in Oslo,
on their official tour of Scandinavian countries. Shehadeh was the founder of the
Palestinian human rights organization Al-Haq, the Palestinian affiliate of
the International Commission of Jurists. According to Ashrawi's account, "Abu
Ammar [Arafat] immediately approved and signed the proposal, and I took it
and ran with it. The Scandinavian countries with their ombudsman tradition
immediately grasped the intention behind the project and extended support.
Sweden was the pacesetter, with funds and expertise, followed by Denmark and
Norway. Abu Ammar gave it his public endorsement as he traipsed around the
world."[32] A preparatory commission headed by Ashrawi was formed, and the institution was crafted based on a systematic look at existing best practices. Human
rights activist Fateh S. Azzam may have been correct in noting that without
Ashrawi's initiative and drive, "the Commission would never have seen the light
of day."[33] A global interlocutor was once again behind regional innovation.

Of all the NHRIs in the Middle East, PICHR is arguably the most active
and substantial. The commitment vested in the institution is apparent in the
composition of the board, which has included prominent figures from within
Palestine and the diaspora, including Hanan Ashrawi and Mahmoud Darwish.
Its mandate is broad, spanning civil and political as well as economic and social
rights, though a few issues fall outside its competence, including violations committed by Israel within its pre-1967 borders. The PICHR's earlier success can also
be attributed partly to its complete financial independence from the Palestinian
Authority. The commission receives all of its funding from international sources,
including European governments (e.g., Norway, the Netherlands, Denmark, Sweden, Switzerland), the European Commission, and the Ford Foundation. As more
recent external assessments reveal, however, institutional maturity will eventually
require state funding and full political independence.[34]

The PICHR's creation reflected a set of overwhelming incentives, occurring
at the juncture of a regulatory moment and ongoing abuses. It was in a sense a
double regulatory moment, both a peace process and the first steps to statehood.
Initially embedded only in an executive decree, the body showed substantial
strengthening over time, even as it has remained hostage to the larger political
conflict. The institution reveals multiple layers of complexity. For instance, while
Arafat may have been most interested in appeasing international critics, the mem-

bers of the preparatory commission may have been motivated by the same intellectual concerns that inspired Ashrawi, the task of building routine state institutions
and strong democratic foundations. Likewise, international funding and support
has been essential for the institution's growth, just as it confirms the incomplete-
ness of the transition, marked by the absence of long-promised implementing
legislation and state funds. Despite the early reaction of local NGOs, some of
which may have feared that the institution was "a political trick to circumvent/
sabotage/centralize/control the NGOs," the institution has managed over time
to earn the hostility of political authorities—and therefore a credible reputation.[35] Forged out of a peace process, the NHRI has shown a high level of international involvement and internal vulnerability. Despite the ongoing challenges
and uncertainties, strong and committed leadership, so crucial in postconflict
transitions, has ensured a way forward.

Institutional Adaptation in Iran

An NHRI was created in Iran in 1995, shortly after the Paris Principles were
formulated.[36] The Iranian Islamic Human Rights Commission (IIHRC) applied
for international accreditation a few years later and was not found to be compliant with the Paris Principles, assigned a C rating in 2000. One year later, within
the Ministry of the Judiciary, a Human Rights Headquarters was formed to coordinate rights activities. Though the Human Rights Commission still did not meet
the basic criteria of independence by the time of Iran's UPR in 2010, the government agreed to create a fully compliant human rights institution. As the government stated in its submission to the Human Rights Council, "The establishment
of the National Human Rights Institution of the Islamic Republic of Iran has
been one of the national priorities."[37]

The decision to create an NHRI in 1995 reflected a broader political opening
initiated in 1993, when Hashemi Rafsanjani was reelected president. This period
saw rising social demands, from a population that was 70 percent young, which
reinforced the government's willingness to make concessions. And as women
and student groups formed, they relied on international human rights standards
and claims specifically. In this context, the government established the Human
Rights Commission in 1995, as well as a parliamentary commission charged with
investigating human rights abuses by public authorities. Some observers have described these bodies as attempts by the regime to build international and domestic legitimacy. For the first time, after years of resistance, the UN Human Rights
Commission's special envoy was also permitted to visit the country in 1996. For

its part, the IIHRC would remain active internationally well into the next decade, sending representatives to participate in conferences (e.g., the APF's annual meeting in Malaysia), and it even became a member of the Asia Network on NHRIs. Its creation signaled to some an "opportunity for beginning a new debate on human rights issues in Iran."[38]

This spirit of greater political openness was merely reinforced with the election of Mohammad Khatami, a reformist, in 1997, especially in terms of freedoms of the press and greater space for NGOs to mobilize. After 2000, closer relations with the EU also led to rising human rights pressures. Since the judiciary was charged by the 1980 constitution with oversight of human rights, the EU moved to engage this particular domestic actor. At this juncture of rising domestic activism, a reformer at the helm, and closer relations with the EU, the government created in 2001 the Human Rights Headquarters. The rationale was one of better coordination, but the fact that the Islamic Human Rights Commission's bid for international accreditation as an NHRI had been unsuccessful one year earlier may also have played a role. In 2001, moreover, Iran entered into negotiations with the OHCHR for technical assistance in the human rights field. Also significant was the creation by Shareen Ebadi, who would go on to win the Nobel Peace Prize, of the influential Defenders of Human Rights Centre in 2000.[39]

Despite the apparent advances, the period just after the Human Rights Headquarters was created in 2001 was marked by internal contradictions. Looking to improve its trade relations with Europe, the government agreed to emphasize human rights concerns. In fact, soon after the Human Rights Headquarters was established, the EU initiated a human rights dialogue with Iran, held between 2002 and 2004. This further elevated the place of human rights, even if mostly symbolically. And the EU commissioner, in his visit to Iran in 2003, explicitly linked economic relations to concrete improvements in human rights. That year, Iran submitted its first report to a human rights treaty body. Yet paradoxically, this was also a period when "unofficial illegal detention centers," including the infamous Prison 59 in Teheran, proliferated.[40]

More domestic political changes came with the election of Mahmoud Ahmadinejad as president in 2005, even while internal debates between reformers and conservatives continued. As the regime clamped down on opponents, civil society groups increasingly turned externally for support and were assisted by a wide range of international actors, including the EU. Direct international pressure intensified, and the UN General Assembly issued critical resolutions in 2005 and 2006.

Perhaps partly in response, in 2005, the Human Rights Headquarters had its statutory profile elevated to a national body, sometimes referred to as the High Council for Human Rights. The head of the judiciary chairs the body, with the ministers of foreign affairs and interior and the commander of the police sitting among its members. In practice, the secretary general of the body functions as its very public spokesperson; and this role has been prominently filled by Mohammad Jawad Larijani, whose articulate skills and political savvy turned him into a public relations force for the regime in the West.[41]

Indeed, Iran's Human Rights Council, perhaps because of its high-profile leader, has acted as a bridge between international actors and the Iranian government on human rights issues. The UN special rapporteur on human rights in Iran asked the council to play a productive role in this regard, referring to it (along with the judiciary) as a potentially "self-correcting" mechanism, a request emphasized by the Asian NGO Network on NHRIs in 2011.[42] The institution, moreover, is the organ that invited Navi Pillay, UN high commissioner for human rights, to visit the country; and it led the country's delegation to the Human Rights Council during the UPR.

Despite multiple governmental human rights institutions in Iran, all have emphasized human rights issues abroad while defending Iran's rights record.[43] This is starkly evident even in the High Council of Human Rights, which resembles a news organization site more than an NHRI. It should also be noted that the IIHRC has continued to exist, and on paper it resembles an NHRI much more so than does the Human Rights Headquarters, though the IIHRC is sometimes referred to as an NGO despite its clear governmental origins and connections. At the APF annual meeting in Malaysia in 2008, in fact, the APF offered associate membership to the IIHRC, which declined. It is likely that the government had decided that the High Council for Human Rights should take central stage as the main candidate for an NHRI: the IIHRC, after all, had failed to be accredited, and its identifying link to Islam may no longer have been viewed in a post-9/11 world as internationally strategic.

With the UPR approaching in 2010, the government enhanced its rhetorical commitment to institutionalizing human rights.[44] In 2010, Iran hosted an international human rights conference; and in 2011, the government referred to its Human Rights Headquarters as a serious sign of Iran's commitments. The government finally submitted its third periodic report to the UN Human Rights Committee in 2011, more than fifteen years late. It accepted the Human Rights Council's recommendations to transform the High Council for Human Rights into an independent NHRI or establish another institution in compliance with the Paris Principles. In its statement to the UPR, the government confirmed that the High Council for Human Rights was drafting relevant legislation to abide by international standards.[45]

Iran began creating NHRIs in the context of external obligations and domestic abuse, largely as a process of appeasement, and shaped by the international diffusion of NHRIs. The domestic political context explains both the timing of the institution's creation and the constraints under which it has operated. The president's decision to liberalize in the early 1990s served as a soft regulatory moment; in turn, the failure of the initial NHRI to be accredited in 2000, combined with closer ties with the EU, led to the creation of alternative governmental structures, from the Islamic Commission to the Council for Human Rights. The UPR process has subsequently pushed the creation of an independent NHRI further along on the government's agenda. The extent of meaningful institutional reform now depends on domestic political change.

Regional Diffusion Takes Off

The proliferation of NHRIs in the region took flight in the second half of the nineties, as another half dozen countries and territories adopted the institution, including Sri Lanka, Hong Kong, Fiji, Nepal, Thailand, and Malaysia. In all instances, the role of regional and international NHRI-diffusing agents was essential, even while the incentives pushing political authorities to create these institutions have varied. Where violence and entrenched authoritarianism characterized political life, the NHRIs were not designed to be especially strong. Significantly, these NHRIs sometimes evolved from earlier institutional precursors, rather than being created entirely from scratch.

Turmoil in Sri Lanka

Sri Lanka created a Human Rights Commission in mid-1996, amid a civil war marked by a high level of human rights abuses and international pressure. Tellingly, the Sri Lankan government announced the creation of the commission at the UN Human Rights Committee in July 1995. Groups like Amnesty International and Asia Watch had already called for a human rights commission. Enacting legislation was passed in July 1996, the same month as the First Asia Pacific Regional Workshop on NHRIs was being held in Darwin, Australia. Domestically, it was a period of limited liberalization, following Chandrika Kumaratunga's election as president in 1994 under a presumed "mandate for peace." That the country was under intense pressure for its human rights record, international actors were calling for the creation of an NHRI, and India had recently created a similar high-profile commission, all pushed Sri Lanka to form a human rights commission.[46]

The country already had experience with ad hoc human rights bodies, as well as an even longer postindependence history of commissions of inquiry.[47] Beginning in 1986, the government established the Commission for the Elimination of Discrimination and Monitoring of Human Rights; and in 1991, the Human Rights Task Force, headed by a retired Supreme Court justice, was formed to investigate cases of extrajudicial detention. The Human Rights Commission was mandated to absorb the work of both bodies. The government had also appointed a Presidential Commission of Inquiry into the Involuntary Removal of Persons. The commission was formed in 1992 in response to transnational human rights pressure, and it held some hearings despite its highly circumscribed mandate.[48] All told, a series of institutional precursors made the NHRI a less threatening proposition.

The Commission for the Elimination of Discrimination and Monitoring of Human Rights, created in 1986, is worth highlighting as a predecessor body of the current commission.[49] When the Sri Lankan government formed this ad hoc body, it did so in response to an intensely critical hearing it had received in February 1985 at the UN Commission on Human Rights. As the government representative stated, "How credible are these reports and how disinterested are their authors as watchdogs of human rights?"[50] This was also a period when some Commonwealth countries were creating and being encouraged to establish antidiscrimination agencies. The commission can be considered an early, albeit ad hoc, NHRI, with a complaints-handling mechanism and conducting promotional activities. The institution indeed reflected the government's attempts to negotiate the tensions between its external human rights obligations and its abusive human rights practices. Creating an institution, which its social peers were adopting, offered the government a way of claiming for itself the role of human rights watchdog while appeasing the regime's critics.

Pressure mounted after 1990, however, for the creation of a permanent human rights commission. In addition to evolving international standards, in 1990, a Sri Lanka NGO (the Law and Society Trust) proposed draft legislation for such a body. A convergence of pressures, including the inadequacy of an ad hoc body, led the government in both 1991 and 1993 to assure the UN Commission on Human Rights that it was in the process of drafting legislation to create a permanent human rights commission. International actors like the United Nations offered technical assistance and advised Sri Lanka's government on relevant legislative matters.[51] After the Sri Lankan government announced it would establish an NHRI, Amnesty International issued a report recommending specific international standards. The regional example of India also seemed to play a substantial role, confirmed both by regional actors and commission insiders. The commission's secretary, D. H. Siriwardene, noted, "We look upon the National Human Rights Commission of India as a role model." "Our constant endeavor is to be like the Indian Commission. We are in close touch with it and try to benefit from its experiences."[52]

The combination of international support and broader domestic liberalization seemed to make some NGOs hopeful about the potential role of Sri Lanka's human rights institution, but the NHRI was soon overcome by government intransigence. According to some accounts, commissioners viewed themselves as part of a "stop-gap arrangement" and did not want to displease their political superiors.[53] Budgetary constraints were significant, with predictable consequences for political independence. Again, international actors—from Amnesty International to the UN Committee Against Torture—pushed for the institution's reform; and again, the government seemed to pander in response. In April 1999, the government chose the UN Commission on Human Rights as its forum for announcing a plan to increase the resources and strength of the HRC. The plan apparently paid off in 2000, when the institution was fully accredited internationally.[54] Some positive measures followed, such as the appointment of a new group of commissioners in 2000, including the first woman. The new commission definitely brought a broader institutional vision, addressing sensitive issues like that of internally displaced persons.[55]

But volatility was in the works, and the institution's course changed after 2006, when a cycle of escalating violence and ongoing impunity ensued. Despite a promise to strengthen the NHRI in June 2006, in the run-up to UN Human Rights Council elections, Sri Lanka's president directly appointed commission members. This basic subversion of the institution's independence, a contravention of the Paris Principles, led to the Human Rights Commission being downgraded in late 2007 from fully to partially accredited (B status), reconfirmed again in March 2009.[56] One observer describes state agents vis-à-vis the NHRI as having a "patently unhelpful and, sometimes decidedly hostile, bureaucracy which seems to feel threatened by the very presence and functioning of the commission."[57] Indeed, as a state implicated in a brutal conflict, Sri Lanka has long been reluctant to address the issue of accountability. It should come as no surprise that despite international support and a committed staff, a civil armed conflict has fundamentally undermined the NHRI's independence and promise.

Hong Kong's Reluctant Compromise

Though not a state, Hong Kong got on the NHRI bandwagon in 1996 when it created the Equal Opportunities Commission. Following the British model of these commissions, the Equal Opportunities Commission was established as a statutory body to implement various antidiscrimination laws: the Sex Discrimination Ordinance, the Disability Discrimination Ordinance, the Family Status Discrimination Ordinance, and the Race Discrimination Ordinance. The commission does not have sufficiently broad jurisdiction or a general human rights mandate to be considered a functioning NHRI. And in practice the institution's independence has been compromised: the government has refused to reappoint activist commissioners who have challenged the government, in favor of inexperienced leaders.[58] The institution is also not to be confused with the Hong Kong Human Rights Commission, an NGO coalition of human rights groups formed in 1988. All told, the NHRI, which earned a C status during international accreditation, is deemed quite weak.

Some legislators and NGOs started proposing a human rights commission in 1990, as part of the debate about enacting a Bill of Rights Ordinance in mid-1991. The bill of rights served to implement the ICCPR in domestic law, so that citizens could seek redress for human rights abuses through the court system. The government nonetheless portrayed a human rights commission as institutionally redundant and dismissed NHRIs elsewhere as ineffective. Instead, partly reflecting the influence of pro-China and pro-business forces, the government opted to create separate discrimination ordinances and the existing equal opportunities commission. Ongoing calls by international treaty bodies and NGOs for a real NHRI have been met with stiff resistance, as the government continuously points to its courts, Ombudsman, and Equal Opportunities Commission as sufficient. Still, despite the rejectionist language, the government submitted its equal opportunity commission for international NHRI accreditation in 2000, an effort that was unsuccessful.

There was a dual impetus behind the 1991 Bill of Rights, which itself led to the debate over creating an NHRI in Hong Kong: the impending transfer of sovereignty, from Britain to China in 1997, and China's crackdown on dissidents in Beijing in 1989. In this unique context of rising social demands, the creation of the equal opportunities commission was a reluctant compromise on the part of the government, who continued to reject calls for a broader human rights commission. The debate echoed similar themes and divergences in Britain.

Overall, the general incentives to establish an NHRI in Hong Kong were weak. Even if the transfer of sovereignty is construed as a regulatory moment, a relatively low level of abuse translated into weak transnational pressures, just as pro-China government forces dampened any interest in localizing authority. A very weak NHRI was instead created almost incidentally, as the events in Tiananmen Square in 1989 combined with the upcoming transfer of sovereignty to unleash a chain of demands for (and resistance to) building a strong NHRI. Given the domestic circumstances, international regime pressures have so far proved insufficient in breaking this cycle and shifting political interests.

Fiji's Reversal

Fiji, Nepal, and Thailand all created NHRIs in 1997. Fiji's Human Rights Commission arose during a regulatory moment, or a constitution drafting process begun in 1993. The commission was included in the 1997 constitution's "world-class" bill of rights, and it was later given implementing legislation in the Human Rights Commission Act of 1999.[59] One year after its creation, Fiji's NHRI was fully accredited internationally, first among Pacific island states.

The constitution was noteworthy in several respects, especially as an attempt to overcome institutionalized racism, which had characterized the previous constitution of 1990, and an effort to move to a multiethnic state, made possible after the election of a new president in 1992. In a divided society, it also represented a social consensus, accepted by various sides. A constitutional review commission headed by Paul Reeves, former governor general of New Zealand, led this consensus-building exercise. It was also no secret that the constitution would have to meet the principles and values of the Commonwealth if Fiji were to rejoin the organization, which had allowed Fiji's membership to lapse after 1987. Indeed, once Fiji's new constitution was enacted in 1997, the country was permitted to rejoin the British Commonwealth. The role of the Commonwealth, especially nearby New Zealand and Australia, were thus crucial in drafting Fiji's bill of rights, including the human rights commission.

Nationalistic extremism nonetheless undermined these efforts after 2000; and in March 2007, as a result of a coup launched a year earlier, Fiji's Human Rights Commission became one of the only ones in the world to lose its accreditation status. In a move that stunned many onlookers (to be replicated in the Honduran context), the commission supported the military's takeover, offering a detailed rationale for doing so. And in April 2007, Fiji resigned from the International Coordinating Committee of NHRIs. After a Court of Appeals ruled that the coup had been illegal, the regime moved to suspend all judges, revoking the 1997 constitution and repealing the 1999 Human Rights Commission Act. In its place, it issued a Human Rights Commission Decree in 2009, establishing a "new" commission, which failed to meet basic international standards relating to independence and mandate. While a relatively strong NHRI had initially been created, during a regulatory moment and with international support, domestic extremism proved overwhelming, pushing the institution to reverse course and subvert democratic gains.

Armed Violence in Nepal

Though both Nepal and Thailand had initiated political transitions in the early 1990s, it was not until mid-decade that each created an NHRI. Nepal established the National Human Rights Commission in 1997, via the Human Rights Commission Act of that year, though the institution did not become operational until 2000. It was fully accredited internationally in 2002 and incorporated into the Interim Constitution in 2007.

When the government announced in 1996 the decision to create the commission, the country was subject to several influences. Most immediately, Nepal was facing intense international criticism as a result of the government's violent suppression of a Maoist uprising.[60] Having accepted human rights treaty obligations, Nepal seems to have created the NHRI largely for international reasons. Regionally, neighboring India had created its own NHRC in 1993 and the Asia Pacific Forum had recently formed. The commission itself emphasizes that its origins lie in the Paris Principles process. What is more, the government's own reluctance in making the institution operational until 2000, despite pressures from political parties and civil society, calls into question its internal commitment to democratic institution building.

Though the institution was formally strong and complied with basic international standards, ongoing political instability—during and after the period of armed conflict—has limited the NHRI in various ways. When a state of emergency was declared in 2005, Commissioner Sushil Pyakunel was forced to leave the country. And despite the move to embed the institution in the 2007 postconflict (interim) constitution, which international actors welcomed, the institution's financial independence remained unclear. Thus, in May 2010, the ICC recommended downgrading the NHRI to "partially compliant," unless evidence of adequate funding and independence were provided. In an example of how threats surrounding accreditation status can lead to institutional strengthening, the NHRI furnished such proof of funding and was indeed able to retain full accreditation.[61]

The postconflict period has been dominated by the challenge of impunity, and the government's determination to avoid accountability. In July 2011, the government sent the commission a written notice, asking them to stop investigating alleged human rights violations committed during the armed conflict. Their rationale was technical: that the peace agreement charged a truth and reconciliation commission with this task; since one had not been established, no other entity was empowered to pursue these investigations. Domestic NGOs and international actors have forcefully challenged this assertion, while international actors like the UNDP and European governments have provided the commission with the resources to enhance its capacities in a postconflict setting.[62]

When Nepal created its NHRI, it did so influenced by international diffusion pressures, which gave it the idea and means to build and strengthen an NHRI, just as it faced incentives to appease transnational critics and localize authority over human rights issues. Yet the NHRI arose in the midst of an armed conflict, rather than in its aftermath. That it has survived into the postconflict period despite government attempts to limit the institution's authority over sensitive accountability issues speaks to international support. As in other conflict situations, the institution has received a higher than average amount of international assistance, giving the institution all the formal hallmarks of an accredited NHRI. As one commentator says, "The problem in Nepal is not so much that the state violates human rights but the absence of the state."[63] Indeed, this is one of the dilemmas of institution building in areas of intense conflict, where the state has been all but dismantled. Nepal's NHRI faces a daunting task, forced to negotiate the tensions of promoting both peace and accountability.

(Bad) Leadership Matters: Thailand's Human Rights Commission

Thailand's National Human Rights Commission was incorporated into the new "People's Constitution" in 1997. Implementing legislation was passed two years later, with the institution becoming operational in 2001—the same year that Thailand was slated to begin its first term on the UN Human Rights Commission.[64] Yet the origins of Thailand's NHRI arguably run much deeper: to the aftermath of "Black May" in 1992, when prodemocracy and military forces confronted one another to produce numerous casualties. Following this catapulting event, NGOs began lobbying for the creation of a national human rights body; and the Cabinet in September 1992 passed a resolution calling for a national mechanism to protect human rights. The process of drafting legislation to create the NHRI proved "highly charged," dragging out over the better part of a decade.[65] Once created, commissioners challenged the government, which responded by withholding funds and resources; indeed, the NHRI did not issue its first annual report until 2004.[66] Despite these delays and challenges, Thailand's NHRI was fully accredited in 2004, even as the selection process for commissioners and the institution's capacities came into question.

Following a coup in 2006, new members were not appointed to the commission, though its head had supported the military takeover.[67] When the appointments were finally made, they were met with a high degree of skepticism by human rights NGOs. The Asian Human Rights Commission said, "The selection process of the new commissioners had been rushed, non-transparent, undemocratic and contrary to the basic principles that the NHRC is supposed to represent." One observer renamed it "the Anti-Human Rights Commission." Of the seven selected, "four had no conceptual understanding of human rights at all, and one had been under investigation for possible human rights violations himself." A rights observer noted that "a more ugly lot of rights commissioners would be hard to find."[68] Brad Adams, Human Rights Watch Asia director said, "The best thing these members can do for human rights is to step down."[69]

The creation of Thailand's NHRI took place during a regulatory moment that took the form of constitution drafting, but it was first placed on the national agenda in 1992, mostly in an effort to appease transnational critics following a highly publicized episode of abuse. Yet the government, which had not accepted major international human rights obligations, resisted making good on its promise of creating an NHRI. Part of this resistance may have reflected an ideological clash between the government's strong economic growth stance and human rights NGOs. The NGOs framed their demands in the same language as the 1993 Bangkok NGO Declaration on Human Rights, calling for participatory democracy and social justice, while invoking marginalized groups and rural areas.[70] A subsequent regulatory moment in 1997 served as an opportunity for popular democratic and human rights demands to make headway. The formation of this NHRI can therefore be understood partly in terms of sequencing, as transnational pressure helped to define an option and place it on the political agenda while a regulatory moment afforded an opportunity to move forward with institutionalization.

The institution's actual strength and sustainability has been compromised by its leadership, just as broader political instability has ultimately eroded institutional capacities. All eyes were on Thailand's new government in August 2011, which claimed to be interested in reform after a year of intense political violence. The extent to which the state's human rights practices will match its rhetoric remains to be seen.[71]

Executive Control in Yemen

A few years after *Yemen* unified and introduced multiparty elections in 1990, the government created a Supreme (or Higher) National Committee for Human Rights by decree in 1997.[72] In 2001, a full-blown Ministry of Human Rights was also established, subsequently supported by international actors like the EU and UNDP; it replaced the human rights committee in 2003. At the same time, the government began adding human rights directorates to various ministries. By the time of the UPR in 2009, government representatives reported that a committee was studying the feasibility of an independent NHRI in conformance with the Paris Principles.

The European Union seems to have played a significant role in these developments. The same year Yemen created the National Committee for Human Rights, the two parties signed a cooperation agreement in November 1997; though the focus was mostly economic, the agreement included a human rights and democracy clause.[73] In 2003, a political dialogue between the two sides was announced. More specifically, in 2005, a five-year project of the European Commission (in partnership with Yemeni NGOs and the Human Rights Ministry) was tasked with strengthening the ministry and beginning a dialogue on a possible NHRI.[74] In its submission to the UPR, even Yemen's government conceded that the idea for an NHRI was the result of an EU initiative.[75]

The Ministry of Human Rights, while active, has not been an independent body. For example, the government made much of the fact that the ministry's first head was a woman. Yet as a former ambassador and Ministry of Information official, al-Suswa seemed more prepared to defend state practices than to champion human rights. With an American graduate degree in communications, Amat al-Aleem al-Suswa worked to project a favorable international image for Yemen, while countering accusations of abuse. As she claimed, "The initiative to correct what is wrong comes from within—not from pressure from outside. . . . These abuses recorded by Amnesty and others do not mean we have systemic abuses. It just means we have something to work on."[76]

Yemen's efforts to create a national human rights committee in 1997 and then replace it with a Ministry of Human Rights in the early 2000s seem to have been driven by efforts to retain executive control over human rights issues while appeasing critics. Yemen had ratified the human rights covenants in 1987, before unification; yet it was only in the context of growing cooperation with the EU and UNDP that the possibility of an NHRI was raised. The government was also highly attuned to transnational criticism of its rights practices. Since unifying in 1990, the country had spiraled into civil war while domestic rights activism had risen, with the formation of groups like the Yemeni Human Rights Organization. In this scheme, the state's human rights bodies represented attempts by the executive to retain tight control and manage national human rights discourse. Alongside ongoing international regime pressures, including the UPR, an independent NHRI in Yemen will depend on broader political reforms. However, after months of street protests by tens of thousands of Yemenis in 2011, and the ouster of President Ali Abdullah Saleh, who ruled for thirty-three years, change at least became imaginable.[77]

Malaysia's SUHAKAM

Malaysia was the last Asian country in the 1990s to create an NHRI, when it established in 1999 a national human rights commission (SUHAKAM). The Human Rights Commission Act of that year gave formal rise to the NHRI, though calls for such an institution had been present since mid-decade. Indeed, domestic NGOs and civil society groups had lobbied unsuccessfully for a human rights institution. Likewise, in 1995, Deputy Prime Minister Tun Musa Hitam, who had been Malaysia's representative to the United Nations and was representing the country before the UN Commission on Human Rights, called for an NHRI; he would go on to be its first leader in 1999. If NGOs and a political leader with ties to the United Nations helped to define a human rights commission as a worthwhile goal, especially in a context of subregional diffusion (as the Philippines, Indonesia, and Thailand had already adopted the institution), state leaders themselves were driven by a desire to appease transnational critics.

Nonstate actors met the institution's creation with widespread skepticism. Once local NGOs learned that the government was creating an NHRI, they convened a forum in July 1999 to offer their recommendations. That same month, Malaysia's parliament considered the bill that would create a human rights commission, passing it in September with no public consultation. The period was generally one of rising opposition and economic turmoil, with the country having entered a recession the previous year. In the words of one local NGO, it was "a source of deflection and providing the international community with a warped view of the state of human rights in the country."[78] Other critics referred to it as "a whitewashing strategy or deflecting shield against the onslaught of mounting domestic and international criticism," especially given the recent political imprisonment (and beating) of Deputy Prime Minister Anwar Ibrahim.[79] The Anwar incident served to galvanize a broader democratic reform movement, out of which arose support for a national human rights commission.[80]

Some analysts warned that the NHRI's creation should not be viewed as a liberal measure by the prime minister. Rather, Malaysia's incentive to create the commission emanated from its interest in appeasing transnational critics (the decision to create an NHRI was announced in April 1999, by none other than the foreign affairs minister), even if the idea had first been introduced by civil society actors. Years after it was created, Deputy Prime Minister Nazri Aziz admitted in 2006, "we have never planned to give any teeth to Suhakam."[81] The body has indeed remained largely a promotional one, but it has also continued receiving international funding and it was fully accredited in 2002.

The state's reluctance to strengthen the human rights commission is putatively tied to ideological gaps between "Asian values" and Western rights discourse, with the former prioritizing development and basic needs. The reality has proved to be more complex, with state actors' interests in evading accountability running deep. As an NHRI created in a nondemocratic context to appease transnational critics, Malaysia's NHRI has had limited scope in which to maneuver and pull off a diplomatic balancing feat; SUHAKAM has had to challenge state actions to maintain its integrity and credibility, but only without risking its own institutional survival.

NHRIs in the New Millennium

After 2000, the range of states that joined the trend of creating an NHRI in the Asia-Pacific region was remarkable: Mongolia, South Korea, Jordan and Qatar, Afghanistan, Timor-Leste, and the Maldives. The role of international and regional actors was significant, especially in the context of democratizing states and in (post)conflict zones. By 2012, all of these institutions were fully accredited as NHRIs, with the exception of the Maldives, which was partially accredited. The experiences of some of these states in creating NHRIs, including those of Mongolia and the Maldives, have remained virtually unknown despite their rich detail. Similarly, South Korea reveals a fascinating account of state-society interactions and tensions in creating an NHRI, though this too has been largely overlooked. The specifics are different, but the overarching framework of strategic emulation still holds.

Diffusion and Convergence in Mongolia

Mongolia created its National Human Rights Commission in 2000, largely as a result of international regime pressures. It was not undergoing a major regulatory moment, it had long ratified the human rights covenants, and it enjoyed a relatively strong human rights record. Indeed, the country had embarked on a peaceful democratic transition in 1990, and the 1992 constitution highlighted the place of human rights; also in 1992, a human rights subcommittee was formed within the parliament's standing law committee. Throughout the 1990s, human rights NGOs began forming as well, serving as conduits for international standards.[82]

Mongolia, moreover, was heavily influenced during this period by UN programs, just as a new government elected in 2000 was intent on consolidating democratic rule and collaborating with international actors to ensure regional security. Mongolia was, after all, a very large country with a small population, sandwiched between Russia and China and highly dependent on foreign debt (especially so after the early 1990s, when it turned to commercial lending). The United Nations, and especially the UNDP, thus took an active role in the country's political and economic reforms under democratization. This fit in with the UNDP's own turn in the late 1990s to integrate human rights more fully into its "sustainable human development" and "good governance" paradigms, represented most directly in the adoption in 1999 of a Global Human Rights Strength Program, commonly known as HURIST, in partnership with the OHCHR.[83] Among the objectives of HURIST was to strengthen national human rights capacities, and NHRIs were mentioned explicitly as an institution to support.

It was in this broader international context that the UNDP and OHCHR reinforced ties with Mongolia in the late 1990s. The UNDP, for its part, had already established in 1996 a Partnership for Progress with the country, focusing on economic growth and capitalizing on the promises of a new government to accelerate democratic reforms. Mongolia was clearly a strong candidate for UNDP support. Not only was the government a willing partner, but the Mongolian government had declared itself a nuclear-free country in 1992. Even Mongolia's location, prone to extreme climactic changes and natural disasters, including a severe drought in 2000, made it a strong target of UN support.[84]

The new government that came to office in 2000 was clearly intent on shedding its former communist mantle and demonstrating its commitment to deepening democratization. An international conference on human security was co-sponsored by Mongolia and the UNDP in May, and the new government's own action plan was titled "Good Governance for Human Security," closely aligning itself with the UNDP's agenda. At the Millennium Summit in August 2000, when the Millennium Development Goals were adopted, Mongolia participated, preparing a memorandum on the UN role in protecting the security interests of small states. This was a government cooperating closely with international actors.

Under these conditions, NHRI-diffusing agents, including the Asia Pacific Forum, proved significant. According to the UNDP, when Mongolia created an NHRI in late 2000, it reflected the influence of three factors that year: UNDP's general role in promoting governance and human rights, technical assistance offered by OHCHR in preparing the draft law, and a visit by former high commissioner Mary Robinson in August.[85] Even so, as early as October 1998, Mongolia's representative had stated before the United Nations in New York that "the establishment of the National Human Rights Commission in Mongolia is under consideration. A relevant draft law has been submitted to the Parliament for its adoption."[86] This first step reflected the role of the newly established Asia Pacific Forum in 1996. Mongolian government representatives had attended the first (1996) and second (1997) annual workshops of NHRIs in the Asia Pacific, hosted by the APF in Australia and India, respectively. By December, at the invitation of the Mongolian government, the APF (with funding from Australia AID) conducted an in-country needs assessment and made a presentation to a parliamentary seminar about the potential role of an NHRI. In February 1998, government representatives attended another regional workshop on NHRIs in Indonesia.[87] By the time the UNDP and OHCHR moved to promote such a body, regional specialized actors had laid the essential groundwork.

Once the NHRI became operational in February 2001, it moved quickly in its work, issuing a highly critical first report in October, and by 2003 it was already fully accredited internationally.[88] Its work was reinforced by international actors, including a five-year project (2001–6) launched by the UNDP and the OHCHR.[89] More recently, Mongolia's NHRI entered into an agreement with the UNDP in December 2011 to further strengthen its institutional capacities.

Mongolia's NHRI reveals how international regime pressures can play a highly effective role when external and internal obligations already converge.

Korean Hunger Strikes and Transnational Campaigning

The Republic of Korea also created a National Human Rights Commission in 2001, quickly moving to play an international leadership role. Since being fully accredited in 2004, it has served as a member of the International Coordinating Committee, in addition to being especially active in the region. As the commission was forged at a time when the government had accepted treaty obligations, but was not experiencing a regulatory moment or high violations, its creation reflected international regime pressures more than anything else. Yet creating an independent NHRI in compliance with the Paris Principles proved a highly contentious process, as a tug of war ensued between the Ministry of Justice and domestic human rights activists in alliance with international actors.

Both domestic human rights organizations and international actors promoted the idea of an NHRI, even before Kim Dae-Jung included it as a presidential campaign promise in 1997. Domestic human rights organizations, which had grown considerably in the 1980s, following the World Conference in Vienna, called for the creation of a national human rights body.[90] Government representatives attended in September 1997 the APF's second regional workshop of NHRIs in India, claiming to explore national models and stating their intent to create a human rights agency.[91] Transnational encounters such as these seem to have been facilitated by the Ministry of Foreign Affairs more than governmental interest in creating an NHRI.[92] More broadly, since joining the United Nations in 1991 and soon after embarking on democratization, South Korea had sought an active role in the international organization. Most notably, it had won a seat on the Human Rights Commission between 1993 and 1998.

In the lead-up to Kim Dae-Jung's election, the long-standing dissident vowed to create a Human Rights Protection Law and an NHRI in accordance with the recommendations of the UN Human Rights Commission. These proposals were made alongside other rights- and democracy-enhancing ideas, including passage of anticorruption legislation and revocation of a national security law, as well as the release of political prisoners. As someone who aspired to be the country's "human rights president" and who would go on to win the Nobel Peace Prize in 2000, the human rights frame was alluring.[93] Creating a national body to complement the work of the United Nations' own commission, on which Korea held a seat at the time, must also have seemed appealing.

The new president did not delay in moving forward with his campaign promise of creating a human rights commission; nor did other actors desist from promoting it. Not long after the president took office in 1998, Amnesty International sent the president detailed suggestions for a human rights commission. Regardless, the Ministry of Justice, which had never advocated for a commission but had had a Human Rights Division since 1962 (under martial law), moved to introduce a draft bill in September for a very weak commission, one subsumed under its own ministry and lacking independence. The bill was supported by politicians responsible for past human rights violations and was not the product of broad consultation.[94]

Immediately, a transnational campaign emerged challenging the draft legislation. Over thirty human rights NGOs established the Joint Committee for Setting Up a National Human Rights Authority and Promoting the Relevant Legislation; the committee was a direct response to the draft legislation introduced by the Ministry of Justice. The Korean Council of Trade Unions referred to the draft bill for an NHRI as an "attempt to make human rights government property."[95] On the international side, Amnesty International and the OHCHR both joined in criticizing the bill, with the former including it in a list of human rights concerns in early 1999.[96] Domestic and foreign critics specifically asserted that the proposed institution did not conform to the Paris Principles, that it had insufficient powers of investigation and lacked independence.

When despite these efforts, the Cabinet approved the bill in March 1999, over two dozen human rights activists went on a hunger strike. In a letter declaring their aims, circulated internationally, they said their intent was "to draw attention to the original purpose of setting up an independent, national institution for human rights and the inadequacy of the existing bill."[97] The following month another four dozen NGOs added their voices to the joint committee. And when Korea hosted the International Conference of NGOs in October 1999, the president of Lawyers for a Democratic Society, himself a former prisoner of conscience, approached Mary Robinson and delivered the following message on behalf of human rights groups: "We are convinced that your meeting with the president will be of great importance to the destiny of the Korean Human Rights Commission. If you even slightly hint that the government bill is acceptable only in the light of the Paris Principles, the president would not hesitate to bulldoze the bill in the National Assembly."[98] Robinson responded by asserting publicly that the Korean Human Rights Commission "could serve as a model for the whole of East Asia if the commission were allowed true independence."[99]

The government responded with minor concessions. In October 1998, it permitted a public hearing about the draft bill, where at least one international expert was invited to comment. Under pressure, they revised the bill somewhat, expanding its jurisdiction and scope, and creating it as a freestanding statutory body, though problems of independence remained. Most of the resistance was still coming from the Ministry of Justice, while the ruling party for its part postponed passage for the remainder of 1999. Following another hunger strike in December 2000, waged by approximately forty activists over the course of thirteen days, the government improved the bill marginally in April 2001. And despite activists' calls for a presidential veto, the law establishing an NHRI was published that May. Even then, NGOs organized a Solidarity Committee in July, which did not stop the government from forming a preparatory and planning committee in August before opening the institution's doors to the public in November.[100]

Despite its contested origins, the NHRI almost immediately proved to be a vibrant body. Some observers even see the institution as a "tipping point" for human rights in the country, ironically helping to transform human rights governance from a top-down affair to a more horizontal and cooperative approach.[101] This may be why there was such an uproar when, beginning in mid-2007, the NHRI's independence came under attack, causing its head to resign. This led the Asian Human Rights Center, among many NGOs, to declare that the institution was no longer in compliance with the Paris Principles. As one editorial lamented in 2011, "An invaluable organization that represented the product of some three decades of fighting for democracy was destroyed in an instant by an administration and figures who hitched a free ride on democracy."[102] Still, the NHRI was reaccredited in 2008, and the country passed its UPR in 2009 with no relevant recommendations, though Amnesty International and regional organizations have continued to resist and mobilize against government attacks on the NHRI.

South Korea's NHRI was first created under a president internationally recognized for his human rights commitments, borne out of his own personal imprisonment and resistance. Yet a ministry of justice, which had long controlled the human rights agenda in the country, was not prepared to cede control to an independent body, regardless of the potential international benefits. A transnational alliance of NHRI supporters applied sufficient pressure to create an institution that managed to play an activist role domestically and internationally among peer institutions. The same political detractors that had been present at the creation, however, returned in different form; and since 2007, they have challenged the institution's role. In some ways, the NHRI served as a flash point of domestic activism, as social opposition to the regime's plans took on unprecedented scope. That the creation of an *independent* institution generated such passionate stances on the part of activists indicates not only the extent to which this NHRI represented societal demands for a democratic, accountable state but also the power of such institutions to galvanize social demands. Even when domestic rights practices appear to converge with external obligations, a closer look below the surface reveals that state institutions still remain vulnerable to the vagaries of political power.

NHRIs in the Middle East: Jordan and Qatar

Jordan's National Centre for Human Rights, fully accredited since 2006, has also played a leadership role internationally and regionally.[103] Created by royal decree in 2002, the institution was proposed by a temporary royal commission established in 2000. Though the body was part of a series of nominal reforms undertaken by the regime, partly in response to rising domestic opposition, international actors initially promoted the idea of institutionalizing human rights. Jordan's NHRI was the product of appeasement, in a context of external obligations and ongoing abuse, as well as international regime diffusion.[104]

King Abdullah, who had taken over the Jordanian monarchy in 1999, agreed to create the Royal Commission for Human Rights in March 2000. The commission was headed by Queen Rania and was charged with assessing the human rights situation, as a prelude to a national action plan. The group functioned until 2002, and among its proposals was the creation of the National Centre for Human Rights. Yet the initial idea for the royal commission had been proposed by the president of Rights and Humanity, a multifaith, British-based NGO that was hired as a consultant by the UNDP and had visited Jordan multiple times between 1999 and 2000. More specifically, in early February 2000, the head of Rights and Humanity and UN high commissioner for human rights Mary Robinson met with Jordan's king and queen. The meeting took place in conjunction with the National Seminar on Developing a Strategy for the Promotion and Protection of Human Rights in Jordan, which Rights and Humanity along with the UN Office of the High Commissioner for Human Rights helped to organize.[105]

The turn to human rights came at a time when Jordan's regime was looking to make symbolic gestures, since it had responded heavy-handedly to rising domestic opposition but its ties to foreign governments and international financial institutions were rapidly growing. In 2001, just as the royal commission was conducting its work and imagining how to institutionalize human rights, a countervailing trend was unfolding: pro-intifada demonstrations were shut down, a controversial election law was passed, the national assembly was dissolved, and parliamentary elections were postponed; after September 11, a series of temporary laws further restricted civil rights. That year also saw new pressures from the United States, a close ally whose actions in the region were opposed by social groups, a World Bank privatization program that required combating corruption, and ongoing fear of political gains by Islamists. Against this backdrop and after having somewhat deliberalized, the king took a series of measures beginning in 2002 to demonstrate the regime's commitment to democratization. The creation of the National Centre for Human Rights fit into this overall scheme.[106]

Almost as soon as the human rights institution was created, the government was keen on having it accredited internationally. While international actors welcomed the NHRI's establishment, they raised questions about its independence and funding. A training program under the auspices of the OHCHR, staffed by New Zealand's Human Rights Commission, offered assistance in complaints handling and human rights education in 2004. When the institution applied for membership in the Asia Pacific Forum that year, the APF approved only an associate membership, calling for numerous reforms and extending technical support. Likewise, when the institution applied for international accreditation, the ICC found it only partially compliant, assigning it a B status in both 2006 and 2007, noting problems of funding, pluralism, and the appointment process. The CRC also called on the institution to make improvements, especially in its resources and by broadening its mandate to include the police and military under its jurisdiction. In partial response to these critiques, the government at last incorporated the NHRI into law in 2006.[107]

The idea for an NHRI in Jordan, then, was proposed by a temporary commission established as a result of a UNDP project in the country. And given the broader context, institutionalizing human rights helped the regime appease potential critics during a period of ongoing abuse. If Jordan did not create an NHRI until then it was because its liberalization heyday came in the early 1990s, before regional regime pressures in the Asia Pacific had taken off. By the time regional diffusion had picked up, Jordan was already deliberalizing. International regime pressures supported the institution throughout its existence and helped to account for basic reforms. But even though Jordan has proven to be a global leader among NHRIs, it was not an innovator per se. Jordan's NHRI illustrates a third-wave institution, which had its origins in a government strategy of appeasement and then evolved into more of a global leader—projecting the image of a rights-protective regime to an international audience.

Around the same time, *Qatar's* emir, Shaykh Hamad bin Khalifa Al Thani, created the National Human Rights Committee by decree in November 2002.[108] The first NHRI in the subregion of any Gulf Cooperation Council state appeared as part of a package of liberalization initiatives that included constitutional and electoral reforms. In this sense, Qatar's NHRI arose mainly as a result of a regulatory moment, since the country had not acceded to major international human rights treaties and human rights abuses were relatively low. The institution was partially accredited in 2006, fully so in 2009.

The small Gulf country embarked on a gradual process of political reform after Hamad bin Khalifa al Thani forcibly took over the country's leadership from his father. One of the most significant steps in the new liberalization program was the Central Municipal Council elections in 1999, the first time women were ever allowed to vote or run in an election; the symbolic significance of the election, held on International Women's Day, was hard to overlook. The NHRI's appearance, then, was part of this "national comprehensive reform policy," just as the government also created in 2003 a human rights office within the Interior Ministry's Legal Department, supplementing a Human Rights Office already under the Foreign Ministry.[109]

Though Qatari government officials emphasize that, unlike other countries, the NHRI was not established "either in response to internal human rights crises or in response to external pressures," there is evidence that international influence did matter. In 2001, when the World Trade Organization held its biannual high-profile meeting in Doha, international NGOs criticized the choice by drawing attention to the country's human rights record. Human Rights Watch described the choice as "an effort by the WTO to avoid the noisy demonstrations of the past year by picking a country that bans demonstrations."[110] It is true that domestic human rights organizations were weak in Qatar, where political parties still are not permitted. But broadly speaking, the government seemed concerned about its international image, and the leadership may have been convinced that developing a reputation as a democratizing state would help protect it in a volatile and insecure region.

According to some accounts, political reforms, of which the NHRI was one example, were intended "to generate international recognition of 'democratic' and 'modern' reforms that seem uncharacteristic in the Arab Gulf. These reforms were to be instrumental in bolstering the legitimacy—and ultimately, security of the new Qatari regime." If "the reform process in Qatar uses institutions regarding elections and women's political rights to bolster the state's international reputation," the same might be true of the regime's use of official human rights institutions. There is little question that, in addition to being part of a more comprehensive set of reforms, the regime had "an eye to Qatar's international image" when it liberalized, including by creating the NHRI.[111]

Yet the role of international regime pressures also was significant. A few months before the emir's decree establishing the NHRI, Qatar joined thirty other countries in Beirut, agreeing to a final statement that concluded the UN Tenth Workshop on Regional Co-Operation for the Promotion and Protection of Human Rights in the Asia-Pacific Region; the statement confirmed states' support for NHRIs in the region, perhaps not surprising given that the Asia Pacific Forum played a leading role in the workshop. Agreeing, along with dozens of other countries in the region, to promote the notion of NHRIs must have shaped the government's decision to announce its own version of the institution eight months later. By 2004, Qatar would be hosting the very same workshop.[112]

The prospect of international accreditation was also significant in strengthening the NHRI. When the NHRI applied for regular membership in the APF in 2005, it was accredited only as an associate member, given concerns over the commission's nonstatutory foundations, as well as questions of independence and representation. The institution later applied successfully for upgraded membership in 2008. Likewise, when the NHRI first applied for international accreditation in 2006, it was found to be only partially compliant. The B rating was changed to an A rating only in 2009. Since then, the institution has been criticized for denying international accusations of human rights violations, especially of human trafficking, though it continues to play an international leadership role. For instance, in 2010, Qatar hosted the First Gulf Forum of Human Rights Institutions, and in 2011 it hosted the Arab-European Human Rights Dialogue. However, Qatar's participation in the UPR process did not raise issues relating to its NHRI, already fully accredited and with its own government sitting on the Human Rights Council.[113]

Qatar's NHRI was created as part of a regulatory moment, leading initially to an institution that was only partially compliant with international standards. International regime pressures defined the NHRI as a body imbued with international legitimacy, reinforcing democratization reforms. Having an internationally recognized and active NHRI, in addition to other signs of democratic commitment, must certainly have seemed an appealing strategy for a small country in an insecure region—the novel use of state institutions as a means of enhancing regional security.

Dodging Bullets: Promoting Rights in War-Torn Afghanistan

Afghanistan created one of the region's best-known NHRIs in 2002, an institution originally envisioned in the Bonn Agreement. The 2002 agreement called on the Interim Administration, with the assistance of the United Nations, to create "an independent human rights commission, whose responsibilities will include human rights monitoring, investigation of violations of human rights, and development of domestic human rights institutions."[114] The Afghanistan Independent Human Rights Commission (AIHRC) was created by presidential decree in 2002, incorporated into the constitution in 2004, and implemented via a presidential decree a year later.[115] Despite a tenuous security situation, weak rule of law, and rampant impunity and corruption, the Commission has complied with the Paris Principles and been exceedingly active. In 2007, it was fully accredited internationally as an NHRI.

Strong assistance from the United Nations and a determined, high-profile leader reinforced the institution from the outset, despite the country being in the midst of ongoing conflict. A special human rights unit of the UN Assistance Mission in Afghanistan aided the institution and placed UN personnel alongside NHRI staff on the ground. International actors welcomed the setup. For instance, in 2003 Human Rights Watch called for even more UN assistance to the commission: "In particular, it should post substantial numbers of its monitors to work side by side with commission staff."[116] Since its inception, the AIHRC has been headed by Dr. Sima Samar, the first Hazara woman to earn a medical degree from Kabul University.[117] The combination of international protection and a resolute leader and staff account for the commission's energetic drive and output for over a decade.

As part of Afghanistan's UPR in 2009, various foreign governments called on Afghanistan's leadership to increase resources to the Commission and strengthen the appointment process. The UN high commissioner for human rights herself reiterated the concerns raised in the UPR process, namely that most of the institution's funding came from foreign sources; indeed dozens of foreign governments and international organizations have subsidized the agency since its inception.[118] Likewise, appointing the head of the commission requires a vote of confidence from the Lower House of Parliament, a potential limitation on the institution's independence.

Afghanistan's NHRI represents the quintessential NHRI created in the midst of violent conflict. Not only was the institution crafted by an internationally brokered peace agreement, but the work of the Commission would not have unfolded in quite the same way without the general presence of UN staff and the weight of foreign funding. The question of institutional sustainability remains, of course, but not because of local incapacity. On the contrary, international actors have been present in the country for so long that it is unclear the extent to which state actors accept the AIHRC or merely acquiesce to international forces that offer protection in a highly insecure environment—one in which the NHRI's head has to rely on armed bodyguards. The deeper challenge the AIHRC faces is that many of the human rights problems it addresses have been created or exacerbated by the same international community that is responsible for its institutional survival. Conflict zones highlight, more starkly than anywhere else, that NHRIs ultimately must rely on their domestic political context.

State Building after Violence: Timor-Leste's Provedoria

East Timor's Provedoria per Direitos Humanos et Justiça was created in 2002, when it was incorporated into the newly independent country's constitution of that year. The country was in the process of accepting international human rights obligations, and it was entering a postconflict situation, with the worst human rights abuses just behind it. Implementing legislation was passed in 2004, the first ombudsman was elected one year later and the office became operational in 2006—fully accredited as an NHRI two years later.[119] The country's primary incentive for creating an NHRI was a regulatory moment, strikingly marked by national independence and constitution making. However, the transition was heavily internationalized, with external actors participating intensely in the NHRI's establishment and direction.

The NHRI cannot itself be separated from the strong international involvement that marked the transition to statehood, including a UN Transition Administration that took over all aspects of basic governance. In fact, the Transition Administration's replacement, UNMISET, helped to set up the Provedor's office. Even the national constitution was internationally driven, pushed through quickly after a UN-sponsored referendum led to independence from almost twenty-five years of Indonesian rule. Widespread retaliation from Indonesian forces and mass violence followed the referendum. A constitutive assembly, organized by international actors, was dominated by one party (Freitlin), and it did not rely on popular consultation.[120]

Even before independence, a workshop was held in Dili in August 2000 on Human Rights and the Future of East Timor, where UN high commissioner for human rights Mary Robinson pledged "concrete support" for a "human rights commission," among other initiatives, to enhance national capacities. The workshop was cosponsored by the United Nations Transitional Administraton in East Timor (UNTAET) and the East Timorese National Jurists Association, cofinanced by UNDP and UNICEF, and attended by a range of international actors from UNTAET, UN bodies, international NGOs, foreign diplomatic missions, and the World Bank.[121] Substantively, the NHRI was modeled on the Portuguese ombudsman, though the human rights mandate of East Timor's was more explicit, as highlighted in the institution's name.

The donor-driven aspects of Timor-Leste's ombudsman were indeed significant, as international actors provided technical and financial support for setting up the Provedor. In the initial group convened by the prime minister's human rights advisor in 2002, UNMISET members were included. And in a consultation workshop that June, the OHCHR's special adviser participated, as did international NGOs.[122] The prime minister's working group looked to NHRI models elsewhere, opting for a hybrid ombudsman with an anticorruption function that would satisfy the criteria stipulated in the Paris Principles. The Timorese ombudsman's anticorruption mandate appealed, in particular, to the World Bank, which had written a paper in mid-1999 about the role of ombudsman agencies as independent auditing bodies that could oversee (potentially corrupt) public officials; and in a subsequent document focused specifically on Timor-Leste, the World Bank linked the Provedor to police oversight.[123]

Once created, the government's weak financial support for the institution—relative to expectations—meant a reliance on external sources of funding, by international donors who were keen on shaping certain aspects of the institution's agenda. As one observer notes rather critically, international involvement skewed the NHRI's agenda: "Within the Office of the Provedor, there are assistance programs from the World Bank, United Nations Integrated Mission in Timor-Leste, UNHCR, OHCHR, USAID and others. The different assistance programs fragment the Office of the Provedor because most donors prefer to support the Human Rights Section and leave out the Governance Section."[124] In particular, the World Bank's insertion into the mix, with its focus on maintaining stability, and therefore investor confidence, pushed it to emphasize anticorruption and oversight of the police, perhaps compromising broader institutional capacities.

The UPR process in 2011 revealed that a decade of ongoing international assistance from the United Nations and other actors had not been sufficient to strengthen the state's commitment to human rights governance. Police abuses remained rampant, past accountability still was unresolved, and state bodies did not heed the majority of the ombudsman's recommendations.[125] Likewise, under pressure to do so, the government established a National Children's Rights Commission in 2009 but did not give it the needed resources to carry out its work. The Provedor has allied with civil society (and even its Indonesian counterpart), but its own calls for state cooperation have fallen on deaf ears.[126]

It is unclear whether international involvement has contributed to a pattern whereby the state merely creates the structural outlines of democracy, establishing institutions and rules according to an internationally approved template and then largely disregards them. The fact that violations were fairly low, and a UN presence was on the ground, may have dampened transnational pressures for change. The Provedor in Timor-Leste is the product of an externally driven regulatory moment, resulting in an accredited and active body. The real test of the *national* institution will come if and when international actors loosen their grip over the Timorese body.

NHRIs across Central Asia

Landlocked *Kyrgyzstan* created an ombudsman in 2002, over a decade after independence in 1991. The human rights ombudsman was established by law and incorporated into the constitution via amendment in 2003.[127] It was part of a wider presidential initiative, in a decade labeled "Human Rights 2002–2010." The country had acceded to most major international human rights treaties in the 1990s and was considered "an oasis of democracy" in an otherwise troubled region, but two factors are worth noting. First, though the constitution embraced the language of human rights, it was also a contradictory document that provided for weak accountability mechanisms; such mechanisms would become the locus of constitutional and public sector reforms.[128] Second, the human rights situation began deteriorating toward the end of the 1990s, with the institutionalization of human rights serving as a partial counterweight to mounting abuses.[129]

When the ombudsman was set up in 2002, it was a few months after a nationwide protest erupted, following the killing of five nonviolent protestors by the police; this incident led to government concessions, including a process of constitutional reform. A predecessor body that had been created in 1998 by presidential decree (the Commission for Human Rights) reflected a similar dynamic following rising human rights abuses. The OSCE, for example, had turned its attention to human rights in the country, including holding a seminar in late 1997 where serious human rights concerns were raised; the United States had also critiqued the regime's human rights practices, though it applied pressure only at the level of rhetoric. As Human Rights Watch warned in a 1998 report, "The international community continued, for the most part, to accept at face value statements in support of human rights from president Akaev, who benefited from the country's liberal democratic image cultivated in the first years after independence; it largely ignored the state of worsening human rights."[130] In this scheme, the creation of a presidential human rights commission must have seemed a viable strategy for deflecting criticism. And starting in 1999, the OSCE began laying the foundations of a draft law for an ombudsman, later providing the institution with start-up funds.

Soon after its creation, international actors called for Kyrgyzstan's ombudsman to be strengthened. Treaty bodies like the CRC, for example, urged the government to establish an NHRI in compliance with the Paris Principles. In 2008, the OHCHR held a series of workshops aimed at strengthening the institution. And during the UPR in 2010, which took place after widespread violence and the president's ousting, the country was pressured to create an NHRI in full compliance with the Paris Principles.[131] Indeed, in 2012, the Kyrgyz Republic submitted for accreditation its National Human Rights Institute of Akyikatch (ombudsman), deemed partially compliant. A combination of external obligations and domestic abuse, along with international regime pressures, help explain the ombudsman's gradual evolution in this Turkic state.

As the last Soviet Republic to gain national independence, *Kazakhstan* also created a commissioner for human rights, or national ombudsman, in 2002. While the former Soviet Republic had become independent in 1991, it followed a very different trajectory in the early posttransition period from those of neighboring states. It took over a decade to create its NHRI, and then only by presidential decree. And it would be yet another decade before Kazakhstan's national ombudsman would apply for accreditation as an NHRI.

The presidential Commission for Human Rights in 1993 may have been modeled on Russia's NHRI. Concerted proposals for an ombudsman were raised in a January 1995 seminar at the United Nations in Geneva attended by government officials, including from the president's human rights commission. They brought the idea with them back to Kazakhstan and considered it in drafting the second postindependence constitution in 1995 (the first had been in 1993), but the institution met with widespread opposition.[132] The parliament would later reject draft legislation for the institution, closely supported by OSCE and UNDP.[133]

In an intriguing aside, illustrating the politics of regional networking, Russia's presidential human rights commission met with its Kazakh counterpart in Akmola in March 1998. The two bodies agreed to meet twice a year and to encourage the formation of similar institutions throughout the CIS, with an eye to creating a subregional grouping of similar bodies.[134] As one of the most stalwart supporters of the CIS, Kazakhstan was an appropriate partner for Russia in this endeavor. And Russia may have been looking for the CIS to play a more prominent role in the world of NHRIs and lead its own regional network.

But in Kazakhstan itself, the president's embrace of human rights rhetoric did not at all match the reality on the ground. The president was firmly an autocrat, essentially exchanging his title of local Communist Party head for Kazakh-stan's president. The 1993 constitution and subsequent ones were top-down instruments, part of an "institutional architecture" erected after independence rather than negotiated at the moment of transition. And the postindependence constitutions served only to enhance the presidency's powers incrementally. The 1990s thus transpired in a climate of rising abusiveness. The regime, moreover, had not yet acceded to the two principal international human rights covenants; it would do so only in 2006.[135]

The creation of the ombudsman in 2002 reflected rising international pres-sure in the aftermath of a notoriously contentious election in 1999 and an alarm-ing increase in human rights abuses. While the idea had been proposed for over a decade, deteriorating human rights conditions pushed the president to offer a symbol of reform. At a meeting in 2002, a few months before the NHRI was announced, EU officials made it very clear that human rights were now an "es-sential condition" of ongoing relations. Pressure from the United States, though mixed, also intensified during this period. In this context, the creation of the ombudsman in 2002 was a response to international human rights pressures, supported by the same state officials that oversaw a policy of repression.[136]

Once created, the president attempted to expand the institution's powers to appease critics while still retaining control over the institution (e.g., directly appointing the ombudsman). Despite the government's assertion that the insti-tution conformed to the Paris Principles, observers like the European Parlia-ment, the OHCHR, and the UN Committee Against Torture were far more critical. Perhaps in response to these growing calls to comply with the Paris Principles, the government asked the Venice Commission to evaluate the om-budsman's statute and see how it might be improved. By the time of the UPR in 2010, numerous countries urged Kazakhstan to strengthen its ombudsman in conformance with international standards.[137] Two years later, the NHRI was submitted for accreditation and found to be partially compliant. International actors had proposed the idea of an ombudsman, while domestic abuses pushed Kazakhstan to create an NHRI when it did. International accreditation pres-sures then led to the institution's strengthening.[138]

Maldives: Social Protests as Tipping Point

The Maldives, Asia's smallest country spanning a vast archipelago, created a Human Rights Commission by presidential decree in 2003. The decision to form the NHRI occurred in the absence of any apparently strong incentives, since the country did not face a regulatory moment, had not yet acceded to the most important human rights treaties, and had a relatively low level of violations. Rather, the decision to create the commission seems to have been in direct response to a series of unprecedented social protests, themselves occasioned by the publicized death of five prisoners, in a country where political parties were not permitted to function and repression of prisoners was commonplace. The idea of creating an NHRI arose from governmental participation in human rights forums sponsored by the Commonwealth and the United Nations, just as the government traced the idea of national human rights action plan to a UN regional workshop on human rights in Bangkok in 1999.[139]

That the Human Rights Commission was intended at least partly for an international audience was clear from the outset. The body was initially created by presidential decree on December 10, 2003, International Human Rights Day, with implementing legislation passed two years later; President Maumoon Abdul Gayoom, who had ruled the country continuously since 1978, announced it in his inaugural address in November 2003. According to a press release by the Foreign Ministry the day the decree was issued, the president vowed that the commission would "function in accordance with the Paris Principles."[140]

The real impetus for the announcement, however, seems to have been an unprecedented wave of civil protests that began unexpectedly in September 2003, when Evan Naseem, a nineteen-year-old boy who was in police custody for drug charges, was killed. After fellow inmates realized he had been tortured, a prison riot broke out and five detainees were killed by the police, within earshot of a nearby tourist beach. Naseem's family displayed their son's body, with his mother speaking out on behalf of her son. This single visceral, representational act (of a mother with her son's body) seemed to catalyze a vocal and public outcry— presumably surrounding this incident but in fact reflecting broader opposition to an entrenched autocratic regime that silenced protestors and did not permit oppositional voices. In a country where people did not express their political grievances openly, five thousand people filled the streets and squares in defiant protest, throwing stones at some government buildings while setting fire to others (including the High Court and the Elections Commission). The president's "reelection" in a yes-no referendum shortly thereafter and his announcement of an "Agenda for Reform, Democracy and Human Rights" proved ineffective in meeting deep-seated social demands.[141]

Two aspects of this incident are quite remarkable in hindsight. First is the fact that human rights groups like Amnesty International had already provided details of repression against prisoners before the fall 2003 episode. For example,

Amnesty International had issued a report that July, titled "Republic of Maldives: Repression of Peaceful Political Opponents." That report, in fact, referenced the torture and death in custody of another nineteen-year-old boy, which had gone largely unnoticed. But it was only when Naseem's scarred, beaten body was displayed and the public was faced with deeply personalized and incontrovertible evidence of abuse that social protest erupted. The second astonishing aspect of this incident is that it led in November, following the protests, to the departure of Mohamed Nasheed. The former prisoner of conscience went into exile in Sri Lanka, where he founded the Maldives Democratic Party; he would later become the Maldives' first democratically elected president in 2008.[142]

Despite international support for the institution, especially from the UN and the APF, the NHRI's early institutional life reflected tight presidential control. This was starkly highlighted by another public protest that broke out in August 2004. This time the government responded with widespread repression, detention of some of the protestors, and a state of emergency lasting two months. Yet the Human Rights Commission itself, which was already functioning based on the initial decree, remained largely silent; and when it did attempt to initiate a public inquiry and hold a meeting symbolically on International Human Rights Day, it was blocked by the government. The first chair resigned less than two years into the job, with others soon following, until the commission had almost no staff; and by 2006, it was essentially nonexistent. The United States during this same period sent U.S. human rights experts to the Maldives to support the NHRI, after arranging for two of the human rights commissioners to travel to the United States as part of an international visitors program. Ironically, during the same period, the U.S. government wanted the Maldives to pass antiterror legislation and to sign an Article 98 agreement, promising not to arrest American citizens or extradite them to the ICC.[143]

In general, international actors continued building the NHRI's capacities. UNDP and the United Nations Population Fund, for example, initiated a four-year project in 2006. And the government responded with more reforms. A new law in 2006 limited the commission's jurisdiction to events occurring after 2000, but gave the commission powers to compel evidence and witnesses and to inspect detention facilities unannounced. The debates surrounding these changes, however, were intense, with some politicians determined to water down the bill, including by reducing the punishment for not cooperating with the commission from dismissal to a fine. If government reforms accelerated in response to international attention, political opposition to the commission did not disappear, just as repression persisted.[144]

The political transition initiated in 2008 was still insufficient to earn the NHRI more than a B status rating, given that the commission required all its members to be Muslim. The UPR process in 2010 further revealed that the commission had its critics; some perceived, for example, that the commission supported only prisoners. The government, for its part, accepted recommendations raised by various states and treaty bodies like the CRC that the NHRI comply fully with the Paris Principles.[145]

In the broader analysis presented here, the Maldives stands as an outlier. In 2003, it was a seemingly small incident of abuse—too small to register as a generalized pattern of egregious abuse likely to trigger transnational protest, as it was limited to a single prison population—that led to the NHRI's creation. It was only when abuse was openly exposed domestically and translated into protest that appeasement efforts by the government followed. The gradual strengthening of the commission has reflected further appeasement on the part of the government pre-2008, and a regulatory moment post-2008. In addition, the influence of international regime pressures has remained consistent since the late 1990s. In this case, unlike in others, social protests preceded—and indeed helped bring about—a significant regulatory moment. While the NHRI was largely inactive initially and did not play a significant role in ushering in democratization, it represented over time the state's complex role vis-à-vis human rights, serving as an institutional setting in which to debate the evolving nature of state-society relations.

NHRI Milestones in the Arab World

Both Iraq and Saudi Arabia took steps in 2004 to establish an NHRI. *Iraq* stands out as a dramatic case of an externally imposed NHRI, proposed in the midst of conflict. An NHRI was part of its 2004 Interim Constitution, signed by the Iraqi Governing Council. Following the trend for posttransitional peace agreements to include an NHRI, Chapter 7 of Iraq's Transitional Administrative Law (The Special Tribunal and National Commissions), stated in Article 50,

> The Iraqi Transitional Government shall establish a National Commission for Human Rights for the purpose of executing the commitments relative to the rights set forth in this Law and to examine complaints pertaining to violations of human rights. The Commission shall be established in accordance with the *Paris Principles* issued by the United Nations on the responsibilities of national institutions.

Occupation authorities also created a Ministry of Human Rights. The OHCHR supported the ministry's work, including by offering training workshops for state officials and assisting with a human rights documentation center. And in 2006, the human rights office within the UN Assistance Mission for Iraq (UNAMI), with support from the OHCHR, organized a series of meetings, including with stakeholders, to lay the groundwork for a draft law and other technical aspects of an NHRI. In the subsequent 2007 International Covenant with Iraq, one of the government's pledges to the international community was "establishing a national human rights institution."[146]

Just as international actors introduced the idea of an NHRI in Iraq, they have also played a strong role in shaping the prospective institution. In 2008, following OHCHR technical assistance, the Council of Representatives passed the Law for the Establishment of an Independent High Commission for Human Rights. UNAMI referred to it as "one of the most significant developments" in the country, while the secretary-general's special representative on Iraq referred to the institution as a "milestone."[147] Likewise, the country director for UNDP stated in December 2011, "A strong and independent Human Rights Commission will be critical for the development of an effective and sustainable national human rights protection system in a democratic Iraq."[148] UNAMI itself was tasked with helping to select the members of the Independent Commission and then assisting the body once it became operational. A workshop cosponsored by APF, UNAMI, and UNDP in Beirut in July 2011 focused precisely on how Iraq's NHRI might select its members.

Setting up an NHRI under occupation represents the strongest instance of coercive state-building. The idea for establishing Iraq's NHRI took place during a crucial regulatory moment and amid violations. The institution was part of an internationally approved set of structures intended to support democratic governance, rights protections, and rule of law. Even the word "independent" in the name suggests a deliberate distancing from executive control. NHRI-diffusing agents in this case were mostly international actors charged with rebuilding state institutions in the occupied country.

Despite not having ratified major human rights treaties, *Saudi Arabia* also created a National Human Rights Association (sometimes translated as the National Society for Human Rights) in 2004. A royal decree that year further established a National Human Rights Committee, operating within the executive and focusing on human rights violations against foreign workers. These steps followed a highly publicized human rights conference held in the country in 2003, producing the Riyadh Declaration. The association was described from the start as the country's first independent human rights organization, though in practice that referred more to formal organizational separateness than political autonomy. Though the institution was sometimes referred to as an NGO, clearly, the government intended it to be part of the state. In 2006, the same year Saudi Arabia joined the Human Rights Council, the association applied (unsuccessfully) for international accreditation as an NHRI.[149]

The establishment of an NHRI came at the same time as a rise in social demands, itself part of more long-standing calls for reform. As one observer sees it, by early 2004, "Saudi Arabia witnessed an unprecedented number of civil initiatives calling for national dialogue and for further integration of women into the workforce."[150] For example, in January 2003, over one hundred intellectuals issued "A Vision for the Present and Future of the Nation," emphasizing civil rights, women's rights, and judicial reform. That April, 450 Shias demanded equal treatment in "Partners for One Nation"; and in February 2004, almost nine hundred elites promoted notions of accountability and reform. Some of this was directly influenced by a post-9/11 wave of domestic terrorist acts that hit the Saudi Kingdom in 2003, but social demands for reform had also been building up for a decade. In the early 1990s, following the first Gulf War, the Saudi government began receiving petitions for reform, both from religious clerics representing dissident voices and from a Shi'a reform movement; despite the varied cast of supporters, many shared a critique of existing government policies and craved judicial reform. The government responded with concessions, especially in the judicial and educational sectors. When a decade later renewed calls for reform followed a wave of terrorist attacks, the government once again initiated liberalization, albeit highly controlled. King Abdullah's ascendancy to the throne in 2005 further accelerated these dynamics.[151]

The role of international actors behind the creation of the NHRI cannot be disregarded. Government officials told the UN special rapporteur on the independence of judges and lawyers, while visiting Saudi Arabia in October 2002, that the country was considering creating an NHRI.[152] In January 2003, in an unprecedented meeting with a delegation from Human Rights Watch, Foreign Minister Prince Said also assured NGO representatives of its intent to create an NHRI, an idea that the delegation encouraged while emphasizing the importance of the Paris Principles.[153] Regionally, this was a period when human rights discourse was acquiring political prominence. Following the first international conference of the Arab Human Rights Movement in Casablanca in April 1999, momentum around the topic built, culminating in the 2004 Arab Charter on Human Rights.[154]

The creation of an NHRI in the early 1990s by Saudi Arabia was therefore mostly a response to transnational human rights pressures. Domestically, calls for reform peaked in the early 2000s, a period that coincided with regional human rights institutionalization. The government responded with concessions, including by accepting foreign human rights delegations. Engagement with international human rights actors, in turn, only intensified demands for further concessions and reforms. The government's decision to seek accreditation for an institution that clearly did not meet international standards reveals the extent to which the NHRI was intended to appease critics. When the APF offered technical assistance and giving the institution partial membership, the government did not even bother responding. Though calls for an NHRI had been raised by the CRC and CEDAW, the subject was given almost no attention in the country's UPR.[155] Appeasement is the overwhelming drive behind Saudi Arabia's NHRI, leading to a very weak institution. Institutional reforms for this powerful state will depend on ongoing international regime pressures, mediated by the political context.

Latecomers in the Asia Pacific

Comparatively, those states in the region that had not established (or at least taken steps to establish) an NHRI by 2005 seemed latecomers. Numbering approximately two dozen countries, some of these states were found in the Middle East (the Persian Gulf region and Syria); many were small island states of the Pacific; and others represented a mix of latecomers (including Bangladesh, Turkey, Pakistan, Cambodia, and Myanmar). The cases continue to reveal that the timing in creating (or agreeing to create) a state accountability mechanism is mostly about when strategic incentives line up with international regime pressures. Put differently, the timing of NHRI creation is partly an accident of history, of when structural conditions change, and of the work of NHRI-diffusing agents who actively promote these institutions. The strength of these institutions, however, remains bound up in the particularities of the domestic context.

Diffusion in the Persian Gulf

NHRIs continued to make headway in the Persian Gulf region. Even *Oman* and the *United Arab Emirates* (UAE), two countries that had not ratified the human rights covenants, took steps to create NHRIs. In both countries, NHRI-diffusing agents had had very few structural opportunities to call for the creation of an

NHRI until then.[156] If global and regional pressures in a post-9/11 world encouraged nominal political liberalization, international regime pressures targeting Gulf countries as well as the new UPR process pushed NHRIs onto the political sphere. Oman's sultan passed a royal decree in late 2008 creating a National Human Rights Commission.[157] In the UAE, the government announced its willingness to create a national human rights commission in direct response to recommendations by the Human Rights Council in 2008. The CRC, moreover, had already called for the creation of an NHRI there and in Oman.[158] It was clear that Human Rights Council pressures, combined with a nascent Gulf network of NHRIs, led both countries to move in the direction of human rights institutionalization. Functional, compliant NHRIs in these countries will depend on broader domestic structural openings, including constitutional reforms or treaty ratifications.

The Gulf country of *Bahrain* was relatively late in creating an NHRI. In 2009, it established by royal decree the National Human Rights Institution, the first in the world with this particular title. The institution began functioning in 2010, but it still was not accredited by early 2012. On one level, the institution was part of a gradual process of reform begun earlier in the decade and symbolized by the National Action Charter, itself a response to antigovernment protests.[159] The reforms were mostly attempts to appease opponents, in a country where political freedom was sharply limited but physical integrity violations were relatively low. Bahrain's human rights institution was established with an international audience very much in mind.

Bahrain had a clear interest in promoting an international image supportive of human rights concerns. It ran for a seat in the newly established Human Rights Council in 2006; and while it did not win that election, it took steps to bolster its human rights credentials. This included, for example, acceding to the two major international human rights covenants in 2006 and 2007, with the cabinet issuing a decree in November 2007 and calling for an NHRI: "Bahrain is committed to establishing a national human rights institution at the earliest opportunity, bearing in mind the relevant United Nations resolutions and, in particular, the Paris Principles."[160] In 2008, Bahrain ran again for a seat on the Human Rights Council, and this time it was elected; as part of its election pledges, it promised to create an NHRI and have it in place by 2009. As the first country in the world to go through the UPR, it announced it would create an NHRI. Shortly thereafter, an agreement between the Foreign Ministry and the OHCHR brought in NHRI experts from Jordan, Morocco, and Northern Ireland to assist Bahrain in laying the institution's early stages.[161]

From the moment of its creation, the institution was immediately beset by strong domestic criticism. Nonstate groups, drawing explicitly on the Paris Principles, offered a detailed analysis of how the institution's leadership irrevocably undermined the NHRI's independence. Even the institution's president resigned in September 2010, when the NHRI's members failed to criticize the government's arrest of pro-democracy activists during the Arab Spring.[162] An institution created mostly on the basis of external obligations proved weak, though it remains to be seen if and how international regime pressures manage over time to shape it, especially if the country's overall political course changes.

Time Lags—Bangladesh to Tajikistan

The idea of an NHRI was first raised in 1995 in both Bangladesh and Tajikistan, though it would be over a decade before either country would take steps to create the institution. Despite reflecting different pathways of institution-building, these countries both faced a mix of strategic incentives and diffusion pressures. *Bangladesh's* government approved a project on the Institutional Development of Human Rights in Bangladesh (IDHRB) in 1995, with the goal of drafting a law for a human rights commission. A joint project with the UNDP in 1996 and the formation of an Action Research Study moved things along; and in mid-1999, the cabinet approved a draft law creating a national human rights commission. Though the government did not consult with civil society, human rights NGOs had long supported the creation of an NHRI and paid close attention. At long last, the National Human Rights Commission emerged in 2008, created by ordinance a year earlier and reconstituted in 2009 with passage of the National Human Rights Commission Act. In 2011, the institution applied for international accreditation and was assigned a B status, due to being insufficiently independent.[163]

The government's willingness to create an NHRI in Bangladesh reflects a strategy of appeasement. With high levels of violation, the regime had come under steady transnational pressure, especially as domestic NGOs began growing in the 1990s. This also combined with pressure from international actors like Amnesty International, which issued critical reports of the government's human rights practices and explicitly supported the notion of an NHRI. The strategic motive was apparent from the start: the Nationalist Party first accepted the idea, though their ideological commitments were not aligned with human rights. Nor did Bangladesh accede to the major international covenants until 1999 and 2000. After it did so, and as the international and regional regimes on NHRIs grew stronger, pressures for a human rights institution intensified. In 2003, Human Rights Watch and the CRC called for a human rights commission; and in 2004, UNDP Bangladesh and the Australian government sponsored a workshop on the role of NHRIs in institutionalizing human rights. When Bangladesh ran for a seat on the first Human Rights Council in 2006, it pledged to institutionalize human rights protections.[164] By all accounts, the government has always been concerned by transnational criticism of its ongoing human rights abuses, and it has been consistently willing to respond with symbolic measures.

These forces help to explain the long delay in establishing the institution and the commission's weakness once it was created. As a Commonwealth study noted,

> The quest for a national human rights institution in Bangladesh also has been slow and beset by delay. The Government set out to establish a National Human Rights Institution in 1995 under much pressure. The process, which has spanned over nearly twelve years, the rule of two political parties and one year of United Nations Human Rights Council membership, has included political deliberation, drafting and redrafting of laws, election manifestos and a pledge to the international community to support the development of a human rights institution.[165]

Appeasement and diffusion, together, account for Bangladesh's long road to establishing an NHRI.

In Central Asia, *Tajikistan's* late arrival to the world of NHRIs can be traced to the fact that it was embroiled in a postindependence war for most of the 1990s. The idea of an ombudsman was nonetheless introduced in 1995 by the Office for Democratic Institutions and Human Rights (ODIHR), part of the Organization for Security and Cooperation in Europe (OSCE). But it was not until after a 1997 ceasefire and elections in 1999 that the idea of an NHRI began to be discussed more consistently, this time by the UN Tajikistan Office of Peace-Building (UNTOP), which had replaced the OSCE on the ground. It was then that the country also ratified the two major human rights covenants in 1999.[166]

Progress toward an NHRI picked up after the mid-2000s, especially following a 2003 constitutional reform that limited the president's power and the subsequent election of Emomalii Rahmon in 2006. During this period, human rights state offices were created within the presidency and parliament; and in 2002, the Commission on Fulfillment of International Human Rights Commitments was formed, reflecting growing attention to recent international obligations. In 2005, a cooperation agreement with the EU included a human rights component. More to the point, in February 2006, the OHCHR and the OSCE cosponsored a conference in Dushanbe on NHRIs, attended by dozens of UN experts and domestic as well as international NGOs. A year later, the UNDP and OHCHR together launched a project aimed at supporting an NHRI. A human rights ombudsman was at last created in 2008 by a legislative act. The government submitted the institution for international accreditation in early 2012; it was found to be partially compliant.[167]

International actors first introduced the idea of an NHRI in Tajikistan in the context of a regulatory moment and ongoing abuse in the mid-1990s; but the politically volatile situation restricted fast progress. By the time the institution was created in 2008, the country had also taken on external human rights obligations. Transnational pressures were themselves not so great, partly due to the country's strategic significance post-9/11, and its use as a staging base for Western assaults into Afghanistan; but appeasement did drive the domestic institutionalization of human rights somewhat, just as the executive had an interest in localizing control over rights issues as much as possible. In fact, this helps to explain the delay in establishing an NHRI. As one assessment notes, "There is a general lack of political will for change, and the few changes that occur are often half-hearted and not followed up by the allocation of new resources. The delay in the appointment of the ombudsman is symptomatic in this respect."[168] Intense involvement by external actors, itself the result of a postconflict situation, meant enormous technical assistance went into crafting an NHRI, eventually paying off in the form of a partially accredited body.

Straddling Identities in Turkey

Turkey was also delayed in creating an NHRI. Though the constitution of 1982 was amended a few times after 2001, it was not until after accession negotiations with the EU began in 2005 and before the country's UPR in 2010 that the Turkish government took concrete steps to establish an NHRI. A reform program announced in 2006 included both an ombudsman and a human rights institution; that year, an ombudsman law was passed, though the constitutional court challenged its legal bases in 2008. A constitutional amendment eventually established the ombudsman, and a draft law was completed in 2011.[169] In its submission to the UPR, the Turkish government stated that it was in the process of completing the legal framework for an NHRI in compliance with the Paris Principles.

These developments need to be placed in the broader context of human rights discourse, which had risen since the early 1990s in Turkey and was closely intertwined with the state's treatment of the Kurdish population. Not only was the Kurdish human rights problem the subject of transnational pressure, but Kurds themselves began adopting the language of human rights in framing their demands. In this sense, the Turkish government found itself stuck between its abuse of the Kurds, arising partly from perceived threats to national identity and security, and recognition of the international legitimacy assigned to human rights norms. In "a political environment in which the advocacy of human rights could be perceived or framed as an assault or threat to the territorial integrity and secular identity of the state," the state attempted to co-opt the language of human rights, including by institutionalizing human rights within the state apparatus.[170] Thus, a parliamentary Human Rights Commission was created in 1990. Throughout the mid-1990s, in fact, human rights institutions within the state seemed to multiply, including a coordinating body known as the Human Rights High Committee alongside human rights boards and units within the presidency, Interior Ministry, and police.[171]

But it was not until after 2000, when treaty obligations grew, that the idea of creating a full-fledged NHRI gained more attention. Turkey's coveted candidacy to the EU was announced in 1999, with the idea of an ombudsman raised in 2001; Turkey then ratified the two international human rights covenants in 2003. One Turkish commentator confirms that the prospect of an NHRI was closely related to the country's hope to join the EU: "In the process of Turkey's candidateship to become a full member of the EU, her preference to constitute both the ombudsman and the human rights institution is in line with the international developments in this field."[172] Indeed, in October 2009 the European Commission on Enlargement to the European Union reminded Turkey that an independent human rights institution and ombudsman were required.[173]

EU demands for national human rights structures reinforced recommendations raised as part of the UPR process. Transnational pressure, in the context of ongoing abuse, led the state to adopt the language of human rights, though somewhat superficially, evident in the country's late ratification of major human rights treaties. Yet once new external obligations were in place, in terms of treaty acceptance and candidacy to the EU, the state's capacity to resist creating an NHRI was far more constrained. Despite a long delay, external obligations linked to membership criteria in a regional organization made the difference in the government's willingness to adopt an NHRI.

Parliamentarians and Politics in Pakistan

Despite the institution's global popularity, an NHRI was evidently not on Pakistan's radar until the 2000s. The original impetus for an NHRI came from a group of parliamentarians who after 2002 organized themselves around the theme of human rights. The group began attending international conferences on NHRIs, bringing the idea back to Pakistan and requesting international technical assistance. This complemented the government's agenda. Though General Pervez Musharraf's government had come to power in a coup, he was committed to holding elections and seemed intent—especially after the 9/11 attacks—to present an aura of democracy. Like the 2002 general elections, which had led to the creation of the parliamentary human rights group, the very notion of an NHRI seemed to satisfy various objectives.

The Parliamentarians Commission on Human Rights (PCHR) was comprised of a cross-section of politicians interested in human rights. Shortly after the group's formation in 2002, the British Council in Pakistan invited and arranged for group representatives to travel to Ireland for an international seminar. The occasion was quite significant for the group, marking "the first official recognition of our work at international level."[174] The seminar focused on the effectiveness of national human rights commissions, and it was attended by participants from twenty-five countries, with Riaz Fatyana (PCHR chair) and Masood Khan (a judge at Peshawar's High Court) representing Pakistan. After Belfast, they attended a one-day seminar on NHRIs in London, organized by the human rights centers of a few universities.[175] Upon returning to Pakistan, not surprisingly, the PCHR drafted a concept paper on NHRIs.

In May 2004, Prime Minister Musharraf endorsed the proposal to create a National Human Rights Commission; and in October the Pakistani Cabinet approved the concept paper, with a draft bill soon prepared. This also initiated a process of more formal consultations with international actors, including the OHCHR, APF, and Commonwealth. Thus, the APF, for example, participated in meetings with a broad segment of stakeholders in 2005, exploring the idea of an NHRI in Pakistan; and the Commonwealth Human Rights Initiative offered its analysis of the NHRI in a paper it published that year.[176] A bill that would establish a "national human rights commission" was introduced to Parliament in December 2008. Both members of the APF and the OHCHR were consulted as the bill went through a series of revisions. At last, in December 2011, Pakistan's National Assembly voted overwhelmingly to create an independent NHRI, with Senate consideration in February 2012.

The bill's Statement of Objects and Reasons provides some insight into the multiple interests driving support for an NHRI:

> In pursuance of UN General Assembly Resolution No. 48/134 of December 20, 1993, and such other relevant resolutions of the UN Commission on Human Rights, the UN member states are under obligation to establish independent national human rights institutions which is considered as a singular criterion to judge a state's commitment towards the protection and promotion of human rights. Presently, the national human rights commissions are functioning in 54 countries of the world out of which 13 are Asian countries, including India. The formation of NCHR would not only fulfil the international obligation of establishment of such a Commission, it shall also serve as driving force for negating the propaganda of human rights violations in Pakistan.[177]

In short, an NHRI could meet Pakistan's international obligations, already adopted by regional peers, simultaneously countering any bad press against the government.

State Promises in Kuwait and Syria

When *Kuwait's* UPR took place in 2010, members of the Human Rights Council called on the government to create an NHRI, a recommendation the government accepted. The UN high commissioner for human rights also visited Kuwait in April 2010, as part of a workshop on NHRIs in the Gulf.[178] With external obligations in place, international actors moved to place the idea of an NHRI on the government's agenda, though the state had long been responding to social activism with limited institutionalization on behalf of human rights.

As early as 1992, a Standing Committee on Human Rights had been created in the National Assembly, hand in hand with growing rights activism in the country. As Mary Ann Tetrault describes it, "These groups irritated the government, not only because they were more efficient that state organizations charged with overseeing efforts to deal with the same problems . . . but also because they were so efficient in building international channels of communication and playing a role independent of the government in international arenas."[179] Though the government apparently attempted to co-opt the groups, the strategy proved unsuccessful. In this sense, "the showdown over human rights activism was and continues to be embedded in the larger struggle of the regime to limit the power of parliament and the civil rights of Kuwaiti citizens."[180] "The parliamentary human rights committee . . . provides a protected space within which the concerns of citizen activists can be articulated and pursued. It also moves issues identified by the popular groups into the National Assembly for consideration."[181] Once the parliamentary committee was established, a cycle followed, as human rights demands were met by regime concessions, including ratification of the major international human rights covenants in 1996.

Other than mild liberalization, however, Kuwait lacked a significant regulatory moment that would serve as an opportunity to promote an NHRI. Its human rights groups were large and active in transnational networks, but the level of egregious violations was relatively low to lead to significant mobilization against the regime. It was not until international diffusion pressures intensified late in the first decade of the 2000s, in the form of the UPR and subregional networking—marked by the first Gulf Forum of Human Rights Institutions in Doha in May 2010—that an NHRI became a distinct possibility.

Syria's turn to consider creating an NHRI came in the summer of 2000, known as the Damascus Spring, following Hafez el Assad's death. Calls for reform flourished, and salons dedicated to liberal discussions were organized. In a climate of possibilities, the CESCR urged the Syrian government in September 2001 to create an NHRI compliant with the Paris Principles.[182] Syria had accepted international human rights obligations in the mid-1970s, so it was already open to calls from treaty and UN bodies to create an NHRI. And by the time of Syria's appearance before the UN Human Rights Committee in 2005, government representatives stated their plans to establish an NHRI; in 2004, they had already created a National Committee for International Humanitarian Law. This was followed up by a UN technical assistance program, launched in early 2006, to support the country's upcoming five-year development plan (2006–10), which specifically included the creation of a national human rights commission among its target goals.[183]

According to the UN Committee on the Rights of the Child in 2011, the government was "looking into creating a Higher Council for Human Rights," "hopefully soon." In Syria's submission to the UPR that year, the government linked this recommendation to a National Dialogue created after the events of 2011. The national dialogue itself, however, was a state-led initiative, so much so that many members of the opposition refused to participate. Interestingly, the government attempted to portray the national dialogue as an instance of its responsiveness to social demands, though in reality it was much more likely an attempt to appease critics. The Human Rights Council recommended an NHRI, as did the CRC in 2011.[184] External obligations and transnational pressures opened the way for international regime proponents to place an NHRI on the list of state promises.

Pacific Island States

By the end of 2011, nine Pacific Island states had still not created an NHRI, though significantly all had accepted doing so as part of the UPR process: Micronesia, Nauru, Palau, Papua New Guinea, Samoa, Seychelles, Solomon Islands, Tonga, and Vanuatu. A few key regional developments, beginning in the late 1990s, led mostly by the APF and reinforcing international regime pressures, were essential. A workshop in Kuala Lumpur in 1997 called for an NHRI in every ASEAN member state; and in 2000, the Working Group for an ASEAN Human Rights Mechanism also proposed that all ASEAN member states create NHRIs.[185] Most directly, in 2004, the Pacific Island Forum supported a regional workshop on NHRIs organized by the APF.[186]

None of these states had experienced a major regulatory moment since the Paris Principles were drafted. The most recent constitution was Seychelles', dating to 1993; and Tonga's constitution was from the nineteenth century (1875). In a few states, including Tonga and Nauru, constitutional reform was on the table in the late 2000s, just as a draft constitution was introduced in the Solomon Islands in 2011.[187] In almost all of these small Pacific states, then, long-standing constitutions limited the opportunity for NHRI diffusion.

If a regulatory moment occurred in any of these countries it was in the Solomon Islands, where a peace process following civil unrest (1999–2000) led to constitutional reform and international involvement. The Townsville Peace Agreement, concluded in 2000, called for constitutional reforms, with the 2004 draft constitution including both a "human rights commission" and an ombudsman; subsequent drafts in 2009 and 2011 retained this feature. The presence of the OHCHR in the country in mid-2001 morphed into a one-year project for national human rights institutional capacities in 2003. And in 2005, the APF sent a high-level delegation to the Solomon Islands, meeting with a range of actors from the prime minister to NGOs. When a national action plan for human rights was presented in 2010, it too included an NHRI. International NGOs like Amnesty International followed up, calling on the government to move forward with the institution.[188] The original impetus, however, was a postconflict setting in which international actors promoted the idea of an NHRI, later reinforced as part of the UPR process.

Human rights treaty obligations have also been quite weak or recent among these small island states, further reducing opportunities for institutional diffusion. Among the nine Pacific Island islands that were latecomers, only two had ratified the international human rights covenants—Papua New Guinea and Palau—and they only did so in 2008 and 2011, respectively. Three additional states had acceded to the ICCPR, but also quite late: Nauru in 2001, Samoa in 2008, and Vanuatu in 2009. While the Solomon Islands was the only state to have ratified one of the human rights covenants (ICESCR) in the early 1980s, it had not accepted the other covenant. Nonetheless, as a general matter, human rights standards are strongly represented in these countries' constitutions; Papua New Guinea, for example, is one of the only countries in the world to have almost all of the rights in the UDHR constitutionally recognized. The reluctance to ratify human rights treaties (indeed, only three of these states, i.e., Nauru, Samoa, and Vanuatu, have ratified the Rome Statute) seems instead to reflect the perceived high costs associated with treaty reporting.[189] Regardless, low levels of treaty acceptance have translated into fewer opportunities for international actors, including treaty bodies, to call for the creation of an NHRI. And even in cases where treaties have been accepted, weak to moderately weak rule of law systems in these countries has made it difficult for external obligations to become domestically embedded in state institutions.

Finally, transnational human rights pressure has been low for these countries. This partly reflects their small size, leading foreign actors to overlook them; in fact, many of these states are omitted from the annual reports of organizations like Amnesty International. Furthermore, with the exception of Papua New Guinea, these countries generally have solid human rights records that, when combined with their size, preclude transnational pressure.

In this sense, it is noteworthy that Papua New Guinea stands out among these states for agreeing to establish an NHRI. As early as 1993, the justice minister at a UN workshop announced plans to create a national human rights commission. A similar announcement by the prime minister in 1994 referred specifically to recommendations made by Amnesty International in a 1993 report.[190] Concurrently, the UN Human Rights Commission issued a resolution critical of the country, and the country moved to invite UN special rapporteurs to visit the country.[191] Interest in a human rights commission was renewed in 1996 in the aftermath of a highly publicized case, when a young woman was sold as "compensation" following a police shooting.[192] In this context, the government approved in 1997 establishing an NHRI, a position it reaffirmed a decade later in a final option paper and then as a draft law. While Papua New Guinea also had a widely praised ombudsman, a bill proposed in 2010 threatened to strip the body's power; the bill was dropped following public protest.[193] The uneven political climate aside, government representatives during the country's UPR expressed their hope that an NHRI would be operational by 2012.

Despite relatively weak incentives, all of these states agreed in principle to establish an NHRI, doing so mostly in the context of the UPR. Even before their appearance before the Human Rights Council, however, international bodies, especially the APF and the OHCHR, promoted the idea of an NHRI. The APF visited various of these countries, including Nauru (2009), Papua New Guinea (2009), and Palau (2011). In Papua New Guinea, it offered expert advice at an OHCHR workshop to finalize the draft law. In 2008, the OHCHR provided Palau with technical assistance on draft legislation.[194] Samoa received assistance from New Zealand's NHRI and the APF, as it conducted a feasibility study and evaluated different models; in the end, the recommendation was for a national human rights commission to be housed in the ombudsman's office, one that could later evolve into a separate body. According to the government, Samoa "was drafting a strategic plan on the requirements for the establishment of a human rights commission based on the report taking into account Samoa's characteristics including its culture, the *fa'asamoa* policies and legislation."[195] Samoa itself was the site of a regional workshop on the establishment of NHRI mechanisms in the Pacific in April 2009.[196]

States in the region regularly report that their reluctance to create an NHRI stems from a lack of resources, as well as low ratification rates and even the ongoing pull of local customary law.[197] For example, in its report to the UPR, Micronesia's government said that, while it recognized the need for a national human rights agency, it faced economic challenges and requested international assistance in creating such a body.[198] All told, a weak structure of incentives explains why so many small Pacific states still lack an NHRI. Ongoing assistance and international regime pressures may evolve into functioning NHRIs. The question of whether these institutions are needed is another one altogether.

Half Steps by Cambodia and Myanmar

Shortly after the Paris Principles were formulated in October 1991, *Cambodia* concluded its peace agreement in the French capital. Yet it was not until 2004 that a new coalition government included in its platform of reforms a pledge to create an independent NHRI. Two years after that, a conference in Cambodia focused on the establishment of an NHRI; sponsored by the government and ASEAN's Working Group for Human Rights Mechanisms, it was attended by a broad range of domestic and international actors. The prime minister himself gave the keynote address, committing to create an independent human rights institution. As a result of the conference, a joint working group composed of civil society and government representatives was formed to draft relevant legislation. During the country's UPR in 2009, members of the Human Rights Council, reinforcing calls made by CESCR, called on Cambodia's government to expedite plans for an NHRI, a recommendation the government formally accepted.[199]

Cambodia's willingness to form an NHRI reflected a coalition government's broader interest in reform, itself occurring in a context of ongoing abuse. A spike in abuses in 1997 had been met with mounting international criticism and calls by NGOs for a national human rights commission, leading the government to create a Human Rights Committee in June 1998, a body that proved largely ineffective. The early 2000s, moreover, were marred by international accusations of the government's unwillingness to hold members of the Khmer Rouge accountable for past abuses. By the time of the national elections in 2003, the government was trying both to improve its relations with ASEAN members and to appease its international critics. The reforms proposed by the new coalition government thus represented a mix of ideas supported by reform-minded members of civil society and accepted by a government intent on controlling the pace and nature of any changes. Though ASEAN was the government's main partner in the path to an NHRI, other international actors like the United Nations and the APF were significantly involved, just as regional networking had been extensive. For example, in 2010, members of the Cambodian Working Group visited the Philippines commission.[200]

Still, on the government side, support for an NHRI seems to have been above all a means of appeasing critics and, insofar as international human rights obligations exist, of localizing control over human rights issues within the executive. As of 2011, however, Cambodia's government still has not kept the pledge it made in 2004 to create an NHRI, despite the existence of a draft bill first proposed by civil society and passed to the OHCHR for comments. Progress will depend on a changing political context that elevates the place of state accountability. Yet institutionalization also has its own momentum, and conceivably an NHRI could itself contribute to crafting a future Cambodia.

Even *Myanmar*, a country considered isolationist and exceptionalist, took steps to create an NHRI. The government created the Human Rights Committee in 2000 and the Myanmar Human Rights Body in 2007; that institution was placed within the Ministry for Home Affairs, and one of its main objectives was to devise a national human rights commission. The Human Rights Body came in the context of a regulatory moment, shortly before a new constitution was issued, and amid ongoing violations. The government then announced in September 2011 that it would create a national human rights commission. The announcement followed a visit of the UN special rapporteur, as well as a (nominal) transition to civilian rule earlier that year. Unlike most states, Myanmar had not ratified either international human rights covenant or accepted the ICC's jurisdiction. International regime pressures placed the notion of an NHRI on the political agenda (including explicit calls from UNCT, CEDAW, and CRC). In 2011, the same year as the country appeared before the Human Rights Council for its first UPR, the government agreed rhetorically to create an NHRI.[201]

Reluctant Institutionalists

Other states in the Asia Pacific were either reluctant or ambivalent about creating an NHRI by the time of their UPR in the late 2000s. This group includes Japan, North Korea, Bhutan, the Marshall Islands, and Brunei Darussalam. In all of these cases, Human Rights Council recommendations that an NHRI be created were met with vague and unclear assurances—that the government would *consider* doing so. The specific motives for delaying institution building varied, but weak incentives to lock in new commitments, localize authority, or appease critics were always present.

Japan has wavered in its willingness to create an NHRI, despite support from civil society groups and international regime pressures. In 2002, the government submitted a Human Rights Protection Bill to the Diet that included the establishment of an NHRI; however, with the dissolution of the House of Representatives a year later, no progress was made.[202] This came at a time when human rights standards were being institutionalized domestically. For example, in 2000 the Act of Promotion of Human Rights Education and Encouragement was passed. More broadly, a Human Rights Bureau was formed within the Ministry of Justice, along with eight human rights divisions, forty-two human rights offices, and fourteen thousand human rights volunteers spread throughout the state bureaucracy.[203] The government also agreed to recommendations by the Human

Rights Council (on which Japan held a seat from 2006 until 2011) that it move to establish an NHRI; similar calls were made by the UN Human Rights Committee and the CRC. In 2009 and 2010, the APF met with the Japanese Bar Association, government representatives, and civil society groups to draft relevant legislation. However, by the time of its midterm UPR report in 2011, the government justified the delay as follows:

> There have been arguments concerning various issues such as the scope of human rights infringements eligible for remedy, the measures to guarantee the independence of the human rights institution, and the details of the authority to investigate infringements. At present, therefore, the bill on a new human rights institution has not yet been re-submitted to the Diet. Japan will continue to work on studies toward the establishment of a national human rights institution in accordance with the Paris Principles in order to realize a more effective remedy for the victims of human rights infringements.[204]

The Japanese state has been subject to regional diffusion pressures and long-standing treaty obligations, but it has not created an NHRI. On balance, the government has used the presence of other domestic human rights structures as an excuse for the non-urgency of an NHRI. Nor has the country's strong rule of law translated into an NHRI, as political leaders have not been interested in re-localizing authority over human rights claims, including by creating an alternative source of autonomy to the courts. Because Japan's legal system is known not to provide individual complainants with ready access, is marked by slowness and high costs, and is generally off-putting for those most likely to submit petitions against the government, an internationally accredited NHRI could seem a threatening option. Especially in a climate of minor violations and no regulatory moments, the government has faced few incentives to do more than engage in delay tactics and excuse making.

The *Democratic Republic of Korea* finally expressed its willingness to consider creating an NHRI and accept UN technical assistance, a recommendation made by the United States (which, ironically, lacks an accredited NHRI) during the UPR process in 2009.[205] Other stakeholders also used the occasion of North Korea's UPR to promote the idea of an NHRI. This openness went hand in hand with a new constitution introduced in 2009, which explicitly included the notion of "human rights"; the country had ratified the human rights covenants in the early 1980s. A regulatory moment in 2009 and ongoing transnational pressures created an opening, through which international regime pressures could attempt to take effect. The government's response has been carefully tepid.

While *Bhutan* had not created an NHRI by the time of its UPR in 2009, the government also expressed a willingness to consider doing so. This was rooted in a broader transition initiated after 2005, when the king unexpectedly announced he would hold parliamentary elections and abdicate the throne to his son. In 2008, the transfer of power occurred, parliamentary elections were held, and a new constitution was enacted. Though the country faced little transnational pressure and had not ratified the human rights covenants, it was subject to international regime pressures. For example, between 1997 and 2001, the OHCHR ran a technical cooperation project aimed at strengthening national human rights structures, while the CRC called explicitly for an NHRI to be created. In the context of a broader regulatory moment, international regime pressures, including the UPR, seemed to make headway, as evident in the government's response to UN recommendations: "Bhutan takes note the recommendations and will consider establishment of an National Human Rights Institution in conformity with the Paris Principles, bearing in mind the small size of the country and its population, and resource constraints. The matter is under the active consideration of the Royal Government."[206]

Another small state that had not agreed to create an NHRI by the time of its UPR review in 2010 was the *Marshall Islands*. Though the government rejected the recommendation that an NHRI be established, it agreed to consider studying its feasibility.[207] With a constitution in place since the late 1970s, little transnational pressure and few external human rights obligations, relatively little opportunity existed for NHRI proponents to be influential. In this context, Human Rights Council recommendations managed only to extract the vaguest of responses from the government.

A similar dynamic was evident with *Brunei Darussalam*. The country's constitution dated to the mid-1980s, when the country had become independent; violations were low; and external human rights obligations remained weak by the time of the UPR in 2009. The CRC, nonetheless, had called for an NHRI. But like the Marshall Islands, the government of Brunei refused to commit to creating an NHRI, though it too expressed a willingness to consider the institution's feasibility.[208] Official state responses, however, cannot always be taken entirely at face value. For small states, facing little incentives to establish an NHRI, government responses to international regime demands may reflect a kind of bargaining, for technical assistance and resources in creating an externally derived institution.

Rejectionist States

A few states in the Asia Pacific have explicitly rejected the notion of adopting an NHRI. These rejectionist states include China, Israel, Kiribati, Laos, Singapore, and Vietnam. In all cases, either strategic incentives for an accountability mechanism have not been strong or the countries somehow escaped the attention of NHRI-diffusing agents. All, moreover, had failed to ratify the International Criminal Court's Rome Statute, suggesting that resistance to an NHRI has far broader bases. Yet even among this small group of rejecters, the variance is greater than it seems, and the details suggest that future NHRI adoption is not entirely off-limits.

The small island state of *Kiribati* resisted the possibility of an NHRI, though the CRC recommended such a body in 2006 and local stakeholders raised the issue as part of the UPR in 2010.[209] The government faced no incentives, confronting no transnational attention and unwilling to ratify either human rights covenant. Though a member of the Commonwealth, Kiribati did not join the United Nations until 1999. In view of its small size, high level of poverty, and the extreme pressures it faced as a result of climate change, the island government has resisted adopting an internationally inspired and potentially costly institution.

Likewise, the city-state of *Singapore* rejected calls for an NHRI, including from local stakeholders and Human Rights Council members during the country's UPR in 2011. Like other "rejectors," it too faced weak incentives: it has not had a regulatory moment or ratified the human rights covenants, and it has a relatively low level of abuse. In a civil-society statement issued on International Human Rights Day in 2011, groups noted how, in the aftermath of the UPR, the government "has rejected recommendations for greater civil liberties, to repeal the death penalty, abolish outdated emergency laws such as the Internal Security Act, as well as the establishment of a National Human Rights Institution and an independent elections commission. Such is the state of our fundamental freedoms."[210] This suggests that rejection of an NHRI is part of a broader pattern of abuse. If transnational pressure were to rise, government concessions might follow.

Two single-party states that also rejected creating NHRIs were *Laos* and *Vietnam*. Unlike other resistors, both had ratified human rights treaties: Vietnam in the early 1980s, and Laos much later in 2000. In the case of Laos, human rights violations increased between 2000 and 2007. And despite pressure from CERD, CEDAW, and the Human Rights Council to create an NHRI, the government rejected calls for the institution.[211] Political leaders did not look to localize treaty commitments, given the weak rule of law and a system of authority already centralized in the executive. Vietnam moved after 2000 to a policy of greater international engagement, but it still resisted the notion of an NHRI. In 2007, the government participated in a regional workshop on NHRIs for Asian countries lacking the institution; it joined other workshop participants in affirming the concluding statement's support for the institution. Yet by the time of its UPR in 2009, the Vietnamese government rejected the idea of an NHRI.[212] It had a high level of abuse, and its external obligations were watered down by a relatively weak rule of law system and strong executive power. Just as both Laos and Vietnam had refused to ratify the Rome Statute, they rejected creating an NHRI.

Israel is another state that rejected the notion of creating an NHRI at its UPR in 2008.[213] Though it has not undergone a regulatory moment in recent years and its acceptance of major human rights obligations dates to the early 1990s, it faces persistent transnational pressure. Yet the government has proven immensely adept at resisting human rights criticism. Given ongoing conflict with the Palestinian people and authorities, an NHRI may seem too threatening a prospect for a nominally democratic state engaged in egregious rights violations.

In *China's* case, the government's position seems to have become more rejectionist over time. Chinese government representatives in the 1990s attempted to gain UN approval for an NHRI at least informally, but they were confronted with push-back and demands for complying with the Paris Principles. Even though during the UPR in 2009 the government rejected recommendations by Human Rights Council members and local stakeholders that it create an NHRI, the government does not seem entirely opposed to the possibility. Resistance may reflect, more accurately, an unwillingness—really, an incapacity—to create a compliant NHRI during this political moment. As a young Chinese scholar asks, "Can we expect an independent NHRI in a country which does not even have an independent judiciary?"[214]

International regime pressures have nonetheless targeted China actively, calling for an NHRI to be created. Beginning with the second international conference on NHRIs in Tunis in 1993, China became involved in the international discourse on NHRIs. And various international conferences focusing on the prospect of NHRIs for China have been held in the country, with international actors like the APF and academic institutions participating. For example, a conference on the Functions and Operations of Chinese National Institutions on Human Rights Protection was held in Beijing in October 2006, while the APF organized a study tour of relevant stakeholders in China. Treaty bodies like the CRC, CESCR, and the Human Rights Committee, moreover, have also applied pressure to create an NHRI.[215]

It seems that the Chinese government sought initially to create an NHRI for the sake of appeasement, recognizing the institution's diffusion and global legitimacy. However, after the difficulties of accreditation became clear, the government retracted its earlier support for an NHRI. This has resulted in government ambivalence, rejecting the notion but continuing to participate in international NHRI forums. The global leader seems tempted by the prospect of an internationally accredited domestic institution, but only on its own terms and if it can avoid risk-filled institutional trappings.

Conclusions: (Re)Localizing Authority and Social Control

The Asia-Pacific region is marked by enormous diversity, and no region-wide human rights regime exists. Despite intense institutionalization within subregions and the presence of vigorous societal groups, it still remains the only area of the world with no human rights treaty or commission or court of its own. While the Middle East is conventionally separated from Asia, the United Nations includes the former in its broad demarcation of the region, spanning from the Middle East to East Asia and encompassing Oceania and small Pacific islands. It is a vast area that includes countries in dire poverty and is home to East Asian economies marked by impressive growth rates and high standards of living. It is culturally diverse, encompassing populous societies from Eastern religious backgrounds to former Western colonies and rich indigenous societies. Politically, strong democracies sit next to entrenched autocracies, just as violent war-torn zones share borders with peaceful states. Given the vastness and divergences that characterize the region, it is striking that NHRIs have diffused to the extent they have.

The diffusion of NHRIs must be understood largely in the context of international and regional pressures. The creation of the Asia Pacific Forum in the 1990s served as a powerful transmitter of NHRI models across borders, complementing the work of the United Nations and other international bodies.

The process of international accreditation, in particular, has pushed states to establish or strengthen NHRIs, just as the relatively recent UPR—with its regularized, mandatory exchanges, requiring states to report on the full range of their
human rights practices, while permitting stakeholders and others to participate—
also has encouraged progress in institution building. Fiji's loss of NHRI accreditation lends credibility to the threats associated with not following an
internationally recognized template. Also noteworthy was Chinese leaders' early
enthusiasm for having a body accredited as an NHRI, shifting over time as the
pressures of accreditation rose and became politically untenable domestically.

It is true that the region, as a whole, after 1990 has not experienced as many
democratic transitions as have other areas of the world, so that NHRI creation
has not revolved around an attempt to lock in commitments. Rather, given relatively high levels of abuse and transnational pressure, state leaders have often
agreed to establish an NHRI as a means of appeasing critics. Moreover, they
have often done so after having accepted external human rights obligations. Yet
because many of these countries lack a strong rule of law, the localization of
authority has really entailed an attempt—especially when faced with new or rising social demands—to relocate authority within the executive. Likewise, even if
in theory, the creation of NHRIs were a precursor to a region-wide mechanism,
for numerous state leaders, building a state human rights institution is really an
effort to localize (or retain) control over a potentially contentious set of issues.

Despite the seeming centrality of the state itself, social forces may constitute
the main subtext. In place after place, the state's attempt to appease is relevant
only in response to shifting social demands and claims to popular authority.
Sometimes this takes the form of vocal and defiant protestors, as the cases of
South Korea and the Maldives uniquely illustrate. Other times, social power is
manifest in violent clashes, evident in conflict zones like Afghanistan, Iraq, Sri
Lanka, or Nepal. Still other times social representatives vested with political authority promote the notion of an NHRI from within the state itself, as in the
Pakistani parliamentarians who travelled to NHRI meetings in Europe and re-
turned ready to transplant a version of the institution at home. And most recently,
NHRIs themselves can play the role of stakeholders challenging the state in international forums to rule legitimately, as the UPR process amply reveals.

Neither cultural nor political resistance has been able to forestall the regional
proliferation of NHRIs in the Asia Pacific. State leaders in the region care about
their international images, and NHRIs have become a symbol of a human-rights-
abiding modern state. The adoption of NHRIs has varied, in terms of its timing
and strength, depending on the incentives facing states and the domestic political

context. While more often than not states in the region have created these institutions to appease critics by relocalizing authority closer to the centers of power,
the process has been vigorously contested by social groups and pushed forward
by regional and international networks—institution builders dedicated to transforming state power.

9

Membership Rites and Statehood in the New Europe

If political transitions and new constitutions serve as key regulatory moments, pushing states to lock in commitments, then no wonder Europe joined the global bandwagon of NHRI diffusion after 1990. With the collapse of the Soviet Union, newly independent states in Eastern Europe moved to create NHRIs in the 1990s. Strikingly, country after country across Eastern Europe established an NHRI as part of either postindependence democratic institution building or constitutional reform; membership in the Council of Europe also proved crucial. While most Eastern European countries failed to meet international standards, a few significant exceptions existed: Russia, Bosnia, Georgia, Ukraine, and Albania. Western European countries that had not already done so also joined the global trend, including Belgium, Greece, the Netherlands, Cyprus, and Northern Ireland.

Subregional diffusion was itself facilitated and reinforced by larger regional trends. The first meeting of European NHRIs was held in 1994 and the second in 1997, marking the formation of a network known as the European Group of NHRIs. The Council of Europe, moreover, issued two relevant resolutions in 1997: Resolution 14, which encouraged the establishment of NHRIs; and Resolution 11, which highlighted cooperation among NHRIs, member states, and the Council of Europe[1] In practice, for many states, the creation of a human rights ombudsman became a condition of membership in European institutions.

Compared to countries in the Global South, a few somewhat surprising trends are evident among European NHRIs. First, a large proportion of NHRIs in Europe are not fully accredited internationally; it is in fact the region of the world with the most B-status institutions. And some states with institutions commonly referred to as NHRIs, moreover, have never applied for international accreditation. Second, the issue of institutional redundancy is significant, as multiple and overlapping accountability structures exist within and across countries; and in many countries, a long delay has marked the period from when the idea of an NHRI was first introduced to when it actually began functioning. Third, the ombudsman model has been the region's preferred type of NHRI, focused largely on individual complaints from national citizens. Finally, in the case of both consolidated democracies and democratizing states, domestic actors have often adopted a post–human rights ideology: the notion that human rights is already institutionalized within the state and therefore somehow irrelevant for today's national debates. In other cases, the rejection has been far more subtle, revealing a deeper assumption that "human rights" constitutes a more appropriate frame of reference for states in other parts of the world—for them, but not us. To invoke Makau Mutua's imagery, the European view stereotypically equates human rights abuses with savage acts of the Other rather than its own barbarities or its mundane degradations and marginalized communities. In still other instances, a human rights framework may have triggered fears of a revolutionary discourse, rooted in the historical memory of communism's fall being driven ideologically, in small but not insignificant ways, by the discourse of human rights. As Russian ombudsman Oleg Mironov said of state officials, "They saw the human rights activists as the dissidents who led to the collapse of the Soviet system, to the demise of socialism."[2]

In Europe, then, NHRIs have come to be part of an institutional checklist of requirements for statehood and/or regional membership in European institutions. The "checklist" has been diffused subregionally, as states have mimicked one another, and through region-wide directives and networks. That the regional system of NHRIs was developing alongside a global one, featuring some European NHRIs as leaders, also was significant. In the case of newly independent and democratizing states, regulatory moments were closely aligned with constitutionalism, external human rights obligations tended to be relatively new, and violence was typically low. In established democracies, NHRIs were adopted almost entirely in response to international regime pressures, leading to inordinately weak institutions.

Newly Independent States in Eastern Europe

NHRIs, especially the ombudsman, appealed to the new states of Eastern Europe. The attraction was not so much human rights, since that discourse was often too embroiled in past struggles. Rather, an NHRI was appealing because it carried the promise of state transformation. For countries that were embarking on a project of state building in a new democratic context, a horizontal accountability institution resonated. A broader project of reconceptualizing national identity, moreover, tended to include a strong European dimension. And in this scheme, the ombudsman (or NHRI) symbolized statehood in the new Europe. More pragmatically, the institution was an actual prerequisite for membership or entry into this Western community of states—and sometimes a condition of economic and security relations with the region's powerful countries. In almost all cases, NHRIs in Eastern Europe after 1990 were forged during a strong regulatory moment, sometimes consisting of both national independence and constitutional drafting.

Asserting Sovereignty in Croatia

The Defender of People's Rights, or the People's Attorney, in *Croatia* was a traditional ombudsman, attached to parliament and given an explicit human rights mandate. Though Croatia's human rights ombudsman did not begin functioning until 1994, its origins were in the 1990 constitution. Following the country's independence in 1991, moreover, it was given statutory life in the Ombudsman Act of 1992; and it gained international accreditation in 2008. With passage of the Anti-Discrimination Act in 2009, it also became an equality body, charged with combating discrimination.[3]

The insertion of the ombudsman into the constitution needs to be understood in the context of the overall document, which was intended as an assertion of state sovereignty. The constitution, in a sense, was part and parcel of statehood, and more specifically of what the Croatian leadership believed should constitute an independent European state, one likely to garner the recognition of other states. The constitution, moreover, was an explicitly liberal, democratic document, inspired by the French model; it was also a rejection of one-party communist rule, laying the foundations for a new set of state institutions that would mark the regime's full transition.[4]

The NHRI had its share of challenges, especially in its early period. In fact, the first ombudsman resigned in protest, after parliament rejected its initial report for being too politicized.[5] In later years, parliament again refused to accept the NHRI's report without offering any explanation.[6] And in a move that might be interpreted as an effort to create an institutional rival, the government established a Human Rights Office in 2001. In its self-description, the

Human Rights Office uses language similar to the Paris Principles, referring to the protection and promotion of human rights. And in practice, the Human Rights Office has purportedly undertaken overlapping activities without consulting the ombudsman, including preparation of the state's report for the UPR.[7]

For its part, the ombudsman seems to have gained limited visibility and networking, though it is difficult to determine the extent to which this is due to inadequacies on the ombudsman's part or broader political opposition to the office. Compared to its counterparts in other Balkan countries, the office seems to have fewer resources. Since the ombudsman was accredited as an NHRI and its mandate was expanded as an equality body, international actors have moved to assess the institution critically, including its capacity to collaborate with state and nonstate actors.[8]

Croatia's NHRI was forged during a regulatory moment and in a context of widespread abuse. The institution was operating in a divisive political context that limited its capacity to demand accountability, and it lacked strong leadership to help it navigate the tense climate. Like other newly democratizing states in the region, it was also functioning in an institutionally crowded environment; the ombudsman is one alongside a series of specialized ombudsmen (children, gender, and disabilities) and other state human rights institutions like the Human Rights Office. While more can be better, it can also produce institutional redundancies and inefficiencies.[9] Croatia's NHRI shows how governments can sometimes create competing human rights institutions, effectively diluting and displacing demands for accountability.

Hungary's Minority Question

Despite its relatively early creation, *Hungary* never attempted to get its NHRI accredited until 2011. Having acceded to the two international human rights covenants as far back as 1976, it moved to create a human rights ombudsman in the context of a democratic transition and constitutional revisions at the end of the 1980s. The offices of Parliamentary Commissioner of Civil Rights and Parliamentary Commissioner for the Rights of Ethnic and National Minorities were included in constitutional reforms drafted in 1989 and entering into force in 1990.[10] Both institutions began functioning in 1995, after implementing statutes were passed and their leaders were selected.

The creation of these institutions needs to be situated within Hungary's particular regime transition, which took the form of a peaceful negotiated pact. The ombudsman was part of a set of institutions designed to ensure democratic governance, especially by serving as checks on the executive's power. Like other features in the "democracy package," the idea of including an ombudsman was proposed by a set of reform socialists, or "academic-bureaucrats" working out of the Ministry of Justice, who were tasked in mid-1988 with recommending constitutional revisions. At first, the introduction of these institutions consisted of a legal academic exercise, drawing on European models of democratic institutions. But when it found its way to political roundtable negotiations, it became part of a concrete democratic bundle of reforms, one that could meet the criteria for membership in the Council of Europe.[11]

International considerations were also significant. In the late 1980s, Western governments were attaching human rights conditions to aid packages, just as the institution of the ombudsman continued spreading. The inclusion of the minorities ombudsman, as it is sometimes called, may also have reflected a more overlooked dynamic: promoting the national rights of minorities as a way of addressing international security concerns, relating to Hungarian (Magyar) minorities in neighboring countries (i.e., Romania, Slovakia, Ukraine, the former Yugoslavia).[12] More generally, the ombudsman institution in Hungary was deemed appropriate both domestically and internationally, just as it promised numerous benefits, such as checking errant executive power, and thereby addressing long-standing parliamentary-presidential tensions; institutionalizing minority and other rights demands within the state, so they would become less likely to turn violent or spill over into neighboring countries with Hungarian minorities; and ensuring membership in a community of liberal, democratic European states.

Unlike other Eastern European states, Hungary never applied for NHRI accreditation until 2011, when it came under pressure to do so during the UPR process. The government put forward for accreditation the broadest of its ombudsman agencies, the civil rights commissioner, though the minorities office seemed to participate most regularly over the years in NHRI forums, including the European Group of NHRIs. The accreditation body was unconvinced, deeming the civil rights commissioner only partially compliant with the Paris Principles. A new constitution in 2012, however, called for a single ombudsman agency, promising in principle to better meet international standards.[13]

The Slovenian Ombudsman's Private Roots

During this period, *Slovenia* also created a human rights ombudsman in 1991. The institution was first incorporated into the postindependence constitution that year. It consisted of a parliamentary ombudsman model, combining the traditional Scandinavian institution with the hybrid form appearing in European countries like Spain.[14] The institution is only partially compliant with the Paris Principles, accredited as a B-status body.

It is noteworthy that the body, despite being a postindependence institution, had a predecessor in the Council for the Protection of Human Rights and Fundamental Freedoms, a mass organization formed by the Socialist Alliance of Working People in 1988. That body was given legislative powers in 1990 to act independently and to examine individual cases. Once the ombudsman began functioning in 1995, the new body took over the archives and cases of the former council, in a fascinating instance of how a private organization morphed into a public NHRI after national independence.[15]

Slovenia's ombudsman has run into similar problems to some of its counterparts in the region, even though it is relatively strong organizationally. There was a delay in getting the ombudsman off the ground, with the first ombudsman not being elected until 1994 and the institution not becoming fully functional until 1995. Throughout the life of the institution, moreover, human rights promotion has been absent from its mandate and the terms and conditions of members have not been fully stipulated, potentially compromising the institution's independence. These gaps explain why the institution, despite its overall stability, is only partially compliant with international standards.[16] It also shows how the international accreditation process places a premium on formal structural changes, as guarantees of institutionalization and enduring effectiveness.[17] The dominant perspective in Slovenia, however, is that the institution does good work so there is no urgency in complying with all of the international requisites.[18]

Slovenia's ombudsman was created during a crucial regulatory moment, encompassing both national independence and constitution making, with a relatively low level of violence. The prospect of membership in European institutions, and European identity, made the ombudsman model a natural candidate for inclusion as a new democratic institution, even while it inherited the work of its predecessor body, the Human Rights Council. Ironically, given the institution's relative strength and its standing in Slovenia and in Europe, pressures to conform fully to the Paris Principles have not yet resulted in reform.

"All Promotion" in Romania

Romania in turn created an NHRI that is exclusively promotional. In 1991, perhaps in anticipation of membership in the Council of Europe and following the

Danish "institute" model, it created the Institute for Human Rights via legislation. That same year, Romania was the first country of the former Soviet Union to incorporate an ombudsman (the People's Advocate) into its constitution. It was also the first country with which the UN Human Rights Centre completed a technical cooperation agreement. During accreditation, however, in 2007 and 2011, Romania's Institute for Human Rights was assigned a C status, given its promotional mandate. After 2011, the country shifted strategies and began characterizing the national ombudsman, which is a hybrid body, as the country's NHRI.[19]

Romania created both an ombudsman and the human rights institute during a regulatory moment, marked by the nominal introduction of multiparty elections and constitutional reform, though democratic consolidation itself did not occur until 1996. It did so partly with its sights on membership in European institutions and all the benefits this might bring; a communist successor party was still at the helm of the regime. As one scholar of the region notes, reflecting on the ombudsman and other horizontal accountability institutions, the government was "merely paying lip service to civil society's demands, while in reality it did not want the ombudsman office to challenge its own authority."[20] This helps to explain why "the Romanian ombudsman's legal powers are modest, . . . and every holder of the office has done even less than the law allows so as not to upset the government."[21] During the process of constitutional drafting, moreover, the ombudsman led to some of the "most contradictory and heated debates" about the usefulness of an institution that was said to have been adopted by "all countries."[22] Some groups in civil society had high hopes for the institution, intended to put a break on a bureaucracy that had known few limits in the past, while others emphasized how the conditions to import and transplant this foreign model were absent in Romania.[23]

In establishing its democratic credentials and drafting a new constitution in 1991, Romania was borrowing foreign models (mostly from Europe) that would provide it with the hallmarks of democratic governance and reform. This is how the creation of the human rights institute and ombudsman were envisaged at the time, not as NHRIs per se. Yet despite international assistance and advice, the institutions remained hostage to the political climate, still dominated by members of the former regime. Prior to its first UPR in 2008, Romania submitted its human rights institute for international accreditation, failing to get a stamp of approval. However, as regional pressures for consolidating and accrediting human rights institutions continued to mount, Romania switched tactics and labeled the People's Advocate its NHRI.

Lithuania's Return to Europe

Lithuania's Seimas Ombudsman, formed in 1992, is another NHRI that has never been brought for accreditation. It was incorporated into the 1992 constitution, was given legal standing in 1994, and began functioning one year later.[24] The idea emerged as part of the overall process of national independence and explicit efforts to align the country with Western Europe: in its self-introduction, the institution traces its establishment to "the practice of many European and world countries."[25] Indeed, if the constitutional court established at the same time is any indicator, these new democratic institutions were established by political elites, with little if any consultation, who were importing institutional models from Western Europe. Mostly in response to regional pressures, Lithuania also went on to establish two specialized ombudsmen institutions in 1999 and 2000, for equal opportunities and the rights of the child, respectively.[26]

As part of the UPR process in 2011, the Lithuanian government reported that it was also considering a proposal to create a comprehensive Human Rights Council, which would coordinate the work of the various human rights institutions and place the country in compliance with the Paris Principles.[27] When Lithuania created its human rights ombudsman, it did so in the context of a regulatory moment marked by national independence and constitution making, as well as in the shadow of human rights treaty obligations and prospects of acceptance into European institutions. Indeed, Lithuania

> could "return to Europe" in the fullest sense only if she met the conditions of membership in the various European and Euro-Atlantic organizations. . . . Acceptance by the community of states meant adopting democratic forms of government and protecting human and minority rights. . . . Nevertheless, the politics of the post-independence period often reveal a divergence between law and practice. The political class mouthed the vocabulary of democracy but sometimes their actions showed either that they did not understand the meaning of the term, or cynically ignored it.[28]

Postindependence Lithuania has faced few incentives to develop a strong and accredited NHRI: a political commitment to accountability that was mostly rhetorical, human rights violations minor enough to escape transnational pressure, and formal democratic structures sufficient to gain European acceptance. Yet with the European Group of NHRIs and the UPR process in place, the creation of a Human Rights Council or other accredited human rights ombudsman is more likely.

Reformers in Russia

Russia also moved to create a human rights ombudsman, the commissioner for human rights, in 1993, incorporating it into the new constitution that year. The institution was formed in the face of strong incentives: a regulatory moment, treaty obligations, and ongoing abuses. A presidential decree led to the appointment of the first commissioner in 1994, though implementing legislation was not passed until 1997. Unlike many other NHRIs in the region, the Russian ombudsman has been fully accredited internationally since 2000.

The establishment of Russia's human rights ombudsman needs to be situated first in the context of an uncertain political transition. Leading up to the collapse of the Soviet Union in 1989 was a power struggle between the Yeltsin presidency and parliament. During this period and in the context of (foreign-assisted) legal reform initiatives, a small group of human rights activists and democratic reformers proposed in 1990 a human rights committee to initiate and review draft legislation.[29] As Emma Gilligan describes it, the notion of an ombudsman—though explicitly rejected by the Soviet state as a European "bourgeois" institution—resonated with the reformists' orientation:

> It was, in many respects, an institution that reflected the intellectual ideals of many within the dissident culture of the 1970s; the goal of which was to provide some justice to those suffering under a fragile state and to facilitate an exit from authoritarianism through rational problem solving and moral persuasion. On another level, it was a gesture that sought to compensate for the absence of criminal punishment, lustration, or a truth and reconciliation commission in post-Soviet Russia.[30]

Yeltsin appointed renowned dissident Sergei Kovalev to head the human rights committee, partly as a strategy to bolster his own credentials as a democratic reformer. Almost immediately, the committee began receiving thousands of letters detailing citizen complaints; given the committee's dearth of resources, it was not long before the creation of a full-blown human rights ombudsman emerged as an urgent matter. The committee itself drew on the classic ombudsman model in Europe, notably from Sweden and Great Britain, in proposing a draft law. Yet these developments were met with mounting opposition, including from the security apparatus and communist majority, who feared the political consequences of state accountability.[31]

In November 1991, the human rights committee issued a Declaration of the Rights and Liberties of the Human Being and the Citizen, elevating the place of individual rights and creating a Parliamentary Commissioner for Human Rights. A draft constitution prepared by the Constituent Assembly in 1993 included both the human rights declaration and the office of the ombudsman. And in September 1993, just after parliament had been temporarily dissolved, President Yeltsin issued a decree forming a presidential human rights commission, with another decree in November detailing the commission's workings.[32] Kovalev was reappointed as human rights commissioner, now taking a more active role as "international spokesman for Russia's new policy on human rights," just as a series of honorary members raised the institution's profile in the public arena.[33] An "ombudsman task force" was also appointed to devise the organization's exact structure and functions.[34]

Though the idea had always been to establish the ombudsman after a new constitution was adopted, an expedited process was accepted in early 1994, as the Duma traded posts in a broad bargaining arrangement, and Kovalev was accepted as its leader. Almost immediately, the ombudsman became the recipient of UN technical assistance and began its work. Kovalev's role as ombudsman would be short-lived after he challenged government policy in Chechnya; and propelled by the nationalist bloc, he was removed from his post in March 1995.[35]

The enacting legislation, which was still under debate, became the subject of even more controversy, not to be fully approved until early 1997. The second ombudsman was elected in mid-1998, the product of another interparty deal struck by parliament. Yet the institution was not provided with funding, premises, equipment, or staff. The ombudsman would eventually surmount these obstacles and build a large state institution, but only after struggling to set the right tone in the institution's reports and overall orientation. By 2001, the "formative years" were almost complete; and the ombudsman began receiving more complaints (e.g., 60,000 in 2000), which were also more representative of the range of abuses in the country, just as it began to confront state policy toward Chechnya.

It also began working more closely with NGOs and the media, broadening the human rights issues it addressed.[36]

A few themes emerge from Russia's adoption of a human rights ombudsman as its NHRI. The idea for the institution came from human rights and democratic reform activists, who were intensely interested in *state* reform; the institution's European lineage and promise to exert popular control over the executive appealed intellectually to this group. The fact that this small group found a supporter in the president was crucial, especially given parliamentary divisions and broad opposition to the idea of state accountability.[37] For his part, President Yeltsin favored the institution partly because it was a marker of democratic reform, setting him apart from the former regime. The ombudsman was indeed viewed as a new, European institution, especially in contrast to the communist-era Office of the Prosecutor-General, which continued operating.[38] With the prospect of membership in the Council of Europe, an ombudsman was a natural option. Still, concerns over holding the state accountable for past abuses, as well as ongoing violence in Chechnya, meant a long delay in fully establishing the institution. In this regard, an initial human rights committee was transformed into a human rights commission, eventually becoming the country's ombudsman. Russia's accredited NHRI was the product of strong incentives to lock in commitments, localize authority, and appease critics, as well as domestic institutional evolution.

The Drive for European Membership: Slovakia and Latvia

Slovakia's National Centre for Human Rights was created by legislation in 1993, the same year as national independence. It was enshrined in the "Agreement between the United Nations and the Government of the Slovak Republic Regarding the Establishment of the Slovak National Centre for Human Rights," which detailed the institution's functioning.[39] In 2004, following passage of the Anti-Discrimination Act in Slovakia, the center also became an equality body. Yet despite external funding and support, including from European governments like the Netherlands, the NHRI's budget remained tied to parliament; and after 2002 it was only partially compliant (B status) with international standards. During the country's UPR in 2009, Slovakia was pushed to comply fully with the Paris Principles. Its accreditation nonetheless lapsed in 2012 after it failed to submit relevant materials.[40]

Just as the National Centre for Human Rights was created during a regulatory moment, a human rights ombudsman—the public defender of rights—was established as part of major constitutional amendments in 2001, sparked by the lead-up to EU membership. The proposal had nonetheless been floated for a long time; indeed, as far back as when Slovakia was still part of Czechoslovakia, a draft bill for the creation of a public defender of rights had circulated.[41] It is always possible that in the future the country will present the public defender for accreditation as an NHRI in lieu of the center.

Slovakia followed a familiar pattern of democratization in Eastern Europe, one undermining the state's interest in supporting human rights. Despite (or perhaps because of) international involvement, democratization has been unable to overcome the political system's basic fragility, made worse by rising nationalism in the context of conflict with ethnic Hungarians.[42] In a public opinion poll in 1995, for example, a majority of people said Slovakia's postindependence government did not respect human rights. The country has a relatively well-developed NGO sector, though its support by foreign actors has often undermined it in the eyes of the government.[43]

Slovakia created its NHRI during a regulatory moment, with heavy international involvement. The institution's mandate has expanded over time in response to region-wide pressures. But despite significant external technical support, transnational human rights pressures against Slovakia have not generally been strong, given a relatively low level of rights violations and a small population. In a regional context where few fully accredited NHRIs exist, the pressures to strengthen the National Centre have not been especially overwhelming.

Latvia created two NHRIs in succession. The National Human Rights Office was created by a Cabinet of Ministers ruling in 1995 and by law in 1996; it most resembled the "national human rights commissions" model. Though the country became independent in 1990 and adopted a new constitution in 1992, the creation of the human rights office seemed to have been linked most closely to joining the Council of Europe in 1995. In 2006, the human rights office was replaced by the Latvian ombudsman, though that institution, like its predecessor, was not given constitutional standing. And unlike the previous body, the ombudsman cannot summon people before it. While it is intended to implement EU antidiscrimination directives, especially important in Baltic states, where up to one-fifth of the national population is stateless, it has no actual powers in this regard.[44]

The shift to an ombudsman office appears closely related to the country's joining of NATO and the EU in 2004. In fact, when the government affirmed as part of its UPR in 2011 that its NHRI already complied with the Paris Principles, treaty bodies and other international actors still pressured the government to seek accreditation.[45] It remains to be seen whether ongoing pressure to follow a regional template for a human rights ombudsman will yield concrete results for an institution that, like so many in the region, was created largely to meet formal membership criteria.

Dualism in Uzbekistan

Uzbekistan was the first member of the Commonwealth of Independent States to establish an NHRI, taking the form of a hybrid ombudsman. In 1995, it created the Authorized Person of the Oliy Majlis of the Republic of Uzbekistan for Human Rights, otherwise known as the Authorized Person for Human Rights, with implementing legislation passed in 1997. Housed within parliament and not accredited internationally, it was created in a broader context of liberalization, which began with national independence in 1991 and a new constitution in 1992. Part of a presidential initiative following the first parliamentary elections in 1994, it was portrayed as a response to the recent Vienna Declaration.[46] In 1996, the government also established a National Centre for Human Rights, identified as an NHRI in the government's submission to the UPR in 2008. That the country remained firmly authoritarian was evident in the ombudsman's structural limitations.

The creation of human rights structures by the state seems to have been heavily internationalized. For example, in 1996, the OSCE had organized a workshop on NHRIs in Tashkent, during which the "experience of foreign ombudsmen and experts was taken into account."[47] Even in the organization's own self-description, the reasons for creating the institution included strong external elements: "A necessity to create a new structure to protect human rights in Uzbekistan was conditioned by a number of factors: establishment of civil society, expansion of democratic reforms, implementation of effective measures to protect citizens' rights, accumulated international experience, as well as requirements associated with the membership of the Republic of Uzbekistan in international human rights organizations." Since that time, the Authorized Person has concluded other cooperation agreements with international organizations and several European countries.[48]

The period after 2000 was one of contradictions. On the one hand, human rights conditions deteriorated, including civil unrest in 2005 that resulted in hundreds of people being killed. At the same time, the government moved to strengthen the NHRI at least on paper.[49] In 2003, it was incorporated into the constitution, with new legislation entering into force in 2005. The 2005 law was portrayed as mirroring "international standards in the area of human rights institutions, and international experience in legal governance of the status of Ombudsmen."[50] When the country underwent its UPR in 2008, the government responded to recommendations that the NHRI be strengthened by claiming it was already fully compliant.[51] Stakeholders, however, had a different view, labeling the ombudsman as "fully dependent on the executive branch."[52] For the 2009–11 period, UNDP thus initiated a project on developing the capacity of the country's NHRIs.[53]

The creation of the hybrid ombudsman in Uzbekistan was no doubt heavily tied up in the country's postindependence links with Europe. In 1995, a set of exploratory talks began with the European Commission over a Partnership and Cooperation Agreement, finalized in 1996. Though the language of democracy and human rights featured centrally in institution building, many observers viewed the motives as commercially driven. A reputation for being a rights-abiding state, with all the expected institutional markers was, after all, a prerequisite for closer relations with European countries. It was in this context that both the ombudsman and Human Rights Centre were created, and 1997 was declared the Uzbek Year of Human Rights, all formal steps to appease prospective international partners.[54] Created at the juncture of a regulatory moment and external obligations, the creation of these institutions was borrowed from an international rule book for how new democracies were supposed to act. Ongoing authoritarianism kept the country from joining the Council of Europe; but in a context of minor violations, international actors still rewarded formal rights institutions that existed mostly on paper.

Bosnia and Herzegovina's Postconflict Ombudsman

Bosnia and Herzegovina's Human Rights Ombudsman was included in the 1995 Dayton Peace Agreements. It was part of the postconflict state building and democratic institutionalization envisioned by Western actors in the aftermath of war.[55] Not surprisingly, the institution—even before it was established—was very heavily internationalized, in a country where NATO troops and the OHCHR were on the ground and overseeing key aspects of governance during the transition. In 1994, the first human rights ombudsman was appointed by the OSCE, beginning its work in January 1995—months before the formal conclusion of the Dayton Accords. Strongly influenced by the Council of Europe's Venice Commission, a law passed in 2004 and amended in 2006 regulates the federal ombudsman, which is fully accredited internationally.[56]

The post-conflict institutional scene was complicated in Bosnia and Herzegovina with the coexistence of three ombudsmen agencies: one at the federal level (1995), one for the state of Bosnia and Herzegovina (1996), and one for Republika Srpska (2000).[57] European authorities pushed for institutional consolidation; in fact, merging the three ombudsman was a "post-accession obligation" of joining the Council of Europe in 2002, one of over a dozen stipulated criteria.[58] The consolidation finally occurred in 2010, proving more controversial than mere reorganization. As Julie Mertus describes it, "The merger decision is intensely personal for the affected commissioners and staff, because the process will necessarily entail cutting positions and laying off staff. It is also incredibly political because any change will affect concentrations of power and control over the domestic human rights agenda."[59]

One of the most daunting challenges for Bosnia and Herzegovina has been moving to localize authority after an overreliance on foreign actors during the postconflict period. In the case of the ombudsman, this has meant managing without an international staff, what some Bosnians came to describe as "internal international actors."[60] However, "[f]ew critics dispute that Bosniafication has had a profound effect on all human rights institutions, leading to a downgrading of their importance and impact, a lessening of their independence, and a weakening of their credibility among the general public. Bosniafication led to a 50 percent pay cut for employees of the institutions and a drastic reduction in benefits. This in turn led many staff members, including the most well trained human rights lawyers, to seek employment elsewhere."[61]

Bosnia and Herzegovina presents another case of a country that faced overwhelming incentives to create an accountability mechanism. The postconflict nature of the situation meant that the role of international actors was extensive, so much so that the transition to self-governance has paradoxically left an institutional vacuum. Given the vibrancy of local NGOs, moreover, state human rights institutions have been partially displaced. Combining the formulaic creation of NHRIs with a local "culture of legal double-talk" has led to an NHRI that is technically competent but still finding its way through the maze of human rights governance.[62]

Institutional Legacies of Independence

More countries across the region continued adopting an NHRI: Georgia, Macedonia, Moldova, Ukraine, Turkmenistan, Albania, and Azerbaijan. These countries showed broadly similar dynamics despite their national differences. For example, *Georgia's* Public Defender's Office was incorporated into the 1995 constitution and created by a parliamentary decree in 1996, one year after Eduard Shevardnadze was elected president.[63] The ombudsman, established in the lead-up to Council of Europe membership in 1999, matched well the country's Western orientation. Supported by numerous foreign donors, as proudly displayed on the institution's website, the Public Defender's Office was fully accredited as an NHRI in 2007.[64]

Still, by the new millennium, Georgia was facing challenges similar to those of other states in the region. As one observer notes, the myth of the political transition was coming under assault, as the regime's autocratic realities were coming head to head with new democratic formalities. If the 1990s had been a period of "democracy without democrats" in Georgia, after 2000 it was a time of "democrats without democracy."[65] At stake was much more than Western-oriented democratization: the country had embarked on an internal project of statehood and identity beginning with independence in 1991. Following the Rose Revolution in 2003 and armed conflict with Russia, Georgia was under strains that were inevitably transposed onto the ombudsman's office, whose independence was not always respected and which lacked the power and resources to perform effectively.[66]

Unlike other neighboring states, Georgia faced higher initial incentives for creating an accountability institution, including a greater level of human rights violence. Western support seems to have reinforced the institution, despite efforts by the government to disregard the ombudsman and even to use force against it; in a state of emergency and one month after it was accredited, its premises were broken into in 2007.[67] Ironically, higher abuse at the time of the institution's creation led to greater international involvement and a stronger institution, better able to withstand subsequent state opposition and broader political volatility.

Macedonia's ombudsman, though not accredited, is also known as a human rights ombudsman. The former Yugoslav republic's constitution of 1991, coinciding with independence that year, referred to the institution as the public attorney, though the first ombudsman was not elected until 1997, when the institution became functional.[68] This followed membership in the Council of Europe in 1995 and coincided with ratification of the European Convention on Human Rights (ECHR) in 1997. In 2001, the ombudsman was incorporated into the national constitution via amendment, as part of the Framework Agreement signed that year between the government and ethnic Albanian representatives; the implementing legislation was itself heavily influenced by the Venice Commission. The ombudsman now includes a nondiscrimination mandate and penitentiary component. Despite this expanding mandate, international treaty bodies (e.g., the Human Rights Committee and CAT) have called on the government to reinforce the ombudsman. More recently, as part of the UPR in 2009, Macedonia was pushed to strengthen the ombudsman to conform to the Paris Principles, including by expanding its powers and respecting its financial independence. The government offered assurances that it would do so.[69]

The fact that the human rights mandate in Macedonia's ombudsman was relatively weak may reflect the particularities of constitution making in 1991, just before rising attention to NHRIs and in a context of relatively low rights abuses. The creation of an ombudsman, charged with protecting citizens' rights vis-à-vis the state, spoke to Western requisites for a democratic constitution. The original name of public attorney, an institution that predated national independence in Macedonia and with deeper roots in the region and common-law systems, alluded to the institution's role in representing the state.[70] Now that the ombudsman has strengthened its formal credentials, ongoing international regime pressures to abide by the Paris Principles may reinforce the institution's human rights dimensions. Whether the institution becomes more widely known in Macedonian society nonetheless remains to be seen.

Moldova also created a human rights ombudsman during the same period, closely tied to international actors. Though abuses were minor, independence in 1991 and a new constitution in 1994, along with the establishment of a constitutional court in 1995 and membership that same year in the Council of Europe, opened the door to democratic institutional change. The most immediate impetus, however, was a UNDP study in the mid-1990s, which called for an NHRI in Moldova; a joint commission of UNDP and government representatives was then created to draft a relevant law. The law was enacted, along with a presidential decree in 1997, the same year as Moldova acceded to the ECHR.

This NHRI, or the Parliamentary Advocates–Centre for Human Rights, commenced its activities in 1998.[71] Since its inception, most of the center's activities seem to be promotional in nature; and though minor incremental reforms have been initiated, the center still does not have constitutional standing. After waiting a relatively long time before seeking international accreditation, Moldova's NHRI was assigned B status in 2009, found to be only partially compliant with the Paris Principles. Yet between the UPR process and the country's strong linkages to Europe, including the EU and the OSCE, reform could be forthcoming.

Ukraine's postindependence transition was almost derailed when a serious economic recession hit the country. This delayed institution building somewhat, and it was five years after independence and shortly after joining the Council of Europe, that the former Soviet republic introduced a new constitution in 1996. This constitution included the office of a human rights ombudsman, or the Parliament Commissioner for Human Rights.[72] Implementing legislation followed in 1997, the same year the country acceded to the ECHR, with the first ombudsman elected in 1998. As the organization describes its influences, "When the Ukrainian model of the Commissioner for Human Rights was devised, allowance was made for the prevalent national and legal traditions, the system of state power, as well as the expertise of the ombudsmen elsewhere, specifically in the Scandinavian nations and in the countries that embarked on the road of reform—Poland, Hungary and Russia."[73]

Ukraine's government has been noticeably responsive to international calls for strengthening its NHRI. Treaty bodies, especially the CESCR and CAT, remanded the institution for lacking independence, not being sufficiently attentive to socioeconomic rights, and providing minorities with inadequate access. These were also among the concerns raised during the UPR procedure in 2008. Ukraine's NHRI was initially found to be only partially compliant with the Paris Principles; but after the necessary changes were made, the institution was fully accredited.[74]

Ukraine thus stands as another example of an NHRI forged during a regulatory moment and in the face of external obligations. The broader political context, marked by the ongoing challenges of new democracies, including corruption and an overly strong presidency, initially constrained full compliance with international standards. Despite having Europe's largest standing army, after Russia, international regime pressures effectively pushed for institutional reform and activism. Maintaining state institutions for democracy and human rights was the price of sustaining economic and other partnerships with more powerful Western countries.

Albania's People's Advocate (or People's Attorney, Avokati i Popullit), a hybrid ombudsman, was first mentioned in the country's 1998 constitution.[75] The institution's appearance, like the constitution, was part of a second political transition that had taken place since the Soviet Union's collapse and that had come to a head when social protests (partly in response to the collapse of widespread pyramid schemes) were met with state violence. It also followed membership in the Council of Europe in 1995 and ratification of the ECHR one year later. Despite these

broader processes, human rights abuses were also relatively high during this period, prolonged by Western powers who in the early 1990s and especially during
the Bosnian War had sought an ally in Albania and were willing to offer high
levels of assistance despite deteriorating human rights conditions.[76]

International actors supported the NHRI from its inception. The OSCE,
Council of Europe, and Danish government were especially active during the
institution's creation. Albania's NHRI further benefitted during its formative
years from the Council of Europe's Stability Pact for South Eastern Europe, a
conflict-prevention program created in 1999 for the subregion that targeted the
strengthening of ombudsman offices and NHRIs among other democratic institutions. Even the Association of the Francophonie helped fund a quarterly bul-
letin published in Albanian and French. In 2003, the institution was provisionally
assigned A status as an NHRI, fully so after 2004.[77] As the country joined
NATO in 2009 and looked toward EU membership, the People's Advocate featured as one of the strongest NHRIs in the region. Paradoxically, the institution's creation during a period of high violations, and in the midst of a regulatory
moment as well as newly acquired human rights obligations, set the incentives
for a strong NHRI.

While *Azerbaijan's* commissioner for human rights, a national parliamentary
ombudsman, was officially created by a parliamentary act in 2001, the NHRI
had first been mentioned in two presidential decrees in 1998. The same year that
the ombudsman was created, Azerbaijan joined the Council of Europe; and the
first human rights commissioner was elected in 2002, also when the country
ratified the ECHR. By 2006, just as Azerbaijan issued a National Human Rights
Plan and joined the Human Rights Council, its NHRI was fully accredited internationally.[78]

President Ilham Aliyev's decrees in 1998 must be understood as part of his
broader attempt to seek international legitimacy and growing integration with
Europe, on the heels of a new constitution in 1995 that strengthened the presidency's powers substantially. Perhaps not surprisingly, one of the limitations of
the human rights ombudsman was that it excluded the head of state from its jurisdiction. Indeed, the period of the late 1990s, when the idea of an ombudsman
institution was first mentioned in Azerbaijan, has been described as "semiau-
thoritarian": "Only genuine political activists and journalists, and the radical
opposition, found themselves systematically in officialdom's line of fire."[79] For
foreign onlookers, however, talk of democracy and of institution building were
welcome signs of a stable state in the volatile region of the Caucasus. It was another instance of a country with a relatively high level of violations, and in the

context of nominal liberalization and rising human rights obligations, producing an active NHRI.

Human Rights Fatigue in the Czech Republic

The public defender of rights, or the ombudsman, was created in the *Czech Republic* as late as 1999, not beginning to function until 2001. Significantly, it was established relatively long after the country's 1992 constitution and its separation from Slovakia in 1993, and having already ratified the major human rights treaties. Though its mandate was gradually expanded, including in 2006 when the ombudsman began addressing detainee issues and in 2009 when it started assisting victims of discrimination, it has never been accredited.[80]

The idea of creating an ombudsman predated the federation's dissolution. The unified government had prepared a bill for an ombudsman, which nonetheless disappeared with the country's separation. In 1995, a parliamentary committee tried to revive the proposal, but it was opposed by the president and failed to gain the support of a majority in parliament. Only in 1999, after a change in government, did the idea at last succeed. The initiative, however, derived almost entirely from civil society, with the Czech Helsinki Committee leading the campaign for creating a comprehensive NHRI. The ombudsman that resulted was not exactly what these actors had envisioned, but it at least served to institutionalize human rights concerns more than may otherwise have been the case.[81]

The role of European pressures was quite significant. By some accounts the Council of Europe's recommendation in 1997 to establish ombudsman offices was "decisive."[82] And in 1999, the year the Czech Republic joined NATO, the transatlantic organization had also called for the institution's creation. Likewise, the process leading up to EU membership in 2004 created pressures for rapid reform. These forces help to explain the establishment of other parallel human rights structures, including a Government Council for Human Rights (created in 1998) and a government commissioner for human rights.[83]

This institutionalization, however, may have had a paradoxical effect. On the one hand, it served to lock in the government's commitment to human rights norms and seal its reputation internationally. On the other hand, it may have stifled domestic actors. In a country where human rights issues had been an integral part of the Velvet Revolution, public distrust of government ran high, so that civic participation was weakened; and society had mostly grown tired of the confrontational discourse of human rights. As one observer notes, "Supporters of human rights tended to view the new mechanisms as the end of human rights activism."[84] Apparently, "[a]fter the Velvet Revolution had reached its initial goals, Václav Havel himself dismissed the need for the creation of the Czech Helsinki Committee, because 'democracy' had taken hold in the new republic, vitiating the need for issue-specific human rights institutions."[85] It was time for the country to move on; human rights and democracy were problems of the past, already resolved. Despite ongoing violations, including hate-related attacks and discrimination against minorities like the Roma, the ombudsman's office to some extent mirrored society, rarely invoking the language of human rights explicitly in its day-to-day functions.[86]

Pressures for accrediting the ombudsman as an NHRI, moreover, have been quite weak. The UPR process in 2008 called mostly on the government to implement the ombudsman's recommendations. The Czech state had already proved that it was willing to alter domestic structures for international benefits. Though it had been the last EU member state not to have ratified the Rome Statute, the government at last acceded to the treaty in 2009, just as it prepared to take over the EU's presidency. External obligations (or more precisely, the need to demonstrate, credibly, commitment to these obligations so as to garner ongoing regional benefits) drove the ombudsman's institutional creation. Yet once formed, the institution minimized its human rights focus, which no longer appealed to domestic groups, and did not seek accreditation, despite (or perhaps due to) the widespread perception internationally that it was already an NHRI.

Western European NHRIs

Unlike diffusion throughout Eastern Europe, dominated by national independence and political transition, in Western Europe NHRIs were adopted by a mix of countries, facing very different incentives. For example, domestic racist incidents help to account for the NHRI's rise in both Belgium and Switzerland. Significantly, these were institutions that were not created self-consciously as NHRIs but were later transformed into this category of bodies through international accreditation. The Equal Treatment Commission in the Netherlands in turn seemed to orient around the country's external obligations and represent a domestic political compromise. In Finland, an institution dating to the early twentieth century (the parliamentary ombudsman) was gradually transformed into an NHRI, with external obligations also featuring centrally. The Mediterranean states of Cyprus and Greece likewise joined the trend, largely in response to regional diffusion mechanisms, magnified by the requirements of membership in European institutions. In the case of Greece, transnational pressure resulting from human rights violations led to a stronger NHRI than in Cyprus. Despite the variations, strategic emulation played a consistently significant role.

Racism and Rights in Small, Liberal States

In Western Europe, other states continued joining the global trend, though they created weakly designed NHRIs. Two of these states (Belgium and Switzerland) were small, liberal countries. In both cases, the creation of an NHRI was linked most closely to racist incidents.

Belgium was the first country in Western Europe to create an NHRI in the 1990s: the Centre for Equal Opportunities and Opposition to Racism (CEOOR) was established in 1993 by a parliamentary act.[87] Substantial constitutional revisions that year, which established Belgium as a federal state, were certainly in the foreground, especially since the constitution carried important implications for immigrant populations and ethnic integration. The country's human rights obligations, which did not include CERD until 1999, seemed to serve as constitutional benchmarks. Likewise, the creation in 1993 of a regional monitoring institution, the European Commission against Racism and Intolerance, as well as the Vienna Conference that year might also have been influential. But the primary interest in creating the CEOOR in 1993 was not to join a regional or global NHRI trend. The institution arose in direct response to domestic racial tensions.

The CEOOR itself replaced the semiofficial Royal Commissariat for Migration Policies that had been established under the prime minister's office to combat racism. According to Dirk Jacobs, this was "the direct result of the electoral success of the extreme right-wing and racist Vlaams Blok in the municipal elections of 1988 (in the city of Antwerp)."[88] Following the 1991 general elections, when Vlaams Blok made further electoral gains, antiracist demonstrations ensued. These tensions were compounded by a seventy-point plan, issued by the extreme right in mid-1992, which outlined "solutions" for dealing with the "problem" of immigration. Years earlier, a similar dynamic had played out: while Belgium had long signed (but not ratified) CERD, a cycle of hate crimes and public demonstrations against racism had led to the Anti-Racism Law in 1981.[89] It was little wonder, then, that in the tense climate of the early 1990s, and given the country's international obligations and new constitution, a permanent state body was created to deal with racism.

Over time, Belgium's parliament expanded the center's mandate. The center was originally set up to support victims of racial discrimination, but a broader range of issues was added incrementally, including migration, human trafficking, poverty, and nonracial discrimination. Since 2003, moreover, an equal opportunity mandate was incorporated in response to European directives. Though the center was not initially created as an NHRI, the Belgian government applied for international accreditation as early as 1999. The institution, still housed under the prime minister's office, was found to be only partially compliant with the Paris Principles, a decision reaffirmed in 2010. As part of the 2011 UPR process, Amnesty International and others called on Belgium to create a fully compliant NHRI. In the official government report submitted for its UPR, the government stated it had not yet created a national human rights commission, though many institutions like the center helped to protect human rights in Belgium.[90] Ongoing international regime pressures, along with the gradual expansion of the institution's mandate, perhaps combined with another high-profile racist incident, could push Belgium to strengthen the institution even further, narrowing the gap between its international obligations and domestic institutional practices.

Shortly after Belgium created a national body to combat racism, *Switzerland* followed suit, establishing the Federal Commission against Racism in 1995. Like neighboring Belgium, postwar immigration in a multiethnic but largely heterogeneous society was met with racist incidents and the resurgence of right-wing extremism in the late 1980s. One of the state's responses to this overt and violent racism was to ratify CERD in 1994.[91]

While the question of ratifying CERD had been raised as far back as 1971, according to the government, "it was the recent increase of acts of terror against foreigners, or committed on the grounds of race, which moved the Swiss authority to take up the issue again."[92] After acceding to CERD, a related antiracism law was passed in 1995 and the Federal Commission against Racism was established to implement CERD domestically. On some level, rising extremism and racism had led to ratification of an international treaty, which in turn sparked domestic implementation measures in the form of an NHRI. These dynamics are further supported by the fact that the government simultaneously updated the mandates of two other federal commissions (for foreigners and refugees), addressing how these commissions might better coordinate with each other and their new counterpart on racism.[93]

Domestic actors later used the fact that the racism commission was only partially accredited internationally to press for a stronger NHRI. As early as 1998, the government had submitted the Federal Commission for international accreditation, which earned B status at that stage. In 2000, NGOs and individuals committed to the creation of an NHRI in Switzerland formed a working group.[94] Shortly thereafter, two parliamentarians launched an initiative for establishing an NHRI; and by 2006, a formal Association for the Promotion of an

NHRI formed to lobby the government. Perhaps in the run-up to Switzerland's UPR in 2008, the government decided to host a meeting with NGOs, where one of the themes that emerged was the importance of an NHRI. According to NGOs, federalism was a key stumbling block to creating an NHRI, requiring all of the cantons to cooperate (after all, one canton, Appenzell Innerhoden, had held out on giving women the right to vote until 1990!).[95]

After the UPR, Switzerland tried to have another institution—its federal women's commission—accredited as an NHRI. This time international standards had evolved and tightened significantly, and the institution was found in March 2009 to be noncompliant with the Paris Principles (a C-status institution). Following that failure, in summer 2009, the government announced it would create a Swiss Competence Centre for Human Rights, a pilot project launched by several universities that would evolve into a full-blown NHRI in four to five years. The institution was the result of a federal contract won by a consortium of universities, including the universities of Bern, Fribourg, Neuchâtel, and Zurich.

Even after the decision to create the Competence Centre was taken, the Federal Commission against Racism reapplied for accreditation in 2010, and it was demoted to C status. It seemed that peer NHRIs on the ICC were looking to pressure the only country in the world that had applied simultaneously to have two different institutions accredited as NHRIs. While international practice moved in the direction of reducing, not creating, institutional redundancies, pressure for Switzerland to establish a single NHRI persisted.

The new Swiss Competence Centre for Human Rights (or Swiss Centre of Expertise in Human Rights) began functioning in 2011. Though it was cautiously welcomed by domestic NGOs, they immediately questioned its independence, resources, and limited role in the cantons.[96] Clearly, the government, which was not an EU member and appeared to be following the Danish model, has resisted the notion of creating an NHRI per se, opting for a "center" housed in a university setting. Facing relatively weak incentives to create an accountability mechanism, the government's response to ongoing pressures has been to buy time and deflect the issue. The politics surrounding the Swiss Competence Centre have yet to play out, as the country's designated NHRI continues evolving and longstanding domestic proponents of an NHRI react.

Dutch Accommodation

When the *Netherlands* created the Equal Treatment Commission in 1994, it did so in the context of international and regional obligations. The institution was putatively created to promote and monitor compliance with that year's Equal Treatment Act, a general document covering discrimination on multiple grounds, including race, gender, and religion.[97] In 2003, passage of an antidiscrimination law for disability expanded the commission's mandate. The Netherlands thus illustrates a process of institutional evolution, as European-wide laws led to national specialized laws, which gradually evolved into more comprehensive laws and a related institutional body, eventually transforming into a standard NHRI.

The commission's creation in 1994 reflected its European and domestic origins. As one commentator notes, the Equal Treatment Commission was "preceded by several specialized equality bodies that were established in the first instance to meet the obligations emanating from the law of the European Community."[98] Some of these specialized bodies dated to the 1980s, addressing issues of pay, working conditions, and gender. A national ombudsman had also been created in 1981, though it lacked an explicit human rights mandate. Yet for domestic political reasons, it took a full decade for requisite compromises to be struck and an accommodation—integral to Dutch policy making—to be reached. One of the main obstacles to creating equality institutions came from the Christian Democrats, who wanted to secure a series of exceptions, including for religious organizations.[99] When the Equal Treatment Act was finally passed in 1994, it represented a compromise of sorts, albeit one rife with exclusions and gaps.

Transnational regime pressures would still prove essential in the Dutch government's willingness to create an NHRI in compliance with the Paris Principles. When the Equal Treatment Commission applied for international accreditation in 1999, it was found to be only partially compliant and assigned a B status, later reaffirmed in 2004 and 2010. The accreditation process nonetheless opened the door for both international and domestic actors to begin calling for institutional reform. In a 2007 evaluation of the commission, it became evident that the Dutch public's awareness of the Equal Treatment Act was relatively low. As the Dutch government admitted, "knowledge of fundamental rights in the Netherlands is not what it should be."[100] Both treaty bodies and NGOs pushed the government on this point as they called for broader reform.[101]

Most significant, however, was the Dutch government's determination to hold a seat on the new Human Rights Council. As one of the leading government proponents of human rights in the world, election to the Human Rights Council was essential in shaping the nascent international institution. Having successfully campaigned for a one-year seat in 2006, just as the new council began operating, the Netherlands won a subsequent three-year term, 2007–10. In its reelection bid, it had pledged to establish a fully compliant NHRI. And by the time of its own UPR in 2008, the government confirmed that it was in the final stages of deciding on the specific nature of the NHRI, which enjoyed widespread support from both members of parliament and NGOs. The proposal leading to the new institution was prepared by a mix of existing state bodies (i.e., the Equal Treatment Commission, National Ombudsman, and Data Protection Authority) as well as the highly regarded academic think tank the Netherlands Institute of Rights.[102]

Finally, in November 2011, the Dutch Parliament approved a new law creating an NHRI, which would transform the Equal Treatment Commission into the National Human Rights Institution for the Netherlands—one of the only bodies in the world to carry the name of a "national human rights institution." One immediate criticism was that litigation would be limited to those rights covered in the Equal Treatment Commission.[103] On balance, however, the Netherlands showed its willingness, in the context of evolving transnational regime pressures, to adapt its domestic institutions to better meet, and shape, its external obligations.

The Nordic Transformation

Finland's parliamentary ombudsman is remarkable for having been created in 1919 and enduring so long, only to be transformed into a human rights ombudsman in 1995. This transformation cannot be understood apart from European institutions, especially membership in the Council of Europe in 1989, ratification of the ECHR in 1990, and accession to the EU in 1995.[104]

The constitutional revisions of 1995, which most notably recognized economic, social, and cultural rights and redefined citizen rights as human rights, were the direct result of Finland's treaty obligations. As the ombudsman's office describes it, the reforms of that year ushered in "a new perspective" for the ombudsman's office. This shift was all the more striking because it represented a historic turn for Nordic countries, from a tradition of legislative supremacy to rights-based constitutionalism driven by EU membership. There is little question that "[h]uman rights treaties binding on Finland, especially the ECHR, featured as the main inspiration and stimulus for this reform."[105]

But what is perhaps most noteworthy about the reform, especially as it relates to NHRI creation, is that the reform was procedural more than substantive. As some analysts describe it,

The significance of the ratification and the incorporation of the ECHR did not relate so much to the substantive rights provisions of the convention. . . . The crucial difference, in relation to the prevailing constitutional culture, was the introduction of an effective international judicial monitoring mechanism that allowed individuals to bring their cases to an international court if they had not succeeded on the domestic level. . . . [F]rom the perspective of national legal orders that are without preexisting rights practice, it was the European human rights system with its extensive case law that first convinced the reluctant national courts to regard human rights as legally binding and enforceable rights.[106]

Put differently, the constitutional reforms of 1995, which were the immediate precursor to the ombudsman's mandate, were sparked not just by regional developments; they also represented attempts to localize authority over human rights issues, so that individuals' claims could be resolved domestically.

Over time, as global attention to NHRIs grew, domestic pressures for the creation of an accredited NHRI likewise increased. Rather than opposing the creation of such a body per se, political leaders often treated the idea of an NHRI as an unnecessary redundancy, given numerous other relevant institutions, namely the Parliamentary Ombudsman, the Advisory Board (operating in the Foreign Ministry since 1988), several specialized ombudsmen (equality, minorities, children, data protection), and relevant academic institutions. Consequently, one proposal that emerged in 2002, from an academic institution, was to adopt a network approach to NHRIs and coordinate the various relevant bodies. By 2006, stronger calls for a traditional NHRI began emerging, including from the Finnish League for Human Rights. In a study commissioned by the Foreign Ministry, the league called for the creation of an NHRI that would conform with the Paris Principles; the current institutional state, they said, was overly fragmentary. Based on this study, the Advisory Board formally moved for the government to take up the issue in its platform. When this failed, Jacob Söderman, former European ombudsman and a member of parliament, proposed in 2008 a legislative motion to create an NHRI.[107]

The result of these mounting domestic pressures was the creation in 2012 of a Human Rights Centre within the office of the Parliamentary Ombudsman. More specifically, the Human Rights Centre would be "operationally autonomous and independent, but administratively a part of the Office of Parliamentary Ombudsman." Included in the center would be a Human Rights Delegation; and together the center, delegation, and ombudsman would compose the country's NHRI—a uniquely nested institutional structure. The ombudsman at the time described the reform as "historic" and the "beginning of a new era." In tracing the need for such an institution, Ombudsman Jääskeläinen revealed the international and domestic incentives: "The human rights institution is needed because of international cooperation. In some international connections, a status in accordance with the Paris Principles can be a downright prerequisite for participation or being entitled to speak. A human rights institution is necessary also to meet purely national needs. It will gather together Finland's fragmented human rights structures and provide a forum for cooperation between them and coordinating their activities."[108] In general, international regime pressures, combined with domestic actors supporting the idea of an NHRI, as well as an earlier constitutional revision, help to explain the transformation of a century-old traditional ombudsman into a modern-day NHRI.

Euro-Mediterranean Trajectories

The late 1990s also saw the creation of NHRIs in Southern Europe, with the institution spreading to Cyprus and Greece. While Cyprus's National Institute (sometimes translated as institution) for the Protection of Human Rights had not applied for international accreditation by the time of its first UPR, Greece's National Commission for Human Rights has been fully accredited since 2000. Despite important domestic differences, European initiatives calling for the creation of NHRIs during this period cannot be discounted. Both governments were keenly aware of these developments, and of each other's plans, and both moved to create NHRIs in 1998.[109]

Regionally, a few significant developments unfolded on the NHRI front that shaped events in Cyprus and Greece. In January 1997, for instance, the second meeting of European NHRIs met in Copenhagen, where recommendations were made and forwarded to the Council of Europe that NHRIs be promoted and that NHRIs in member states cooperate with the council.[110] The Council of Europe also adopted resolutions later that year calling on all states to create an NHRI, especially a "national human rights commission." These recommendations were especially important for at least two reasons. First, the Council of Europe had considered, and dismissed, the idea of promoting NHRIs as early as the 1980s. In 1985, it opted instead, given regional trends, for issuing a recommendation about the role of the ombudsman.[111] Second, the shift in the council's attention in the 1990s reflected rising global attention to NHRIs, following the Paris Principles and the Vienna World Conference, as well as the first meeting of NHRIs in Europe held in Strasbourg in early November 1994. In this context of NHRI diffusion, the Council of Europe itself joined the global bandwagon.

By September 1998, *Cyprus* issued a Council of Ministers decision to form a National Institution for the Protection of Human Rights. The institution was established by decree and placed within the office of the Law Commissioner; it was designed as an "umbrella" body, bringing together government agencies working on human rights and NGOs.[112] It is noteworthy that Cyprus already had an ombudsman, created in 1991 and including human rights in its mandate. Yet other than long-standing human rights treaty obligations, it did not face strong incentives to create an NHRI. In addition to the Council of Europe's growing attention to NHRIs, other regional pressures threatened to expose human rights abuses. While this may not have been of foremost consideration in the decision to establish the National Institution, it reflected how regional pressures to institutionalize the protection and promotion of human rights were on the rise. For example, the European Commission against Racism and Intolerance, established in 1994, would soon prepare country reports—the first report on Cyprus was completed in 1998. These developments might have carried some weight with a country seeking EU membership. The institution's own dual mandate was to protect and promote human rights, its name closely mirrored the very concept of an NHRI, and the body participated in NHRI networks and forums. The government's intent to create an NHRI per se seemed clear. Tellingly, at a meeting of the UN Committee on Economic, Social, and Cultural Rights, the government representative justified the institution's creation by decree "principally to save time," since it was "felt necessary to set up the Institution immediately."[113]

Over time, international and regional actors pressured Cyprus to create an institution in compliance with the Paris Principles. For example, the advisory committee on the Framework Convention for the Protection of National Minorities raised the issue in 2007, while treaty bodies like the CESCR and the CRC also made similar calls. This pressure intensified during the country's UPR process in 2009, when numerous countries urged the Cypriot government to establish an accredited NHRI.[114] Though government officials were aware that the institution fell short of international standards, they still faced weak incentives to strengthen it.

Greece's National Human Rights Commission (the only NHRI in Europe to adopt that name) was also created in 1998, and it reflected regional pressures and an accommodating domestic context. After the election of a socialist leader in 1996, human rights organizations noted positive steps taken by the regime, such as ratifying the ICCPR in 1997. That same year, Greece also ratified the Framework Convention for the Protection of National Minorities, though with reservations. These steps did not just reflect an ideological commitment to human rights norms. To the contrary, 1996 had been a year of human rights abuses in Greece, met by severe international criticism. Human Rights Watch described violations that year as "alarming," involving minority rights, maltreatment of immigrants, and freedom of expression. In September, the European Parliament issued a critical report, just as the European Court of Human Rights that year found Greece to have violated religious freedoms. In 1997, the European Committee for the Prevention of Torture visited Greece and expressed its concerns about irregular detentions; that year, the European Roma Rights Center also began monitoring rights abuses in Greece.[115]

In apparent response, the government created a human rights ombudsman in 1997, which became operational one year later. Some analysts trace the ombudsman's creation to the fact that the country was one of the only ones in the region that lacked a national ombudsman, which might connect to the European Ombudsman—a region-wide body formed in 1995. This may well be true, but given the government's broader human rights problem, the matter may also have taken on some urgency. Greece thus moved to create a human rights commission via legislation in December 1998, designating it as its NHRI; it earned almost immediate accreditation. That European dynamics were pushing Greek institution building during this period is further evident in another commission established by the same legislative act: the National Bioethics Commission, created in apparent response to the European 1997 Convention on Human Rights and Bioethics.[116]

Overall, both Greece and Cyprus created NHRIs in 1998 largely in response to regional diffusion pressures, especially a Council of Europe recommendation issued one year earlier, calling on all member states to create an NHRI. That Cyprus's accession process to the EU began in 1997, with requirements for harmonizing domestic laws and institutions with European ones, may help explain the rush to create an NHRI via decree and as an umbrella body of existing agencies, weakening it from the outset. If the prospect of European membership ironically led to a weaker NHRI in Cyprus, Greece's government also faced regional diffusion pressures but may have been more interested—in the recent aftermath of an abusive period—in creating an institution that would be accredited internationally and appease critics credibly.

Postconflict Scenarios

Among the most noteworthy instances of NHRI creation in Europe in the 1990s were those appearing in the region's postconflict zones, namely those resulting from the Belfast Peace Agreement, which created NHRIs in Ireland and Northern Ireland, and those following Yugoslavia's dissolution in the Balkans, leading to NHRIs in Kosovo as well as in Serbia and Montenegro. As NHRIs have become standard fare in contemporary peace agreements, these cases serve as important illustrations of the possibilities and limits of this kind of institution building. Despite being externally imposed to some extent, these NHRIs also reveal how local institutions and resistance can shape and constrain the institutional environment in which accountability mechanisms operate.

Building Twin Institutions

The human rights commissions of both *Northern Ireland* and the *Republic of Ireland* had their origins in the Belfast (Good Friday) Peace Agreement of 1998. The agreement required creating two comparable and closely interacting human rights commissions—what the UN Human Rights Commissioner referred to as the "'twin' national institutions," an apparent model for postconflict societies.[117] The Northern Ireland Act served to establish the Human Rights Commission of Northern Ireland, which began operating in 1999. Though initially found to be only partially compliant with the Paris Principles, by 2006 it was fully accredited. In Ireland, the Irish Human Rights Commission was created by statute in 2000, and shortly thereafter was fully accredited internationally. Arising out of a peace agreement in the aftermath of conflict, but with deeper local roots, both human rights commissions are relatively active, strong institutions.

The predecessor to both bodies was the Standing Advisory Commission on Human Rights, created in 1973 by the Northern Ireland Constitution Act and mentioned explicitly in the Belfast agreement as the forerunner institution.[118] Though the commission was largely a promotional agency, its origins are instructive of the complex politics underlying state institutions. When support in the early 1970s for a bill of rights in Northern Ireland threatened the British government, the idea of a human rights commission was proposed as an alternative. It would be "charged with the duty of keeping in touch with the activities of all public agencies in the field of human rights and of producing an annual report, including recommendations as to any further statutory provision which it considers should be made."[119] By the time the commission was created in 1973, it was given both a narrow mandate and limited independence. Despite these challenges, members of the commission managed to push the boundaries of their power and to place some issues on the government's agenda, especially those relating to discrimination law.[120]

Even before the peace agreement, moreover, it is telling that the idea of a human rights commission was proposed as part of an extensive constitutional review completed in Ireland in 1996. The Constitutional Review Group's report included a section on human rights commissions, referring to the institution's diffusion across Europe and Western democracies. It referred at length to the experience of Australia and South Africa, and in passing to Canada and France. Significantly, it also highlighted the example of Northern Ireland's Standing Advisory Commission on Human Rights, recommending in the end a commission that was not as broad as Australia's and that left the work of adjudication to the courts.[121]

As the peace agreement was being drafted, the Committee on the Administration of Justice—an NGO based in Northern Ireland—pushed for inclusion of a human rights commission so that rights on paper might be translated to rights in practice. Expectations were high from the outset, especially in Northern Ireland, where the commission was charged with drafting a bill of rights. Whereas creating the NHRI in Ireland was a more straightforward exercise, in Northern Ireland the early years proved challenging. Controversies broke out over the appointment of the initial commissioners. And with the powers and resources of the commission highly strained, conflict over financial limitations led to several publicized resignations.[122]

The apparent problems of Northern Ireland's NHRI reflected on the one hand, Britain's own reluctance to adopt a rights-based approach. But it also revealed deeper societal rifts, as might be expected after years of ongoing conflict. Though all parties agreed to create a human rights commission, the reality was that the equality agenda, which included human rights concerns, was favored by some parties more than others, including Sinn Féin.[123] For the Unionists, the human rights commission was considered a bête noire, a disturbingly biased institution.[124] As one observer notes, "There is tension between the international narrative of human rights as universal and local Northern Ireland perceptions of human rights as privileging one community over another."[125] The weight of the past was simply too heavy to wish away.

Like so many other NHRIs, equipping both commissions with sufficient re-sources to carry out their work proved an ongoing challenge. Though the British government eventually increased the power of Northern Ireland's commission (e.g., to compel information and initiate judicial proceedings), the institution still suffers from insufficient resources. Likewise, while Northern Ireland's com-mission continues working actively to promote NHRIs in other postconflict states, its own role at home has been somewhat constrained by the conflict's legacy. In the Irish Republic, drastic budget cuts led to a government proposal in 2011 that the Human Rights Commission and the Equality Authority be merged into an Irish Human Rights and Equality Commission. The commission itself and civil soci-ety groups cautiously supportive of the merger insisted that the new body remain the country's designated NHRI and retain international accreditation.[126]

Both commissions were created in the aftermath of conflict, drawing on an institutional form that was increasingly popular throughout the Commonwealth and that signified a democratic, rights-abiding state on the global stage. But the idea of a human rights commission already resonated locally, both in Northern Ireland and Ireland, given the long-standing experience of the Standing Advi-sory Commission on Human Rights. A postconflict regulatory moment thus worked in tandem with the various governing authorities' attempts to localize control over human rights issues. While peace agreements can lead to relatively strong institutions, bodies crafted under these conditions also remain especially vulnerable to their broader context, including unresolved lingering conflicts.

Balkan Dissolution

In another postconflict situation, a human rights ombudsman was created in *Kosovo* in 2000. After a decade of conflict between the majority Kosovar Alba-nians who wanted independence on the one hand and Serbia and Montenegro on the other, a draft peace agreement concluded in Rambouillet, France, in 1999 first mentioned the idea of an ombudsman institution for Kosovo.[127] It was not until the United Nations Interim Administrative Mission in Kosovo (UNMIK) was established as the territory's interim governing authority, following the collapse of the peace talks and a seventy-eight-day air campaign by NATO, that the Ombudsperson Institution of Kosovo (also known as the Human Rights Ombudsman) came into existence in 2000. Its legal foundations were, first and foremost, a set of UNMIK regulations, though the institution was later incorpo-rated into Kosovo's constitution in 2008. The ombudsman, moreover, was also part of the formal duties assigned to the OSCE Mission in Kosovo. In fact, it was the OSCE that drafted the regulation establishing the ombudsman, influenced partly by the peace agreement's provisions on the institution.[128]

Like the Bosnian ombudsman included in the Dayton Accords, Kosovo's also had to be run by someone of international origin; that is, the ombudsperson could not be a national of any state that formed part of the former Yugoslavia or Albania. Unlike the Bosnia and Herzegovina ombudsman, however, or most ombudsman offices in Central and Eastern Europe for that matter, Kosovo's institution was not authorized to pursue cases in the courts for the purposes of assessing the conformity of domestic laws with international ones. As Linda Reif notes, "It is regrettable that the UN did not provide the Kosovo Human Rights Ombudsperson with the powers to launch cases before the courts to provide legally binding decisions on the conformity of UNMIK regulations and domestic laws with the international human rights standards referred to in Regulation 2000/38, similar to the powers given to a number of Central and Eastern European human rights ombudsmen."[129]

Kosovo's ombudsman met with significant resistance almost from its inception. The deeper problem may have reflected ongoing ethnic tensions, of course, but the international (coercive) administrative apparatus was also at fault. It is no secret, as documented by international human rights organizations, that UNMIK and NATO's Kosovo Force did an infamously poor job of protecting human rights. They, in turn, just like local Kosovar authorities, failed to cooperate effectively with the ombudsman. In 2010, a law was passed further limiting the ombudsman, though this did not stop the institution from challenging human rights abuses. In general, Kosovo's ombudsman has enjoyed an inordinately low level of support and poor financing; it was even evicted from its office space, after the building was privatized and the government failed to find an alternative location. Not surprisingly, an EU Progress Report in 2011, described the institution as weak, "due to the lack of political support to ensure its proper functioning and financial independence."[130] It is little wonder that Kosovo's ombudsman still was not accredited after a decade of existence.

Kosovo's case reveals that peace agreements and highly intensive international involvement are insufficient to ensure a strong NHRI. After the peace process collapsed and an international administration was introduced—in a territory that has declared independence but is not yet formally a state—authorities opted for a weaker institution. Even drafting the original regulation was delayed when NATO opposed that KFOR fall under the ombudsman's jurisdiction.[131] Any accountability institution can prove threatening, especially for those engaged in or committing contested acts.

The creation of Kosovo's ombudsman coincided with the collapse of the Milosevic regime in *Serbia and Montenegro*. Once that political transition was under way, domestic reforms quickly followed, with an eye to membership in the Council of Europe. There was another more tangible connection linking the conflict in Kosovo with the need to protect human rights in Montenegro, as tens of thousands of people fled Kosovo and were living in tents.[132] The cross-border effects could not have been more real.

The OSCE played an especially active role in supporting the creation of NHRIs in Serbia and Montenegro after 2001. It was essential in setting up an ombudsman in the Serbian autonomous province of Vojvodina in 2002 and then in forming a network of local ombudsmen, attached to cities and municipalities. It also supported the creation of an ombudsman in Montenegro in 2003, the Protector of Human Rights and Freedoms; in that ombudsman's first annual report, the institution was billed as permitting Montenegro to join other modern, democratic states and to align its laws with European and international human rights standards. After Serbia and Montenegro joined the Council of Europe in 2003, moreover, the OSCE helped prepare a draft law for a Serbian ombudsman, following up with technical assistance and capacity building, just as the Venice Commission reviewed the draft legislation.[133]

Though legislation creating an ombudsman in Serbia was passed in 2005, it was not until after Montenegro's secession in 2006 that agreement on an actual ombudsman was reached. Thus, the Protector of Citizens (or People's Advocate) began functioning in Serbia in 2007. Interestingly, in an agreement brokered by the OSCE, the Catalan ombudsman was to provide comprehensive support to Serbia's new institution. Thus, the Catalonian deputy ombudsman was placed for an extended stay within the Serbian ombudsman's office in 2008, leading to subsequent exchanges. By 2010, the Protector of Citizens was accredited internationally as a fully compliant NHRI. While Montenegro's older ombudsman continued receiving support from the EU and OSCE, and it was incorporated into the national constitution of 2007, it did not apply for accreditation. In fact, by the time of the country's UPR in 2008, the ombudsman was recognized favorably as an NHRI, but not pressured to apply for accreditation.[134]

International support for creating ombudsman offices began almost as soon as the Milosevic regime collapsed. The prospect of joining the Council of Europe was a powerful incentive; and once they were members, pressure to create and strengthen NHRIs persisted. While Serbia's institution was more captive to domestic political conflict, and therefore took longer to establish, it gained accreditation rather quickly. A regulatory moment, joined by intense international pressure to implement external obligations, helped to create two relatively strong NHRIs. The question remains of why Montenegro's ombudsman has not been accredited, perhaps suggesting that accreditation is not as crucial for small states with an apparently strong accountability institution.

European Latecomers

The relatively late arrival of NHRIs to some European countries generally reflects a weak set of incentives, rather than outright opposition to the idea. In a few cases, NHRIs resembling research institutes and loosely following the Danish model, appeared; these included Germany, Luxembourg, and Norway. In the United Kingdom, in the 1990s, the wisdom of merging existing rights bodies into a single NHRI was debated extensively, resolving itself only in the new millennium. There were also a few latecomers in Eastern Europe and the Caucasus. Bulgaria's delays reflected broader holdups associated with the political transition, itself impeded by rampant corruption. In Armenia, a predecessor body filled in for an NHRI, though regime pressures eventually proved influential.

Think Tanks or NHRIs?

Other Western European countries created NHRIs after 2000, even absent regulatory moments or organized opposition to abuse: Germany (2000), Luxembourg (2000), and Norway (2001). In the case of these NHRIs, the institutions have been fully accredited despite their variously nontraditional nature. For example, both Germany's Institute for Human Rights and Norway's Centre for Human Rights resemble think tanks and research sites more than standard NHRIs. In Norway's case, the center was originally incorporated into the University Senate and functioned as a research institute.

Referring to the Paris Principles, *Germany's* parliament decided in 2000—in the fiftieth anniversary of the ECHR—to establish a German Institute for Human Rights (Deutsches Institut für Menschenrechte). Two years later, the body was internationally accredited. As an NHRI that follows the Danish model of an "institute," the German body conducts research and serves as a policy institute. It was created by a parliamentary resolution, not legislation, following pressure from civil society in the mid-1990s. Groups from civil society, including representatives of the Human Rights Forum, an influential network of domestic NGOs, remained involved in setting up the institute. And apparently, "in the groundswell of enthusiasm for the Vienna Declaration, German politicians and human rights activists signaled their approval for an NHRI."[135]

Despite societal groups' long-standing support for a governmental human rights institution, the NHRI was not created until 2000. In part, this reflected the fact that Germany's human rights policies were focused almost entirely on foreign policy. Even before Germany's participation in NATO's 1999 intervention in Kosovo, justified by the government on human rights grounds, the state had taken steps to institutionalize human rights in foreign policy. For example, in 1998, it created a federal government Commission for Human Rights Policy and Humanitarian Aid within the Foreign Ministry. Within the Bundestag, Germany also had a long tradition of parliamentary petitions committees, which played a role similar to an ombudsman, so the need for an NHRI may not have seemed as pressing despite calls for creating such a body.[136]

Though the NHRI's long-awaited establishment is often described as the product of an enthusiastic consensus, reflected in the parliament's unanimous, nonpartisan support for the resolution, sufficient evidence suggests that the government was not entirely committed to the idea of a *national* human rights institution, that is, one devoted to promoting and protecting human rights at home. Following a long delay in establishing an institution for which there was strong domestic and international support, the government still opted for a weak model. Having erected human rights mechanisms for foreign policy, an NHRI itself was postponed. Perhaps most tellingly, the institute's first executive director was forced to resign before completing his term, after pushing too hard to look at human rights issues domestically, compared to others who wanted to focus on human rights abroad.[137]

Not everyone, moreover, views the institute as strongly as its international accreditation might suggest. For example, the UN Committee on Economic, Social, and Cultural Rights, in examining Germany's fourth periodic report, recommended that given the NHRI's limited functions and powers, either the institution be strengthened substantially or an altogether new NHRI be erected.[138] According to the government commission's own website, human rights protection does not figure into the Institute's role: "Protection of individual human rights in Germany is in principle the responsibility of the courts. . . . In addition to the courts, Germany has a whole range of government and non-government bodies and organizations working to protect human rights. Petitions committees and commissioners for citizens' affairs provide people with a contact point where they can lodge their complaints."[139] Even the Human Rights Forum, an organization that strongly supported the NHRI's creation, conceded in its submission to the UPR process that government institutions focused too much on "human rights outside Germany." To this day, the institute is partly financed out of the Ministry of Foreign Affairs.[140]

Rather, Germany's government seems to have created an NHRI quite reluctantly, only following calls from civil society. The unanimous parliamentary acclaim that greeted it may have been more akin to a collective sigh of relief from skeptics: satisfying a proposal for an NHRI with a minimalist institution, which matched Germany's interest in portraying an image of itself as a country pursuing a "moral foreign policy," including through extensive development assistance. Human rights at home, however, raised thorny issues about the treatment of noncitizens and the inequitable results of the state's welfare policy, especially for a country that post-unification had tried so intently to break free of its past. External obligations led to adoption of a weak NHRI. What remains to be seen is how exactly the government responds to future accreditation pressures, as the limitations of its NHRI are more fully exposed.

Luxembourg adopted the NHRI model of its neighbor France, creating a National Consultative Commission for Human Rights in 2000. Influenced by the Paris Principles, Luxembourg's prime minister mentioned the idea of creating such a commission in 1997, though talk of one had already been taking place. In 1999, the government included the proposal in its platform, and it issued a ruling in 2000 establishing the Commission consultative des droits de l'homme (Consultative Commission on Human Rights). In the opening lines of the ruling, the institution's creation was justified in terms of democratic values and the importance of horizontal politics for human rights.[141] External obligations, oriented around the country's leadership role within European institutions, were the driving force behind the NHRI.

Beyond the Paris Principles, several factors shaped the context in which Luxembourg's prime minister decided to announce support for a human rights advisory commission. Prime Minister Jean-Claude Juncker, who had taken office in 1995, was intent on raising the country's profile in Europe. Indeed, in 1997, Luxembourg took over the rotating presidency of the European Council (EC), the same year he announced the NHRI's creation. The prime minister made his announcement in December, just as he hosted an important EC meeting in Luxembourg that month. At the EC meeting, held on the eve of the fiftieth anniversary of the UDHR, the European body called on all member states to enhance their human rights policy efforts. At the same meeting, moreover, the prime minister opposed Turkey's potential membership in the EU on the basis of human rights concerns.[142]

The NHRI's creation was also linked to European efforts to address racism and xenophobia, a particular focus of the French NHRI. In June 1997, the European Monitoring Centre on Racism and Xenophobia had been created. In the regulation establishing Luxembourg's NHRI, the body was designated the national counterpart of the new European institution. Luxembourg's stated commitments to the issue were quite public, also hosting in December 1997 a conference marking the end of the European Year against Racism. European governments had already negotiated and signed in October the Treaty of Amsterdam, which elevated the place of human rights and antidiscrimination. In this spirit, Luxembourg also reformed its penal code in July 1997, prohibiting discrimination on the basis of race and other social categories. Issues of human rights, nondiscrimination, and equality, as well as the monitoring of racist and xenophobic incidents, were high on the regional—and therefore national—agenda.[143]

The formation of a national ombudsman in Luxembourg offers some instructive parallels. While a *médiateur*, modeled on the French ombudsman, was proposed in 1976, the government resisted establishing one unless it could retain control over the post's appointment. In a similar way to the skepticism that had met the notion of an EU ombudsman, the government in Luxembourg feared an independent ombudsman appointed by parliament. It was only long after the EU ombudsman was created in 1995 and Luxembourg stood out as one of the only member states (along with Germany and Italy) lacking the institution, that the prime minister proposed creating a *médiateur* in 2001.[144]

Though the NHRI itself was fully accredited in 2001, the government continued anticipating and responding to suggestions made in the accreditation process. After accreditation criteria were changed in 2006, for example, the NHRI was given legislative standing, equal to other rights protective institutions like the ombudsman.[145] Furthermore, in 2009, the ICC's accreditation subcommittee expressed concerns over the provisions regulating the dismissal of members, which was addressed so that the institution maintained its accreditation status in 2010.

Luxembourg's decision to create an NHRI can be traced most closely to the country's leadership in European institutions, which in the late 1990s increasingly turned their attention to human rights issues, including questions of racism and xenophobia as well as antidiscrimination. In this regard, the influence of the Paris Principles along with France's own institution, which served as a model given that commission's particular focus and international stature, and historical linkages between the neighboring countries, is quite clear. The NHRI's initial weakness may have reflected the government's own external orientation as well as executive skepticism of parliament, a similar story to the late appearance of the ombudsman in Luxembourg. The government's external orientation, however, meant that retaining international accreditation mattered a great deal, pushing the government to adapt and strengthen the independent watchdog agency.

The *Norwegian* Centre for Human Rights, in turn, illustrates the challenges of locating an NHRI within an academic research institute. The center was created by a royal decree in 2001, though it had a predecessor in the Norwegian Institute of Human Rights. That institute was established in 1987 and moved to the University of Oslo in 1995. A 1999 government white paper, "Focus on Human Dignity," announced the decision to have the institute designated an NHRI, part of the National Plan of Action for Human Rights for 1999–2004. The decree creating the institution explicitly proposed a "national institution for the protection and promotion of human rights"; and it referred to the Paris Principles, though it gave the Foreign Ministry responsibility for designing the institution's mandate and organizational structure. The decision was made, moreover, not to attach a complaints mechanism to the institution, given the existence of a well-established ombudsman body since 1962. The name was changed to the Norwegian Centre for Human Rights in 2003, and the institution's mandate was expanded in 2005 to include broader monitoring functions.[146]

The international accreditation process has proved consequential for the NHRI's development. The body was accredited as an A status NHRI in 2003, but with reservations. The ICC proposed that national funding be earmarked for the NHRI, not funneled through university funding, and that a representative advisory board be created. Both adjustments were made, and the center received full accreditation in 2006. However, as part of the UPR process in 2009 and in view of upcoming reaccreditation in 2011, the center and government agreed to review the institution and committed to making the necessary changes to retain accreditation status, especially given what it recognized to be a "more rigorous international accreditation process."[147] One of the central challenges was how to sustain its dual identity as an NHRI and a research institute; and indeed, housing the NHRI within an academic institution proved to be a matter of internal debate even within the center.[148]

This dilemma was resolved through an external review and the reaccreditation process. The external reviewers submitted their report on March 2011, recommending most notably that the NHRI be separated from the university, a position that the center's board approved. The review further called on the government to create a fully independent NHRI by legislation. Still, the ICC decided in October 2011 to recommend demoting the center to a B status NHRI. According to established practice, the institution would retain its current status and have one year to provide evidence of fuller compliance with the Paris Principles. The Norwegian government and the center's staff appeared committed to ensuring a broad process of consultation, which would lead to a new NHRI. In the interim, the center promised to "ensure continuity in its NI-function until a solution for a reorganized NIHR has been agreed on the national level."[149]

The dominant incentive Norway faced when it decided to designate an NHRI in 1999 was its external human rights obligations. This shaped its national action plan for human rights, one of whose main proposals was to ensure that the country had an NHRI. The national action plan was itself a response to the government's political platform and the entry into force of the Human Rights Act in 1999, as well as more broadly to the Vienna World Conference that had called on all states to create such plans. Norway, moreover, reflected a common trend in the 1990s among dualist countries in Europe, including its Scandinavian neighbors, of incorporating the ECHR domestically.[150] At the same time, Norway's strong leadership in promoting human rights through its development program overseas was a hallmark of its national identity on the global stage. As NHRIs diffused throughout the 1990s, addressing human rights concerns at home became necessary to maintain credibility internationally. According to the government's white paper, "Norway's international efforts will always be viewed in the light of the way in which the Norwegian authorities protect the human rights of their own citizens. If we fail to put our own house in order, Norway's international commitment to the promotion of human rights efforts will lose its credibility."[151]

The decision to designate a research institute as its NHRI may have reflected the extent to which the decision really was externally driven. Grafting onto an existing body, like passing a royal decree rather than a legislative act, bypassed the hard work of creating an institution from scratch. With a strong ombudsman system already in place, the Norwegian government's preference was for a largely promotional body. Maintaining international standing, however, also meant responding to pressures associated with the accreditation process. Thus, the same international motives that led to creating a weak NHRI in 2001 led to the resolve to strengthen the institution one decade later, if only to maintain national standing as a "global good Samaritan" with a fully accredited NHRI.[152] Despite the efforts, the NHRI's status was downgraded in 2012 to partially compliant.

Transitional Delays and Anticorruption in Bulgaria

It took over a decade after Bulgaria's political transition began and a new constitution was approved in 1991 for the country to create an NHRI. In 2003, the Law on the Ombudsman was passed; and after agreement was reached on a candidate for the office, the institution started functioning in 2005, being incorporated into the constitution (via amendment) one year later. Also, in 2003, the Commission of Protection against Discrimination was created as an institution that, along with the ombudsman, the Bulgarian government would designate as one of its NHRIs, seeking accreditation for both in 2011.[153]

The seeming delay in creating an NHRI may seem puzzling, coming years after the country both joined the Council of Europe and ratified the ECHR in 1992. Why did Bulgaria escape the European trend to create NHRIs in the 1990s? The possibility of an ombudsman had in fact been mentioned twice in the course of constitution making. Two of the fifteen proposed drafts referred to the institution, though lack of local awareness about the ombudsman may have meant it was overlooked and dropped from the constitutional agenda. Delayed reforms seemed to be common in Bulgaria, perhaps reflecting the particular nature of the country's transition, marked by ongoing support for a Communist Party that had not entirely fallen into disrepute in the decade before the transition and a weak and inexperienced political opposition. Partly for these reasons, the prospect of membership in European institutions was not so fully on Bulgaria's radar during the early process of constitution making as it was elsewhere in the region, where the transition marked a more complete break with the past.[154]

When the idea for an ombudsman in Bulgaria was picked up again in the late 1990s, it was by civil society. In particular, the Center for the Study of Democracy, an NGO, resurrected the idea in 1998 and then inserted it into Coalition 2000—an anticorruption campaign launched by civil society. Corruption had reached very high levels in the country, including the judiciary, partly attributed to the weakness of accountability mechanisms. In this regard, the center issued a concept paper, "Opportunities for Establishment of Ombudsman Institution in Bulgaria," and prepared draft legislation for the institution. Thus, Bulgaria's ombudsman was created as part and parcel of an anticorruption campaign.[155] This was also a period when the prospect of European membership and international activism dominated the political agenda. Indeed, Bulgaria won a seat on the UN Security Council in 2002–3, and it joined NATO in 2004, signing an accession agreement with the EU in 2005 and joining that organization in 2007. Domestic NGOs linked the notion of an ombudsman to the issue of anticorruption, during a receptive period of Europeanization, which in turn facilitated the creation of both the ombudsman and the equality body.

Almost immediately after the institution was created, international bodies like CAT called on Bulgaria's government to create a Paris Principles–compliant NHRI. The UPR in 2010 led to numerous similar calls, with the government accepting the recommendation and stating that it would seek international accreditation.[156] One year later, in 2011, Bulgaria submitted two NHRIs for accreditation. If the domestic context helps to explain the apparent delay in creating an NHRI in Bulgaria, civil society and Europeanization (as well as external obligations, more generally) account for institutional creation and strengthening, including the institution's incorporation into the constitution. International regime pressures, from treaty bodies and as a result of the UPR, pushed the government to seek accreditation for its oversight mechanism.

Merger and Devolution in the United Kingdom

Great Britain's Commission for Equality and Human Rights was long in coming when the Equality Act of 2006 established it. The commission combined three preexisting bodies, with an explicit human rights mandate grafted onto it: the Commission for Racial Equality, the Equal Opportunities Commission, and the Disability Rights Commission. The subject of an intense decade-long national debate, the decision was finally made to establish a single body that treated equality and human rights as interdependent concerns.[157] The main impetus was to incorporate domestically the European Convention on Human Rights, a drive that began in the 1990s; virtually no attention was paid to the international context or even the notion of NHRIs. The commission began functioning in 2007 and was accredited as an NHRI in 2008, with its right to participate in international bodies shared equally by the three constituent bodies of Great Britain, Northern Ireland, and Scotland.

The idea of a Human Rights Commission reflected a longstanding effort to incorporate the ECHR into British law. Though calls were made for incorporating the ECHR domestically as early as the 1960s, it was not until a 1993 speech by Labour Party leader John Smith, the introduction of a subsequent bill in 1994, and a 1996 paper by the Labour Party on the subject, "Bringing Rights Home," that the subject generated serious attention. The paper raised the possibility of a human rights commission, but the party remained noncommittal. Then, after Labour won the national elections of May 1997, the government issued an influential white paper on a revised bill introduced that February. The skeptical title of the section addressing the possibility of a human rights commission served to frame the debate: "Should There Be a Human Rights Commission?" As the paper commented, "The Government's priority is implementation of its Manifesto commitment to give further effect to the Convention rights in domestic law. . . . Establishment of a new Human Rights Commission is not central to that objective and does not need to form part of the current Bill. . . . However, the Government has not closed its mind to the idea of a new Human Rights Commission at some stage in the future."[158] In a theme that would dominate the debates to come, the government claimed that it was especially concerned about the implications of a human rights commission for the existing equality bodies.

Though support for a human rights commission was not altogether absent, when the bill was debated in 1997 and 1998, the government remained unconvinced. A think tank, the Institute for Public Policy Research, pushed for the idea of a comprehensive commission, as did NGOs working on rights issues that were not covered by the current equality bodies (the so-called new strands of rights, including discrimination on the basis of age, sexuality, and religion). Some parliamentarians also offered support, often emphasizing how a rights commission would be uniquely positioned to shape public awareness and the cultural ethos. The Commission for Racial Equality and the Equal Opportunities Commission, both created in the mid-1970s, responded cautiously. These bodies had been forged during a seminal moment in the country's struggle over racial and gender equality, and they were understandably reluctant to lose control over their respective agendas.[159] The government itself remained unpersuaded, passing the issue off to the new Joint Committee on Human Rights. When the Human Rights Act entered into force in 2000, it did not include a human rights commission.

The focus shifted after 2001 away from the notion of a human rights commission and to a single equality body without a human rights mandate. One reason for this change was 9/11, since challenges to the government antiterrorism measures often referred to the Human Rights Act. In this controversial climate, a human rights commission may have seemed especially threatening. Another source behind support for a single equality body was an organizational restructuring that followed the 2001 election; human rights governance was moved from the Home Secretary's office to the Lord Chancellor's Department. Still another factor was an employment directive issued in 2000 by the European Commission, which required enforcing equality legislation outside the scope of the existing national bodies. By this time, moreover, a third equality body, the Disability Rights Commission, had been created in 2000; and it too would not be prepared to let go of its specialized mandate so soon after it had secured it.[160]

In deliberating over whether a human rights or equality commission was needed, the joint committee began amassing evidence that the Human Rights Act was not working, that it was not reaching the public and it was leaving the most vulnerable members of society untouched.[161] It was at this stage that the equality bodies shifted their own positions, now open to the idea of a human rights commission, though ideally one distinct from their own. Aware that the momentum for a human rights body was growing, the government struck a compromise by supporting the notion of including human rights in a single body. By late 2003, an agreement was reached that "human rights and equality are two sides of a single coin."[162]

The next challenge was to sort out the myriad organizational details involved in a merger and the creation of a comprehensive institution. Having agreed on the overall agenda, this stage was marked by a high level of consultation with the relevant stakeholders.[163] Among the major agreements was the decision to pursue a Single Equality Act, since harmonization among the three laws would prove far too complicated and inadequate. Despite outstanding questions, including devolution issues relating to Scotland and Wales, participants worked hard to resolve matters before an upcoming election. The Equality Act thus passed in 2006, establishing the Equality and Human Rights Commission, which began operating the following year.

Despite the commission's accreditation as an NHRI in 2008, it has faced several challenges. Internally, problems of leadership led to a series of resignations in 2009, including that of its chair. The government has accused the commission of not handling well the merger and not meeting sufficiently its central mandate of building a human rights culture. After 2010, the conservative government cut funding to the commission and threatened to narrow its mandate and remove some of its functions, confirming the ongoing precariousness faced by so many accountability institutions.[164]

Great Britain's NHRI serves to illustrate a few key dynamics. First, the origins of the NHRI reflect an attempt to localize authority; they arose almost entirely in relation to a national debate about how to incorporate the ECHR. While the case for incorporation emphasized practical matters, including the costs and delays for

British citizens in having to access justice via the court in Strasbourg, there was also an expressed interest in claiming national control over human rights conflicts. Thus, in its 1997 white paper, the Labour Party noted the unnecessarily high number of rulings by the court against the United Kingdom: "It is plainly unsatisfactory that someone should be the victim of a breach of the Convention standards by the State, yet cannot bring any case at all in the British courts. . . . For individuals, . . . the road to Strasbourg is long and hard. . . . We therefore believe that the time has come to enable people to enforce their Convention rights against the State in the British courts."[165] Second, the commission's creation highlights the political hurdles associated with merging long-standing domestic institutions and other postconsolidation organizational challenges, as well as the ongoing vulnerability of any NHRI to government opposition and poor funding.

The creation of a human rights commission in Great Britain was intensely contested for over a decade, driven by the state's interest in relocating authority over rights issues from Strasbourg to London and shaped by the apparent ineffectiveness of state institutions after the Human Rights Act was passed. The Equality and Human Rights Commission (EHRC) was later designated an NHRI, but international regime pressures did not have much to do with its establishment. While this did not impede the body from meeting the criteria for international accreditation, the full legacies of this genesis remain to be seen.

The same year as Britain created the EHRC, *Scotland* also passed in 2006 the Scottish Commission for Human Rights Act, though that body did not begin operating until 2008. The institution was accredited in 2010 as a fully compliant NHRI, and its orientation and experience were very different from Britain's. For Scotland, the human rights commission contributed to expanding powers that the government was already accumulating as the result of a broader process of devolution from the United Kingdom. The Scottish Commission, moreover, was immediately and explicitly focused on the international context, opening its doors symbolically on December 10, International Human Rights Day.[166]

In a conference held as early as June 1999, the idea of a human rights commission for Scotland had been discussed. International actors shared their experiences at the meeting, including the potentially unique advantages of an NHRI. The key impetus was passage of the Human Rights Act in 1998, which was met enthusiastically. Caught up in the excitement, the Scottish Human Rights Centre, an NGO, issued in December 1998 a popular Scottish Declaration of Human Rights. The adoption of the Scotland Act in 1998 was also essential. The act created a Scottish parliament, which would oversee human rights issues, and introduced the issue of devolution. The Human Rights Act and the Scotland Act together reinforced Scottish interests in localizing authority over human rights issues. And by June 2000, the Scottish executive announced it would release "consultation proposals" for a Scottish Human Rights Commission. Despite this early support for a human rights commission, the idea got lost in broader debates over devolution.[167] Yet by the time Britain was negotiating the details of a single commission, Scotland had already resolved to establish its own human rights commission.

Once established, the commission was keen on playing an international leadership role. In 2010, it hosted the tenth international conference on NHRIs in Edinburgh, and in 2011 the commission took over chairing the European Group of NHRIs.[168] This activism partly reflected Scottish interests, especially in the context of devolution. In this sense, incorporation of the ECHR offered Scotland an opportunity to exert its national independence, by both claiming authority over human rights governance as much as possible and playing a global leadership role, differentiating itself from Britain in the process.

By all accounts, Scotland's NHRI has proven to be a stronger institution that Britain's EHRC. One might attribute this to several factors, including a simpler context not overwhelmed by the challenge of a merger. There was also a stronger tradition in Scotland of working cross-sectionally on a range of rights and equality issues, with stronger networking among relevant organizations already in place.[169] But it is also true that the Human Rights Act presented both states with very different opportunities. For the British government, a commission was far more contested nationally, offering it an opportunity to wrestle control away from the European court in Strasbourg but also carrying the risk of greater legal challenges at home. Long-standing institutions that were already in place at least promised to maintain the status quo, not broaden the rights agenda unnecessarily. In contrast, for Scotland, the commission—in conjunction with the enhanced international opportunities it offered—promised to reinforce the broader process of devolution and thus state power.

Armenia's Human Rights Defender

In 2003, *Armenia* moved to establish the Human Rights Defender, a hybrid ombudsman. The NHRI, which was accredited internationally in 2006, had its origins in a 1998 presidential human rights commission and was very closely shaped by membership in the Council of Europe. Indeed, the timing of the institution's creation appears to have been more linked to the process of membership in European institutions than to the political transition started in 1991.

Armenia initiated its application for membership in the Council of Europe in 1996. In April 1998, the new president—following international condemnation of the elections one month earlier, and in a context of ongoing abuse—created a human rights commission as part of his office. The office was headed by Paruyr Hayrikyan, a former prisoner of conscience during the Soviet era; and it was quickly apparent that it lacked independence and was a government mouthpiece.[170] Amnesty International proposed to the president in June 1998 that he create an ombudsman, later following up with the president's Human Rights Commission. As the international organization described it, "Amnesty International noted that the existence of such an office could form a significant building block of a human rights culture in Armenia, and therefore urged that it be designed with care and consideration—with powers and objectives which are consistent with international standards."[171] What is more, Amnesty International provided the government with detailed suggestions about designing the ombudsman's office. The presidential human rights commission took up the international recommendations and proposed in 1999 that an ombudsman be created. Despite the efforts, the idea was firmly rejected for domestic political reasons.[172]

After 2000, the Council of Europe insisted that an ombudsman be part of a broader process of constitutional revision, which it stipulated as a criterion for membership in the European organization. A couple of months after Armenia joined the Council of Europe in 2001, the Venice Commission vetted a draft law for the creation of the office. In mid-2003, a referendum for constitutional revision was held, which included a national ombudsman, though the referendum failed to pass. Some analysts maintain that opponents were actually challenging the president and his holding of the referendum, more than the content of the proposed reforms. With strong backing from the EU, the Venice Commission, and the United States, a package of constitutional reforms in line with European requirements was finally passed in another referendum in late 2005.[173] A Council of Europe resolution described the constitutional revisions of 2005, as a "precondition for the fulfillment of some of the most important commitments that Armenia undertook upon its accession to the Council of Europe. These include the reform of the judicial system, the reform of local self-government, the introduction of an independent ombudsman."[174]

The post of Human Rights Defender was at last created by legislation in 2003, with the office beginning to function one year later.[175] Coinciding with subsequent international accreditation, the Council of Europe and European Commission initiated a joint project fostering human rights in the region, which undertook ongoing strengthening of Armenia's ombudsman.[176] The NHRI's creation thus reflected external obligations, including membership in regional institutions, more than anything else, as indicated by a precursor body from the late 1990s. Opposition along the way to establishing a full-blown accountability institution was partly the product of domestic resistance to the presidency, who both permitted abuses and allowed external actors to play a heavy-handed role in institution building.

European Holdouts

By the time of their UPR, only four countries in Europe still had not set up an NHRI: Iceland, Malta, Estonia, and Belarus. With the exception of Belarus, all of them had institutional alternatives that precluded or delayed the introduction of an NHRI. In all cases, however, these countries did not reject the notion of establishing a state accountability mechanism; to the contrary, they agreed during the UPR process to create one. Regional diffusion was significant. In this regard, it is noteworthy that neither Iceland nor Belarus is an EU member, while Belarus is not a member of the Council of Europe. The others, Malta and Estonia, both joined as late as 2004; weak regional networking could therefore explain their status as holdout states.

Iceland and Malta

It may seem puzzling that *Iceland* does not have an NHRI, given its broader normative commitments. Though the Minister of Foreign Affairs announced in April 2007 that establishing an NHRI in compliance with the Paris Principles was an urgent matter, by the time of the UPR in 2011, the government stated that it was still considering the institution's creation. In the interim, international actors had called on the government to establish the institution, including the High Commissioner on Human Rights and treaty bodies like CERD and CEDAW.[177] New external obligations and a domestic regulatory moment, nonetheless, may at last lead to an NHRI. Following the economic crisis in 2008, Iceland at long last applied to the EU in 2009, despite long-standing resistance. Likewise, a new constitution was in the works, the first draft of which was completed in 2011.

Part of Iceland's delay in creating an NHRI may reflect its status as a small country with a relatively strong human rights record, but it also has to do with the fact that an alternative institutional body informally substituted for an NHRI since the mid-1990s. The Icelandic Human Rights Centre (IHRC) was created in 1994 by a group of NGOs who joined forces to promote human rights nationally and internationally. This was in the immediate aftermath of the Vienna World Conference, and right before the constitution was revised in 1995 to incorporate human rights standards (including the ECHR).[178] Significantly, similar institutions were also established during this period, including the parliamentary ombudsman (1997), an ombudsman for children (1994), and a gender equality office (1996). Given the country's strong human rights record, pressure for NHRI accreditation was predictably low.

The IHRC quickly rose to prominence as a leading NGO in Iceland, though it received substantial funds annually from the Ministries of Justice and Foreign Affairs. It functioned in this manner for ten years, until late 2004 when the government unexpectedly announced that it would eliminate its funding, expressing concern that government funding could undermine its independence. The center would have to apply for government funding (at much lower amounts) on an ad hoc basis, though this would introduce uncertainty in programming and potentially compromise the organization's capacity to criticize public authorities. Intense criticism followed the government's decision, both domestically and abroad, coinciding with the formation of a committee in 2005 to consider constitutional reforms. Labor unions, NGOs, and celebrities denounced the government's move and appealed for a return of the funding to the IHRC. The Council of Europe's Human Rights Commissioner made a similar plea in a mid-2005 report: "Iceland, along with every other Council of Europe member state, merits an effective national human rights body. I urge the Government to take measures to ensure that Iceland continues to benefit from the services of an independent national human rights institution either through supporting and developing existing structures or by the establishment of a statutory institution fully in line with the Paris principles."[179] The Danish Institute for Human Rights, with which IHRC collaborated closely, and the Association for Human Rights Institutions also joined the appeal to restore support of the IHRC, but without success—even after a new government took office in 2007.[180]

Since the high point of the conflict in 2005 and 2006, the IHRC itself began assessing the potential value of having a fully accredited NHRI in Iceland, issuing a report in December 2008. Fittingly drawing on the models of human rights institutes in Denmark and Norway, the IHRC was clearly prepared to step in and adopt the formal role of NHRI, since it already had the infrastructure for doing so.[181] From the government's perspective, in its report to the UPR, the IHRC was one of a few institutions listed under the category of "ombudsman." The state report also referenced the possibility of a national human rights body.[182]

It remains to be seen whether the government of this small country, with one of the highest levels of gender equality in the world but persistent racism, will opt for transforming the IHRC into its official NHRI. Tellingly, the initial creation of the IHRC as an NGO, the government's withdrawal of funding in 2005, and the potential creation of a formal NHRI coincided with a regulatory moment marked by constitutional reforms. International regime pressures, especially through the United Nations OHCHR, treaty bodies, and UPR, have helped place the importance of a formal NHRI on the agenda for Iceland. The prospect of membership in the EU may require it as a rite of passage.

Malta has not bothered responding one way or another to international recommendations that it establish an NHRI. Proposals to this effect were raised both as part of the UPR process in 2009 and by the CESCR.[183] The government established an ombudsman in 1995—with the advice of New Zealand's ombudsman—included by constitutional amendment in 2007, shortly after it joined the EU; but it does not have a human rights mandate. This period also coincided with a slight shift in Maltese foreign policy, as the country amended its long-standing neutrality to engage in a Partnership for Peace, or limited relations with NATO.[184] As Malta is a small country facing no transnational pressure and having met the requirements of European membership with its ombudsman, its government's incentives to create an accredited NHRI have been relatively low.

Resistance in Estonia and Belarus

In Eastern Europe, Estonia and Belarus had not yet created an NHRI by the time of their UPR, though both accepted doing so as part of that process. Estonia had a long-standing ombudsman, the chancellor of justice, created in 1938 (third after Sweden's and Finland's). Though suspended during Soviet rule, it began functioning again in 1993, the same year as Estonia joined the Council of Europe and one year after its new constitution.[185] Despite Estonia's ratification of the ECHR and the ombudsman's work on antidiscrimination and some rights issues, the country did not bother having the institution accredited as an NHRI.

Interestingly, in late 1992, after a controversial Aliens Law was passed and Western actors criticized the Estonian regime for its treatment of the Russian minority, the president created—on International Human Rights Day—the Estonian Human Rights Institute. A cynical view characterized the president's motives as one of assuring "the world that such an institution in Estonia was unnecessary, because there were no human rights abuses."[186] Though the president established the institute, which continues receiving state funds, it is nonetheless characterized as an NGO. Most significantly, the institute itself began appealing annually after 2004 to the government that it create an independent NHRI, though nothing came of it.[187] State excuses tended to emphasize that there was no need for such a body, especially given existing institutions like the chancellor of justice.

As part of the UPR process, numerous recommendations were made that Estonia create an NHRI, or at least consider transforming the existing ombudsman. These proposals reinforced similar calls already made by treaty bodies, including CERD, the Human Rights Committee, and CAT. The Estonian government at last agreed to establish an NHRI, reversing its previous resistance to the idea. International regime pressures, most closely associated with the UPR, building on previous calls by treaty bodies and local NGOs pushed the government to concede. If Estonia did not do so until rather late despite its external obligations, it may have been because the country had a long-standing institution and a low level of human rights violations, escaping intense pressures to create an NHRI.

Belarus also accepted recommendations made during its UPR to create an NHRI, but it faced very different circumstances, engaging in a higher level of violations and operating under a closed political system, with the same president in office since 1994. Significantly, Belarus was not a member of the Council of Europe, barred from applying since 1997 due to electoral irregularities and human rights abuses. Neither had the country ratified the ECHR. Still, the OSCE's Office for Democratic Institutions and Human Rights had promoted the creation of an ombudsman. Human rights treaty bodies and other UN actors also called for establishing an NHRI, including CERD in 2004 and the special rapporteur for human rights in Belarus in 2007.[188] The future of an NHRI in Belarus remains highly uncertain, though the government's nominal agreement was a significant step. Despite having acceded to the international human rights covenants, Belarus's broader resistance to the ECHR and its exclusion from the Council of Europe—a reflection of a closed political system, for a government intimately allied with Russia and enjoying a high human development index— has blocked more intense international regime pressures. External obligations and organized abuse proved insufficient incentives, revealing how important it is to be linked into regional networks.

Conclusions: Western Convergences, Global Discourses

Despite the institution of the NHRI originating historically in Europe and spreading widely across the continent, accreditation rates have remained relatively low in the region. Even when an institution considered an NHRI exists, governments have not always sought accreditation. And of all the world's regions, this one contains the highest percentage of "partially compliant" (or B-status) NHRIs. In some ways, of course, this is unsurprising. When France adopted the world's first NHRI in the 1940s, human rights were viewed largely as a foreign matter, an idea to be projected internationally more than a set of principles to bind internal practices.

Rather, the history of NHRI diffusion in Europe seems to be one of disjointed convergences, of countries tapping into, adopting, and exporting a global discourse without entirely making it their own. In reflecting on the rise of European states more generally, Charles Tilly notes how "formal organizational characteristics of the world's states have, in fact, converged dramatically over the last century or so; the adoption of one Western model or another has become a virtual prerequisite for recognition by prior members of the state system."[189] The NHRI's diffusion across Europe, often really that of the ombudsman, confirms this long-standing dynamic. In some cases, notably in Western Europe, states created specialized bodies that reflected the domestic politics of inequality more than anything else, only later "converting" these into NHRIs. In Eastern Europe and the CIS, states often adopted an NHRI halfheartedly, associating human rights discourse with the past and anxious to move on with the business of freedom. In other cases, even states that were fierce advocates of human rights on the global stage were reluctant to create self-restraining NHRIs, preferring to focus on research and on the world's human rights problems more than their own. In the end, though, impressively, the various pathways and experiences somehow converged into a region filled with NHRIs.

One persistent puzzle is why states that have these institutions do not always seek accreditation. If state leaders borrow the idea from regional institutions and actors, why have so many European governments not bothered acquiring a formal stamp of approval? Strategic emulation still seems to be involved. Political leaders do not engage in institution building in a vacuum; they are looking for socially appropriate models, which will help them retain or gain authority (i.e., legitimate power). Ombudsman and national human rights bodies have featured centrally on the checklist of requirements for European membership and compliance; and states have dutifully moved to conform. Once they have attained the status they wanted, however, there may be little to be gained—absent further incentives or regime pressures—from seeking accreditation. Many of the states that have a nonaccredited NHRI also have relatively strong human rights records and are not having the issue of accreditation raised in any strong sense during the UPR process. And in some cases their NHRIs would have to be strengthened, which could prove politically costly (and risky), in order to meet today's more stringent requirements of accreditation.

When NHRIs arise out of dramatic regulatory moments, like national independence or regime transition, the process can get caught up in broader exercises of statehood. This can become part of a project of transforming the state into an accountable actor. In the context of globalization and regionalization, it can further entail the transformation of state and national identity, an attempt to attach both to something external but socially resonant. It can also represent an effort, at least partially so, to overcome and sometimes even forget the past. Like other states, European ones may have created NHRIs during varying conditions of ambiguity, but the particular form the institution has taken in the birthplace of these institutions has created its own historical ambiguities: embracing a global discourse, nominally and as a form of membership rite, to join an exclusive community of nation-states.

10

How Accountability Institutions Matter

A friend had just taken the man to a local meeting where there was talk of "derechos humanos" and of how the police can't do certain things to you; if they do, you can report them to La Comisión. The man took the pamphlet they gave him and put it in his shirt pocket (he couldn't read, but he knew his children would like the bright colors). As he was driving home, the police stopped him on a mountain road. They pulled him out of his truck, shoved him roughly—for no reason. He remembered he still had the pamphlet in his pocket. He took it out, waving it and saying, "I have human rights. You can't do this, or I'll go to La Comisión." The police, looking disgusted, let him go; and the man continued on his way home. His friend later told us about it.

—Human rights worker, Chiapas, Mexico,
interview with author, August 1996

Institutional assessment is always rife with dilemmas. How does one capture the full array of what an institution does? How does one accommodate relative successes and failures alongside a coherent narrative of the institution's overall effects? That institutional outcomes can be conceptualized (and measured) in vastly different and contested ways, only adds to the complexity of the task. In the anecdote above, was the human rights commission successful in equipping one person with the means to resist police violence? Was the incident isolated, or did it indicate some broader pattern? Should we evaluate the institution's work in terms of how it empowers people on the street, based on the behavior of a police officer representing the state, or both? These questions are consequential in revealing the multiple ways in which an institution's influence can be interpreted (and misinterpreted).

In the case of accountability institutions, assessment requires that we settle on the notion of "accountability," on how to conceptualize and measure the term.[1] For NHRIs, how exactly does one assess human rights "protection" or "promotion," and how does one represent contradictory trends? Despite the challenges, assessing the work of institutions—directly and indirectly—is important. It may not be that we arrive at a final and conclusive sense of the institution's value. Institutions, after all, are social in nature, simultaneously reflecting and reconstituting a world of actors and structures. In this shifting and complex environment, assessment exercises are always necessarily limited and imperfect, but they serve to document and to mold—reinforcing, altering, reimagining—what the institution does and how social groups co-act with it, as well as how it might be improved.

I open the chapter with an overview of how the research on NHRIs has evaluated questions of institutional influence. I then present a framework for assessing the impact of accountability institutions, focusing on how institutions both constrain and empower actors. I touch on the conceptual and methodological challenges associated with assessing any institution, and accountability ones in particular. Rather than focusing on enforcement or punishment, I am attentive to the broader social dimensions of accountability, especially the ways in which accountability offers actors a public, discursive, and normative space in which to confront and engage one another. I also move to outline various stages of accountability (documentation, remediation, and prevention), which I use as a metric of sorts in discussing the work of NHRIs. The overall approach is unorthodox in some ways, though it builds on prior work on NHRIs. Throughout the chapter, I draw on numerous examples from around the world to illustrate my claims. The objective is to show a range of influence—parts of it already considered, some of it new—from which others might draw upon and zero in on while conducting in-depth examinations of particular accountability institutions. As long as institutions are complex and evolving spaces in which various actors come together, assessing their role remains a necessary if partial and ongoing exercise.

"Impact" and the Research on NHRIs

The literature on NHRIs has existed for just over a decade, with the first generation of work on these institutions focusing mostly on the question of institutional creation. This first wave of work sought to establish that NHRIs existed, both individually and as a broader category of actors, sometimes in a given region of the world. It also set out to describe the contours of these institutions' design and functions, as well as to examine both the international standards defining them and the evolving connections and networks linking them. As these institutions have accumulated history, and the international regime on NHRIs has deepened, attention has gradually shifted to exploring their broader effects.[2] In this sense, multiple catchphrases have been used to describe outputs, including impact, influence, performance, effectiveness, outcomes, and consequences. I review here, in broad strokes, the dominant strands of this body of work, some of it academic in orientation and much of it closely linked to the policy world.

A few themes emerge across the diverse approaches. First, some of the work in this area has sought to identify "benchmarks," or indicators of influence, often linked to international standards. According to this view, assessment requires evaluating how well various international standards have been met. Second, much of the work has grappled with the complexity of what exactly is being assessed, with analysts identifying various dimensions across which an NHRI's effectiveness can be assessed. Third, though not always articulated explicitly, widespread recognition exists of the tension between the direct and indirect effects of an NHRI, including the extent to which an institution's actions can be linked to changes in human rights practices more broadly.[3] Fourth, like many studies of assessment, various authors have struggled between the use of qualitative indicators of impact and quantitative measures, each of which involves particular trade-offs. Finally, though constituting a minority view, some work has called critical attention to the importance of adopting a more "holistic" perspective that takes seriously the voices of vulnerable populations—arguably, those most needing these institutions. Together, the small but growing body of studies, illustrated below by some of the leading work, yields important insights about how we might evaluate the impact of NHRIs going forward.

One of the first systematic attempts to offer a rubric for assessing the effectiveness of NHRIs was a detailed report drafted by Richard Carver for the International Council on Human Rights Policy in 2005.[4] The report identified a dozen elements that contribute to the effectiveness of NHRIs (e.g., public legitimacy, accessibility, diverse staff, broad mandate, power to monitor compliance with recommendations, adequate resources, effective institutional links); its focus was on identifying benchmark standards and related indicators. According to the report, "Measuring the *impact* of NHRIs is even more difficult. To do this it will be important to reach firm conclusions not only about the general state of human rights, but about the effect of NHRI's actions."[5] In offering guidelines for NHRI self-assessments, the report provides quantitative and qualitative indicators, and it differentiates between output, performance, and impact. Output refers to what the institution has done in a functional, concrete sense. Performance refers to how well functions are executed, whereas impact concerns "how far the activities had a positive impact on the enjoyment of human rights."[6] Carver's efforts to identify systematic dimensions and indicators of an NHRI's influence were a valuable step in conducting disciplined assessments, and they set an important marker for future research.

Stephen Livingstone and Rachel Murray have also done valuable work on determining benchmarks of NHRI effectiveness.[7] Their contribution lies partly in recognizing thoughtfully the difficulties inherent in assessing NHRIs according to universal criteria in a world of local variance: "Given the variety in the character of NHRIs and the different contexts within which they operate it is difficult to develop a single set of criteria which can be applied to all of them to assess their effectiveness. Even among those organizations that fund the establishment of national institutions, there does not appear to have been clear guidelines or benchmarks against which the funding is assessed."[8] Drawing on a broad range of relevant literature, Livingstone and Murray opted for eighteen benchmarks against which NHRIs can be evaluated, across three main categories: capacity, performance, and legitimacy. In the end, most of the benchmarks refer to functions and attributes of NHRIs, closely resembling existing international standards, but serving as a systematic checklist of influence.

In a related vein, though focusing on local human rights commissions in the United States, Mila Versteeg addresses the role of performance measures, this time emphasizing outputs and outcomes.[9] Like others studying an NHRI's impact, Versteeg concurs that outcomes are difficult to measure and trace to an institution. She cites the work of the Iowa Civil Rights Commission, which has a system of performance assessment consisting of three steps: defining a strategic goal, identifying a performance measure to evaluate when the goal is reached, and recommending actions to reach the performance measure. While framed in terms of local commissions in the United States, the issues raised could easily be applied to the world of NHRIs:

> Once a commission focuses on measuring performance, it faces some difficult issues and choices. How can the commission adequately capture the *value* of the many things the commission does? Can

things such as value and effectiveness be measured at all? Is it possible the measurement will be used against the commission? Should a commission see performance measurement as a tool to improve its performance, as a tool for fundraising, or as part of its service to the public—and are there trade-offs among these? Is it sufficient to keep simple counts of *activities*, such as the number of complaints answered or the attendance generated at trainings, or should the commission try to measure the *impact* of these actions?[10]

Asking methodologically and politically informed questions such as these offers an important corrective to the assumption that the role of NHRIs is altogether straightforward, even as the answers remain elusive.

In my own research on NHRIs, I have emphasized the need to assess an NHRI's effects across a range of issues and dimensions, highlighted the twin goals of human rights protection and promotion, introduced broader categories of evaluation like agenda setting and socialization, and cautioned about the possibility of perverse effects.[11] Since NHRIs operate across a spectrum of issues, it is important to remember that effectiveness in one area will not necessarily amount to effectiveness in another. An NHRI that is especially active in protecting disability rights, for example, may be relatively unresponsive to the abuse of indigenous rights. Furthermore, given how central the notions of protection and promotion are to international human rights standards, these twin goals can serve as fundamental organizing categories when assessing NHRI influence. I have also drawn a parallel between these categories and an NHRI's regulative (i.e., protective) and constitutive (promotional) effects.[12] For greater specificity, I have examined the work of NHRIs across an expanded list of categories, including rule creation, agenda setting, socialization, and accountability. And I have tried to introduce a critical dimension to NHRI studies, checking for the possibility that accountability institutions sometimes have unintended and negative consequences. Arguably, the advantage of such demarcations is in permitting us to connect an institution's outputs to its broader social impact.

Finally, Obiora Okafor introduced a forgotten and essential dimension to scattered writings on an NHRI's impact when he and Shedrack Agbakwa called eloquently in a 2002 article for a more "holistic" conceptualization of NHRI impact, one more attuned to human agency and "voices of suffering."[13] Okafor argued that "in addition to envisioning an ideal NHC as making a difference because of 'what it does,' observers of these institutions should also envision such an ideal NHC as one that might be valuable because of 'what other agents are able to do with it' (as a resource that is valuable in the hands of popular agents such as civil society groups)."[14] By "voices of suffering," Okafor and Agbakwa follow Upendra Baxi's conception, describing these voices as "persons or groups whose need for protection is greatest, who are society's most vulnerable, and who survive at the bottom end of the scale of human freedom from want and deprivation."[15] This overlooked touchstone introduced a more highly socialized and overtly ethical lens through which to assess NHRIs.

Beyond these various contributions, there is something to be said for commonsense views of NHRIs and their influence. Most activists and scholars engaged with these institutions would concur with Livingstone and Murray's depiction of what constitutes a generally effective and ineffective institution:

> Those that are seen as effective display a willingness to engage with the most serious human rights issues in a society, are prepared to challenge powerful groups (especially government) where they feel such groups are failing to fulfil their responsibility to protect human rights, enjoy a prominent place in public discourse on human rights, are well respected both nationally and internationally (especially by human rights NGOs and also by government even if it does not always agree with the NHRI) and are professional in their dealings with others. Those viewed as ineffective at worst become simply apologists for government abuses of human rights.[16]

On some level, few would disagree with occasionally reducing the impact of an NHRI to a more commonsensical touchstone of success: whether the institution's representatives make a good-faith effort to fulfill their mandate given their particular circumstances.

Accountability Institutions and the Public Sphere

In an age of institutional assessment, fueled by scarce resources and competing demands, it is not enough to create institutions. Donors and other constituencies want to know how effective the institution is. What impact does it have, and how influential is it? Does it really make a difference, and exactly how so? Academics who study institutions have also turned in recent years to evaluating effects, following a wave of earlier research on institutional origins and design.[17] Despite the differences, a few recurrent challenges—conceptual and methodological—are evident across efforts to assess institutional influence.

Conceptually, the dominant touchstones of institutional performance and impact tend to be rooted in a rationalist view of institutions.[18] That is, the general tendency is to evaluate how well an institution solves the problems it was created to address or how well the institution fulfills its core purpose and mandate. There is a functionalist logic on display here: the institution is assumed to be an agent, evaluated in terms of what it *does*. While sensible in many respects, this strategy is also an incomplete metric. Institutions are both structures and agents. As "structures," they serve as spaces in which social interaction and communication occurs; as agents, they "do things." The conceptual challenge is to assess an institution's influence in a way that captures its twofold nature, or its dual role as structure and agent.

Methodologically, other challenges confront the attempt to measure an institution's influence, including a basic problem of "multiple and sufficient" causation: since outcomes can be caused by a host of factors, it is virtually impossible to isolate or unravel the institution's contributions.[19] This is very common in the human rights field, where the links between any single institution or actor and changes in abuse can be difficult, if not impossible, to trace. The temptation is often to adopt crude measures, which may be reliable but tell us little of real interest. Another common trap is to focus wholly on how well an institution meets its intended goals. The problem is that institutions can also have unintended effects, obscured from view, including negative or perverse consequences.

To address these basic challenges, I evaluate accountability institutions based on process as much as output or performance, attentive to how they constrain *and* empower actors. This strategy opens the door to accommodating potentially contradictory types of effects, while focusing on both the institution's actions and the social context in which it operates. I offer a more specific framework below for exactly how to evaluate these varied effects in the case of accountability institutions and NHRIs. Before doing so, however, the notion of "accountability" needs to be clarified and conceptualized in its broadest sense.

A Social Conception of Accountability

Accountability is what joins NHRIs and democracy to one another. Most scholars writing in this vein have emphasized how NHRIs offer horizontal accountability, as one set of actors within the state holds another set accountable; democracies, in turn, are assumed to require both horizontal and vertical forms of accountability.[20] For many, not only are NHRIs to be celebrated for this reason, but accountability institutions in general are viewed as essential means of bolstering democratic governance, through regularized and representative channels that uphold individual rights. This kind of claim, while useful in some ways, fails to capture another, more basic dimension of accountability institutions and their connection to democracy: their potential to create a social space for public deliberation over wrongdoing.[21]

Accordingly, accountability institutions also permit social actors to confront political authority, that is, to push norm violations into the public sphere. These confrontations, which are deliberative and discursive in nature, are arguably an essential contribution to democratic governance. According to this view, accountability institutions no longer revolve centrally around notions of enforcement or punishment, as conventional views often assert. As administrative agencies, they stand apart from executive or judicial authority, charged instead with the unique purpose of holding public authorities responsible for abuse.

More specifically, this alternative take on accountability has five key characteristics. First, accountability denotes a social relationship, as actors are accountable only before one another. Accountability, then, does not just concern individual wrongdoing. Rather, definitionally, accountability cannot occur outside the context of a particular set of social interactions. It is a social phenomenon. Second, as the term itself partly reveals, accountability reflects a regularized pattern, not a one-time, single-frame event. In practice, this means that accountability is usually part of a broader agreed-on process, which gives actors the ability to pursue accountability in a sustained manner. This might entail a common set of rules and procedures, just as it may indicate the existence of offices, staff, and material resources. Third, accountability is centrally preoccupied with and oriented around, in a normative sense, the notion of wrongdoing. There is a presumption that wrongdoing has occurred or is a distinct possibility; and social responsibility for the wrongdoing, whatever form it may take, should be pursued. Fourth, just as accountability denotes a social relationship, it reflects a discursive exchange, which is worth highlighting as a separate if related aspect. Communication is a key feature of accountability in any setting, marked by standard setting, interpretation, documentation, accusations, defenses, debate, and other back-and-forth exchanges. Unlike judiciary contexts, accountability does not necessarily entail a highly circumscribed adversarial approach (though it can). It is instead marked by more fluid social participation. Fifth, and closely related, accountability typically involves a public aspect, as actors conduct at least some of their discursive exchanges in the open; this process of public exchange and deliberation can be as important as any discrete outcome. Together, these characteristics depict accountability as a social, communicative process revolving around wrongdoing, a depiction that widens substantively the criteria for assessment.

Stages of Accountability

The process of accountability can occur in various phases, including *documentation, remediation*, and *prevention* (see Table 7). These activities serve to differentiate accountability from other institutionalized practices, and they are consistent with the key aspects of accountability outlined above: accountability as regularized social phenomenon, marked by public, discursive exchanges and revolving around the notion of wrongdoing. In each stage, institutional effects can be examined broadly, in terms of how the activities in question serve to constrain and empower various actors.

Documentation is integral to the broader process of accountability, so that without it, accountability is not even possible. Documentation refers to the means by which "accounts" of wrongdoing are collected, transcribed, represented, and disseminated.[22] Since approaches to documentation can vary, the process itself can privilege some actors and exclude or further marginalize others. Far from being a neutral endeavor, the act of documenting wrongdoing can be influential, helping to define whose account matters, what is defined as official truth, and which issues make it onto the political agenda.

Remediation is an accountability institution's response to wrongdoing (an attempt to right wrongs), usually involving some possible restructuring of social relations. Proposed changes can be quite narrow, focusing on a very small set of actors, or much broader, encompassing large segments of society. Remediation can take various forms, from asking something of contending parties to proposing that the rules of interaction be altered or individual culprits be punished. If documentation is about establishing social truths, remediation revolves around defining justice within politically acceptable parameters. Processes of remediation can be deeply contested, as groups are challenged—or appeased—in the face of purported wrongdoing.

Beyond establishing and addressing past wrongdoing, accountability can also mean preventing future wrongdoing. Some accountability institutions therefore engage in prevention, in addition to documentation and remediation. Prevention consists of an accountability institution itself taking steps to address the likelihood of future wrongdoing, whereas remediation involves the institution making

Table 7

The Influence of Accountability Institutions: Critical Assessment Indicators

Stages of accountability	Description	Possible indicators	Criteria of influence
Documentation	Process by which accounts of wrongdoing are collected, transcribed, represented, and disseminated	Accessibility	Do physical, economic, or cultural barriers restrict various groups' access to the institution?
		Narratives of abuse	Are new wrongs (or rights) being introduced? Is official state discourse being challenged?
		Inquiries, investigations, and reports	Are public inquiries used? Are investigations obstructed? How widely diffused are the institution's reports?
Remediation	Institutional responses to wrongdoing, past or ongoing	Compensation	Is compensation paid? Is it a substitute for broader systemic reform?
		Rules and recommendations	Does the institution promote rule changes? To what extent are recommendations implemented?

(continued)

Table 7
(Continued)

Stages of accountability	Description	Possible indicators	Criteria of influence
		Threat cycles	Do authorities threaten or coerce the institution? Are discrete improvements in abuse evident?
Prevention	Steps taken to minimize the likelihood of future wrongdoing	Socializing authorities	Does perverse learning occur? Do socialization efforts vary across types of authority?
		Popular education	Is the public more aware of what constitutes a wrong? Is the public aware of the institution, and how does it perceive its role? Has the public adopted the institution's discourse?

other actors answer or correct for their wrongdoings. Prevention can entail a range of activities, such as socializing actors about the inappropriateness of wrongdoing or otherwise altering the presumed sources of abuse.

Documentation: Voice, Truth, and Agenda Setting

Complaints and reports often feature centrally in the work of many NHRIs, often constituting the bulk of their activities. These actions are often overlooked in the drive to move beyond them and evaluate their impact. Dismissing these activities, however, is a mistake if the goal is to understand the full influence of an NHRI. Documentation is significant both as a process and outcome. For example, the process by which an NHRI goes about documenting complaints and abuses is often the main point of contact between an NHRI's representatives and members of society. In this regard, the means by which complaints are collected and the ways in which they can give privileged access to some people and issues, whether deliberately or not, are an essential basis of assessment. In addition, documentation is also an outcome in its own right. When NHRIs document abuses in their reports, they offer an account of the truth, whether supporting the official truths of the state or offering a counternarrative. In some cases, documentation can define an issue not previously considered or emphasized, thereby putting it on the political agenda. In general, documentation serves to give voice to particular actors, renders a version of the truth, and places some issues and matters before a polity. Assessing the work of an NHRI or accountability institution requires taking seriously the full scale of these documentation activities and efforts.

The Geography of NHRIs: Making and Handling "Complaints"

When an accountability institution handles complaints, influence cannot be assessed only in terms of the number of complaints processed or the successful resolution of cases, though these are clearly common and important markers of influence. On a more fundamental level, the question of *access* needs to be addressed. Can people needing the institution access it? More specifically, do they have the knowledge and capacity to access the institution and demand accountability? If they do not, focusing on the institution's formal complaints process will not reveal the full scope of activities. Hard data will tell us about changes over time, and across space, in the number or type of complaints. But they will not tell us about barriers to access—the invisible data undergirding official statistics.

Access, moreover, taps into issues of social equity, a criterion for evaluating how well the institution meets broader social goals. In contrast, focusing exclusively on the number of complaints submitted or resolved offers an incomplete and ultimately inadequate metric of influence.

Despite the limitations of quantitative trends, the growth of human rights complaints to NHRIs still remains impressive. In India, for example, complaints to the NHRC doubled in its early years between 1996 and 1999, from 20,000 to 40,000, many initiated by NGOs rather than individuals. In Indonesia, "[s]oon after its creation," the commission "became a lightning rod for complaints from every corner of Indonesia."[23] Indeed, in the case of NHRIs, rising complaints can reflect growing awareness, both of the institution and of human rights standards. Complaints mechanisms are therefore crucial in providing members of society with new and alternative spaces in which to engage the state, whether about past abuses (real or imagined) or current practices. Such enhanced access can be especially significant in transitional polities. As Slovenia's former ombudswoman notes, "People who in the past were unable or did not dare to complain have begun to make full use of this new opportunity. . . . Some people describe actual or supposed injustices committed decades ago. Others feel themselves to be utterly powerless and more than anything just want advice on what they should do and who they should turn to. Some realize that in their particular case it is too late to put things right, but it seems important to them to explain their problem to a high ranking representative of the state."[24] A staff attorney at the Czech ombudsman likewise reflects, "That is part of our function . . . to give people the sense that they can complain to the state and that we will listen."[25] Halfway around the world, when indigenous peoples in remote Latin American villages access NHRIs, they tend to view the institution as a state agency capable of controlling *state* actions.[26] If complaints make new encounters between the state and society possible, it is often because they are less expensive and onerous to approach than other state bodies including the courts.

Even with a robust number of complaints, issues of accessibility can still vary. As studies in other fields, including rural health show, access has several, sometimes overlapping dimensions, including physical, economic, and cultural.[27] These are all variously at play in the case of NHRIs. For instance, an NHRI's physical location affects the ease actors have in accessing the institution, just as it signals to some extent the state's perception of the institution's standing and value. Some NHRIs have been located in highly symbolic sites, which often invoke past abuses and represent the transformation of a space—really, of the state itself—from a place of violence to one of accountability. Thus, Uruguay's NHRI came to occupy the premises of SIDE (Secretaría de Información y Defensa), a notorious former detention center. The Council of Ministers, which approved the location, described it as a symbolic site straddling memory and future.[28] Germany's Human Rights Institute was located deliberately on a historically significant street, near Checkpoint Charlie. After the Palestinian Authority moved from Ramallah to Jerusalem in the late 1990s, the NHRI too shifted its seat to be in the center of power.[29] In some instances, NHRI premises can become symbolically charged, as occurred in Algeria. When mothers of the disappeared began manifesting on a weekly basis, they chose to do so outside the headquarters of the NHRI, symbolizing the state in the eyes of victims and the public.[30]

Even so, an institution's physical location can be a barrier to access. It can be especially difficult for rural populations or those away from capital cities to access an NHRI. This is a pervasive problem, disproportionately affecting poor and indigenous populations living in remote areas, just as it affects NHRIs operating under scarce resources. In places like Tanzania and South Africa, among countless others, an NHRI can be inaccessible to many segments of the population, including areas of the country far from provincial offices. This is why regional offices can be so significant, enhancing public outreach and access. When the Palestinian NHRI opened offices in Nablus and Bethlehem, they were able to reach new populations in the northern and southern West Bank, respectively.[31] In Nicaragua, the absence of regional offices, attributed to budget issues, is said to disproportionately exclude indigenous populations.[32] In other words, those who most need the services of an NHRI may not be able to access it, even when they are otherwise aware of and willing to do so. One innovative approach to the question of limited access has been the use of mobile offices, where units of an NHRI travel out to people rather than being confined to traditional office spaces. For example, in Egypt, the ombudsman's office has a mobile van, just as NHRIs in both Costa Rica and Bolivia have opted for mobile offices.[33]

Sometimes even in an urban setting, an NHRI may be located so as to limit its accessibility. Colombia's NHRI aptly illustrates this: "The complaints department was tucked far in the back of a cavernous brick and tile building in an old residential neighborhood in Bogotá, through a painted metal gate, past the security guard (later a metal detector) and the receptionist, across an interior parking lot, up a flight of stairs, and down a seemingly empty hallway."[34] In other urban settings, central offices can be part of large, off-putting government offices. Even if buildings are technically open to anyone, imposing government structures are not especially inviting. And in some cases, NHRIs can be difficult to locate, with few public transportation options and even limited signage available. Once there, the number of "barriers," in terms of gates and checkpoints can be equally daunting. Though rarely discussed, physical access presents a particular problem for people with disabilities. A consultancy report on Croatia's NHRI recognized that "the location should be chosen with due consideration to the availability of public transportation and should be fully accessible to persons with disabilities."[35]

In violent contexts, moreover, traveling to an NHRI can present its own dangers. These challenges have been raised in the case of the Palestinian NHRI, where travel and curfew restrictions have limited people's capacity to access the Ramallah office.[36] In Sri Lanka, difficult and dangerous travel also limits access to the human rights commission. And in Ecuador, people living in remote areas or border zones where violence is heightened, often prefer not complaining "for fear of exposing themselves to even greater danger."[37] Even when there is no physical hardship associated with accessing an NHRI, a climate of violence can be stifling, making people too fearful to approach an NHRI.

Since states are complex actors, issues of physical space often play out in intrastate disputes. For example, the space the NHRI occupies can itself become the source of state contestation. In Northern Ireland in 2011, the NHRI was co-located next to seven other institutions, undermining its sense of institutional autonomy and standing.[38] And in an act of government retaliation, the Zambian NHRI's office in 1996 was summarily relocated to the Electoral Commission, losing the premises that had been promised to it, after it had accused the government of torture during coup-related detentions. While Chad's offices were initially placed within the prime minister's quarters, the NHRI demanded its own space. Across these examples, the NHRI's location became a source of friction within the state.[39]

A related issue concerns the capacity of NHRI themselves to access other state bodies that it is charged with monitoring, including detention facilities. In Kenya, the NHRI is permitted to visit detention centers, but military camps remain off-limits. Inmates in Russia are often discouraged from applying to the NHRI; and apparently, in some cases, inmates have been moved in anticipation of an NHRI visit. The Afghani Human Rights Commission has the power to monitor detention facilities without prior notice, though coalition forces' detention centers are exempt.[40] Prisons and detention centers, which in many contexts are already treated as exceptional spaces, play a varied role in the world of NHRIs, as a space the NHRI is permitted to monitor to widely varying degrees.

Economic costs are another, perhaps more obvious, barrier to accessing NHRIs. For example, in Russia, those with the least resources seem to prefer the office of the procurator-general, which is less expensive to access.[41] Sometimes costs relate to the distance that must be traveled to reach the institution. Even in a small country, the costs of traveling some distance can prove prohibitive. One critic reflects on the costs of accessing the ombudsman in Belize:

> [I]n reality, in a country that has a per capita average income of $2000 per person (by government figures), the services of the Ombudsman is restricted mainly to the one district capital town, out of the six district capitals and to perhaps three nearby villages. . . . The cost of availing oneself of Ombudsman services for the rest of the six district nation towns are estimated to run from $75 to $400 dollars in travel expenses, hotels, meals, days lost and taxi fares. If you had to make more than one trip to his brand new office, it would cost astronomical portions of your average annual income for the average citizen.[42]

Technology can further magnify the economic costs of accessing an accountability institution. Complaints do not always have to be submitted in person; they can sometimes be made by telephone or online via the Internet. Yet access to computers, in terms of both physical access and know-how, is obviously variable and intersects closely with economic resources. Telephones are more accessible but can entail hidden barriers to access, including cultural ones. For example, in Eastern Europe, a former ombudsperson notes that people in new democracies are not always comfortable making claims or denunciations by phone.[43] The point may well apply to other settings, where state policing is or has been high in the relatively recent past.

Beyond physical and economic barriers, then, cultural factors sometimes stand in the way of accessing an NHRI. This is quite apparent in the case of indigenous peoples, who can be reluctant to access institutions they perceive to be "foreign" even in a national context.[44] The problem often relates to staffing, since offices for indigenous issues or NHRI branches located in indigenous regions can lack staff members from indigenous communities. Moreover, given people's multiple and cross-cutting identities, those who find it difficult to access an NHRI are already likely to be facing other structural barriers in their everyday lives. As one study of NHRIs and indigenous people asserts, indigenous women are triply marginalized and discriminated against, for being women, indigenous, and poor. Cultural barriers can also take other forms, as in Eastern European countries where a weak culture of complaint making keeps people away from an NHRI.[45]

While access barriers can keep particular categories of people from seeking the services of an NHRI, they can affect whether certain issues (e.g., the types of abuse, perpetrators, locations) remain invisible or not—not by coincidence, but as a result of the institution's systemic framing of principles. For example, registered complaints do not always seem to mirror human rights abuses. In Mongolia, CEDAW noted critically that most complaints were originating in one particular area (Ulaanbaatar), expressing concern about "the lack of complaints about discrimination based on sex despite the prevalence of violence against women."[46] And for Colombia, in one sample year, most complaints revolved around the public health system and the right to petition public authorities, with very few referencing the armed violence.[47] Most complaints to NHRIs, moreover, tend to be individualized, which works against collective petitions that might reference economic and social rights or abuses against marginalized groups, including indigenous peoples.[48]

Even after a complaint is submitted, it has to be deemed admissible for the NHRI to consider it. In some instances, gaps in an institution's mandate mean that numerous complaints filed will never proceed beyond the complaint stage, and this can be a source of contestation. In Russia, for example, only between 28 and 40 percent of complaints are accepted.[49] And an ongoing source of discontent among indigenous communities in the Americas is that complaints detailing serious violations are often rejected because private actors are charged with the wrongdoing; these abuses can include house and crop burnings, death threats, murders, and persecution at the hand of mercenaries hired by powerful groups. Sometimes NHRIs provide access to petitioners, but without following up to investigate or challenge the state. This is illustrated by Mexico's human rights commission, which responded to the crisis in Chiapas in the mid-1990s mostly by collecting complaints. In stark contrast, a reformed NHRI a few years faced feminicide in Juárez by challenging the state more forcefully.[50] The patterns underlying admission rates of complaints thus need to be explored much more closely.

In general, evaluating accountability mechanisms and their influence requires considering how information about wrongdoing is collected and processed. For accountability institutions that have a complaints mechanism, one must determine the extent to which the institution provides access so that its constituencies can report wrongdoing and the degree to which access to the NHRI (physical, economic, or cultural) may be blocked. Questions of access should be included in any assessment of an NHRI's influence. They help to explain the profile of complaints received, including who tends to submit them and what abuses are reported. They also serve to guard against marginalized communities being inadvertently excluded from the institution's reach.

Narratives of Abuse and Protection

In documenting abuses, accountability institutions present very particular accounts or narratives of wrongdoing. They highlight certain things but not others; they adopt a given tone, telling stories of who did what to whom. When these accounts come from an NHRI, they take on a semiofficial status. In some cases, an NHRI can be complicit in government denial of wrongdoing; in other cases, they offer an alternative truth. While accountability narratives can take numerous forms, they are especially valuable in introducing new narratives of abuse and protection (i.e., defining new wrongs, rights, and remedies) and in challenging official discourses (or re-creating existing narratives).

On a macro-level, NHRIs, as an international set of actors, have moved to explore how human rights intersect with a range of issues: indigenous peoples, persons with disabilities, the prevention of torture, the rights of the child, women's rights, enforced disappearances, corporate responsibility, as well as more recent issues like LGBT rights, national security post-9/11, and the Responsibility to Protect doctrine.[51] These issues, often addressing marginalized groups or overlooked topics, are now attached to an NHRI's realm of activities, even as they generate knowledge about and awareness of these issues among potentially broader audiences.

At the most general level, NHRIs can introduce or elevate the rhetoric of human rights. Human rights discourse, in turn, can empower people or act as a flash point of contention; regardless, it can enhance a "public space" or make possible a "new public transcript."[52] In Malawi, one observer comments to that effect, "Although an empirical evaluation of the impact of these institutions on the promotion, protection and enforcement of human rights is yet to take place, their role in shaping the rhetoric of human rights cannot be doubted. The domestic and international protection of human rights has been of direct benefit to Malawians by creating and protecting public space."[53]

Indeed, accountability institutions sometimes place new issues on the political agenda. India's NHRI has brought into the spotlight a broad spectrum of unexamined problems, from questions of deaths in custody and prison conditions to the rights of the mentally ill and problems of child labor. The NHRI has also been instrumental in proposing systemic reform of the police and a paradigm shift away from punishing to rehabilitating prisoners.[54] In Mongolia, the

NHRI "raised new human rights issues that were not considered in the public domain . . . but have the potential to profoundly affect large numbers of persons, such as human trafficking."[55] In contexts as varied as South Africa, Poland, and El Salvador, NHRIs have turned attention onto economic and social rights, or poverty, defining human rights beyond the traditional civil and political categories. For example, in Thailand, the NHRI's first chair focused on nontraditional issues like corporate human rights abuses and the impact of development projects on rural well-being.[56]

NHRIs have sometimes pushed the state's agenda by pursuing issues that are socially taboo but linked to global discourses, such as HIV/AIDS and sexual diversity or harassment. Costa Rica's NHRI, for instance, has publicized complaints against state agencies on topics like sexual harassment or discrimination against cohabitation.[57] And Nicaragua's NHRI was the first in the region to create a special ombudsman on rights of sexual diversity.[58] In Thailand, a commissioner began referring to sexual orientation as a human rights issue, leading the NHRI to cooperate with relevant NGOs and hold a workshop on sexuality rights, revealing how important the leadership's interests and initiative can be.[59] Some NHRIs have also promoted the issue of HIV/AIDS, challenging entrenched social taboos. Sometimes these issues are addressed in a special office or unit of the institution. In Uganda, a "vulnerable persons desk" works on HIV/AIDS, though it has still proven difficult to connect this work to human rights more broadly.[60] Despite the challenges, promotion of HIV/AIDS awareness can empower social groups to oppose discrimination more generally.[61]

Some NHRIs have incorporated transitional justice, or past abuses, into their work. Afghanistan's commission, in cooperation with the United Nations, collected evidence of violations since 1978. Though transitional justice issues were not included in the Bonn Agreement, a national human rights workshop in 1992, attended by President Hamid Karzai as well as leaders of civil society and religious organizations, gave the NHRI its mandate: to "undertake national consultations and propose a national strategy for transitional justice and for addressing the abuses of the past."[62] Significantly, this expanded mandate, which led to extensive documentation, was largely initiated by local actors responding to a perceived gap in the international mandate. In 2005, the UN high commissioner for human rights hand delivered the final report, "Call for Justice," to President Karzai himself, which led to a task force and eventual action plan. Likewise, Colombia's ombudsman was charged with designing the Trujillo Commission, which turned into an opportunity for the institution to display its capacities on a national level.[63]

Accountability institutions can also challenge official state discourse with particular accounts of wrongdoing. Kosovo's ombudsman noted how important it is to challenge the state, even if no one seems to be listening. The institution's influence, he indicated, derives partly from the *act of challenging*.[64] One dramatic example occurred in Kenya. After commissioners there heard of abuses in a remote part of the country, they chartered a plane, took media representatives along, and later issued a report accusing the security forces in direct, powerful language: "[T]he current approach is unsustainable, unconstitutional and dehumanizing" and "various human rights violations have been perpetrated against people living in northern Kenya under the guise of security operations."[65] Another anecdote comes from Peru, where the "ombudsman openly sided with the opposition and accused Fujimori of electoral fraud in the 2000 elections; after Fujimori left office, the NHRI participated in the country's truth and reconciliation commission.[66] Some NHRIs have spoken out on behalf of indigenous populations. For example, after a newspaper reported in Bolivia that several communities in the Alto Parpetí region were being held captive on gated, private properties and were not allowed to leave, even to attend school, Ombudsman Sonia Soto was so moved that she vowed publicly to do everything in her power to help free the people, labeling it a discriminatory act on the part of the current government. Similar steps have been taken in terms of minority rights. In the notorious Danish cartoon controversy, depicting images of the Prophet Muhammad, the head of Denmark's NHRI played a constructive role, consistently speaking out on behalf of nondiscrimination and minority rights beyond one-sided freedom of speech.[67]

NHRIs can also challenge the state by demanding that the state respect the institution's independence.[68] India's NHRI warned the government that, unless it empowered it to inquire more effectively into human rights violations by the armed forces, this would "erode the credibility of the Government of India in its [more general] commitment to respect human rights."[69] As one observer remarks about the Malaysian commission's first few years, it managed both "to irritate the government and disappoint sectors of civil society," as "a body which is both anti-government and an instrument of government, both a creature of the state and its watchdog."[70] Who the accountability institution sides with can certainly affect broader perceptions of its credibility. An expert on South Korea's NHRI captured well the institution's responsibility in taking on the state: "The National Human Rights Commission is the national institution whose role it is to constantly criticize the government's wrongful acts and human rights violations. In its nature, it is inevitable for the Commission to have a conflict with the government. If there is no more tension between an NHRI and the government, such institution is not an NHRI anymore."[71]

While the language an NHRI uses in documenting wrongdoing often may seem innocuous or insignificant, an institution's staff makes particular choices about which issues to emphasize and how to engage the state rhetorically. This can be particularly consequential in identifying new wrongs and rights (e.g., those dealing with marginalized populations or taboo topics), inserting them into national discourses and agendas, and challenging or reinforcing official state narratives. As quasi-state actors, these institutions are uniquely situated to shift the human rights narrative of the state, and it is one of the areas in which an NHRI's leadership seems to matter most. An accountability institution's willingness to challenge the state is therefore another important if overlooked indicator of influence, as the institution uses its voice to promote change. So much of what an accountability institution does occurs in the narrative or discursive realm that it is high time such rhetorical interventions were taken more seriously.

The Place of Public Inquiries and Reports

Accountability institutions can document wrongdoing in other ways, including through public inquiries and in the course of conducting investigations and producing annual or special reports. These aspects of documentation can be quite significant. For example, public inquiries and hearings are crucial as participatory processes, in which societal actors are convened to report directly and verbally to the state, either in public forums or privately. Inquiries and reports reflect some initiative on the part of the NHRI, which identifies a set of issues requiring further exploration and attention. Sometimes these issues arise from patterns observed in the complaints process; other times, they are responses to press stories and media sources. Given their participatory nature, public inquiries and reports bring both visibility to an NHRI and a certain degree of legitimacy.

Public hearings can be initiated for various reasons, sometimes in response to civil society groups. In Kenya, a lawyer-activist for Stones of Hope, a local NGO, organized a pressure campaign against the NHRI, to hold a public hearing into the practices of salt farm owners, including the role of private corporations.[72] In Mongolia, a public inquiry on the use of torture led to changes in the administration of justice.[73] And of course, one of the countries in the world whose NHRI has used public hearings most visibly and productively is Australia. Acclaimed inquiries have been held on the separation of Aboriginal and Torres Strait Islander children from their families, same-sex marriage, homeless children, and children in immigrant detention facilities. The first of these issues found its way into a groundbreaking set of public hearings, where stories were collected from children and communities devastated by the forced removal of indigenous children from their families between 1910 and 1970. The powerful final report, "Bringing Them Home," was released in 1997; it called for numerous measures, including a formal national apology and an annual commemorative holiday.[74] Such inquiries, probing into neglected situations of abuse, can be invaluable social processes, helping forge historical memory out of collective recollections and input.

An NHRI sometimes initiates an investigation or takes other steps in conjunction with ongoing monitoring activities. Afghanistan's commission, quite notably, undertook a survey in 2003–4 of over six thousand Afghanis in thirty-two provinces and refugee populations. Respondents were asked for their views of the twenty-three-year conflict and how to provide justice. About 70 percent of people identified themselves as having directly experienced serious human rights violations, expressing deep distrust of the government and the international community.[75] These voices and views, otherwise unknown, were revealed. Far away in the Seychelles, the National Human Rights Commission responded to two successive waves of incidents in Montagne Posée Prison in March 2009, in which several prisoners were hospitalized, by conducting an investigation and preparing a report, detailing concrete changes that should be made urgently; the changes were implemented within two weeks of the report's conclusion.[76]

India, which can initiate *suo motu* investigations, also illustrates potential challenges. On the one hand, India's human rights commission is generally well endowed to investigate abuses. It has the power to summon and compel witnesses to appear before it and then examine them under oath. It also can compel the discovery and production of relevant documents. And in its proceedings, the NHRI has all the powers of a civil court.[77] To cite one example, the Human Rights Commission identified from numerous complaints that equality in education was a pervasive if unexamined problem. It consequently set out to investigate the problem and prepare a set of reports, addressing diverse issues like initiation practices at educational institutions and racism and discrimination in education. Despite these real advances, the Indian NHRI's investigatory machinery has been overburdened and partly staffed by former state security officials. Investigations have also been hampered by restrictions on the NHRI's mandate—including cases involving the military, rights that are not civil and political in nature, or complaints that occurred more than a year earlier.[78] It is also worth noting, more generally, that commissions of inquiry have not always accomplished their public goals in India, used instead by the state to appease critics and deflect more meaningful accountability. As one retired judge from Bombay's High Court suggests,

> Whenever any matter of serious violations of human rights arises, governments promptly announce an inquiry by a sitting or retired judge. The immediate impact is to silence the press, the public and the people affected by the violations. It also stops any inquiry by the human rights commissions, because under the act, if any inquiry is announced by the government, the commission will not inquire into that incident. It also stops further inquiries by the police or other investigating agencies. Having achieved this objective of silencing all concerned, the government waits for the completion of the inquiry and the report. If the report is favourable to the government, it is accepted. If it is against the government it just refuses to accept it or to act on its recommendations.[79]

Likewise, while investigations can expose wrongdoing and lead to concrete improvements, paradoxically they can also stifle further inquiry into an issue, creating the illusion that accountability has been satisfied. Broader-scale, open public inquiries may be more successful since they engage social groups actively and transparently in the process of documenting wrongdoing, closer to a participatory notion of accountability.

One of the main forms of NHRI documentation, closely related to inquiries and investigations, is the preparation of reports. Reports, whether annual or specialized, should be judged partly on how widely diffused they are. Especially in the case of annual reports, NHRIs often seem to target foreign audiences, with glossy and thick tomes in English. In addition to documenting wrongdoing, reports can be records or logs of institutional activities, self-justifications before external audiences, including donors. Regardless, they can also prove valuable for international NGOs, who may rely on local documentation (alongside other NGO reporting) to apply transnational pressure. In general, reports are viewed as instruments of transparency, which is why they are virtually required for international accreditation.

In the case of research-oriented NHRIs, prevalent in the human rights "institute" model associated with countries like Denmark and Germany, reports and documentation feature centrally in the institution's mandate. In these cases, documentation tends to be more specialized and an opportunity to examine an issue in depth. For institutions that do not have complaints mechanisms, research can provide a way of being "informed of the situation on the ground," even if critics might charge the opposite—that research in fact documents abuses in a top-down fashion, removed from street-level reality.[80]

Still more critically, the production of reports does provide the state with information, and it gives the NHRI some control over the data—data traditionally in the realm of NGOs. When the Maldives announced it would create an NHRI, a foreign ministry press release conceded that the commission would act "as a source of human rights information for the Government and the people of the country."[81] Information can obviously be used for highly divergent purposes, so it is important to remain vigilant of the multiple uses of human rights reports by official bodies.

Unlike complaints, which typically are registered privately by individuals or organizations, investigations, inquiries (generally underutilized by NHRIs), and reports are more broadly shared social forms of documentation. Evaluations of an NHRI's impact should therefore be attentive to how many opportunities the institution offers for public inquiries, how restricted its investigations are, and how widely diffused are its reports. Put differently, one must question how many opportunities exist for social groups—beyond individual claimants—to participate in an NHRI's documentation activities, whether by contributing to accounts of wrongdoing or themselves accessing existing documents.

Remediation: Contested Authority and Organizational Identity

After wrongdoing is identified, whether as something that happened in the past or as an ongoing practice, an accountability institution moves to define and in some instances secure a remedy. Remedies can be framed broadly, not necessarily arising from specific complaints or petitions. NHRIs, moreover, have a wide spectrum of remedies available to them; and since typically NHRIs do not have extensive if any powers of enforcement, remediation very often includes a discursive dimension, or an exercise in persuasion. Thus, NHRIs may attempt to mediate between the state and civil society, propose new rules or changes to legislation, or call on the state to issue compensation as well as recommend other actions.

Remediation by an NHRI often consists of challenging the state. It can be a necessarily confrontational act, as the institution accuses the state of wrongdoing and attempts to persuade state agents that the wrong must somehow be made right. In contesting the state's authority to act with impunity, an NHRI is representing social claims for justice and essentially opening a space for the public within the state. Remediation therefore has important constitutive effects, including shaping an NHRI's own organizational identity and, by extension, social perceptions of its capacity to deliver accountability. This becomes especially important in the case of institutions emphasizing mediation. While notions of mediation, arbitration, compromise strike a democratic chord, they can also be viewed critically. When serious human rights abuses are at stake, those most marginalized want a state accountability agency to "take sides." A commentator of indigenous rights in the Americas attests provocatively that an NHRI should not mediate, but rather it should side with the most impoverished, discriminated against, and excluded populations. According to this view, there is no such thing as a neutral position, and the politics of mediation can become a way of eluding confrontations with power.[82]

Rather than mediator or advocate, in devising remedies, an NHRI can occasionally play the role of something more akin to facilitator. Sometimes this involves facilitating the implementation of international human rights standards. Kenya's Human Rights Commission, for example, decided to challenge discriminatory inheritance practices by supporting "local" solutions. As new threats like HIV/AIDS displaced women from their homes after their husbands died, the commission facilitated a discussion with rural elders. This led to an arrangement where a woman could stay on her land and become its legal trustee. While the remedy did not represent full equality, it constituted a partial improvement; and it did so in a workable way and without imposing a universal standard that may have met resistance.[83] One might also imagine the role of facilitator as being especially valuable in contexts where an independent judiciary is weak, or "institutional mechanisms for the effective representation of citizens in the judiciary" are absent.[84]

One of the most well-known types of remedy that an accountability institution can provide is compensation. Not all NHRIs call for state compensation, but some of them have been quite successful in doing so. India's National Human Rights Commission is one of the leading examples, mandated by law to recommend that the state grant "immediate interim relief" to a victim of human rights abuse or their family. Significantly, the Indian NHRI can recommend compensation as soon as it ascertains there has been a human rights violation, without prejudice to any subsequent court rulings.[85] According to even its staunchest critics, the commission has managed well to persuade the state to pay compensation to human rights victims. In one noteworthy case, the Indian commission wrestled compensation from the state for the families of 250 children who had died from manipulated starvation.[86] According to India's NHRI, compensation constitutes an implicit admission by state officials of wrongdoing. Claimants themselves have occasionally rejected monetary compensation from the commission on the grounds that it failed to address broader issues of state responsibility.[87]

Compensation, then, is another remedy that cuts both ways. On the one hand, it clearly constitutes a form of accountability, albeit a monetary one. On the other hand, precisely because the exchange is mostly monetary, it may reflect an "easy" form of accountability, which does not necessarily have to be accompanied by an official apology, individual punishment, or broader systemic reform. And in most cases, it is true, compensation does not tend to be accompanied by more comprehensive forms of redress. On balance, the dilemma is this: is compensation, as a weak form of accountability, better than the alternative of no accountability? This question needs to be debated more explicitly, as NHRIs and international actors grapple with how precisely compensation fits into a broader package of concrete remedies.

Crafting Rules and Recommendations

Much NHRI work revolves around proposing new rules and issuing recommendations. Unlike mere agenda setting, these steps are not oriented around documenting wrongdoing. Instead, they consist of requests that the state initiate specific actions to counter abuse. Because NHRIs tend to lack enforcement powers, state leaders are largely free to follow or disregard the institution's proposals. In cases where they do heed an NHRI's recommendations, the institution has succeeded in helping to create new rules or practices. However, even when the state ignores an NHRI's recommendations, as it so often does, the NHRI still has succeeded in defining specific remedies and imagining alternative courses of state action. Nothing may result in a direct or visible sense, but the accountability institution has performed an important role, which can be picked up again in the future. Concrete recommendations can thus shape the discursive and political arenas in which state and non-state actors interact.

In the world of NHRIs, recommendations that are relatively targeted and specific are most likely to be implemented. This explains why recommendations relating to imprisonment or conditions of detention have proved relatively successful, across a broad range of contexts. Prison authorities in the Seychelles accepted NHRI recommendations to improve prison conditions. And in Afghanistan, fifty private prisons were closed as a result of NHRI monitoring, while over thirty-six hundred people who were found to be arbitrarily detained were released.[88] Likewise, following publication by Jordan's NHRI of a report on prisons in 2006, King Abdullah visited Al Jafr Prison, whose conditions of brutality were detailed in the report. He ordered its immediate closure, transforming it symbolically into a school and vocational training center.[89] Likewise, a complaint from an NGO in India alleging that twenty people, including children, were being kept in a stone quarry in the northern state of Haryana led to an investigation by the NHRI and the group's eventual release.[90]

In some cases, complaints submitted to an NHRI can be used to bring about statutory changes. For example, Costa Rica's legislative assembly extended rights protections to cohabiting couples, after the NHRI publicized the topic based on a pattern of complaints it had received and called for reform.[91] Russia's NHRI also discovered as a result of complaints that the rate of pensions given to the elderly, veterans, and the disabled was disproportionately low in a northern region of the country. The institution proposed a decree implementing equal pay, and it succeeded in raising benefits for over one million people.[92] After Mongolia's National Human Rights Commission took a petition to the Supreme Court, it too made significant strides in securing rights for thousands of Tsaatans, the smallest ethnic minority in the country, residing in an isolated mountainous area.[93]

Many of the rules created by India's NHRI focused on issues of criminal justice like custodial deaths and police arrests, are also instructive.[94] Rule creation in India sometimes has shaped fairly bureaucratic tasks, such as devising forms for state officials to use in reporting human rights abuses. Sometimes, the commission has used its statutory power of taking certain issues before the Supreme Court to create new rules; thus new guidelines were developed for interpreting the widely abused Armed Forces (Special Powers) Act. In other instances, the commission has helped to establish new state institutions, such as the creation in 1999 of human rights units within various police headquarters. The NHRI promoted the idea of these units and then issued guidelines, compatible with international human rights standards, for how these offices should function.[95] Likewise, the commission specified guidelines requiring state authorities to change their standard operating procedures: state authorities were to report any deaths in custody within twenty-four hours as well as submit post-mortem reports to the Commission, using forms prepared by the NHRI.[96] Though it is true that the number of custodial deaths rose during this same period, the potential longer term effects of changing rules should not be discounted. NHRIs push states to make self-binding rules, even if the process seems in practice messy and contradictory.

In many cases, however, state agents disregard NHRI recommendations entirely, with institutions variously pushing back or caving in to these affronts. Nepal, for instance, has an "alarmingly low" implementation rate, with fewer than 9 percent of all recommendations made by the NHRI between 2000 and 2010 implemented. Nor do the authorities tend to cooperate with the Nepalese commission's investigations.[97] In South Africa, the NHRI has failed to demand that state actors, from parliamentarians to local police, enforce its recommendations. And Thailand is another country where the government has not taken well to recommendations and reports by the NHRI. Ousted Thai premier Thaksin Shinawatra, for example, condemned the human rights commission for its scathing report of the "war on drugs."[98] The chair of Thailand's NHRI described the challenges: "Government negligence in not taking into consideration our reports and recommendations is the biggest problem. We investigated over 3,000 cases, but the Thai government took only one for consideration, the Thai-Malaysian gas pipeline, and sent it to parliament. It was very discouraging during our first three years in office as the government did not even inform us if they received our reports."[99] NHRIs in countries as diverse as Uganda, Lithuania, Ecuador, Zambia, and Russia also commonly face resistance from various departments and offices.[100]

Rule creation is clearly not rule implementation, but what is important is that an NHRI reframes the structural context in which the broader state apparatus operates. In this regard, different avenues to rule creation by an NHRI exist, including draft legislation; specific guidelines and rules for implementing human rights protections; and specifically targeted recommendations, including the creation of particular mechanisms or concessions (e.g., prisoner releases and detention facility closures). All of these remedies have in common an attempt by the NHRI to get other state actors to do something in response to wrongdoing. In some cases, low levels of remediation can of course reflect the NHRI's own organizational weaknesses, which impede its capacity to move beyond documentation. Regardless of the source, weak remediation lies at the root of some of the harshest critiques against NHRIs: their inherent incapacity to fulfill their central purpose and control state actors by holding them accountable. But NHRIs also enhance state accountability when they define and promote specific remedies, regardless of whether the remedies are accepted or implemented. The very act of constructing them changes the playing field in important if subtle and underappreciated ways.

Threat Cycles as Indicators of Influence

Human rights institutions face inordinately high expectations. In fact, the overwhelming temptation is to assess a human rights institution's influence in terms of human rights violations. The conventional and understandable assumption is that a human rights institution should result, however indirectly, in less abuse. Anecdotally, however, there is little to suggest that creating an NHRI leads to a dramatic decline in violations, though there are numerous situations in which discrete instances of abuse are improved.

Even if NHRIs are not always associated with a decline in violations, ironically, their influence may be evident when the state uses threats to silence or punish it. In some contexts, especially armed conflict zones like those of Colombia and Nepal, physical assaults against the NHRI have taken place. This has also been the fate of the Palestinian Commission, which has come under attack by the Palestinian Authority. In 2004, police assaulted the head of the Jaffa office and a UN volunteer, who were investigating a complaint of torture at a local police station. Commissioner-General Eyad Sarraj was himself arrested multiple times and attacked. And after the Al-Aqsa Intifada in 2000, the Ramallah offices of the Palestinian NHRI were ransacked and their equipment was destroyed.[101] Threatening to cut off funding, or actually cutting it, is another common coercive response by the state to an NHRI it finds threatening. In Cameroon, for example, the state cut the NHRI's funding extensively for two years after it issued a critical, albeit confidential, report on the police.[102] Some states have formally threatened to close NHRIs. This happened in Uganda in 2004, in conjunction with efforts to undermine the institution's independence.[103] In other cases, state hostility has led to NHRIs that have simply become less outspoken in challenging the government, a trajectory taken at various times by NHRIs in Cameroon, Chad, and Togo.[104]

In a world of perfect compliance, NHRIs would be unnecessary. Their efforts to protect and promote human rights target the abusive practices of a state, practices that themselves reflect perceived threats to national security or identity.[105] Especially in places where democratic modes of governance and accountability are weakly institutionalized, states may respond to NHRI activism with coercion. Such instances of abuse, perpetrated against the state's own watch-dog agency, paradoxically confirm the NHRI's influence. When a state threatens or coerces an NHRI, it shows that the institution is threatening state leaders' sense of impunity and invulnerability—that they are doing something right. Yet from the institution's perspective, it also means that working for an NHRI can be a dangerous business. As a former Hungarian ombudsman said following a back-lash against the NHRI's staff, "Who safeguards the guardians?"[106]

Prevention: NHRIs as Socializing Agents

Accountability institutions are sometimes forward looking, attempting to pre-vent the outbreak of wrongdoing. Most of the preventive work that NHRIs do is at the level of socialization, both socializing members of the state, through train-ing and other programs, and conducting human rights education for the general population. These activities reflect the promotional functions of an NHRI, and promotion of human rights has always been one of the key tasks of any human rights institution, in the classic language of UN treaties and bodies. Promotion, in turn, is directly linked to the notion that much of human rights work is neces-sarily aspirational. While prevention in theory could relate to the more material-ist bases of human rights abuses, in the case of NHRIs, prevention usually refers to direct action taken by the institution to minimize the likelihood of abuse.

Regardless of the longer term effects of promoting human rights, which are difficult if not impossible to gauge, one basic impact of socializing efforts by NHRIs is the "the legitimization of rights discourse as local discourse."[107] As one observer notes, "The importance of this cannot be discounted in states where the idea of human rights has been delegitimized by projecting it as an alien, imperi-alistic discourse."[108] This type of discursive influence is fundamental: once the language of human rights is inserted nationally, it can be used as a source of empowerment, cooptation, contestation, or other local appropriation. Localized discourse reflects rising awareness of human rights, wherever it may lead.

If social awareness is key to preventing human rights abuses, socialization of state officials—those most directly responsible for many human rights violations—is considered essential. A student of Russia's NHRI agrees that "changing behavioral patterns within state agencies unaccustomed to the de-mands of accountability through persuasion and public pressure" is of paramount significance.[109] While training agents of the state as to what is prohibited and what it means to have (and claim) rights is at the heart of NHRI activities target-ing state actors, the impact of these efforts is often most evident in attitudes and expectations toward the NHRI itself. Thus, Belize's former ombudsman reflects, "In 1999 when I became Ombudsman of Belize, one of the major road blocks that had to be removed was resistance by the public bureaucracy, especially the Police, who perceived that the Ombudsman would be the defender of the complainant even if he or she were dead wrong."[110]

India's NHRI again showcases how state agents can be socialized through training programs. In addition to preparing training materials for police personnel, for example, the commission has helped to organize seminars on specialized subjects like forensic science and prison management. It also has networked with other state agencies that play a role in human rights socialization, including senior officers charged with training police personnel and paramilitary forces. In other cases, the commission has supported innovative efforts, including a "postcard" system of human rights "dos and don'ts" that army personnel can carry with them, and even an annual human rights debate competition for members of the security and armed forces.[111] That state officials are aware of the NHRI's power on some level is clear. For instance, to avoid receiving public subpoenas, many Indian officials reportedly agree to cooperate with the NHRI after the mere threat of a subpoena.[112]

Assessing the success of training efforts targeting state officials, however, is not straightforward. State officials might comply, but on the margins, just enough to avoid detection and charges of wrongdoing. Put differently, state officials exposed to human rights training can learn the wrong lessons, even the limits of what they can get away with. To further complicate things, given the multiplicity of state actors, training might succeed with some groups more than others. In Bolivia, human rights training seemed to be more successful against the armed forces, but it ran up against more serious impediments from the police and local municipalities.[113] In federal systems, human rights training of state officials can prove even more challenging.[114] Yet at a minimum, training of local officials enhances awareness of rights discourses and alters understandings among state agents—of what constitutes abuse and the repercussions that might follow. The extent to which awareness on the part of state officials translates into concrete improvements remains an empirical question, depending on broader circumstances, but very often it leads to not-altogether insignificant concessions or cooperation.

Human Rights Education

One of the major activities of NHRIs is to undertake human rights education (HRE). Shortly after the Paris Principles were enacted and NHRIs proliferated globally, the United Nations named 1995 to 2004 the United Nations Decade for Human Rights Education. The international organization defines HRE as "training, dissemination and information efforts aimed at the building of a universal culture of human rights through the imparting of knowledge and skills and the moulding of attitudes."[115] Indeed, the term refers, on the one hand, to the human right *to an education* and, on the other, to being *educated about* human rights issues. To the extent that the former is partly encompassed within the broader right to general education, it is the latter that has dominated the work of most actors in the field.[116]

Among NHRIs themselves, a widespread consensus exists that socialization is a key to overcoming human rights abuse. In personal interviews, most members of India's commission identified the lifting of "entrenched attitudes" as the single greatest obstacle to human rights reform.[117] Still, socialization efforts by India's NHRI have shied away from broad public campaigns, in the face of government intransigence, a large population, and a cumbersome bureaucracy.[118] In other places, human rights abuses are also traced to deep-seated prejudices that pervade society. As a human rights ombudsman in Slovenia said, "They really don't understand they are using discriminatory speech."[119] In South Africa, as elsewhere, HRE is often equated with the promotion of a "culture of human rights," a fundamental if daunting task.[120] Sometimes a divergence exists so that NGO awareness of an NHRI and its work does not match the public's. Thus, in Sri Lanka, the human rights movement's high expectations were not matched initially by public awareness. In this sense, the NHRI had "a marginal impact on the advancement of human rights in the country."[121]

Cross-regionally, it is noteworthy that NHRIs in the Asia Pacific—the region of the world with the lowest relative concentration of NHRIs—have been most active in promoting HRE.[122] NHRIs there have used their status as quasi-state bodies to mediate usefully with government officials on behalf of HRE. Examples of active NHRIs in the region abound—from Afghanistan's NHRI, which has trained over tens of thousands of individuals over thousands of workshops to South Korea's NHRI that has innovatively prepared a series of films to Mongolia's NHRI, which holds annual national forums on Human Rights Day.[123] In other regions, in contrast, nonstate actors have taken the lead on HRE more than NHRIs.[124]

The case of South Africa's NHRI, which has been especially active in the realm of HRE, is worth highlighting. South Africa's NHRI is arguably "one of the best-funded and most active human rights commissions" in Africa, and it is especially known for its promotional work.[125] The government's interest in promoting

HRE has always been framed in terms of broad long-term gains, including conflict resolution; even high crime rates in the country have been linked to the need for HRE.[126] Yet less than one-tenth of the SAHRC's budget has been devoted to HRE in past years, a figure that may appear disproportionately low given the centrality of HRE in the commission's mandate.[127] Like any actor involved in HRE, moreover, the SAHRC has had to confront the challenge of "normative transfer," or tailoring international human rights norms to match local standards and needs.[128] This has entailed practical steps like translating documents into local languages and disseminating human rights norms via local interlocutors who have access to and legitimacy among distinct communities. It is one of the rationales for training community leaders, or "training the trainers," who can then transfer knowledge about human rights to a mass audience, sometimes targeting vulnerable groups: community organizations, trade unions, women's and rural groups, and those who are HIV-positive.[129]

As part of its HRE initiatives, the South African commission—like so many of its counterparts around the world—has also diffused human rights norms through more informal means, including use of media outlets. The SAHRC has taken out radio advertisements, sometimes with international funding (e.g., USAID). Local newspapers occasionally carry NHRI advertisements on particular themes, such as children's rights or domestic violence. Much more frequently, workshops and conferences form part of the commission's informal outreach work.

One organizationally innovative step taken by South Africa's NHRI, bridging formal and informal efforts, was to create a Human Rights Education and Training Centre.[130] The center, created in 2000 with permanent offices and a staff at the SAHRC's Johannesburg headquarters, institutionalized HRE within the commission. The center trains groups, organizing courses, seminars, and workshops; and it prepares relevant instructional materials and pedagogical models to disseminate broadly.[131] Funding for the center, like funding for the commission itself, derives from a combination of national and international—governmental and private—donors, with South Africa's Department of Education and other government offices providing resources alongside the likes of UNESCO and the Commonwealth Secretariat. Significantly, the decision to create the center arose not only out of a perceived gap in services, but purportedly in direct response to international guidelines associated with the International Decade for HRE.[132]

As the South African example and countless others affirm, raising public awareness, both of an NHRI and of human rights more generally, often involves interfacing with the media. It is quite common for NHRIs to have public service announcements and to work with the media to make sure its campaigns, reports, and initiatives receive publicity. In the Czech Republic, the ombudsman has even been the subject of a reality television show, featuring cases before the NHRI. Recognizing the media's potential role in raising social awareness, some experts have suggested using newspaper coverage of an NHRI as an indicator of social awareness about the institution—or the NHRI's broader social influence.[133]

Though the value of HRE can seem limited, especially in the face of ongoing abuse, its effects must be evaluated in broader terms, especially as international actors devote resources to promote HRE. When Norway initiated a project after 2002 to strengthen HRE in Indonesian legal institutions, did it really make a difference that the number of human rights centers at academic institutions jumped from three to forty-one?[134] HRE certainly raises awareness of "human rights" and its discourses, procedures, debates, and opportunities. For this reason alone, social awareness—across various constituencies, including marginalized ones—should be a touchstone of an accountability institution's impact, regardless of ensuing state action.

The (Perverse) Power of Accountability Institutions

Understanding the impact of an NHRI or accountability institution is complicated by the possibility of perverse consequences. This caveat is rooted in the basic assumption that states are the principal violators and guarantors of human rights. Even as NHRIs acquire moral authority in a domestic context, state officials may disregard the majority of the institution's recommendations. In some contexts, moreover, NHRIs are structurally constrained in what they can do. As a commentator remarked about the Malaysian NHRI, "In a country where human-rights violations are systemic rather than discrete, where state institutions commit egregious human-rights violations through acts of commission or omission, there is a limit to what an NHRI can accomplish."[135] When the creation of a human rights commission was being debated in the Kenyan parliament, one parliamentarian honed in on the crucial dilemma: "[T]he assumption in creating a National Commission for Protection of Human Rights is that the State itself is the principal guarantor and protector of human rights. But the reality on the ground is different. On the ground, we all know that governments all over the world, are the worst violators of human rights. So, how can we trust a government which is the worst violator of human rights to be the protector and guarantor of human rights?[136]

One implication of this dualism—of the state as human rights violator and protector—is that NHRIs can have perverse consequences, sometimes limiting the space in which NGOs operate. Ideally, of course, if NHRIs are independent, they should not be working at cross-purposes with NGOs; the relationship should be symbiotic and positive. The Czech ombudsman, for example, helped civil society "negotiate more effectively with the state on issues of accountability and responsibility."[137] Yet evidence of perverse effects, while difficult to document systematically, is extensive. In India, NGOs "virtually stopped filing cases with the commission, learning relatively quickly that it is better to go to the courts or to politicize a human rights campaign."[138] In other instances, the incapacitation of nonstate actors seems deliberate state policy more than unintended consequence. The case of Chiapas, Mexico, is sobering in this regard: "Federal and state officials . . . appear less concerned with investigating and prosecuting complaints of human rights violations by government security forces and their paramilitary allies (although they have made recommendations in such matters), than with limiting the powers of indigenous authorities."[139] State authorities pursued these seemingly contradictory goals, implementing restrictive legislation even while embracing the language of human rights.[140]

The connections between NHRIs and NGOs, though often overlooked, can take quite tangible forms, as funding and staffs circulate back and forth. Winifred Tate summarizes the exchanges in the case of Colombia:

> Highly trained professionals circulate between NGOs, state agencies, and international institutions, while the same bodies fund all three. State agencies cannot help but develop the same funding dynamic as NGOs, becoming project driven and tailoring their programs to the funding interests of foreign governments and international agencies. . . . In the final twist, their competition becomes NGOs, as state agencies apply to the same sources of funding for many similar kinds of projects.[141]

And the hostility can be quite palpable. To work for a state human rights institution in Colombia is to be a sellout or an "NGO-traitor," though the view from a staffer can be quite different: "We didn't go there to work as infiltrators. We didn't have any commitment to any actor or political force. We were trying to position human rights work within the state. There were changes, imperceptible but important to those of us who lived it."[142] Occasionally NGO reactions to

NHRIs reflect their own internal contradictions. In Uganda, some NGOs perceived the human rights commission as monopolizing the field, even while they themselves seemed to fear broaching controversial issues.[143]

Perverse institutional consequences, moreover, can be dynamic, shifting substantially over time. In some cases, such as in Tanzania, an NHRI can be created with good intentions and become highly politicized over time. Or as in Colombia, the NHRI may initially issue critical reports and have strong alliances with NGOs and then lose its credibility.[144] In the process, state authorities can use an NHRI they created to reinforce impunity, substituting the institution for fuller accountability and creating the illusion that "someone in the government is doing something."[145] When this occurs, an NHRI can become a vehicle of the state's active (re)production of impunity.[146]

NHRIs also interface with other institutions like the courts. Time and again, we see in debates leading up to the creation of NHRIs concerns over the necessity of an accountability institution, given alternative and potentially competing bodies like the judiciary.[147] Though the drive to create NHRIs can complement alternative dispute resolution forums, it can also reflect the high costs associated with accessing courts in many places and for many people.[148] An anecdote from Tanzania illustrates how the courts and NHRIs can be vitally connected. An NGO, the Tanzanian Legal and Human Rights Centre, made a strategic decision in 2001 to take a case to the country's NHRI rather than to the courts. The case involved a land dispute, leading to the displacement of over one hundred people next to Serengeti National Park, the killing of livestock, and the burning of houses and fields. Loudspeakers had abruptly announced one day that people had four days to leave their homes; and less than a week later, they were forcibly removed. In 2004, Kenya's NHRI issued a detailed report, exposing state violations and ordering compensation. After the government refused to comply, the NHRI recommended that the case be taken to the courts. Yet in the end, according to one account, both the NHRI and the courts were insufficient; they represented individualistic, rationalist, bureaucratic responses to problems that were far more socially and structurally embedded.[149]

In fact, the quasi-judicial nature of NHRIs can limit the types of claims deemed acceptable. Even when the institution serves as a valuable new space for accountability claims, it restricts those demands to legalized areas; generally, only rights recognized by law can be brought before an NHRI. In the case of rights not yet recognized, for instance those relating to sexuality, social groups have limited room to maneuver, though they can still submit claims and work to influence the institution's agenda. Expecting systemic progress to result directly from individual submissions, however, is more often than not a losing proposition.

Conclusions: Expressing Accountability in New Spaces

Like the influence of other human rights institutions, NHRIs are often depicted in binary terms, as highly significant or a mere tool in the hands of cynical states. Writing about the classic ombudsman in the 1960s, Walter Gellhorn tapped into a similar dynamic: "The Ombudsman has in recent years been so rapturously regarded abroad that his achievements have not often been evaluated. What he is supposed to accomplish is taken as the equivalent of what he has in fact accomplished."[150] NHRIs are not universally adored, but their influence is often assumed. The reality tends to be a complex mix of influence. More so than other institutions, accountability agencies serve to open new spaces for state-society interaction, including new criteria by which to judge governments. And although legalism can impede the organizational freedom of some NHRIs, these institutions' legal standing can give them concrete access to government files, investigations, and recommendations with the force of law, or at least the possibility of institutionalized change.

Assessing the influence of any institution depends in large part on initial expectations. Following this logic, it seems that a lot of NHRIs have been set up to fail, with mandates that would essentially require them to undo systemically entrenched patterns of oppression. In Panama, one observer recounts how in public forums leading up to the ombudsman's creation, it was common to idealize the figure to the point of giving it an overwhelming amount of responsibilities, which could only doom it to disappoint. The key to the institution's success may instead be to carefully delimit its actions.[151] In other words, assessment does not happen in a vacuum; it is constructed against a set of baseline premises and expectations, only sometimes articulated. If NHRIs often disappoint, they sometimes can exceed initial expectations, even where leaders' motives in creating human rights institutions seemed clearly suspect. Against the backdrop of expectations, NHRIs may have their greatest impact where they are least expected—not because of what they do, but because so little was initially expected of them.

While an NHRI's influence is partly the result of institutional origins and design, and even expectations, there is still room for significant variation. In some instances, for example, leadership clearly matters; this can be especially true in monocratic institutions (e.g., ombudsman), where a central figure defines the institution, and in contexts where resources are constrained and institutional success is therefore more open to initiative and creativity. An NHRI that stands out as relatively successful in this regard is the Ugandan one. Despite a shortage in resources, it managed to challenge both the government, including the security forces, and the opposition. It also showed a capacity for learning, shifting from an almost exclusive focus initially on civil and political rights to rights to health and food and the condition of child soldiers. The role of leadership, under the impressive direction of Margaret Sekaggya, no doubt was crucial.[152]

Countries where human rights abuses are relatively minor and democratic openness is high face other challenges, including the possibility that the NHRI will underperform. NHRIs in the EU, for example, often lack political support, have overlapping mandates, and are only weakly independent.[153] But it is also the story behind NHRIs in Benin and Senegal, where political openness has backfired in terms of institutional activism. And even in the case of highly effective NHRIs, such as Canada's Human Rights Commission, problems of funding threaten the capacity of these institutions to supply the human rights protection increasingly demanded of them.[154]

An NHRI's standing can be contingent on broader political openness, with somewhat paradoxical effects for the relationship between NHRIs and NGOs. In countries where political freedom is curtailed and NGOs are weak, as in Nigeria, nonstate groups might use the state institution strategically for credibility and cover. However, when NHRIs operate in freer climates, as it does in Kenya, NGOs may not need the state institution to the same extent. Despite similarities across the Nigerian and Kenyan NHRIs, then, the state institution has enjoyed a better working relationship with NGOs in Nigeria.[155] That ordinary people have a new means of accessing the state is of course also significant. Sometimes *that* seems the goal, as confirmed by a staff lawyer at the Czech ombudsman: "[T]hat is part of our function . . . to give people the sense that they can complain to the state and that we will listen."[156] And where human rights abuses are relatively minor, moreover, NHRIs can face an added burden of having to demonstrate their ongoing relevance.

Another way to conceive of an NHRI's influence is in terms of the multiple roles it can play, such as advocate, mediator, facilitator, watchdog, representative, or catalyst. For example, in conflict zones, one observer notes that "the regulatory role an NHRI can play . . . may be limited to that of a catalyst at best, and at worst, playing the role of a 'canary down the coalmine.'"[157] In Malaysia, some have questioned whether the NHRI's role is that of watchdog or lapdog.[158] And in Russia, the ombudsman is said to have been "both an advocate of human rights and an objective voice established to deal with human rights complaints."

Thus, Russia's ombudsman saw itself as "free to privilege certain human rights concerns at particular historical moments regardless of whether these concerns matched the percentage of complaints entering the office."[159]

Despite the tendency to dichotomize the effects of an NHRI, in terms of overall success and failure, the impact of an accountability institution is necessarily multifaceted. Is an NHRI "a simple decoration in the architecture of democracy?"[160] Or as a critic of Belize's ombudsman stated, are NHRIs a cover for political strategy? "Like Ombudsmen appointments worldwide, the post is a political gambit and rear guard action by political parties to defend their turf against complaints from citizens. . . . Nor will the Ombudsman make any difference. He may satisfy some citizens in the home base of power politics in the port town and a couple of villages, but otherwise the whole Ombudsman affair is a "red herring," a distraction. A piece of cosmetic tinkering to give the appearance that the parties controlling the country really care."[161] Cynics might go a step further and critique the "endless loop of efforts resulting in remarkably little forward motion. . . . These efforts appear to exist largely to satisfy international pressure for governmental action, and they often succeed in deflecting public scrutiny."[162] And they might mock the effects of an NHRI that do not seem sufficiently serious, as one observer of Costa Rica's NHRI defined the institution's victories: "It has had some immediate successes such as persuading the Health Ministry to close several noisy dance halls and a pig farm polluting a river."[163]

Yet even when NHRIs seem to fail in some respects, they can still localize human rights discourse, in all its ambiguities and contradictions. As a leading NGO activist in India remarked to me, perhaps the most noteworthy contribution of India's NHRC is that the subject of human rights is no longer perceived as being "anti-national."[164] Ideally, an accountability institution should be relevant to the people who most need it. In the parliamentary debates preceding the creation of an NHRI in Kenya, Dr. Anangwe raised this issue: "If we are going to create an institution like the Kenya National Commission on Human Rights, it must be adding value to the lives of Kenyans. . . . Its job will not merely be to tell the international community that Kenya is very good at the protection of human rights. We want to see it on the ground. We want the Commission to be bold in its actions, especially against the Government."[165]

Assessing the influence of NHRIs requires conceptualizing outputs across the various stages of accountability—documentation, remediation, prevention— while treating accountability as a broad social process. Those intent on shaping and strengthening these institutions' influence must insert themselves into these same spaces, moving to promote fuller access to all members of society, challenging official narratives as required, and pushing for public deliberations. The dominant tendency of pressuring governments to conform to international standards of institutional design (i.e., the Paris Principles) is important but incomplete. Accountability is not the province of individual punishment or enforcement, as it so often is made out to be. Accountability institutions provide discursive, public spaces for state and society to communicate and confront contested norms of wrongdoing. This requires thinking about institutional impact in broader terms than the lists of benchmarks that have dominated the field. Determining how well an NHRI conforms to international standards is significant, though often it says more about the institution's strength (from a design standpoint) than the full range of its influence. Assessing an NHRI's impact requires, instead, considering overlooked dynamics, including questions of accessibility, truthtelling, and socialization. Accountability institutions like NHRIs matter in the end because of how they empower *and* constrain various state and societal actors. Those wishing to improve these institutions must target the institutions themselves, beyond the government, calling on NHRIs to be socially accountable.

11

Adaptive States: Making and Breaking International Law

Karl Polanyi asserted in *The Great Transformation* that "[n]o mere declaration of rights can suffice: institutions are required to make the rights effective."[1] Polanyi was highlighting the necessity of public institutions, their role in translating rights into practice. Yet Polanyi also saw institutions as social products, "embodiments of human meaning and purpose" in a given historical moment.[2] In this view, institutions are the engines of change, just as they are shaped and constrained by their particular context. While Polanyi was commenting most directly on the nature of institutions, he was also implying that the origin of any right lies in a parallel "wrong." Rights, that is, enter the political imagination precisely because people's ideals of what is owed them (or someone else) fail to live up to the reality of their circumstances. Thus, rights declarations can never suffice, as Polanyi notes, since the wrongs animating them are themselves the product of historically and socially embedded institutions—one set of institutionalized practices must be transformed into another.

The great paradox for human rights is that institutional transformation, even when it occurs, will itself not suffice. This is because international and national human rights institutions have social contradictions embedded into them, evolving in the shadow of a state that both defines and violates international human rights norms. This presents us with two overlapping ironies. On the one hand, activists most prepared to work for institutional change must believe in the transformative power of institutions, in their capacity to turn ideals into practice and improve human lives, even while the institutions may camouflage state motives and produce perverse consequences. On the other hand, even the most cynical of state efforts to manipulate institutions can feed back and reinforce social demands, occasionally taking unexpected turns and engendering longer lasting reform. Neither state nor society always gets what it wants out of human rights institutions, but occasionally they do.

This is the story I have tried to tell in tracking the global rise of NHRIs, an account of how the modern state creates self-restraining mechanisms as a way of retaining, not abdicating, its authority. During periods of norm ambiguity, when the state's normative commitments are in question, state leaders have an incentive to adopt socially appropriate ideas. After the fact, normative discourses and institutions can appear so certain, even morally arrogant, that we forget the ambiguities leading to them, including moments of transition, new obligations, or contested practices that open space for norm-diffusing agents to promote their ideas. Beyond human rights, ambiguity may also underlie broader patterns of global diffusion in world affairs, helping to explain why new normative orders so often get locked in after wars or why global commitments can spark localizing trends. Strategic emulation is a powerful driving force, rooted in the dualities of the modern state.

The picture that emerges of the state is that it is adaptive more than self-restraining. State leaders, propelled by strategic emulation, follow external scripts, latch on to myths, and perform membership rites. They do these things because their social peers do them, as they look to lock in commitments or localize authority or appease critics. This is the background against which over a hundred of the world's states have created in the past half century self-restraining, accountability mechanisms taking the form of "national human rights institutions." Despite enormous diversity and variance, the institution has diffused globally and NHRIs have become an internationally recognized actor in their own right. Though cast as a modern democratic institution, enabling horizontal accountability, the unstated dynamic is that state leaders today still resemble political authorities of the past, in their willingness to institutionalize self-restraint as a means of retaining more than relinquishing authority. Today's NHRIs have something in common with Jahangir's seventeenth-century Mughal "chain of justice": symbols of accountability, warnings to dissenting authorities, means of connecting with a populace and preventing rebellion—now embedded in a global context of similarly interlinked institutions, representing the state's dual role as maker and breaker of international law.

Ambiguity, Path Dependencies, and Dynamic Diffusion

The role of ambiguity in international politics has not been sufficiently explored.[3] Yet the theory and evidence here point to the ways ambiguity shapes strategic emulation, itself a complex mechanism of diffusion. Unlike certainty, which centers on probability, ambiguity revolves centrally around questions of interpretation and multiple meaning. During such circumstances, I have argued, public authorities have an incentive to adopt socially appropriate ideas and norm-diffusing agents have greater space to promote their ideas.

As NHRIs have diffused globally, the theme of ambiguity has manifested itself in other ways. In particular, the history of NHRI diffusion, perhaps like other historicized accounts of diffusion, is one that in some cases can only be read back in retrospect. At the time of their creation, many NHRIs were not perceived as such; states were merely establishing specialized institutions. This is especially true of the early adopters and those states creating ombudsman agencies, given the latter's long-standing pedigree. Likewise, many of the countries that showed a delay in creating an NHRI were not really resisting or defying the global trend. Where institutional alternatives, or closely related institutions that could essentially stand in for an NHRI already existed, states faced weaker incentives to create an NHRI, or at least the decision was more contested. In accounts of diffusion, then, delays cannot always be interpreted as indicating resistance. Diffusion—marked by converging ideas and institutions—is itself an interpretive judgment. Whether or not an institution is an NHRI, accredited or not, is partly an act of labeling. NHRIs have converged and diffused globally, but only following labeling and accreditation and other practices of social recognition.

Path dependencies have also been prevalent, but not so much in terms of origins leading neatly to impact.[4] An institution's initial conditions do leave a legacy, generally speaking. Above all, countries facing overwhelming incentives (a regulatory moment, external obligations, *and* organized abuse) have tended to create relatively strong NHRIs. Those facing only external obligations or no incentives at all, in contrast, established the weakest institutions. On balance, however, institutional origins have not proven determinative. More striking are the numerous examples of institutions overcoming their starting point and playing a role that exceeded initial expectations, often as a result of bold leaders, fiercely persistent social activists, and transnational professionals promoting the idea of an NHRI.

Two further related aspects of diffusion—time and place—are especially worth noting. Political scientist Paul Pierson is correct in reminding us of the value of bringing time into politics and considering institutions as moving pictures more than static snapshots.[5] The history of NHRIs cannot be recounted adequately without such a conception of time, as I have tried to capture somewhat in the book's organization. Human rights institutions that were created around the same time shared important similarities with others during the same period. As Chapter 3 shows, the international regime on NHRIs shifted and evolved over time. This did not just affect the attention given to NHRIs or the amount of assistance offered during any given period; it meant that the very idea and meaning of an NHRI has shifted over time. In a world of dramatic changes in technology and in the international system itself, diffusion is necessarily dynamic: the number of potentially available adopters was different in the 1940s than in the 1970s and after the 1990s, as states collapsed and others acquired independence. Internally, moreover, the conditions of diffusion, ambiguity, and strategic emulation that I have highlighted were fundamentally a product of a particular historical moment. Put simply, time matters.

Likewise, place, especially in terms of regional and cultural configurations, has been crucial. One of the strongest statistical findings was that regional diffusion always seemed to be significant; that is, no matter what else was at play, whether one's regional peers had an NHRI was relevant. If place matters, however, it is only because of its social content. Social peers, whether in a regional context of relatively close proximity or from common cultural zones (like the Commonwealth and the Francophonie), promoted the idea of an NHRI quite actively, sometimes aggressively, through their contacts, exchanges, and modeling.

Time and place, obvious as they may seem, are therefore at the crux of how NHRIs diffused worldwide. While human rights mechanisms are assumed to spread mostly through social emulation (compared to other issues in international politics and economy, which depend on more strategic processes like competition or coercion), the rise of NHRIs demonstrates that both strategic and social diffusion processes go hand in hand, what I have called strategic emulation. And strategic emulation itself is very much bound up in time and place. Whether a regulatory moment occurs, new external obligations exist, or organized abuse is present necessarily depends on the particularities of time and place, on a broader

context that shapes the very conditions of ambiguity and makes global norm diffusion possible.

The Spatial Politics (and Ethics) of State Accountability

One of the most significant consequences of accountability institutions is to
provide new spaces of interaction. These reconfigurations can be quite significant
in shaping power relations, as discussed most directly in Chapter 10 in terms of
the geography of complaint making. This is precisely what gives rise to another
set of considerations, about the ethics of state institutions. Once an institution
has become socially recognized, it essentially inhabits its own space in global
politics and law. Occupying such a space can mean that these institutions acquire a taken-for-granted quality, assumed to be benevolent, necessary, or desirable. Yet given local resistance and adaptation, and the reluctance of some states
to adopt them or seek accreditation, it is important to ask a harder set of questions. Are NHRIs always necessary, and should they be promoted so uniformly?

Accountability institutions are quite often, understandably, assessed in terms
of their functions. But institutions like NHRIs also alter the spaces in which
state and society interact, as the NHRIs reviewed here so frequently show. Indeed, much of the impact of accountability mechanisms and NHRIs concerns
the (re)configuration of state power and its implications for nonstate actors. For
example, NHRIs provide members of society with new access points to the state,
as people literally queue up to submit their complaints (a scene I first witnessed
in Mexico City, which piqued my interest in these institutions), at the same time
that they perpetuate barriers for some groups—from indigenous members of
society to the urban poor and those living in remote parts of the country to those
with disabilities or who are already marginalized. In another instance of NHRIs
restructuring the spaces between state and society, NHRIs can help the state
interpenetrate societal groups, whether co-opting or otherwise controlling them,
or acting as a connecting gateway, as countless examples around the world also
demonstrate. Likewise, an NHRI itself can constitute a new public, discursive
space where state and society engage and confront one another, evident in the
women defiantly protesting outside Algeria's NHRI or young political activists
in South Korea who used the NHRI to confront the state.

Another set of configurations revolves around the state itself. In one of the
most popular images associated with NHRIs, these institutions serve as horizontal connectors among state actors, helping to transform the state.[6] On another
level, horizontal linkages extend out into a global context, as networks of NHRIs

serve to connect state actors to one another across national borders, comparable to the transgovernmental networks Anne-Marie Slaughter first identified.[7] In still another variation, NHRIs can bring international norms into the domestic arena, implementing and embedding them in local structures. Such localization of the international or global is a key feature of NHRIs, most apparent in countries with a strong rule of law like Canada and Australia but also Senegal in the 1970s and India more recently.

Ultimately, institutional structures would themselves be meaningless were they devoid of actors, who occupy and imbue them with significance. In the case of NHRIs, political leaders shape and respond to these accountability mechanisms, while state bureaucrats staff and interact with these institutions, as do societal groups and individual claimants and all those who unknowingly are on the receiving end of radio announcements and school curricula prepared by these agencies. The leaders of the institutions themselves can be crucially important, as every practitioner knows, but the question is how. The evidence amassed here suggests that an NHRI's leadership can matter most under crisis conditions and when resources are strained—when creativity is at a premium—and in monocratic institutions where one individual is the key figure (e.g., the ombudsman).

Because state accountability institutions can reconfigure power relations, the ethics of building these institutions is indeed open to question. Some states already have numerous accountability mechanisms, so the addition of an NHRI may not have sufficient value added to justify the costs. Though not discussed very often in the literature, institutional substitutes are one of the key factors impeding or delaying NHRI creation. In other cases, NHRIs appear to exist in form and function, sometimes for all intents and purposes, but they remain unaccredited. Given these confounding trends, a broader argument might claim that state leaders have a principled obligation to buck the global tide and resist imposed uniformities that do not promise, given their costs, to improve the daily life conditions of people. If creating another NHRI is an exercise mostly in conformance, why should it be encouraged?

A noteworthy case in this regard is the United States, which has resisted the global trend, has institutional alternatives that arguably may suffice, and often claims exceptionalism on the world stage. Though the U.S. Civil Rights Commission might seem to satisfy the criteria of a domestic human rights body, the institution has not participated in relevant NHRI forums internationally. Moreover, as a recent report notes, "during the last decade, the Civil Rights Commission suffered from over-politicization, under-funding and under-staffing, and lost much of its capacity to investigate instances of discrimination."[8] The commission is also framed in terms of "civil rights," revealing a national reluctance to adopt the language of human rights, which includes economic and social rights. Despite the existence of local human rights bodies, a national institution devoted to human rights does not exist in the United States. Certainly, arguments about added value should be taken seriously, especially when resources are relatively scarce. For powerful countries, however, the ethical boundaries are more indeterminate. Would the United States gain from embracing a discourse of human rights, beyond civil rights, and transforming its current commission to reflect this? The debate still is contentiously polarized, but the findings in this volume indicate that domestic resistors will not have an incentive to concede until the country ratifies both international human rights covenants and then moves to localize authority. For those wishing to transform the long-standing U.S. Civil Rights Commission into an NHRI, charged with symbolic value and practical consequences, they should push simultaneously for treaty ratification—itself contingent on daunting changes, wrapped up in the nation's historically embedded contradictions and requiring a transformation of the discourses and practices surrounding economic and social equality.

Negotiating Sovereignty

As an overarching meta-norm and principle of organization in world politics, state sovereignty is often presented in opposition to human rights standards and practices. But to what extent do emerging human rights trends really challenge deep-seated notions of the sovereign state? At first glance, NHRIs do not seem to threaten state sovereignty as significantly as other human rights developments, if at all. In contrast to humanitarian intervention or international legal institutions, NHRIs do not lie beyond the state or its purview; technically, they are located within the state itself, and most often NHRIs lack enforcement powers against the broader state apparatus. These institutions do not seem to constitute a dramatic assault on state sovereignty. For states that systematically abuse human rights, moreover, a state bureaucracy devoted to human rights may seem cosmetic pretense. And for states that generally respect human rights, the creation of such an institution may seem unnecessary or superfluous.[9]

Yet it is precisely the seemingly mundane nature of NHRIs, enmeshed in the modern state's bureaucracy, that makes these institutions consequential for sovereignty. The post-Cold War diffusion of NHRIs signals a historic normative shift: the implementation of international human rights norms, or their institutionalization in domestic structures, has become a measure of state legitimacy.

Neither human rights nor NHRIs displace state sovereignty, or serve as an alternative focal point of authority. Rather, human rights and NHRIs constitute historically coevolving standards, infusing the state's sovereign legitimacy and authority with new meaning in a changing world. Indeed, if the Cold War saw the internationalization of human rights norms, the end of the Cold War gave way to their internalization.[10] The global proliferation of NHRIs aptly illustrates this broad development.

Internalization, of course, has often been symbolic and aspirational, when looked at in terms of state practice. But the view is altogether different when examined through a societal lens. When states violate human rights norms today, social forces react in protest, making claims and challenging the state's actions and the state's *right* to act in a certain way; and they often do so appealing to the language of authoritative human rights standards. These discursive and often physical confrontations and clashes are significant in historical terms. Indeed, the power of human rights, and of NHRIs in particular, is often better gauged through the politics of contention than by the state's compliance with evolving standards. State sovereignty is still robust, though it has also come under assault and challenge, and it increasingly occupies unsettled terrain.

This is because sovereignty, like human rights or the impact of NHRIs, is not an all-or-nothing phenomenon; it needs to be unbundled.[11] And insofar as sovereignty can have various dimensions, NHRIs challenge state sovereignty in partial and complex ways.[12] On the one hand, NHRIs represent an attempt by the state to retain its sovereign authority by creating an internationally sanctioned self-restraining mechanism. On the other hand, these institutions are altering the ways in which state and societal actors encounter one another around questions of human rights. The implications for evolving notions of state sovereignty are thus quite significant.

Still, NHRIs rarely seem to constrain state authority dramatically, in the sense of leading to a noted decline in violations. But as recounted in Chapter 10, they can be influential in a range of ways that do challenge the state, directly and indirectly. Directly, they can document abuses (giving voice to people, officializing truths, and setting political agendas), push the state to offer remedies for wrongdoing, and attempt to prevent future abuses via socialization and education. Indirectly, moreover, even limited and symbolic institutions can serve as political opportunities for social actors to mobilize.[13] And when the state itself is disaggregated into various actors (such as the executive versus legislature, police versus military, government ministries), an NHRI's complex effects become even more apparent. Interestingly, all of these effects can take place even when NHRIs are originally created mostly to appease critics. Those wishing to strengthen these agencies must therefore push at the margins, getting accountability institutions to be broadly accountable. Such social pressures, from domestic and international actors, may be as consequential as more obvious or formulaic efforts to promote the Paris Principles.

The multiplicity of NHRI experiences since the end of the Cold War suggests that sovereignty itself is an evolving institution, whose meaning is variegated and contested as a result of interactions among actors.[14] The crucial point is not that the state is no longer sovereign; it is that the notion of what constitutes sovereign authority in world politics is changing. NHRIs are centrally involved in the construction and reconstruction of state sovereignty. When through processes of strategic emulation states create NHRIs, or alter their internal structures and move to implement international norms, precisely to retain broader sovereign control, this reveals just how states are attempting to negotiate the shifting contours of their sovereignty.

The interactions of NHRIs with state and nonstate actors—each making claims and counterclaims of one another—are processes by which the scope of legitimate sovereign authority acquires meaning and changes over time. Recognizing these multiple contingencies, Richard Falk notes that "sovereignty and human rights are linked in complex, contradictory ways."[15] Indeed, the notion of state sovereignty often refers to the legitimate scope of state practice. In the human rights sphere, this has usually included an implicit catalogue of prohibitions on state action. When state authorities cross a certain line, ensuing social challenges can represent varying threats to the state's sovereignty. Stephen Krasner thus observes that human rights have challenged the norm of state sovereignty but not its practice, or notions about what the state should do but not what it actually does, leading him to describe the international system as one of "organized hypocrisy." But sovereignty today appears to be more about process than fixed outcome. In this evolving context, state actions falling short of full compliance are at the very least signs of adaptation and, occasionally, partial progress.

Perversity and Possibility

The global rise of NHRIs exposes the contradictions of the modern state, as the principal maker and breaker of international law. Not only has the state long resorted to a mix of coercion and consent to rule, and rein in dissent, but rights themselves appeal to these state dualities. Michel Foucault incisively reveals the tensions:

The essential role of the theory of right, from medieval times on-
wards, was to fix the legitimacy of power; that is the major problem
around which the whole theory of right and sovereignty is organ-
ised. When we say that sovereignty is the central problem of right in
Western societies, what we mean basically is that the essential function of the discourse and techniques of right has been to efface the
domination intrinsic to power in order to present the latter at the
level of domination in two different aspects: on the one hand, as the
legitimate rights of sovereignty, and on the other, as the legal obligation to obey it.[16]

Accordingly, states in the West extended rights to enhance their own authority,
imbuing power with legitimacy. They did it when confronted with new social
demands, and they defined rights as possessions or entitlements, offering a path
to individual freedom—and enlightenment. The unexpected twist was that rights
had no real meaning unless and until they were *claimed* by social groups, transforming them into a political weapon or tool of social change. State and society
both became locked into the discourse of human rights, which has nonetheless
meant different things to different groups. NHRIs are situated at this exact crucible.

If rights are understood as socially legitimate claims, in some places and for
some people, then institutions are the structures through which these claims can
be fulfilled or channeled. But sometimes institutions fail, underperform, or back-
fire. This is why it is useful, and even necessary, to remember that protecting and
promoting rights—the basic purpose of NHRIs—must ultimately be aimed at
making concrete improvements in people's lives. Amartya Sen echoes the broader
view, reminding us that justice should not be pursued transcendentally but
grounded in the actualized realities of ordinary living: "The importance of
human lives, experiences and realizations cannot be supplanted by information
about institutions that exist and the rules that operate. Institutions and rules are,
of course, very important in influencing what happens, and they are part and
parcel of the actual world as well, but the realized actuality goes well beyond the
organizational picture, and includes the lives that people manage—or do not
manage—to live."[17]

Human rights as a concept is passionately contested, by both adherents who
embrace it as almost a creed and skeptics who dismiss it on divergent grounds—
from charges of naïve idealism or moral arrogance to claims of neo-imperialism
and nationalist hypocrisy.[18] Often missing is recognition that contestation is
itself the key.[19] That human rights ideas have become the subject of opposing

claims in world and local politics, and occasionally a source of empowerment, is significant. For NHRIs to matter, they too must potentially become sites of contestation. The basic dualities that are historically embedded in the modern state have been transposed on NHRIs, so it cannot be any other way.

NHRIs are set up to promote and protect human rights, but they can never protect human rights per se. This is because rights abuses often reflect deep conditions of structural violence.[20] If NHRIs can be faulted as a group for one thing, it is an insufficient challenge to the material conditions that perpetuate human rights violations. Attention to economic and social rights and the role of corporate actors does not take us far enough.[21] Nor should we overlook the ethical implications of international financial institutions like the World Bank that promote the notion of an NHRI (fitting it into a broader package of democracy, human rights, and good governance reforms), while aggressively pursuing restructuring policies that marginalize people and engender social inequality.[22] NHRIs, despite their global rise, recognition, and promise, should not automatically be assumed to be *just:* "To ask how things are going and whether they can be improved is a constant and inescapable part of the pursuit of justice."[23] Ongoing critical scrutiny is always required in the face of such globalizing, inherently contradictory projects as human rights, NHRIs, sovereignty, or statehood.

Notes

Chapter 1

1. *Tuzuk-Jahangiri* [Memoirs of Jahangir], ed. Alexander Rogers and Henry Beveridge, vol. 1 (London: Royal Asiatic Society, 1909–14), 7. While this translation appears to be widely cited today, consider this older version: "If the officers of the courts of justice should fail in the investigation of the complaints of the oppressed, and granting them redress, the injured persons might come to this and shake it, and so give note of their wrongs." Syed Hossain Bilgrami and C. Willmott, *Historical and Descriptive Sketch of His Highness the Nizam's Dominions,* vol. 2 (Bombay: Times of India Steam Press, 1884), 563.

2. See Ellison Banks Findly, *Nur Jahan, Empress of Mughal India* (Oxford: Oxford University Press, 1993), 70. According to Bilgrami and Willmott, "the chain was probably meant as a show, a circumstance of which petitioners were probably well aware." Bilgrami and Willmott, *Historical and Descriptive Sketch,* 563. E. S. Holden says that another Mughal emperor (Humayaun of Hindustan) had drums for the same purpose in the sixteenth century, while Sultan Shamsuddin Altansch (A.D. 1211) had "two marble lions with iron chains round their necks from which hung great bells." E. S. Holden, *The Moghul Emperors of Hindustan,* A.D. 1398–A.D. 1707 (Westminster: Constable, 1895), 242. Radhey Shyam, in turn, maintains that Murtaza Nizam Shah ordered in the sixteenth century a "chain of justice" on the plains of Kala Chabutra. Radhey Shyam, "Kingdom of Ahmadnagar" (Ph.D. diss., University of Allahabad, 1996).

3. Put differently, an NHRI is "a body which is established by Government under the constitution or by law or decree, the functions of which are specifically defined in terms of the promotion and protection of human rights." United Nations, *National Institutions: A Handbook on the Establishment and Strengthening of National Institutions for the Promotion and Protection of Human Rights* (New York: United Nations, 1995).

4. See International Coordinating Committee of National Institutions for the Promotion and Protection of Human Rights, "Chart of the Status of National Institutions," http://nhri.ohchr.org/.

5. Sonia Cardenas, "Human Rights and the State," in Robert Denemark, ed., *International Studies Encyclopedia* (Oxford: Wiley-Blackwell, 2010), 3518–35.

6. Sonia Cardenas, "Adaptive States: The Proliferation of National Human Rights Institutions," Working Paper Series T-01-04 (Carr Center for Human Rights Policy, Kennedy School of Government, Harvard University, December 2010). See also Thomas Pegram, "Diffusion across Political Systems: The Global Spread of National Human Rights Institutions," *Human Rights Quarterly* 32, 3 (August 2010): 729–60.

7. Richard Carver, "A New Answer to an Old Question: National Human Rights Institutions and the Domestication of International Law," *Human Rights Law Review* 10, 1 (2010): 1–32.

8. Anne Smith, "The Unique Position of National Human Rights Institutions," *Human Rights Quarterly* 28, 4 (2006): 904–46.

9. Some of the most important work in this area includes Linda Reif, "Building Democratic Institutions: The Role of National Human Rights Institutions in Good Governance and Human Rights Protection," *Harvard Human Rights Journal* 13 (Spring 2000): 1–69; Cardenas, "Adaptive States"; Kamal Hossain, Leonard F. M. Besselink, Haile Selassi Gebre Selassie, and Edmond Völker, eds., *Human Rights Commissions and Ombudsman Offices: National Experiences throughout the World* (The Hague: Kluwer, 2001); Sonia Cardenas, "Emerging Global Actors: The United Nations and National Human Rights Institutions," *Global Governance: A Review of Multilateralism and International Organizations* 9, 1 (Winter 2003): 23–42; Linda Reif, *The Ombudsman, Good Governance and the International Human Rights System* (Leiden: Martinus Nijhoff, 2004); Julie Mertus, *Human Rights Matters: Local Politics and National Human Rights Institutions* (Stanford, Calif.: Stanford University Press, 2009); and Ryan Goodman and Thomas Pegram, eds., *Human Rights, State Compliance, and Social Change: Assessing National Human Rights Institutions* (Cambridge: Cambridge University Press, 2012). See also Office of the United Nations High Commissioner for Human Rights, *National Human Rights Institutions: History, Principles, Roles and Responsibilities* (New York and Geneva: United Nations, 2010).

10. On human rights as a "site of struggle," see Alice M. Miller and Carole S. Vance, "Sexuality, Human Rights, and Health," *Health and Human Rights* 7, 2 (2004): 5–15.

11. See Rudra Sil and Peter J. Katzenstein, "Analytic Eclecticism in the Study of World Politics: Reconfiguring Problems and Mechanisms across Research Traditions," *Perspectives on Politics* 8 (2010): 411–31. Also Sil and Katzenstein, *Beyond Paradigms: Analytic Eclecticism in the Study of World Politics* (New York: Palgrave Macmillan, 2010).

12. UN General Assembly, "Strengthening of the United Nations: An Agenda for Further Change" (A/57/387, report of the secretary-general, September 9, 2002), para. 50, p. 12.

13. United Nations, "Report of the Secretary-General on National Institutions for the Promotion and Protection of Human Rights" (E/CN.4/1997/41, Fifty-Second Session of the UN Commission on Human Rights, 1997).

14. "Address by United Nations High Commissioner for Human Rights at the Workshop on the Role of the National Institutions in the Promotion and Protection

of Human Rights in Line with Paris Principles: Challenges, Achievements and Aspirations for the Gulf Cooperation Council (GCC) States" (Doha, Qatar, April 20, 2010), http://www.ohchr.org/.

15. "The Road to Rights: Establishing a Domestic Human Rights Institution in the United States" (report, Global Exchange on National Human Rights Commissions at the Rockefeller Foundation Center, Bellagio, Italy, August 2–6, 2010); Columbia Law School, Human Rights Institute and International Association of Official Human Rights Agencies, "State and Local Human Rights Agencies: Recommendations for Advancing Opportunity and Equality through an International Human Rights Framework" (n.d.); Shubhankar Dam, "Lessons from National Human Rights Institutions around the World for State and Local Human Rights Commissions in the United States," Executive Session Papers: Human Rights Commissions and Criminal Justice (Harvard University, Kennedy School of Government, Cambridge, Mass., August 2007); Kenneth L. Saunders and Hyo Eun (April) Mang, "A Historical Perspective on U.S. Human Rights Commissions," ed. Marea L. Beeman, Executive Session Papers: Human Rights Commissions and Criminal Justice (Harvard University, Kennedy School of Government, Cambridge, Mass., June 2007).

16. Sonia Cardenas, "Transgovernmental Activism: Canada's Role in Promoting National Human Rights Commissions," *Human Rights Quarterly* 25, 3 (2003): 775–90; Jeong-Woo Koo and Francisco O. Ramirez, "National Incorporation of Global Human Rights: Worldwide Expansion of National Human Rights Institutions, 1966–2004," *Social Forces* 87 (2009): 1321–54; Pegram, "Diffusion across Political Systems"; Chris Sidoti, "National Human Rights Institutions and the International Human Rights System," in Goodman and Pegram, *Human Rights, State Compliance, and Social Change.*

17. See especially Guillermo O'Donnell, "Horizontal Accountability in New Democracies," in Andreas Schedler, Larry Diamond, and Marc F. Plattner, eds., *The Self-Restraining State: Power and Accountability in New Democracies* (Boulder, Colo.: Lynne Rienner, 1999), 38.

18. Christopher S. Elmendorf, "Advisory Counterparts to Constitutional Courts," *Duke Law Journal* 56, 4 (February 2007): 953–1045.

19. Anne-Marie Slaughter, *A New World Order* (Princeton, N.J.: Princeton University Press, 2004); and Slaughter, "The Real New World Order," *Foreign Affairs* 76 (September/October 1997): 183–97.

20. For example, Li-Ann Thio, "Panacea, Placebo, or Pawn? The Teething Problems of the Human Rights Commission of Malaysia (SUHAKAM)," *George Washington International Law Review* 40, 4 (2009): 1271–1342; and Human Rights Watch, *Protectors or Pretenders? Government Human Rights Commissions in Africa* (New York: Human Rights Watch, 2001).

21. Cardenas, "Emerging Global Actors"; Brian Burdekin and Anne Gallagher, "The United Nations and National Human Rights Institutions," in Gudmundur Alfredsson, Jonas Grimheden, Bertrand G. Ramcharan, and Alfred de Zayas, eds., *International Human Rights Monitoring Mechanisms: Essays in Honour of Jakob Th. Möller* (The Hague: Kluwer, 2001), 815–25; Anna-Elina Pohjolainen, *The Evolution of National Human Rights Institutions: The Role of the United Nations* (Copenhagen: Danish Institute for Human Rights, 2006).

22. The fifteen states are Bahamas, Bhutan, Brunei Darussalem, China, Cuba, Israel, Japan, Kiribati, Laos, Marshall Islands, North Korea, Singapore, St. Vincent and the Grenadines, the United States, and Vietnam. This assessment, reviewed in subsequent chapters, reflects material from the first full round of the Universal Periodic Review, 2006–11. UPR documents can be accessed at http://www.ohchr.org.

23. See Cardenas, "Adaptive States."

24. Excluding the criteria that make an NHRI effective from the NHRI's definition is also important for avoiding circularity.

25. One UN survey found 58 percent of NHRI respondents to be human rights commissions. United Nations, Office of the High Commissioner for Human Rights, "Survey on National Human Rights Institutions" (report on the findings and recommendations of a questionnaire addressed to NHRIs worldwide, Geneva, July 2009), 9. In Europe, where ombudsmen abound and are not always viewed as NHRIs, the term "national human rights structure" is gaining ground. Reif, "The Shifting Boundaries of NHRI Definition in the International System," in Goodman and Pegram, *Human Rights, State Compliance, and Social Change.*

26. See generally Ann Abraham, "The Future in International Perspective: The Ombudsman as Agent of Rights, Justice and Democracy," *Parliamentary Affairs* 61, 4 (2008): 681–93; Harley Johnson, "Ombudsman—Essential Elements," in Hossain et al., *Human Rights Commissions and Ombudsman Offices*; Gerald E. Caiden, Niall Macdermot, and Ake Sandler, "The Institution of Ombudsman," and I. E. Nebenzahl, "The Direct and Indirect Impact of the Ombudsman," both in Gerald E. Caiden, ed., *International Handbook of the Ombudsman: Evolution and Present Function* (Westport, Conn.: Greenwood, 1983); and Hing Yong Cheng, "The Emergence and Spread of the Ombudsman Institution," *Annals of the American Academy of Political and Social Science* 377 (May 1968): 20–30. For the intersections with NHRI, see Reif, *The Ombudsman*; and Linda Reif, "Transplantation and Adaptation: The Evolution of the Human Rights Ombudsman," *Boston College Third World Journal* 31, 2 (2011): 269–310. See also Defensor del Pueblo, *The Book of the Ombudsman* (Madrid: Defensor del Pueblo, 2003), 180–95.

27. "Principles Relating to the Status of National Institutions" (hereafter Paris Principles) (UN General Assembly Resolution 48/134, December 20, 1993).

28. On the Canadian Commission, see, for example, John Hucker, "Antidiscrimination Laws in Canada: Human Rights Commissions and the Search for Equity," *Human Rights Quarterly* 19 (1997): 547–71.

29. UN Economic and Social Council, "The Role of National Human Rights Institutions in the Protection of Economic, Social, and Cultural Rights" (E/C.12/1998/25, December 10, 1998).

30. These dual functions are based on the distinction between regulative and constitutive types of norms. For the application of this distinction in international relations, see David Dessler, "What's at Stake in the Agent-Structure Debate?," *International Organization* 43 (Summer 1989): 454–58; and Friedrich Kratochwil, *Rules, Norms, and Decisions: On the Conditions of Practical and Legal Reasoning in International Relations and Domestic Affairs* (Cambridge: Cambridge University Press, 1989). I first discussed these categories in Cardenas, "Adaptive States."

31. The remainder of this section draws on Cardenas, "Emerging Global Actors: The United Nationas and National Human Rights Institutions," *Global Governance* 9, 1 (2003): 125–27, copyright © 2003 by Lynne Rienner Publishers, Inc., by permission of the publisher. On national human rights action plans, see Sergio Pinheiro and David Carlos Baluarte, "National Strategies—Human Rights Commissions, Ombudsmen, and National Action Plans" (background paper for *Human Development Report*, 2000).

32. In discussing regulatory functions, I have relied partly on John Hatchard's useful survey of national human rights commissions in the Commonwealth. Hatchard, "National Human Rights Commissions in the Commonwealth" (background paper, Conference on Commonwealth Human Rights Initiative, Institute for Public Policy Research, London, October 16–17, 1997).

33. On institutionalism in international relations, see, for example, R. A. W. Rhodes, Sarah A. Binder, and Bert A. Rockman, eds., *The Oxford Handbook of Political Institutions* (New York: Oxford University Press, 2006), especially Elizabeth Sanders, "Historical Institutionalism," 39–55; John L. Campbell, *Institutional Change and Globalization* (Princeton, N.J.: Princeton University Press, 2004); and Robert O. Keohane and Lisa L. Martin, "Institutional Theory as a Research Program," in Colin Elman and Miriam Fendius Elman, eds., *Progress in International Relations Theory: Appraising the Field* (Cambridge, Mass.: MIT Press, 2001), 71–108.

34. See in particular Beth A. Simmons, Frank Dobbin, and Geoffrey Garrett, eds., *The Global Diffusion of Markets and Democracy* (Cambridge: Cambridge University Press, 2008).

35. E.g., Paul Pierson, "When Effect Becomes Cause: Policy Feedback and Political Change," *World Politics* 45, 4 (July 1993): 595–628.

36. The UPR was started by the new Human Rights Council in 2006, representing a system of regular review of all states' human rights records. By the end of 2011, all of the world's states had been reviewed. A review requires that states submit a comprehensive report, along with one prepared by the United Nations and one submitted by stakeholders. The Human Rights Council submits a final assessment, including a set of recommendations, to which states must respond. See www.upr-info .org for overview and statistics.

37. On treating the use of (historical) narratives as data and evidence, see Tim Büthe, "Taking Temporality Seriously: Modeling History and the Use of Narratives as Evidence," *American Political Science Review* 96, 3 (2002): 481–93.

38. Reif, *The Ombudsman*; and Hossain et al., *Human Rights Commissions and Ombudsman Offices*.

Chapter 2

1. Samuel Moyn makes a similar point about human rights generally. Moyn, *The Last Utopia: Human Rights in History* (Cambridge, Mass.: Belknap, 2010).

2. I borrow here and in the first section from my essay "Human Rights and the State, 3518–20."

3. See, for example, Upendra Baxi, *Human Rights in a Posthuman World: Critical Essays* (Oxford: Oxford University Press, 2009); Makau Mutua, *Human Rights: A Political and Cultural Critique* (Philadelphia: University of Pennsylvania Press, 2008); and Costas Douzinas, *Human Rights and Empire: The Political Philosophy of Cosmopolitanism* (New York: Routledge, 2007).

4. Jack Donnelly, *Universal Human Rights in Theory and Practice*, 2nd ed. (Ithaca, N.Y.: Cornell University Press, 2003); David Held, *Political Theory and the Modern State: Essays on State, Power, and Democracy* (Stanford, Calif.: Stanford University Press, 1989); and R. J. Vincent, *Human Rights and International Relations* (New York: Cambridge University Press, 1986).

5. Rhoda E. Howard and Jack Donnelly, "Human Dignity, Human Rights and Political Regimes," *American Political Science Review* 80, 3 (1986): 801–17.

6. R. Nordahl, "A Marxian Approach to Human Rights," in Abdullahi Ahmed An-Na'im, eds., *Human Rights in Cross-Cultural Perspectives: A Quest for Consensus* (Philadelphia: University of Pennsylvania Press, 1995), 162–87.

7. Y. Barzel, *A Theory of the State: Economic Rights, Legal Rights, and the Scope of the State* (Cambridge: Cambridge University Press, 2002); Charles Tilly, *Coercion, Capital, and European States AD 990–1992* (Malden, Mass.: Blackwell, 1992).

8. A. Svensson-McCarthy, *The International Law of Human Rights and States of Exception* (The Hague: Martinus Nijhoff, 1998); G. Agamben, *State of Exception*, trans. K. Attell (Chicago: University of Chicago Press, 2005).

9. See Perry Anderson, *Lineages of the Absolutist State* (London: Verso, 1979); Lynn Hunt, *Inventing Human Rights: A History* (New York: Norton, 2007); J. M. Headley, *The Europeanization of the World: On the Origins of Human Rights and Democracy* (Princeton, N.J.: Princeton University Press, 2007); M. R. Ishay, *The History of Human Rights: From Ancient Times to the Globalization Era* (Berkeley: University of California Press, 2004).

10. James Ron, "Varying Methods of State Violence," *International Organization* 51, 2 (1997): 275–300.

11. Hannah Arendt, *The Origins of Totalitarianism* (New York: Harcourt, Brace and World, 1996); and Seyla Benhabib, *The Rights of Others: Aliens, Residents and Citizens* (Cambridge: Cambridge University Press, 2004).

12. Upendra Baxi, "Politics of Reading Human Rights: Inclusion and Exclusion within the Production of Human Rights," in S. Meckled-García and B. Cali, eds., *The Legalization of Human Rights: Multidisciplinary Perspectives on Human Rights and Human Rights Law* (New York: Routledge, 2006), 182–200.

13. Stephen D. Krasner coined the term "organized hypocrisy" in international relations. Krasner, *Sovereignty: Organized Hypocrisy* (Princeton, N.J.: Princeton University Press, 1999).

14. Michael Ignatieff, ed., *American Exceptionalism and Human Rights* (Princeton, N.J.: Princeton University Press, 2005); and Julie Mertus, *Bait and Switch: Human Rights and US Foreign Policy*, 2nd ed. (New York: Routledge, 2008).

15. See especially Reif, *The Ombudsman*, 7–12.

16. Caiden, Macdermot, and Sandler, "Institution of Ombudsman," 4.

17. See generally Chapter 1, note 26; as well as Caiden, Macdermot, and Sandler, "Institution of Ombudsman."

18. A brief historical illustration suggests how power rivalries may be important for understanding the ombudsman. Sweden's first ombudsman in 1809 was created by parliament and mentioned in the country's constitution that year. Recognized as the world's first ombudsman, the 1809 institution actually borrowed its name and underlying premise from a similar institution created in Sweden a century earlier. In 1713, Sweden's King Charles XII created, while in exile in Turkey, a Supreme Ombudsman, renamed in 1719 the Chancellor of Justice; over the next century, this institution was part of the executive or the parliament depending on shifting power relations. In 1809, a parliamentary version of the Chancellor of Justice was created, with the Chancellor remaining a separate entity, still in existence today. Frank Orton, *The Birth of the Ombudsman* (Sarajevo: Human Rights Ombudsman of Bosnia and Herzegovina, June 2001). A few additional details are worth noting. Apparently, the name "ombudsman" was selected after much deliberation, since no existing word captured the exact meaning of the institution. "Ombudsman" itself is from the Old Norse *umbodhsmadr*, meaning "man of commission," while a Danish law from 1241 also referred to *umbozma*, denoting a royal civil servant at the local level; in both cases, the ombudsman was a representative of the ruler. The idea for the institution, moreover, was borrowed from Ottoman administration and had long existed in Islamic law (*Qadi al-Qadat*, found in sharia, is the idea that in a decentralized administration, a central figure is able to spot wrongdoing and hold everyone responsible, including the ruler). For a concise summary, see Reif, *The Ombudsman*, 4–5; and Caiden, Macdermot, and Sandler, "Institution of Ombudsman," 9–10.

19. Elmendorf, "Advisory Counterparts to Constitutional Courts."

20. Joshua Toulmin Smith, *Government by Commissions: Illegal and Pernicious* (London: S. Sweet, 1849).

21. Napoleon's Consultative Commission followed the 1851 coup. See the 1877 account by Victor Hugo, "The Consultative Commission," in *History of a Crime* (Rockville, Md.: Wildside Press, 2007), pt. 2, chap. 6, 43–49.

22. On local human rights commissions in the United States, see Chapter 1, note 15. Also Risa E. Kaufman, "State and Local Commissions as Sites for Domestic Human Rights Implementation," in Shareen Hertel and Kathryn Libal, eds., *Human Rights in the United States: Beyond Exceptionalism* (Cambridge: Cambridge University Press, 2010), 89–110; and Angela Arboleda and Robin Toma, "Strengthening Relations between Local Police and Immigrant Communities: The Role for Human Rights Commission," Executive Session Papers: Human Rights Commissions and Criminal Justice (Harvard University, Kennedy School of Government, Cambridge, Mass., June 2008). The IAOHRA can be accessed at www.iaohra.org.

23. See more broadly Cynthia Soohoo, Catherine Albisa, and Martha F. Davis, eds., *Bringing Human Rights Home: A History of Human Rights in the United States*, 3 vols. (New York: Praeger, 2007).

24. For the dynamics of race riots, see Ann V. Collins, *All Hell Broke Loose: American Race Relations from the Progressive Era through World War II* (New York: Praeger, 2012); Jan Voogd, *Race Riots and Resistance: The Red Summer of 1919* (New York: Peter Lang, 2008); David Fort Goodshalk, *Veiled Visions: The 1906 Atlanta Race Riot and the Reshaping of American Race Relations* (Chapel Hill: University of North Carolina Press, 2005); James S. Hirsch, *Riot and Remembrance: America's*

Worst Race Riot and Its Legacy (New York: Houghton Mifflin, 2003); and Allen D. Grimshaw, ed., *A Social History of Race Relations* (New Brunswick, N.J.: Transaction, 1969).

25. This body brought together both novices and long-standing activists; most were Christians, and a religious discourse clearly framed the project. Each committee consisted of a "small group of not over six to ten white and Negro leaders as a permanent committee of counsel and cooperation." George Madden Martin, "Race Cooperation," *McClure's* 54, 8 (October 1922): 13. The committees were to cooperate with public government agencies to gain concrete improvements in race relations—from boards administering education to health agencies to even sewage service. George Madden Martin was the pen name of a southern female author and social activist; in her home state of Kentucky, she was a member of the interracial commission and led the Association of Southern Women for the Prevention of Lynching. See Martin, "Rights of Man," *Harper's* 106 (February 1903): 415–23.

26. Local committees would be complemented by a state-level interracial committee, often with government cooperation. Government participation took various forms, including funding, promotion, and membership by state officials on the state committee. The Commission on Inter-Racial Cooperation—an overarching body of local and state interracial committees—was headquartered in Atlanta, where the first local committee had formed. Earlier, this body was known as the Southern Commission on Inter-Racial Cooperation. On the Commission on Inter-Racial Cooperation, see Gunnar Myrdal (with Sissela Bok), *The American Dilemma: The Negro Problem and Modern Democracy*, 7th printing, vol. 2 (1944; repr., New Brunswick, N.J.: Transaction, 2009), 842–50. Also Edward Flud Burrows, *The Commission on Interracial Cooperation, 1919–1944: A Case Study in the History of the Interracial Movement in the South* (Madison: University of Wisconsin, 1954).

27. For example, of the fifty-eight members of the Southern Commission, only five were African Americans.

28. "Fair Play for the Negro," *New York Times*, September 26, 1922.

29. The Connecticut Commission was also a response to the beating of a Hartford pastor by white supremacists while on a train traveling through Alabama. Stacey Close, "Fire in the Bones: Hartford's NAACP, Civil Rights and Militancy, 1943–1969," *Journal of Negro History* 86, 3 (Summer 2001): 228–63. See also Gerald Benjamin, *Race Relations and the New York City Commission on Human Rights* (Ithaca, N.Y.: Cornell University Press, 1974).

30. Neil R. McMillen, *Remaking Dixie: The Impact of World War II on the American South* (Jackson: University Press of Mississippi, 1997), 87.

31. A young Martin Luther King, Jr. says in his autobiography, "After that summer in Connecticut, it was a bitter feeling going back to segregation." Martin Luther King, Jr., *The Autobiography of Martin Luther King, Jr.* (New York: Grand Central, 2001); and http://mlkinsimsbury.org.

32. U.S. President's Committee on Civil Rights, "To Secure These Rights" (chapter 4, Executive Order 9981, 1947). See also Azza Salama Layton, *International Politics and Civil Rights Policies in the United States* (New York: Cambridge University Press, 2000).

33. The South Carolina Human Affairs Commission was created in 1972.

34. Southern Regional Council, "SRC History Timeline 1919–2000," http://www.southerncouncil.org/history.html. For the rise of human rights discourse during this period, see Thomas F. Jackson, *From Civil Rights to Human Rights: Martin Luther King, Jr., and the Struggle for Economic Justice* (Philadelphia: University of Pennsylvania Press, 2007).

35. These were in Alabama, Arkansas, Georgia, Mississippi, and South Carolina.

36. Myrdal, *American Dilemma*, 847.

37. UN Economic and Social Council (ECOSOC), "Seventh Meeting of the Nuclear Commission on Human Rights, Hunter College, NY" (E/HR/15, May 10, 1946).

38. Pohjolainen, *Evolution of National Human Rights Institutions*, 31.

39. Ibid., 31.

40. "René Cassin," in Frederick W. Haberman, ed., *Nobel Lectures, Peace 1951–1970* (Amsterdam: Elsevier, 1972), 408–12.

41. ECOSOC Resolution 2/9 (June 21, 1946).

42. On Cassin, see Antoine Prost and Jay Winter, *René Cassin* (Paris: Rayard, 2011); Marc Agi, *René Cassin, fantassin des droits de l'homme* (Paris: Plon, 1979); and Eric Pateyron, *La contribution française à la rédaction de la Déclaration universelle des droits de l'homme: René Cassin et la Commission des Droits de l'Homme* (Paris: La Documenttion Française, 1998).

43. République Française, Commission Nationale Consultative des Droits de l'Homme, "Introduction" (Paris, n.d.), 4, available from the author.

44. Ibid., 3.

45. Ibid., nn3–4.

46. Christine Fauré, "Réflexions sur la Déclaration Universelle des Droits de l'Homme de 1948" (December 6, 2008), 3.

47. Moyn, *Last Utopia*, 11.

48. John Braithwaite, "The Regulatory State?," in Rhodes, Binder, and Rockman, *Oxford Handbook of Political Institutions*, 407–30.

Chapter 3

1. Beth Simmons and Z. Elkins, "On Waves, Clusters and Diffusion: A Conceptual Framework," *Annals of the American Academy of Political and Social Science* 598 (2005): 33–51; and Simmons, Dobbin, and Garrett, *Global Diffusion of Markets and Democracy*. Also Fabrizio Gilardi, "Transnational Diffusion: Norms, Ideas, and Policies," in Walter Carlsnaes, Thomas Risse, and Beth Simmons, eds., *Handbook of International Relations,* 2nd ed. (London: Sage, 2012), 453–77; as well as David Strang and John W. Meyer, "Institutional Conditions for Diffusion," *Theory and Society* 22, 4 (1993): 487–511; David Strang and Sarah A. Soule, "Diffusion in Organizations and Social Movements: From Hybrid Corn to Poison Pills," *Annual Review of Sociology* 24 (1998): 265–90; and Rebecca Kolins Givan, Kenneth M. Roberts, and Sarah A. Soule, eds., *The Diffusion of Social Movements: Actors, Mechanisms, and Political Effects* (Cambridge: Cambridge University Press, 2010). More broadly, Everett M. Rogers, *Diffusion of Innovations*, 5th ed. (New York: Free Press, 2005). For NHRIs, see Pegram, "Diffusion across Political Systems."

2. Stephen D. Krasner, "Structural Causes and Regime Consequences: Regimes as Intervening Variables," in Krasner, ed., *International Regimes* (Ithaca, N.Y.: Cornell University Press, 1983), 1–21.

3. For example, Simmons and Elkins, "On Waves, Clusters and Diffusion."

4. In addition to ibid., see political applications of clustering in Halvard Buhaug and Kristian Skrede Gleditsch, "Contagion or Confusion? Why Conflicts Cluster in Space," *International Studies Quarterly* 52, 2 (2008): 215–33; selections in Simmons, Dobbin, and Garrett, *Global Diffusion of Markets and Democracy*, including Kristian Skrede Gleditsch and Michael D. Ward, "Diffusion and the Spread of Democratic Institutions," 261–302; also Kristian S. Gleditsch and Michael D. Ward, "Diffusion and the International Context of Democratization," *International Organization* 60, 4 (2006): 911–33.

5. The diffusion curve, in general, predicts a similar pattern: innovators 2.5 percent, early adopters 13.5 percent, early majority 34 percent, late majority 34 percent, laggards 16 percent. Rogers, *Diffusion of Innovations*.

6. There are 165 parliamentary human rights bodies in 109 countries, according to the PARLINE Database (www.ipu.org). The International Committee of the Red Cross (ICRC) reports 101 national committees for international humanitarian law, typically interagency bodies. ICRC, "Table of National Committees and Other National Bodies on International Humanitarian Law" (October 23, 2011), http://www.icrc.org. Interestingly, these institutions show a diffusion pattern similar to that of NHRIs, despite the more long-standing nature of international humanitarian law. Cardenas, "Adaptive States," 12–13.

7. In international relations, scholars have also pointed to "tipping cascades" and "norm cascades" as similar phenomena. See, for example, Kathryn Sikkink, *The Justice Cascade: How Human Rights Prosecutions Are Changing World Politics* (New York: Norton, 2011); and Ellen Lutz and Kathryn Sikkink, "International Human Rights Law and Practice in Latin America," *International Organization* 54, 3 (2000): 633–59.

8. The classic work on international human rights regimes is Jack Donnelly, "International Human Rights: A Regime Analysis," *International Organization* 40, 3 (Summer 1986): 599–642; for an update, see Donnelly, *International Human Rights* (Boulder, Colo.: Westview, 2012), chaps. 5 and 6. See also Emilie Hafner-Burton, "International Regimes for Human Rights," *Annual Review of Political Science* 15 (June 2012): 265–86; and for widely cited region-specific work, Andrew Moravcsik, "Explaining International Human Rights Regimes: Liberal Theory and Western Europe," *European Journal of International Relations* 1, 2 (June 1995): 157–80, and Tom J. Farer, "The Rise of the Inter-American Human Rights Regime: No Longer a Unicorn, Not Yet an Ox," *Human Rights Quarterly* 19, 3 (August 1997): 510–46.

9. On transnational advocacy networks, Margaret E. Keck and Kathryn Sikkink, *Activists Beyond Borders: Advocacy Networks in International Politics* (Ithaca, N.Y.: Cornell University Press, 1998).

10. Donnelly, "International Human Rights: A Regime Analysis."

11. ECOSOC, Resolution 9 (II) (June 21, 1946). A brief historical background on NHRIs can be found in United Nations, *United Nations Action in the Field of Human Rights* (New York: United Nations, 1983), 344–45.

12. ECOSOC Resolution 772 B (XXX) (July 25, 1960); ECOSOC Resolution 888 F (XXXIV) (July 24, 1962); and UN General Assembly Resolution 2200 C (XXI) (December 16, 1966).

13. Moyn, *Last Utopia*. The remainder of this section draws from Cardenas, "Emerging Global Actors: The United Nations and Human Rights Institutions," *Global Governance* 9, 1 (2003): 28–29, copyright © 2003 by Lynne Rienner Publishers, Inc., by permission of the publisher.

14. Letter from the Representative to the UN Commission on Human Rights (Tree) to Secretary of State Rusk, New York, May 14, 1962, National Archives and Records Administration, RG 59, Central Files 1960–63, 341.7/5–1462. For U.S. opposition to the creation of a UN Commissioner for Human Rights, see, for example, Memorandum from the Director of the Office of United Nations Political Affairs (Sisco) to the Deputy Assistant Secretary of State for International Organization Affairs (Gardner), Washington, D.C., 4 September 1963. National Archives and Records Administration, RG 59, Central Files 1960–63, SOC 14 ECOSOC.

15. UN General Assembly, "National Institutions for the Promotion and Protection of Human Rights" (UN General Assembly Resolution A/RES/33/46, December 14, 1978).

16. UN General Assembly Resolution 41/129 (December 1986) was perhaps the most important UN statement in the 1980s.

17. Term used by Louis Joinet, chairman of the UN Working Group on Arbitrary Detention, at the second annual workshop on NHRIs (Tunis, December 1993). UN General Assembly, "Human Rights Questions."

18. UN General Assembly, "Vienna Declaration and Programme of Action" (UN General Assembly Resolution A/CONF.157/23, July 12, 1993), para. 36.

19. This section draws on Sonia Cardenas, "Sovereignty Transformed? The Role of National Human Rights Institutions," in Noha Shawki and Michaelene Cox, eds., *Negotiating Sovereignty and Human Rights: Actors and Issues in Contemporary Human Rights Politics* (Farnham: Ashgate, 2009), 27–40. The World Conference on Human Rights was held in Vienna between July 14 and 25, 1993. For assessments of the World Conference, see Ann Marie Clark, Elizabeth J. Friedman, and Kathryn Hochstetler, "The Sovereign Limits of Global Civil Society: A Comparison of NGO Participation in U.N. World Conferences," *World Politics* 51, 1 (October 1998): 1–35; Kevin Boyle, "Stock-Taking on Human Rights: The World Conference on Human Rights, Vienna 1993," *Political Studies* 43, 1 (August 1995): 79–95; and Donna J. Sullivan, "Women's Human Rights and the 1993 World Conference on Human Rights," *American Journal of International Law* 88 (January 1994): 152–67.

20. United Nations, "Vienna Declaration," para. 36.

21. Paris Principles.

22. Cardenas, "Sovereignty Transformed?"

23. See Linda Reif, "The Shifting Boundaries of NHRI Definition in the International System," in Goodman and Pegram, *Human Rights, State Compliance, and Social Change*.

24. See Geraldine van Bueren, *The International Law on the Rights of the Child* (The Hague: Martinus Nijhoff, 1998).

25. Mario Gomez, "Social Economic Rights and Human Rights Commissions," *Human Rights Quarterly* 17, 1 (February 1995): 155–69; and C. R. Kumar, "National Human Rights Institutions (NHRIs) and Economic, Social and Cultural Rights: Toward the Institutionalization and Developmentalization of Human Rights," *Human Rights Quarterly* 28, 3 (August 2006): 755–79.

26. On some of these broader linkages, see Thomas W. Pogge, *World Poverty and Human Rights*, 2nd ed. (Cambridge: Polity, 2008); Philip Alston and Mary Robinson, eds., *Human Rights and Development: Towards Mutual Reinforcement* (Oxford: Oxford University Press, 2005); and Paul Farmer, *Pathologies of Power: Health, Human Rights, and the New War on the Poor* (Berkeley: University of California Press, 2003).

27. UN General Assembly, "National Institutions for the Promotion and Protection of Human Rights" (A/56/255, report of the secretary-general, August 1, 2001); Burdekin and Gallagher, "United Nations and National Human Rights Institutions"; Danish Centre for Human Rights, "Support for Emerging and Developing National Human Rights Institutions" (n.d.); and Cardenas, "Emerging Global Actors."

28. From the mid-1950s, UN human rights assistance took the form of "advisory services." This program provided experts, funded fellowships, and organized human rights seminars. See United Nations, "Fact Sheet No. 3 (Rev. 1), Advisory Services and Technical Cooperation in the Field of Human Rights" (Geneva: United Nations, August 1996).

29. ECOSOC, "Advisory Services in the Field of Human Rights: Technical Cooperation in the Field of Human Rights" (E/CN.4/1998/92, report of the secretary-general, March 3, 1998).

30. See UN General Assembly, Resolution 48/134 (December 20, 1993).

31. See C. Raj Kumar, "National Human Rights Institutions: Good Governance Perspectives on Institutionalization of Human Rights," *American University International Law Review* 19, 2 (2003): 259–300.

32. Cardenas, "Emerging Global Actors," 784–77.

33. See Noha Shawki, "A New Actor in Human Rights Politics? Transgovernmental Networks of NHRIs," in Shawki and Cox, eds., *Negotiating Sovereignty and Human Rights*; and Cardenas, "Sovereignty Transformed?"

34. These included Tunis (1993), Manila (1995), Merida, Mexico (1997), and Marrakesh (2000), Copenhagen and Lund (2002), Seoul (2004), Santa Cruz, Bolivia (2006), Nairobi (2008), Edinburgh (2010), and Amman (2012).

35. See "International Coordinating Committee of National Institutions for the Promotion and Protection of Human Rights (ICC)," available at http://nhri.ohchr.org.

36. Irish Human Rights Commission, "European Group of NHRIs," www.ihrc.ie.

37. Catherine Renshaw and Kieren Fitzpatrick, "National Human Rights Institutions in the Asia Pacific Region: Change Agents under Conditions of Uncertainty," in Goodman and Pegram, *Human Rights, State Compliance, and Social Change*; Andrea Durbach, Catherine Renshaw, and Andrew Byrnes, " 'A Tongue but No Teeth'? The Emergence of a Regional Human Rights Mechanism in the Asia Pacific," *Sydney Law Review* 31, 2 (2009): 211–38; Andrew Byrnes, Andrea

Durbach, and Catherine Renshaw, "Joining the Club: The Asia Pacific Forum of National Human Rights Institutions, the Paris Principles, and the Advancement of Human Rights Protection in the Region," *Australian Journal of Human Rights* 14, 1 (2008): 63–98; Brian Burdekin, *National Human Rights Institutions in the Asia-Pacific Region* (Leiden: Martinus Nijhoff, 2007); and Kieren Fitzpatrick, "The Asia Pacific Forum: A Partnership for Regional Human Rights Cooperation," in Birgit Lindsnaes, Lone Lindholt, and Kristine Yigen, eds., *National Human Rights Institutions: Articles and Working Papers* (Copenhagen: Danish Centre for Human Rights, 2001), 141–48.

38. Staff, Danish Institute for Human Rights, interview, June 2006.

39. Canadian Human Rights Commissions, *Annual Report* (1996).

40. The ICC Rules of Procedure adopted on April 15, 2000 are now part of the ICC Statute. The first Rules of Procedure of the ICC Sub-Committee on Accreditation date to September 2004. ICC reports and records are posted on the UN's NHRI portal: www.nhri.ohchr.org.

41. UN General Assembly, "National Institutions for the Promotion and Protection of Human Rights" (A/54/336, report of the secretary-general, September 9, 1999).

42. See Sidoti, "National Human Rights Institutions."

43. For early assessments of the UPR process, see Lawrence C. Moss, "Opportunities for Nongovernmental Advocacy in the Universal Review Process at the UN Human Rights Council," *Journal of Human Rights Practice* 2, 1 (2010): 122–50; Matthew Davies, "Rhetorical Inaction? Compliance and the Human Rights Council of the United Nations," *Alternatives: Global, Local, Political* 35, 4 (October 2010): 449–68; Elvira Dominguez Redondo, "The Universal Periodic Review of the UN Human Rights Council: An Assessment of the First Session," *Chinese Journal of International Law* 7, 3 (2008): 721–34; and Felice D. Gaer, "A Voice Not an Echo: Universal Periodic Review and the UN Treaty Body System," *Human Rights Law Review* 7, 1 (2007): 109–39.

44. See Amrei Müller and Frauke Seidensticker, *The Role of National Human Rights Institutions in the United Nations Treaty Body Process* (Berlin: German Institute for Human Rights, December 2007). On the role of NHRIs as national preventive mechanisms for OPCAT, see NHRI Torture Prevention and Response Project, http://nhritortureprevention.org.

45. Sidoti, "National Human Rights Institutions."

46. Ibid., 120.

47. On institutional nesting, see generally Vinod K. Aggarwal, ed., *Institutional Designs for a Complex World: Bargaining, Linkages, and Nesting* (Ithaca, N.Y.: Cornell University Press, 1998).

48. See Byrnes, Durbach, and Renshaw, "Joining the Club."

49. In describing the role of UNESCO, Martha Finnemore recounts how national science policies were "supplied" by UNESCO more than they were "demanded" by domestic constituencies. There are interesting parallels with the international promotion of NHRIs. See Martha Finnemore, "International Organizations as Teachers of Norms: The United Nations Educational, Scientific, and Cultural Organization and

Science Policy," *International Organization* 47 (Autumn 1993): 565–97. I first raised this point in Cardenas, "Adaptive States," 54.

50. Sidoti, "National Human Rights Institutions."

Chapter 4

1. Václav Havel et al., *The Power of the Powerless: Citizens against the State in Central-Eastern Europe* (London: Hutchinson, 1985), 27.

2. For a similar argument, see Mark Goodale and Sally Engle Merry, eds., *The Practice of Human Rights: Tracking Law between the Global and the Local* (Cambridge: Cambridge University Press, 2007).

3. Sonia Cardenas, "State Compliance and National Human Rights Institutions," in Goodman and Pegram, *National Human Rights Institutions, State Compliance, and Social Change*, 29–51.

4. Byrnes, Durbach, and Renshaw, "Joining the Club."

5. The most succinct overview of these mechanisms in international relations is presented in Beth A. Simmons, Frank Dobbin, and Geoffrey Garrett, "Introduction: The Diffusion of Liberalization," in Simmons, Dobbin, and Garrett, *Global Diffusion of Markets and Democracy*, 1–63. See also Gilardi, "Transnational Diffusion"; and for a concrete application of multiple diffusion mechanisms at work, Witold J. Henisz, Bennet A. Zelner, and Mauro F. Guillen, "The Worldwide Diffusion of Market-Oriented Infrastructure Reform, 1977–1999," *American Sociological Review* 70, 6 (2005): 871–97.

6. For the close linkages between competition and the diffusion of economic ideas and institutions, see Simmons, Dobbin, and Garrett, *Global Diffusion of Markets and Democracy*, including Zachary Elkins, Andrew T. Guzman, and Beth A. Simmons, "Competing for Capital: The Diffusion of Bilateral Investment Treaties, 1960–2000," 220–60.

7. For a "world society" (social emulation) perspective on the diffusion of international human rights norms, see Christine Min Wotipka and Francisco O. Ramirez, "World Society and Human Rights: An Event History Analysis of the Convention on the Elimination of All Forms of Discrimination against Women," in Simmons, Dobbin, and Garrett, *Global Diffusion of Markets and* Democracy, 303–43. In the case of NHRIs, Koo and Ramirez, "National Incorporation of Global Human Rights." More broadly, Ryan Goodman and Derek Jinks, "How to Influence States: Socialization and International Human Rights Law," *Duke Law Journal* 54, 3 (December 2004): 621–703. For studies of NHRIs that take seriously the domestic context, see Carver, "New Answer to an Old Question"; and Mertus, *Human Rights Matters*.

8. For similar notions of regulation and power, see works by Michel Foucault, especially *Discipline and Punish: The Birth of the Prison*, 2nd ed. (1977; repr., New York: Random House, 1995), e.g., "The regulation imposed by power is at the same time the law of construction of the operation" (153).

9. On state regulation generally, Braithwaite, "The Regulatory State?" The self-restraining state is discussed in Schedler, Diamond, and Plattner, *Self-Restraining State*. A related line of inquiry concerns the relationship between bureaucracy and demo-

cratic governance. For a relevant review, see Johan P. Olsen, "The Ups and Downs of Bureaucratic Organization," *Annual Review of Political Science* 11 (2008): 13–37.

10. See especially William E. Connolly, *Politics and Ambiguity* (Madison: University of Wisconsin Press, 1987). Also, James Mahoney and Kathleen Thelen, *Explaining Institutional Change: Ambiguity, Agency, and Power* (New York: Cambridge University Press, 2009). For interesting applications in international political economy, Jacqueline Best, *The Limits of Transparency: Ambiguity and the History of International Finance* (Ithaca, N.Y.: Cornell University Press, 2005) and Benjamin J. Cohen, "The International Monetary System: Diffusion and Ambiguity," *International Affairs* 84, 3 (May 2008): 455–70. On peacekeeping, Michael Lipson, "Performance under Ambiguity: International Organization Performance in UN Peacekeeping, *Review of International Organizations* 5, 3 (2010): 249–84.

11. The term "regulatory moment" has been used infrequently, though typically implying new opportunities for state transformation, e.g., Henk Overbeek, ed., *Restructuring Hegemony in the Global Political Economy: The Rise of Transnational Neo-Liberalism in the 1980s* (New York: Routledge, 1993), 28. I am instead adapting the term from the widely used notion of "constitutional moments," advanced by Bruce Ackerman, especially in Ackerman, *We the People: Foundations* (Cambridge, Mass.: Harvard University Press, 1991) and *We the People: Transformation* (Cambridge, Mass.: Harvard University Press, 2000). Regulatory moments, as I use the term, tend to be more formal than constitutional moments (even though they are embedded in the informal processes integral to constitutional moments) and norm ambiguity and strategic emulation feature centrally. Like constitutional moments, however, regulatory ones are "constitutive" of interests and identities, and they can represent instances of "punctuated equilibrium" in a broader process of institutional change.

12. For a related discussion of how political leaders in democratizing contexts look to lock in preferences and, in a self-binding mechanism, reduce future uncertainty by accepting international human rights agreements, see Andrew Moravcsik, "The Origins of International Human Rights Regimes: Democratic Delegation in Postwar Europe," *International Organization* 54, 2 (Spring 2000): 217–52. Locking in is also integral to path-dependent processes. For general discussions of the latter, see Paul Pierson, "Increasing Returns, Path Dependence, and the Study of Politics," *American Political Science Review* 94, 2 (2000): 251–67; as well as Georg Schreyögg and Jörg Sydow, *The Hidden Dynamics of Path Dependence: Institutions and Organizations* (New York: Palgrave Macmillan, 2010); Scott Page, "Path Dependence," *Quarterly Journal of Political Science* 1, 1 (2006): 87–115; Ian Greener, "The Potential of Path Dependence in Political Studies," *Politics* 25, 1 (2005): 62–72; and James Mahoney, "Path Dependence in Historical Sociology," *Theory and Society* 4, 4 (2000): 507–48.

13. Michelle Parlevliet, *National Human Rights Institutions and Peace Agreements: Establishing National Institutions in Divided Societies* (Geneva: International Council on Human Rights Policy, 2006).

14. Treaties are commonly portrayed as instances of international delegation, seemingly puzzling because of the potential loss of sovereignty. Andrew Moravcsik, in particular, has argued that state leaders are willing to delegate authority externally to reduce domestic uncertainty. Moravcsik, "Origins of International Human Rights Regimes." My claim is that implementing external obligations also creates problems

of domestic delegation. See, more generally, J. Bendor, A. Glazer, and T. Hammond, "Theories of Delegation," *Annual Review of Political Science* 4 (2001): 235–69.

15. See especially, Beth A. Simmons, *Mobilizing for Human Rights: International Law in Domestic Politics* (Cambridge: Cambridge University Press, 2009).

16. I adapt this term from Stephen Krasner's use of "organized hypocrisy." Krasner, *Sovereignty*.

17. Another study of international diffusion that emphasizes domestic incentives (albeit economic liberalization and political fragmentation) is Daniel R. Kelemen and Eric C. Sibbitt, "The Globalization of American Law," *International Organization* 58, 1 (2004): 103–36. Contrary to my argument, however, Kelemen and Sibbitt treat diffusion as a spurious outcome, reflecting domestic factors rather than processes of international competition or emulation. In my argument, domestic conditions provide norm promoters with structural openings.

18. In related fashion, David Marsh and J. C. Sharman discuss how the literature on diffusion tends to be structural, whereas research on policy transfer tends to be agent centered; they call for greater fusion. See Marsh and Sharman, "Policy Diffusion and Policy Transfer," *Policy Studies* 30, 3 (2009): 269–88. For a relevant discussion of how international regime actors promote domestic institution building, see Finnemore, "International Organizations as Teachers of Norms." And for how diffusion can be cause as much as consequence, see Detlef Jahn, "Globalization as 'Galton's Problem': The Missing Link in the Analysis of Diffusion Patterns in Welfare State Development," *International Organization* 60 (2006): 402–31; more generally, Pierson, "When Effect Becomes Cause."

19. On the importance of cultural linkages for diffusion, see Strang and Meyer, "Institutional Conditions for Diffusion." The role of Europeanization (including conditionality) is discussed in Walter Mattli and Thomas Plumper, "The Internal Value of External Options: How the EU Shapes the Scope of Regulatory Reforms in Transition Countries," *European Union Politics* 5, 3 (2004): 307–30. For diffusion among trading partners, see Brian Greenhill, Layna Mosley, and Aseem Prakash, "Trade-Based Diffusion of Labor Rights: A Panel Study, 1986–2002," *American Political Science Review* 103, 4 (2009): 669–90.

20. E.g., Emilie Hafner-Burton and James Ron, "Seeing Double: Human Rights Impact through Qualitative and Quantitative Eyes," *World Politics* 61, 2 (April 2009): 360–64.

21. For how the stages of diffusion can matter, see, for example, Jacint Jordana, David Levi-Faur, and Xavier Fernandez Marin, "The Global Diffusion of Regulatory Agencies: Channels of Transfer and Stages of Diffusion," *Comparative Political Studies* 44 (2011): 1343–69.

22. Settling on a date of institutional creation is not as straightforward as it may seem, and existing efforts to collect systematic data on NHRIs have not tended to adopt explicit criteria, leading to datasets that are internally inconsistent and of limited comparative value. When classifying the year when an NHRI was created, I focus on foundational documents (e.g., constitutional inclusion, presidential decree, legislative act). I treat the year in which the institution began operating as a distinct point. I do not include the year when political leaders first mentioned the idea of creating an NHRI, though I address this and other related issues in the case narra-

tives. Likewise, I include institutional precursors to current NHRIs only when these represent clear and uninterrupted name changes. Country-specific details are discussed in the case chapters.

23. In this chapter and throughout the book, I rely on accreditation data from the International Coordinating Committee of National Institutions for the Promotion and Protection of Human Rights, especially the "Chart of the Status of National Institutions" (http://www.ohchr.org).

24. For the classic work on "speech acts," John R. Searle, *Speech Acts: An Essay in the Philosophy of Language* (Cambridge: Cambridge University Press, 1969).

Chapter 5

1. Global interlocutors are somewhat related to "social entrepreneurs," though the former tend to enjoy some official capacity. They are also likely to be key members of epistemic communities, or experts in their particular field. On social entrepreneurship, see, for example, David Bornstein, *How to Change the World: Social Entrepreneurs and the Power of New Ideas* (Oxford: Oxford University Press, 2004). The literature on epistemic communities is large; for a useful, interdisciplinary overview, Elias G. Carayannis, Ali Pirzadeh, and Denisa Popescu, *Institutional Learning and Knowledge Transfer across Epistemic Communities: New Tools of Global Governance* (New York: Springer, 2011).

2. On Cassin in general, see Prost and Winter, *René Cassin*; Agi, *René Cassin*; and Pateyron, *La contribution française*.

3. Commission nationale consultative des droits de l'homme, "Historique," http://www.cncdh.fr.

4. Fauré, "Réflections sur la Déclaration Universelle."

5. Aurelia Kergueno, "L'engagement français dans le processus d'internationalisation des droits de l'homme," Université Pierre Mendès-France (1996).

6. United Nations Treaty Collection, http://treaties.un.org.

7. Kergueno, "L'engagement français."

8. The "commissions" model (applied, for example, to the regulation of railways) was popular during the nineteenth century, including in Great Britain and Japan. See generally Bernard S. Silberman, *Cages of Reason: The Rise of the Rational State in France, Japan, the United States and Great Britain* (Chicago: University of Chicago Press, 1993).

9. See, for example, Yves Beigbeder, *Judging War Crimes and Torture: French Justice and International Criminal Tribunals and Commissions (1940–2005)* (The Hague: Martinus Nijhoff, 2006); Sir Alistair Horne, *A Savage War of Peace: Algeria 1954–1962* (New York: Viking, 1978); as well as James D. Le Sueur, "Torture and the Decolonization of French Algeria: Nationalism, 'Race' and Violence during Colonial Incarceration," in Graeme Harper, ed., *Colonial and Post-Colonial Incarceration* (New York: Continuum, 2001), 161–75.

10. Commission nationale consultative des droits de l'homme website, http://www.cncdh.fr/; and International Coordinating Committee accreditation records.

11. British Guiana Commission of Inquiry, "Report of the British Guiana Commission of Inquiry, constituted by the International Commission of Jurists: Racial Problems in the Public Service" (Geneva: International Commission of Jurists, October 1965).

12. See Justice S. Y. Mohamed, "The Role of the Ombudsman and Human Rights Institutions in Guyana," in Victor Ayeni, Linda Reif, and Hayden Thomas, eds., *Strengthening Ombudsman and Human Rights Institutions in Commonwealth Small and Island States* (London: Commonwealth Secretariat, 2000), 79–90.

13. See Howard Tolley, *The International Commission of Jurists: Global Advocates for Human Rights* (Philadelphia: University of Pennsylvania Press, 1994), especially 125–27.

14. Guyana Constitution, Article 191(1). "Non-Appointment of Ombudsman a Mockery of the Institution," *Kaieteur News*, August 27, 2012.

15. For the Caribbean, see Ayeni, Reif, and Thomas, *Strengthening Ombudsman and Human Rights Institutions*.

16. United Nations Division of Human Rights, "Seminar on National and Local Institutions for the Promotion and Protection of Human Rights" (Geneva, September 18–29, 1978).

17. UN General Assembly, Human Rights Council, "Report of the Working Group on the Universal Periodic Review: Guyana" (A/HRC/15/14, Fifteenth Session, Agenda Item 6, June 21, 2011).

18. Mbaye had been head of the Supreme Court since 1964. He was first to articulate the notion of a "right to development" in the early 1970s, and he would be one of the key drafters of the African Charter on Human and Peoples' Rights. In general, see Cheikh Yim Seck, *Kéba Mbaye: Parcours et combats d'un grand juge* (Paris: Karthala, 2009).

19. Human Rights Watch, *Protectors or Pretenders?* For the influence of early UN documents on NHRIs, see Comité senegalais des droits de l'homme, http://www.csdh.sn.

20. "Pour que l'on puisse parler de protection des droits de l'homme, il est nécessaire que le systême en cause prévoit en cas de violation desdits droits, une forme de sanction qui frappe l'auteur de la violation déplorée et signalée." Kéba Mbaye, *Les Droits de l'Homme en Afrique* (Paris: Editions Pedone and Commission Internationale des Juristes, 1992), 76.

21. For politics in Senegal during this period, see Donald B. Cruise O'Brien, *Saints and Politicians: Essays in the Organisation of a Senegalese Peasant* Society (Cambridge: Cambridge University Press, 2009); Sheldon Gellar, *Democracy in Senegal: Tocquevillian Analysis in Africa* (New York: Palgrave Macmillan, 2005); Frederic Charles Schaffer, *Democracy in Translation: Understanding Politics in an Unfamiliar Culture* (Ithaca, N.Y.: Cornell University Press, 2000).

22. See Reif, "Transplantation and Adaptation."

23. Provedor de Justiça, "Criação do Provedor de Justiça," http://www.provedor-jus.pt.

24. Branca Amaral, "Portugal," in Caiden, *The International Handbook of the Ombudsman*, 345–7.

25. See, for example, Omar G. Encarnación, *Spanish Politics: Democracy after Dictatorship* (Cambridge: Polity, 2008); Richard Gunther, José Ramón Montero, and Joan Botella, *Democracy in Modern Spain* (New Haven, Conn.: Yale University Press, 2004); Jon Cowans, *Modern Spain: A Documentary History* (Philadelphia: University of Pennsylvania Press, 2003), 262–85; and Laura Desfor Edles, *Symbol*

and Ritual in the New Spain: The Transition to Democracy after Franco (Cambridge: Cambridge University Press, 1998).

26. Spanish Constitution and Defensor del Pueblo, www.defensordelpueblo.es. Also Defensor del Pueblo, *The Book of the Ombudsman*, 196–219.

27. Julián Ribera, *Orígenes del justicia de Aragón* (Zaragoza: Tip. Y Lib. De Comas Hermanos, 1897). See also the website of the Justicia de Aragón, http://www.eljusticiadearagon.com.

28. See Laura Díaz Bueso, "Spain's Parliamentary Ombudsman Scheme," in Roy Gregory and Philip Giddings, eds., *Righting Wrongs: The Ombudsman in Six Countries* (Amsterdam: IOS Press, 2000), 323–38; and Juan Vintó Castells, "The Ombudsman and the Parliamentary Committees on Human Rights in Spain," in Hossain, *Human Rights Commissions and Ombudsman Offices*, 393–422.

29. Spanish Constitution, Article 54, and Organic Law 3, April 6, 1981.

30. The Human Rights Act superseded the Human Rights Commission Act of 1977 and the Race Relations Act of 1971. See New Zealand Human Rights Act 1993, Public Act 1993, No. 82, August 10, 1993.

31. New Zealand Human Rights Amendment Act 2001. New Zealand's Human Rights Commission was fully accredited as an NHRI in 1999.

32. See generally Linda Reif, "The Domestic Application of International Human Rights Law in Canada: The Role of Canada's National Human Rights Institutions," in Oonagh E. Fitzgerald, ed., *The Globalized Rule of Law: Relationships between International and Domestic Law* (Toronto: Irwin Law, 2006), 467–517. For overviews, see Michelle Falardeau Ramsy, "Canadian Human Rights Commission" and Gerard Savard, "Complaint Handling at the Canadian Human Rights Commission," in Hossain et al., *Human Rights Commissions and Ombudsman Offices*, 453–510.

33. Robert Brian Howe and David Johnson, eds., *Restraining Equality: Human Rights Commissions in Canada* (Toronto: Toronto University Press, 2000), 6–7.

34. Ibid., 39–42.

35. See, for example, the critical blog "Canadian Human Rights Commissions Exposed!" http://canadianhumanrightscommission.blogspot.com. In 2010, funding cuts led to office closures in Toronto and Vancouver. "Stephen Harper's Democracy Prize a Sad Joke," *The Star* (Toronto), September 12, 2012.

36. See, for example, Hucker, "Antidiscrimination Laws in Canada."

37. Walter Gellhorn, *Ombudsmen and Others: Citizens' Protectors in Nine Countries* (Cambridge, Mass.: Harvard University Press, 1967), 103.

38. Regula Stämpfli, "Direct Democracy and Women's Suffrage: Antagonism in Switzerland," in Barbara J. Nelson and Najma Chowdhury, eds., *Women and Politics Worldwide* (New Haven, Conn.: Yale University Press, 1994), 697.

39. UN General Assembly, Human Rights Council, "Report of the Working Group on the Universal Periodic Review: Switzerland" (A/HRC/8/41, Eighth Session, Agenda Item 6, May 28, 2008).

40. Interviews, Geneva, Switzerland, August 2002.

41. Gabriele Kucsko-Stadlmayer, ed., *European Ombudsman-Institutions: A Comparative Legal Analysis* (New York: Springer, 2008), 96. See also Nikolaus Schwärzler, "The Ombudsman Institutions in Austria," in Hossain et al., *National Human Rights Commissions and Ombudsman Offices*, 247–67.

42. Ursula Kriebaum, "The Austrian Human Rights Advisory Council," University of Vienna–Austria (n.d.).

43. Office of the High Commissioner for Human Rights (OHCHR), "Chart of the Status of National Institutions: Accredited by the International Coordinating Committee of National Institutions for the Promotion and Protection of Human Rights" (Accreditation Status as of August 2011).

44. Kucsko-Stadlmayer, *European Ombudsman-Institutions.*

45. Università degli studi di Padova, "Istituzioni italiane peri diritti umani" (February 2001–January 2002), 28.

46. See the annual reports of Amnesty International during this period, available from http://www.amnesty.org.

47. Database of the Ombudsman in Italy, through October 2008, results of a project by the Human Rights Centre of the University of Padua for the Italian Presidency of the Council of Ministers, http://unipd-centrodirittiumani.it. Ombudsmen at the local level (i.e., regions, provinces, and municipalities) were created after 1980, though they are not widely known. See Sondra Z. Koff and Stephen P. Koff, *Italy: From the First and the Second Republics* (New York: Routledge, 2000), 162.

48. See Comitato per la promozione e protezione dei diritti umani, http://www.comitatodirittiumani.net.

49. Ibid.

50. Jude Wallace and Tony Pagone, eds., *Rights and Freedoms in Australia* (Sydney: Federation Press, 1989), 245.

51. The Human Rights Commission was also charged with implementing the Racial Discrimination Act (1975) and the Sex Discrimination Act (1984). Over time, new specialized commissioners were added: Privacy Commissioner (1989–2000), Disability Discrimination Commissioner (1992), Aboriginal and Torres Strait Islander Social Justice Commissioner (1993), and Age Discrimination Commissioner (2005). In 1993, the Human Rights Commission was also charged with monitoring the country's compliance with the Convention on the Rights of the Child. Note also that in 1998 a coalition government tried to have the name changed to Human Rights and Responsibilities Commission. Annemarie Devereux, *Australia and the Birth of the International Bill of Human Rights, 1946–1966* (Sydney: Federation Press, 2005), 243.

52. South Australia created an antidiscrimination body in 1966, joined by New South Wales and Victoria in 1977.

53. Neil Reiss, Katherine Lindsay, and Simon Rice, *Australian Anti-Discrimination Law: Text, Cases and Materials* (Sydney: Federation Press, 2008), 22.

54. Yoram Dinstein and Mala Tabory, *The Protection of Minorities and Human Rights* (The Hague: Martinus Nijhoff, 1992), 334.

55. For reference to the Special Adviser on Human Rights, see Susan Magarey and Kerrie Round, *Roma the First: A Biography of Dame Roma Mitchell*, rev. ed. (Kent Town, South Australia: Wakefield Press, 2007), 277. In the United States, a Human Rights Bureau was created in 1977 within the State Department, by an activist Congress, which had incorporated human rights concerns into foreign policy earlier in the decade. See Clair Apodaca, *Understanding U.S. Human Rights Policy: A Paradoxical Legacy* (New York: Routledge, 2006); and Mertus, *Bait and Switch.*

56. A new coalition government of the Liberal and National Parties in 1996 led to budget cuts and ultimately futile attempts to undermine the institution's independence. Rhonda Case Evans, "National Human Rights Institutions in the Courts: Evaluating the Promise of International Human Rights Entrepreneurship" (unpublished manuscript, 2011).

57. Australian Human Rights Commission, "History of the Commission," http://www.hreoc.gov.au. See also John von Doussa, "The Protection Role of the Australian Human Rights Commission," in Ramcharan, *The Protection Role of National Human Rights Institutions*, 1–21.

58. For politics during this period in Australia, see Rodney Smith, Araiadna Vromen, and Ian Cook, eds., *Contemporary Politics in Australia: Theories, Practices and Issues* (Cambridge: Cambridge University Press, 2012); and Louise Chappell, John Chesterman, and Lisa Hill, *The Politics of Human Rights in Australia* (Cambridge: Cambridge University Press, 2009).

59. Department of External Affairs opinion, submitted by C. S. Harders to the attorney general, "Draft International Covenants on Human Rights" (NAA 432/68, Item 68/2797, Pt. 4, November 30, 1966), cited in Devereux, *Australia and the Birth of the International Bill of Human Rights*, 243.

60. Devereux, *Australia and the Birth of the International Bill of Human Rights*.

61. This was suggested in the negotiations over the ICESCR, where Australia opposed including an antidiscrimination clause. Australian representative statement on draft of ICESCR (NAA A 432/68, Item 68/2797, Pt. 3, ca. January 12, 1955), cited in Devereux, *Australia and the Birth of the International Bill of Human Rights*, 152.

62. Daniela Piana, *Judicial Accountabilities in New Europe: From Rule of Law to Quality of Justice* (Aldershot, UK: Ashgate, 2010), 106.

63. David Ost, *Solidarity and the Politics of Anti-Politics: Opposition and Reform in Poland since 1968* (Philadelphia: Temple University Press, 1990), 176.

64. Kazimierz Poznański, *Poland's Protracted Transition: Institutional Change and Economic Growth, 1970–1994* (Cambridge: Cambridge University Press, 1996), 148.

65. See annual reports, posted on Poland's Human Rights Defender website, http://www.rpo.gov.pl/index.php?s=3.

66. See, for example, its bilingual annual reports, available from the International Ombudsman Institute, http://www.theioi.org.

67. For example, Caiden, Macdermot, and Sandler, "Institution of Ombudsman," 10.

68. OHCHR, "Chart of the Status of National Institutions." See Morten Kjaerum, "The Protection Role of the Danish Human Rights Commission," in Ramcharan, *The Protection Role of National Human Rights Institutions*, 23–42.

69. Danish Human Rights Institute, http://www.humanrights.dk/.

70. Ibid.

71. Mertus, *Human Rights Matters*.

72. See especially Jennifer Schirmer, *The Guatemalan Military Project: A Violence Called Democracy* (Philadelphia: University of Pennsylvania Press, 1999).

73. For the longer term effects, see J. Mark Ruhl, "The Guatemalan Military since the Peace Accords: The Fate of Reform under Arzú and Portillo," *Latin American*

Politics and Society 47, 1 (April 2005): 55–85. Also, Stephen C. Ropp and Kathyrn Sik-kink, "International Norms and Domestic Politics in Chile and Guatemala," in Thomas Risse, Stephen C. Ropp, and Kathryn Sikkink, eds., *The Power of Human Rights: International Norms and Domestic Change* (Cambridge: Cambridge University Press, 1999), 172–204.

74. I.e., Honduras in 1982 and El Salvador in 1983. Frederick Drake, *Between Tyranny and Anarchy* (Stanford, Calif.: Stanford University Press, 2009), 220.

75. Reif, *The Ombudsman*, 192.

76. Schirmer, *Guatemalan Military Project*, 129–30.

77. Ibid., 128.

78. See Guatemala, Procurador de los derechos humanos, http://www.pdh .org.gt/.

79. OHCHR, "Chart of the Status of National Institutions."

80. Abraham F. Sarmiento, *Journey of a Retired Supreme Court Justice* (Quezon City: University of the Philippines Press, 2008), 29. In *Radical Evil on Trial*, Carlos Santiago Nino offers another take: Aquino's presidential committee was following the model of a truth commission in Argentina. Nino, *Radical Evil on Trial* (New Haven, Conn.: Yale University Press, 1996), 30.

81. See, for example, Robin Broad, *Unequal Alliance: The World Bank, the International Monetary Fund, and the Philippines* (Berkeley: University of California Press, 1998).

82. Canadian Human Rights Foundation, *Working with National Human Rights Commissions Overseas: The Role of Canadian Expertise and Resources* (Ottawa: CHRF, 1998), 8. In general, see Purificacion C. V. Quisumbing, "The Protection Role of the Philippines Human Rights Commission," in Ramcharan, *The Protection Role of National Human Rights Institutions*, 155–63.

83. Cardenas, "Adaptive States," 32.

84. Ravi Nair, interview, New Delhi, 2001.

85. Sarmiento, *Journey of a Retired Supreme Court Justice*, 29.

86. Asian NGOs Network on National Institutions (ANNI), "Report on the Performance and Establishment of National Human Rights Institutions in Asia" (2008).

87. Amnesty International, *The Philippines—Not Forgotten: The Fate of the "Disappeared"* (London: Amnesty Publications, 1996), 15–16. And Anja Jetschke, "Linking the Unlinkable? International Norms and Nationalism in Indonesia and the Philippines," in Risse, Ropp, and Sikkink, *Power of Human Rights*, 134–71.

88. House of Representatives, Republic of the Philippines, House Bill No. 5039 (Manila, 1998), Section 9.

89. Sarmiento, *Journey of a Retired Supreme Court Justice*, 29.

90. Organization of African Unity, African Charter on Human and Peoples' Rights, Article 26 (1996).

91. Jennifer C. Seely, *The Legacies of Transition Governments in Africa: The Cases of Benin and Togo* (New York: Macmillan), 50.

92. John E. Jessup, *An Encyclopedic Dictionary of Conflict and Conflict Resolution, 1945–1996* (Westport, Conn.: Greenwood, 1998), 742.

93. Seely, *Legacies of Transition Governments in Africa*, 50.

94. For example, in 1988, the UN Centre for Human Rights, based in Geneva, held a relevant seminar in Togo. "Fourth Judicial Colloquium on the Domestic Application of International Human Rights Norms," in *Developing Human Rights Jurisprudence*, vol. 4 (London: Commonwealth Secretariat, June 1992), 107.

95. In terms of pressures, the United States had imposed restrictions on Benin, following accusations that it was permitting Libya to use its territory as a terrorist base. David Lea and Annamarie Rowe, eds., *A Political Chronology of Africa* (London: Taylor & Francis, 2005), 33. In addition to negotiations with international financial institutions during the period, domestically an attempted coup and a series of public strikes upped the ante for the regime. Human Rights Watch, *Protectors or Pretenders?*

96. Human Rights Watch, *Protectors or Pretenders?*

97. Ibid., 31.

98. "Commission nationale des droits de l'Homme du Malu: Me Moussa Maiga dénonce le lanque de soutien de l'Etat," *Le Républicain* (Mali), September 17, 2008. Also, OHCHR, "Chart of the Status of National Institutions."

99. African Commission on Human and Peoples' Rights, "Resolution on the Establishment of Committees on Human Rights or Other Similar Organs at National, Regional or Sub-Regional Level" (Fifth Ordinary Session, Benghazi, Libya, April 3–14, 1988), para. 3, reprinted in Christof Heyns, ed., *Human Rights Law in Africa* (The Hague: Kluwer Law International, 2002), 197.

100. The link between the committee and the 1988 reforms is from Hugo Stokke, Astri Suhrke, and Arni Tostensen, eds., *Human Rights in Developing Countries: Yearbook 1997* (The Hague: Kluwer Law International, 1998), 230.

101. *Al-lijna al-'arabiyya al-libiyya lihouqouq al-insan*, translation from Dejo Olowu, *An Integrative Rights-Based Approach to Human Development in Africa* (Pretoria, South Africa: Pretoria University Law Press, 2009), 107. On the reforms, see Amnesty International, "Libya: Amnesty International's Prisoner Concerns in the Light of Recent Legal Reforms" (MDE 19/02/91, 1991), 1.

102. Dejo Olowu, for example, is puzzled as to why Human Rights Watch in its report on NHRIs in Africa (*Protectors or Pretenders?*) excludes the Libyan Committee: "It is curious to note that the Human Rights Watch survey, as extensive and deep as it appears, excluded the Libyan experience." Olowu, *Integrative Rights-Based Approach*, 107n523.

103. Badredine Arfi, "North Africa," in Edward A. Kolodziej, ed., *A Force Profonde: The Power, Politics, and Promise of Human Rights* (Philadelphia: University of Pennsylvania Press, 2003), described the body as "cosmetic," 97. On when the committee attained observer status, Rachel Murray and Malcolm Evans, eds., *Documents of the African Commission on Human and Peoples' Rights* (Oxford: Hart, 2001), 240.

Chapter 6

1. Olowu, *Integrative Rights-Based Approach*, 107.

2. For a relevant discussion, see Murray, *The Role of National Human Rights Institutions at the International and Regional Levels: The Experience of Africa* (Oxford: Hart, 2007), chap. 4.

3. Olowu, *Integrative Rights-Based Approach*, 106.

4. African Commission on Human and Peoples' Rights, "Resolution on Grant-ing Observer Status to National Human Rights Institutions in Africa" (24th Ordi-nary Session, Banjul, Gambia, October 22–31, 1998), para. 4, in Heyns, *Human Rights Law in Africa*, 217–18.

5. See Sandra Fullerton Joireman, "Inherited Legal Systems and Effective Rule of Law: Africa and the Colonial Legacy," *Journal of Modern African Studies* 39, 4 (December 2001): 571–96.

6. September 30 to October 2, 1992. For a more recent discussion of NHRIs in Anglophone Africa, see Obiora Chinedu Okafor, "National Human Rights Institu-tions in Anglophone Africa: Legalism, Popular Agency, and the 'Voices of Suffer-ing,'" in Goodman and Pegram, *Human Rights, State Compliance, and Social Change*, 124–49.

7. I have chosen to define the decade in standard terms, beginning with 1990. Starting with the Paris Principles or the Vienna World Conference (1991 or 1993) would also have made theoretical sense. But I am emphasizing instead the transition to a post–Cold War world, with its more generalized attention to human rights issues and democratic governance. Given activism on behalf of NHRI before this decade, examining the full decade together is also reasonable.

8. Eve Sandberg, "Theories of Democratization and the Case of Donor-Assisted Democratization in Namibia," in Stuart S. Nagel, ed., *Handbook of Global Political Policy* (New York: Marcel Dekker, 2000), 100. An ombudsman had been created briefly in 1986 via legislation. Victor O. Ayeni, "Evolution of and Prospects for the Ombudsman in Southern Africa," *International Review of Administration Science* 63 (December 1997): 551–52. See also J. Malan, "The Office of the Ombudsman in Namibia," in Hossain et al., *Human Rights Commissions and Ombudsman Offices*, 331–42.

9. Some have viewed this as a liability in dealing with transnational corpora-tions. See Michael K. Alddo, *Human Rights Standards and the Responsibility of Trans-national Corporations* (The Hague: Martinus Nijhoff), 295.

10. Abdullahi Ahmed An-Naim, ed., *Human Rights under African Constitutions: Realizing the Promise for Ourselves* (Philadelphia: University of Pennsylvania Press, 2002), 64.

11. The assessment about the government's rising fear of human rights pressures is from the Centre for the Independence of Lawyers and Judges (1989), as cited in Peter R. Baehr, Hilde Hey, Jacqueline Smith, and Theresa Swinehart, eds., *Human Rights in Developing Countries, Yearbook 1994* (The Hague: Kluwer, 1994), 210–11.

12. Reif, *The Ombudsman*, 226; and Hossain et al., *Human Rights Commissions and Ombudsman Offices*, 189.

13. Baehr et al., *Human Rights in Developing Countries*, 211.

14. See generally Emile Short, "The Development and Growth of Human Rights Commissions in Africa—The Ghanian Experience," in Hossain et al., *Human Rights Commissions and Ombudsman Offices*, 187–210; Anna Bossman, "The Protection Role of the Ghana Human Rights Commission," in Bertrand G. Ramcharan, ed., *The Protection Role of National Human Rights Institutions* (Leiden: Martinus Nijhoff, 2005), 57–85; and Kofi Quashigah, "The Ghana Commission on Human Rights

and Administrative Justice," in Birgit Lindsnaes, Lone Lindholt, and Kristine Yigen, eds., *National Human Rights Institutions: Articles and Working Papers* (Denmark: Danish Centre for Human Rights, 2000), 199–207.

15. John Dugard, "The Influence of International Human Rights Law on the South African Constitution," 49, 1 *Current Legal Problems* (1996): 305–24; Tiyanjana Maluwa, "International Human Rights Norms and the South African Interim Constitution 1993," *South African Yearbook of International Law* 19 (1993–94): 14–42; Philip Alston and James Crawford, *The Future of UN Human Rights Treaty Monitoring* (Cambridge: Cambridge University Press, 2000), 273; Heinz Klug, *Constituting Democracy: Law, Globalism and South Africa's Political Reconstruction* (Cambridge: Cambridge University Press, 2000).

16. Kristin Henrard, *Minority Protection in Post-Apartheid South Africa: Human Rights, Minority Rights, and Self-Determination* (Westport, Conn.: Praeger, 2002). Broad overviews of the commission are offered in David McQuoid-Mason, "The Role of Human Rights Institutions in South Africa" and N. Barney Pityana, "The South African Human Rights Commission," in Hossain et al., *Human Rights Commissions and Ombudsman Offices*, 617–38. Also, Jonathan Klaaren, "A Second Look at the South African Human Rights Commission, Access to Information, and the Promotion of Socioeconomic Rights," *Human Rights Quarterly* 27 (2005): 539–61.

17. Justice Elton Singini and ombudsman James Chirwa. See generally Justice E. M. Singini, "Malawi's Human Rights Commission," in Hossain et al., *Human Rights Commissions and Ombudsman Offices*, 527–32.

18. Constitutionalism was complemented by "liberalization of the legal regime for the registration of voluntary associations." Fidelis Edge Kanyongolo, "The Rhetoric of Human Rights in Malawi: Individualization and Judicialization," in Harri Englund and Francis B. Nyamnjoh, eds., *Rights and the Politics of Recognition in Africa* (London: Zed Books, 2004), 64.

19. Ibid.

20. Robert I. Rotberg, ed., *Corruption, Global Security, and World Order* (Baltimore: Brookings Institution Press, 2009), 320. A report by the British Department of International Development reached a similar conclusion. Ibid.

21. The Constitutional Commission requested input from the commission of inquiry in 1991. Eric Wiebelhaus-Brahm, *Truth Commissions and Transitional Societies: The Impact on Human Rights and Democracy* (New York: Routledge, 2010), 112.

22. Uganda Constitutional Commission, *Report of the Uganda Constitutional Commission* (Entebbe: Uganda Printing and Publishing, 1993), 185–88.

23. Reif, *The Ombudsman*, 232. See generally, Edmond R. B. Nkalubo, "Uganda Human Rights Commission," in Hossain et al., *Human Rights Commissions and Ombudsman Offices*, 579–611; and Marcus Topp, "Uganda: Human Rights Protection by the State in Uganda," in Lindsnaes, Lindholt, and Yigen, *National Human Rights Institutions*, 169–97.

24. An-Naim, *Human Rights under African Constitutions*, 417. For how, in cases of torture, the commission experienced delays but then improved over time, see Human Rights Watch, *State of Pain: Torture in Uganda* (New York: Human Rights Watch, March 2004), 73.

25. Uganda had ratified the African Charter in 1986, the ICESCR in 1987, and the ICCPR in 1995. *UN Treaty Collection*, http://treaties.un.org. In 2002–3, it chaired African NHRIs. According to John Hatchard, the Ugandan NHRI was one of the most powerful in all of the British Commonwealth.

26. The commission was created by Decree 22 on September 27, 1995, most often referred to as the National Human Rights Commission Act. Nigeria had already ratified the two international covenants in 1993 and the African Charter 1983. See Muhammed Tabiu, "National Human Rights Commission of Nigeria," in Hossain et al., *Human Rights Commissions and Ombudsman Offices*, 553–59.

27. Obiora Chinedu Okafor and Shedrack C. Agbakwa, "On Legalism, Popular Agency and the 'Voices of Suffering': The Nigerian National Human Rights Commission in Context," *Human Rights Quarterly* 24, 3 (2002): 665.

28. Olowu, *Integrative Rights-Based Approach*, 113.

29. Amnesty International, *Annual Report 1996* (London: Amnesty Publications, 1996).

30. Among the nine members of the Movement for the Survival of the Ogoni People was Kenule Saro Wiwa, a widely regarded environmental activist. See Ken Saro-Wiwa, *A Month and a Day: A Detention Diary* (New York: Penguin, 1996).

31. Bukhari Bello was dismissed in June 2006 and Kehinde Ajoni in March 2009. R. Iniyan Ilango, *Easier Said Than Done: A Report on the Commitment and Performance of the Commonwealth Members of the U.N. Human Rights Commission* (New Delhi: Commonwealth Human Rights Initiative, 2007), 113; and Amnesty International, "Nigeria: Independence of National Human Rights Commission Under Threat," AFR 44/009/2009 (March 20, 2009).

32. The 2011 reform is known as the National Human Rights Commission Amendment Act. See Amnesty International, "Nigerian President Signs Landmark Human Rights Bill" (News release, March 9, 2011).

33. In April 1994, the Constitutional Commission held a two-day seminar, attended by foreign experts, on the formation of an ombudsman. Thomas P. Ofcansky and Laverle Berry Page, eds., *Ethiopia Country Study Guide* (Washington, D.C.: International Business, 2005), 128.

34. The commission was required by Article 55 (14) of the 1995 constitution, later established by Parliamentary Proclamation 210/2000. See EHRC, http://www.ehrc.org/et. Ethiopia also acceded to the two international human rights covenants in 1993 and to the African Charter in 1998. *UN Treaty Collection.*

35. "Sterilised Independence," *The Reporter* (Addis Ababa), 1998, 3, cited in Bertus Praeg, *Ethiopia and Political Renaissance in Africa* (New York: Nova Science, 2006), 205.

36. Human Rights Watch, *World Report 2011* (New York: Human Rights Watch, 2011), 125.

37. Article 25 was amended. Like most other East African countries, Zambia already had a more long-standing traditional ombudsman office.

38. *Europa World Year Book 2*, vol. 2 (London: Taylor & Francis, 2004), 4720.

39. Human Rights Watch, *Protectors or Pretenders?*; and Commonwealth Secretariat, *Comparative Study on Mandate of National Human Rights Institutions in the Commonwealth* (London: Commonwealth Secretariat, 2007), 76.

40. Originally in "Zambia: Editorial Says Zambian Rights Commission 'Toothless,'" *The Post* (Zambia), October 8, 1998; Human Rights Watch, *Protectors or Pretenders?*, 38.

41. For instance, in 2006 CERD pressured the government to strengthen the NHRI. Ilango, *Easier Said Than Done*, 71.

42. Human Rights Watch, *Protectors or Pretenders?*

43. *Europa World Year Book 2*, 2433. Also, in July 1995, Moi had announced a KANU Standing Human Rights Committee, two days before a donor meeting in Paris where human rights was to be raised. Hans Peter Schmitz, "Transnational Activism and Political Change in Kenya and Uganda," in Risse, Ropp, and Sikkink, *Power of Human Rights*, 64.

44. The standing committee, headed by a well-meaning academic (Professor Murungi), apparently conducted some investigations, but its work was blocked by the president's office. National Assembly, "Official Report, Kenyan National Commission on Human Rights Bill, Parliamentary Debates" (April 9, 2002), 441, hereafter Kenyan Parliamentary Debates. Human Rights Watch draws an interesting contrast between Nigeria and Kenya, both of which had repressive regimes and weak human rights bodies; however, the freer climate in Kenya after 1992, which gave NGOs more room to organize, meant that they could afford to ignore the government institution. The Kenyan Human Rights Commission is an NGO created in 1992. Prof. Kiraitu Murungi referred to the standing committee as a "bogus institution." Kenyan Parliamentary Debates, 441.

45. Hatchard, "National Human Rights Commissions," 210, says it cannot be considered an NHRI because it did not at all conform to international standards. In May 1998, for example, Murungi and the chair of the Standing Committee on Human Rights went to an international seminar on national human rights commissions in Belfast. Kenyan Parliamentary Debates, 441.

46. Dr. Anangwe, Kenyan Parliamentary Debates, 443.

47. Kenyan Parliamentary Debates, 439–40.

48. Ibid.

49. Schmitz, "Transnational Activism and Political Change," 64.

50. Kenya had acceded to the international human rights covenants in 1972, the African Charter in 1982, and the Convention Against Torture in 1997. *UN Treaty Collection*.

51. Cameroon ratified the two international covenants in 1984 and the African Charter in 1989. *UN Treaty Collection*. See S. Nfor Gwei, "The Cameroon Experience in Creating and Running a National Commission for the Promotion and Protection of Human Rights," in Hossain et al., *Human Rights Commissions and Ombudsman Offices*, 169–85.

52. The Comité national des droits de l'homme et des libertés was created by Decree 90/1459.

53. "What of Our So-Called Human Rights Commission?," November 19–25, 1992, in Godfrey B. Tangwa, ed., *No Trifling Matter: Contributions of an Uncompromising Critic to the Democratic Process in Cameroon* (Bamenda, Cameroon: Langaa, 2011), 209.

54. Human Rights Watch, *Protectors or Pretenders?*

55. The 2004 act was No. 2004/016 of July 22, 2004; enabling legislation was also passed on July 7, 2005 (No. 2005/254). Ulrik Spliid, *The Compliance of the Constituent Documents of West African and Central African National Human Rights Institutions with the Paris Principles: A Descriptive Analysis* (Copenhagen: Danish Institute for Human Rights, March 2009), 52–56. The national elections in 2004 were held in October.

56. For example, the subcommittee on accreditation emphasized the institution's failure to comply with the international prohibition granting voting rights to representatives of the executive. Spliid, *Compliance of the Constituent Documents.*

57. CERD, for instance, referred to the institution's B rating and called for the body's independence. Cameroon's NHRI received technical assistance from the Commonwealth and La Francophonie (it was a member of both groupings) and from the UNDP. For a review of some of the institution's design weaknesses at the time, see Eric Ngonji Njungwe, "A Brief Comparison between the South African and the Cameroon National Human Rights Commissions," *Cameroon Journal on Democracy and Human Rights* 1, 1 (June 2007): 24–27.

58. Amnesty International, "Equatorial Guinea: Torture," AFR 24/05/90 (1990).

59. Amnesty International, "Equatorial Guinea: Arrests of Pro-Democracy Activists—A Changing Pattern of Human Rights Violations" (November 1, 1991).

60. The UN special rapporteur was for the Right to Freedom of Opinion and Expression. UN General Assembly, Human Rights Council, "Compilation Prepared by the OHCHR: Equatorial Guinea" (A/HRC/WG.6/GNQ/2, September 18, 2009), 3.

61. Sonia Cardenas and Andrew Flibbert, "National Human Rights Institutions in the Middle East," 59, 3 *Middle East Journal* (Summer 2005): 414–17.

62. Susan Waltz, *Human Rights and Reform: Changing the Face of North African Politics* (Berkeley: University of California Press, 1995), 190.

63. Anthony Chase and Amr Hamzawy, eds., *Human Rights in the Arab World* (Philadelphia: University of Pennsylvania Press, 2008), 187.

64. In contrast, the Diwan al Madhalim, which is more of a traditional ombudsman, does accept individual complaints.

65. Comité Supérieur des Droits de l'Homme et des Libertés Fondamentales, created by Decree No. 54 on January 7, 1991.

66. "Tunisia Speech by Ben Ali on Human Rights; Committee Set Up," British Broadcasting Corporation (April 11, 1991), cited in Cardenas and Flibbert, "National Human Rights Institutions," 419.

67. Human Rights Watch, *Protectors or Pretenders?*, 37.

68. Anna Würth and Claudia Engelmann, "Governmental Human Rights Structures and National Human Rights Institutions in the Middle East and North Africa," in Hatem Elliesie, ed., *Beiträge zum Islamischen Recht VII: Islam and Menschenrechte/ Islam and Human Rights* (Frankfurt: Peter Lang, 2010), 255.

69. Würth and Engelmann, "Governmental Human Rights Structures," 200.

70. Ibid.

71. Farhat Rajhi, "Mise à niveau du Comité Supérieur des Droits de l'Homme et des Libertés Fondamentales (CSDHLF) de Tunisie," www.leaders.com.

72. "Tunisian Ex-minister Loses Rights Post after Coup Remark," *AFP*, May 7, 2012.

73. The ministry disappeared with the ONDH's creation. Heyns, *Human Rights Law in Africa*, 230.

74. Comité algérien des militants libres de la dignité humaine et des droits de l'homme, *Livre blanc sur la répression en Algérie, 1991–1994* (Algeria: Hoggar, 1995), 96.

75. Benjamin MacQueen, *Political Culture and Conflict Resolution in the Arab Middle East: Lebanon and Algeria* (Melbourne, Australia: Melbourne University Press, 2009), 118.

76. Human Rights Watch, *Algeria—Time for Reckoning: Enforced Disappearances in Algeria*, 15, no. 2 (New York: Human Rights Watch, February 2003), 50n14.

77. MacQueen, *Political Culture and Conflict* Resolution, 119.

78. John P. Entelis, "Civil Society and the Authoritarian Temptation in Algerian Politics: Islamic Democracy vs. the Centralized State," in Augustus Richard Norton, ed., *Civil Society in the Middle East*, vol. 2 (Leiden: Brill, 1996), 73.

79. Würth and Engelmann, "Governmental Human Rights Structures," 255.

80. Algeria, Presidential Decree No. 01–71 (March 25, 2001) created the NHRI. Alkarama, "Algeria: The National Institution for Human Rights (CNCPPDH) in the Hot Seat" (May 15, 2009).

81. Alkarama, "Algeria: The National Institution for Human Rights (CNCP-PDH) in the Hot Seat." Alkarama, an Arab human rights organization, submitted a detailed statement of problem areas to the ICC. See http://www.alkarama.org. A new constitution in 1996 did not include the NHRI. For reaccreditation materials, see ICC, "Algeria: Summary, Re-Accreditation of the National Advisory Commission for the Promotion and Protection of Human Rights of Algeria to the International Coordinating Committee of National Human Rights Institutions (March 2010), http://nhri.ohchr.org.

82. Reed Brody, *Chad: The Victims of Hissène Habré Still Awaiting Justice* (New York: Human Rights Watch, 2005), 16. National Commission on Human Rights of Chad, Act No. 3/PR/94 is reprinted in Heyns, *Human Rights Law in Africa*, 445. The 1996 implementing decrees are also reprinted in ibid.

83. Human Rights Watch, *Protectors or Pretenders?*, 142.

84. Ibid., 145.

85. Ibid., 45.

86. OHCHR, "Chart of the Status of National Institutions."

87. OHCHR, "Report of the Special Rapporteur on the Situation of Human Rights in Zaire" (E/CN.4/1997/6, January 28, 1997).

88. "Zaire: UN Human Rights Report" (E/CN.4/1996/66, report on the human rights situation in Zaire presented by Special Rapporteur Roberto Garretón, in compliance with Resolution 1995/69 of the UN Human Rights Commission, January 29, 1996).

89. Ibid. Amnesty International had issued a critical report in 1997; and the UN secretary-general's Investigative Team, which had withdrawn in April, released its final report in late June. The government vigorously rejected its findings.

90. *Africa South of the Sahara* (London: Europa Publications, 1999), 350.

91. Article 33 of Niger's National Constitution (1996 and 1999); for implementing legislation, Law No. 98–55 (December 29, 1998), amended in Law No. 2001–05 (August 20, 2001).

92. Law No. 2010–001 (February 20, 2010). Niger's UPR was formed in February 2011.

93. "Niger's Responses to Recommendations" (November 22, 2011), http://upr-info.org.

94. Article 40. Madagascar had ratified the two international covenants in 1971 and the African Charter in 1992. I date this NHRI to the 1996 decree, since the wording in the constitution was sufficiently vague and the initial decision in 1994 was for an ombudsman (le Médiateur).

95. Decree No. 96-1282 (December 18, 1996).

96. Note that the U.S. State Department dates the institution to 2000. On Madagascar's NHRI rating, see OHCHR, "Chart of the Status of National Institutions."

97. See Richard Sandbrook, "Mauritius: Evolution of a Classic Social Democracy," in Richard Sandbrook, Marc Edelman, Patrick Heller, and Judith Teichman, eds., Social Democracy in the Global Periphery (Cambridge: Cambridge University Press, 1998), 123–46.

98. The NHRI was created by the Protection of Human Rights Act 1998 (December 1998), which entered into force by a proclamation in February 1999. See Veda Bhadain, "The Institution of the Ombudsman in Mauritius," in Hossain et al., Human Rights Commissions and Ombudsman Offices; L. A. Darga, "The Ombudsman and the National Human Rights Commission of Mauritius" (South Africa: Electoral Institute for Sustainable Democracy in Africa/EISA, December 2009); and UN Treaty Collection for ratification details and OHCHR, "Chart of the Status of National Institutions" on accreditation.

99. Mauritius Plan of Action, Section E, 64–68, reprinted in Heyns, Human Rights Law in Africa, 26.

100. Olowu, Integrative Rights-Based Approach, 112.

101. Mauritania's Commission on Human Rights, Poverty Reduction and Integration seems to have become inactive after 2007.

102. See founding documents (e.g., Decree 036-2010, June 12, 2006) on Mauritania's National Human Rights Commission website, http://www.cndh.mr.

103. UN General Assembly, "National Report, Submitted by Government of Mauritania" (A/HRC/WG.6/9/MRT/1, August 23, 2010).

104. "Lomé Peace Accord, Peace Agreement between the Government of Sierra Leone and the Revolutionary United Front of Sierra Leone" (July 7, 1999), Article XXV.

105. Rwanda's NHRI was included in the Arusha Accord ("Peace Agreement between the Government of Rwanda and the Rwandese Patriotic Front"; August 4, 1993), Law No. 4/99 (March 1999), and Rwanda's 2003 Constitution. In addition to the Human Rights Commission, Rwanda also established other parallel institutions, including an ombudsman.

106. For example, the European Union gave the commission $1.28 million toward this end. Human Rights Watch, Human Rights Watch Report, 2003 (New York: Human Rights Watch, 2003), 66.

107. Human Rights Watch, "Liberia: President Should Act on Rights Commission" (News release, May 19, 2010); and ICC, "Report and Recommendations of the

Session of the Sub-Committee on Accreditation (Geneva: ICC, March 26–30, 2012), 26–28.

108. Liberia's NHRI was created by Act No. 2004–302 (May 3, 2004) and presidential decree No. 205–08/PR (July 15, 2005). See the joint letter submitted by Human Rights Watch and Amnesty International, "Letter to Liberian President Ellen Johnson-Sirleaf Urging Creation of Rights Commission," May 19, 2010. Also UN General Assembly, Human Rights Council, "Report of the Working Group on the Universal Periodic Review: Liberia" (A/HRC/16/3, June 4, 2011).

109. Linas-Marcoussis Agreement, February 2003, available in the Peace Agreements Digital Collection of the U.S. Institute of Peace, http://www.usip.org; UN General Assembly, Human Rights Council, "Report of the Working Group on the Universal Periodic Review" (A/HRC/13/9, January 4, 2010) and "National Report Submitted by the Government of Côte d'Ivoire" (A/HRC/WG.6/6/CIV/1, September 3, 2009).

110. Spliid, *Compliance of the Constituent Documents*, 61.

111. On coercive diffusion in world politics, see Simmons, Dobbin, and Garrett, *Global Diffusion of Markets and Democracy*, 17; and G. John Ikenberry and Charles A. Kupchan, "Socialization and Hegemonic Power," *International Organization* 44, 3 (June 1990): 283–315.

112. See Michelle Parlevliet, "National Human Rights Institutions and Peace Agreements: Establishing National Institutions in Divided Societies" (International Council on Human Rights Policy, Review Meeting on Role of Human Rights in Peace Agreements, Belfast, March 7–8, 2005).

113. Pius Msekwa, *Reflections on Tanzania's First Multi-Party Parliament: 1995–2000* (Dar es Salaam, Tanzania: Dar es Salaam University Press, 2000), 19.

114. Ernest T. Mallya, "Promoting the Effectiveness of Democracy Promotion Institutions in Southern Africa" (Research Report No. 40, EISA, Johannesburg, South Africa, 2009), 26.

115. The United Republic of Tanzania, Government Paper No. 1, "Government Views on the National Constitutional Reforms" (Regular Report No. 483, 1998).

116. World Bank, "Tanzania: Support to the Government of Tanzania's Anti-Corruption Program" (Poverty Reduction and Social Development Unit, Africa Region, October 1998), 8.

117. Issa G. Shivji, *Where Is Uhuru? Reflections on the Struggle for Democracy in Africa* (Cape Town, South Africa: Fahamu Books, 2009), 24. The Danish International Development Agency provided substantial assistance. Report submitted to the U.S. Agency for International Development, *Democracy and Governance Assessment of Tanzania: Transitioning from the Single-Party State*, November 2000, 44.

118. Rick Stapenhurst, Niall Johnston, and Riccardo Pelizzo, eds., *The Role of Parliament in Curbing Corruption* (Washington, D.C.: World Bank, 2006), 144.

119. See World Bank, "Tanzania: Support to the Government."

120. Msekwa, *Reflections on Tanzania's First Multi-Party Parliament*, 11.

121. Ernest T. Mallya, *The State of Constitutional Development in Tanzania—2000* (Kampala, Uganda: Kituo Cha Katiba, 2001), 3.

122. United Republic of Tanzania, "Government Views on the National Constitutional Reforms." On the Kisanga report, see Robert V. Makaramba, *The State of*

Constitutional Developments in Tanzania (Kampala, Uganda: Kituo Cha Katiba, 2000).

123. World Bank, "Tanzania: Support to the Government."

124. Shivji, *Where Is Uhuru?* 24.

125. OHCHR, "Chart of the Status of National Institutions."

126. See, for example, *Africa South of the Sahara 2004*, 33rd ed. (London: Europa Publications, 2004), 115–16.

127. "Bamako Declaration" (Regional Conference on Impunity, Justice, and Human Rights in West Africa, December 2011). Also, Ministère de la Promotion des Droits Humains, Secrétariat Général, Burkina Faso, *Rapport sur la création et le fonctionnement de la Commission nationale des droits humains du Burkina Faso* (2011), http://afrique.apf-francophonie.org.

128. International Monetary Fund, "Burkina Faso: Poverty Reduction Strategy Paper Progress Report" (IMF Country Report No. 04/78, March 2004), 70; and *Africa South of the Sahara 2004*, 116.

129. African Peer Review Mechanism, *Country Review Report of Burkina Faso* (Report No. 9, May 2008), 110. Decree No. 2001-628/PRES/MIPDH (November 20, 2001) established the NHRI. Burkina Faso also had an ombudsman dating to 1994, but it too had been given limited resources.

130. UN Office for the Coordination of Humanitarian Affairs, *Burkina Faso: Human Rights Promotion Ministry Created* (Ouagadougou: IRIN, June 12, 2002).

131. ICC, Report and Recommendations of the Session of the Sub-Committee on Accreditation (Geneva: ICC, March 26–30, 2012), 17; and UN General Assembly, Human Rights Council, "National Report Submitted by the Government of Burkina Faso" (A/HRC/WG.6/3/BFA/1, August 21, 2008).

132. Tamir Moustafa, "Protests Hint at New Change in Egyptian Politics," *Middle East Report* (April 9, 2004), http://www.merip.org.

133. OHCHR, "Chart of the Status of National Institutions."

134. Christof H. Heyns and Fran Viljoen, *The Impact of the United Nations Human Rights Treaties on the Domestic Level* (The Hague: Kluwer, 2002), 227.

135. "Euro-Mediterranean Partnership: Commission Proposes Package of Measures to Invigorate Barcelona Process" (IP/10/975, Brussels, September 6, 2000).

136. Amira Howeidy, "Rights at a Crossroads," *Al-Ahram Weekly*, No. 482 (May 18–24, 2000); Cardenas and Flibbert, "National Human Rights Institutions," 424–28; and Joshua Stacher, "Rhetorical Acrobatics and Reputations: Egypt's National Council for Human Rights," *Middle East Report* 235 (Summer 2005), http://www.merip.org.

137. Stacher, "Rhetorical Acrobatics and Reputations." Also, Cardenas and Flibbert, "National Human Rights Institutions."

138. Cardenas and Flibbert, "National Human Rights Institutions."

139. Karima Kamal, "National Council for Human Rights or Security Council?," *Egypt Independent*, February 16, 2010.

140. See UN General Assembly, Human Rights Council, "Report on the Working Group on the Universal Periodic Review: Egypt" (A/HRC/14/17, March 26, 2010).

141. Act No. 5, January 13, 2003. The constitution, drafted in 2001, was adopted by a referendum in January 2002. It discussed the NHRC in Chapter 14, Articles 167–69.

142. See generally, John Frank Clark, *The Failure of Democracy in the Republic of Congo* (Boulder, Colo.: Lynne Rienner, 2008).

143. Spliid, *Compliance of the Constituent Documents.*

144. UN General Assembly, Human Rights Council, "Report on the Working Group on the Universal Periodic Review: Congo" (A/HRC/12/6, June 5, 2009), 4.

145. African Police Oversight Forums, *An Audit of Police Oversight in Africa* (Cape Town, South Africa: African Minds, 2008), 23; and Permanent Mission of the Republic of Djibouti to the United Nations, "Aide Mémoire: Djibouti's Voluntary Pledges and Commitments in Accordance with Resolution A/RES/60/251 (April 2006).

146. UN General Assembly, Human Rights Council, "National Report Submitted by the Government of Djibouti for Universal Periodic Review" (A/HRC/C/WG.6/4/DJI/1, November 14, 2008), 18. The decree was No. 2008–013/PR/MJAP, April 23, 2008.

147. The OHCHR regional office had also recommended an interministerial body to coordinate treaty submissions. See the website of the OHCHR, Regional Office for East Africa (Addis Ababa), http://eastafrica.ohchr.org/.

148. Djibouti Peace Accord, Peace Agreements Database, Transitional Justice Institute, University of Ulster; and *UN Treaty Collection.*

149. Decree No. 001037/PR, November 7, 2000.

150. For historical background, see David E. Gardinier and Douglas A. Yates, *Historical Dictionary of Gabon*, 3rd ed. (Methuen, N.J.: Scarecrow Press, 2006); and Léon Guiral, *Le congo français du Gabon à Brazzaville* (Charleston, S.C.: Nabu Press, 2011).

151. U.S. Department of State, *Country Reports on Human Rights Practices* (2000), 258; United Nations/Human Rights Internet, *For the Record 1997—The UN Human Rights System*, vol. 1 (Minneapolis: University of Minnesota, Human Rights Internet, 1998), 41. The Francophonie Summit was held in Moncton, New Brunswick.

152. "Gabon Human Rights Commission Will Not Be Independent," *Le Gabon Enervant*, October 1, 2011, http://gabonenervant.glogspot.com.

153. See Decree Law No. 19/2001, Ministry of Justice. The ombudsman, or Provedor de Justiça, was created via constitutional amendment.

154. The country's first multiparty elections were held in 1992; the coup in 2003 was apparently backed by France, the former colonial power. The landlocked country, moreover, has been embroiled in four decades of intense instability, with a strong UN presence.

155. For critical overviews, see UN General Assembly, Human Rights Council, "Summary of Stakeholders' Submissions" (A/HRC/WG.6/12/SWZ/3, July 22, 2011).

156. UN General Assembly, Human Rights Council, "Report of the Working Group on the Universal Periodic Review: Swaziland" (A/HRC/19/6, December 12, 2011).

157. Democratic Republic of the Congo (Lusaka) Ceasefire Agreement, July and August 1999, USIP Digital Peace Agreements Collection, http://www.usip .org.

158. Bertrand G. Ramcharan, *The United Nations High Commissioner for Human Rights: The Challenges of International Protection* (The Hague: Martinus Nijhoff, 2002), 114 and 116.

159. Decree 007/01, February 23, 2001. Democratic Republic of the Congo, Human Rights Ministry, "Report to the African Commission on Human and Peoples' Rights: Initial Report of the Democratic Republic of the Congo" (April 30, 2002), 24.

160. Ibid.

161. Global Integrity, "DRC Scorecard Report," *Global Integrity Report*, 2006, http://www.globalintegrity.org. The observatory's legal basis was Law 04/20, July 2004, Article 154. There had been a new constitution in 2000.

162. UN General Assembly, Human Rights Council, "National Report Submitted by the Government of the DRC for Universal Periodic Review" (A/HRC/WG.6/6/COD/1, September 3, 2009), 27.

163. "Response to Recommendations: Democratic Republic of the Congo" (May 11, 2012), http://www.uprinfo.org.

164. UN General Assembly, Human Rights Council, "National Report Submitted by the Government of the DRC for Universal Periodic Review," 3.

165. Angola 1992 Constitution, Articles 142–44. The institution is detailed as well in Article 192 of the 2010 constitution. See also "Statute of the Judicial Ombudsman and the Organic Law" (2005, published 2006: Law 4/06 and Law 5/06, April 28, 2006).

166. See, for example, W. Martin James, *A Political History of the Civil War in Angola: 1974–1990* (New Brunswick, N.J.: Transaction, 2011).

167. Zoë Wilson, *The United Nations and Democracy in Africa: Labyrinths of Legitimacy* (New York: Routledge, 2006), 179–81.

168. Human Rights Watch, *Angola Unravels: The Rise and Fall of the Lusaka Peace Process* (New York: Human Rights Watch, August 1999), 246.

169. UN General Assembly, Human Rights Council, "Survey Prepared by the Office of the High Commissioner for Human Rights: Angola" (Stakeholder Submissions) (A/HRC/WG.6/7/AGO/3, November 6, 2009); Electoral Institute for the Sustainability of Democracy in Africa, "Angola: Office of the Ombudsman" (Johannesburg: EISA, August 2009), available at http://www.eisa-org.za; and Provedor de Justiça de Angola website, www.provedor-jus.co.ao.

170. Provedor de Justiça, "Relatório anual de actividades apresentado à Assembleia da República: 2006," www.provedor-jus.pt.

171. See UN General Assembly, Human Rights Council, "Compilation Prepared by the OHCHR: Angola" (A/HRC/WG.6/7/AGO/2, November 11, 2009).

172. France, Canada, Pakistan, Philippines, and Malaysia called for a compliant NHRI. UN General Assembly, Human Rights Council, "Review of the Working Group on the Universal Periodic Review: Angola" (A/HRC/14/11, March 24, 2010).

173. UN General Assembly, Human Rights Council, "Review of the Working Group on the Universal Periodic Review: Burundi" (A/HRC/10/71, January 8, 2009).

174. See Human Rights Watch, "Burundi: Strengthen Support for National Human Rights Commission" (October 6, 2011).

175. UN General Assembly, Human Rights Council, "Review of the Working Group on the Universal Periodic Review: Guinea" (A/HRC/15/4, June 14, 2010).

176. See UNDP-Lesotho, "Establishment of the Human Rights Commission in Lesotho" (December 20, 2010), www.undp.org.ls; and UN General Assembly, Human Rights Council, "National Report, Submitted by the Government of Lesotho for the UPR" (A/HRC/WG.6/8/LSO/1, February 22, 2010), 19.

177. Libya, General People's Committee, Decision No. 557 (2007).

178. UN General Assembly, Human Rights Council, "Review of the Working Group on the Universal Periodic Review: Libyan Arab Jamahiriya" (A/HRC/16/15, January 4, 2011).

179. UN General Assembly, Human Rights Council, "National Report, Submitted by the Government of Botswana for the UPR" (A/HRC/WG.6/3/BWA/1, September 5, 2008); and UN Human Rights Committee, Botswana First Report, 92nd Session, March 19–20, 2008 (available from the International Service for Human Rights, Human Rights Monitor Series).

180. UN General Assembly, Human Rights Council, "Compilation Prepared by the OHCHR: Eritrea, for the UPR" (A/HRC/WG.6/6/ERI2, September 18, 2009); and U.S. Commission on International Religious Freedom, *Annual Report to Congress* (Washington, D.C.: U.S. Commission on International Religious Freedom, 2010), 53.

181. According to Hassan Bubacar Jallow's résumé, available from the Commonwealth, in 1993 he chaired the Group of Experts to Advise on the Establishment of a National Human Rights Commission for the Gambia. See the Commonwealth website, www.thecommonwealth.org.

182. See "Final Communiqué" (Consultative Meeting of NHRIs in West Africa, Banjul, Gambia, November 8–10, 2006).

183. Assan Martin, "National Human Rights Commission: A Mechanism to Monitor Human Rights Activities," *The Point* (Banjul, Gambia), May 18, 2010.

184. UN Press Release, "Somalia: Continued Deterioration in Human Rights Situation" (September 27, 2007); and UN General Assembly, Human Rights Council, "Compilation Prepared by OHCHR: Somalia, for the UPR" (A/HRC/WG.6/11/SOM/2, February 21, 2011).

185. "Response to Recommendations: São Tomé" (November 24, 2011), upr-info.org.

186. Note that Mozambique was the first country to join the Commonwealth, in 1996, without having been part of the British Empire. See UN General Assembly, Human Rights Council, "National Report, Submitted by the Government of Mozambique for the UPR" (A/HRC/WG.6/10/MOZ/1, November 11, 2010); UN General Assembly, Human Rights Council, "Review of the Working Group on the Universal Periodic Review: Mozambique" (A/HRC/17/16, March 28, 2011);

and "Response to Recommendations: Mozambique" (November 22, 2011), upr-info .org.

187. James C. Scott, *Domination and the Arts of Resistance: Hidden Transcripts* (New Haven, Conn.: Yale University Press, 1990), 28.

Chapter 7

1. Rodrigo Alberto Carazo, "The Ombudsman of Costa Rica," in Hossain et al., *Human Rights Commissions and Ombudsman Offices*, 308.

2. Jorge Luis Maiorano, "El Defensor del Pueblo en América Latina: La Necesidad de Fortalecerlo," in Luis Armando Carello, ed., *Derecho constitucional y administrativo*, vol. 3 (Madrid: Centro de Estudios Financieros, 2002), 170. For regional overviews, see Thomas Pegram, "National Human Rights Institutions in Latin America: Politics and Institutionalization," in Goodman and Pegram, *Human Rights, State Compliance, and Social Change*; Gonzalo Elizondo and Irene Aguilar, "The Ombudsman Institution in Latin America: Minimum Standards for Its Existence," in Lindsnaes, Lindholt and Yigen, *National Human Rights Institutions*, 209–20; and Comisión Andina de Juristas (CAJ), *Defensorías del pueblo en la Región Andina: Experiencias comparadas* (Lima, Peru: CJ, 2001).

3. Leo Valladares Lanza, "The Challenges Facing the Ombudsman in Latin America," in Linda C. Reif, ed., *The International Ombudsman Yearbook 1998*, vol. 2 (The Hague: Kluwer, 1999), 159–65.

4. Fredrik Uggla, "The Ombudsman in Latin America," *Journal of Latin American Studies* 36 (2004): 423–50, 449.

5. Kathryn Sikkink, "Human Rights, Principled Issue-Networks, and Sovereignty in Latin America," *International Organization* 47 (Summer 1993): 430–31; Ellen L. Lutz, "Human Rights in Mexico: Cause for Continuing Concern," *Current History* 92 (February 1993): 78–82; and Grupo Parlamentario del Partido de la Revolución Democrática, Cámara de Diputados, *Legislación de los derechos humanos en México: Avances y retrocesos* (Mexico City: Congreso de la Unión, 1993).

6. *Dirección para la defensa de los derechos humanos del estado de Nueva Leon*, in Gregory and Giddings, *Righting Wrongs*, 264.

7. Organization of American States (OAS), *Annual Report of the Inter-American Commission on Human Rights 1989–1990* (Washington, D.C.: OAS General Secretariat, 1990); and Americas Watch, *Human Rights in Mexico: A Policy of Impunity* (New York: Human Rights Watch, 1990).

8. U.S. House of Representatives, Committee on Foreign Affairs, Subcommittees on Human Rights and International Organizations and on Western Hemisphere Affairs, *Current Developments in Mexico*, 101st Congress, 2nd sess. (September 12, 1990); and Americas Watch, *Human Rights Watch World Report 1992* (New York: Human Rights Watch, 1991).

9. Government of Mexico, "Decreto constitucional," *Diario oficial de la Federación* (Mexico City, January 28, 1992). See Mexican Constitution, Article 102, Section B. See also Jorge Madrazo, "New Policies on Human Rights in Mexico: The

National Commission for Human Rights, 1988–1993," *Ombudsman Journal* 12 (1994): 19–39. For the post-1993 period, see also José Luis Soberanes Fernández, "The Protection Role of the Mexican Human Rights Commission," in Ramcharan *The Protection Role of National Human Rights Institutions*, 107–15; and Alejandro Anaya Muñoz, "Transnational and Domestic Processes in the Definition of Human Rights Policies in Mexico," *Human Rights Quarterly* 31, 1 (February 2009): 35–58.

10. The constitution of 1983 was being amended; the ombudsman was embedded in legislation in 1992. Michael Dodson and Donald Wilson Jackson, "Horizontal Accountability in Transitional Democracies: The Human Rights Ombudsman in El Salvador and Guatemala," *Latin American Politics and Society* 46, 4 (Winter 2004): 1–27.

11. In the constitution of 1886, the office of *procuradores* was created, attending to vulnerable members of society. In the 1939 constitution, the Procurador General de la República was placed within a new Ministerio Público o Fiscal, as a representative of the state and society, drawing on antecedents in Spanish legal history; again, the focus was on the most vulnerable members of society, and the office developed a mediating role. In the 1945 constitution, it was given full independence and was made a protective body. In 1950, the Procuraduría General reverted back to poverty, as established in the 1886 constitution, but also as a way of differentiating itself from the Mexican Procuraduría General, which was an accusatory body. In El Salvador, two institutions were created: attorney general (fiscal general) and Procuraduria General (a protective body). Procuraduría General de la República de El Salvador, *Historia de la Procuraduría General* (San Salvador, El Salvador, 2011).

12. This was in addition to the attorney general (fiscal general) and a general ombudsman (Procuraduria General).

13. Michael Dodson, "The Human Rights Ombudsman in Central America: Honduras and El Salvador Case Studies," *Essex Human Rights Review* 3, 1 (2006): 29–45, 39.

14. Ibid., 40.

15. Uggla, "Ombudsman in Latin America," 434.

16. Beatrice de Carrillo was reelected in 2004.

17. Winifred Tate, *Counting the Dead: The Culture and Politics of Human Rights Activism in Colombia* (Berkeley: University of California Press, 2007), 226. See generally Jose F. Castro Caycedo, "The Defender of the Public of the Republic of Colombia," in Hossain et al., *Human Rights Commissions and Ombudsman Offices*, 289–97.

18. Consejero Presidencial para los Derechos Humanos. The highly personalized institution of *personeros* was inherited from colonial times. Tate, *Counting the Dead*, 61, 223, and 226.

19. Tate, *Counting the Dead*, 226–27. For an in-depth discussion of the institutionalization of human rights within Colombia's military, see "Human Rights and the Colombian Military's War Stories," chap. 7 in ibid.

20. Tate, *Counting the Dead*, 228.

21. Ibid., 229.

22. Ibid., 223, and 140–41.

23. Ibid., 64.

24. Ibid., 231.

25. Ibid., 219. International NGOs (e.g., International Crisis Group) called for large amounts of foreign funds to strengthen accountability mechanisms, including the ombudsman.

26. Executive Decree No. 26–92 (June 8, 1992) and Executive Decree No. 51–92; and Dodson, "Human Rights Ombudsman in Central America," 31–32.

27. Dodson, "Human Rights Ombudsman in Central America," 31–38.

28. Inter-American Commission on Human Rights, Organization of American States, "Honduras: Human Rights and the Coup d'État" (2009), para. 175; and Misión Internacional de Observación de Derechos Humanos en Honduras, "Gobierno de facto viola derechos humanos en Honduras: Informe Final" (July 6, 2009).

29. Gustavo Veiga, "De defensor a negador de los derechos humanos," *Pagina 12* (Argentina), September 7, 2009.

30. It was incorporated into the Defensoría de los Habitantes in mid-1993. Hossain et al., *Human Rights Commissions and Ombudsman Offices*, 300. On the ombudsman for children, see Reif, *The Ombudsman*, 309.

31. Law 7319, November 17, 1992. See Rodrigo Alberto Carazo, "The Ombudsman of Costa Rica," in Hossain et al., *National Human Rights Commissions and Ombudsman Offices*, 299–314.

32. The institution was referred to by its current name in the constitution. See Paraguayan Constitution, Chapter IV, Section 1, Articles 276–80 and Law No. 631 (1995). Relevant legislation was passed in 1995.

33. The Defensoría highlights the role of both El Justicia (a mediator among neighbors) and El Protector de Naturales (for indigenous issues). See Defensoría del Pueblo, República del Paraguay, "Historia," http://www.defensoriadelpueblo.gov.py.

34. The IACHR also sent a follow-up note in July 2000. For full details, see IACHR, "Third Report on the Situation of Human Rights in Paraguay" (OEA/Ser.L/V /II. 110, March 9, 2001).

35. The amendment was to the constitution of 1853. Decree 1.786 was repealed when Law No. 24.284 was passed on December 1, 1993, and then was amended in Law No. 24.379 in 1994. For an overview, see Luis Maiorano, "The Ombudsman Institution in Argentina," in Hossain et al., *Human Rights Commissions and Ombudsman Offices*, 233–46; and Gabriella Dalla Corte, "El Defensor del pueblo en la redefinición del estado argentino: Los conflictos sociales del fin de siglo," *Scripta Nova* 45 (August 1999), http://www.ub.eto/geocrit/nova.htm.

36. See, for example, Rebecca Bill Chavez, *The Rule of Law in Nascent Democracies: Judicial Politics in Argentina* (Stanford, Calif.: Stanford University Press, 2004); and Jonathan R. Barton and Laura Tedesco, *The State of Democracy in Latin America: Post-Transitional Conflicts in Argentina and Chile* (New York: Routledge, 2005).

37. Enrique Peruzzotti, "The Societalization of Horizontal Accountability: Rights Advocacy and the Defensor del Pueblo de la Nación in Argentina," in Goodman and Pegram, *Human Rights, State Compliance, and Social Change*, 243–69.

38. Senators Eduardo Menem and Libardo Sánchez, both of the Partido Justicialista. Gregory and Giddings, *Righting Wrongs*, 65. These included the provinces of San Juan, La Rioja, Salta Córdoba, and Rio Negro and the Federal Capital.

39. Maiorano, "El Defensor del Pueblo en América Latina."

40. Andrea Paula Botto, *Quién defiende a los consumidores? La regulación de los servicios públicos residenciales en Argentina y en Brasil despues de las privatizaciones* (Buenos Aires: Prometeo Libros, 2007), 104.

41. Reif, *The Ombudsman*, 200–205. Ombudsman Organization Act, Act No. 26,5120 (August 4, 1995), enacting legislation in 1995.

42. Uggla, "Ombudsman in Latin America," 436. See also Thomas Pegram, "Accountability in Hostile Times: The Case of the Peruvian Human Rights Ombudsman, 1996–2001," *Journal of Latin American Studies* 40, 1 (February 2008): 51–82.

43. Uggla, "Ombudsman in Latin America," 438.

44. Ibid., 441.

45. Ibid., 446.

46. Charles D. Kenney, "Horizontal Accountability: Concepts and Conflicts," in Scott Mainwairing and Christopher Welna, eds., *Democratic Accountability in Latin America* (Oxford: Oxford University Press, 2003), 66.

47. Part V of the 1981 constitution addressed the institution of the ombudsman.

48. The institution has had links with the Danish Centre for Human Rights, the Inter-American Institute of Human Rights, the Caribbean Human Rights Network, and the International Ombudsman Institute. The ombudsman was not appointed until 1995.

49. UN General Assembly, Human Rights Council, "Compilation Prepared by the OHCHR, for Antigua and Barbuda's UPR" (A/HRC/WG.6/12/ATG/2, July 25, 2011); and "Report of the Working Group on the Universal Periodic Review: Antigua and Barbuda" (A/HRC/19/5, December 14, 2011).

50. Larry J. Diamond, *Developing Democracy: Toward Consolidation* (Baltimore: Johns Hopkins University Press, 1999), 4. Power was transferred from Vere Bird to his son Lester; the Labour Party continued to rule, but with a smaller majority.

51. It ratified the ICESCR in 2000, along with CEDAW and CERD in 2001. *UN Treaty Collection.*

52. UN General Assembly, Human Rights Council, "Compilation Prepared by the OHCHR, for Belize's UPR" (A/HRC/WG.6/5/BLZ/2, March 9, 2009).

53. For how the institution could offer an alternative system of dispute resolution, given the ongoing problem of accessing justice via the courts in Belize, see Albert K. Fiadjoe, "Access to Justice—Where Does the Ombudsman of Belize Fit In?" (Paper presented at the Belize Country Conference, University of West Indies, November 21–24, 2001, www.cavehill.uwi.edu.)

54. The 2009 constitution retained the institution.

55. In 1999, shortly after the institution's creation, it applied for international accreditation and was deemed "partially compliant" with the Paris Principles, though this certification was quickly reversed. This section draws mostly from Fredrik Uggla, "Through Pressure or Persuasion? Explaining Compliance with the Resolutions of the Bolivian Defensor del Pueblo," in Goodman and Pegram, *Human Rights, State Compliance, and Social Change*, 270–94.

56. The 1996 amendments followed on earlier amendments (in 1982 and 1992) to the 1979 constitution. Section II, para. 2 (1996), Article 96 (1998), and Article 214 (2008).

57. Defensoría del Pueblo Ecuador, *Breve recuento de la historia del ombudsman y el nacimiento de la defensoría en Ecuador*, YouTube, posted on December 17, 2012.

58. As the Inter-American Commission notes in its 1997 report on Ecuador, "During 1995 and into 1996, relations between the branches of Government were strained, with the then-ruling party holding fewer than ten of 77 seats in the Congress." IACHR, "Report on the Situation of Human Rights in Ecuador" (OEA/Ser.L/V/II.96, April 24, 1997), chap. 2.

59. According to the IACHR's 1997 report on Ecuador, "The right to judicial protection is impeded by: pervasive delay in the judicial system; barriers to the impartial and independent administration of justice, including corruption and the impermanence of certain judicial appointments; and the lack of access to judicial protection due to the dearth of public defenders and the unresponsive distribution of facilities in certain rural areas. Reports indicate that the judicial system is substantially underfunded, and that the scarcity of resources contributes to each of the foregoing problems." Ibid.

60. Unger, *Elusive Reform*, Chapter 2.

61. John M. Ackerman, "Understanding Independent Accountability Agencies," in Susan Rose-Ackerman and Peter L. Lindseth, eds., *Comparative Administrative Law* (Cheltenham, UK: Edward Elgar, 2010), 273. Complaints committed by the police forces are under the purview of the Ministry of Government's National Human Rights Directorate. UN General Assembly, Human Rights Council, "Summary Prepared by the OHCHR, for Ecuador's UPR" (A/HRC/WG.6/11/ECU/3, March 6, 2008).

62. The other "functions" were executive, legislative, judicial and indigenous justice, and electoral. Ackerman, "Understanding Independent Accountability Agencies," 273.

63. Law No. 7 was passed on December 2, 1996, entering into force on February 5, 1997. See Xenia Solis Bravo, "El Defensor del Pueblo de la República de Panamá y el Ombudsman Nacional del Reino de los Paises Bajos de Holanda en una perspectiva comparativa" (Costa Rica: Instituto Interamericano de Derechos Humanos, 2001).

64. Someone who worked in 1991 on the creation of a human rights ombudsman was Luis Adolfo Corró Fernández, a lawyer who had studied comparative law in Spain until 1986 and who served in 1991 as the chief of staff for the president of Panama's National Assembly, going on to work on refugee issues within Panama and running unsuccessfully for the post of ombudsman in 2004. See the biography posted on the website of Corró Fernández & Asociados, http://www.corrfernandezlawfirm.com. In 1982, a thesis was also apparently written on the topic. "Ley N° 7 de 5 de febrero de 1997 por el cual se estableció la Institución en la República de Panamá," 1. Panama's constitution is from 1972, with revisions in 1978, 1983, 1993, 1994, and 2004.

65. Panama's army was converted in 1990 to a police force. See Orlando J. Pérez, *Post-Invasion Panama: The Challenge of Democratization in the New World Order* (Lanham, Md.: Lexington Books, 2000), 12.

66. "Ley N° 7 de 5 de febrero de 1997 por el cual se estableció la Institución en la República de Panamá," 1.

67. Executive Decree No. 172 (April 1995).

68. "Un ejercicio ejemplar de democracia participativa, que debe servir de ejemplo a procesos similares en el resto del mundo." Oscar Ceville, "Ley No 7, por el cual

se estableció la Institución en la República de Panáma" (Statement to Panama's National Assembly, February 5, 1997).

69. "Ley N° 7 de 5 de febrero de 1997 por el cual se estableció la Institución en la República de Panamá," 2.

70. President Ernesto Pérez Balladares. Amnesty International, "Panama Amnesty Law to Be Debated in Legislative Assembly" (AMR44/01/96, February 15, 1996).

71. Red de Derechos Humanos—Panama, *Alternative Report on Human Rights Situation in Panama* (Panama City, March 2008), 14.

72. Gonzalo Elizondo and Irene Aguilar, *La institución del Ombudsman en América Latina: Requisitos mínimos para su existencia* (Costa Rica: IIDH, 2009). The Central American group was formed in 1994, linked closely to the subregion's peace processes, supported by the European Community.

73. Panamanian Constitution, Chapter 9, Articles 129–30; and OHCHR, "Chart of the Status of National Institutions."

74. Nicaraguan Constitution, Article 17, Part VIII. The implementing legislation was Act No. 212, which entered into force in 1996.

75. The announced formation in 1992 of a government human rights body within the attorney general's office was postponed. Peter R. Baehr, ed., *Human Rights in Developing Countries: Year Book 1995* (Leiden: Kluwer, 1995), 211.

76. Procuraduría para la Defensa de los Derechos Humanos, República de Nicaragua, "Cómo nace la PPDH" (http://www.procuraduriaddhh.gov.ni/).

77. Decree No. 438 (March 3, 1980).

78. The preamble refers to Resolutions 23 (XXXIV) and 24 (XXXV) of the UN Human Rights Commission, from March 1978 and March 1979, respectively, as well as Resolution 33/46 of the General Assembly from December 4, 1978. The decree can be accessed on the website of Nicaragua's National Assembly, http://demoan.cadimo.com. For the argument that the institution was created to counterbalance the outspoken NGO, see Roger Miranda and William Ratliff, *The Civil War in Nicaragua: Inside the Sandinistas* (New Brunswick, N.J.: Transaction, 1994), 172. The IACHR speaks positively of the commission in its 1981 report following an in-country visit. See IACHR, "Report of the Situation of Human Rights in the Republic of Nicaragua" (OEA/Ser.L/V/ II.53, doc. 25, June 30, 1981), chap. 8. Likewise, Donnelly and Howard-Hassmann note that despite its political biases, the institution did defend human rights. Jack Donnelly and Rhoda E. Howard-Hassmann, eds., *International Handbook of Human Rights* (Westport, Conn.: Greenwood, 1987), 254. For U.S. government funding of the Permanent Commission on Human Rights, see James Peck, *Ideal Illusions: How the U.S. Government Co-opted Human Rights* (New York: Metropolitan Books, 2010), 314n147.

79. Miranda and Ratliff, *Civil War in Nicaragua*, 172.

80. Procuraduría General de la República de Nicaragua, "Breve reseña historica," www.pgr.gob.ni.

81. Mark Ungar, *Elusive Reform: Democracy and the Rule of Law in Latin America* (Boulder Colo.: Lynne Rienner, 2002), 38.

82. This citizen branch includes the ombudsman, comptroller, and attorney general (fiscal general). Together, the heads of these agencies make up the Republican Moral Council, charged with combating corruption and the abuse of power. Ackerman, "Understanding Independent Accountability Agencies," 273.

83. Decree No. 1034 (January 24, 1996).

84. www.pgr.gob.ni.

85. *South America, Central America and the Caribbean* (New York: Routledge, 2006), 156–63. Also, Walton Brown, Jr., *Bermuda and the Struggle for Reform: Race, Politics, and Ideology, 1944–1998* (Bermuda: Cahow, 2011).

86. For example, the human rights act was amended in 1988, 1992, 1995, and 2000.

87. Bermuda Human Rights Commission, *Annual Report of the Human Rights Commission* (Bermuda: Bermuda Human Rights Commission, 1982), 3. As early as 1953, an ad hoc race relations committee was created, perhaps influenced by similar bodies in the United States. "House to Consider Setting-Up Race Relations Council," *Bermuda Recorder*, May 9, 1964. Originally set for review in 2011, the accreditation process was deferred.

88. Professor Jorge Mario Quinzio. See Juan Domingo Milos, "La idea del defensor del pueblo en Chile: Los inicios del Capitúlo Chileno del Ombudsman" (April 21, 2009), http://www.defensorpueblo.blogspot.com.

89. Constitutional reforms took place in 1989, 1991, 1997, 1999, 2000, 2003, 2005. See Ana María Moure Pino, "El Defensor del Pueblo y su establecimiento en Chile" (Universidad de Alcalá, January 27, 2004); and Elia Parra, "La lenta implementación de Ombudsman en Chile" (June 21, 2007), http://www.elciudadano.cl.

90. UN General Assembly, Human Rights Council, "National Report, Submitted by the Government of Chile for UPR" (A/HRC/WG.6/5/CHL/1, February 16, 2009), 3. At the time of the UPR, the government also affirmed its commitment to passing a constitutional amendment creating an ombudsman and to devising a national action plan for human rights.

91. For the founding bill, see Law No. 20, 405. There was one abstention; and the vote was unanimous in the Chamber of Deputies. See Instituto Nacional de Derechos Humanos, http://www.indh.cl.

92. Capitulo Chileno del Ombudsman, "Indicaciones a Proyecto de Ley Que Crea el Instituto Nacional de Derechos Humanos," May 17, 2007.

93. Note that local ombudsman bodies also exist. Parra, "La lenta implementación"; and Capitulo Chileno del Ombudsman, "Encuentro ciudadano: Defensoría del Pueblo: Ahora más que nunca" (August 27, 2011), http://www.derhumano.blog spot.com.

94. For an overview of the CDDPH's history, see Secretaria de Direitos Humanos, "CDDPH: Historico," http://www.sedh.gov.br/.

95. See Célia Costa, "A atuação de Lysâneas Maciel no campo dos direitos humanos na década de 1970," in Angela María de Castro Gomes, ed., *Direitos e cidadania: Justiça, podar e mídia* (Rio de Janeiro: FGV Editor, 2007), 282. Law no. 4319, March 16, 1964 established the institution.

96. *Direito à memoria e à verdade* (Brasília: Secretaria Especial de Direitos da Presidência da República, 2007), covering events between 1961 and 1988.

97. See Office of the United Nations High Commissioner for Human Rights, "National Plans of Action for the Promotion and Protection of Human Rights," http://www.ohchr.org. The Brazilians, moreover, had consulted the Australian human rights plan. James Louis Cavallaro, "The Brazilian National Human Rights Program in Context" (Encontro Anual de ANPOCS, n.d.).

98. UN General Assembly, Human Rights Council, "National Report, Submitted by the Government of Brazil for UPR" (A/HRC/WG.6/11/BRA/1, March 7, 2008); and Susan Ariel Aaronson and Jamie M. Zimmerman, *Trade Imbalance: The Struggle to Weigh Human Rights Concerns in Trade Policymaking* (Cambridge: Cambridge University Press, 2008), 99.

99. UN General Assembly, Human Rights Council, "Compilation Prepared by the OHCHR, for Brazil's UPR" (A/HRC/WG.6/11/BRA/2, March 31, 2008), 3.

100. Secretaria Especial dos Direitos Humanos da Presidência da República, "Programa Nacional de Direitos Humanos" (2009).

101. Pinheiro and Baluarte, "National Strategies." Also Paulo Sérgio de Moraes Sarmento Pinheiro, "Brazil and the International Human Rights System" (Working Paper CBS-15-00, University of Oxford, Centre for Brazil Studies, 2000). Pinheiro was a UN special rapporteur and human rights secretary.

102. See invitation by OHCHR for a side event on "national human rights institutions in federal states" and presentation by Lyal S. Sunga, May 18, 2011, http://nhri .ohchr.org. Other federal states that in 2011 had not established an NHRI included Comoros, Ethiopia, Micronesia, Pakistan, St. Kitts and Nevis, the United States, and the United Arab Emirates.

103. For example, São Paulo has the Conselho de Defesa dos Direitos da Pessoa Humana.

104. The military tried unsuccessfully to draft a new constitution in 1980. Luis Roniger and Mario Sznajder, *The Legacy of Human Rights Violations in the Southern Cone: Argentina, Chile and Uruguay* (Oxford: Oxford University Press, 1999), 177.

105. The remainder of this section draws on UN General Assembly, Human Rights Council, "National Report, Submitted by the Government of Uruguay for UPR" (A/HRC/WG.6/5/URY/1, February 24, 2009) and "Compilation Prepared by the OHCHR, for Uruguay's UPR" (A/HRC/WG.6/5/URY/12, March 13, 2009).

106. UN General Assembly, Human Rights Council, "Compilation Prepared by the OHCHR, for Dominican Republic's UPR" (A/HRC/WG.6/6/DOM/2, August 11, 2009).

107. UN General Assembly, Human Rights Council, "National Report, Submitted by the Government of St. Kitts & Nevis for UPR" (A/HRC/WG.6/10/KNA/1), November 10, 2010.

108. "Caribbean Regional Seminar on the Role of the Ombudsman in the Fostering of Good Governance and Democracy" (Basseterre, St. Kitts, January 12–15, 2004; communiqué issued by the Commonwealth, January 15, 2004).

109. People's Democratic Movement (Press release, 2008).

110. UN General Assembly, Human Rights Council, "Report of the Working Group on the Universal Periodic Review: Grenada" (A/HRC/15/12, June 16, 2010).

111. Report of the Grenada Constitutional Review Commission (November 1985), 19; UN General Assembly, Human Rights Council, "Compilation Prepared by the OHCHR, for Grenada's UPR" (A/HRC/WG.6/8/GRD/2, February 22, 2010); and *UN Treaty Collection*.

112. "Responses to Recommendations: Suriname" (January 6, 2012), http://upr -info.com.

113. CARICOM Initiative, "Forward Together Suriname National Consultation: Involving Civil Society in Caribbean Development" (Paramaribo, October 12), 4 and 8.

114. "Responses to Recommendations: Suriname"; and UN General Assembly, Human Rights Council, "Compilation Prepared by the OHCHR, for Suriname's UPR" (A/HRC/WG.6/12/ATG/2, July 25, 2011).

115. "Responses to Recommendations: Cuba" (February 5, 2009), http://upr-info .com; and *UN Treaty Collection.*

116. See discussion in Chapter 2; International Association of Official Human Rights Agencies, www.iaohra.org; and author interviews with multiple NHRI leaders abroad.

117. Catherine Powell, *Human Rights at Home: A Domestic Policy Blueprint for the New Administration* (Washington, D.C.: American Constitution Society for Law and Policy, October 2008); and "Road to Rights."

118. Isabel Allende, *Eva Luna* (1985; repr., New York: Dial Press, 1987), 16.

119. Marguerite Feitlowitz, *A Lexicon of Terror: Argentina and the Legacies of Torture* (Oxford: Oxford University Press, 1998).

Chapter 8

1. South Asia Human Rights Documentation Center (SAHRDC), *National Human Rights Institutions in the Asia Pacific Region*, "Report of the Alternate NGO Consultation on the Second Asia-Pacific Regional Workshop on Human Rights Institutions" (New Delhi: SAHRDC, March 1998), 37, cited originally in Cardenas, "Adaptive States," 2. For regional overviews of NHRIs, see Chapter 3, n36. Also, Abul Hasnat Monjurul Kabir, "Establishing National Human Rights Commissions in South Asia: A Critical Analysis of the Processes and Prospects," *Asia-Pacific Journal on Human Rights and the Law* 2, 1 (2001): 1–53; and Hugo Stokke, "Taking the Paris Principles to Asia: A Study of Three Human Rights Commissions in Southeast Asia (Norway: Chr. Michelsen Institute, 2007).

2. Arun Ray, *National Human Rights Commission of India: Formation, Functioning and Future Prospects*, 2nd rev. ed. (New Delhi: Khama, 2004), 81–82; and Charles H. Norchi, "The National Human Rights Commission of India as a Value-Creating Institution," in John Montgomery, ed., *Human Rights: Positive Policies in Asia and the Pacific Rim* (Hollis, N.H.: Hollis Publishing, 1998), 113. These commissions had been established, along with institutions like the Election Commission and the Auditor General, in the postindependence 1949 constitution and began functioning in 1950. In 1978, after the emergency period had ended, government resolutions transformed these bodies into multimember institutions. A survey of India's NHRI is also provided in Vijayashri Sripati, "India's National Human Rights Commission: A Shackled Commission?" *Boston University International Law Journal* 18, 1 (Spring 2000): 1–33; and A. S. Annand, "The Protection Role of the Indian Human Rights Commission," in Ramcharan, *The Protection Role of National Human Rights Institutions*, 87–105.

3. Manoranjan Mohanty, "The Fight for Rights, Race of Civil Liberties Groups," *The Statesman* (New Delhi), September 1985.

4. Personal communication with Australian judge, Hon. Michael Kirby, November 2011. Judge Kirby does not recall discussing with him the commission, though he thinks it is possible that he met with Dame Roma Mitchell, who was chair of the Human Rights Commission at the time and herself a former distinguished judge (coincidentally, Australia's first woman judge). In 1988, Justice Bhagwati chaired (at a Commonwealth-sponsored meeting) the drafting of the influential Bangalore Principles, which asserted that judges in common-law systems can invoke international human rights law, even when the laws in question have not been formally incorporated domestically, in cases where an ambiguity or gap exists. In more recent years, Judge Bhagwati said he made a mistake in supporting the emergency decrees in the 1970s, after which time he became a forceful proponent of human rights. Michael Kirby, "PN Bhagwati—An Australian Appreciation" (December 20, 1998), http://www.lawfoundation.net.au/; Maneesh Chhibber, "35 Years Later, a Former Chief Justice of India Pleads Guilty," *Indian Express* (New Delhi), September 16, 2011.

5. See IPHRC, "Report of the Indian People's Human Rights Tribunal on Arwal Massacre" (New Delhi: IPHRC, 1987).

6. Ray paraphrasing V. N. Gadgil, Congress Party spokesperson. Ray, *National Human Rights Commission of India*, 83.

7. Ibid., 82–84.

8. Ibid., 85 and 87.

9. Ibid., 85.

10. Norchi, "The National Human Rights Commission of India as a Value-Creating Institution," 113–14.

11. D. S. Aswal, "Human Rights Body: Why," *The Patriot* (New Delhi), June 21, 1993, cited in Roy, *National Human Rights Commission of India*, 89.

12. Ravi Nair, cited in Edward A. Gargan, "Indian Rights Group's Cry: Police Rape and Torture," *New York Times* (October 14, 1992): A10. See also Cardenas, "Adaptive States," 38–10.

13. Rajeev Dhavan, "More Is Not Always More: Unto Us a Human Rights Commission Is Given—But Why?" (Working Paper No. 18, Public Interest Legal Support and Research Centre, New Delhi, May 1993), cited in Norchi, "National Human Rights Commission of India," 116.

14. Ministry of Home Affairs, Government of India, "Background Note on Setting Up of a National Commission on Human Rights—Issues and Tentative Framework" (n.d.), cited in Norchi, "National Human Rights Commission of India," 116.

15. S. B. Chavan, "India: The National Human Rights Commission Bill, 1993" (New York: Lawyers' Committee for Human Rights, 1993).

16. V. Vijayakumar, "The Working of the National Human Rights Commission: A Perspective," in C. J. Nirmal, ed., *Human Rights in India: Historical, Social, and Political Perspectives* (Oxford: Oxford University Press, 2000), 216.

17. Norchi, "National Human Rights Commission of India," 113. The head of the minorities commission was to be an ex officio member of the NHRC.

18. Vijayakumar, "Working of the National Human Rights Commission," 215.

19. Ray, *National Human Rights Commission of India*, 82. The report was that of a tribunal formed by the IPHRC and headed by two retired judges of Bombay's Higher Court.

20. National Human Rights Commission of Indonesia, "Komnas Ham History," *Annual Report 1994* (Jakarta: Komnas Ham, 1995); and International Council on Human Rights Policy, "Indonesia," in *Performance and Legitimacy: National Human Rights Institutions* (Switzerland: ICHRP, 2000), 22. See also Cardenas, "Adaptive States," 35–37.

21. Jetschke, "Linking the Unlinkable?," 156.

22. National Human Rights Commission of Indonesia, "Komnas Ham History," in *Annual Report 1994* (Jakarta: Komnas Ham, 1995).

23. SAHRDC, *Komnas HAM—The Indonesian Human Rights Commission: The Formative Years* (New Delhi: SAHRDC, 2000), 36–37.

24. Amnesty International, *Indonesia: An Audit of Human Rights Reform* (London: Amnesty Publications, March 1999).

25. Cardenas, "Transgovernmental Activism," 784–87.

26. While Oslo's Declaration of Principles from 1993 did not mention human rights, both subsequent interim agreements (Oslo I and II) as well as the Wye Memorandum did so. As Article XIV ("Human Rights and the Rule of Law") notes, due regard would be paid by both sides to "internationally-accepted norms and principles of human rights and the rule of law." In fact, it was the exclusion of human rights issues from the declaration of principles, despite earlier rhetorical commitments, that led some members of the Palestinian delegation to push for their inclusion as part of the negotiations for the Gaza/Jericho agreement (Oslo I) in 1994.

27. Decree No. 59/1994. Article 31 reads, "An independent Commission for Human Rights shall be established by law, which shall specify its formation, duties and jurisdiction. The Commission shall submit its reports to the President of the National Authority and the Palestinian Legislative Council."

28. International Coordinating Committee of National Institutions for the Promotion and Protection of Human Rights, "Specific Recommendations—Re-Accreditation Application: Palestine" (Report and recommendations of the session of the Sub-Committee on Accreditation, Geneva, March 26–30, 2009). See also, Byrnes, Durbach, and Renshaw, "Joining the Club," 83–84.

29. The original decree's title used the word "citizen," though that document also used "National Supreme Commission on Human Rights." See the Independent Commission for Human Rights website, www.ichr.ps.

30. Amnesty International, "Israel and the Occupied Territories: Chairman Arafat Affirms Palestine Liberation Organization Commitment to Human Rights" (News Service 124/93, October 5, 1993). In its news release, Amnesty International dates the decree to October 3, though the decree itself appears to be stamped September 30.

31. Hanan Ashrawi, *This Side of Peace: A Personal Account* (New York: Simon and Schuster, 1996), 280.

32. Ibid., 280–81.

33. Fateh S. Azzam, "Update: The Palestinian Independent Commission for Citizens' Rights," *Human Rights Quarterly* 20, 2 (1998): 341.

34. Cardenas and Flibbert, "National Human Rights Institutions," 422–23.

35. Ashrawi, *Side of Peace*, 281.

36. The Cairo Declaration on Human Rights in Islam had been issued in 1990. It is available at http://www.oic-oci.org/.

37. UN General Assembly, Human Rights Council, "National Report, Submitted by the Government of Iran for UPR" (A/HRC/WG.6/7/IRN/1, November 18, 2009), 12.

38. Hassan Davoodfard and Jayum Anak Jawan, "Effectiveness of International Actions in Debate of Human Rights in Iran 1990–2008," *Australian Journal of Basic and Applied Science* 5, 5 (2011): 519–36.

39. See UN General Assembly, Human Rights Council, "National Report, Submitted by the Government of Iran for UPR," Annex IV.

40. Davoodfard and Jawan, "Effectiveness of International Action in Debate of Human Rights in Iran," 525; and Human Rights Watch, *World Report 2002* (New York: Human Rights Watch, 2002), 423–30.

41. One of his brothers chaired parliament in 2012, while another one was the chief justice.

42. ANNI, Regional Conference on the Engagement with the Asia Pacific Forum of National Human Rights Institutions, September 5–6, 2011, Bangkok. ANNI was created in 2006.

43. Amnesty International, "Iran: Submission to the Human Rights Committee" (October 17–November 4, 2011).

44. In March 2010, the UN Human Rights Council issued a resolution on the protection of human rights defenders, including NHRIs in this category. See A/HRC/RES/13/13.

45. UN General Assembly, Human Rights Council, "National Report, Submitted by the Government of Iran for UPR."

46. Act No. 21 (1996). See " 'Embedded in the State': The Human Rights Commission of Sri Lanka" (Colombo, Sri Lanka: Law and Society Trust, August 2012), 23, 298. Also, Commonwealth Human Rights Initiative, *The Human Rights Commission of Sri Lanka—The First Year* (New Delhi: CHRI, 1999).

47. For example, Kishali Pinto-Jayaawardena, ed., *A Legacy to Remember: Sri Lanka's Commissions of Inquiry 1963–2002* (Colombo, Sri Lanka: Law and Society Trust, 2010).

48. Human Rights Watch, *World Report 1992* (New York: Human Rights Watch, 1992), 463.

49. The commission was created as part of the Sri Lanka Foundation, itself formed in 1973 to promote human rights.

50. Statement by H. W. Jayawardene, Sri Lanka, UN Commission of Human Rights (41st Session, Agenda Item 12, Question 5 of the Violation of Human Rights, March 8, 1985).

51. More specifically, UNICEF, UNDP, UNHCR, NORAD, Canadian International Development Agency, Swedish International Development Agency, and the British Commonwealth have offered assistance.

52. Apratim Mukarji, *Sri Lanka: A Dangerous Interlude* (Elgin, Ill.: New Dawn Press, 2005), xxxi. For further confirmation of this argument, see Renshaw and Fitzpatrick, "National Human Rights Institutions in the Asia Pacific Region."

53. Mukarji, *Sri Lanka*, xxxi. See also Mario Gomez, "Sri Lanka's New Human Rights Commission," *Human Rights Quarterly* 20 (May 1998): 281–302.

54. Amnesty International, *Sri Lanka: Torture in Custody* (London: Amnesty Publications, 1999); Amnesty International, *Sri Lanka: Scrutiny by the Human Rights Committee* (London: Amnesty Publications, 1995); Gomez, "Sri Lanka's New Human Rights Commission; SAHRDC, *National Human Rights Institutions in the Asia Pacific Region;* and Commonwealth Human Rights Initiative, *The Human Rights Commission of Sri Lanka.*

55. Mario Gomez, "National Human Rights Commissions and Internally Displaced Persons: Illustrated by the Sri Lankan Experience" (Washington, D.C.: Brookings Institution, July 2002). A critical perspective is also offered in U.K. Foreign and Commonwealth Office, "Annual Report on Human Rights" (2009).

56. Ilango, *Easier Said Than Done*, 62; and OHCHR, "Chart of the Status of National Institutions."

57. Mukarji, *Sri Lanka*, xxxi.

58. This section draws on Hong Kong Human Rights Monitor, "A Project on the Establishment of a Human Rights Commission in Hong Kong" (consultation document for Asia Pacific Forum meeting, August 10, 2007).

59. George Williams, "Constructing a Community-Based Bill of Rights Model," in Tom Campbell, Jeffrey Goldsworthy, and Adrienne Stone, eds., *Protecting Human Rights: Instruments and Institutions* (Oxford: Oxford University Press, 2003), 247. This section draws from John D. Kelly and Martha Kaplan, *Represented Communities: Fiji and World Decolonization* (Chicago: University of Chicago Press, 2001), 143–200; Catherine Renshaw, Andrew Byrnes, and Andrea Durbach, "Implementing Human Rights in the Pacific through National Human Rights Commissions: The Experience of Fiji," *Victoria University of Wellington Law Review* 40 (2009): 251–78; and UN General Assembly, Human Rights Council, "Report of the Working Group on the UPR: Fiji" (A/HRC/14/8, March 23, 2010). See also Shaista Shameem, "The Protection Role of the Fiji Human Rights Commission," in Ramcharan, *The Protection Role of National Human Rights Institutions*, 43–56.

60. SAHRDC, *National Human Rights Institutions in the Asia Pacific Region*, 2. On the NHRI's early work, see Nayan Bahadur Khatri, "The Protection Role of the Nepalese Human Rights Commission," in Ramcharan, *The Protection Role of National Human Rights Institutions*, 117–34.

61. ICC, "Report and Recommendations of the Session of the Sub-Committee on Accreditation" (Geneva, May 23–27, 2011), 23–24. Also, Andrea Durbach, "Human Rights Commissions in Times of Trouble and Transition: The Case of the National Human Rights Commission of Nepal," UNSW Law Research Paper No. 2010–18 (Sydney: University of New South Wales, December 2009).

62. See UN General Assembly, Human Rights Council, "Compilation Prepared by the OHCHR, for Nepal's UPR" (A/HRC/WG.6/10/NPL/2, September 30, 2010). A peace agreement was signed in 2006, ending a decade-long conflict, and the long-standing monarchy ended in 2008.

63. Emma Lantschner, "Set-Up and Challenges of National Human Rights Commissions in India and Nepal," in Rainer Hofmann and Ugo Caruso, eds., *Minority Rights in South Asia* (Frankfurt: Peter Lang, 2011), 174.

64. Articles 199 and 200 of the 1997 constitution. The National Human Rights Commission Act was passed in 1999. The NHRC was part of other watchdog institutions that were intended to check executive excesses, including the Officer of Auditor General and the National Counter Corruption Commission, as well as a constitutional court and ombudsman.

65. Douglas Sanders, "The Rainbow Lobby: The Sexual Diversity Network and the Military-Installed Government in Thailand," in Peter A. Jackson, ed., *Queer Bangkok: 21st Century Markets, Media, and Rights* (Aberdeen: Hong Kong University Press, 2011), 235.

66. Naruemon Thabchumpon, "Human Rights in Thailand: Rhetoric or Substance on 'Asian Values,'" in Damien Kingsbury and Leena Avonius, eds., *Human Rights in Asia: A Reassessment of the Asian Values Debate* (New York: Palgrave Macmillan, 2008).

67. The commission was included in the 2007 constitution.

68. David Streckfuss, *Truth on Trial in Thailand: Defamation, Treason, and Lèse-majesté* (New York: Routledge, 2011), 293.

69. Ibid., 294.

70. Sanders, "The Rainbow Lobby." Note that Thailand ratified the ICCPR in 1996 and the ICESCR in 1999. *UN Treaty Collection.*

71. UN General Assembly, Human Rights Council, "Report of the Working Group on the Universal Periodic Review: Thailand" (A/HRC/19/8, December 8, 2011).

72. Decree No. 1995 (1997). See Cardenas and Flibbert, "National Human Rights Institutions," 430–31.

73. November 25, 1997, replacing a cooperation agreement from 1984.

74. Cardenas and Flibbert, "National Human Rights Institutions," 430–31.

75. Ibid.

76. Ibid., 430.

77. Sheila Carapico, "Some Yemeni Ideas about Human Rights," in Anthony Chase and Amr Hamzawi, eds., *Human Rights in the Arab World: Independent Voices* (Philadelphia: University of Pennsylvania Press, 2006).

78. Thio, "Panacea, Placebo, or Pawn?," 1275. For a general overview, see Amanda Whiting, "Situating Suhakam: Human Rights Debates and Malaysia's National Human Rights Commission," *Stanford Journal of International Law* 39 (2003): 59–98.

79. Thio, "Panacea, Placebo, or Pawn?," 1275.

80. On the Anwar affair, see, for example, David Capie, "Globalization, Norms, and Sovereignty: ASEAN's Changing Identity and Its Implications for Development and Security," in David B. Dewitt and Carolina G. Hernandez, eds., *Development and Security in Southeast Asia*, vol. 3, Global (Surrey, UK: Ashgate, 2003), 87–114.

81. Cheah Boon Kheng, *Malaysia: The Making of a Nation* (Singapore: Institute of Southeast Asian Studies, 2002), 216.

82. For example, the Voluntary Committee for the Protection of Human Rights formed in July 1990, followed by the Mongolian Human Rights Committee in December 1991; in 1994, a national coordinating committee of Amnesty International

was established; and the Movement for Human Rights and Justice, along with the Mongolian Human Rights Center, both appeared in 1998. Alan J. K. Sanders, *Historical Dictionary of Mongolia* (Plymouth, UK: Scarecrow Press, 2010), 343–15.

83. Influenced by the Vienna World Conference and broader UN reforms by the secretary-general that were to mainstream human rights throughout UN bodies in the 1990s, the UNDP elaborated this approach in a paper in 1998 ("Integrating Human Rights with Sustainable Human Development").

84. Being nuclear-free was a goal recognized by the United Nations in 1998, leading to passage in 2000 of a denuclearization national law.

85. For UNDP project details, see http://www.undp.mn/dghr-cdnhrc.html. HURIST, according to the *Yearbook of the United Nations* (http://unyearbook.un.org), was very active in Mongolia in 2000.

86. Statement by Mrs. Ts. Nymsuren, UN General Assembly (Agenda Item 110(a), Human Rights Questions: Implementation of Human Rights Instruments, New York, October 30, 1998).

87. For example, Asia Pacific Forum, "Background Paper, Third Meeting of the Asia Pacific Forum of National Human Rights Institutions," Jakarta, September 7–9, 1998." See, in general, www.asiapacificforum.net.

88. In 2002 it was provisionally accredited.

89. The ILO and New Zealand AID were other partners.

90. Choe Hyondok, *South Korea—Human Rights as Part of the Democratization Process* (Aachen: Missio, 2004), 9. A few elite organizations, closely aligned with the state, had been formed in the 1950s and 1960s, e.g., the Korean Human Rights Protection Organization in 1961. Ian Neary, *Human Rights in Japan, South Korea, and Taiwan* (New York: Routledge, 2002), 90. The Korean Human Rights Network was also formed in 1994.

91. Asia Pacific Forum, "Second Regional Workshop of NHRIs" (New Delhi, India, September 1997).

92. Neary, *Human Rights in Japan, South Korea, and Taiwan.*

93. Nora Hui-Jung Kim, "Framing Multiple Others and International Norms: The Migrant Worker Advocacy Movement and Korean National Identity Reconstruction," *Nations and Nationalism* 15, 4 (October 2009): 678–95.

94. Amnesty International, "South Korea: Legislation to Establish Human Rights Commission Is Seriously Flawed" (ASA 25/37/1998, October 23, 1998); and Neary, *Human Rights in Japan, South Korea, and Taiwan.*

95. Neary, *Human Rights in Japan, South Korea, and Taiwan*, 90.

96. Amnesty International, "South Korea: Government Proposal Will Set Up a Weak National Human Rights Commission without Proper Consultation with Civil Society" (ASA 25/017/1999, April 9, 1999).

97. Korean Confederation of Trade Unions, "Hunger Strike Exposes the Tarnished Human Rights Integrity of the Kim Dae Jung Government" (April 12, 1999).

98. Ranjiv Devraj, "Rights Activists Pin Hopes on UN Rights Chief" (Inter Press Service, Seoul, October 16, 1999).

99. Ibid.

100. Buhm-Suk Baek, "Do We Need National Human Rights Institutions? The Experience of Korea" (Cornell Law School J.S.D./Doctoral Student Papers No. 4,

October 19, 2010), 12. There is also a Korean dissertation on this legislative process: Baek Woon-Jo, "A Study of the Legislative Process Behind the Law of Human Rights Commission in the Republic of Korea" (Ph.D. diss., Inha University, South Korea, 2002). See "Protest Letter to President Kim Dae-Jung and His Ruling Party from Representative of Human Rights Organizations in South Korea," January 5, 2001 (http://www.humanrights.asia/).

101. Baek, "Do We Need National Human Rights Institutions?"

102. "Human Rights in Crisis," *The Hankyoreh* (South Korea), November 22, 2011.

103. For example, in 2007, Jordan's NHRI organized the Arab-European Human Rights Dialogue, along with the Danish Institute. See Cardenas and Flibbert, "National Human Rights Institutions," 428–29.

104. Royal Decree, December 19, 2009 was approved by a Council of Ministers decision on December 3. The NHRI adapted international norms to the local cultural context, as it did in other countries in the Middle East, stating that the institution's objectives were to "promote the principles of human rights within the Kingdom by drawing from the tolerant teachings of Islam and the heritage of Arab Islamic values as well as the rights enshrined in the Constitution." National Centre for Human Rights, http://www.nchr.org.jo; and Cardenas and Flibbert, "National Human Rights Institutions," 428.

105. Rights and Humanity, www.rightsandhumanity.org. Prof. Julia Häusermann was the founder and president.

106. See Curtis R. Ryan, "Governance, Reform and Resurgent Ethnic Identity Politics in Jordan," in Abbas Kadhim, ed., *Governance in the Middle East and North Africa: A Handbook* (New York: Routledge, 2013).

107. United Nations General Assembly, Human Rights Council, "Compilation Prepared by the OHCHR for Jordan's UPR" (A/HRC/WG.6/4/JOR/2, November 21, 2008); and Byrnes, Durbach and Renshaw, "Joining the Club," 76–77.

108. Decree Law No. 38, November 11, 2002.

109. Mohamed Saeed M. Eltayeb, "The Qatari National Human Rights Committee: A Search for Evaluation" (Focus 47, Asia-Pacific Human Rights Information Center, March 2007).

110. Human Rights Watch, "WTO Sends Wrong Message with Qatar Choice" (News release, January 23, 2001).

111. Jennifer Lambert, "Political Reform in Qatar: Participation, Legitimacy and Security," *Middle East Policy* 18, 1 (Spring 2011): 89–101.

112. Asia Pacific Forum, *Annual Report 2001–2002*, http://www.asiapacificforum.net.

113. United Nations General Assembly, Human Rights Council, "Report of the Working Group on the UPR: Qatar" (A/HRC/14/2, March 15, 2010); and Byrnes, Durbach and Renshaw, "Joining the Club," 78–79.

114. United Nations, "Agreement on Provisional Arrangements in Afghanistan Pending the Re-Establishment of Permanent Government Institutions" (Bonn Agreement) (December 5, 2001).

115. Article 58, constitution, Decree of the Presidency of the Interim Administration on the Establishment of an Afghan Independent Human Rights Commission

(June 6, 2002). The Presidential Decree on Enforcement of the Law on Structure, Duties and Mandate of the Afghanistan Independent Human Rights Commission (Decree No. 16, May 12, 2005) endorsed the law approved by the Cabinet Ministers.

116. Human Rights Watch, *"Killing You Is a Very Easy Thing for Us": Human Rights Abuses in Southeast Afghanistan* (New York: Human Rights Watch, July 29, 2003), 93.

117. Sima Samar was nominated for the Nobel Peace Prize in 2009; and she had worked in exile in Pakistan for almost twenty years. See Sally Armstrong, *Veiled Threat: The Hidden Power of the Women of Afghanistan* (Jackson, Tenn.: Seal Press, 2003).

118. E.g., Denmark, Switzerland, Finland, Norway, Canada, the United Kingdom, the United States, New Zealand, Australia, the Netherlands, Ireland, UNHCR, and OHCHR. UN General Assembly, Human Rights Council, "Report of the Working Group on the Universal Periodic Review: Afghanistan" (A/HRC/12/9, July 20, 2009).

119. Constitution, Section 27, Law 7/2004, Statute of the Office of the Ombudsman for Human Rights and Justice (May 26, 2004).

120. See Geoffrey Robinson, *"If You Leave Us Here, We Will Die": How Genocide Was Stopped in East Timor* (Princeton, N.J.: Princeton University Press, 2010). Note that representatives of Komnas HAM, who were "deeply partisan" were used to staff the KPS (Komisi Pengamanan dan Stabilitas, or Commission on Peace and Stability), part of the government's public disinformation campaign in East Timor. Ibid., 113.

121. The keynote address was titled "Building the Future of East Timor on a Culture of Human Rights." "Human Rights and the Future of East Timor" (Report on Joint UNTAET Human Rights Unit and East Timor Jurists Association workshop, Dili, East Timor, August 7–8, 2000).

122. República Democrática de Timor-Leste, Primero Governo Constitucional de Timor-Leste, "Establishment of the Office of the 'Provedor de Direitos Humanos e Justiça' in East Timor" (7th annual meeting, Asia Pacific Forum of National Human Rights Institutions, New Delhi, India, November 11–13, 2002).

123. World Bank, "Using an Ombudsman to Oversee Public Officials" (PREM Note No. 19, April 1999). "Putting in Place Independent Oversight and Audit" (n.d., filed with the World Bank).

124. Guteriano Nicolau, "Ombudsman for Human Rights: The Case of Timor-Leste" (Focus 47, Asia-Pacific Human Rights Information Center, March 2007).

125. See UN OHCHR, "Joint Submission from the Office of the Provedor for Human Rights and Justice and Civil Society Organizations in Timor-Leste to the United Nations Universal Periodic Review" (March 21, 2011); and "Responses to Recommendations: Timor-Leste" (June 7, 2012), http://upr-info.com.

126. In 2010, both NHRIs concluded a memorandum of understanding to implement the findings of two transitional justice bodies. Amnesty International, "Kyrgyzstan," in *Annual Report 2011* (London: Amnesty International, 2011).

127. See Act of August 2, 2002, and Article 40(2) of the Kyrgyzstan Constitution.

128. In 2003, for example, when the ombudsman was incorporated into the constitution, the country also passed an Anti-Corruption Law. On the weakness of accountability mechanisms throughout the public sector, see Mahabat Baimyrzaeva, "Kyrgyzstan's Public Sector Reforms: 1991–2010," *International Journal of Public Administration* 34, 9 (2011): 555–66.

129. Eugene Huskey, "Kyrgyzstan: The Fate of Political Liberalization," in Karen Dawisha and Bruce Parrott, eds., *Conflict, Cleavage and Change in Central Asia and the Caucasus* (Cambridge: Cambridge University Press, 1997), 242.

130. Human Rights Watch, *Annual Report 1999* (New York: Human Rights Watch, 1999), 274. See also Brigitte Kofler, "Kyrgyzstan," in Kucsko-Stadlmayer, *European Ombudsman-Institutions*, 263–67.

131. UN General Assembly, Human Rights Council, "Report of the Working Group on the Universal Periodic Review: Kyrgyzstan" (A/HRC/15/2, June 16, 2010).

132. The country had become independent in 1991. Kazakhstan Ombudsman, "History," www.ombudsman.kz. In 1996, within the Prosecutor General's office, the Department for Supervising the Protection of Human and Civil Rights was created, though it was disbanded one year later. Charles Buxton, *The Struggle for Civil Society in Central Asia: Crisis and Transformation* (Sterling, Va.: Kumarian Press, 2011), 37.

133. Decree 947, September 19, 2002.

134. Vladimir Kartashkin, "Powers and Activities of the Human Rights Commission of the President of the Russian Federation," in *Israeli Year Book of Human Rights*, vol. 28 (The Hague: Martinus Nijhoff, 1998), 112.

135. R. Hrair Dekmejian and Hovann H. Simonian, *Troubled Waters: The Geopolitics of the Caspian Region* (London: I. B. Taurus, 2003), 52; and Sally N. Cummings, *Kazakhstan: Power and the Elite* (London: I. B. Taurus, 2005).

136. Human Rights Watch, "Kazakhstan," *Human Rights Watch World Report 2003*, http://www.hrw.org.

137. UN General Assembly, Human Rights Council, "Report of the Working Group on the UPR: Kazakhstan" (A/HRC/14/10, March 23, 2010) and "Compilation Prepared by the OHCHR for Kazakhstan's UPR" (A/HRC/WG.6/7/KAZ/2, November 30, 2009); and Joachim Stern, "Kazakhstan," in Kucsko-Stadlmayer, *European Ombudsman-Institutions*.

138. While *Turkmenistan* did not have an internationally accredited NHRI by the time of its UPR in 2008, it had created an official human rights body in 1996: the National Institute of Democracy and Human Rights, under the office of the presidency, which was empowered to receive individual complaints. Creating the institution was seen as "an apparent attempt to deflect international criticism of Turkmenistan's treatment of political opponents of the regime." It was viewed as a strategic response by the government, following a period of unrest. As the time of the UPR approached in 2008, international actors applied more pressure to create an NHRI. For example, in mid-2009, an international seminar on NHRIs, focusing on the investigation of individual complaints, was held in Ashgabad, sponsored by the local office of the OSCE. *Europa World Year Book 2*, 4254; and OSCE-Turkmenistan, "International Seminar on NHRIs: Exchange of Good Practices on the Investigation of Individual Complaints" (July 2009).

139. See Republic of Maldives, "Human Rights Action Plan" (2008), http://plan ning.gov.mv/.

140. Human Rights Commission Act (August 18, 2005); Act No. 6/2006, Presidential Decree (December 10, 2003); and Ministry of Foreign Affairs, Male, Republic of Maldives, "Establishment of the 'Human Rights Commission of the Maldives' " (Press release, December 10, 2003).

141. On the Evan Naseem case, see especially "Uncuffed: Torture Victims of Maldives," http://uncuffedmv.com. More broadly, Shahinda Ismail, "The National Human Rights Commission—The Maldives" (Focus 47, Asia-Pacific Human Rights Information Center, March 2007).

142. See Amnesty International, "Republic of Maldives: Repression of Peaceful Political Opponents" (July 29, 2003); and Randeep Ramesh, "Maldives Human Rights Activist Wins Presidential Election," *The Guardian* (October 29, 2008).

143. Aditya Pandey, ed., *South Asia: Polity, Literacy and Conflict Resolution* (New Delhi: Isha Books, 2005), 290; and Paul Close and David Ashew, *Asia Pacific and Human Rights: A Global Political Economy Perspective* (Aldershot, UK: Ashgate, 2004), 104.

144. UNDP, UNFPA, UNICEF, and World Health Organization, "Support to the Human Rights Commission of the Maldives, 2006–2009" (October 31, 2006), http://www.undp.org; and Ismail, "National Human Rights Commission."

145. Byrnes, Durbach and Renshaw, "Joining the Club," 81–82; UN General Assembly, Human Rights Council, "Report of the Working Group on the UPR: Maldives" (A/HRC/16/7); and International Federation for Human Rights (FIDH), "From Sunrise to Sunset: Maldives Backtracking on Democracy" (Paris: FIDH, December 2012).

146. UN General Assembly, Human Rights Council, "National Report, Submitted by the Government of Iraq for UPR" (A/HRC/WG.6/7/IRQ/11, January 18, 2010).

147. UN Assistance Mission for Iraq, "Human Rights Report" (July 1–December 31, 2008), 21; and "Iraq: UN Official Welcomes Creation of Human Rights Committee" (UN News Centre, November 18, 2008).

148. Peter Batchelor (Country Director, UNDP Iraq), "Opening Remarks," United Nations Country Team Iraq, Human Rights Day Speech (December 13, 2011), http://iq.one.un.org/.

149. The conference was titled Human Rights in Peace and War in took place in October 2003. See Saudi Embassy in the United States, "First Independent Human Rights Organization in Saudi Arabia" (Press release, March 7, 2004), http://www .saudiembassy.net; Cardenas and Flibbert, "National Human Rights Institutions in the Middle East," 432–33; and Byrnes, Durbach, and Renshaw, "Joining the Club," 80–81.

150. Muhammad I. Ayish, *The New Arab Public Sphere* (Leipzig, Germany: Frank & Timme, 2008), 139.

151. See especially Leigh Nolan, *Managing Reform? Saudi Arabia and the King's Dilemma* (Washington, D.C.: Brookings Doha Center, May 2011); and Joseph Kéchichian, *Legal and Political Reforms in Sa'udi Arabia* (New York: Routledge, 2013).

152. UN General Assembly, Human Rights Council, "Compilation Prepared by the OHCHR for Saudi Arabia's UPR" (A/HRC/WG.6/4/SAU/2, November 20, 2008), 3.

153. Human Rights Watch, "Saudi Arabia: Human Rights Groups Emerging" (August 9, 2003).

154. Also that year, a regional conference on democracy, human rights, and the role of the ICC produced the Sana'a Declaration of January 2004. See generally, Chase and Hamzawy, *Human Rights in the Arab World.*

155. Saudi Arabia does not have a constitution, though a basic law introduced in 1992 has similar effects. See UN General Assembly, Human Rights Council, "Compilation Prepared by the OHCHR for Saudi Arabia's UPR" and "Report of the Working Group on the UPR: Saudi Arabia" (A/HRC/11/23, March 4, 2009); and Byrnes, Durbach, and Renshaw, "Joining the Club," 80–81.

156. Oman's constitution was from 1996, while the UAE's 1971 constitution had undergone amendment in 1996 and 2008.

157. Oman had ratified CERD and CEDAW in 2003 and 2006, respectively. *UN Treaty Collection*; and UN General Assembly, Human Rights Council, "National Report, Submitted by the Government of Oman for UPR" (A/HRC/WG.6/10/OMN/1, November 18, 2010).

158. "UAE's Human Rights Report," *Khaleej Times* (Dubai), December 7, 2008; and UN General Assembly, Human Rights Council, "Compilation Prepared by the OHCHR" (A/HRC/WG.6/10/OMN/2, November 12, 2010) and (A/HRC/WG.6/3/ARE/2, September 29, 2008).

159. See UN General Assembly, Human Rights Council, "National Report, Submitted by the Government of Bahrain for UPR" (A/HRC/WG.6/1/BHR/1, March 11, 2008).

160. Ibid., 11.

161. UN General Assembly, Human Rights Council, "Letter Dated 29 February 2008 from the Permanent Representative of Bahrain to the United Nations" (A/62/739, March 13, 2008); and OHCHR, "Mark of Progress" (August 19, 2008), http://www.ohchr.org.

162. See, for example, Bahrain Center for Human Rights, "Press Statement on the Establishment of the 'National Human Rights Institution' in Bahrain" (May 2, 2010), http://bahrainrights.org/; and Amnesty International, "Bahrain," *Amnesty International Annual Report 2011*, http://www.amnesty.org.

163. A. H. Monjurul Kabir, "A National Human Rights Commission for Bangladesh," *Focus* 18 (December 1999), http://www.hurights.or.jp/. Also, ICC, "Report and Recommendations of the Session of the Sub-Committee on Accreditation (Geneva, May 23–27, 2011), 7–8.

164. Amnesty International, "Bangladesh: Proposed Standards for a National Human Rights Commission" (ASA 12/003/1997, January 6, 1997); UN General Assembly, Human Rights Council, "Compilation Prepared by OHCHR" (A/HRC/WG.6/4/BGD/2, December 12, 2008) and "Summary of Stakeholders' Submissions" (A/HRC/WG.6/4/BGD/3, November 24, 2008); and Permanent Mission of Bangladesh to the United Nations, "Aide Mémoire on Bangladesh's Voluntary Pledges Towards Human Rights" (April 2006), http://www.upr-info.org/

165. Ilango, *Easier Said Than Done*, 15.

166. The UNHCR established an in-country presence in 1993. Arie Bloed, ed., *The Conference on Security and Co-Operation in Europe: Basic Documents, 1993–1995* (The Hague: Martinus Nijhoff, 1997), 60; and UNDP-OHCHR, "Case Study— When a National Government Requests UN Support: Establishing a NHRI in Tajikistan, 2006–2008," toolkit available at www.unssc.org.

167. U.S. Department of State, "Country Report on Human Rights Practices 2003—Tajikistan" (2004), http://www.state.gov; Human Rights Watch, "Tajikistan," *World Report 2005*, http://www.hrw.org; UNDP-OHCHR, "Case Study;" and ICC, "Chart of the Status of National Institutions."

168. Danish Institute for Human Rights, "Background Information, Tajikistan," www.humanrights.dk.

169. Engin Saygin, "Turkey's Ombudsman: A Real Ombudsman?" (European Group for Public Administration annual conference, Bucharest, Romania, September 7–10, 2011). On reform program, see UN General Assembly, Human Rights Council, "National Report, Submitted by the Government of Turkey for UPR" (A/HRC/WG.6/8/TUR/1, February 22, 2010).

170. Zehra F. Kabasakal Arat, "Collisions and Crossroads: Introducing Human Rights in Turkey," in Arat, ed., *Human Rights in Turkey* (Philadelphia: University of Pennsylvania Press, 2007), 3.

171. UN General Assembly, Human Rights Council, "National Report, Submitted by the Government of Turkey for UPR" (A.HRC.WG.6/8/TUR/1, February 22, 2010), 4–5; and Arat, *Human Rights in Turkey*.

172. Abdurrahman Eren, "National Human Rights Institutional Models in Comparative Law and the Case of Turkey" (Gazi Üniversitesi Hukuk Fakültesi Dergisi, L XV, Y. 2011, Sa 3), 27.

173. Commission of the European Communities, "Turkey 2009: Progress Report" (Brussels, October 14, 2009).

174. Riaz Fatyana, "Time for Action!" (Parliamentarians Commission for Human Rights), www.pchr.org.pk.

175. Queen's University, the University of Essex, and the University of Notre Dame.

176. "Analysis of the Pakistan National Commission for Human Rights Bill, 2005" (Commonwealth Human Rights Initiative, June 2005).

177. "Rights Commission Bill to Be Tabled in National Assembly," *Dawn* (Pakistan), English edition, November 21, 2011.

178. Bahrain, UAE, and Oman were further stops to promote NHRIs.

179. Mary Ann Tetrault, *Stories of Democracy: Politics and Society in Contemporary Kuwait* (New York: Columbia University Press, 2000), 200.

180. Ibid., 201.

181. Ibid. In 2011, Kuwait was elected into the Human Rights Council.

182. ECOSOC, "Concluding Observations of the Committee on Economic, Social and Cultural Rights: Syrian Arab Republic" (E/C.12/1/Add.63, September 24, 2001). On the Damascus Spring, see Alan George, *Syria: Neither Bread nor Freedom* (London: Zed, 2003).

183. UN Committee on Civil and Political Rights, "Concluding Observations of the Human Rights Committee: Syrian Arab Republic" (CCPR/CO/84/SYR, August 9, 2005); and Syrian Arab Republic, "UN Development Assistance Framework, 2007–2011," http://www.undp.org.

184. OHCHR, "Committee on the Rights of the Child considers the Report of the Syrian Arab Republic" (September 22, 2011); and UN General Assembly, Human Rights Council, "National Report, Submitted by the Syrian Arab Republic for UPR" (A/HRC/WG.6/12/SYR/1, September 2, 2011), 20–24 and "Report of the Working Group on the UPR: Syrian Arab Republic" (A/HRC/19/11, January 24, 2012).

185. NHRIs were not necessarily a precursor to the regional mechanism, but they complemented it.

186. Also in 2004, the Vietiane Action Programme (VAP) (available at http://www.aseansec.org) identified NHRI networking as one of its program areas. This was created in 1993 in preparation for the Vienna World Conference.

187. G. Powles and Alisi Taumoepeau, "Constitutional Change in Tonga" (Paper, Australian Law Reform Agencies conference, Port Vila, Vanuatu, September 10–12, 2008). Dates of existing constitutions are as follows: Micronesia (1979, independence 1986), Nauru (1968), Palau (1981), Papua New Guinea (1975), Samoa (1962), Solomon Islands (1978), Tonga (1875), Tuvalu (1986), and Vanuatu (1980).

188. Amnesty International, "Solomon Islands: Weak Human Rights Infrastructure, Discrimination" (ASA43/001/2010, November 8, 2010); Jennifer Corrin, "Breaking the Mould: Constitutional Review in Solomon Islands," *Revue juridique polynésienne* 13 (2007): 143–68; http://www.asiapacificforum.net; and http://www.ohchr.org.

189. UN General Assembly, Human Rights Council, "National Report, Submitted by the Government of Papua New Guinea for UPR" (A/HRC/WG.6/11/PNG/1, May 9, 2011), 4; and Pacific Islands Forum Secretariat, *National Human Rights Institutions: Pathways for Pacific States* (New Zealand: New Zealand Human Rights Commission, July 2007).

190. Amnesty International, "Papua New Guinea: 'Under the Barrel of a Gun'" (1993).

191. They invited the UN Special Rapporteur on Extrajudicial, Summary or Arbitrary Executions and the UN Special Rapporteur on Torture. See Amnesty International, "Papua New Guinea: Human Rights Commission Mooted" (ASA/34/001/1994, October 4, 1994).

192. David Robie, "The Trials of a Tribal Girl: Dilemmas of Human Rights in the Pacific" (Inter Press Service and New Zealand Political Review, May 21, 1996).

193. See UN General Assembly, Human Rights Council, "Summary Prepared by the OHCHR, for Papua New Guinea's UPR" (A/HRC/WG.6/1/PNG/3, January 28, 2011).

194. UN General Assembly, Human Rights Council, "Compilation Prepared by the OHCHR, for Palau's UPR" (A/HRC/WG.6/11/PLW/2, February 17, 2011), 5.

195. UN General Assembly, Human Rights Council, "National Report, Submitted by the Government of Samoa for UPR" (A/HRC/WG.6/11/WSM/l, February 14, 2011).

196. The Samoa Declaration was issued at the Regional Workshop on the Establishment of National Human Rights Mechanisms in the Pacific. The participants included Samoa, Micronesia, Palau, the Solomon Islands, and Vanuatu.

197. Joy Liddicoat, "National Human Rights Institutions: Pathways for Pacific States" (Pacific Islands Forum Secretariat, 2007). The author was a member of New Zealand's Human Rights Commission. For the clash between custom and human rights, see New Zealand Commission, "Converging Currents: Custom and Human Rights in the Pacific" (2006).

198. UN General Assembly, Human Rights Council, "National Report, Submitted by the Government of Micronesia for UPR" (A/HRC/WG.6/9/FSM/1, August 23, 2010), 17.

199. UN General Assembly, Human Rights Council, "Compilation Prepared by the OHCHR, for Cambodia's UPR" (A/HRC/WG.6/6/KHM/2, September 18, 2009). Also, "Conference on the Establishment of a National Human Rights Institution in Cambodia" (September 25–27, 2006), http://www.asiapacificforum.net; and Kek Galabru, "We Need an Independent National Human Rights Commission" (Phnom Penh: Cambodian League for the Promotion and Defense of Human Rights, May 2004), http://www.licadho-cambodia.org.

200. Tynna Mendoza, "Cambodia Joint Working Group Commits to Undertake Serious Work for an Independent National Human Rights Institution" (2010), http://www.seanf.asia; and Galabru, "We Need an Independent National Human Rights Commission." See also Craig Etcheson, "Dealing with Human Rights Violations from a Previous Regime: Dilemmas of Accountability in Cambodia;" in Hossain et al., *Human Rights Commissions and Ombudsman Offices*, 115–29.

201. UN General Assembly, Human Rights Council, "Compilation Prepared by the OHCHR, for Myanmar's UPR" (A/HRC/WG.6/10/MMR/2, November 5, 2010).

202. Government midterm report to UPR (2011). The bill was introduced in March 2002, and the House of Representatives was dissolved in October 2003.

203. UN General Assembly, Human Rights Council, "National Report, Submitted by the Government of Japan for UPR" (A/HRC/WG.6/2/JPN/1, April 18, 2008).

204. Government of Japan, "Mid-Term Progress Report on Its Implementation of Recommendations Made in May 2008, to Human Rights Council for UPR" (March 2011).

205. Roberta Cohen, "Human Rights: A Means of Engaging North Korea" (Washington, D.C.: Brookings Institute, June 2010).

206. "Responses to Recommendations: Bhutan" (June 18, 2012), http://upr-info.com; and UN General Assembly, Human Rights Council, "Report of the Working Group on the Universal Periodic Review: Bhutan" (A/HRC/11/Add.l, March 10, 2010). Also, UN General Assembly, Human Rights Council, "Compilation Prepared by the OHCHR for Bhutan's UPR" (A/HRC/WG.6/6/BTN/2, September 18, 2009).

207. "Responses to Recommendations: Marshall Islands" (July 7, 2011), http://upr-info.com.

208. UN General Assembly, Human Rights Council, "Compilation Prepared by the OHCHR for Brunei Darussalam's UPR" (A/HRC/WG.6/6/BRN/2, August 7,

2009); and "Responses to Recommendations: Brunei Darussalam" (May 1, 2012), http://upr-info.com.

209. UN General Assembly, Human Rights Council, "Compilation Prepared by the OHCHR for Kiribati's UPR" (A/HRC/WG.6/8/KIR/2, February 19, 2010) and "Summary of Stakeholders' Submissions" (A/HRC/WG.6/8/KIR/3, January 28, 2010).

210. Singapore Unity Project, "Civil Society Joint Statement: Advancing Human Rights in Singapore" (December 10, 2011).

211. UN General Assembly, Human Rights Council, "Compilation Prepared by the OHCHR" (A/HRC/WG.6/8/LAO/2, February 12, 2010) and "Report of the Working Group on the UPR: Lao People's Democratic Republic" (A/HRC/15/5); and "Responses to Recommendations: Laos" (September 8, 2012), http://upr-info.com.

212. UN General Assembly, Human Rights Council, "Compilation Prepared by the OHCHR" (A/HRC/WG.6/5/VNM/2, March 16, 2009, 6; and "Responses to Recommendations: Vietnam" (November 5, 2012), http://upr-info.com.

213. "Responses to Recommendations: Israel" (March 19, 2009), http://upr-info .com.

214. Sanzhuan Guo, "China and an Independent National Human Rights Institution in Compliance with the Paris Principles: A Critical Analysis" (Paper, National Human Rights Institutions Workshop, Melbourne Law School, July 22, 2009); "Responses to Recommendations: China" (September 5, 2012), http://upr-info.com; and United Nations, OHCHR, Interviews (Geneva, August 2002).

215. Likewise, the third international conference on NHRIs in China was held in Beijing in October 2004, hosted by the China University of Political Sciences and Law in cooperation with the Raoul Wallenberg Institute. Xu Xianming, Ziang Liwei, and Zhang Wei, "National Human Rights Institutions Discussed at International Workshop" (Beijing: China Society for Human Rights Studies, 2004). Also, UN General Assembly, Human Rights Council, "Compilation Prepared by the OHCHR for PRC's UPR" (A/HRC/WG.6/4/CHN/2, December 16, 2008); and asiapacificforum.net. Note that NGOs began calling for an NHRI in Taiwan after 1999. See, for example, Fort Fu-Te Liao, "Establishing a National Human Rights Commission in Taiwan: The Role of NGOs and Challenges Ahead," *Asia-Pacific Journal on Human Rights and the Law* 2, 2 (2001): 90–109.

Chapter 9

1. The resolutions were issued by the Committee of Ministers. Regional overviews of NHRIs are provided in Richard Carver, "One NHRI or Many? How Many Institutions Does It Take to Protect Human Rights?—Lessons from the European Experience," *Journal of Human Rights Practice* 3, 1 (2011): 1–24; European Union Agency for Fundamental Rights (FRA), "National Human Rights Institutions in the EU Member States" (Belgium: FRA, 2010); Gauthier de Beco, "National Human Rights Institutions in Europe," Working Paper, Cellule de Recherche Interdisciplinaire en Droits de 'Homme, Université Catholique de Louvain (2007); and Carver,

"National Human Rights Institutions in Central and Eastern Europe: The Ombudsman as Agent of International Law," in Goodman and Pegram, *Human Rights, State Compliance, and Social Change*, 181–209.

2. Emma Gilligan, "The Human Rights Ombudsman in Russia: The Evolution of Horizontal Accountability," *Human Rights Quarterly* 32 (2010): 592. See Makau Mutua, *Human Rights: A Political and Cultural Critique* (Philadelphia: University of Pennsylvania, 2008).

3. Article 92 of Croatian constitution. In 2001, the ombudsman's mandate was extended to cover the Minister of Defense, military forces, and security services. Kucsko-Stadlmayer, *European Ombudsman-Institutions*, 134; and European Network of Equality Bodies, "Office of the Ombudsman—Croatia" (June 12, 2012), http://www.equineteurope.org.

4. Cindy Skach, *Borrowing Constitutional Designs: Constitutional Law in Weimar Germany and the French Fifth Republic* (Princeton, N.J.: Princeton University Press, 2005), 120. As the 1990 constitution expresses this sovereign drive: "At the historic turning-point marked by the rejection of the communist system and changes in the international order in Europe, the Croation nation reaffirmed . . . its freely expressed will, its millennial statehood and its resolution to establish the Republic of Croatia as a sovereign state."

5. Denis J. Galligan and Daniel M. Smilov, *Administrative Law in Central and Eastern Europe 1996–1998* (Budapest: Central European University Press, 1999), 30.

6. Human Rights Watch, *World Report 2011*, 418.

7. See, for example, John Hucker, "The Ombudsman Institution in Croatia: An Expert Analysis" (OSCE Mission to Croatia, June 6, 2003).

8. UN General Assembly, Human Rights Council, "Summary Prepared by the OHCHR: Hungary, for the UPR" (A/HRC/WG.6/11/UN.3, January 28, 2011).

9. UN General Assembly, Human Rights Council, "National Report, Submitted by Croatia's Government for UPR" (A/HRC/WG.6/9/HRV.1, August 12, 2010). Also, Carver, "One NHRI or Many?"

10. Hungary also has parliamentary commissioners for data protection and freedom of information and for future generations (addressing environmental issues). See Joachim Stern, "Hungary," in Kuckso-Stadlmayer, *European Ombudsman-Institutions*, 221–31; and Reif, *The Ombudsman*, 166–68.

11. Rudolf L. Tökés, "Institution Building in Hungary: Analytical Issues and Constitutional Models, 1989–90," in András Bozóki, *The Roundtable Talks of 1989: The Genesis of Hungarian Demcoracy* (Budapest: Central European University Press, 2002), 107–36. Hungary joined the Council of Europe in 1990 and ratified the European Convention on Human Rights in 1992.

12. See Ignác Romsics and Béla K. Király, eds., *Geopolitics in the Danube Region: Hungarian Reconciliation Efforts, 1848–1998* (Budapest: Central European University, 1999).

13. See ICC, "Report and Recommendations of the Session of the Sub-Committee on Accreditation" (Geneva, May 23–27, 2011), 8–9.

14. Ivan Bizjak, "The Human Rights Ombudsman of Slovenia," in Hossain et al., *Human Rights Commissions and Ombudsman Offices*. Bizjak was Slovenia's first

ombudsman. Also, Brigitte Kofler, "Slovenia," in Kuckso-Stadlmayer, *European Ombudsman-Institutions*, 395–400; and Reif, *The Ombudsman*, 163–66.

15. Law No. 71/1993. See Republic of Slovenia, Human Rights Ombudsman, "History of the Institution in Slovenia," http://www.varuh-rs.si.

16. ICC, "Report and Recommendations of the Session of the Sub-Committee on Accreditation" (March 29–April 1, 2010).

17. For example, the ICC said in its 2010 accreditation report on Slovenia, "[The ICC has received] advice from the Ombudsman that recent domestic legislative changes in Slovenia have annulled the provision in the Law of the Human Rights Ombudsman that entitled the Ombudsman to a salary equal to that of the President of the Constitutional Court, and entitled the Deputies to a salary equivalent to Constitutional Court judges. This change may impact the independence and efficiency of the institution and affect the security of tenure of the current Ombudsman and Deputies." Para. 4. ICC, "Report and Recommendations of the Session of the Sub-Committee on Accreditation" (October 11–15, 2010), 8–9.

18. FRA, "National Human Rights Institutions in the EU Member States," 30.

19. Law No. 29 (1991) created the Institute for Human Rights. See Kucsko-Stadlmayer, *European Ombudsman-Institutions*, 358; and Romanian Institute for Human Rights, www.irdo.ro. The ombudsman was nonetheless not given implementing legislation until 1997. The country gained membership in the Council of Europe in 1993. Regarding accreditation, see ICC, "Report and Recommendations of the Session of the Sub-Committee on Accreditation" (Geneva, May 23–27, 2011), 20–21. In the OHCHR's Directory of NHRIs, Romania now lists the Advocate of the People as its NHRI. See http://nhri.ohchr.org.

20. Alina Mungiu-Pippidi, "Poland and Romania," in Larry Diamond and Leonardo Morlino, eds., *Assessing the Quality of Democracy* (Baltimore: Johns Hopkins University Press, 2005), 218.

21. Ibid., 217–18.

22. Laura Hossu and Radu Carp, "A Critical Assessment of the Role of the Romanian Ombudsman in Promoting Freedom of Information," *Transylvanian Review of Administrative Sciences*, no. 33 E (2011): 90–108.

23. Ibid.

24. Article 73 of the 1992 constitution. I-363-11/1/1994 is the implementing law. A new law in 1998 made the ombudsman's salary no longer equal to that of a Supreme Court judge. Act VIII-950-3/12/1998.

25. The Seimas Ombudsman's Office of the Republic of Lithuania, www.lrs.lt.

26. Nida Gelazis, "Defending Order and Freedom: The Lithuanian Constitutional Court in Its First Decade," in Wojciech Sadurski, ed., *Constitutional Justice, East and West: Democratic Legitimacy and Constitutional Courts in Post-Communist Europe in a Comparative Perspective* (The Hague: Kluwer Law, 2002), 397; and UN General Assembly, Human Rights Council, "National Report, Submitted by Government of Lithuania for UPR" (A/HRC/WG.6/12/LTU/1, July 19, 2011).

27. UN Human Rights Council, "National Report by Lithuania," 3.

28. Thomas Lane, *Lithuania: Stepping Westward* (New York: Routledge, 2001), 131.

29. The proposal was advanced at the first Congress of People's Deputies in May 1990. Gilligan, "Human Rights Ombudsman in Russia," 580.

30. Ibid., 578 and 582n33.

31. Ibid., 581.

32. Decree No. 1458 (September 1993) and Decree No. 1798 (November 1993). Gilligan, "Human Rights Ombudsman in Russia," 584–85.

33. Gilligan, "Human Rights Ombudsman in Russia," 585.

34. The task force was assisted by the Russian-American Project Group, formed by Andrei Sakharov in 1987. Ibid., 586–87.

35. Ibid., 587.

36. Oleg Mironov was a law professor and former police investigator, supported by the Our Home Is Russia group; the communists supported the appointment, in exchange for the right to select the head of the defense committee. Ibid., 588–91.

37. According to Gilligan, "Without Yeltsin, the resurrection of the old committee in the form of the new presidential commission would never have been approved by the parliament." Ibid., 585.

38. The office was known as having a strong prosecutorial bias; during the communist period, it was considered a fourth branch of government. Council of Europe, Parliamentary Assembly, "Documents: Working Papers, 2005 Ordinary Session (June 20–24, 2005), 53.

39. Act No. 308/1993, entering into force in 1994. See Slovak National Centre for Human Rights, "The Role, Functions, and Competences" (http://www.snslp.sk).

40. Slovak National Centre for Human Rights, Council of Europe, www.coe.int.

41. Joachim Stern, "Slovakia," in Kuckso-Stadlmayer, *European Ombudsman-Institutions*, 388.

42. Kevin F. F. Quigley, *For Democracy's Sake: Foundations and Democracy Assistance in Central Europe* (Washington, D.C.: Woodrow Wilson Center Press, 1997), 64.

43. Minton F. Goldman, *Slovakia since Independence: A Struggle for Democracy* (Westport, Conn.: Greenwood, 1999), 87.

44. See UN General Assembly, Human Rights Council, "National Report, Submitted by the Government of Latvia for UPR" (A/HRC/WG.6/11/LVA/1, February 14, 2011); and Joachim Stern, "Latvia," in Kuckso-Stadlmayer, *European Ombudsman-Institutions*, 269–74. See more broadly, Caroline Sawyer and Brad K. Blitz, eds., *Statelessness in the European Union: Displaced, Undocumented, Unwanted* (Cambridge: Cambridge University Press, 2011).

45. UN General Assembly, Human Rights Council, "Report of the Working Group on the UPR: Latvia" (A/HRC/18/9, July 7, 2011).

46. Akmal Saidov, "Country Study: Uzbekistan," *Human Development Report* (UNDP, 2000).

47. "Establishment of the Institute of the Authorized Person," Uzbekistan Ombudsman website, www.ombudsman.gov.uz.

48. These include Poland, Sweden, Russia, Azerbaijan, Latvia, Slovakia, Spain, and France. See "International Cooperation in the Field of Human Rights," Uzbekistan Ombudsman website, www.ombudsman.gov.uz.

49. See Human Rights Watch, "Saving Its Secrets: Government Repression in Andijan" (New York: Human Rights Watch, 2008).

50. "Establishment of the Institute of the Authorized Person."

51. "Responses to Recommendations: Uzbekistan" (February 24, 2010), http://upr-info.org.

52. UN General Assembly, Human Rights Council, "Summary Prepared by the OHCHR: Uzbekistan, for the UPR" (A/HRC/wG.6/3/UZB/3, September 16, 2008).

53. UNDP Uzbekistan, "Development of Capacities of the National Human Rights Institutions in Uzbekistan," www.undp.uz.

54. Resul Yalcin, *The Rebirth of Uzbekistan: Politics, Economy and Society in the Post-Soviet Era* (Reading, UK: Ithaca Press, 2002), 273–77.

55. Amanda Lee Wetzel, "Post-Conflict National Human Rights Institutions: Emerging Models from Northern Ireland and Bosnia & Herzegovina," *Columbia Journal of European Law* 13 (2006–2007): 427–70.

56. The Council of Europe's European Commission for Democracy through Law, known as the Venice Commission, is an advisory body on constitutional matters that promotes heavily the office of the ombudsman.

57. At the state level, a Human Rights Chamber also existed; given that it was much quicker to access, the public often bypassed the ombudsman and applied directly to the chamber.

58. UN General Assembly, Human Rights Council, "National Report, Submitted by the Government of Bosnia and Herzegovina for the UPR" (A/HRC/WG.6/7/BIH/1, December 8, 2009), 10.

59. Mertus, *Human Rights* Matters, 61.

60. Ibid., 73.

61. Ibid., 83.

62. Ibid., 80.

63. Organic Law No. 230 (May 1996). A constitutional court was also established that year.

64. The EU, UNDP, SIDA, Council of Europe, USAID, UNICEF, and the governments of Liechtenstein, Denmark, Lithuania, and Switzerland.

65. Ghia Nodia and Alvaro Pinto Scholtbach, *The Political Landscape of Georgia: Political Parties: Achievements, Challenges and Prospects* (Delft, Netherlands: Eburon, 2006), 28.

66. For a list of reforms, see for example, Public Defender of Georgia, *Annual Report* 2004, 96 (http://www.ombudsman.ge/). Kucsko-Stadlmayer, *European Ombudsman-Institutions*, 201.

67. UN General Assembly, Human Rights Council, "Compilation Prepared by the OHCHR, for the Government of Georgia for the UPR" (A/HRC/WG.6/10/GEO/2, November 15, 2010), 2.

68. Macedonian Constitution, Article 77.

69. Ombudsman Act, Law No. 07-4502/1 (September 2003), implementing legislation was not enacted until 2003. Brigitte Kofler, "FYR Macedonia," in Kucsko-Stadlmayer, *European Ombudsman-Institutions*, 297–302; Venice Commission (http//www.venice.coe.int/); and "Responses to Recommendations: Macedonia (September 25, 2009), http://upr-info.org.

70. With roots in the *advocatus fisci* during Roman times, created to represent the state in legal proceedings after the state and emperor's treasuries were separated,

the institution appeared in Serbia as early as the nineteenth century: in 1842 the administrative lawyer, from 1848 to 1928 the protector of administrative rights, and, after 1934, a public attorney. "History," Public Attorney's Office of the Republic of Serbia website, www.rjp.gov.rs.

71. Law No. 1349-XII and Presidential Decree No. 381-II-28/11/1997. Parliamentary Decision No. 1484 XIII in February 1998 led directly to the opening of the Centre for Human Rights that year. Kucsko-Stadlmayer, *European Ombudsman-Institutions*, 310.

72. Ukrainian Constitution, Articles 55, 85, 101, 150; the body is also known as the Authorised Human Rights Representative of the Verkhovna Rada.

73. "The Ukrainian Parliament Commissioner for Human Rights—The Ukrainian Model of Ombudsman," Ukrainian Ombudsman website, www.omb.gov.ua.

74. See UN General Assembly, Human Rights Council, "Compilation Prepared by the OHCHR for Ukraine's UPR" (A/HRC/WG.6/2/UKR/2, April 10, 2008) and "Report of the Working Group on the UPR: Ukraine" (A/HRC/8/45, June 3, 2008).

75. Albanian Constitution, Articles 60–63. For an overview of the institution, especially in its first three years, see this account by Albania's first ombudsman: Ermir Dobjani, "The Establishment and Operation of the People's Advocate: The Ombudsman in Albania," in Linda C. Reif, ed., *The International Ombudsman Yearbook* (Leiden: Martinus Nijhoff, 1998), 64–75.

76. Human Rights Watch, "Albania," in *World Report 1998* (New York: Human Rights Watch, 1998), http://www.hrw.org.

77. Joachim Stern, "Albania," in Kucsko-Stadlmayer, *European Ombudsman-Institutions*, 69–76; and Stability Pact for South Eastern Europe, "Regional Meeting of Ombudsman Institutions" (Belgrade, September 28–29, 2004).

78. Though Azerbaijan is in Central Asia, it is a member of the Council of Europe and the European Group of NHRIs. Azerbaijan Ombudsman, "On the Actions in Provision of Human Rights and Freedoms" (February 22, 1998) and "State Program on Protection of Human Rights" (June 18, 1998), http://www.ombudsman.gov.az; UN General Assembly, Human Rights Council, "National Report, Submitted by the Government of Azerbaijan for UPR" (A/HRC/WG.6/4/AZE/1, November 4, 2008); and Brigitte Kofler, "Azerbaijan," in Kucsko-Stadlmayer, *European Ombudsman-Institutions*, 101–5.

79. Svante E. Cornell, *Azerbaijan since Independence* (Armonk, N.Y.: M. E. Sharpe, 2011), 93.

80. Law on the People's Advocate 349/1999, as amended 342/2006. The office is sometimes translated as public protector. UN General Assembly, Human Rights Council, "National Report, Submitted by the Government of the Czech Republic for UPR" (A/HRC/WG.6/1/CZE/1, March 6, 2008).

81. Mertus, *Human Rights Matters*, 97.

82. Joachim Stern, "Czech Republic"; Kucsko-Stadlmayer, *European Ombudsman-Institutions*, 146.

83. Mertus, *Human Rights Matters*, 91; and UN Human Rights Council, "National Report by Czech Republic," 6.

84. Mertus, *Human Rights Matters*, 93.

85. Ibid., 93–94.

86. Ibid., 97. Most of the issues brought to the ombudsman's office concern economic and social rights.

87. The parliamentary act was replaced in 2007. See Equinet, "Centre for Equal Opportunities an Opposition to Racism" (http://www.equineteurope.org).

88. Dirk Jacobs, "Immigrants in a Multinational Political Sphere: The Case of Brussels (Belgium)," in Alisdair Rogers and Jean Tillie, eds., *Multicultural Policies and Modes of Citizenship in European Cities* (Aldershot, UK: Ashgate, 2001), 111.

89. See Anja Detant, "The Politics of Anti-Racism in Belgium: A Qualitative Analysis of the Discourse of the Anti-Racist Movement Hand in Hand in the 1990s," *Ethnicities* 5, 2 (June 2005): 183–215; and Cas Mudde, *The Ideology of the Extreme Right* (Manchester: Manchester University Press, 2000), 97–8.

90. UN General Assembly, Human Rights Council, "National Report, Submitted by the Government of Belgium for UPR" (A/HRC/WG.6/11/BEL/1, February 16, 2011) and "Stakeholders' Submissions to Belgium's UPR" (A/HRC/WG.6/11/BEL/3, February 16, 2011).

91. Damir Skenderovic, *The Radical Right in Switzerland: Continuity and Change, 1945–2000* (New York: Bergahn Books, 2009), 310.

92. The government message was from 1992, referring to the intent to ratify CERD. S. J. Roth, "The Legal Fights against Anti-Semitsim: Survey of Developments in 1992," in Yoram Dinstein and Mala Tabory, eds., *Israel Yearbook on Human Rights* (Leiden: Kluwer, 1993), 382.

93. Skenderovic, *Radical Right in Switzerland.*

94. "Working Group for a National Human Rights Institution" (Information Platform, Switzerland, www.humanrights.ch).

95. See UN General Assembly, Human Rights Council, "National Report, Submitted by the Government of Switzerland for the UPR" (A/HRC/WG.6/2/CHE/1, April 9, 2008).

96. Amnesty International, *Annual Report 2011* (London: Amnesty International, 2011).

97. The act was passed on March 2, 1994; a decree from July 29, 1994, outlined its procedures. For an interesting discussion of the commission's references to intersectionality, see Susanne Burri, "Promises of an Intersectional Approach in Practice? The Dutch Equal Treatment Commission's Case Law in European Union Non-Discrimination," in Dagmar Schiek and Anna Lawson, eds., *European Union Non-Discrimination Law and Intersectionality: Investigating the Triangle of Racial, Gender and Disability Discrimination* (Surrey, UK: Ashgate, 2011), 97–110.

98. Jenny Goldschmidt, "Anti-Discrimination Law in the Netherlands," in Yuwen Li and Jenny Goldschmidt, eds., *Taking Employment Discrimination Seriously: Chinese and European Perspectives* (Leiden: Brill, 2009), 253.

99. Martin Moerings, "The Netherlands," in Donald T. West and Richard Green, eds., *Sociolegal Control of Homosexuality: A Multi-Nation Comparison* (New York: Springer, 1997), 306.

100. UN General Assembly, Human Rights Council, "National Report, Submitted by the Government of Netherlands for the UPR" (A/HRC/WG.6/1/NLD/1, March 7, 2008), 9.

101. UN General Assembly, Human Rights Council, "Compilation Prepared by the OHCHR for the UPR of the Netherlands" (A/HRC/WG.6/1/NLD/2, March 19, 2008) and "Summary of Stakeholders' Submissions to the UPR" (A/HRC/WG.6/1/NLD/3, March 13, 2008).

102. UN Human Rights Council, "National Report of the Netherlands."

103. Amnesty International, "Netherlands: Protecting Human Rights at Home," Amnesty International Submission to the UN Universal Periodic Review (EUR 35/001/2011, May–June 2012). A related criticism was that certain Caribbean territories (e.g., Aruba, Curaçao, and Saint Martin) would be unable to access the NHRI.

104. See Joachim Stern, "Finland," in Kuckso-Stadlmayer, *European Ombudsman-Institutions*, 179–88.

105. Juha Lavapuro, Tuomas Ojanen, and Martin Scheinin, "Rights-Based Constitutionalism in Finland and the Development of Pluralist Constitutional Review," *International Journal of Constitutional Law* 9, 2 (2011): 505–31. Also, Parliamentary Ombudsman of Finland, "Fundamental and Human Rights" (http://www.oikeusasiamies.fi/).

106. Lavapuro, Ojanen, and Scheinin, "Rights-Based Constitutionalism," 513.

107. Tuomas Ojanen, *Thematic Legal Study on National Human Rights Institutions and Human Rights Organisations Finland* (Helsinki: Institute for Human Rights of Abo Akademi University, September 2008).

108. All quotes are from Parliamentary Ombudsman of Finland, "Ombudsman Presents Annual Report for 2010 to the Speaker of the Eduskunta" (press release, http://www. oikeusasiamies.fi/).

109. For the claim that Greece was following the Council of Europe's 1997 recommendation, see George Papadimitriou, "The Greek National Commission for the Protection of Human Rights," in Linos-Alexandre Sicilianos and Christiane Bourloyannis-Vrailas, eds., *The Prevention of Human Rights Violations: Contributions on the Occasion of the Twentieth Anniversary of the Marangopoulos Foundation for Human Rights* (Leiden: Martinus Nijhoff, 2001), 250.

110. The relevant part of the recommendation, in sections a and b, calls on the governments of member states to consider establishing effective national human rights institutions, in particular human rights commissions, which are pluralist in their membership, or ombudsmen institutions and to draw on experience gained by existing national human rights institutions and to be attentive to the Paris Principles. Steering Committee for Human Rights, "Explanatory Memorandum to Recommendation No. R (97) of the Committee of Ministers to Member States on the Establishment of Independent National Human Rights Institutions (Strasbourg: Council of Europe, June 16, 1997), Appendix V, 39–42.

111. This was especially the case within the council's Steering Committee for Human Rights, following a 1982 seminar the council cosponsored with the University of Siena on Non-Judicial Means for the Protection and Promotion of Human Rights (October 28–30). Ibid., 39.

112. It consists of monitoring and steering committees; the first committee monitors treaty obligations, and the second investigates abuses. Press and Information Office, Republic of Cyprus, 2005. See Brigitte Kofler, "Cyprus," in Kucsko-Stadlmayer, *European Ombudsman-Institutions*, 139–44.

113. ECOSOC, "Summary Record of the Second Part (Public) of the 35th Meeting" (E/C.12/1998/SR.35/Add.1, Cyprus, November 23, 1998). Cyprus became a member of the EU in 2004. See also European Commission against Racism and Intolerance, "Country Monitoring Work—Cyprus" (http://www.ecri.coe.int).

114. Advisory Committee on the Framework Convention for the Protection of National Minorities, "Second Opinion on Cyprus" (ACFC/OP/II (2007)004, June 7, 2007); and UN General Assembly, Human Rights Council, "Compilation Prepared by the OHCHR" (A/HRC/WG.6/6/CYP.2, August 24, 2009) and "Report of the Working Group on the UPR: Cyprus" (A/HRC/13/7, January 4, 2010).

115. Human Rights Watch (HRW), "Greece," *World Report 1997: Events of 1996* (New York: HRW, 1997), 221–23; and HRW, "Greece," *World Report 1998*, http://www.hrw.org.

116. Law 2667/1998 (December 18, 1998). This was a groundbreaking treaty also known as the Oviedo Convention. See Council of Europe (COE), *Biomedicine and Human Rights: The Oviedo Convention and Its Additional Protocols* (Strasbourg, COE, 2009); and Reif, *The Ombudsman*, 152.

117. Mary Robinson, speech at Queen's University of Belfast, December 2, 1998, quoted in Stephen Livingstone, "The Northern Ireland Human Rights Commission," *Fordham International Law Journal* 22, 4 (1998): 1465. In general, see Brice Dickson, "The Protection Role of the Northern Ireland Human Rights Commission," in Ramcharan, *The Protection Role of National Human Rights Institutions*, 135–54.

118. The Belfast Peace Agreement also called for a bill of rights and incorporating the ECHR into Northern Ireland law. Antidiscrimination commissions also played a complementary role during this period. See Livingstone, "Northern Ireland Human Rights Commission," 1477–79.

119. Ibid., 1470–71.

120. Ibid.

121. Republic of Ireland, "Report of the Constitutional Review Group" (Dublin: Stationery Office, 1996), 403–8.

122. Mertus, *Human Rights Matters*, 49–50; and Livingstone, "The Northern Ireland Human Rights Commission," 1480.

123. Cornelia Albert, *The Peacebuilding Elements of the Belfast Agreement and the Transformation of the Northern Ireland Conflict* (Frankfurt: Peter Lang, 2009).

124. Brice Dickson, *The European Convention on Human Rights and the Conflict in Northern Ireland* (Oxford: Oxford University Press, 2010), 333.

125. Mertus, *Human Rights Matters*, 57.

126. For example, in June 2006 it hosted a meeting of twenty-five NHRIs from countries in conflict. See Northern Ireland Human Rights Commission, "International Round Table on the Role of National Institutions in Conflict and Post Conflict Situations" (Belfast: June 20–22, 2006), http://www.nihrc.org. Also, Working

Group on the Irish Human Rights and Equality Commission, "Report to the Minister of Justice and Equality and Defence" (Dublin: April 19, 2012), http://www.upr.ie.

127. Interim Agreement for Peace and Self-Determination in Kosovo (Rambouillet Agreement) (1999), chap. 6.

128. UNMIK Regulations No. 2000/38, 2006/06, and 2007/15. Reif, *The Ombudsman*, 273–82.

129. Ibid., 278–79.

130. Christopher Waters, "Human Rights in an International Protectorate: Kosovo's Ombudsman," in Linda C. Reif, ed., *International Ombudsman Yearbook*, vol. 6 (Leiden: Martinus Nijhoff, 2000); Amnesty International, "Kosovo (Serbia and Montenegro) United Nations Interim Administration Mission in Kosovo (UNMIK), Briefing to the Human Rights Committee, 87th Session, July 2006" (EUR 70/007/2006); and Safet Kabashaj, "Lack of Support Weakens Kosovo's Ombudsman," *Southeast European Times*, December 12, 2011.

131. Reif, *The Ombudsman*, 276.

132. See Matthew McAllester, *Beyond the Mountains of the Damned: The War Inside Kosovo* (New York: New York University Press, 2002).

133. Republic of Montenegro, Protector of Human Rights and Freedoms, *Annual Report 2004* (Podgorica: Protector of Human Rights and Freedoms, March 2005), 10; Organization for Security and Co-operation in Europe, Mission to Serbia, "Ombudsperson Institutions in Serbia" (September 2011); and Venice Commission, Commissioner for Human Rights, and General Directorate of Human Rights of the Council of Europe, "Draft Joint Opinion on the Law on the Ombudsman of Serbia," Opinion no. 315/2004 (Strasbourg: November 24, 2004).

134. UN General Assembly, Human Rights Council, "Report of the Working Group on the UPR: Montenegro" (A/HRC/10/74, January 6, 2009); and Síndic de Greuges de Catalunya, "Support to Serbian Ombudsman, 2008" (http://www.sindic.cat/).

135. Mertus, *Human Rights Matters*, 118. The Forum Menschenrechte (Human Rights Forum) was founded in 1994 in preparation for the Vienna World Conference. Scott Calnan, *The Effectiveness of Domestic Human Rights NGOs: A Comparative Study* (Leiden: Martinus Nijhoff, 2008), 83. For a general overview, see Beate Rudolf, "The German Institute for Human Rights," *Nova Acta Leopoldina* NF 113, 387 (2011): 19–24.

136. Brigitte Kofler, "Germany," in Kucsko-Stadlmayer, *European Ombudsman-Institutions*, 203–13; Mertus, *Human Rights Matters*; and UN General Assembly, Human Rights Council, "National Report, Submitted by the Government of Germany for UPR" (A/HRC/WG.6/4/DEU/1, November 10, 2008).

137. Mertus, *Human Rights Matters*, 121–23.

138. UN Committee on Economic, Social and Cultural Rights, Germany, "Concluding Observations" (4th Periodic Report, August 30–31, 2001).

139. Germany, Federal Foreign Office, "The Commission for Human Rights Policy," www.auswaertiges-amt.de.

140. Forum Meschenrechte, Joint Submission to the UN Human Rights Council for Germany's UPR (Berlin: September 8, 2008), available on http://www.ohchr

.org; and Deutsches Institut für Menschenrechte, "The Institute's Structure," http://www.institut-fuer-menschenrechte.de.

141. "Historique," Commission consultative des droits de l'homme website, www.ccdh.public.lu: "C'est à l'image de la Commission nationale consultative française que la Commission luxembourgeoise s'est créée"; and "Règlement du Gouvernement en Conseil du 26 mai 2000 portant création d'une Commission consultative des Droits de l'Homme."

142. European Council Meeting, "Presidency Conclusions" (Luxembourg: December 12–13, 1997), http://www.consilium.europa.eu/.

143. UN Committee on Civil and Political Rights, "Third Periodic Report: Luxembourg" (CCPR/L/LUX/2002/3, May 28, 2002); and European Union, "Closing Conference of European Year Against Racism" (press release; Luxembourg: December 19, 1997).

144. A law was passed in 2003, though the office was not incorporated into the constitution. See Joachim Stern, "Luxembourg," in Kucsko-Stadlmayer, *European Ombudsman-Institutions*, 292.

145. "Historique," Commission consultative des droits de l'homme.

146. Decree, September 21, 2001. Norway, Royal Ministry of Foreign Affairs, "Terms of Reference for the Review of the Norwegian Centre for Human Rights in Its Capacity as Norway's National Human Rights Institution" (Oslo: Government of Norway, June 23, 2010); and Ministry of Church Affairs, Education and Research, royal decree, September 21, 2001.

147. Norway, Royal Ministry of Foreign Affairs, "Terms of Reference." In fact, as part of UPR, the Norwegian Centre for Human Rights submitted a stakeholder report proposing the government conduct a review, which it accepted. Note, moreover, that the review was written in English so it could be submitted as part of reaccreditation. See UN General Assembly, Human Rights Council, "Summary Prepared by the OHCHR: Norway, for the UPR" (A/HRC/WG.6/6/NOR.3, July 21, 2009).

148. "The two perspectives—one as seen from the Paris Principles, the other as seen from the university—illustrate that a *comprehensive* review of Norway's NHRI in the current situation is a rather complex task since it involves concerns on two different yet interdependent and institutional levels." Norway, Royal Ministry of Foreign Affairs, "Terms of Reference," 4n2.

149. Norwegian Centre for Human Rights, "Compliance with the Paris Principles of the Norwegian Centre for Human Rights, NHCR's Summary of and Comments to the Report Submitted by the National Institutions Review Team in March 2011" (Oslo, June 7, 2011), 1.

150. Denmark (1992), Iceland (1994), Sweden (1995), and Norway (1999). See Ed Bates, *The Evolution of the European Convention on Human Rights* (Oxford: Oxford University Press, 2010), 162.

151. Government of Norway, "Some Aspects of the Norwegian Plan of Action for Human Rights, White Paper No. 21 (1999–2000)," 3–4 (available from http://www.ohchr.org).

152. Alison Brysk, *Global Good Samaritans: Human Rights as Foreign Policy* (Oxford: Oxford University Press, 2009).

153. The Law on the Ombudsman, SG 48 (May 23, 2003), entered into force in 2004. See Bulgarian Constitution, Article 91a. See Joachim Stern, "Bulgaria," in Kucsko-Stadlmayer, *European Ombudsman-Institutions*, 127–32; and UN General Assembly, Human Rights Council, "National Report, Submitted by the Government of Bulgaria for UPR" (A/HRC/WG.6/9/BGR/1, August 12, 2010).

154. Marko Škreb, *Transition: The First Decade* (Cambridge, Mass.: MIT Press, 2002). Bulgaria, Latvia, Czech Republic, and Slovakia did not incorporate an NHRI into their posttransition constitutions.

155. Southeast European Legal Development Initiative, *Anti-Corruption in Southeast Europe: First Steps and Policy* (Sofia, Bulgaria: Center for the Study of Democracy, 2002), 72.

156. UN General Assembly, Human Rights Council, "Compilation Prepared by the OHCHR, for the Government of Bulgaria for the UPR" (A/HRC/WG.6/9/BGR/2, July 30, 2010), 3; and "Report of the Working Group on the UPR: Bulgaria" (A/HRC/16/9, January 4, 2011), 4.

157. Sarah Spencer, "Equality and Human Rights Commission: A Decade in the Making," *Political Quarterly* 79, 1 (January–March 2008): 6–16; Sarah Spencer and I. Bynoe, *A Human Rights Commission: The Options for Britain and Northern Ireland* (London: Institute for Public Policy Research, 1998); Jenny Watson, *Something for Everyone: The Impact of the Human Rights Act and the Need for a Human Rights Commission* (London: British Institute of Human Rights, 2002); Government of the UK, Women and Equality Unit, "Fairness for All: A New Commission for Equality and Human Rights," White Paper (May 2004); Colin Harvey and Sarah Spencer, "Equality and Human Rights Commissions in the UK and Ireland: Challenges and Opportunities Compared" (School of Law, Queen's University Belfast and Centre on Migration, Policy and Society, Oxford University, November 2011). On the racial equality commission, see Christopher Boothman, "The Commission of Racial Equality," in Hossain et al., *Human Rights Commissions and Ombudsman Offices*, 691–730.

158. Calls for incorporation were made in 1968, 1974, 1976, 1978, and 1986. The possibility of a human rights commission had also been raised in the early 1990s. Spencer, "Equality and Human Rights Commission," 6. See Government of the UK, "Rights Brought Home: The Human Rights Bill," White Paper No. Cm 3782 (London: Stationery Office, 1997).

159. The Equal Opportunities Commission was created in 1975 to implement the Sexual Discrimination Act of that year. The Commission for Racial Equality was formed in tandem with the Race Relations Act of 1976; Britain had ratified CERD in 1969. An earlier race relations act dating to 1965 had led to the Race Relations Board and Community Relations Commission.

160. The Disability Rights Commission implemented the 1995 Disabilities Discrimination Act.

161. One influential report in this regard was "Something for Everyone," from the British Institute of Human Rights. See Spencer, "Equality and Human Rights Commission," 8.

162. Spencer, "Equality and Human Rights Commission," 9, citing a statement by Patricia Hewitt and Lord Chancellor Charlie Falconer.

163. This included meeting regularly with the Equality and Diversity Forum, an umbrella group of all equality and human rights organizations. Spencer, "Equality and Human Rights Commission," 9. For full details of these negotiations, see the excellent survey by Spencer, "Equality and Human Rights Commission," 9–14.

164. See House of Lords/House of Commons, Joint Committee on Human Rights, "Equality and Human Rights Commission" (Thirteenth Report of Session 2009–10, March 25, 2010); and Randeep Ramesh, "Equality and Human Rights Commission Has Workforce Halved," *The Guardian* (May 15, 2012).

165. Labour Party, "Rights Brought Home: The Human Rights Bill" (1997).

166. Sarah Spencer and L. Chauhan, "A Human Rights Commission for Scotland" (London: Institute for Public Policy Research, 1999); Scottish Executive, "Protecting Our Rights: A Human Rights Commission for Scotland" (2001); and Scottish Human Rights Commission, http://www.scottishhumanrights.com.

167. Audrey Osler, ed., *Citizenship and Democracy in Schools: Diversity, Identity, Equality* (Oakhill, UK: Trentham Books, 2000), 30; Spencer and Chauhan, "A Human Rights Commission for Scotland"; and Lynne Robertson, "Wide Support for Human Rights Event," *The Herald* (Edinburgh), December 7, 1998.

168. Scottish Human Rights Commission, http://www.scottishhumanrights.com.

169. Harvey and Spencer, "Equality and Human Rights Commissions in the UK and Ireland," 26.

170. Simon Payaslian, *The Political Economy of Human Rights in Armenia: Authoritarianism and Democracy in a Former Soviet Republic* (London: I. B. Taurus, 2011), 119. Abuses included the physical abuse of conscripts and religious intolerance. See Human Rights Watch letter to Armenia's president, Robert Kocharian, regarding the treatment of Jehovah's Witnesses (January 15, 1999).

171. Amnesty International, "Armenia: Comments on the International Report Submitted to the United Nations Human Rights Committee" (1998), 2.

172. Ibid., and Amnesty International, *Annual Report 2000* (London: Amnesty International, 2000).

173. Erik S. Herron, *Elections and Democracy after Communism?* (New York: Palgrave Macmillan, 2009), 101–2; and Council of Europe, Venice Commission, "Ombudsman in the Republic of Armenia," CDL (2001) 26 (Strasbourg: March 2, 2001).

174. Council of Europe, Parliamentary Assembly, "Constitutional Reform Process in Armenia," Resolution 1458 (2005).

175. Law, October 21, 2003. Brigitte Kofler, "Armenia," in Kucsko-Stadlmayer, *European Ombudsman-Institutions*, 85–90.

176. Council of Europe and European Commissions, "Ukraine and South Caucasus States—Fostering a Culture of Human Rights" (May 2006–April 2009), www.jp.coe.int.

177. UN General Assembly, Human Rights Council, "National Report, Submitted by the Government of Iceland for the UPR" (A/HRC/WG.6/12/ISL/1, July 19, 2011) and "Compilation Prepared by the OHCHR" (A/HRC/WG.6/12/ISL/2, July 25, 2011).

178. Iceland, Constitutional Act No. 97/1995. See Icelandic Human Rights Centre, "History and Mandate," http://www.humanrights.is/.

179. Council of Europe, "Report by Alvaro Gil-Robles, Commissioner for Human Rights, on His Visit to the Republic of Iceland, 4–6 July 2005."

180. See, for example, Icelandic Human Rights Centre, "Notes on ECRI's Second Report on Iceland," http://www.humanrights.is/

181. Icelandic Human Rights Center, "Civil Society Report on the Implementation of the ICCPR" (April 20, 2011), 3.

182. UN Human Rights Council, "National Report, Submitted by the Government of Iceland."

183. UN General Assembly, Human Rights Council, "Compilation Prepared by the OHCHR, for the Government of Malta for the UPR" (A/HRC/WG.6/5/MLT/2, March 12, 2009), 3.

184. Brigitte Kofler, "Malta," Kucsko-Stadlmayer, *European Ombudsman-Institutions*, 304. Malta joined the EU in 2004. Also, NATO, "Malta Re-Engages in the Partnership for Peace Program" (April 13, 2008), http://www.nato.int/.

185. Estonia ratified the ECHR in 1996. See Joachim Stern, "Estonia," in Kucsko-Stadlmayer, *European Ombudsman-Institutions*, 161–64.

186. Anatol Lieven, *The Baltic Revolution: Estonia, Latvia, Lithuania, and the Path to Independence* (New Haven, Conn.: Yale University Press, 1994), xxiv.

187. Estonian Human Rights Institute, "Replies of the Estonian Institute for Human Rights to the List of Issues to Be Taken Up in Connection with the Consideration of the Third Periodic Report of Estonia to the Human Rights Committee" (July 6, 2010).

188. UN General Assembly, Human Rights Council, "Compilation Prepared by the OHCHR for the UPR of Belarus" (A/HRC/WG.6/8/BLR/2, February 17, 2010); and "Responses to Recommendations: Belarus" (January 13, 2011), http://www.upr-info.org.

189. Tilly, *Coercion, Capital, and European States*, 195.

Chapter 10

1. On human rights accountability, see Francesca Lessa and Leigh A. Payne, eds., *Amnesty in the Age of Human Rights Accountability: Comparative and International Perspectives* (Cambridge: Cambridge University Press, 2012); Kathryn Sikkink, "The Age of Accountability: The Global Rise of Individual Criminal Accountability," in Lessa and Payne, *Amnesty in the Age of Human Rights Accountability*, 19–41; Steven R. Ratner, Jason S. Abrams, and James L. Bischoff, *Accountability for Human Rights Atrocities in International Law: Beyond the Nuremberg Legacy*, 3rd ed. (Oxford: Oxford University Press, 2009); and United Nations Development Programme, "Using Indicators for Human Rights Accountability," in *Human Development Report* (2000).

2. For example, Goodman and Pegram, *Human Rights, State Compliance, and Social Change,* especially Julie Mertus, "Evaluating NHRIs: Considering Structure, Mandate, and Impact," 74–90.

3. E.g., Sonia Cardenas, "National Human Rights Institutions and State Compliance," in Goodman and Pegram, *Human Rights, State Compliance, and Social Change.*

4. International Council on Human Rights Policy (ICHRP), *Assessing the Effectiveness of National Human Rights Institutions* (Geneva: International Council on Human Rights Policy, 2005). Closely related to benchmarks of effectiveness are efforts to identify "best practices." See for example, Commonwealth Secretariat, *National Human Rights Institutions: Best Practices* (London: Commonwealth, 2001).

5. ICHRP, *Assessing the Effectiveness of NHRIs.*

6. Ibid., 33.

7. Stephen Livingstone and Rachel Murray, "The Effectiveness of National Human Rights Institutions," in Simon Halliday and Patrick Schmidt, eds., *Human Rights Brought Home: Socio-Legal Perspectives on Human Rights in the National Context* (Oxford: Hart, 2004), 137–64.

8. Ibid., 139–10.

9. Mila Versteeg, "Performance Measures for Human Rights Commissions" (Executive Session Papers: Human Rights Commissions and Criminal Justice, Marea L. Beeman, series ed., August 2007).

10. Ibid.

11. See especially Cardenas, "Adaptive States"; and Cardenas, "National Human Rights Institutions and State Compliance."

12. Cardenas, "Adaptive States."

13. Okafor and Agbakwa, "On Legalism, Popular Agency."

14. Ibid., 687–88. NHC refers to a national human rights commission.

15. Ibid., 694.

16. Livingstone and Murray, "Effectiveness of National Human Rights Institutions," 140.

17. See in general Rhodes, Binder, and Rockman, *Oxford Handbook of Political Institutions.*

18. For example, Kenneth A. Shepsle, "Rational Choice Institutionalism," in Rhodes, Binder, and Rockman, *Oxford Handbook of Political Institutions*, 23–38.

19. Cingranelli and Richards, in discussing how to measure the impact of human rights organizations (NGOs and INGOs), likewise note that one "must isolate the effects of NGOs and INGOs from the effects of other types of human rights organizations working toward similar goals in a given target state." David L. Cingranelli and David L. Richards, "Measuring the Impact of Human Rights Organizations," in Claude E. Welch, Jr., ed., *Non-Governmental Organizations and Human Rights: Promise and Performance* (Philadelphia: University of Pennsylvania Press, 2001), 26.

20. O'Donnell, "Horizontal Accountability in New Democracies"; and Peruzzotti, "Societalization of Horizontal Accountability."

21. Richard L. Sklar, "Democracy and Constitutionalism," in Schedler, Diamond, and Plattner, *Self-Restraining State.*

22. See Craig Calhoun, ed., *Habermas and the Public Sphere* (Cambridge, Mass.: MIT Press, 1992). This also taps into a social, discursive view of

institutions. See Vivien A. Schmidt, "Discursive Institutionalism: The Explanatory Power of Ideas and Discourse," *Annual Review of Political Science* 11 (2008): 303–26.

23. SAHRDC, *National Human Rights Institutions in the Asia Pacific Region*, 35.

24. I. Bizjak, "The Role and Experience of an Ombudsman in a New Democracy," in Linda C. Reif, ed., *International Ombudsman Yearbook*, vol. 2 (Leiden: Martinus Nijhoff, 1998), 60.

25. Mertus, *Human Rights Matters*, 98.

26. Instituto Interamericano de Derechos Humanos, *Ombudsman y Acceso a la Justicia de los pueblos indígenas: Estudios de caso en Bolivia, Colombia, Guatemala y Nicaragua* (Costa Rica: IIDH, 2006), 11.

27. Studies on barriers to access cover a broad range of topics, including access to education, information, healthcare, water, justice, medicine, and banking services. In human rights generally, see International Council on Human Rights Policy, *Access to Human Rights: Improving Access for Groups at High Risk* (Geneva: ICHRP, 2004).

28. Javier Miranda, "Gran expectativa de organismos internacionales en creación de Institución Nacional de DDHH" (August 24, 2011), www.presidencia.gub.uy.

29. Mertus, *Human Rights Matters*, 123; and PICCR, "Report Submitted to the Tenth Annual Meeting of the Asia Pacific Forum of National Human Rights Institutions (Mongolia)" (August 24–26, 2005), 3.

30. "Algeria: The National Institution for Human Rights (CNCPPDH) in the Hot Seat" (May 15, 1999), www.alkarama.org.

31. PICCR, "Report Submitted to the Tenth Annual Meeting."

32. IIDH, *Ombudsman y Acceso a la justicia*, 664.

33. Sarika Arya, "A Day in the Life of the Ombudsman Unit," *Yale Journal of Human Rights* (June 24, 2009), http://yjhr.blogspot.com; and IIDH, *Ombudsman y Acceso a la justicia*, 54.

34. Tate, *Counting the Dead*, 215–16.

35. Hucker, "Ombudsman Institution in Croatia," 14.

36. PICCR, Report Submitted to the Tenth Annual Meeting," 3. The office had moved between 1997 and 2000 to Ramallah from Jerusalem, after the seat of the Palestinian Authority changed.

37. Freedom House, *Countries at the Crossroads 2007: A Survey of Democratic Governance* (Lanham, Md.: Rowman & Littlefield, 2008), 228.

38. Harvey and Spencer, *Equality and Human Rights Commissions*, 5.

39. Commonwealth Human Rights Initiative, *Police Accountability: Too Important to Neglect, Too Urgent to Delay*, CHRI 2005 Report (New Delhi: CHRI, 2005), 64; and Human Rights Watch, *Protectors or Pretenders?*

40. See Human Rights First, "Detained and Denied in Afghanistan: How to Make U.S. Detention Comply with the Law" (May 2011).

41. Gilligan, "Human Rights Ombudsman in Russia," 598.

42. Belize Development Trust, "A Different Look at the New Ombudsman" (Report 106, September 1999).

43. Bizjak, "Human Rights Ombudsman of Slovenia," 62.

44. IIDH, *Ombudsman y acceso a la justicia*, 665.

45. Ibid., 124.

46. UN General Assembly, Human Rights Council, "Compilation Prepared by the OHCHR, for the Government of Mongolia for the UPR" (A/HRC/WG.6/9/MNG/2, August 10, 2010), 4.

47. Uggla, "Ombudsman in Latin America," 433.

48. IIDH, *Ombudsman y acceso a la justicia*, 78.

49. Gilligan, "Human Rights Ombudsman in Russia," 598.

50. The transnational dimension was strong in both Chiapas and Juárez. Sonia Cardenas, "State Institutions for Human Rights: Latin America in Comparative Perspective," International Studies Association meeting, Chicago, February 2007, 12–16; and IIDH, *Ombudsman y acceso a la justicia*, 125.

51. See International Coordinating Committee of National Institutions for the Promotion and Protection of Human Rights, "Themes," www.nhri.ohchr.org.

52. Tate, *Counting the Dead*, 295.

53. Kanyongolo, "Rhetoric of Human Rights in Malawi," 75.

54. National Human Rights Commission, *Human Rights Newsletter* and *Annual Report* (New Delhi: NHRC, multiple issues, 1990s–present).

55. UNDP, "Capacity Development of National Human Rights Commission of Mongolia," www.undp.mn.

56. Sanders, "Rainbow Lobby," 235.

57. Mavis Hiltunin Biesanz, Richard Biesanz, and Karen Zubris Biesanz, *The Ticos: Culture and Social Change in Costa Rica* (Boulder, Colo.: Lynne Rienner, 1999), 79.

58. See Amnesty International, "Nicaragua," in *Annual Report 2010* (London: Amnesty International, 2010).

59. Sanders, "Rainbow Lobby," 236.

60. UN OHCHR and Joint United Nations Programme on HIV/AIDS, *Handbook on HIV and Human Rights for National Human Rights Institutions* (Geneva: UN OHCHR, 2007), 18; and Lisa Karanje, *Just Die Quietly: Domestic Violence and Women's Vulnerability to HIV in Uganda* (New York: Human Rights Watch, August 2003), 64.

61. UN OHCHR and Joint United Nations Programme on HIV/AIDS, *Handbook on HIV and Human Rights.*

62. Afghanistan Independent Human Rights Commission, "Peace, Reconciliation and Justice in Afghani Action Plan," www.aihrc.org.af.

63. Ibid.; and Tate, *Counting the Dead*, 295.

64. Kabashaj, "Lack of Support Weakens Kosovo's Ombudsman."

65. Ben Rawlence, *"Bring the Gun or You'll Die": Torture, Rape and Other Serious Human Rights Violations by Kenyan Security Forces in the Mandera Triangle* (New York: Human Rights Watch, 2009), 46.

66. Uggla, "Ombudsman in Latin America," 444.

67. IIDH, *Ombudsman y acceso a la justicia*, 82. On the Danish debate, see DIHR, "Balancing Freedom of Speech with Respect for Minorities" (Copenhagen: 2006), http://www.humanrights.dk; and John Cerone, "The Danish Cartoon Row and the International Regulation of Expression," *ASIL Insights* 10, 2 (February 7, 2006), http://www.asil.org.

68. Asian Human Rights Commission, "Nepal: Independent National Human Rights Commission Needed" (July 8, 2011).

69. NHRC, *Human Rights Newsletter* (New Delhi: January 2001), 3.

70. Thio, "Panacea, Placebo, or Pawn?," 1340.

71. Baek, "Do We Need National Human Rights Institutions?," 19.

72. Lucie E. White and Jeremy Perelman, eds., *Stones of Hope: How African Activists Reclaim Human Rights to Challenge Global Poverty* (Stanford, Calif.: Stanford University Press, 2011).

73. UNDP Mongolia, "Capacity Development of the National Human Rights Commission of Mongolia" (December 2001–June 2006), www.undp.mn.

74. Australia Human Rights and Equal Opportunity Commission, "Bringing Them Home: Report of the National Inquiry into the Separation of Aboriginal and Torres Strait Islander Children from Their Families" (1997).

75. Human Rights Watch, "Blood-Stained Hands: Past Atrocities in Kabul and Afghanistan's Legacy of Impunity" (2005), especially 7–9.

76. UN General Assembly, Human Rights Council, "National Report, Submitted by the Government of Seychelles for the UPR" (A/HRC/WG.6/11/SYC/1, March 2, 2011), 16.

77. NHRC, Protection of Human Rights Act 1993, chap. 3.

78. Sonia Cardenas, "National Human Rights Commissions in Asia," *Human Rights Review* 4, 1 (October–December 2002): 30–51.

79. Justice H. Suresh, Bombay High Court, retired, "The Right to a Public Hearing" (Asian Human Rights Commission, n.d.), http://www.humanrights.asia/.

80. Azzam, "Update," 342.

81. Maldives, Foreign Ministry, "Establishment of the Human Rights Commission of the Maldives" (December 12, 2003).

82. IIDH, *Ombudsman y acceso a la justicia*, 126.

83. Milena Stefanova and Nicholas Mezies, "Book Review," *Journal of Legal Pluralism* 60 (2011): 185.

84. Payaslian, *Political Economy of Human Rights in Armenia*, 120.

85. NHRC, Protection of Human Rights Act 1993, section 18(3).

86. Cardenas, "National Human Rights Commissions in Asia," 46.

87. NHRC, *Human Rights Newsletter* (New Delhi, January 2001).

88. AIHRC, "Report on the Situation of Economic and Social Rights in Afghanistan" (November–December 2009), 9.

89. King Abdullah, "Initiatives: Human Rights," www.kingabdullah.jo.

90. Cardenas, "National Human Rights Commissions in Asia," 46.

91. Biesanz, Biesanz, and Biesanz, *The Ticos*, 79.

92. Gilligan, "Human Rights Ombudsman in Russia," 592.

93. United Nations, "Actors for Change: The Growth of Human Rights Institutions" (2006).

94. For example, NHRC, *Human Rights Newsletter* (New Delhi, multiple issues, 2000).

95. NHRC, *Human Rights Newsletter* and *Annual Report* (New Delhi, multiple issues, 1990s–2000).

96. NHRC, *Human Rights Newsletter* (New Delhi) 7, 9 (September 2000): 1.

97. Asian Human Rights Commission, "Nepal Must Respect Its Commitment to a Strong and Independent National Human Rights Commission" (July 7, 2011).

98. Hsien-Li Tan, *The ASEAN Intergovernmental Commission on Human Rights: Institutionalizing Human Rights in Southeast Asia* (Cambridge: Cambridge University Press, 2011), 93; and Human Rights Watch, "Not Enough Graves: The War on Drugs, HIV/AIDS, and Violations of Human Rights," 16, 8 (June 2004).

99. Sanders, "Rainbow Lobby," 235.

100. Human Rights Watch, *Protectors or Pretenders?;* and Gilligan, "The Human Rights Ombudsman in Russia." For Lithuania, see Kucsko-Stadlmayer, *European Ombudsman-Institutions*, 287. On Ecuador, UN General Assembly, Human Rights Council, "Summary Prepared by the OHCHR: Ecuador," for the UPR, March 6, 2008 (A/HRC/wG.6/1/ECU.3).

101. PICCR, "Report Submitted to the Tenth Annual Meeting."

102. Commonwealth Human Rights Initiative, *Police Accountability*, 64.

103. Larry Diamond and Marc F. Plattner, *Democratization in Africa: Progress and Retreat*, 2d ed. (Baltimore: Johns Hopkins University Press, 2010), 234; and Report of the Human Rights Committee, 48.

104. Human Rights Watch, *Protectors or Pretenders?*, 5.

105. See Sonia Cardenas, *Conflict and Compliance: State Responses to International Human Rights Pressure* (Philadelphia: University of Pennsylvania Press, 2007).

106. Máté Szabó. See MS, "The Philosophy of a Hungarian Ombudsman: Human Dignity without Barriers" (Budapest, Hungary: Office of the Parliamentary Commissioner, n.d.), 4.

107. Thio, "Panacea, Placebo, or Pawn?," 1285.

108. Ibid., 1285, 1338.

109. Gilligan, "Human Rights Ombudsman in Russia," 600.

110. "The Ombudsman of Belize & the Human Rights Mandate" (n.d.), the Commonwealth, http://www.thecommonwealth.org.

111. NHRC, *Human Rights Newsletter* and *Annual Report* (New Delhi, multiple years); and former chief justice of India's Supreme Court and former NHRC chair Ranganath Misra, interview, New Delhi, March 2001.

112. SAHRDC, *Komnas HAM*, 24–25; anonymous sources and NHRC members, interviews, New Delhi, March 2001.

113. Uggla, "Ombudsman in Latin America," 441.

114. Ibid., 440–41.

115. United Nations General Assembly, "United Nations Decade for Human Rights Education (1995–2004) and Public Information Activities in the Field of Human Rights" (A/52/469/Add.1, report of the secretary-general, addendum, October 20, 1997), 5.

116. Cardenas, "Constructing Rights?" 365.

117. NHRC members, interviews, New Delhi, March 2001.

118. Ibid.

119. Nicholas Wood, "Hounding of Gypsies Contradicts Slovenia's Image," *New York Times*, November 13, 2006.

120. For example, Zonke Majodine, "Shaping a Society Based on a Human Rights Culture," *Sunday Times* (South Africa), October 20, 2002, 20. More broadly,

Jeremy Sarkin, "The Development of a Human Rights Culture in South Africa," *Human Rights Quarterly* 20, 3 (August 1998): 628–65.

121. Ujjwal Kumar Singh, ed., *Human Rights and Peace: Ideas, Laws, Institutions and Movements* (New York: Sage, 2009), 303.

122. See Cardenas, "Constructing Rights? Human Rights and the State," *International Political Science Review* 26, 4 (2005), 369.

123. On Mongolia, see Altangerel Choijoo, "Human Rights Education Program of the National Human Rights Commission of Mongolia," in *Human Rights Education in Asian Schools* (Osaka: Hurights Osaka, n.d.), 15–25. For a list of films produced by Korea's NHRI, see http://www.koreafil.or.kr.

124. In the Americas, for example, HRE has fallen mostly under the purview of ministries of education not NHRIs. Cardenas, "Constructing Rights?," 368.

125. Human Rights Watch, *Protectors or Pretenders?*

126. Ibid. Unless noted otherwise, the remainder of this section relies on SAHRC annual reports and interviews with commission staff, June–July 2003; and Cardenas, "Constructing Rights?"

127. Cardenas, "Constructing Rights?," 371.

128. Claudia Lohrenscheit, "International Approaches in Human Rights Education," *International Review of Education* 48 (July 2002): 181.

129. Cardenas, "Constructing Rights?" 372.

130. See introductory discussion in SAHRC, "Fourth Annual Report December 1998–December 1999," 35–36.

131. See, for example, the SAHRC report by Sherri Le Mottee (assisted by André Keet), "Human Rights and Inclusivity in the Curriculum" (September 2003).

132. SAHRC, "Fourth Annual Report December 1998–December 1999," 35.

133. Mertus, *Human Rights Matters*, 101.

134. See Norwegian Centre for Human Rights, "Indonesia Programme," www.jus.nio.no.

135. Thio, "Panacea, Placebo, or Pawn?," 1277.

136. Kenyan Parliament, "Debate on Kenya National Commission on Human Rights Bill" (Murungi), April 9, 2002, 439.

137. Mertus, *Human Rights Matters*, 104–5.

138. Ravi Nair, executive director of the South Asian Human Rights Documentation Center, interview, New Delhi, March 2001.

139. Shannon Speed and Jane F. Collier, "Limiting Indigenous Autonomy in Chiapas, Mexico: The State Government's Use of Human Rights," *Human Rights Quarterly* 22, 4 (2000): 877–905.

140. Ibid.

141. Tate, *Counting the Dead*, 233.

142. Ibid., 253.

143. Human Rights Watch, "Hostile to Democracy: The Movement System and Political Repression in Uganda" (October 1, 1999), 43–44; Schmitz, "Transnational Activism and Political Change," 70.

144. Tate, *Counting the Dead*, 222.

145. Biesanz, Biesanz, and Biesanz, *The Ticos*, 79.

146. Tate, *Counting the Dead*, 217.

147. For example, Kenyan Parliament, "Debate," 443.

148. Joe Oloka-Onyango, "NGO Struggles for Economic, Social, and Cultural Rights in UTAKE: A Ugandan Perspectives," in Makau Mutua, ed., *Human Rights NGOs in East Africa: Political and Normative Tensions* (Philadelphia: University of Pennsylvania Press, 2009), 105.

149. Ruth Buchanan, Helen Kijo-Bisimba, and Kerry Rittich, "The Evictions at Nyamuma, Tanzania: Structural Constraints and Alternative Pathways in the Struggles over Land," in White and Perelman, *Stones of Hope*, 91–121.

150. Gellhorn, *Ombudsman and Others*, 239–40.

151. "Ley N° 7 de 5 de febrero de 1997 por el cual se estableció la Institución en la República de Panamá (Con Exposición de Motivos)," 2.

152. For a critique of the commission's focusing too much on civil and political rights, see Oloka-Onyango, "NGO Struggles for Economic, Social, and Cultural Rights," 104–5. And Margaret Sekaggya, "The Protection Role of the Uganda Human Rights Commission," in Ramcharan, *The Protection Role of National Human Rights Institutions*, 165–77.

153. See European Union Agency for Fundamental Rights, "National Human Rights Institutions in the EU Member States: Strengthening the Fundamental Rights Architecture in the EU" (2010).

154. See Human Rights Watch, *Protectors or Pretenders?;* and Howe and Johnson, *Restraining Equality.*

155. Human Rights Watch, *Protectors or Pretenders?*, 26.

156. Mertus, *Human Rights Matters*, 98.

157. Susan Harris Rimmer, "Building Democracy and Justice after Conflict: The Afghanistan Independent Human Rights Commission" (Working Paper No. 5, Australian National University, March 2010).

158. Thio, "Panacea, Placebo, or Pawn?," 1287.

159. Gilligan, "Human Rights Ombudsman in Russia," 589.

160. Hossu and Carp, "Critical Assessment," 9.

161. Belize Development Trust, "Different Look at the New Ombudsman."

162. Tate, *Counting the Dead*, 227.

163. Biesanz, Biesanz, and Biesanz, *The Ticos*, 79.

164. Ravi Nair, interview, New Delhi, March 2001.

165. Kenyan Parliament, "Debate" (Dr. Anangwe), 443.

Chapter 11

1. Karl Polanyi, *The Great Transformation* (1944; repr., Boston: Beacon Press, 2001), 256.

2. Ibid., 254.

3. More broadly, see Chapter 4, note 10. For a related critical approach to NHRI trajectories and legacies, see Peter Rosenblum, "Tainted Origins and Uncertain

Outcomes: Evaluating NHRIs," in Goodman and Pegram, *Human Rights, State Compliance, and Social Change*, 297–323.

4. The literature on path dependence in politics is voluminous. See Chapter 4, note 12.

5. Paul Pierson, *Politics in Time: History, Institutions, and Social Analysis* (Princeton, N.J.: Princeton University Press, 2004).

6. See Peruzzotti, "Societalization of Horizontal Accountability"; Evgeny Finkel, "The Authoritarian Advantage of Horizontal Accountability: Ombudsman in Poland and Russia," *Comparative Politics* 44, 3 (2012): 291–310; Gilligan, "Human Rights Ombudsman in Russia"; Dodson and Jackson, "Horizontal Accountability in Transitional Democracies."

7. Slaughter, *New World Order*. For Slaughter's earlier references to a transjudiciary network for human rights, see Slaughter, "The Long Arm of the Law," *Foreign Policy* (Spring 1999): 34–35; and "Real New World Order."

8. "Road to Rights."

9. This section borrows material from my "Sovereignty Transformed?"

10. Cardenas, "Adaptive States."

11. E.g., Krasner, *Sovereignty;* and Jack Donnelly, "State Sovereignty and Human Rights," *Human Rights & Human Welfare*, Working Paper no. 21 (June 23, 2004).

12. See Cardenas, "National Human Rights Commissions in Asia."

13. Beth Simmons offers a similar argument regarding the influence of treaties. Simmons, *Mobilizing for Human Rights*.

14. Cardenas, "Sovereignty Transformed?"

15. Richard Falk, "Sovereignty and Human Rights: The Search for Reconciliation," *Issues of Democracy* 5, 1 (2000): 31. Also Falk, *State Sovereignty and Human Rights* (New York: Holmes and Meier, 1981).

16. Michel Foucault, *Power/Knowledge: Selected Interviews and Other Writings 1972–1977*, ed. Colin Gordon (New York: Pantheon Books, 1980), 95.

17. Amartya Sen, *The Idea of Justice* (Cambridge, Mass.: Harvard University Press, 2009), 18.

18. For an introduction to critical perspectives, see Baxi, *Human Rights in a Posthuman World;* Mutua, *Human Rights: A Political and Cultural Critique;* and Douzinas, *Human Rights and Empire*.

19. On the centrality of contestation for human rights in world politics, see, for example, Sonia Cardenas, *Conflict and Compliance: State Responses to International Human Rights Pressure* (Philadelphia: University of Pennsylvania Press, 2007), 137. Likewise, Martha Finnemore notes that "normative contestation is in large part what politics is all about." Finnemore, *National Interests in International Society* (Ithaca, N.Y.: Cornell University Press, 1996), 135.

20. See especially Farmer, *Pathologies of Power*; and Pogge, *World Poverty and Human Rights*.

21. For studies of how NHRIs promote economic and social rights, see especially Gomez, "Social Economic Rights and Human Rights Commissions"; and Kumar, "National Human Rights Institutions (NHRIs) and Economic, Social and Cultural Rights." In terms of business, the UN Human Rights Council issued a resolution (A/HRC/17/L.17/Rev.1) on June 5, 2011, highlighting the role of NHRIs vis-à-vis

business. The International Coordinating Committee's first thematic group, more-over, focuses on the relationship between business and human rights. For related materials and records, see the ICC's website, http://nhri.ohchr.org/EN/Themes /BusinessHR/Pages/Home.aspx.

22. In general, see Galit A. Sarfaty, *Values in Translation: Human Rights and the Culture of the World Bank* (Stanford, Calif.: Stanford University Press, 2012); David Cingranelli and M. Rodwan Abouharb, *Human Rights and Structural Adjustment* (Cambridge: Cambridge University Press, 2008); and Ngaire Woods, *The Globaliz-ers: The IMF, the World Bank, and Their Borrowers* (Ithaca, N.Y.: Cornell University Press, 2007).

23. Sen, *Idea of Justice*, 86.

Index

pre-1990s emergence of NHRIs, 14,
74–105; in Africa, 80–82, 100–103; in
Asia-Pacific region, 97–100; in
Australia, 90–92; in Austria, 87, 88;
in Benin, 100, 101, 383n95; in Canada,
84, 85–87, 90, 91; in Caribbean
countries, 78–80; commissions-model
institutions in, 82, 84–87; in
Commonwealth countries, 84–87,
90–92; in Denmark, 90, 94–95;
diffusion of, 89–90, 103–5; in Europe,
22, 28–29, 75–78, 82–89, 92–95; in
France, 22, 28–29, 75–78; global
interlocutors and, 75–82, 377n1; in
Global South, 95–103; in Guatemala,
96–97; in Guyana, 78–80; hybrid
ombudsman institutions in, 82–84; in
Iberian countries, 82–84, 87; in Italy,
87, 89; in Latin America, 96–97; in
Libya (not technical NHRI), 100,
102–3, 383n102; in Mali, 100, 102; in
New Zealand, 78, 84–85, 86–87, 90,
91; organized abuse and, 90, 100; in
Philippines, 97–100; in Poland,
92–94; in Portugal, 82–83, 84;
retroactive labeling of, 87–89; in
Senegal, 80–82, 87, 100, 355; in
Spain, 82, 83–84; in Sweden, 87,
88–89; in Switzerland, 87–88; in
Togo, 100–101, 101–2

1990s expansion of NHRIs, 14, 384n7
1990s expansion of NHRIs in Africa, 74,
107–31; in Algeria, 117–18, 119,
122–23, 389n81; in Cameroon,
117–19; in Chad, 117–18, 123–24; in
Commonwealth states, 107, 108–17,
126, 386n25, 395n186; in Côte
d'Ivoire, 128, 129–30; in Equatorial
Guinea, 119; in Ethiopia, 108, 113, 114,
115, 386n34; in Francophone
countries, 107, 117–28; in Ghana, 108,
109–10; in Kenya, 108, 113, 115–17; in
Liberia, 128, 129; in Madagascar,
117–18, 125–26, 390n94; in Malawi,
108, 111–12; in Mauritania, 117–18,
127–28; in Mauritius, 117–18, 126–27;
in Morocco, 117–18, 119–20, 138; in
Namibia, 108–9, 110; in Niger, 117–18,
125; in Nigeria, 108, 113–14, 115,
386n26; prompted by external
obligations, 113–17, 130; prompted by
regulatory moments, 108–13, 115, 130;
in Rwanda, 128–29, 130, 390n105; in
Sierra Leone, 128; in South Africa,
107, 108, 110–11; in Sub-Saharan
Africa, 128–31; in Sudan, 128,
130–31; in Tunisia, 117–18, 120–22,
199; in Uganda, 108, 112–13, 115,
386n25; in Zaire, 124–25; in Zambia,
108, 113, 115

Acknowledgments

It was summer 1996 when I felt as if I had discovered national human rights institutions. I was in Mexico City, doing preparatory work for dissertation chapters on Latin America when I heard a radio announcement that caught my attention. It was an advertisement for "human rights," informing people they had rights by virtue of being human and, interestingly, they could claim these rights at the "National Human Rights Commission." I was both impressed and bemused by the thought that the language of human rights was being openly promoted (something that would not happen in the United States). I was also intrigued by the seeming simplicity and assuredness of it all: human rights as commodity, to be sold and consumed in a neat exchange. Later that week, walking through the basement stacks of a research library, a large collection of reports caught my eye: they were the annual reports of Mexico's National Human Rights Commission, voluminous tomes, filled with data. As a researcher, I couldn't help but get excited by the wealth of material, and the obvious paradox on display, as state actors who violated human rights were also placing themselves as central defenders of these rights.

I was soon off to see for myself the offices of the National Human Rights Commission. What impressed me immediately was the line of people, many of them of obviously modest means, holding "complaint forms," detailing how their various human rights had been violated. There were no protests, no banners or chants; it was all very bureaucratic and controlled. I found my way to the Research Department, collected materials, and set up interviews for another day. Before long I was heading to Chiapas to see how the NHRC was faring in the midst of the violent conflict there. Speaking to a mix of state and NGO representatives,

I was soon convinced that the NHRC opened up a complex and unexplored world of state-society interaction.

When I returned to New York, I researched enough to learn that the NHRC was part of a new class of global actors, "national human rights institutions." Though a seminal document had been issued just a few years earlier, virtually nothing was written on these institutions—certainly nothing in my own discipline of political science. I knew that most human rights students had never heard of these nascent bodies. I also knew that this would be the subject of a postdissertation book.

Here, at long last, is the book I set out to write, though it is fundamentally different from the one I would have written back then. Working on uncharted ground, I nonetheless discovered a growing body of reports by international organizations and NGOs and work by a few legal scholars. Foremost among these was Linda Reif, whose groundbreaking article in 2000 on the links between NHRIs and democracy helped establish the field.

When Linda's article appeared, I was in the middle of a postdoctoral fellowship at Harvard's Carr Center for Human Rights Policy. I would not have been able to devote myself to full-time research that year had it not been for Jack Montgomery, who was first to believe in this project. I am forever grateful for his generosity, supporting me as if I had been his own student. The group he convened around shifting notions of sovereignty in Asia opened up a world of possibilities for me. At our meetings in Cambridge and Laguna Beach, and in follow-up conversations, I was given invaluable advice in those early days.

Other special thanks go to Ryan Goodman, who convened a remarkable group of people working on and at NHRIs over the course of a few years at Harvard Law School. For someone writing on NHRIs, it was a who's who of personalities all gathered in one room. While the Chatham House Rule applied to those closed-door discussions, the insights and contacts I gained enriched the book immeasurably. Ryan's own work on international human rights, no less than his unparalleled promotion of the study of NHRIs, has always set a high bar; and I am very thankful for his ongoing support of my work. From those meetings, I would especially like to thank Richard Carver, Jim Cavallaro, Kieren Fitzpatrick, Mario Gomez, C. Raj Kumar, Julie Mertus, David Meyer, Obiora Okafor, Tom Pegram, Mindy Roseman, Peter Rosenblum, Margaret Sakaggya, Sima Samar, and Chris Sidoti. I also gained valuable insights from Raymond Atuguba, Brian Burdekin, Hyo-Je Cho, Brice Dickson, Katerina Linos, Michael O'Flaherty, Mohammad-Mahmoud Ould Mohamedou, Enrique Peruzzoti, Miguel Sarre, Justice Emile Francis Short, Michael Stein, Tseliso Thipanyane, and Mark Ungar. Among those at the Carr Center, where I first worked extensively on this project, I wish to thank in particular Jacob Cogan, Michael Ignatieff, Samantha Power, Sarah Sewell, Terezinha da Silva, and Sergiu Troie. And for their comments, feedback, or other assistance at various stages of the project, I am grateful to Kerry Buck, Alison Brysk, Christine Chinkin, Rhonda Evans Case, Richard Descagne, Jack Donnelly, Gérard Fellous, Dave Forsythe, Nat Glazer, Michael Goodhart, Ian Hamilton, Susan James, Rashid Kang, Justice Michael Kirby, Ronnie Lipschutz, Mahmoud Monshipouri, Rosemary Morales-Fernholz, Charles Norchi, Orest Nowosad, Michael Peletz, Francisco Ramirez, Jan Aart Scholte, Kathryn Sikkink, Beth Simmons, Vijaya Sripati, and Paul Wapner. Despite benefiting from so much support, in navigating this vast institutional terrain, all errors and omissions are of course mine.

In India, where I first saw the work of an NHRI close up (and discovered a seventeenth-century "chain of justice"), I am especially indebted to Justices J. S. Verma, Sujata Manohar, and Ranganath Mishra, as well as to Upendra Baxi, N. Gopalaswami, Harish Khare, Ravi Nair, and Virendra Dayal. Rahul Mukherji and his family offered their friendship and opened their home to me, making my work in India all the more memorable. My time in South Africa would have been very different had it not been for Laurel Baldwin Ragaven, Nono Dihemo, Jacqueline Gallinetti, Justice Richard Goldstone, Karthy Govender, Rudolph Jansen, André Keet, Daphney Khuzwayo, Zonke Majodina, Mmathari Mashao, Justice Sandile Ngobo, Michelle O'Sullivan, Barney Pityana, and Jeremy Sarkin. In Denmark, I owe special thanks to Lis Dhundale, Thomas Trier Hansen, Birgitte Kofod Olsen, Henrik Lindholt, Birgit Lindsnaes, and Hans-Otto Sano. And in Mexico, openness from the staff of various organizations sparked my interest in this project, especially the National Human Rights Commission's Headquarters, library, and documentation center in Mexico City, along with their office in San Cristobal de las Casas, Chiapas; the Human Rights Committee of Mexico's Chamber of Deputies; and the Centro de Derechos Humanos "Fray Bartolomé de las Casas" and CONPAZ, both in Chiapas.

I also benefited on this project from substantial financial and institutional support. In particular, I am thankful for funding from Harvard's Center for Business and Government and Soka University of America; a Canadian Studies Research Grant from the Canadian Government; as well as the Academic Council of the United Nations System and the American Society of International Law, which funded participation at a workshop at Warwick University. I am also appreciative of Harvard's Carr Center for Human Rights Policy, where I spent an engaging year as a postdoctoral fellow, and the Lauterpacht

Centre of International Law at Cambridge University, which hosted me for a one-month visit. My home institution of Trinity College was exceedingly generous, including providing me with multiple faculty research grants and a two-year Dana Research Chair that offered me invaluable time and space for completing the book. Various Trinity undergraduate students served ably as research assistants over the years, including Anna Borchert, Jessica Gover, Meredith Hubbell, Rebecca Landy, and Monica Rober. I have also been fortunate, as always, to work with Peter Agree and his first-rate editorial team.

Even before that summer in Mexico, my partner Andrew Flibbert joined me at every step of the way. For his patience in enduring another decade-long project, I am grateful—even more so for sharing our everyday life together. Alex and Samantha, both wise beyond their years, give me abiding perspective and joy; I hope they will forgive their mother for making them suffer through these *Chains of Justice*. My parents, too, tolerated the deadlines and absences, at a difficult time, just as they have taught me to live intensely and laugh freely. For this, and so much more, I dedicate the book to them.